ELEVENTH EDITION

Dynamic Social Studies

George W. Maxim

West Chester University

330 Hudson Street, NY NY 10013

Dedication

To Libby

You gave me the strength to push through the self-doubt and fatigue.
This book could not have happened without you!

Vice President and Editor in Chief: Kevin M. Davis
Portfolio Manager: Drew Bennett
Content Producer: Miryam Chandler
Portfolio Management Assistant: Maria Feliberty
Executive Product Marketing Manager: Christopher Barry
Executive Field Marketing Manager: Krista Clark
Development Editor: Bryce Bell
Procurement Specialist: Deidra Smith
Cover Designer: Carie Keller, Cenveo Publisher Services
Cover Art: eve/Fotolia
Media Producer: Allison Longley
Editorial Production and Composition Services: SPi Global
Full-Service Project Manager: Jason Hammond
Printer/Binder: LSC Communications
Cover Printer: LSC Communications
Text Font: Stone Serif ITC Pro

Library of Congress Cataloging-in-Publication Data: [CIP data is available at the Library of Congress.]

1 16

ISBN-10:   0-13-428671-5
ISBN-13: 978-0-13-428671-6

About the Author

George W. Maxim began his elementary school teaching career in rural Appalachia and ultimately taught in varied settings and at different levels from preschool through Grade 6. After completing a very enjoyable elementary school teaching career, Dr. Maxim pursued a PhD in elementary education from Pennsylvania State University, specializing in social studies and early childhood education. He accepted a position at West Chester (PA) University immediately after completing the requirements for the degree, teaching graduate and undergraduate courses in social studies education, creative thinking processes, literacy, and early childhood education. Dr. Maxim served as Director of the Early Childhood program for several years. He has lectured, conducted in-service programs, and offered workshops for teachers throughout the country and has also been invited to speak to audiences in locations as distant as Seoul, South Korea.

Dr. Maxim is the recipient of a number of teaching awards, including the Certificate of Excellence in (College) Teaching Award from the Pennsylvania Department of Education. As an active member of the National Council for the Social Studies, he has served on the Educational Publishing Advisory Committee and has chaired the Early Childhood/Elementary Advisory Committee. He was instrumental in helping to launch NCSS's elementary education journal, *Social Studies and the Young Learner*, serving on its editorial board for several years.

His articles have appeared in *Social Studies and the Young Learner, Social Education, The Social Studies, Childhood Education,* and other relevant professional journals. He has written books other than this text, including *The Very Young, The Sourcebook, and Learning Centers for Young Children.* In addition, he contributed a chapter to Loretta MacAlpine's *Inside Kidvid,* a parent's guide to video.

Dr. Maxim's wife, Libby, is a highly accomplished reading specialist (now retired), having helped scores of children throughout the West Chester area to become successful readers. His oldest son, Mike, is head of infrastructure at a corporation located in New York City, and his youngest son, Jeff, is a computer programmer in New York City.

Dr. Maxim enjoys writing and teaching; he particularly likes creating new and exciting approaches to classroom instruction. And he will never turn down a chance to play a good game of golf!

Contents

12 Economics: Thinking and Choosing Responsibly   369

13 Sociology and Anthropology: Social Structures and Culture   386

Preface

As I worked on this eleventh edition of *Dynamic Social Studies*, I continuously asked myself, "Why are you still doing this?" My question had nothing to do with a lack of enthusiasm for the project; actually, I love writing. Although I will not write the next great novel, I truly enjoy immersing myself in a textbook world. Textbook authors don't simply select a topic to write about and begin punching away at the keyboard, but they must discover ways to capture and sustain a reader's interest in topics that aren't always self-motivating. So, the reason I asked, "Why are you still doing this?" is because I wanted to find ways to grab your attention, arouse your curiosity, and engage you in the content. My answer to the question is also based on a conviction that social studies is crucial for the development of informed, rational, and culturally responsive citizens. I needed to best communicate to you the essential role that social studies plays in bringing pride, responsibility, and meaning to your students' lives as citizens of our nation in the 21st century.

This is not a text steeped in research and theory, although research and theory are an important part of it. Nor is it a "cookbook" text full of delicious classroom recipes, although it does contain a wealth of teaching examples and suggested strategies. It does build bridges between theory and practice with the hope that future teachers understand that no single method of instruction, by itself, can help us achieve all the important goals of social studies instruction. The text is designed to help you find ways to inspire children to want to learn the things they need to know in order to understand and participate in the world around them. To accomplish these goals you must be bold; you cannot be afraid to make mistakes. You must constantly struggle to find the method that works best for your students by seeking out answers to the most important question of all: "Why am I doing this?"

How Is the Text Organized?

The chapters in this edition are arranged into four sections. Section One provides an overview of the purposes, problems, and possibilities of social studies in the elementary school curriculum as well as guidance and direction in planning lessons and units—choosing objectives, assessment procedures, and learning activities. Section Two addresses a key feature of effective teaching—the selection of instructional resources that meet the needs and interests of students as well as satisfy social studies content standards. Section Three describes teaching practices that are supported by constructivist learning theory. The constructivist view of learning can be translated into a number of active teaching practices, running the gamut from teacher-guided instruction to inquiry and problem solving. Section Four focuses on the six core disciplines and their respective content, tools, and investigative processes, from which students will draw as they attempt to uncover and discover significant curricular content about human beings and the ways in which they function: history, geography, civics, economics, anthropology, and sociology.

New to This Edition

This eleventh edition maintains the focus of previous editions, but it has been thoroughly revised and updated.

- In response to the prevailing standards scene and other trends in the field, four new chapters are now included in Section Three:

  CHAPTER 5 Beyond the Ordinary: Teaching and Learning with Concrete Instructional Resources

  CHAPTER 6 Beyond the Ordinary: Teaching and Learning with Representational Instructional Resources

  CHAPTER 7 Beyond the Ordinary: Teaching and Learning with Informational and Persuasive Text

  CHAPTER 8 Beyond the Ordinary: Teaching and Learning with Narrative Text

- Several new classroom scenarios have been introduced at chapter openings. The scenarios, each having taken place in actual elementary school classrooms, work as advance organizers that place the content into a meaningful context. In addition, a number of fresh scenarios have been inserted throughout the chapters to help you understand and visualize how teachers have actually used suggested teaching strategies in their classrooms.

- Numerous new photographs, illustrations, and figures help to illuminate and reinforce the information presented.

- Several important topics have been added, expanded, and updated: diversity and differentiated instruction as an underlying premise of instruction; the College, Career, and Civic Life (C3) Framework for Social Studies State Standards; the Common Core State Standards; creating, using, and managing appropriate technological processes and resources; inquiry strategies based on the C3 Inquiry Arc; a useful framework that strengthens the teaching of the core social studies disciplines; acquiring knowledge through reading complex content area fiction and nonfiction text; guided reading and close reading strategies, as well as suggestions for integrating good children's literature into the social studies program; and expanded discussion of the literacy strategies and skills that help students acquire information and communicate their learning.

- Distributed at strategic points throughout each chapter are open-ended, Reflection on Learning questions that have no clear-cut answers, but require reflection through which you extract personal meaning. Sometimes, reflection will be as simple as thinking about what you've learned and associating it to past experiences. At other times, reflection may become a part of class discussion. Either way, the purpose of reflection is to help personalize the learning experience.

- The eleventh edition is powered by Pearson's new eText technology, which creates a powerful and personal online learning experience. The e-book version is interactive, containing study and review questions, appropriate videos, and questions requiring personal reflection. These features enhance the overall technology movement that is the future of our schools and our society.

- Finally, references have been updated throughout the text. The latest ideas from the social studies profession have been included, and appropriate citations have been made.

eText Features

The eText version of the eleventh edition provides instant access on smartphones, tablets, and laptops. The eText allows you to highlight text, take and share notes, search keywords, and print pages. The eText brings you the following features:

- *Check Your Understanding:* As you read the material, you can use embedded quizzes called "Check Your Understanding" to enhance your grasp of the content. Feedback will be provided to ensure comprehension after you complete each multiple choice question.
- *Video Exploration:* Interactive videos help create interactive lessons. You are invited to answer video quizzes (called *Video Explorations*) as you watch the selected video clip. Feedback is provided after you answer each question.
- *Video Example:* Additional videos provide examples of concepts discussed in the text.

Supplements

Instructor's Manual

For each chapter, the Instructor's Manual contains Key Questions, a Chapter Outline, and eText information. It also includes a combination of Print Resources (books, journals, and current event publications), Electronic Resources (websites), Video Resources, and Organizations. There is also a list of the chapter's vocabulary terms and their definitions.

Test Bank

The Test Bank contains multiple choice questions, essay, and true or false questions, as well as the answer keys for each chapter.

PowerPoint

The PowerPoint slides first explain how the book will help you create a dynamic social studies classroom through its features, such as NCSS standards integration, text sets, and classroom activities. Each chapter is then outlined by topics and terms, which you can read to follow along with the book.

Acknowledgments

This eleventh edition would not have been possible without the encouragement and support of my family. Enormous appreciation is extended to my wife Libby, whose selfless help was given freely and affectionately, and accepted with deep appreciation; my son Mike, head of infrastructure at a major New York City corporation, who has spread his wings and worked hard to make his dreams come true; and my son Jeff, a computer programmer in New York City who boldly exercised courage and integrity to live his dream. They may not be aware of how much they helped, but I thank them for being my strength.

I am also indebted to my parents, Rose and Stanley Maxim. Their honorable work ethic instilled in me the value of determination in tackling a job as overwhelming as writing a book. Their love of parenthood was a valuable inspiration for me throughout my life and my career.

I am grateful for the opportunity to work with a highly talented, supportive, and friendly team of editors at Pearson. First, I would like to thank Meredith Fossel, Executive Editor, Teacher Education, for her vision, extraordinary insights, and personable leadership as she guided this revision. I deeply appreciate Meredith's confidence in me and her support of my work throughout this project. I also consider myself lucky to have had an opportunity to work with Bryce Bell as our Developmental Editor. Bryce was a superb "coach" who provided the best possible conditions for our team to maximize its performance. Hoorah, Bryce! A note of appreciation is also extended to Karen Mason and Tania Zamora, Rights and Permissions specialists, who managed all matters related to the time-consuming process of reviewing photos, text quotes, and other outside materials contained in the manuscript. And, Jesika Bethea, Product Marketing, applied her sound judgment to create a strong marketing strategy for this edition. I think the world of the cover of this edition, a wonderful choice provided by Miryam Chandler, Content Producer. As I express my gratitude to those at Pearson, I must never forget the kindness and patience of Maria Feliberty, Editorial Assistant. You are special, Maria! Finally, I want to send out a big word of thanks to Jason Hammond, Project Manager at SPi Global, who respectfully and affably employed his creativity and craftmanship to organize and monitor the production responsibilities of this project. Doumo arigatou gozaimasu, Jason! Working with Jason at SPi Global, copy editor Susan McIntyre of Essential Edits expertly took hold of my original copy, organized it, cleaned it up, and prepared it for production. This entire team was not only competent and professional, but friendly as well; I owe much to them.

I thank the following reviewers for their helpful suggestions and insights: Judy Britt, Winthrop University; Katherine Condon, Framingham State University; and Amy Saks Pavese, St. Michael's College.

Finally, seven people deserve special thanks for their support and encouragement throughout this project: Dan "Yogdah" Darigan for helping me more fully understand and appreciate the potential of integrating literacy and social studies, as well as for his refreshing inspiration and professional support during our weekly faculty meetings; John "Pogo" Ogborn for his appreciation of and interest in my professional achievements; Ellen and Bernard Tenenbaum and Jane and George Barker for connecting our families through accepting our sons as their daughters' lifemates; and my unnamed junior high school social studies teacher who once motivated me in a way she'll never know with her derisive castigation, "You're never going to amount to anything, Maxim!"

SECTION ONE

Foundational Principles

Learn what it is like to be a social studies teacher in an elementary school. Begin your path to successful teaching by acquiring a deep understanding of social studies as a school subject and learning how to draw on its central concepts and structures to plan classroom instruction for elementary school children. Discover the importance of integrating content and processes from various disciplines as you plan assessment-based, engaging, and effective social studies lessons. Ask yourself, what do I know about social studies and what do I need to learn in order to teach it well?

wavebreakmedia/Shutterstock

CHAPTER 1

Social Studies:
The Subject You Will Teach

Learning Outcomes

Have you ever stopped to think what makes some social studies teachers more successful than others? There is no simple answer, of course, but one characteristic that separates successful social studies teachers from the rest of the pack is that they are students of their profession. That is, they know and understand the nature of the subject they are teaching—its fundamental concepts, structure, and learning processes. Therefore, after completing this chapter, you will be able to:

- Appraise how your past elementary school recollections enhance and shape your future as a social studies teacher.

- Describe the nature of social studies as an elementary school subject.

- Explain how past approaches to teaching social studies have evolved into contemporary instructional practices.

- Identify the general strategies that exemplify best practices in contemporary social studies classrooms.

- Explain how democratic ideals are infused into daily classroom life.

Classroom Snapshot

Dorothy Holzwarth's fourth graders in Upper Darby, Pennsylvania, were about to wind up a thematic unit on their state when Naisha brought in a newspaper story about Maryland having recently adopted the monarch butterfly as its state insect. "Does Pennsylvania have a state insect, too?" inquired several interested youngsters. That was all it took to launch Mrs. Holzwarth's class into one of the most enjoyable social studies learning adventures it had ever tackled.

The students got the ball rolling by looking up information from various sources; they found a state flower, a state song, a state tree, a state nickname, and various other official state symbols but no official "state bug." The children wanted to write to the president of the United States to see if they could have one, but Mrs. Holzwarth explained that since this was a state matter, they should direct their query to their district legislators in Harrisburg, the state capital.

Before they did so, however, the class decided to conduct a regular democratic election to determine what insect would be the most fitting state symbol. Several insects were nominated, and each nominee became the subject of careful study. The students explored the pros and cons of an assortment of bugs, such as the praying mantis, dragonfly, ladybug, and grasshopper. After weighing the advantages and disadvantages of each, a class vote settled the matter: the firefly was their selection. Why? One reason was that the scientific name, Photuris pennsylvanica, closely resembled the name of their state. Students also liked the fact that these insects dotted their backyards on summer evenings and they spent many a summer night running around in pursuit of these elusive "lightning bugs."

After the vote, the students wrote a letter to their state representatives, asking how they might make their actions official. The lawmakers were extremely impressed with the children's civic energy and arranged to visit Mrs. Holzwarth's classroom to answer the children's questions and personally thank them for their interest in state issues. The awestruck youngsters listened intently as the legislators discussed the process of introducing a law in the state legislature and advised the students how to proceed with their project. Their next step would be to persuade other legislators to support their cause. Undaunted, these 26 children wrote more than 250 letters—203 to the House, 50 to the Senate, and 2 to the governor and his wife. The children also learned that they needed popular support from voters in their area, so they canvassed their neighborhoods and shopping malls until they obtained more than 2,100 signatures.

The students printed more than 600 bumper stickers proclaiming "Firefly for State Insect." They also kept up their letter writing campaign, asking legislators to vote YES when the bill came onto the floor. The children were invited to Harrisburg for the House Government Committee hearings on their bill.

When they arrived in Harrisburg, they were met head-on by television crews and reporters. The hearing was held according to established decorum, with the children testifying about fireflies for about 2 hours. The committee reported its unanimous support of the bill to the House of Representatives, and eventually the bill passed the House by a vote of 156 to 22. The Senate passed the bill by an overwhelming vote of 37 to 11. When the governor finally signed the bill (Act 59), the children were again in Harrisburg to watch the institution of a new state law. Photuris pennsylvanica officially took its place alongside the whitetail deer, ruffed grouse, and Great Dane as official state animals.

For Mrs. Holzwarth's class, this was much more than an exercise in choosing a state insect. It was an authentic, purposeful learning experience in which the children took direct political action and participated in legislative processes. They learned about petitioning and writing letters to their representatives, and they saw firsthand how government works. One child noted, "Now we have something to tell our grandchildren." Another, when asked if she would like to get another law passed, blurted, "Darn right! I'd like a law against homework. Homework gives you pimples!"

Successful social studies teachers like Mrs. Holzwarth enjoy their work and value the lives they touch. There are no secret recipes or mystical formulas to duplicate the Mrs. Holzwarths of our profession; each is one of a kind. As much as possible, they try to make social studies an inspiring, productive, and memorable experience for their students. They eagerly combine time-tested, traditional "best practices" with novel, groundbreaking approaches in an effort to encourage deep understandings, enhance curiosity, and provoke critical thinking. They value their role in the lives of children and realize that teachers—not books, not technology, not lesson plans, not buildings, and not even class size—are what really matter. They know and love our nation and hold bright hopes for its future. Their sense of democratic values influences everything they do in their social studies classrooms. Successful teachers know that young children are our future, and the way they live and learn today becomes the way they will live and learn tomorrow. They expertly handle with keen insight and skill all the subtle professional responsibilities that contribute to a quality social studies program, and their instructional choices are based on a maze of complicated decisions.

Few individuals are more meaningful in the lives of elementary school children than their parents, close relatives, and teachers. For that reason, elementary school social studies teachers should be among the finest people we know. But being a fine person does not in itself guarantee success. Successful teachers must also possess a set of professional skills founded on sound theoretical and research-based principles. They welcome the challenge of creating superb social studies classrooms and boldly demonstrate that they would rather be challenged than safe and bored. They work hard to acquire a "can-do spirit" early in their careers, for succeeding in complex situations is as much about attitude and self-confidence as it is about knowledge and skill.

As you strive for success, think of yourself much as an artist preparing to create an oil painting. Certainly, all artists must follow certain basics, acquire specialized painting skills, and practice a lot. But a common element among the artists who stand out seems to be that they have found a distinctive technique that transports their works beyond the ordinary. They are the ones who explore and experiment until they come up with a matchless style that expresses their inner feelings and touches the lives of others. Much like standout artists, successful social studies teachers are the product of a unique vision; they have a special *something* that makes students pause, look closer, and want to take part in the excitement of their classrooms. So work hard, dream a lot, and muster the grit to establish a point of view. However, you cannot, and should not, take risks unless your fundamentals are solid. Successful social studies teachers never take risks blindly; their decisions are based on a strong professional foundation. Build that foundation in social studies education and take your risks there, for it is the one area of the elementary school curriculum that most openly invites the ideas and dreams of adventurous and creative young teachers.

Reflection on Learning

You may simply scribble rough notes or jot down something more polished and complete. The point is to simply start recording your ideas spontaneously and candidly.

I've seen some pre-service teachers work for hours on a lesson plan only to fail miserably, and I've seen others glance over their material for 5 minutes before walking into a classroom and carry out a creative, spontaneous, and highly productive lesson. It makes you think . . . in the end, what makes a great teacher? What qualities would *you* expect a successful social studies teacher to demonstrate? Which do you currently possess? Which do you lack? Which are you in the process of developing?

Memories of Elementary School Social Studies

Our quest to understand how to teach social studies must reach into the past; analyzing threads of the past gives us the insight to examine current conditions. Whether we minimize their importance or cling to them throughout our professional lives, there is little doubt that our past elementary school experiences have shaped us as people and will cause us to behave in certain ways as teachers. All of us tend to attach ourselves to exemplary role models we hope to take after or to classroom conditions we hope to replicate. And, undoubtedly, there have been teachers we have vowed not to model ourselves after and scenarios we have promised to avoid. So go back to your elementary school days and take a close look. What do you remember about social studies from your elementary school days? Who was the *best* elementary school social studies teacher you ever had? Now, try to picture the *worst* elementary school social studies teacher you ever had. What memories do you have of those teachers? Can you single out any of these noteworthy individuals as having contributed to the person you are today? Jot down a list of three or four strong feelings or clear events (good and bad) that first pop into your mind and share your list with your classmates.

I enjoy doing this activity on the first day of a semester with my students. I find it instructive both for them and for me. Although I hesitate to describe this category first, the "dislike" category usually includes memories such as reading assigned pages from a textbook and answering questions at the end of the section (while the teacher corrected weekly spelling tests at his or her desk), listening to a teacher lecture about latitude and longitude (without the benefit of a map or a globe), memorizing facts about the early explorers of North America (where they came from, when they left their homeland, the date they arrived here, and where they explored), and copying facts word for word from a teacher's endless parade of PowerPoint slides (with an oversupply of information on slide after slide of small text). After discussing the "disliked" experiences, I ask students to suggest word labels that best sum up those types of educational experiences. "Boring," "lifeless," "dull," "mind-numbing," "a waste," and "humdrum" are some of the expressions I remember. The power of an ineffective teacher is something almost all of us have experienced on a personal level and, although they are a significant minority, it is a frustrating reality that there are ineffective teachers in some social studies classrooms.

Unfortunately, when they have such negative recollections of their past encounters with social studies, pre-service teachers tend to underestimate the hard work that goes into successful classroom instruction: "Is that all there is to it? Why, anybody can teach social studies to elementary school kids! Who can't tell them to take out their textbooks, read a few pages, and answer the questions at the end of the section? Why does anyone need to take a college methods course to learn to do something so simple?" When facing such satirical feedback from my students, I find that the best way to cope is to admit its legitimacy. It's true . . . anybody *can* tell children to take out their textbooks to read a few pages. And, yes, anybody *can* ask them the questions printed at the end of a reading selection. While these accusations are reasonable, they are missing the whole point of teaching in today's elementary school social studies classroom. Social studies is not meant to be taught that way.

In contrast to the "dislike" category, the "like" category usually includes memories such as "Writing our own classroom constitution and holding elections," "Making web-based travel brochures to interest students from other states to visit our state," "Once we had firefighters, who assisted in recovery efforts, to speak about their impressions and experiences at Ground Zero," "Role-playing a historical figure for a pageant of great people who lived during the Civil War," "Drawing hieroglyphics that represented our names," "Cooking venison stew as we read the book *Sign of the Beaver*," "Hearing a Peace Corps volunteer talk about his experiences in Sierra Leone," and "Taking food and clothing to a homeless shelter." Several students gave detailed explanations of favorite social studies teachers. One particularly striking remembrance was a story of Mrs. Dunbar:

> *I had a fifth-grade teacher, Mrs. Dunbar, who made social studies one of my favorite subjects. We always looked forward to social studies class because Mrs. Dunbar always had something special for us to do. Once, we were studying prehistoric life. Although health and safety regulations would probably not allow teachers to do this today, Mrs. Dunbar asked us to strip everything off and bring in bones left over from our dinners at home. You could probably guess that the next day we had a pile of all kinds of bones—fish, chicken, beef. . . . Our first job was to scrub them thoroughly with soap and water. Then we boiled them in vinegar water, soaked them in a bleach and water solution to make them white, dried them off, and put them in a large box called 'The Boneyard.' We were organized into groups and Mrs. Dunbar encouraged us to select any of the bones we wanted and glue or wire them together in the general shape of the dinosaurs we were studying. We gave our dinosaurs their scientific names and displayed an information card next to the models. Mrs. Dunbar called us paleontologists. I still remember the word because it was a real thrill to have such an impressive title at the time. She was such a talented teacher. As a matter of fact, Mrs. Dunbar is the reason I wanted to become a teacher.*

As the student related this story, I could not help but think how we all need a story of special teachers such as Mrs. Dunbar to remind us of the kinds of creative and inspirational behaviors that make individuals stand out from the crowd.

When asked to suggest words that best summed up these favorable kinds of experiences, students unfailingly come up with expressions such as "fun," "exciting," "interesting," "worthwhile," "rewarding," "active," and "creative." I bring closure to the activity by asking the students to think about these questions: "Which set of words would you want students to use when they describe *you* and *your* social studies program?" and "What will you need to know or be able to do for that to happen?"

The resulting discussion usually raises questions about the professional know-how required to carry out social studies programs that are fun, exciting, interesting, lively, rewarding, and active and, at the same time, instructive. A small number of students worry that using "fun-type" activities might create serious classroom management problems: "I'd like my social studies class to be fun and exciting, but I'm worried that the children, and I, will lose control." "Won't children think of the 'fun' activities as 'playtime' and just fool around in class, not learning anything?" Their concerns suggest a perception that "fun-type" activities are frivolous, lack challenge, or, at best, serve as convenient rewards for accomplishing the more serious stuff of classroom life.

Most of my students, however, tend to feel that being strictly serious about content can do just the opposite—result in a dull and boring social studies program. They fear that "serious-type" social studies programs can become trivial and tedious for both the teacher and the children. "It's a mistake to think of fun learning as wasted learning effort," they counter. "Fun does not mean easy; as teachers, we certainly need to encourage hard work. But self-motivated discovery and play are the most natural ways children learn. Children like to solve problems; they like to think. The problem is that educators often get in the way of this natural process by teaching a meaningless curriculum in an industrial factory setting."

As the class discussion draws to a close, my students typically ask these questions: "How can I make social studies fun and still maintain control over what the children do and understand?" "How can I get across the important social studies content without being run-of-the-mill or ordinary?" "How can I teach content without communicating to the children that we think they're unskilled or ignorant?" "Is it possible to blend both styles to achieve the greatest results?" One of the most significant challenges future social studies teachers face is, on the one hand, ensuring that children acquire the knowledge, skills, and values that help prepare them for constructive participation in a democratic society, and on the other hand, organizing and conducting lessons that offer a blend of pleasure, intrigue, variety, active involvement, and excitement.

Students benefit from fun, active social studies lessons designed with their unique needs and interests in mind.

Pressmaster/Shutterstock

As far back as 1933, John Dewey addressed this dilemma and offered some sage advice that remains relevant today. In speaking to the serious–fun dilemma of social studies instruction, Dewey (1933) wrote that if either is used exclusively, we end up with a double-edge sword: "Play degenerates into fooling [around] and work into drudgery" (p. 286). Instead of planning instruction at either end of the play–work continuum, Dewey suggested a delicate balance between seriousness and fun. That is, our social studies classrooms must be places where students play with ideas, think deeply about content, make connections to their lives, and become energized as active, eager learners. The key to successful teaching is creating a lively, playful, experiential curriculum that informs students about things that matter. If your curriculum is meaningful and fun for your students, it will be meaningful and fun for you, too.

The rest of this chapter will consider some of the defining attributes of social studies as a school subject and how to help make social studies a meaningful and vibrant experience for your students. They are not meant to be all inclusive, but the defining attributes have been organized as ***four dimensions of content***: (1) *knowing about the nature of social studies as a school subject;* (2) *understanding the origin, erosion, and rebirth of social studies as a school subject;* (3) *developing instructional practices that promote and support learning;* and (4) *creating a democratic classroom community that serves an array of diverse students.*

 CHECK YOUR UNDERSTANDING 1.1 **Click here** to check your understanding of this section of the chapter.

Attribute 1: Social Studies as a School Subject

As an elementary school teacher, you will be responsible for teaching a variety of subjects including math, language arts, reading, science, and social studies (and sometimes art, music, or physical education). And teaching those subjects well to a classroom full of 5- to 12-year-olds demands hard work, dedication, skill, and loads of knowledge. That is why you will be taking a number of methods courses that focus on specific subject areas. Those courses will vary in content and methodology, but social studies is part of your course lineup because it is the only class that offers specialized techniques explicitly intended to help children become active, responsible citizens in a diverse democratic society.

Being able to share with you a definition of social studies having general consensus is quite significant for those of us who have been in the field for a while, as it took over 75 years of controversy, disagreement, and debate before this deceptively uncomplicated task was completed by the professional community. Many find it incomprehensible that the field labored from 1916 to 1993 to ultimately agree on the nature of this school subject! (You will read more about this later in this chapter.) However, when you think about a subject responsible for achieving a goal as extensive as "educating good citizens," such a significant responsibility is bound to raise disputes among experts holding strong opinions about sensitive educational issues. That is why coming to an agreement on its definition can be arguably much more contentious than defining school subjects such as math or reading. With that in mind, the confirmed National Council for the Social Studies definition (NCSS, 1993) is a good place to start your investigation into the nature of social studies as an elementary school subject:

> *Social studies is the integrated study of the social sciences and humanities to promote civic competence. Within the school program, social studies provides coordinated, systematic study drawing upon such disciplines as anthropology, archaeology, economics, geography, history, law, philosophy, political science, psychology, religion, and sociology, as well as appropriate content from the humanities, mathematics, and natural sciences. The primary purpose of social studies is to help young people develop the ability to make informed and reasoned decisions for the public good as citizens of a culturally diverse, democratic society in an interdependent world.* (p. 3)

Clearly, the definition highlights two main characteristics that distinguish social studies from other subjects you will teach. That is, social studies (1) is *integrative*—by its nature, social studies incorporates content and processes from many disciplines—and (2) is the main school subject that assumes the *major goals* of preparing students with the knowledge, skills, and attitudes required for civic competence. Although civic competence is not the exclusive responsibility of social studies, it is more fundamental to social studies than to any other subject in the elementary school curriculum.

Integrative Social Studies

What is an integrated social studies curriculum? Basically, it is a way of connecting separate school subjects with social studies to focus upon unifying concepts or skills. This unity can be commonly brought about in either, or both, of two major ways: *intra*disciplinary integration and *inter*disciplinary integration. *Intradisciplinary integration* happens when the knowledge and skills of the disciplines that make up one school subject are fused together for instruction. For example, reading, writing, listening, speaking, viewing, and visually representing have been merged into the elementary school subject we call "language arts." Disciplines such as biology, chemistry, astronomy, zoology, meteorology, botany, and geology have been combined as the elementary school subject known as "science." Similarly, history, geography, civics, economics, sociology, and anthropology have been joined into a subject we know well as "social studies."

The process of *interdisciplinary integration*, on the other hand, combines the various school subjects for the purpose of examining a central theme, issue, problem, topic, or experience. To help your students better understand a complex issue such as global warming, for example, you may plan learning experiences that include content, skills, and processes from science, technology, language arts, art, and social studies.

SOCIAL STUDIES AS AN INTRADISCIPLINARY SCHOOL SUBJECT

To help you understand the connections among the different sub-disciplines of social studies, it is essential to look into two seemingly similar terms that people often confuse: *social science* and *social studies*. Although the terms are often used interchangeably, they are quite different.

Let us first examine the term *social science*. The word *social* indicates that we are dealing with people living together in organized groups, or societies. The word *science* is derived from the Latin word *Scientia*; it means "knowledge." So, if we combine the separate words *social* and *science*, we can define a *social science* as any of several disciplines that examine how people interact and develop as social beings. If you're interested in learning about the exercise of authority in India, for example, you would want to consider a social science that explains governing systems. If you want to know where the finest coffee growing regions of the world are located, it would be wise to look into a social science that describes places on Earth and how those places influence human activity. Social sciences cover a variety of disciplines; each has its own investigative methodology and specialized field of knowledge.

Six major social sciences contribute to most elementary school social studies programs: geography, history, political science, anthropology, sociology, and economics. Each discipline is distinctive, but specialists from one discipline often find that their research overlaps with work being done in another. *Social studies* is an umbrella label for the curricular area that brings together the subarea social sciences into a single coordinated, systematic school subject area called social studies (see Figure 1.1).

Geography "What is the Ring of Fire?" "Why does New York City have so much traffic?" and "How does global warming affect ocean life?" are but three of the countless questions geographers ask about places on Earth and their relationship to the people who live there. Geographers study people and places by investigating Earth's physical dimensions (such as mountains, deserts, rivers, and oceans) and its human dimensions (the impact of Earth's physical features on people and vice versa).

History Historians systematically investigate, analyze, and interpret the past by asking questions such as "What happened?" "Why did it happen?" and "What can we learn from what has

FIGURE 1.1 The Social Sciences

happened?" Historians use various tools to help them answer their questions. Some of these tools are called *primary sources*—something written or created by people who were present during a historical event. Letters, diaries, speeches, interviews, or photographs are examples of primary sources. Artifacts such as government documents, weapons, tools, or toys are also considered primary sources. Historical evidence, such as books or paintings, produced after a historical event by someone not actually present at the event, is called a *secondary source*. In general, primary or secondary historical evidence can be separated into three groups: what has been written, what has been said, and what has been physically preserved.

Civics   Civics is the study of the rights and responsibilities of citizenship, including the ways governments and political systems operate—how people get power, what their duties are, and how they carry out their duties. Civic education in our nation's democratic society focuses on understanding the ideals of democracy and a reasoned commitment to its values: "What are the purposes and function of governments?" "How is power justified, created, exercised, and challenged?" "What are the rights and duties of citizenship?"

Anthropology   Anthropologists study people and their physical, social, and cultural development. They examine the total pattern of human behavior and its products particular to a special group (language, tools, beliefs, social forms, art, law, customs, traditions, religion, superstitions, morals, occupations, and so on). Anthropologists usually concentrate in one of four specialties—archaeology, cultural anthropology, linguistic anthropology, or biological–physical anthropology. *Archaeology* is the scientific study of earlier civilizations carried out by recovering and examining material evidence of the past, such as skeletal remains, fossils, ruins, implements, tools, monuments, and other items from past human cultures, to determine their history, customs, and living habits. *Cultural anthropology* is the study of customs, cultures, and social lives in settings that vary from nonindustrialized societies to modern urban centers. *Linguistic anthropology* examines the role of language in various cultures. *Biological–physical anthropology* studies the evolution of the human body and analyzes how culture and biology influence one another. Because of this immense scope of study, anthropology has often been described as a universal discipline. Anthropologists ask basic questions such as "When, where, and how did humans evolve?" "How have societies developed and changed from the ancient past to the present?" "How do people obtain food, prepare it, and share it?" "How do people in various cultures dress or communicate?" "How do its rituals and ceremonies define this group of human beings?"

Sociology   Sociologists study society and social behavior by examining the groups and social institutions people form, such as families, governments, religions, businesses, or schools. They also study the behaviors and interactions of groups, analyzing the influence of group activities on individual members. Sociologists investigate the values and norms of groups to discover why group members behave as they do. They study how groups form, how they operate, and how they change. Sociologists organize their study of groups around many questions such as "What kinds of groups of people form in any given society?" "What are the expectations of group members?" "What problems do group members face?" and "How do groups exert control over their members?"

Economics   Economists study the production, distribution, and consumption of goods and services by asking questions such as "What goods and services best meet market needs?" "How should those goods and services be produced?" "Who is willing and able to get the goods and services?" From youngsters who save their allowance for a special toy, to college students who must scrape together enough money for tuition, to newlyweds who apply for a mortgage as they buy their first home, all people face situations in which they attempt to satisfy unlimited wants with limited resources. It is from this idea, the *scarcity concept*, that economics emerges. Because of scarcity, humans have attempted to find ways to produce more in less time with less material, thus developing specialization of labor. Specialization led to the idea of interdependence, a reliance of people on one another that necessitates monetary, transportation, and communication systems. From the interactions of these factors, a market system developed through which buyers and sellers produce and exchange goods or services. Finally, governments, responsible for controlling segments of the market system, ensure the welfare of all their citizens.

SOCIAL STUDIES AS AN INTERDISCIPLINARY SCHOOL SUBJECT

As an elementary school teacher, I often questioned the conventional practice of teaching school subjects as separate classes. My main questions had to do with sensed similarities among individual subjects in terms of subject matter, instructional strategies, and learning processes. Why is it that when my students read a story about Sojourner Truth at 9:30 in the morning and I use a graphic organizer to strengthen their comprehension skills, they label it *reading*? Why is it that when we read about Abraham Lincoln at 2:30 in the afternoon and I use a graphic organizer to help students organize information, they label it *social studies*? I'm essentially doing the same thing. The only difference between the two classes is the time of day and the person we are reading about! Considering the overlap of literacy and social studies, wouldn't instruction have been more meaningful and efficient if it were organized across the disciplines? How could anyone possibly teach social studies without teaching reading, too (and art, and science, and math, and music, and writing, and every other school subject)? Have you ever thought about these things, too? Elementary school students often do, in their own way. For example, curious about how my students comprehended what we were doing in school, I once asked my third graders to define both reading and social studies. One student, Gina, mirrored my questions about separate subjects with her response: "Reading is what we do at 9:00 in the morning and social studies is what we do at 2:30 in the afternoon."

Thankfully, in today's elementary school curriculum, teachers are encouraged to integrate learning across the disciplines. They bring together the common learnings from the separate subjects to help build targeted skills and concepts. As you progress through your methods coursework, you will find that social studies applies many strategies you will be learning about, such as storytelling, read alouds, readers' theater, shared reading, guided reading, independent reading, and all types of writing opportunities from the *language arts*; how specialized geography and anthropology topics can tie in beautifully with *science* and *math*; how *art* and *music* help children understand other cultures. An ideal interdisciplinary subject, social studies in the elementary grades enables our emerging citizens to actively confront the complex dynamics underlying critical social issues by integrating what they learn from other classes into satisfying problem-solving and decision-making experiences. You will find that interdisciplinary instruction commonly employs project-based learning, a strategy through which students work for an extended period of time to investigate and respond to an engaging and complex question, problem, or challenge that cuts across two or more disciplines.

Despite the advantages of interdisciplinary learning, it can become a disaster if planning is hasty, narrow, or uninformed. Newscasts and web sources in mid-January 2012, for example, reverberated with the story of a suburban Atlanta teacher who resigned in shame and embarrassment after it was found that his students were given math homework that included offensive word problems about slavery. One problem read: "Each tree has 56 oranges. If eight slaves pick them equally, then how much would each slave pick?" Another was: "If Frederick [who apparently was Frederick Douglass] got two beatings each day, how many beatings did he get in one week? Two weeks?" News of these "slavery math problems" left parents, educators, and the general public in disbelief: How could a qualified teacher pose such outrageous questions? According to a district spokesperson, the teacher did not write the homework to be malicious or offensive; he was trying to *integrate social studies into the math curriculum.* The "Frederick" math problem, for example, was a misguided attempt to help students explain the hardships Douglass had to overcome before he ultimately became a hero. The incident was especially confounding because it took place in a school where 88% of the students were either African American or Hispanic and half the staff was non-Caucasian.

To be able to plan and carry out integrated learning competently, you must select *proper* learning contexts that trigger student interests and meet their instructional needs. To avoid serious problems like the one in suburban Atlanta, it is important to know what makes interdisciplinary learning work and whether the experience will be beneficial to students. The material that follows is planned to challenge you to find ways to integrate literacy and social studies in purposeful and meaningful ways.

Interdisciplinary and intradisciplinary integration have been important missions of social studies since its inception as a school subject. It would be instructive to return to the definition of social studies to examine how both types of curriculum integration are incorporated.

 Video Exploration 1.1

Major Social Studies Goals

As a nation, we have traditionally placed social studies at the core of the elementary school curriculum because we are a proud people—a democratic republic of nearly 320 million citizens, each of whom is part of a unique political venture. We prize our political processes, our institutions, our shared heritage, and our freedom. To preserve and protect this inheritance, we have called on our schools to fully prepare our youngsters to participate in and maintain our democratic nation. We want our future citizens to respect our past as a democratic society and recognize the rich contributions of all groups who have made modern America a free and powerful nation. We want students to take active roles as champions of freedom who stand up for the rights and responsibilities of citizenship. We want students to speak with their voices, actions, and votes for the improvement of the quality of life in our families, communities, nation, and world.

We will look at goals much more closely in Chapter 2, but for now, think of a goal as something important you seek to accomplish. The overriding goal of social studies is now and always has been to prepare students for the most important duty they will be entrusted with as adults—accepting a post that Thomas Jefferson called *the office of citizen*. Jefferson viewed the office of citizen not as a place of employment but as a responsibility of all citizens to accept active involvement in governance. Surely, Thomas Jefferson is best known for drafting the Declaration of Independence but he also wrote volumes on education. He viewed education as an indispensable component of American democracy because, he argued, it is impossible for a nation to be both ignorant and free. According to Jefferson, then, preparing citizens to take an active role in the affairs of our democracy has *education* at its heart. NCSS (2010) has mirrored Jefferson's emphasis on an educated citizenry by stressing that "the aim of social studies is the promotion of civic competence—the knowledge, intellectual processes, and democratic dispositions required of students to be active and engaged participants in public life. By making civic competence a central aim, NCSS emphasizes the importance of educating students who are committed to the ideas and values of democracy" (p. 9).

What do students need to know or be able to do to develop civic competence? Although several professional organizations have issued outcome statements for K–12 social studies programs, the NCSS Task Force on Early Childhood/Elementary Social Studies (1989) compiled a list specifically targeting the early childhood and elementary school grades. The task force emphasized that although the basic skills of reading, writing, and computing are indispensable, they are incapable, by themselves, of addressing the complex social, economic, ethical, and personal matters of contemporary society. The responsibility of enabling children to productively participate in their world must be shouldered by a systematically planned social studies program. The task force recommended that the program's essential goals be divided into three broad areas: knowledge, skills, and values and beliefs.

KNOWLEDGE

A social studies program should help students construct a rich and accurate background of information about the world at large and the world at hand, the world of the past and the world of the future. This knowledge base provides the necessary foundation for emerging reflective thought.

Think for a moment about all the social studies knowledge you have accumulated over the years. Some, like the name of the 17th president of the United States or the major exports of Bolivia, may have been long forgotten. However, there may be other knowledge you believe that every literate American should know. What five specific facts do you feel are indispensable for today's youth? Write them down. Compare your list with those of your classmates. Should children learn about important *people* such as Benjamin Franklin, Confucius, or Harriet Tubman? What about important *places* such as the Gobi Desert, the Fertile Crescent, or the rainforests of the Amazon? Should we include important *things*, such as pueblos, railroads, or the Great Wall of China? And how about including significant *events*, such as the Battle of Bull Run, the rise of Christianity, or the discovery of Mohenjo-Daro? Did anyone suggest significant *ideas*, such as Henry Ford's assembly line, Hinduism, or the Bill of Rights? Like the suggestions you furnished for this brief exercise, school districts must describe specific social studies content for each grade level.

SKILLS

The skills that are primary to social studies are those related to maps and globes, such as understanding and using locational and directional terms. Skills that are shared with other parts of the curriculum but may be most powerfully taught through social studies include communication skills such as writing and speaking; research skills such as collecting, organizing, and interpreting data; reading skills such as reading pictures, books, maps, charts, and graphs; and technology skills such as keyboarding, word processing, digital citizenship, online safety, and information literacy skills.

VALUES AND BELIEFS

The early years are ideal for children to begin to understand core civic principles, or core democratic values (i.e., justice, individual rights, truth, the common good, equality of opportunity, and diversity), especially in terms of the smaller social entities of the family, classroom, and community. Children can also develop, within the context of social studies, positive attitudes toward knowledge and learning and develop a spirit of inquiry that will enhance their understanding of their world so that they will become rational, humane, participating, effective members of a democratic society.

Social studies provides students with the knowledge, skills, and values and beliefs that enable them to become informed, active, and responsible citizens.

bikeriderlondon/Shutterstock

Over the past few decades, teachers have been bombarded with terms such as "goals," "objectives," "outcomes," "competencies," and "standards" as approaches to education have shifted from *objectives*-based, to *competency*-based, to *outcomes*-based, to *standards*-based. These shifts in approach were intended to improve our schools, but the process of change has been perplexing. Rapid shifts have often resulted in great difficulty grasping the precise meanings of associated terms. For the purposes of this text, however, think of *goals* as long-range, general statements of what your social studies program intends to accomplish—the end results of instruction expressed in broad terms (e.g., preparing active, responsible citizens). Goals provide a framework on which the more specific *standards* of an educational program can be affixed. Standards are the brief, defining statements spelling out the specific skills, values, and attitudes linked with the broader goals of instruction. Goals and standards both describe the intended results of instruction; the major difference between the two terms is that goals communicate long-range, unmeasurable end results in general terms while standards communicate short-term, measurable results in specific terms.

 Video Exploration 1.2

 CHECK YOUR UNDERSTANDING 1.2 **Click here** to check your understanding of this section of the chapter.

Attribute 2: The Origin, Erosion, and Rebirth of Social Studies

The phrase "Phoenix rising from the ashes" popped into my head one day, and I didn't understand why until I started planning this chapter. Those of you familiar with the Harry Potter books and movies undoubtedly know about the amazing power of the phoenix, but for those not familiar with the idiom, it refers to a mythical Egyptian bird that lived in the Arabian Desert. Every 500 years, the phoenix would build its own funeral pyre (nest) and set it on fire with a single clap of its wings. From the pile of ashes, a young and more powerful phoenix would rise anew. That was it! "Phoenix rising from the ashes" was suddenly the burst of inspiration I needed to help me symbolize the fascinating transformation of social studies from the time it was born, to when it was almost consumed by the searing fires of neglect, to when it rose up again in hope.

Social Studies Is Born

To understand how this scenario evolved, join me on a simulated trip back to 1916 to share in the joy and excitement of seeing social studies first enter this world as an elementary school subject. In addition to observing events such as Pershing raiding Mexico in search of Poncho Villa, Enrico Caruso recording *O Solo Mio* for the Victor Talking Machine Company, and Boston's Rube Forster no-hitting the New York Yankees, we will also witness the National Education Association (NEA) searching for fresh new educational approaches to address the unprecedented wave of immigration that took place at the turn of the 20th century. Most immigrants didn't know English and had very little education, so a movement to educate and Americanize these millions of foreign-born families was approached with considerable intensity. To help the flood of immigrant children understand the history and way of life in their new land, schools were expected not only to teach them to speak the English language, but also to provide drill and practice in the three "Rs" (reading, 'riting and 'rithmetic) and to instill American customs, standards of behavior, and morals. This was accomplished by reading stories about prominent historical figures as well as about the early formation of the United States. Schools addressed standards of behavior through the messages contained in moralistic stories from the McGuffey Readers, a series of graded readers that were widely used as textbooks in American schools from the mid-19th century to the mid-20th century. The McGuffey Readers helped form the nation's character, encouraged allegiance to country, and forged American values through stories stressing virtues such as always telling the truth; working hard; resisting the temptation to lie, steal, or cheat; and honoring one's father and mother. McGuffey values were reinforced by patriotic symbols in the classroom—the American flag, which hung at the front of bare elementary classrooms, flanked by portraits of Presidents Washington and Lincoln. This process became known as "Americanization." However, most children attended school for only a few years, if at all. They often opted out for work in factories, coal mines, and on farms in order to help support their struggling families.

During this time, John Dewey challenged the rigidity that characterized many American classrooms by claiming that these practices were inadequate for preparing young citizens well for life in a vibrant democracy. He insisted that the stern practices (for example, immigrant children were struck on their knuckles with rulers or paddles for using their native language, or had their mouths washed out with soap) should be replaced by a caring community, commitment to diversity, learning-by-doing approaches (hands-on projects and thematic units), democratic classroom relationships, and an integrated curriculum. Dewey was a harsh critic of "dead" knowledge, which he characterized as any learning that was disconnected from practical life.

After much deliberation about whether existing instructional practices or the innovative approaches of the emerging Progressive Education movement would best promote effective citizenship, the NEA surprisingly suggested that reform could best be achieved with a brand-new school subject called *social studies*. Making this proposal was a bold move, since never before had a school subject called *social studies* existed in the United States or anywhere else in the world. The major mission of this completely new school subject was to promote the "social efficiency" of citizens in a rapidly changing society. The "subject matter" was to be drawn from the three most influential social sciences of the time—history, geography, and civics—and blended together as one school subject for the purpose of helping children understand their American heritage and acquire the skills and sensitivities basic to constructive participation in our nation's democratic society. (It has now expanded to include the six social disciplines described earlier.)

Although the promise of this new subject called "social studies" was widely discussed among educators, it encountered a highly unreceptive school bureaucracy and failed to be widely implemented. Citizenship education continued to be carried out into the 1930s and 1940s with teacher lectures as well as readings of moralistic stories.

A "PROGRESSIVE" SOCIAL STUDIES CURRICULUM

By the early 1930s, Lucy Sprague Mitchell (1934) became one of the first educators to popularly apply Dewey's Progressive Education philosophy to NEA's new conception of social studies instruction when, at the Bank Street College of Education in New York City (part of Columbia University), she designed her famed "Here-and-Now" curriculum. Mitchell contended that traditional instruction was completely disconnected from students' young lives and proposed that children's immediate life experiences should form the basis of the curriculum. Mitchell asserted that the best way for children to learn about the world was to first explore the familiar (here-and-now) and to apply what they learned through follow-up projects such as recording their observations on graphs, charts, original stories, drawings, and murals. The learnings from children's firsthand explorations (usually well-planned field trips) would then serve as the base on which students could establish connections with increasingly remote people, places, and events; therefore, Mitchell's social studies curriculum contained several themes that expanded from self-knowledge, to family, to neighborhood, and to community.

The basic tenet of Progressive Education subscribed to by Mitchell was that real-world situations and problems provide the best context for learning because they provoke deep thinking

Children must be actively engaged in developmentally suitable activities through which they learn about the world in which we live and their place in it.

in a problem-solving framework. The teacher was no longer considered to be the center of instruction, but a facilitator who nurtured and supported the students' efforts. Consider this series of events, for example: The 6-year-olds are building a model farm out of blocks; laying out the land for pastures, meadows, or grain fields; experimenting by planting corn in cotton and in soil; and husking and cooking corn obtained on a visit to a farm. The 7-year-olds are studying prehistoric life in caves they constructed, while their 8-year-old friends are role-playing the lives of Phoenician merchants and traders inventing, adopting, or adapting a system of measurements and weights, a numerical system, and a system of records. The 9- and 10-year-olds are studying colonial history, building a replica of a room that might have been found in an early American house. Teachers give the children raw wool. They examine the wool, and they spin it with their fingers and wind it on a stone. Although you could expect to see these experiences carried out in today's best schools, they actually took place in Progressive laboratory classrooms at the University of Chicago in the early 1900s. Dewey (1896) asserted that, "the child comes to school to *do*; to cook, to sew, to work with wood and tools in simple constructive acts; within and about these acts cluster the studies—writing, reading, arithmetic" (p. 245).

THE "EXPANDING ENVIRONMENTS" CURRICULUM MODEL

Now that the "social studies" movement and Progressive Education were gaining momentum as wary partners, heated rivalries soon cropped up about what kind of curriculum would best advance well-informed, responsible, and engaged citizenship for our changing nation. Traditionalists claimed that elementary school social studies programs should remain controlled by the established subjects of American history, geography, and civics. Others suggested that social studies, especially during the early elementary grades, should be taught in a child-centered, integrated style advocated by progressive educators. In the midst of this debate, teachers went about their work with very little consequential change through the 1930s and into the 1960s. Progressive education was virtually abandoned in the 1950s, and it fell apart as a distinguishable movement by the end of that decade. However, during the ensuing years, a number of educators held onto or rediscovered Dewey's ideas. He has been widely referenced and his recommendations have been broadly implemented even into this century.

The NEA's 1916 concept of "social studies" received major support in the early 1960s with Paul R. Hanna (1963). Hanna conceived of an "Expanding Communities" approach to elementary school social studies that mirrored Lucy Sprague Mitchell's belief that social studies should be thought of as a coordinated, integrated study of people that starts with what is familiar to children and progressively moves outward to expanding human communities. Have you ever thrown a pebble into a quiet pond and watched the ripples radiate outward? Much like watching the ripples of a pond, Hanna visualized social studies content as a series of concentric circles starting with the self at the center and progressively radiating out to wider communities: *home and school* in Grade 1, the *neighborhood* in Grade 2, *community* in Grade 3, *state and region* in Grade 4, *United States* in Grade 5, and the *hemisphere (or world)* in Grade 6.

Hanna's concept quickly became the accepted curriculum framework that nearly every school district, textbook company, and curriculum leader used to organize the elementary school social studies program; Hanna's *Expanding Communities* textbook-centered approach, supplemented with Progressive Education's child-centered projects and periodic inquiry episodes, defined social studies instruction from the 1960s to the turn of this century. Now better known as the *Expanding Environments approach*, the framework has dominated elementary school social studies for well over 50 years.

The Expanding Environments approach has been scrutinized over the years with varying degrees of acknowledgement. Into the 1980s, Diane Ravitch (1987), one of Expanding Environments' sharpest critics, called the approach anti-intellectual, redundant with what children learn outside school, trivial, and boring. Into the new millennium, Bruce Frazee and Samuel Ayers (2003) claimed that while this approach appears to provide an organized curricular sequence, it lacks meaningful content, especially in the early elementary grades, and children tend to find it deeply trivial and repetitious. The authors say that students in grades K–3 are taught about community helpers such as mail carriers and firefighters, but those lessons are superfluous (what kindergartener or first grader is unfamiliar with mail carriers and firefighters?). Even the National Council for the Social Studies (2009) claimed in its position statement "Powerful and Purposeful Teaching and Learning in Elementary School Social Studies": "The [Expanding Environments] curriculum model of self, family, community, state, and nation is insufficient for today's young learners" (p. 31). While daunting at times, the sharp criticism has been successfully deflected and most social studies curricula, and social studies textbooks, are still based on variations of the Expanding Environments approach.

 Video Exploration 1.3

THE "SPIRAL" CURRICULUM

Numerous federally funded curriculum projects during the 1960s and 1970s (a trend known as "New Social Studies") stressed the use of inquiry, critical thinking, primary documents, and multimedia data sources that they claimed had been missing from the Expanding Environments textbook programs. Several were published as textbook series, but most fizzled after two or three years of use. Most all of these suggested replacements for Expanding Environments were described as a form of *Spiral Curriculum*. The Spiral Curriculum is based on a cognitive theory proposed by cognitive psychologist Jerome Bruner during the 1960s. A single sentence from his writings may have influenced educational change at that time more than any other stimulus: "We begin with the hypothesis that any subject can be taught in some intellectually honest form to any child at any stage of development" (1960, p. 33). Although Bruner's intent was to argue for more science in our elementary schools, many educators used the statement to claim that even highly complex material, if properly structured and presented, can be grasped by young children. This idea supported the concept of the spiral curriculum, ". . . in which ideas are first presented in a form and language . . . which can be grasped by the child, ideas that can be revisited later with greater precision and power until, finally, the student has achieved the reward of mastery" (Bruner, 1966, p. 107). Using this approach, a key concept is introduced during the early grades and students return to that concept repeatedly and in more depth throughout the grades. So, a key concept introduced by a first-grade teacher will continue to be taught throughout Grade 5 or 6, but with greater complexity and difficulty as the children develop and mature.

Key concepts for the Spiral Curriculum, such as *culture, heritage, authority, interdependence,* and *scarcity,* are selected for their ability to synthesize a large amount of information and for ease of use on different levels of complexity or abstraction. For example, Figure 1.2 shows that as time goes on (each loop is a full year), students learn about the same concept but in more complex contexts. For example, suppose that *interdependence*—people *depend* on others for certain things—is a targeted concept for your school. So in Grade 1, the concept may be taught within the context of a family system, where each member of a family has an effect on the other members' thoughts, feelings, and actions, and that these are reciprocal—when one family member changes, it affects the entire family. In Grade 3, the concept may grow to other social contexts, such as the community; for example, although farmers grow fruits and vegetables or obtain meat, milk, and eggs from pigs, cows, and chickens, they remain *dependent* on others for hoes, rakes, tractors, and other tools. Likewise, unless they live on a farm, those suppliers are *dependent* on farmers for their food. In Grade 5, children learn that Botswana is the largest producer of diamonds in Africa. It earns 80% of its revenue by exporting this mineral to countries such as the United States, the United Kingdom, and Germany. In return, Botswana imports vehicles, electrical appliances, household utensils, and other materials from the international community.

In summary, the Expanding Environments approach selects grade-level content according to the developmental characteristics of the students while the Spiral Curriculum selects topics, themes, and problems unrestricted by developmental concerns. Students are exposed to the same concepts through all the grades during the elementary school years, repeatedly building on these concepts as their knowledge becomes deeper. A dynamic social studies curriculum, whether Expanding Environments or Spiral, provides, in its own way, for consistent and cumulative learning from kindergarten through the middle school years. Content is extended and enriched at each grade level, with students building on knowledge and skills already learned while preparing for what is to come.

FIGURE 1.2 The Spiral Curriculum

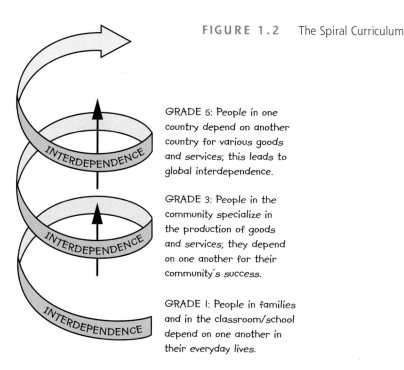

GRADE 5: People in one country depend on another country for various goods and services; this leads to global interdependence.

GRADE 3: People in the community specialize in the production of goods and services; they depend on one another for their community's success.

GRADE 1: People in families and in the classroom/school depend on one another in their everyday lives.

Reflection on Learning

You may simply scribble rough notes or jot down something more polished and complete. The point is to simply start recording your ideas spontaneously and candidly.

If you were to look in on an elementary school social studies classroom today, which of the ground-breaking reform recommendations of the past would you expect to see?

Social Studies in Decline

In its various forms, social studies remained a powerful and important part of the elementary school curriculum until the new millennium when educators faced pressures to hop on a new bandwagon. For some reason, educators have been habitually enticed to jump on bandwagons. The most recent bandwagon appears to be the modern standards movement that gained much initial attention with the publication of *A Nation at Risk* (National Commission on Excellence in Education, 1983). The report examined the quality of education in the United States and reported in its first sentence that, "Our nation is at risk:" (p. 1): "If an unfriendly foreign power had attempted to impose on America the mediocre instructional performance that exists today, we might well have viewed it as an act of war" (p. 9). As far as social studies was concerned, many feared that America's students did not have the necessary knowledge to make informed decisions about issues that affected them. Tests of social studies knowledge brought our nation's attention to just how devastating the situation had become. Richard Paxton (2003) reported some alarming results—for example, 14% of America's teens identified Abraham Lincoln as our country's first president. The same percentage said that our country celebrates its independence from France each July 4; 11% named John Adams, our second president (succeeding Abe Lincoln?), as the composer of *The Star-Spangled Banner*, and 9% believed it was Betsy Ross! *A Nation at Risk* drummed up popular interest in the quality of public education in the United States and the public demanded more stringent educational *standards*. A new bandwagon was under way in the United States and continues to the present!

PROFESSIONAL STANDARDS

In 1989, the National Council of Teachers of Mathematics (NCTM), a professional organization of mathematics educators, started the trend by publishing a set of professional standards for teaching mathematics. The NCTM standards served as a model for similar efforts in other school subjects, and soon the importance of social studies surged to the forefront: "What should be taught?" "How should it be taught?" and "How should student achievement be assessed?" Using these questions as a guide, a task force of the National Council for the Social Studies (1994) published *Curriculum Standards for Social Studies: Expectations of Excellence*, which specified what students should know and when they should know it. The standards were meant to provide a framework for professional curriculum planning and development. These initial NCSS standards were revised in 2010 (NCSS, 2010). The current NCSS social studies curriculum standards focus on 10 themes, as did the original standards:

1. Culture
2. Time, continuity, and change
3. People, places, and environments
4. Individual development and identity
5. Individuals, groups, and institutions
6. Power, authority, and governance
7. Production, distribution, and consumption

8. Science, technology, and society
9. Global connections
10. Civic ideals and practices

The themes constitute the organizing strands that should weave their way through social studies programs from pre-kindergarten through Grade 12. You can request a copy of the *National Curriculum Standards for Social Studies* (Bulletin 111) by writing to the National Council for the Social Studies or visiting the NCSS website.

In addition to the NCSS standards, most of the individual social sciences created separate reports to provide a consistent, clear understanding of what students were expected to learn or be able to do. You may wish to access the Internet to visit sites that contain standards from the individual social sciences (but note that, as of this publication, standards for anthropology and sociology are not available):

National Center for History in the Schools
National Council for Geographic Education
Center for Civic Education
Council for Economic Education

NO CHILD LEFT BEHIND (NCLB)

During the early 2000s, public education was immersed in waves of standards proposals to address the concerns raised in *A Nation at Risk*. The whole conundrum seemed to reach its decisive moment in 2002 with the introduction of *No Child Left Behind* (U.S. Department of Education, 2002). As a matter of fact, our story of the "Social Studies Phoenix" picks up again at this point as a proud and vibrant social studies began to slowly wither away in a nest of dying embers stoked by a steady reduction of instructional time resulting from the unintended effects of NCLB. Under NCLB law, states were directed to set standards for grade-level achievement and to test students in reading and math in Grades 3 through 8 and once in high school. Schools that regularly missed yearly achievement targets could be penalized in several ways, including state intervention or school closing; thus, the tests were labeled as "high stakes." Facing such pressure, schools struggled to improve reading and math test scores and soon were desperate to find extra time to spend teaching those tested subjects . . . something else had to go. In most cases, it was social studies. Social studies was considered a nonessential subject that was taught only after the basics of reading and mathematics were thoroughly addressed. "We were lucky if we found a total of an hour per week to squeeze in social studies during those days," recalled fifth-grade teacher Jeff Barker. "And, when we did jam social studies into the end of a day's schedule, all we had time for was a round robin reading of a few pages from the textbook followed up with a brief 'interrogation' to see if they learned anything. We tended to overlook, ignore, or wholly neglect social studies. And, to be honest, many classroom teachers did not support efforts to increase time spent on social studies because they were too worried about their reading and math test scores. Actually, we were forced to stop teaching social studies entirely when testing time came around! Why take the time?" The brutal NCLB testing cycle, then, appeared to cheat Mr. Barker and other teachers of their dream-building time; they were convinced that their days of experiencing the joy and satisfaction of active social studies were long gone. Social studies was placed on a pyre of neglect with the hope that it would just sit there quietly until reduced to a pile of ashes. Why waste time with social studies when there are so many more important things to be done? Out of sight, out of mind was the general idea.

Although facing such a disheartening outlook, the social studies profession refused to simply slowly disintegrate in the pyre. That was no place for a proud and distinguished school subject! The National Council for the Social Studies (2007) was especially determined to bring social studies back to life by insisting that it was a core subject that needed to be considered on equal footing with literacy and mathematics: "Since the introduction of NCLB, there has been a steady reduction in the amount of time spent in the teaching of social studies, with the most profound decline noticed in the elementary grades. . . . That such a situation has evolved is untenable in a nation that prides itself on its history, its system of government and its place as a leader in the global community." Because citizenship had been considered the central purpose of social studies, as well as the cornerstone of public schooling, social studies education advocates felt it was vital to convince policymakers and legislators that citizenship proficiency was equal to proficiency in reading and math and should be given shared emphasis in the curriculum: How can we morally deny our youth quality social studies instruction and fail to provide the knowledge, skills, and attitudes prerequisite of effective citizenship in our proud democratic society?

COMMON CORE STATE STANDARDS (CCSS)

In 2009, the push for social studies rebirth received a surprising shot in the arm from a second influential standards initiative—the *Common Core State Standards* (National Governors Association, 2010). There have been many bandwagons in education during the last 50 years, but few have been as imposing as the *Common Core State Standards Initiative*. Being rushed into nearly every school district in the country, CCSS hoped to transform a big, ailing chunk of our nation's K–12 educational system by outlining the knowledge and skills in English language arts (ELA) and mathematics required for students to ultimately be successful in college and in their careers. Those who supported this effort believed that having a common standards framework would be helpful in minimizing the confusion caused by numerous professional and governmental standards documents.

"I understand the rationale behind CCSS," acknowledged Jeff Barker, a fifth-grade teacher at the Inwood Academy for Leadership Charter School in New York City (serving primarily Hispanic and African-American children in the Washington Heights neighborhood of Upper Manhattan). "The goal of holding American students to higher expectations is certainly legitimate and I support it for our students at Inwood Academy." As creative, passionate teachers seeking ways to serve their students well, the faculty at Inwood Academy has faced many school-related challenges, many of which include the staggering influence of poverty on the lives of their children. Mr. Barker continued, "With appropriate nurturing and support, these students can and will thrive. Poverty does not mean ignorance; my children do have a deep thirst for knowledge and can be high achievers when I implement strategies that facilitate success."

Mr. Barker was worried, however, that the computer-based testing of CCSS would ultimately drive curriculum and instruction; if the tests were to be used for high-stakes outcomes as they were with *No Child Left Behind*, the teachers were concerned that their lessons would become so scripted that they could be robbed of their professional autonomy. "Will we have no other choice than to teach to the test using direct, simplistic 'drill and kill' strategies?" "Will testing, and practice for test-taking, demand so much time for language arts and math that it will continue to reduce or eliminate time from one or more untested subjects or activities (social studies, science, art and music, physical education, lunch, or recess)?" As with Inwood Academy's teachers, social studies educators around the country were wary not only of the potentially destructive practice of high-stakes testing, but also of diminishing the freedom of teachers to develop teaching methods that value inquiry over the straightforward accumulation of facts. Where else, other than social studies, they wondered, would our young citizens develop the intellectual power to recognize problems, ask good questions, develop meaningful investigations, and consider possible solutions or consequences?

COLLEGE, CAREER, AND CIVIC LIFE FRAMEWORK (C3)

Such fears were quelled somewhat with an understanding that, unlike NCLB, CCSS recommended *general, cross-disciplinary literacy* outcomes as a shared responsibility among all disciplines within the school, including, but not limited to, social studies. Ironically, social studies was de-emphasized in our schools because it was not assessed on the state standardized tests associated with NCLB but, since informational text comprehension *is* tested on CCSS-based tests, what better way is there to teach associated reading strategies than through relevant social studies print sources?

In 2013, a time when CCSS was being hastily adopted by nearly all state departments of education, the NCSS released its *College, Career, and Civic Life Framework (C3)* in response to further clarify what CCSS should look like in social studies classrooms (National Council for the Social Studies, 2013). In many ways, the C3 Framework merged nicely with the Common Core; like CCSS, the C3 Framework took direct aim at *college* and *career* readiness. However, the C3 Framework added a third critical "C" to its document—a focus on preparation for *civic life*. The C3 Framework envisioned social studies as valuable context for supporting the literacy emphasis of the Common Core Standards. Therefore, the *College, Career, and Civic Life Framework (C3)* fully incorporated and extended the expectations of CCSS, and outlined how the C3 Framework connected to and elaborated on the Common Core State Standards for social studies inquiry. The C3 Framework presented a great opportunity to embrace new ways of doing things and adapting social studies instruction as a literacy-based, content-area investigative process.

In recognizing the need for this interdisciplinary perspective, the C3 Framework developers explained: "We like to say 'literacy for a social studies purpose,' as social studies content provides the context and inspiration for wanting to read, write, and communicate with others" (NCSS, 2013, p. 224). With this in mind, the C3 Framework has envisioned social studies instruction as an *inquiry arc* made up of the following components:

1. Developing questions and planning inquiries;
2. Applying disciplinary concepts and tools;
3. Evaluating sources and using evidence; and
4. Communicating conclusions and taking informed action. (NCSS, 2013, p. 12)

The C3 Framework (fully discussed in Chapter 4) advocated the inquiry arc as a way to engage students in meaningful and purposeful interdisciplinary experiences that help develop the critical thinking, problem-solving, and participatory skills expected of engaged citizens in the 21st century.

 Video Exploration 1.4

IMPLEMENTING NATIONAL AND PROFESSIONAL STANDARDS

Professional and national standards have been widely and successfully used by state departments of education as a framework to organize teaching, learning, and assessment in social studies. To help you better understand how these three standards sources (professional, national, and state) are noticeably intertwined, let us return to the experiences of the teachers at Inwood Academy. In 2011, the New York State Board of Regents established its overall standards document called the *Common Core Learning Standards* (New York State Education Department, 2011). It included the *Common Core State Standards* (CCSS) and a small number of additional standards unique to New York State (NYS). Soon after the development and approval of those overall state standards, the New York State Education Department (2013) elected to single out and retool its social studies standards. The three major standards documents we have been examining up to this point served as the backbone for the NYS three-part social studies document:

1. *The Common Core State Standards* (CCSS) served as the basis for the NYS "Common Core Literacy Skills" component;
2. NCSS's *Ten Themes of Social Studies* helped organize the NYS "Key Ideas and Conceptual Understandings" component; and
3. NCSS's *College, Career, and Civic Life (C3) Framework for Social Studies State Standards* helped develop the "Social Studies Practices" component, particularly its C3 inquiry arc as the major approach to student learning.

The teachers at Inwood Academy were heartened throughout this standards implementation process after reading a CCSS recommendation that, "Teachers are . . . free to provide students with whatever tools and knowledge their professional judgment and experience identify as most helpful for meeting the goals set out in the Standards" (National Governors Association, 2010, p. 1). It was important for teachers to recognize that the social studies standards were intended only to define what students were expected to know and be able to do; lesson design and effective instruction would continue to be guided by their firm understanding of pedagogical best practices. The standards revision process has convinced Inwood Academy's teachers that if students are to develop the skills appropriate for active citizenship in a democracy, they must be capable of thinking about complex social problems in a classroom environment that promotes decision making and problem solving. Thinking and content are clearly inseparable in quality social studies programs.

Advocates for more social studies now lift their voices in unison to answer the question, "Where does social studies fit into this new era of education?" with the resounding cry, "At the forefront!" They contend that social studies is just as appropriate a setting for integrating the elementary school curriculum as the burning nest is for supporting the rebirth of the phoenix.

 CHECK YOUR UNDERSTANDING 1.3   **Click here** to check your understanding of this section of the chapter

---

Reflection on Learning

You may simply scribble rough notes or jot down something more polished and complete. The point is to simply start recording your ideas spontaneously and candidly.

   Are standards and standardized testing improving education in America? Why or why not?

Attribute 3: Instructional Practices That Promote and Support Learning

The general goals for social studies education during the elementary school years are not unlike the goals for social studies education during the middle grades and high school, but the environment in which these goals are achieved is much different for elementary school youngsters than for students in the upper grades. Elementary school children come to school with a high degree of natural energy, curiosity, and imagination. They are adventurous, curious, eager to learn, energetic, always in motion, loud, and emotional. Elementary school children are also great socializers and eager to fit in. Consequently, they like group activities and projects. These are but a few of the characteristics that lead elementary school teachers to establish a one-of-a-kind, developmentally appropriate learning environment for their young students.

If the young people of our democratic nation are to grow into the office of citizen, then social studies must be delivered in a developmentally appropriate way during the elementary years. Knowledge, skills, and attitudes necessary for informed and thoughtful participation in society require an active, engaging, enjoyable, and rewarding system of instruction that results in meaningful and substantial learning. I like to call an approach to carrying out this mission *dynamic social studies,* largely because it places students in a classroom environment that encourages them to rediscover the "young social scientists" within. Much like adult social scientists, they hold a powerful desire to answer questions about their world and are captivated by the spectacular phenomena of their social surroundings. One of the greatest joys of practicing adult social scientists, for example, is to answer a question with the words "I don't know" because it gives them the opportunity to discover the unknown. Not knowing is the fuel for their furnace; and, if my social scientist friends are telling the truth, most would keep doing what they do even if they weren't paid for it. Isn't that just like the natural curiosity of childhood?

We encourage and support this sense of wonder when we open children's minds to the creative spirit that floods the social sciences. Just think about the deep sense of wonder young-sters display as they operate on their world like "young social scientists": a "geographer" bends down to study the effect of sand sifting through her fingers; an "economist" helps determine how the class will obtain the money necessary to buy a sapling for the school playground; a "political scientist" petitions the principal to provide a schoolwide program aimed at prevent-ing bullying; an "anthropologist" leafs through an old yearbook and marvels at the hairstyle and clothing differences; a "historian" watches and listens as her grandfather augments stories of the Vietnam War with fascinating memorabilia. These children have not acquired the pro-fessional credentials of practicing social scientists. However, they were curious enough about their social world to act on their curiosities. That is the basic premise of this text: Children are curious about their world and strive to seek answers to their questions so they can obtain knowledge about their wondrous social environment.

Powerful and Purposeful Social Studies Instruction

A position statement of the National Council for the Social Studies (2009) titled "Powerful and Purposeful Teaching and Learning in Elementary School Social Studies" provides guidelines for engaging students in significant learning and encourages them to connect what they are learn-ing to authentic situations. According to NCSS, we are teaching social studies powerfully when instruction is meaningful, integrative, value-based, challenging, and active.

MEANINGFUL

In order for social studies instruction to be meaningful, teachers must understand and meet the needs of their students. Teachers should capitalize on the diversity of their students and on students' natural interests in the world around them. Increasingly, elementary teachers have students of diverse backgrounds and differing abilities in their classes and must differentiate instruction in order to better meet individual needs. Successful elementary teachers possess both a command of the subject matter and the ability to engage students in the learning pro-cess through a variety of instructional methodologies.

INTEGRATIVE

Social studies is integrative by its very nature; earlier in this chapter, you learned how social studies became a distinct school subject by bringing together the social sciences. In addition, elementary school instruction often capitalizes on connections among the other curricular areas as well, such as merging language arts or science and social studies. Integrative learning combines content and processes from two or more disciplines, primarily through the use of project-based learning or other student-centered approaches, allowing students to see how ideas are connected. Integrating social studies throughout the curriculum eases competition for time in an increasingly crowded elementary school day.

VALUE-BASED

Becoming active, responsible citizens does not happen on its own as young students are taught subject matter content. Children must also participate in learning experiences that involve the core values of our democracy—the fundamental beliefs and constitutional principles of American society that unite all Americans, including freedom of speech, equality of opportu-nity, justice, patriotism, rule of law, and diversity. Exploring core values, discussing them, and making connections between those values and your students' lives are keys to developing a true understanding of active citizenship.

Students integrate concepts and skills from various disciplines as they learn more about themselves and the human condition.

Pavel Losevsky/Fotolia

CHALLENGING

Challenging elementary school social studies instruction provides students with opportunities for in-depth investigation of a few engaging concepts rather than superficial treatment of many topics. Challenging social studies instruction requires the application of higher-order thinking skills that are part of activities such as debates, discussions, projects, and simulations. And teachers should ask children the kinds of questions that stimulate decision making, problem solving, and issue analysis rather than those that elicit isolated factual knowledge.

ACTIVE

In effective social studies programs, elementary teachers use a variety of approaches, strategies, and materials to support children's interests and abilities. Processes such as problem solving, debates, simulations, project-based learning, and creative writing are active strategies that can lead to new opportunities for discovery and engagement. Consider active learning as a wide range of activities that involve students in doing things and in thinking about what they are doing.

 Video Exploration 1.5

Constructivist Teaching Practices

How can powerful and purposeful social studies instruction best be carried out? Competing theories and philosophies of learning and teaching have been proposed throughout the years, but the constructivist model appears to have convincingly rushed to the forefront and will serve as the model for successful social studies instruction in this textbook. Constructivism is neither radical nor revolutionary. Jean Piaget and Lev Vygotsky developed the theories that support constructivism almost 80 years ago. John Dewey advocated an instructional system that supports constructivism at the turn of the 20th century; Jerome Bruner did the same a few decades later.

Constructivists tell us that children build their own knowledge of the world as they strive to establish connections between that which they already know and that which is new to them. Sometimes, children can fit the demands of a new learning task into their existing cognitive frameworks. When that happens, the children enter a state of "cognitive satisfaction." At other times, children's existing conception of the world can be so far removed from the new learning experience that it creates a state of "cognitive conflict"; in these cases, the children have some difficulty associating what they already know and cannot use their existing knowledge to immediately unlock meaning from a learning task. At this point, children become driven to resolve the difference: "Why doesn't this new information fit in with what I already know?" When this discrepancy challenges their expectations, children will try to unearth the requisite knowledge to aid in reconstructing their existing model of the world (making sense out of the learning task). Building new concepts by altering existing cognitive structures is at the center of constructivism.

If you carefully consider this constructivist portrayal of the learning process, you can see that the emphasis on mental activity corresponds very closely with the way practicing social scientists carry out their investigations (although practicing social scientists obviously use more highly coordinated and unified processes). Puzzling problems that grow from a conflict between what a social scientist already knows and what she or he is confronted with creates an element of interest that launches an inquiry. Once the problem is recognized and captures a social scientist's interest, she or he sets in motion a series of powerful investigative processes until the conflict is resolved and new understandings are constructed.

Constructivists refer to "interest" as the energy required to instigate the constructive process; even with adults, a lack of interest can thwart strong effort. But, when one's interests are fully engaged, effort becomes highly productive. To make constructivism work in social studies classrooms, then, you must be able to create and present *intriguing situations* (challenging tasks, questions, or problems) that inspire our young classroom social scientists to want to figure something out. For these intriguing situations to work properly, you must be fully aware of the existing knowledge background of their students. If students encounter situations that are too far removed from their existing background of understanding, for example, they will become frustrated and bewildered. Conversely, if the intriguing situation lies comfortably within the children's existing background of understanding, they will not be challenged and will not have the interest to explore the situation any further. The key to effective instruction is to gear the intriguing situation slightly in advance of the children's existing background of understanding. This way, children will be energized to use their prior knowledge to make the new experience understandable. As they proceed through the learning experience, children steadily restructure prior knowledge to make the new experience fit in. The change that occurs in the mental structure of the child is referred to as *constructivist learning*. The new information is not simply stored in the mind; rather, new information is integrated into the knowledge that already exists as the children continuously reframe their world.

As students participate in intriguing situations, teachers in constructivist classrooms must also function as facilitators or guides to make certain that the children can capably navigate their way through. Therefore, constructivism can be thought of as having both *cognitive* and *social* components. The cognitive component describes learning as the process of resolving intriguing situations; however, that resolution process is rarely accomplished in isolation. It is difficult for children to change their thinking on their own; intriguing situations alone are not enough. Therefore, it is important for children to enter into educational dialogues with teachers and other children. Children construct new knowledge as they collaborate with adults or peers to work their way through puzzling tasks or problems. Constructivism begins with the principle that the primary role of teaching is not to lecture, explain, or otherwise attempt to pass on knowledge, but to guide, facilitate, and support children as they pull together their own ideas and conclusions. One of the most familiar strategies teachers use to assist children in connecting their current knowledge to a new learning experience is teacher-facilitated discussions. Oftentimes, teachers find it helpful to assist their students' thinking during these discussions with attention-grabbing graphic representations such as diagrams, charts, drawings, and other visual displays. These help-ful illustrations are popularly called *anticipation guides* because they help students graphically connect their past experiences to the targeted concepts under study. A conventional anticipation guide is a knowledge chart. The following classroom exemplar demonstrates how one teacher used an anticipation guide to help her students access their current understandings of the topic and process any new information associated with the learning experience.

What child wouldn't want to study something as tasty and fun as yummy, fluffy popcorn? That's the question Amy Carr asked herself as she initiated a constructivist classroom experience that helped integrate four major disciplines history, geography, science, and reading. Ms. Carr began the lesson by bringing the children's attention to a table display that included a large popcorn bucket. "Hmmmm . . . a popcorn bucket," Ms. Carr said in pretend surprise. "I wonder what in the world a popcorn bucket has to do with what we're going to do in school today!"

The children picked up on Ms. Carr's seemingly genuine confusion and offered a number of possible explanations. Then, holding the bucket on her lap so that all could see, Ms. Carr reached in and held up a cup of unpopped popcorn. "Look," said Ms. Carr. "What could you tell me about this?" To help them keep track of all their suggestions, Ms. Carr recorded the students' comments on a knowledge chart: "That's popcorn before you pop it." "It turns fluffy and white after you pop it." "Some people put butter on it." "I like lots of salt on mine." "I think the American Indians invented it." Ms. Carr listed everything they knew (or thought they knew) about popcorn in a column labeled "What We Know about Popcorn." Then, Ms. Carr pulled The Popcorn Book *by Tomie de Paola out of the popcorn bucket, introduced it, and read it aloud. It is a delightfully illustrated picture book that tells children everything they want to know about popcorn. The book takes them through the history of popcorn, tells where it is grown, explains how the Native American Indians made popcorn, and describes how Native Americans in Massachusetts brought bowls of popcorn to the first Thanksgiving potluck feast. It even reveals the secret of how those hard little kernels suddenly burst into the feathery globules we call popcorn. After reading the book, Ms. Carr coordinated a group discussion during which the children talked about all that they had learned. Ms. Carr helped the students record their new information in the second column ("What We Learned about Popcorn") and corrected any information in the first column that was inaccurate.*

The book experience satisfied the need to know for some youngsters, but there remained several who were personally driven to find out even more information about popcorn. Ms. Carr directed them to the classroom computers, where they explored a wealth of information obtainable from the Jolly Time® popcorn company (http://www.jollytime.com). All the relevant information they uncovered was added to the information chart.

Teachers in constructivist social studies classrooms do not commit themselves to any single method as the exclusive "right way to teach." They understand that there are many ways to help children unlock the mysteries of life and that the heart of solid social studies instruction is balance and proportion. Sometimes, as *collaborators*, social studies teachers "bring the action to the children" by demonstrating, assisting, and explaining in order to help their students con-struct new knowledge or refine skills. At other times, as *facilitators*, teachers guide the children as they personally "initiate the action," supporting students emotionally and intellectually as they independently strive to explain a puzzling question or problem. The classroom is no lon-ger a place where a traditionally stereotypic teacher (content expert) passes on knowledge to a group of empty-headed students who wait for each fact like hungry guppies in a feeding frenzy. As I once heard a wise educator say, "The road to learning is always under construction." It is because constructivists think of learning as a dynamic process that I have titled this text ***Dynamic Social Studies***.

 CHECK YOUR UNDERSTANDING 1.4 **Click here** to check your understanding of this section of the chapter.

Attribute 4: Democratic Classroom Communities

American youngsters are spending their elementary school years in classrooms that have become increasingly diverse, housing a complex combination of cultures, genders, skills, talents, and interests. In many ways, classrooms can be viewed as a microcosm of society—places where a rich mixture of children work together to build the social and participatory skills required of citizens in our American democracy. In all societies, however, it seems that one group of citizens enjoys a preponderance of privileges, often because of social and cultural factors such as race, gender, and socioeconomic status, while others are handicapped by diminished privileges. As leaders in a microcosm of American democracy, you have a responsibility to recognize and overcome any such inequities and provide all students with equal opportunities to learn. The ability to eventually participate as active adults in a diverse democratic society begins with equitable social studies education during the early elementary grades; the early years are important antecedents of later attitudes toward social and cultural responsibility. For this reason, it is important to create the conditions that draw on the talents and strengths of all children, regardless of their culture, social class, gender, talents, or other defining characteristics; your classroom must be productive, supportive, and free of bias. Children in such environments tend to become more engaged in classroom activities, have more positive attitudes about school, welcome and confront new challenges, get along better with peers, and experience more success while learning new academic content and skills.

A Democratic Classroom

Almost everything that takes place within a democratic social studies classroom contributes to children's *sense of self*—that is, how much they value themselves, how important they think they are, and whether they believe they are worthy of high regard and acceptance. Most children achieve a healthy sense of self and visualize themselves as worthy, capable individuals. However, some children are threatened when their sense of self does not match what they perceive as the school "norm"; something happens that makes them think of themselves as inept or unworthy. These are the children who often find their classroom to be the epitome of anxiety and frustration—"I'm stupid" and "I just don't fit in" are the kinds of comments that seem to capture their lack of confidence and loss of hope. And those agonizing thoughts are often accompanied by alarming feelings such as sadness, anger, or worthlessness. What can be done to help all children acquire a healthy sense of self?

The path to a positive sense of self begins with teachers who provide warm, nurturing relationships and developmentally appropriate instruction; these are clearly the essential ingredients of democratic classroom life. Your decisions about the ingredients of such an environment will be greatly influenced by what you know of child development. The field of child development has tended to focus on *developmental milestones*, or the relatively stable, predictable developmental changes that typically occur in the years from birth through the elementary school grades. Children tend to follow stable, predictable patterns of growth during the elementary school years, but a complex combination of heredity and environment will influence variations in temperament, personality, intelligence, ability, and achievement: Lakeisha starts writing neatly in first grade; Barbara lacks the fine motor coordination to produce legible letters in third grade. Matthew asks politely for things that he wants by first grade; Ramon screams to get his way in third grade. There is nothing unusual about these differences. Every classroom includes a broad spectrum of skills and abilities. Some students will be a grade level or two behind, while others could probably teach the class. So, in addition to developmental milestones, you must recognize that individual variation is not only to be expected but valued. So use developmental milestones only as general guidelines; do not make the mistake of thinking that "earlier" or "faster" is "better" development. For example, Einstein was 4 years old before he could speak and 7 before he could read!

Some children will experience delays in a single area or in multiple areas; other children will acquire basic skills more quickly and with less practice. At times, however, differences can be more extreme than simply having a child be a little behind or a bit more advanced. Some children may be visually or physically impaired, have ADHD, speak a different language, experience a behavioral disorder, or be extremely gifted and talented. What influences variation? In some cases, it is heredity; in others, it may be physical health factors, mental health issues, a traumatic event, abuse or neglect, poverty, poor nutrition and health care, or gender role expectations. An understanding of individual differences and their causes helps you recognize both normal variations in growth as well as extreme differences, thereby aiding you in the process of identifying those who may have special needs. Expect to find a wide range of differences in the children you teach, and just think how boring teaching would be if every student were the same!

A good place to start building and reinforcing the ideals of social studies education is to help students sense personal connections between their own lives and what is going on in school. So at the beginning of each new school year, create an all-inclusive learning environment that nurtures trust and respect for all people—celebrating and valuing diversity—from the color of one's skin to intellectual or physical abilities to the language spoken. Children who understand and appreciate the glorious diversity among their peers will more likely grow up as wise citizens who respect our nation's rich mix of cultures, heritages, abilities, and interests. The overall goal of a democratic classroom is to establish a trusting, caring, and supportive *classroom community* built on recognition of and respect for students' unique individual backgrounds and strengths. Children function best when they feel they are part of a democratic classroom community where everyone feels accepted and where individuality is encouraged.

Democracy in the classroom can mean many things, but for the purposes of this book, it means creating a learning environment in which trust and respect exist between teacher and children and among children themselves; it involves a sense of community where people work together harmoniously to achieve a common goal. Democratic classroom communities are firmly supported by a foundation of democratic principles—liberty, freedom, justice, fairness, equality, and equal opportunity—and celebrate diversity while eradicating racial, ethnic, cultural, and gender stereotypes. Some long-established models of education have tended to overlook the ways in which classroom conditions can affect the lives of children; therefore,

Instead of simply teaching the basics of democracy as part of the formal curriculum, a growing number of social studies teachers are taking steps to make the teaching and learning process a more democratic experience. These students, for example, are voting on an issue very important to the class—they are "doing democracy."

Racorn/Shutterstock

they operate with a conviction that there is "one best path for all." However, all good social studies teachers stand firm and declare, "The belief that a singular approach is applicable to all children tends to render education practically useless to almost everyone. There is diversity in every classroom!"

   CHECK YOUR UNDERSTANDING 1.5   **Click here** to check your understanding of this section of the chapter.

> ### Reflection on Learning
>
> *You may simply scribble rough notes or jot down something more polished and complete. The point is to simply start recording your ideas spontaneously and candidly.*
>
> If you become a *successful* social studies teacher, what will you need to do in order to become an *outstanding* social studies teacher? What will be the first step in your drive to become an outstanding social studies teacher?

A Final Thought

At the roots of a democracy are knowledgeable and thoughtful citizens. Of course, they have many other qualities, too, but high on the list of behavior for democratic citizens is thinking for themselves. Democracy requires individuals who are able to search for and examine the facts whenever they must make up their minds about important issues. These issues might relate to one's personal life or to complex international concerns; in any case, the protection of our freedom lies in the hands of rational people. Such skills must be learned during the early years with a dynamic social studies curriculum that offers meaningful experiences to all. All youngsters must find something to excite their interest and stimulate their thinking. A one-dimensional approach to social studies instruction cannot do this. We fail our children with narrowness; if our myopic view of teaching has caused them to feel stupid or to be bored, we have lost. Learning for an informed citizenry is too important to be thought of as something that everyone must be able to do in any single way. The danger to our future is great when we restrict the adventuresome, "can-do" spirit of childhood. Therefore, dynamic social studies programs must employ various teaching strategies and promote functional thinking skills. The probing, wondering minds of childhood must be freed. The society of tomorrow starts in your classroom today.

Successful teachers welcome the challenge of creating superb social studies classrooms and look to sound theory as the basis for their instruction. They deliberately build their programs on their best knowledge of who they are teaching, what they are teaching, and how they are teaching. Successful social studies teachers have what it takes, in spirit and skill, to tailor their classrooms to fit the children who come to them. They demonstrate, without timidity, that they would rather be challenged than safe and bored.

In addition to what we have considered up to this point, one of the most helpful ways of keeping up with current trends is to review the activities and publications of professional organizations. The largest and most influential professional organization for social studies educators is the National Council for the Social Studies (NCSS). The council produces several publications of interest to social studies teachers: *Social Education*, the primary journal, focuses on philosophical, theoretical, and practical classroom application articles involving K–12 instruction; *Social Studies and the Young Learner*, a separate journal for elementary teachers, offers articles primarily designed to provide relevant and useful strategies for elementary school classrooms. The NCSS also periodically publishes "how-to" pamphlets that offer in-depth suggestions for implementing specific instructional responsibilities (e.g., using creative dramatics or current affairs strategies) in the social studies classroom. You should also become familiar with *The Social Studies*, a peer-reviewed journal that publishes articles on new directions and approaches to social studies education. The relevant addresses follow:

National Council for the Social Studies
8555 Sixteenth Street
Silver Spring, MD 20910
www.socialstudies.org
(301) 588-1800

The Social Studies
1319 Eighteenth Street, NW
Washington, DC 20036
http://www.tandfonline.com/action/journalInformation?journalCode=vtss20#
.VzYng5ErJaQ
1-800-354-1420

References

Bruner, J. S. (1960). *The process of education.* New York, NY: Vintage.

Bruner, J. S. (1966). *On knowing: Essays for the left hand.* Cambridge, MA: Harvard University.

Dewey, J. (1933). *How we think.* Boston: D.C. Heath.

Dewey, J. (1971). A pedagogical experiment. In *Early Works of John Dewey* (Vol. 5, pp. 244–246). Carbondale, IL: Southern Illinois University Press. (Original work published 1896).

Frazee, B., & Ayers, S. (2003). Garbage in, garbage out: Expanding environments, constructivism, and content knowledge in social studies. In J. Leming, L. Ellington, & K. Porter (Eds.), *Where did social studies go wrong?* (pp. 111–123). Washington, DC: Thomas B. Fordham Foundation.

Hanna, P. R. (1963). Revising the social studies: What is needed? *Social Education, 27,* 190–196.

Mitchell, L. S. (1934). *Young geographers.* New York, NY: John Day.

National Commission on Excellence in Education. (1983). *A nation at risk: The imperative for educational reform.* Washington, DC: Author.

National Council for the Social Studies. (1993, January/February). Definition approved. *The Social Studies Professional, 114,* 3.

National Council for the Social Studies. (1994). *Curriculum standards for social studies: Expectations of excellence* (Bulletin 89). Washington, DC: Author.

National Council for the Social Studies. (2007). *Social studies in the era of No Child Left Behind: A position statement of National Council for the Social Studies.* Retrieved from http://www.socialstudies.org/positions/nclbera

National Council for the Social Studies. (2009). Powerful and purposeful teaching and learning in elementary school social studies. *Social Education, 73,* 252–254.

National Council for the Social Studies. (2010). *National curriculum standards for social studies: A framework for teaching, learning, and assessment* (Bulletin 111). Washington, DC: Author.

National Council for the Social Studies (2013). *The college, career, and civic life (C3) framework for social studies state standards: Guidance for enhancing the rigor of K–12 civics, economics, geography, and history.* Washington, DC: Author.

National Council for the Social Studies Task Force on Early Childhood/Elementary Social Studies. (1989). Social studies for early childhood and elementary school children preparing for the 21st century. *Social Education, 54,* 16.

National Governors Association Center for Best Practices & Council of Chief State School Officers. (2010). *Common core state standards for English language arts and literacy in history/social studies, science, and technical subjects.* Washington, DC: Authors.

New York State Education Department (2011). *New York State P–12 common core learning standards.* Retrieved from https://www.engageny.org/resource/new-york-state-p-12-common-core-learning-standards

New York State Education Department (2013). *New York State common core K–12 social studies framework.* Retrieved from https://www.engageny.org/sites/default/files/resource/attachments/ss-framework-k-12-intro.pdf

Paxton, R. (2003). Don't know much about history—Never did. *Phi Delta Kappan, 85,* 264–273.

Ravitch, D. (1987). Tot sociology: Or what happened to history in the grade schools. *The American Scholar, 56,* 343–355.

U.S. Department of Education. (2002). *Executive summary: No Child Left Behind Act of 2001.* Washington, DC: Author.

CHAPTER 2

Effective Instructional Planning

Learning Outcomes

An old saying cautions that "those who fail to plan, plan to fail." Like many old sayings, this one imparts a lot of wisdom. By planning ahead, you increase the likelihood that your social studies lessons will run smoothly and that students will receive quality instruction. Knowing how to craft effective instructional plans is a fundamental competency to strengthen at this stage of your pre-professional development because plans not only help you outline your intended strategies clearly and logically, but they also help provide early focus on just how many gaps you have in content-area expertise or skills associated with successful teaching. So as you delve into the remaining chapters of this text, try to relate new understandings and skills to any specific challenges you faced throughout this chapter. After completing this chapter, you will be able to:

- Explain what is involved in the instructional planning process.

- Describe how unit plans are constructed in a standards-based social studies curriculum.

- Identify the steps involved in planning an effective social studies lesson.

- Explain how to design differentiated lesson and unit plans that address students' diverse cultural backgrounds, interests, skills, and abilities.

Classroom Snapshot

Marge Feeney, a student teacher eager to spread her teaching wings, had spent her first two weeks in Mr. Wilmore's fifth-grade classroom restlessly observing the daily routine, checking student work assignments, taking lunch count, getting to know the children, and assisting individuals in need of special help. At last, the day she had been longing for had arrived. Mr. Wilmore asked Marge to teach her first lesson— a social studies lesson! The class had been involved in an interdisciplinary unit on Important People in Colonial America, and the students were fascinated about the events that led patriots down the "Road to Revolution." To add to their understanding of notable leaders, Marge's job was to prepare a lesson about Benjamin Franklin. In a twinkling of an eye, her eager anticipation turned to sudden alarm. "Benjamin Franklin?" Marge shrieked silently. "Why, I hardly know anything about Benjamin Franklin! The only thing I can think of is that he flew his kite during a thunderstorm and is considered a Founding Father. How does Mr. Wilmore expect me to teach about someone I know so little about about? Even worse, what kind of activity can I possibly pull out of my hat to teach about someone I know so little about?" Trying to maintain a coolness that wouldn't betray her inner panic, Marge swallowed hard and choked out the words, "I'd love to teach tomorrow's lesson about Benjamin Franklin!"

Although Mr. Wilmore eased the demands of Marge's planning task by explaining the overall goals, targeted standards, and instructional objectives of the lesson, Marge knew her work was far from over. "There are so many more things for me to do," Marge reflected. "Assessment, how to 'hook' the students, key ideas, instructional strategies. What if everything doesn't go exactly as I've planned?" Marge was surprised by the content she needed to gather for her lesson plan. She was jolted into a sudden realization that social studies teachers need a lot of information to achieve their objectives—much more than they can store in their minds. In order to be effective, they must be ready to say many times a day, "I don't know. I'll look it up." So Marge went back to her room, sat down at the computer, and found several useful websites with the information for her lesson. When Marge felt she knew the content inside and out, she took on the next challenge: finding a developmentally appropriate instructional strategy. She knew that her students would come to the lesson expecting Mr. Wilmore's customary way of doing things, so Marge tried not to disrupt his normal lesson routine. Mr. Wilmore's students were quite skilled at conducting Internet research, so Marge decided it would be advantageous to have them work in small groups to research and compose a short paragraph about one of Benjamin Franklin's many accomplishments. However, rather than having the students simply collect facts about Benjamin Franklin, Marge realized it was important that they use the information in some way. How could the students not only learn the content, but actually do something with it? Although she had already worked for well over an hour on her planning, Marge wasn't close to being finished. "Who said teaching was easy?" she joked.

Mr. Wilmore required his student teachers to write detailed daily plans. "With a plan in place," he advised, "you'll feel better prepared to face the students." Therefore, Marge set to writing a rough draft, detailing the content as well as the step-by-step procedures intended to bring life to her lesson. After another hour of jotting down and organizing ideas, a lesson finally began to take shape. "I can do it," Marge acknowledged with growing confidence. "It's not easy, but like 'The Little Engine That Could,' I think I can . . . I think I can . . . I think I can do it."

The day had finally arrived when Marge found herself standing alone in front of her very first group of real children . . . ready to take her first wide-eyed, shaky-kneed, Bambi-like steps as a teacher. She could hardly contain her excitement: "Now, if I can just relax and get a feel for being in front of a class."

"It worked!" Marge bellowed to no one in particular when she came back from school the next day. "The lesson really went well. It wasn't perfect, but it went better than expected. I almost lost my train of thought once or twice, but the lesson plan kept me on track. When I noticed my students were having trouble at one point, we paused and went back to review. I had the children explore events in Benjamin Franklin's life using the SweetSearch search engine; they completed their paragraphs and made illustrations depicting the events they had written about. Then we connected the illustrated paragraphs into a large Benjamin Franklin Time Line. They loved it so much that we decided to extend the lesson to tomorrow by inviting other fifth-grade classes to our room to see the time line and hear the students read their paragraphs. I feel like a real teacher now, like I'm ready to step in and take over my own classroom. After all the coursework, and all the worries, and all the dreaming, and all the hard work, I think I'm ready to take the next step."

Can you imagine a lawyer going to court without a legal summary (brief) of the case? How about a football coach going into the Super Bowl without a game plan? Would you allow a contractor to build your house without a detailed set of blueprints? Teaching a group of students without planning is like taking a cross-country trip without consulting a road map. Yet, whenever the topic of instructional planning comes up in my social studies methods courses, students are likely to put on their gloomiest hangdog faces and sulk, "Do we *have to* write lesson plans?" The more adventurous ones have gone so far as to try to convince me that writing lesson plans is a bad idea. It seems that college students, much like the rest of us, tend to dig in their heels if they know that something is important, but do not fully understand why. Their resistance presented a major challenge faced by all teachers at one time or another: "How do I get my students to do something they don't want to do?" I am always tempted to feign displeasure and cajole or threaten them, "You have to; it's my job to make sure you understand the process of instructional planning. Now get to work!" Instead, I reasoned that because I was the person inflicting the pain, it was my job to ease it. Surely, they were too savvy for psychological "tricks," so I tried to help them know why their work mattered by tapping into issues that were important to the students and to demonstrate the significance of the content to their intended professions. And, reasoning that the thought of being assigned the responsibility of writing a detailed unit or lesson plan can be overwhelming to the uninitiated, I staged the planning tasks into discrete, achievable chunks to make the job seem more manageable. In time, they actually became eager to spread their teaching wings, soared with their ideas, and constructed extraordinary plans of instruction. Planning brought a sense of excitement and satisfaction to their pre-professional lives. They learned that instructional planning can be fascinating, rewarding, and highly enjoyable, but also that it requires lots of work. However, it's no secret that many of the most worthwhile things in life require work hard. The most successful teachers I know work very, very hard; unsuccessful teachers, on the other hand, seem to avoid hard work like the plague. Successful teachers subscribe to the belief expressed in Thomas Jefferson's wise observation, "Far and away the best prize that life offers is the chance to work hard at work worth doing." It is practically impossible to be lazy or unenthusiastic when tackling a job as challenging and rewarding as teaching.

I think a major reason students tend to shy away from instructional planning is that teaching can look so easy to individuals who spend upwards of 15,000 hours with classroom teachers by the time they graduate from high school. From this student-oriented perspective, teaching often appears so natural, smooth, and effortless that some are left with the impression that they don't need to work hard to get positive results. However, deliberate planning brings about such a command of teaching that a well-prepared teacher's actions appear effortless and instinctive. Don't be fooled . . . teachers have to work very hard to make something so difficult look so simple. This message comes across loud and clear to cynics who stand in front of a classroom for the very first time. They are often shocked to realize that when the spotlight is on them, the classroom (which they previously saw as an orderly domain) suddenly starts spinning, with confusion and chaos lurking at every turn. I'm not so naïve as to advise that a plan in itself *guarantees* success, but a key ingredient of a recipe for failure is having no plan to follow and saying or doing whatever feels natural at the time—in other words, "winging it." If you want to be successful, don't be a "winger!"

What Is Instructional Planning?

What is *instructional planning*? In general terms, instructional planning is the process of painting the "big picture" of what to teach and how to teach it in ways that help all students reach their potential. The instructional planning process is fundamentally carried out on three major levels, or tiers. The most comprehensive, wide-ranging level is a school district's grade-specific *social studies curriculum guide*s that outline the overall philosophy, goals, standards, objectives, assessments, themes and topics of instruction, and instructional resources for each subject. Most of what we find in curriculum plans focuses on *learning*: What do we want the students to know or be able to do? Why are these learnings important? The second level of planning helps pinpoint how we will *teach* what we have determined the learning outcomes to be—two- to four-week *unit plans* based on topics and themes outlined in each curriculum guide. One way that teachers plan units is around a single topic; these are called *single-topic units*. Single-topic units are normally found in schools where social studies is taught as a class separate from other subjects; instruction is guided by goals centered on a clear-cut social studies content or skill area (for example, learning about the community in which the students live). A second, more common way elementary school teachers plan social studies units is to integrate content and processes from several subjects. Called *thematic units*, these plans organize the social studies curriculum around a central theme that cuts across subject matter lines, thereby breaking down walls isolating the subjects. For example, you might develop a thematic unit about *West African Village Life* to teach sociology (celebrations, family life, sharing and helping each other), geography (climate and the land), history (African storytellers and oral histories), science (tools), math (counting games, geometric patterns), reading (West African prose tales), art (batik, wood carvings, and sculpture), music (musical instruments, rhythm, and dance), and writing skills (composing original "animal tales"). Thematic units stress authentic, real-life learning during which students create tangible, useful products such as a book, a play, a trip, or a presentation that they can share with others. Both single-topic and thematic unit plans are further subdivided into a series of daily lesson plans, which comprise the third level of planning. *Lesson plans* clearly spell out how short-range instruction will be carried out (see Figure 2.1). Although experienced teachers often abridge lesson plans to mental maps or even scribbled notes on scrap paper, you will be expected to write detailed lesson plans for every lesson you teach during field experiences or student teaching. Your college supervisor will expect to see your plans when he or she visits you; your cooperating teacher/mentor will expect a plan before you teach any lesson.

 Video Exploration 2.1

 CHECK YOUR UNDERSTANDING 2.1   **Click here** to check your understanding of this section of the chapter.

How Are Unit Plans Constructed?

Planning, then, can be *long-term* (curriculum guides), *medium-term* (unit plans), or *short-term* (daily lessons). *Long-term curriculum guides* are usually developed by a committee consisting primarily of experienced teachers, administrators, and, perhaps, members of the public. You will

FIGURE 2.1   Relationship of Curriculum, Units, and Lessons

CURRICULUM	UNIT	LESSON
• a standards-based guide that includes the philosophy, content, themes or topics, approach, and assessment practices of the district's social studies program	• a collection of related lessons organized around a single theme or topic, often included in the curriculum guide	• a detailed description that guides instruction for a single class period (sometimes more)

probably not be asked to serve on a curriculum development committee until you have accrued a year or more of teaching experience. *Short-term daily plans* and *medium-term unit plans* will receive most of your attention during the earliest stages of your professional career. An Internet search is a great way to start investigating what lesson and unit plans are like; the plans you uncover will serve as excellent models to guide your efforts as you begin to write your own. Most of these sites are designed by teachers and other educators and contain collections of excellent lessons. However, nothing can replace a plan that you tailor to the individual needs and interests or strengths and weaknesses of your students. It is one thing to surf the Internet to retrieve instructional plans, but to become a successful elementary school social studies teacher, you need to do more. When you put together your own plans, it means you have attained a high level of competency in the content you teach and the methods you use. Arriving at that level is far more worthwhile and fulfilling than simply reproducing lesson plans contrived by others, and is one of the important milestones along the way to becoming a true and successful professional.

In this book, you will learn about social studies unit planning through a process called *task analysis*, a deliberate, one-step-at-a-time approach for breaking down any task into subtasks. The subtasks can be thought of as sequential links that become connected to form a task chain; the initial link is performed first, and then the second link is attached to the first, the third to the second, and this continues until the entire task is fully connected. With that in mind, I will break down the unit planning task into its separate subtask links and encourage you to contribute to each link as you read about it. Since one of the greatest challenges for new teachers can be planning a unit alone, let's start planning a successful unit together—one that does not feel like a gold medal winner in a megaflop contest!

Every principal, teacher, school district, and professor has a favored way of putting together unit plans. Unquestionably, a variety of long-range planning frameworks (templates) offer much to choose from. However, *my* personal choice is based on a mechanism called *backward design* (Wiggins & McTighe, 2006). The mechanism is referred to as being *backward* because it reverses the path teachers often take while planning units. Wiggins and McTighe claim that teachers traditionally have started the planning process by looking for materials and activities—*the input*—rather than the desired results—*the output*. They seem to be on the lookout for dazzling activities or exemplary lessons that challenge and engage students before they

Planning is the cornerstone of effective instruction; it provides a road map that keeps you going in the right direction.

Monkey Business/Fotolia

are familiar with the learning expectations and requirements. Instead, teachers must not consider instructional materials and activities until they have a clear vision of what the students are expected to learn (*output*). Although we will not apply *backward design* in its entirety, we will adapt its three-link "backward planning" chain for our unit planning responsibilities:

1. *Desired Results* ("What do I want students to know or be able to do?")
2. *Assessment Strategies* ("What will I accept as evidence of understanding and proficiency?")
3. *Learning Experiences and Instruction* ("What instructional strategies and learning activities can best bring about the desired results?")

Figure 2.2 illustrates these three links in a straightforward template you can use as a framework on which to build your social studies unit.

Link 1: Desired Results

Let's begin our chain-building exercise by tracking the work of Cheryl Walker, a fifth-grade teacher who developed a standards-based thematic unit, *Great Inventors and Inventions*, for several reasons: (1) the topic is required by her school district's fifth-grade social studies curriculum guide; (2) her state's social studies standards are based on the *Common Core State Standards* and the *College, Career, and Civic Life (C3) Framework for Social Studies State Standards*, both of which call attention to the advantages of using interdisciplinary thematic units; (3) the textbook treatment of the topic is outdated, dry, and sketchy; and (4) her students have a passionate interest in inventors and inventions. Before she started building the first link of her planning chain, Ms. Walker wrote an introductory paragraph to furnish a general snapshot of the vision and focus of the unit. The introductory paragraph usually follows the unit's title and grade-level designation. Examine Ms. Walker's introductory paragraph in Figure 2.3.

After extracting the theme or topic of your social studies unit from the curriculum guide and writing the introductory paragraph, the next step is to review expectations from the curriculum guide and determine three important *output considerations*: (1) goals, (2) content standards (national, state, and professional), and (3) instructional objectives.

FIGURE 2.2   Unit Planning Template

Unit Plan
Grade 5
Introductory Paragraph
I. Desired Results
a. *Established Goals*
b. *Standards*
c. *Instructional Objectives*
II. Assessment Strategies
a. *Diagnostic*
b. *Formative*
c. *Summative*
III. Learning Experiences and Instruction
a. *Introductory Experiences*
b. *Developmental Experiences*
c. *Culminating Experiences*

INSTRUCTIONAL GOALS

An *instructional goal* is an overarching statement that describes, in very broad terms, the knowledge, skills, work habits, and character traits that schools should be fostering in students over time—for months, years, or throughout their lifetimes (the more concise term "goal" may be used at any point throughout this text). Goals convey the unit's grand vision; they furnish the overall frame onto which the more highly specific *standards* and *instructional objectives* of the unit will be attached. For her unit, *Great Inventors and Inventions*, Ms. Walker selected the following from the district curriculum guide as one of her established goals: *The students will integrate ideas from several disciplines to identify problems affecting society.*

STANDARDS

Acknowledging their enormous influence, standards did not descend from the skies on stone tablets in a show of angelic music, smoke, and fire. The modern standards movement actually began years ago with the publication of *A Nation at Risk* (1983), a report that stated America's schools were failing and compared the urgency of addressing the dismal state of education with a virtual state of war. The report touched off a wave of reform efforts that dramatically increased the role of the federal government in addressing the quality of public education for all children in the United States. To meet the challenge, schools were strongly encouraged to adopt rigorous standards as a means of increasing student achievement.

Standards are meant to narrow down instructional goals by offering concise descriptions of what students are expected to know and be able to do at each specific *grade level*; goals, by contrast, communicate possible *lifetime* targets. So think of standards primarily as a bridge between the overarching *goals* and the more highly definitive statements we will examine next—*instructional objectives*. To illustrate, Ms. Walker used the following subordinate *content standard* (among a few others) from the Pennsylvania standards (Pennsylvania Department of Education, 2002) to help clarify her established goal: "Know how human ingenuity and technological resources satisfy specific human needs and improve the quality of life" (p. 29). The content standard was still too broad to provide a clear picture of what she intended to accomplish, so Ms. Walker included more highly focused statements, or intended learning outcomes. She found that the Pennsylvania standards (Pennsylvania Department of Education, 2002) added focus to the content standard by including these intended learning outcomes:

> *Know how human ingenuity and technological resources satisfy specific human needs and improve the quality of life.*
>
> > *Identify and distinguish between human needs and improving the quality of life.*
> > *Identify and distinguish between natural and human-made resources.*
> > *Describe a technological invention and the resources that were used to develop it.* (pp. 29–30)

In social studies—which contains an overwhelming volume of facts, concepts, and skills along with a wide range of controversial issues—standards will likely be broader than in skills-based subjects like reading and math, whose expectations are somewhat more definitive and conforming.

INSTRUCTIONAL OBJECTIVES

Generally, the most sharply focused targets of instruction are referred to as either *intended learning outcomes*, often called *instructional objectives*; regardless of what they're called, they answer the same question: "What *specifically* do you want your students *to know* or *be able to do*?" and provide a clearer idea of what students will attain from a unit (or lesson). Think of *instructional objectives* as more detailed outcomes than either goals or standards. I like to distinguish among goal, standard, and objective by thinking of a *standard* as a middle ground—broader than an *objective*, but narrower than a *goal*. In other words, a single goal may have many subordinate standards and a standard may have many subordinate instructional objectives. Although it is easy to become intimidated by all the confusing jargon, the bottom line is that, in most instances, learning outcome designations flow from the general to the specific—goals, standards, objectives—and those will be the terms used in this book. Let your brain, nerves, every part of your body wrestle with those ideas!

Instructional objectives are the heart of a unit plan. As our hearts are responsible for just about everything that gives our bodies life, instructional objectives are the lifeblood of social studies unit plans. Every learning activity, every instructional strategy, every teaching resource, and every means of assessment is driven by instructional objectives. Just as heart disease can be prevented by addressing certain risk factors, understanding what makes instructional objectives "tick" can help you create effective and appropriate unit plans. Because a wide array of desirable learning outcomes is expected from today's social studies, instructional objectives must represent dimensions of learning and performance that go beyond simple knowledge acquisition and skill development. The oldest and most detailed structure for identifying and writing instructional objectives on various levels of learning is Benjamin Bloom's *Taxonomy of Educational Objectives* (Bloom et al., 1956). To be discussing Bloom's 1956 taxonomy in a 21st-century text is testimony to the fact that it has stood the test of time. Bloom categorized learning behaviors into three interrelated and overlapping domains:

- *Cognitive*—knowledge and intellectual skills
- *Affective*—student motivation, attitudes, perceptions, and values
- *Psychomotor*—physical movement, coordination, and motor skills

Bloom arranged the cognitive domain as a hierarchy, and classified the intellectual skills by levels of cognitive difficulty, from simpler to more complex forms. The intellectual skills range from *knowledge* (remembering or retrieving previously learned material) to *evaluation* (the ability to judge the value of methods, ideas, people, products). As significant as it is, however, the cognitive domain does not stand alone as a category of instructional objectives. The affective domain can significantly enhance, inhibit, or even prevent social studies learning, too; it includes factors such as motivation, attitudes toward learning, and feelings of acceptance or rejection. If you plan on selecting instructional objectives from the affective domain, your target will be to enhance student learning by including factors such as student motivation, attitudes, emotions, and feelings—to inspire them to respond to what they learn, to value it, to organize it, and to become so highly energized to engage in the subject matter that they become virtual "mini-social scientists." The psychomotor domain covers the acquisition of fine and gross motor skills such as using scissors to complete an art project or playing the piano. Fine motor skills involve the small muscles of the hands, which allow you to do things such as write, build a model, use scissors, sew, and manipulate small objects. Gross motor skills are big motor skills such as those involved in running, jumping, or dancing. They require balance and coordination. Development of fine and gross skills requires practice and is measured in terms of speed, precision, distance, procedures, or techniques in execution. In addition to these general psychomotor skills, there are specialized skills that social studies students need to master. These include reading maps and globes, analyzing graphic data, critical thinking and reading, group work, reference and information search skills, and technical skills related to computers and other electronic devices. It may be interesting to note that Bloom's three domains correspond very closely to the three major goals of the NCSS Task Force on Early Childhood/Elementary Social Studies presented in Chapter 1: knowledge, skills, and attitudes necessary for informed and thoughtful participation in society. You may hear Bloom's three domains referred to as *KSA* (*knowledge, skills,* and *attitudes*) or as *knowing/head, doing/hands,* and *feeling/heart.* However you decide to refer to them, the three domains help teachers focus on different outcomes of learning, creating a more holistic form of education.

There are a number of acceptable formats to guide you while composing instructional objectives but, to prevent overkill, I prefer to draft objectives in a way commonly used by most school districts. I call this the "SOS" method. If you examine school district unit plans carefully, you will find that their instructional objectives are *student centered* (the first "S" in SOS). They customarily begin with the words "The *student* will (or shall or will be able to). . . ." Next, their well-stated instructional objectives describe the intended learning *outcome* (the "O" in SOS);

Breaking goals down into specific standards and objectives will facilitate the process of aligning assessment and determining the pathways of instruction.

Monkey Business Images/Shutterstock

the outcome spells out the particular knowledge, skills, or attitudes associated with the broader instructional goals and standards: *"The student will be able to work collaboratively in small groups to research and gather information about an inventor and his or her inventions."* Finally, school district unit plans will break down and further clarify the instructional objective by providing a sample of the *specific performances* (the final "S" in SOS) that shed light on what we mean when we say that a student will "know this," or be able to "do that." If we fail to include these clarifications, it may be virtually impossible to determine whether or not the instructional objectives are being met. For example:

> *The student will be able to work collaboratively in small groups to research and gather information about an inventor and his or her inventions.*
> > *Each group will:*
>
> - *cooperatively select an inventor or invention;*
> - *use a selection of books and/or the Internet to research and record information on the inventor or invention; and*
> - *plan a Google Drive presentation about the inventor or invention.*

In addition to proper framing (phraseology), it is important to remember that since the purpose of your instructional objectives is to clearly describe what you want your students to know or be able to do, you must make sure that each is subordinate to and connected with your stated goals and standards. To illustrate how this all fits together, examine Figure 2.3; it illustrates how Ms. Walker completed the responsibilities for Link 1 of the unit plan, *Great Inventors and Inventions*.

Reflection on Learning

You may simply scribble rough notes or jot down something more polished and complete. The point is to simply start recording your ideas spontaneously and candidly.

Add to Ms. Walker's unit by selecting one more goal; identifying two related standards from national, state, or professional sources; and breaking down each of the standards into one or two instructional objectives.

FIGURE 2.3   The First Link of Ms. Walker's Unit Plan

Great Inventors and Inventions

Grade 5

Introductory Paragraph:

This is a thematic unit based on knowledge of inventors and their inventions. The students will research the lives of great inventors by focusing on two major questions: "How did these inventors get their ideas?" and "How did they make their ideas a reality?" The students will take a look at the genius of inventors by examining the ways inventions we now take for granted amazed people in the past; how inventions have changed the course of history; how inventors have come up with ideas; and how inventions continue to change the way we live and work. Further emphasis will be placed on the problem-solving and analytical skills involved in inventing. The culminating event will be an invention convention that will give students an opportunity to synthesize and apply knowledge and skills to create an invention or innovation to solve a problem, just as "real" inventors would.

I. Desired Results

Established Goal:

The students shall integrate ideas from several disciplines to identify problems affecting society.

Standard:

Know how human ingenuity and technological resources satisfy specific human needs and improve the quality of life.

Identify and distinguish between human needs and improving the quality of life.
Describe a technological invention and the resources that were used to develop it.

Instructional Objective (Performance Outcomes):
The students shall create a new invention for the 21st century.

- *Develop a list of problems in school or outside that require a new approach or solution.*
- *Select one problem to solve.*
- *Analyze the problem and create an invention to make life easier, safer, or more fun.*
- *Complete a patent application for the invention.*
- *Describe and apply advertising techniques to market the invention.*

Link 2: Assessment Strategies

Link 1 of your unit-building chain pinpointed the desired results: the goals, standards, and instructional objectives. Now, Link 2 will supply answers to these questions: "What counts as evidence of successful learning?" "How can I measure the progress my students are making (or have made) toward achieving the desired results?" Assessment is the process you will use to answer those questions as your students progress through three major lesson components: (1) *developing readiness for learning* (at the beginning), (2) *attaining desired results* (along the way), and (3) *assessing outcomes of instruction* (end result). A balanced assessment system requires diagnostic, summative, and formative assessments as components of a comprehensive data-gathering process. *Diagnostic assessment* is implemented at the beginning of a new unit (or learning activity) to determine what students already know about a theme or topic, to get an idea about their skill sets and capabilities, and to target any misconceptions the students may have before the unit is launched. This information is gathered through common assessment tools such as *pre-tests* (to determine what students already know or can do); *self-assessments* (students estimate their own skills and competencies); *graphic organizers* (visual maps and diagrams, such as KWL charts, that help students organize their thinking); and *discussion responses* (comments in reply to content-specific prompts). *Summative assessment* is used to "sum up" the progress made in achieving the intended outcomes at the *completion* of a unit of instruction. Summative assessments may include tests but should include other evidence, such as results of demonstrations, portfolios, or projects. *Formative assessment*, on the other hand, may be used *throughout* the unit to determine the degree to which your students are "getting it." The results are used to improve instruction and student learning *while it is happening.* What classifies an assessment tool as diagnostic, formative, or summative is not the assessment tool itself, but the way it is used—whether to get an idea of existing knowledge or misconceptions before beginning the unit, along the way to see how well your desired results are being met, or at the end of the unit to measure achievement. Regardless of how you combine diagnostic, formative, and summative assessment, it is important to connect assessment processes to the learning targets outlined in Link 1 of the unit plan. By gathering data from contexts in which the students are learning, the results may be more meaningful to you, to the students, and to the students' families. Some units focus on the creation of tangible products, so they tend to utilize a wide range of performance tasks, demonstrations, and portfolios. Content-oriented units, on the other hand, will rely on quizzes or tests among the primary means of assessment, and these tests will often be focused on essential information. Regardless of the assessment tool selected, you must carefully examine the results. If students do not adequately meet the desired outcomes, you will need to look for alternative approaches to achieve your goals.

AUTHENTIC ASSESSMENT

Although some people may associate assessment with assigning grades and taking tests, especially standardized or standards-based tests, successful social studies teachers use an elaborate assortment of strategies and techniques called *authentic assessment*. Rather than simply gauging the degree to which students are able to store and retrieve information on tests administered at the end of a lesson or unit, authentic assessment (sometimes called *alternative assessment, comprehensive assessment,* or *performance assessment*) analyzes students' abilities to apply what they have learned in "real-world" contexts, such as exhibitions, demonstrations, interviews, rubrics, portfolios, journals, and, yes, even teacher-made tests. If you want to find out if Lamont can apply creative thinking skills to solve problems, for example, you will want to encourage him to come up with an original invention. And if you wanted to know if Darla can fill out a patent application, observing how she fills one out is a self-evident assessment strategy. Can Belinda select what she believes are the 10 greatest modern inventions and list them chronologically? It would help to observe her efforts as she constructs a computer-generated time line. Authentic assessments require students to be performers. *Evaluation* is often confused with assessment, but it is important to note that they are two different processes. You can *evaluate* a student's progress toward some goal, standard, or objective by gathering assessment data; think of evaluation as the process of making judgments, such as grades, after interpreting the assessment data. Wiggins and McTighe (2006) recommend four major classifications of authentic assessment:

- Informal checks for understanding
- Academic prompts
- Performance tasks
- Quiz and test items

Informal Checks for Understanding   *Informal checks for understanding* are occasional assessments during daily lessons that provide feedback about student progress toward the desired results: "Do I need to clear up any confusions or misconceptions or is it okay to move on?" Informal checks include common strategies such as brief challenging tasks, informal observations, and teacher questioning.

   Brief challenging tasks that take place throughout a lesson are instant barometers for instruction; they help teachers identify favorable results or areas of concern and use that knowledge to modify teaching and learning strategies. For example, Ms. Walker chose to assess her students' ability to distinguish between *inventions* and *not inventions* by giving pictorial examples of each (a tree and an umbrella, for example). She asked students to hold up one finger if they thought the example was an invention and two fingers if they thought it was not. She also liked to use hand signals as a way for students to indicate their understanding of specific concepts or processes: "Turn your thumbs up if you understand how to file a patent for your idea." "Turn your thumbs down if you're unsure about how to design a web ad for your invention." Also, Ms. Walker found that individual whiteboards were handy as informal checks for understanding. She asked a question to pairs of students and directed them to discuss it and write or draw their responses on whiteboards: "How did the invention of the Internet change people's lives?" The students held the whiteboards up toward Ms. Walker so that she could take a quick look around the room and assess whether they were on task. Ms. Walker spiced up the use of whiteboards by playing a game based on the TV game show *Jeopardy*. She gave an answer ("He invented the first conveyor belt-based assembly line"), and each student wrote a response in the form of a question on his or her whiteboard ("Who is Henry Ford?").

For years, teachers have used brief challenging tasks like these to check for understanding during ongoing instruction. It is important to understand that these strategies should not be used for grading purposes, but primarily to provide feedback about learning so that, if needed, adjustments to instruction can be made.

Informal Observations   Informal observation ("kidwatching") includes various procedures for viewing and listening to students and making judgments about their behavior and learning. Take time to circulate among your students and observe them as they work alone and in groups; listen to their conversations and note what they understand or have difficulty with. Jot down what you learn from these experiences and interactions: "What clues have I picked up about the student's skills, understandings, strengths and challenges, work habits, or motivation?" Whenever possible, carry a small notebook and pencil and when you see something interesting, write it down in one or two sentences. It is helpful to look for patterns; your notes may show that a student is not listening carefully to others or that some concepts are difficult to grasp. A sequence of anecdotes can serve as a record of individual development and be used as a basis to adapt instruction. Record only what you observe; an anecdotal record should deal with nothing but the facts. This data can be used as feedback for students about their learning or as anecdotal data shared with them and/or their parents during conferences.

With a glut of time-consuming responsibilities facing them each day, jotting down and analyzing anecdotal records can be a real challenge for many elementary school teachers. Observation checklists, however, make it possible to collect anecdotal information even when confronted with demanding workloads. Checklists provide a quick, easy, and time-efficient tool to observe and record student progress toward desired results. To construct a checklist, first list the specific outcomes to be assessed and then record the occurrences of each. A sample checklist of behaviors for participating in a cooperative learning group is shown in Figure 2.4.

 Video Exploration 2.2

Asking Good Questions   While asking questions may seem like a fairly routine teaching activity, purposeful questioning can be the most powerful assessment tool we have at our disposal. You will find yourself routinely using a variety of questions to encourage dialogue with and among your students; a general knowledge question will require one answer ("Who invented the telephone?") and at other times you will expect unique responses ("Would you be more excited if your invention made the world a healthier place, or if it made the world a little more fun?"). Questioning enables you to check students' knowledge as you ask factual questions, as well as their ability to think at a higher level as you ask open-ended questions, so a key to asking

FIGURE 2.4   Observation Checklist for Cooperative Learning

	Sometimes Present	Mastered
Assists co-workers when needed		
Follows group-established rules		
Does fair share of group work		
Respects group decisions		
Shares materials willingly		

Directions:

(✓) Place a check in the "Sometimes Present" column if the characteristic is occasionally observed.

(+) Place a plus in the "Mastered" column if the characteristic occurs habitually.

( ) Make no mark if the characteristic is observed seldom or not at all.

purposeful questions is to know what you want for an answer: "What kind of information am I seeking?" Your questions will help you to analyze the degree to which your students are achieving well-defined learning goals; questions are there to provide you with a solid decision-making point: "Is it okay to move on or must I further scaffold student understanding?" Simply quizzing students about the facts may give the illusion of teaching to the uninitiated, but successful social studies teachers know that questions must be arranged according to their level of complexity; this is called *taxonomy*. An imposing stockpile of questioning taxonomies inhabit the educational literature, but developing your own scheme will furnish you with a reliable cache from which to choose. I have found John Dewey's (1933) time-honored "art of questioning" to be particularly helpful in this regard:

- Questions should not elicit fact upon fact but should be asked in such a way as to delve deeply into the subject—that is, to develop an overall concept of the selection.
- Questions should emphasize personal interpretations rather than literal and direct responses.
- Questions should not be asked randomly so that each is an end in itself but should be planned so that one leads into the next throughout a continuous discussion.
- Teachers should periodically review important points so that old, previously discussed material can be placed into perspective with that which is presently being studied.
- The end of the question-asking sequence should leave the children with a sense of accomplishment and build a desire for what is yet to come.

Acquiring the ability to ask good questions doesn't happen overnight or even during student teaching; it often takes years of practice—a long road of trial, error, and success. Chapters 3 and 4, on instructional methods, will provide more detailed information about how to frame and use good questions.

Academic Prompts   Good questions require students to do something more than simply give back facts; students must make sense of what they've learned, connect what they've learned to other material, apply what they've learned to solve problems or challenges, use what they've learned while deciding what to believe or do, or employ what they've learned as a basis for judging actions or ideas. At times, students may become "stuck" while trying to respond to a particular questioning type, so you must be ready to react in ways that help to improve understandings, address misconceptions, or elaborate on ideas. This support mechanism consists of a system of academic prompts; cues or questions that guide students toward increased success.

For example, after reading the book *Louis Braille: The Boy Who Invented Books for the Blind* by Margaret Davidson and Janet Compere (Scholastic, 1991), Ms. Walker asked a variety of questions to check their understanding: "Who is Louis Braille?" simply required students to give back facts. To promote higher-order thinking, Ms. Walker asked, "Which has been more important for the blind, guide dogs or the Braille writing system?" Obviously, this question prompts a more thoughtful response that calls for students to synthesize and evaluate information. Recognizing errors and misconceptions in the students' responses, Ms. Walker provided prompts and cues to scaffold their ideas:

- How did you know that?
- What exactly do you mean?
- Is there another explanation?
- What do you think would happen if . . . ?
- How was _____ different from (like) _____?
- What information did you use to come up with that conclusion?
- Could you please tell me more about _____?
- I'm not certain what you mean. Could you give me some examples?
- This is what I thought I heard you say. Did I understand you correctly?

Performance Tasks   Imagine that your college's theater group has just issued a casting call for actors, dancers, singers, and other talent for an upcoming stage show. Do you think the casting process would be more effective if it involved a series of auditions in front of a casting director or if scores on a true/false test were the primary selection criterion? Although a casting director's choice is obvious, teachers find that they, too, are better able to assess some goals and standards if their students perform tasks that apply the targeted content knowledge or skills to "real-world" situations—portfolios, essays, presentations, exhibitions, and large projects carried out over a period of time. Of course, tests remain an important part of authentic assessment, but only if they are the most appropriate source of evidence.

Performance tasks are goal-directed activities that require students to perform or demonstrate what they have learned. *Performance assessment* is the process of judging performance tasks with a clear-cut set of criteria. Performance assessment is commonly carried out with tools such as scoring rubrics, portfolios, and student work samples. A *rubric* is a scoring guide that bases an evaluation of a product or performance on a range of criteria. Rubrics consist of three primary components: (1) a stated objective, which is a product or performance; (2) a range of scores to indicate degree of performance quality; and (3) criteria defined for each level. The criteria, or characteristics of a product or performance, are usually listed in the left-hand column of a rubric. A number or other indicator of the quality of work is often placed at the top of the rubric. The rubric shown in Figure 2.5 may give you a sense of one way rubrics are used to assess a written report. It was created online at RubiStar, a free website supported by a grant from the U.S. Department of Education (http://rubistar.4teachers.org/).

Portfolios are collections of student work that document their efforts, progress, and achievements over a period of time. There is no single list of items recommended for portfolios; they may include items such as student writings, art products, photographs, independent research reports, projects, favorite books, and work samples. Cheryl Walker liked the idea of using portfolios to assess her students' progress in the unit *Great Inventors and Inventions* but felt that the students required a model before they would be able to put together a portfolio of their own. Ms. Walker wrote the word *portfolio* on a whiteboard. She asked if anyone had an idea of what a portfolio might be. Anticipating that not many would have a clue, Ms. Walker brought out a box containing items that, in effect, created her biographical sketch. She informed her students that portfolios tell a story and that she chose objects that helped tell a story about herself as a person.

The first item Ms. Walker took from her portfolio was a photograph of her family. "I love my family," she announced proudly and pointed out her husband and young children

FIGURE 2.5   Rubric for Written Research Report

Category	4	3	2	1
Organization	Information is very organized with well-constructed paragraphs and subheadings.	Information is organized with well-constructed paragraphs.	Information is organized, but paragraphs are not well constructed.	The information appears to be disorganized.
Quality of Information	Information clearly relates to the main topic. It includes several supporting details and/or examples.	Information clearly relates to the main topic. It provides 1–2 supporting details and/or examples.	Information clearly relates to the main topic. No details and/or examples are given.	Information has little or nothing to do with the main topic.
Sources	All sources (information and graphics) are accurately documented in the desired format.	All sources (information and graphics) are accurately documented, but a few are not in the desired format.	All sources (information and graphics) are accurately documented, but many are not in the desired format.	Some sources are not accurately documented.
Internet Use	Successfully uses suggested Internet links to find information and navigates within these sites easily without assistance.	Usually able to use suggested Internet links to find information and navigates within these sites easily without assistance.	Occasionally able to use suggested Internet links to find information and navigates within these sites easily without assistance.	Needs assistance or supervision to use suggested Internet links and/or to navigate within these sites.
Paragraph Construction	All paragraphs include introductory sentence, explanations or details, and concluding sentence.	Most paragraphs include introductory sentence, explanations or details, and concluding sentence.	Paragraphs include related information but are typically not constructed well.	Paragraphing structure is not clear and sentences are not typically related within the paragraphs.
Mechanics	No grammatical, spelling, or punctuation errors.	Almost no grammatical, spelling, or punctuation errors.	A few grammatical, spelling, or punctuation errors.	Many grammatical, spelling, or punctuation errors.
Diagrams & Illustrations	Diagrams and illustrations are neat and accurate and add to the reader's understanding of the topic.	Diagrams and illustrations are neat and accurate and add to the reader's understanding of the topic.	Diagrams and illustrations are neat and accurate and sometimes add to the reader's understanding of the topic.	Diagrams and illustrations are not neat and accurate OR do not add to the reader's understanding of the topic.

(along with Barkley and Betty Basset Hound, the family pets). Next came a not-so-new golf ball: "I got my first hole-in-one the summer after I graduated from college," she said proudly. Several ribbons followed—they were awarded to her as a youngster for winning a local geography bee. Ms. Walker then held up a tablet computer and explained, "In my spare time, I enjoy exploring the Internet, writing and receiving email, watching movies, listening to music, looking at photos, reading books, playing games, and using all kinds of apps." The most fascinating items came next—a photo of Ms. Walker taken when she was a fifth grader and her report card from the same grade. "I wanted to show you the best report card I ever received," she explained. "I had a fabulous fifth-grade teacher." The last article she removed from the box was a children's book, *The Little Engine That Could*. "This is one of my favorite books. From the first time my parents read it to me as a child, I loved it. It taught me that a person could accomplish almost anything if he or she tried hard enough."

Comparing her collection of personal memorabilia to a social studies portfolio, Ms. Walker asked the class what might be included in their portfolios for the unit. She received several suggestions: daily assignments, drawings, illustrated plans, writings and reports, group projects, individual projects, journal entries, and so on. The class then discussed the format of a good portfolio. They decided it should be housed in a suitable container—boxes, file folders, or binders. All agreed that file folder "inventor's portfolios" would make excellent containers for this unit. The class also decided that the portfolio should be neat and include a table of contents. Furthermore, each item should have with it a short personal statement about why it was important to the learner.

Although portfolios can effectively organize paper or print-based materials, it is difficult to include the more contemporary multimedia resources that have become the latest rage. And, although assessing student progress is greatly enhanced by collecting work samples in binders, folders, or boxes, these portfolios often become massive and cumbersome. Boxes and binders, cassettes, pictures, drawings, projects, and objects such as satellite images and maps are not only hard to handle but take up a lot of space. With an *electronic portfolio*, however, evidence of a student's work would take up very little physical space. And the electronic portfolio could be accessed in a short time with minimal effort when stored on a computer hard drive, flash drive, or CD. Electronic portfolios can hold a great deal of information; work samples such as murals, outdoor projects, large models, and writing samples can be photographed, scanned, and saved. Oral interviews can be recorded. Collaborative group work that otherwise would not be included in each student's hands-on portfolio fits easily into separate electronic portfolios. And electronic portfolios can be embellished with sound, music, pictures, graphics, and video.

There are countless ways to put together portfolios; the important consideration is that students take an active role in selecting material for and organizing them. Of course, the portfolios must address instructional standards and goals. When students create their portfolios, their exhibits become a means through which you may provide evaluative feedback and monitor progress. You should hold individual conferences with the students, during which you guide portfolio review with questions such as the following:

- "How has your work in social studies changed since last year (or last month)?"
- "What do you now know about _____ that you didn't know before?"
- "What are the special items in your portfolio?"
- "What would you most like me to understand about your portfolio?"
- "How did you decide to organize the items?"
- "What are the strengths as displayed in the portfolio? What needs to be improved?"

The conference should focus not just on subject-matter accomplishments but also on planning strategies, personal reflections, and evidence of progress. Assuming an active role in the learning process goes beyond simply recognizing making a mistake to receiving feedback from others and finding practical ways to do something about it. Portfolios provide evidence of performance that goes far beyond command of factual knowledge by offering a clear and understandable picture of how a student's work has evolved. While this is all important, however, the greatest benefit of portfolios may be in self-evaluation. Portfolio assessment offers students the opportunity to set individual goals, select items for evaluation, and reflect on their work. In this way, it encourages pride in learning and helps students develop the motivation to improve.

An important point to remember about assessment is that no single instrument or technique can adequately measure the range of performances and behaviors contained in social studies units. For this reason, educators today strongly recommend obtaining a variety of assessment data and making assessment an integral part of the learning process rather than something that happens at the end.

A teacher asked these students to raise their hands so she could take a quick look around the room to see if they understood the directions for accomplishing a learning task. What form of assessment did the teacher employ?

Hurst Photo/Shutterstock

Quiz and Test Items   Without debate, students must acquire a rich content background in social studies. If we expect them to become productive citizens in our democratic nation, then core social studies content is as basic to their success as the ability to shoot, pass, and dribble are to success in basketball. High-level thinking demands a high degree of knowledge: How can we expect young students to become high-level thinkers if they are unfamiliar with underlying facts and procedures? If used for the proper reasons, content-oriented quizzes and tests can provide important feedback to students as they seek to identify their content-associated strengths and weaknesses. They can furnish you with convenient data on student learning: used at the beginning of a unit, tests or quizzes will tell you what the students currently know and don't know; used at the end of a unit, tests or quizzes can help you find out if they have achieved the desired results; and, used as the unit is progressing, tests and quizzes can help you modify teaching and learning activities to meet student needs. Two of the most commonly used and potentially confusing terms in testing today are "standardized test" and "standards-based test". What do each of these mean?

Standardized Tests   While classroom quizzes and tests yield important information regarding the achievement of unit-specific content outcomes, standardized achievement tests are used to monitor a student's content learning over time and compare their achievement level to students of the same age group or grade level. Anyone who has gone through the public school system will have likely taken several standardized tests. Almost every school district requires and administers them. These include readiness tests, which are used to determine whether a child is ready for the kindergarten program offered by a school or for promotion to first grade; screening tests, to determine if a child will be labeled as learning disabled or, at the other extreme, as gifted and talented; intelligence tests, which are widely used to measure intellectual ability; and achievement tests, which measure a range of skills and content knowledge. The SAT test you probably took as part of your college entrance package is a standardized test. How are standardized tests used in social studies? What do these tests offer that we can't get without them? Comparability in the context of the "big picture" is the major thing: "In general, are my fourth graders learning basic social studies content as well as other fourth graders in our school district?" "Compared to fifth graders throughout the United States, how well are those in our school district doing in map skills?" "How does our district's social studies curriculum compare with others in the state?"

Standards-Based Tests   Assessment is a key component of the standards movement, so states have used *standards-based tests* as part of the outcome-based standards cycle. The first part of the cycle is to establish new, higher standards describing what each child must know or be able to do, along with guidelines for proficiency in a particular subject area or grade level. Next, the curriculum is aligned to these new standards. The cycle is completed when students take standards-based tests to determine the degree to which they have developed proficiency in the knowledge and skills essential for success in school and life. The rationale behind standards-based testing is that test results supply the evidence needed to improve our schools; the data generated by the standardized tests act like a "report card," demonstrating how well local schools are performing.

Standards-based testing is among the most hotly debated education topics today. Although its overriding purpose is to ensure that students are successful in school and life, critics complain that performance on a test alone falls far short of providing a complete picture of what students have learned or how well teachers have taught them. Some complain that the primary responsibility of today's teachers has been reduced to training students to take standardized and standards-based tests. Everything else—creativity, critical thinking, problem solving, questioning—has become secondary. Despite the fact that standards-based tests can determine only a small portion of any student's total achievement, the public assigns test scores great weight: "Are our students making 'normal' progress?" "Is their overall achievement above or below average?" When the answers to these questions have serious consequences ("high stakes")—and they often do—teachers are forced to teach to the test. This devalues good classroom instruction and undercuts the authenticity of scores as measures of what children really know. "Test-generated" instruction often leads to repeated drill and practice on skills and content because teachers are pressured to prove that what they are doing produces good test scores: "If the child hasn't learned, the teacher hasn't taught."

In addition to influencing classroom instruction, standards-based and standardized tests have been criticized for being biased in favor of those who have been exposed to White, middle-class culture and live in metropolitan areas. The more obvious biases have disappeared in recent years, as stereotypes have been eliminated in an effort to be more "politically correct." However, standardized tests are still accused of carrying an inherent bias for today's extraordinarily diverse students.

 Video Exploration 2.3

Despite the testing controversy, tests and quizzes, if used properly, play an important role in learning and offer a number of important benefits for teachers and students. Figure 2.6 shows the tools Ms. Walker proposes to use while assessing understanding and performance throughout her unit.

REFLECTION ON LEARNING

You may simply scribble rough notes or jot down something more polished and complete. The point is to simply start recording your ideas spontaneously and candidly.

There are various ways to gather assessment data. Among other tools, Ms. Walker chose to analyze student work samples, observe student performance, and ask timely questions. Add one or two tools to Ms. Walker's list to indicate how you would gain additional assessment data.

FIGURE 2.6   Adding the Assessment Link to Our Evolving Unit Plan

Great Inventors and Inventions

Grade 5

Introductory Paragraph:

I. Desired Results

Established Goals:

Standards:

Instructional Objectives:

II. Assessment Strategies

Diagnostic

- *Use a KWL chart to determine what the students currently know*

Formative

- *Daily teacher observations to monitor the children's progress*
- *Oral responses to literature discussions*
- *Class and individual discussions to check knowledge, concepts, or assignment tasks; provide opportunities for students to think critically and share ideas*
- *Rubrics to judge core performance tasks, such as a Rube Goldberg machine, a group inventor report, and an individual invention design*

Summative

- *Portfolios containing evidence of projects and other performance tasks*

 CHECK YOUR UNDERSTANDING 2.2   **Click here** to check your understanding of this section of the chapter.

Link 3: Learning Experiences and Instruction

You have now established what your students will be expected to learn and how you will determine the degree to which they are learning it; for each intended learning outcome, you have installed appropriate assessment practices. At this point, it is your responsibility to ask yourself, "What instructional strategies best correspond with my intended learning outcomes and associated assessment practices?" As you can see, the key to effective planning is to connect instructional strategies with the previous two links of our planning chain—goals and assessment. Although this can be the most highly anticipated part of planning, it is also the most pivotal section, especially for first-year teachers. Since learning experiences form a strong connection between you and your students, the instructional strategies you select often determine the level of interest students will have in the unit and the amount of energy they will apply toward achieving the intended outcomes. What a thrilling adventure you are about to embark on!

Wiggins and McTighe (2006) explain that for a unit plan to be considered a good outline of instruction, its activities and learning experiences must be *engaging*—truly thought provoking, fascinating, energizing—and *effective*—students become more competent and productive as a result of worthy work. How do you design learning experiences so that they are engaging and effective? That is where *organization* comes into the picture. It is important to think of a unit plan as a series of connected lessons. In effective *lesson sequencing*, learning experiences are strung together in a well thought-out sequence rather than as a mishmash of disconnected events. Lesson sequencing is the process of logically organizing the lessons so that they offer a clear *direction* toward the attainment of the selected goals. There are many alternatives that you might consider to sequence your learning experiences. I prefer arranging learning experiences much like the story structure arranges the events of a book. In a book, story structure determines the order by which the events of a story are presented to a reader. You can think of story structure as the building blocks of a good story; the simplest story structure includes a *beginning* that catches a reader's attention with a glimpse into the problem or plot, a *middle* that presents a sequence of events forming the bulk of the story, and an *ending* that summarizes or brings the story to a close and keeps the reader thinking about the story after it is finished. We can use the same idea to break down unit activities into small "chapters": *Introductory Experiences, Developmental Experiences,* and *Culminating Experiences.* You must carefully orchestrate these three major chapters because, when woven together, they shape a "literary masterpiece." The specific learning activities you select for each "chapter" can be explained briefly with *activity blueprints*—short descriptions, in paragraph form.

CHAPTER 1: INTRODUCTORY EXPERIENCES

The major purpose of the introductory experience is to clearly communicate what students are going to learn, why it is important to learn these things, how these new learnings relate to what they already know, and how learning is going to be carried out. To be effective, the introductory experience must engage your students: "What kind of bait can I cast out to 'hook' my students on the topic so they will participate as purposeful and involved learners?" (If you prefer educational jargon to the more informal term "hook," substitute "preteaching strategy" here.) A preteaching strategy provides a motivating opening experience that connects to previous learning and stimulates interest in the unit. During the first lesson or two, then, you will want to seize the students' attention and pull them into the topic with an interesting artifact, an amazing fact, an odd quirk, a challenge, or some type of brain teaser, such as sharing a real item the students can inspect and speculate about before reading a story about the person who invented it. You can get the students on the right track by activating their prior knowledge, introducing the topic and main ideas to be covered, making clear how the current unit builds on past learning, and show how it can lead to future learning. Some teachers accomplish this by starting out with a KWL chart or concept map, which they display throughout the whole unit. On the first day, for example, they ask students to share what they already know about inventions and inventors (K), and what they want to learn about inventions and inventors (W), and at the end, what they learned about inventions and inventors (L).

I have found that one of the most important elements of an interest-building introductory experience is a good book. Whether it is a heartwarming bedtime storybook our parents read to us as children, or, as we became independent young adults, an inspiring novel that uncovers deep visionary truths, books have a way of transforming our lives. I call these powerful stories, either read aloud or told, *literature launchers*. Good children's stories can sweep up the students and carry them off into a captivating, enchanting world through well-written and illustrated expository texts; picture books and novels can be the vehicle to transport learners into other cultures, places, and eras. As powerful as they are, however, good stories should not be limited only to introductory experiences. They are effective instructional tools when used at strategic points throughout a unit. With careful searches, such as looking for blogs or websites dealing with the use of children's literature in a social studies classroom, you can find children's trade books through which any of the social studies standards can be taught. A good unit is rich in literature, both fiction and nonfiction.

Ms. Walker started her unit by relating the new material to students' previous knowledge and experiences. She then decided to use an enjoyable hands-on inductive strategy to familiarize her students with the concept of "inventions" by differentiating them from "noninventions." She followed up the activity by reading aloud Emily Arnold McCully's *Marvelous Mattie: How Margaret E. Knight Became an Inventor* (Farrar, Straus and Giroux, 2006). With her sketchbook labeled *My Inventions* and her father's toolbox, Mattie's childhood fascinations with how everyday things worked inspired her to figure out ways to improve the way machines functioned. The outline of how Ms. Walker planned to carry out both learning adventures during the Introductory Experience phase is presented in Figure 2.7.

These children are being "hooked" by a mystery object—something nearly all of them had never seen before. Exploring real objects such as this piece of bamboo immediately challenges their curiosity and stimulates deep interest to act on that curiosity.

Monkey Business Images/Shutterstock

CHAPTER 2: DEVELOPMENTAL EXPERIENCES

Following the introductory phase, you turn to a section that is often described as the "brass tacks" of the unit—the point in time when learner and teacher engagement abounds with "rising action." Your students were prepared for this step because you captured their attention, informed them about what was coming, and helped them make connections between their prior knowledge and the new information. Now, you are responsible for selecting the learning materials and activities that reflect the intended outcomes of the unit and are appropriate for the needs and interests of your students. But what specific teaching methods, materials, and activities are best suited for different learners? Technology? Print resources? Hands-on items? Artifacts? Field trips? Guest speakers? Textbooks? Project-based? Problem-based? Inquiry-based? Directed instruction? Textbook-based? Literature-based? Cooperative learning? Collaborative learning? Interdisciplinary learning? Social models? Radical models? All these choices can set even the calmest mind spinning! Which model works best? This question has baffled educators since the onset of formal education, and it has not yet been persuasively answered to this day. It is important to consider that teaching social studies is such a multifaceted mission that it is impossible to identify any "best way" to teach in all situations and for all purposes. Successful teachers do not draw on just one model of instruction, but make choices from among the rich repertoire of alternatives after analyzing educational goals, the needs and interests of their students, standards, and the linked assessment strategies. Clearly, neither this chapter nor this book can hope to explore the hundreds and hundreds of instructional options from which you might choose. However, the remainder of this text will describe some of the more common instructional methods and materials that help strengthen and support student learning in the social studies curriculum. As you set this phase in motion, the students go to work; you may retreat a bit since your initial teaching responsibilities as a stimulator and arranger are now over. You will have more teaching to do, but in other ways.

At this point, Ms. Walker will sequence instruction in a way that leads each student to achieve intended learning goals. Obviously, not all her students are alike, so it was important for Ms. Walker to tailor unit instruction to meet individual needs. Differentiated instruction is a teaching strategy based on the premise that instructional approaches should vary and be adapted in relation to individual and diverse students in classrooms (Tomlinson, 2014). The model of differentiated instruction requires teachers to be flexible in their approach to teaching and adjust a unit's content, processes, and products to students rather than expecting students to modify themselves for the demands of the unit; all students must have the opportunity to get what they need. (There will be more on differentiated instruction after the section on lesson planning.) With that in mind, examine Ms. Walker's developmental experiences in Figure 2.7.

CHAPTER 3: CULMINATING EXPERIENCES

While the preceding chapters of our "literary masterpiece" outlined the introductory and developmental learning experiences, the culminating experience aims to review, summarize, or bring a sensible "conclusion" to the unit. This concluding portion of the unit usually takes the form of a whole-class or group project that gives students an opportunity to make publicly known what they have learned by producing a concrete end product, such as a digital slide show or e-book, class mural, social action project, festival of dance performance, creative skit, cultural meal, "quilts" with badges representing significant people or places, or commemorative stamps honoring important inventors.

Ms. Walker helped her students make known to others the products of their ingenuity by holding an "Invention Convention"—a display of student-generated inventions and patent certificates (See Figure 2.7). She sent home an invitation so parents could enjoy seeing what can happen when their children's creative juices really get flowing. At the end of the event, Ms. Walker awarded an Invention Convention Certificate of Achievement to each young inventor. The students enjoyed the pats on the back and encouragement that poured their way on this big day!

Did you notice the many ways in which Ms. Walker used the spirit of the *Common Core State Standards (CCSS)* and the *College, Career, and Civic Life (C3) Framework for Social Studies State Standards (C3 Framework)* to carry out interdisciplinary instruction? An overall philosophy associated with standards-based instruction emphasizes that a thorough understanding of today's real-life problems requires an interdisciplinary focus. In Ms. Walker's case, bringing together academic areas such as science, language arts, and social studies enhanced the meaning of what was being taught and provided a rich context for literacy instruction.

 Video Exploration 2.4

Reflection on Learning

You may simply scribble rough notes or jot down something more polished and complete. The point is to simply start recording your ideas spontaneously and candidly.

Keeping in mind the goals, standards, objectives, assessment techniques, and Ms. Walker's teaching strategies, suggest at least one activity or strategy you can add to the *introductory experiences, developmental experiences*, and *culminating* experiences. Be sure that your suggestions allow students increased responsibility for learning—critical thinking, research skills, problem solving, group decision making, and so on.

How Are Lesson Plans Constructed?

While unit plans show the big picture, individual lesson plans, in very basic terms, are guides for carrying out daily instruction. Lesson plans incorporate many of the same features as unit plans, but on a smaller scale—goals, standards, and objectives (desired outcomes), a way of

FIGURE 2.7 The Third Link of Ms. Walker's Unit Plan

Unit Plan

Grade 5

Introductory Paragraph

I. *Desired Results*

II. *Assessment Strategies*

III. *Learning Experiences and Instruction*

Introductory Experiences

1. *Put together a "puzzle box" that contains examples of both inventions and noninventions. Some may be items (e.g., comb, toy telephone, lightbulb, pencil, chocolate chip cookie, rock, twig, small container of soil) and others pictures (e.g., airplane, car, lake, sky, mountain). Bring the students to their group conversation area and ask, "What do you suppose is in this box?" Inform the students that you have a puzzle you want them to try to solve; the puzzle is called "In or Out." Select one of the items and identify it as a positive example, saying, "The lightbulb is 'in.'" Repeat with the rock, saying, "The rock is 'out.'" Continue in this manner, randomly selecting two additional items. Next, divide the students into groups of three and give each group an item. Ask the students to classify the items as positive or negative examples. If they are unable to do that properly, continue the demonstration until the students unlock the mystery. Then invite the students to suggest their own examples of inventions and noninventions. Write on the whiteboard: "An invention is . . ." and ask the students to complete the definition. Some suggestions may be, "Something new," "Something thought up by a person," and "Something thought up by a person that helps people." Students come up with a final definition and compare it with a dictionary definition.*

2. *Read aloud Emily Arnold McCully's Marvelous Mattie: How Margaret E. Knight Became an Inventor (Farrar, Straus and Giroux, 2006). The story tells about how Mattie's childhood fascination with how everyday things worked inspired her to figure out ways to improve the way machines functioned. Based on the book's title and brief summary, have the students infer what the book is about and what they predict about Mattie. After reading the story, have your children retell the story in chronological order as a group. Be sure to review and clarify any confusing parts of the story. Talk together about the character traits of Mattie, and successful inventors in general.*

Developmental Experiences

1. *Rube Goldberg was a popular cartoonist who created new "inventions" that used a series of chain reactions to accomplish a simple task in a very complex manner. Share some famous Rube Goldberg inventions with the students by visiting the website https://www.rubegoldberg.com/. Discuss: Who was Rube Goldberg? What is a Rube Goldberg invention? Why do people find his inventions so fascinating? Do Rube Goldberg's inventions remind you of anything in your life?*

   The students can put what they have learned into action by building their own Rube Goldberg machine. Small groups can choose a simple task and then brainstorm for creative and complicated ways to accomplish that task. The students will upload a video of their finished project for others to see at

   https://diy.org/skills/physicist/challenges/389/make-a-rube-goldberg-machine.

2. *The students research various inventors and their inventions by reading text sets. Text sets are collections of books, at various reading levels, grouped together because they have something in common. The commonality in this case is inventors and inventions. Why not instead carry out a web search? Ms. Walker regularly does this and often combines library and web research, but for this unit, she felt that the library offered more control over the learning process. Ms. Walker used these books:*

   ● *Laurie Carlson's Boss of the Plains: The Hat That Won the West (DK Publishing) is a story of how John Batterson Stetson invented the "10-gallon hat." As a boy, John Stetson dreamed of going west. When at last he went, he found that everyone wore whatever hats they'd worn back home: knit caps, wool derbies, straw sombreros. Stetson found that the sun blistered his face because his derby did not provide enough protection, so the young hat maker invented the wide-brimmed "Boss of the Plains." Others struck gold or blazed trails through unknown territory, but John Stetson made his mark with a hat.*

FIGURE 2.7 (Continued)

- Catherine Thimmesh's Girls Think of Everything: Stories of Ingenious Inventions by Women *(Houghton Mifflin) is a compilation of inspiring stories of successful female inventors. Students will learn about what inspired these women and girls and how they turned their ideas into reality.*

- Eva Moore's The Story of George Washington Carver *(Scholastic) is a biography of one of the most distinguished individuals of our time. Born into slavery, Carver grew up to become a world-famous scientist and inventor. Carver is best known for his invention of hundreds of ways to use peanuts and sweet potatoes.*

- Keith Elliot's Steven Jobs & Stephen Wozniak: Creating the Apple Computer *(Blackbirch Marketing Partners Series) highlights the importance of cooperation and teamwork in the invention process. The book tells the story of two contemporary inventors who were daring leaders in the personal computer revolution.*

- Bruce Koscielniak's Johann Gutenberg and the Amazing Printing Press *(Houghton Mifflin) is a fact-filled book that starts out by explaining how books were handmade and individually penned to order in 15th-century Europe. After this overview, Gutenberg's revolutionary idea for a printing press is introduced, and the story of this famous printer's successes and difficulties is told.*

3. *To carry out the text set process, assign small groups of students to each text set. As they read, direct the students to uncover the following information:*

   a. *When the inventor lived*

   b. *The inventor's most famous invention*

   c. *Why she or he invented it*

   d. *The details of the invention*

   e. *Other interesting inventions by the inventor (if there were any)*

   f. *An explanation of the significance of the invention*

4. *Each group is responsible for writing a research report and delivering it orally to the class. The students in each group work together to design a costume that one member might wear to share the group's information. Did the highlighted inventor have a moustache? If so, the speaker should have one, too. Did she wear a hat? So should the speaker. In addition to looking and acting like the inventor, the students should try to use some type of aid in describing the invention. Would a large illustration work? What about a model or the actual invention?*

5. *The students are involved in the actual steps of inventing something. First, the groups brainstorm problems about their home, school, neighborhood, or any other location. Next, each group selects the most compelling problem and focuses on it. Focusing on that problem, students brainstorm ideas for an invention that could solve it. (For example, in one case, the members of a group eventually decided that they were very uncomfortable playing outdoors on cold winter days because, after running around for a while, their noses inevitably began to run. It was not easy for them to sort through layers of coats and sweaters to find a tissue or handkerchief. So, after considering several alternatives, including a handkerchief that could be attached temporarily to a coat sleeve and used to swipe away the drops—and removed to wash—the group suggested an invention called the "Stop Dripping Mitten." The mitten carried a supply of tissues inside a dispenser built into its palm.)*

6. *The students plan and design their inventions. Distribute large sheets of drawing paper for sketching the designs. Show students examples of actual sketches made by their inventors. Students may be interested to learn that there are regulations for the size of the paper and the format, the color of the drawings, their proportions, how they are numbered and referred to, and how they are included in the patent application. You can find the specific guidelines on the official website of the U.S. Patent and Trademark Office (http://www.uspto.gov/web/offices/pac/design/index.html#drawings). Sample illustrations drawn by actual inventors can be found on various other sites, too. They serve as effective models for students.*

7. *After the groups plan and design their inventions, they give them names. Students should not underestimate the importance of coming up with a good name, for the name has a very important purpose: It helps sell the product. A good product name will draw attention, especially if it is catchy, easy to remember, or clever. When students create a name, they should make sure it will bring attention to the product:*

   a. *Does the name adequately describe the product?*

   b. *Will the name project the idea you want people to get?*

   c. *Is the name easy to remember?*

FIGURE 2.7 (Continued)

8. *The next step is applying for a patent. A patent is an agreement between the U.S. government and an inventor that protects the inventor from anyone else stealing his or her idea. For the purposes of this unit, however, group members file a joint "application" for their invention—a simplified version of an application on which they name their invention, describe it, explain the things they feel are unique and useful, attach the sketches, and verify that the works are theirs by placing their signatures in the spaces provided: "We, the undersigned, affirm that we are the original and first inventors of the _____." As with a real patent application, the inventors must obtain signatures from two witnesses who can substantiate their claims.*

9. *When the applications are complete, they are sent to the Commissioner of Patents and Trademarks at the U.S. Patent Office (Ms. Walker) who checks them to see if everything was completed and done according to the rules. The teacher signs the applications, issues the inventions' "official" patent serial numbers, and stamps them with the "official" acceptance date.*

   No one will come knocking at the door of our new patent holders to buy their new inventions unless they find a way to promote them. One way to find potential buyers is to advertise the product, and one of the best ways to advertise it is for students to examine newspaper or magazine ads to find items that are similar to theirs. Then, using advertising techniques described earlier, the students should find examples of persuasive techniques. Discuss the ads with these prompts:

   a. *Does the ad attract attention?*

   b. *Does it show the benefits of buying the product?*

   c. *Does it create a desire to buy the product?*

10. *To help make students aware of the power advertising has in the success of a new product, Ms. Walker asked each group to select one technique that they thought would help make their product successful. Then they designed and displayed their own advertisements.*

Culminating Activity

An Invention Convention is the culminating event. It gives students an opportunity to demonstrate what they have learned in an experiential way by displaying their inventions to the public. Students will bring their inventions to the selected display site and be available to answer questions about their inventions.

determining the degree to which the intended outcomes were attained (assessment strategies), and how intended outcomes will be achieved (instructional materials and activities). Creating your own lesson plan is a significant pre-professional assignment. It is a practical way to demonstrate that you are becoming everything that you are capable of being—to show you have what it takes to stand out from the rest. Some of your peers may be content to surf websites for completed lesson plans, but it is one thing to use the plans of others and entirely another to create your own. When you do so, you demonstrate that you are good at what you do, you have the skills and know-how of a successful professional, you understand exactly what you are talking about, and you are committed to your work. Acquiring top-notch lesson planning skills won't happen overnight, but it is one of the important markers along the road to becoming a teacher who stands out.

Your lesson plans are intended to guide your efforts while helping your students achieve intended learning outcomes. To start, it is important that you select a lesson plan template that guides your efforts, but there are many plan formats to consider. It is easy to be puzzled by the various lesson plan formats recommended today, but variations among them have more to do with terminology and presentation style differences than with substance. When selecting a format, pick one that is clear, understandable, and readable. You may prefer to record your ideas in a traditional lesson plan book, create a Word document, or share ideas with a colleague on

Google Doc. Whichever way you choose, every effective lesson plan should connect to long-term instructional goals and be guided by the authentic performance assessment tasks. This connection helps focus your instruction and affirms that your planning efforts will guide students toward favorable outcomes. Not every lesson looks alike, but the easiest way to create a lesson plan is to use a template that contains these key features:

1. The plan should communicate a clear idea of the desired outcomes (goals, standards, and objectives).

2. The plan should outline the assessment tasks and criteria that will help determine whether students have "gotten it."

3. The plan must have a "hook" to grab the students' attention and motivate them, a strategy to access their prior knowledge, and a way to establish clear connections to new learning.

4. The plan should outline the strategies or activities that will be used to help students master the desired results.

5. The plan should include a culminating activity, which generally takes place at the end of the lesson or sequence of related lessons. The learners apply the information and skills that they have acquired to the completion and real-world, concrete end project.

6. The plan must accommodate and challenge the diverse learning needs of all students. This may include alterations to the content, methods and materials learning environment, or assessment practices.

As you reflect on the list, have you noticed how the components of lesson plans mirror those of unit plans? It is important to note at this point that there is no need to adhere firmly to your lesson plan, even if you have created a world-class product. As we discussed in Chapter 1, flexibility is an important characteristic of good teaching, so when situations justify it, it is appropriate and expected that you alter or diverge from your plan.

The sample lesson plan shown in Figure 2.8 demonstrates how Ms. Walker intended to carry out the Rube Goldberg activity outlined earlier. It is not meant to serve as an exclusive model of a lesson plan. Keeping in mind the six common features listed above, Ms. Walker simply created a format to make lesson plan writing easier for her. Now is your opportunity to either find a lesson plan format that you like or complete a lesson plan template that your instructor or field experience teacher wants you to try. Because this may be your first social studies lesson plan, it would be helpful to examine previously written lesson plans. You can do this by looking at the countless model plans available on the web.

This brings our discussion of unit and lesson planning to an end. Planning at both levels is a crucial element of dynamic social studies instruction. Planning, either formally or informally, is a continuous process for everyone, for there is a constant need to keep materials, activities, and techniques up to date. As a new teacher, you will work hard to accumulate a rich teaching repertoire; models for your ideas can be found in magazines and journals, and ready-made file cabinets (virtual file cabinets) are out there on the Internet, free for the taking. So dive into the planning process, examine the many planning sources that are popping up regularly, and experience the joy and satisfaction of creating a plan for a topic that has captured your interest. Perhaps you will make an important professional contribution that will become a rich source for future generations of teachers and students in your school district to enjoy.

▶ **Video Exploration 2.5**

FIGURE 2.8   Sample Lesson Plan

Goal

People create new things to make their lives better, easier, and more enjoyable.

Standard

The students shall understand that technology is closely linked to creativity, which has resulted in innovation.

Instructional Objectives

1. Students shall understand the qualities of a good inventor.
2. Students shall work in teams to design and build a small Rube Goldberg machine.
3. Students shall gain an understanding of simple machines and how they may be used to make our lives easier.

Procedure

1. Display the popular children's game *Mousetrap*. Make a connection to the fanciful contraptions of Rube Goldberg. Students will research several websites to learn about Rube Goldberg and how he became a celebrity with his outrageous cartoon contraptions. The cartoons of Rube Goldberg will be introduced to illustrate how his inventions make a simple task even harder to complete.
2. Print a few copies of Rube Goldberg inventions and eliminate the verbal descriptions. Have students work in groups to try to explain what is happening.
3. Gather a few things from around the classroom, your house, a junk drawer, or your garage. Balls, marbles, dominoes, string, toy cars, magnets, cardboard tubes, rubber bands, spools, paper cups, jar lids; any junk will do. However, avoid fire, potentially harmful objects, and dangerous chemicals.
4. Divide the class into groups of three and give each group a "junk box" (referred to as "Inventor's Kit"). Explain to the students that their challenge is to use their Inventor's Kits to create a Rube Goldberg contraption that will move a ping-pong ball into a plastic cup in five steps (the last step of the contraption).

Activity Procedure:

- There must be five steps and at least three different types of simple machines to accomplish the task.
- The events must be clearly visible.
- The goal is to move the ping-pong ball into a plastic cup.
- Safety is important.

5. Encourage the students to play with the items in their Inventor's Kits. What can the toy car bump into or knock down? Can the string pull something up or down? Can something push the ball down a cardboard ramp and set something in motion? Actual student-constructed samples may be viewed on the web.
6. Once they brainstorm a few good ideas for their machines, students should write down the steps or draw a simple illustration of the process. Some may want to use mapping software like *Kidspiration* to assist with the mapping stage. Some students may want to develop at least a few parts of the machine around a theme: toy tractors and animals for a farm?
7. Start building the machine. Be sure not to overlook a major element of Rube Goldberg's inventions—wackiness! Modify the materials and construction of the contraption to achieve the desired result. Option: You may want students to write a short description of what was happening within each stage of the machine, as Goldberg did in his cartoons.
8. Creativity cannot be doled out in short parcels. The students may need two to three class periods to complete this project.
9. The groups will display and demonstrate their inventions. Parents, students from other classrooms, teachers, and community members are welcomed and encouraged to attend this public showing.
10. More able students can be challenged to think about scientific principles they may be able to incorporate into their inventions: simple machines, cause and effect, Newton's Laws, acceleration, momentum, gravity, electromagnetism, and more.

FIGURE 2.8   (Continued)

Less able students may need to incorporate only three simple machines, or not be required to consider simple machines at all. Allow students who are unable to carry out construction activities to demonstrate their creativity in other ways, including media and technology to create new things in new ways.

Assessment

1. Review and discuss the activity with the class to gauge student mastery of what it takes to create an invention.
2. Check to see if the five simple machines were incorporated in the design.
3. Use the following three-point rubric to evaluate students' work:
   - **Three points:** Students built a machine that followed all stated procedures and successfully moved the ping-pong ball into the plastic cup in five steps.
   - **Two points:** Students designed a somewhat creative machine that followed most stated procedures and used four or five steps to move the ping-pong ball into the plastic cup.
   - **One point:** Students failed to follow the rules; they built a machine that used three or fewer steps and/or failed to move the ping-pong ball into the plastic cup.

Reflection on Learning

Your first social studies lesson plan will be a landmark in your professional career and you will probably spend more time planning it than you will ever spend planning another social studies lesson.

Select any single experience outlined in Stage 3 of Ms. Walker's unit (including your suggested additions) and construct a lesson plan that will guide you in achieving intended learning outcomes. Whether your lesson plan fits a particular format is not as relevant (although your instructor may feel it is) as whether it is a high-quality, on-target road map of what students need to learn and how it will be accomplished.

 CHECK YOUR UNDERSTANDING 2.3 Click here to check your understanding of this section of the chapter.

What Is Differentiated Instruction?

In many ways, classrooms can be viewed as a microcosm of society—places where a rich mixture of children work together to build the social and participatory skills required of citizens in our American democracy. As leaders in a microcosm of American democracy, you have a responsibility to recognize and overcome any inequities and provide all students with equal opportunities to learn. The ability to eventually participate as active adults in a diverse democratic society begins with equitable social studies education during the early elementary grades; the early years are important antecedents of later attitudes toward social and cultural responsibility. For this reason, it is important to create unit and lesson plans that draw on the talents and strengths of all children; their learning experiences must be productive, supportive, and free of bias.

Teachers in differentiated classrooms accept and act on the fact that elementary school students are alike in many ways, but that they also have important differences that necessitate essential adjustments to instruction.

Wavebreakmedia/Shutterstock

Tomlinson (2014) describes *differentiated instruction* as the manner through which a teacher responds to the diversity of students in a classroom. She explains that students vary in *at least three ways* that make modifying instruction a reasonable and necessary strategy:

1. *Readiness:* Are there any gaps in learning that will prevent a student from moving ahead?
2. *Interest:* What is a student's level of curiosity or passion for a particular concept or skill?
3. *Learning Profile:* How has learning been shaped by gender, race, culture, physical or mental condition, learning style, or a combination of other complex factors?

Tomlinson (2014) goes on to suggest that there are four ways teachers can differentiate instruction based on student readiness, interest, or learning profile:

1. the **content** (what the students are expected to learn),
2. the **process** (strategies and activities to help students master the content),
3. the **product** (how students demonstrate what they have learned), and
4. the **learning environment** (how the classroom looks and feels).

Based on the readiness, interest, and learning profiles of her students, Ms. Walker plans to adapt the four curricular elements at any point throughout a lesson or the unit, with the goal of increasing the likelihood that students will be more successful as a result:

1. the **content**: *using materials of varying reading ability; meeting with small groups to reteach a particular understanding or skill;*
2. the **process**: *providing learning centers to reinforce or extend understandings or skills; varying the times students have to complete tasks;*
3. the **product**: *giving students options for how they express targeted learning; allowing students to work alone or in small groups;*
4. the **learning environment**: *arranging areas where students can work individually or in collaborative groups; providing materials that reflect the many aspects of classroom diversity.*

Effective differentiation happens throughout a lesson or unit any time you assess students' need in order to create the best learning experience possible. Why should you differentiate your planning? To be a successful social studies teacher, you must encourage each of your students to be all that they can be. Inspire them to take risks with the knowledge that they have your interest and support. Children thrive when they sense that you respect them for who they are and are willing to help them grow to their potential. Every child must know that he or she is appreciated; a good teacher embraces and nurtures differences. The students' experiences will last a lifetime—they help make our world. It is my sincere hope that as you take your place among those meeting the challenge of improving our nation's schools, diversity will remain as the keystone supporting a transformed teaching profession.

REFLECTION ON LEARNING

You may simply scribble rough notes or jot down something more polished and complete. The point is to simply start recording your ideas spontaneously and candidly.

There are various ways to differentiate learning. Ms. Walker settled on two differentiation strategies for each of the four curricular elements described above. Add one or two items to Ms. Walker's list to indicate what else could be done for each curricular element.

 Video Exploration 2.6

 CHECK YOUR UNDERSTANDING 2.4 **Click here** to check your understanding of this section of the chapter.

A Final Thought

Imagine for a moment that we "fast forward" to the end of your first year of teaching and I ask your students to describe you. What words do you think they will use? In all those years of being a student, you shaped mental and verbal pictures of your teachers. Some made a profound difference in your life; others not so much. What kind of image will your students form of you? What would you like that image to be? Let's say that your students described their journey through fifth grade as a delightful voyage because of you. They found significance in almost every lesson you worked so hard to plan; through your sterling efforts, they even established strong emotional connections to long dead presidents and barren, treeless terrains. Most assuredly, you provided students with boundless academic passion and success as well as solid emotional support. Like the best social studies teachers, you impressed others with the warmth you connected to the special times you shared with your students—the stories you talk about and laugh about over and over: "Henry came up to me holding his finger as if it were hurt. When I asked him what was the matter, he replied, 'An elephant bit my finger,' and then turned and walked away!"

You have clearly demonstrated a key element of first-rate social studies instruction—a characteristic I call "stick-with-it-ness." This is a persistent, intense commitment to what you are doing. Teachers with stick-with-it-ness are thrilled with their professional responsibilities. Teaching is not only their job—it is their passion. Teaching leaves successful teachers virtually starry eyed and eager to plan experiences that activate children's learning. All children must believe that their teachers are consumed by what they are doing. In social studies, this means that teachers view their world with fascination and inspire their children to accept theirs as a never-ending mystery. To do this, you must plan significant learning situations in which children experience a little mystery, a bit of magic, and a dash of magnificence. Elementary school children respond to these things; that is what makes their classrooms different from those of any other age group.

You achieve magic in your elementary school social studies program when you help each child become challenged by the activities and emotionally involved in the subject matter. You deliver the best for each youngster and make the most of their time every day. You adapt instruction to meet the special needs and interests of all your students. In short, you are fully sold on the idea that the first step to becoming a successful social studies teacher is to be a good planner.

References

Bloom, B. S., Engelhart, M. D., Furst, E. J., Hill, W. H., & Krathwohl, D. R. (1956). *Taxonomy of educational objectives: The classification of educational goals. Handbook I: Cognitive domain.* New York, NY: Longmans, Green.

Dewey, J. (1933). *How we think.* Boston, MA: D.C. Heath.

National Council for the Social Studies. (2010). *National curriculum standards for social studies: A framework for teaching, learning, and assessment* (Bulletin 111). Washington, DC: Author.

National Council for the Social Studies (2013). *The college, career, and civic life (C3) framework for social studies state standards: Guidance for enhancing the rigor of K–12 civics, economics, geography, and history.* Washington, DC: Authors.

National Governors Association Center for Best Practices & Council of Chief State School Officers. (2010). *Common core state standards for English language arts and literacy in history/social studies, science, and technical subjects.* Washington, DC: Authors.

Pennsylvania Department of Education. (2002). *Academic standards for science and technology* (Appendix B). Harrisburg, PA: Author.

Tomlinson, C. A. (2014). *The differentiated classroom: Responding to the needs of all learners* (2nd ed.). Alexandria, VA: Association for Supervision and Curriculum Development.

Wiggins, G., & McTighe, J. (2006). *Understanding by design.* Upper Saddle River, NJ: Pearson Education, by arrangement with the Association for Supervision and Curriculum Development.

SECTION TWO

Methods and Strategies to Reach and Teach Your Students

Social studies teachers have unlimited possibilities when it comes to selecting methods and strategies for teaching students about their world. Faced with choices ranging from conventional teacher-centered strategies to more active teaching models such as collaborative teamwork and project-based learning, finding a balance is what you should aim for. Be an innovator; combine the strengths of conventional methods with active teaching models to create a unique approach that engages and inspires all students of our uniquely new digital generation. Have the courage to resist the "normal" and make the learning experiences in your social studies classroom productive, exciting, and fun. The methods and strategies described in Chapters 3 and 4 are not meant to be exhaustive; they are intended only to offer a few basic tools that new or inexperienced teachers may find helpful while properly stocking their educational toolboxes at the start of their careers. You will find it productive and rewarding to continually acquire up-to-date and more effective tools as new needs are addressed and your overall skill level grows.

Arkady Chubykin/Fotolia

Social Constructivism:
Constructing Meaning via Collaborative Encounters

Learning Outcomes

The various forms of constructivism have different implications when it comes to instructional decisions. Social constructivism, heavily influenced by Vygotsky and sociocultural theory, proposes that learning takes place through the interaction between people and their environment. Therefore, in social constructivist classrooms, learning is considered a process of collaboration that is facilitated and modeled by the teacher. Learning is assisted by instructional strategies as diverse as direct, explicit concept instruction, effectively directed classroom discussions, and organized group work. So in today's social studies classrooms, you will be expected to master practices based on a commonly accepted belief that concepts evolve through social influences such as modeling, guided learning, and interacting with other people and the environment.

After completing this chapter, you will be able to:

- Define the term *social constructivism*.

- Explain the need for a meaningful and purposeful learning context.

- Describe how to engage students with a wide variety of instructional resources.

- Relate how to use language—especially discussing, questioning, and explaining—to promote learning.

- Detail the process of classifying and communicating ideas with graphic organizers.

- Explain how to break down concepts into explicit, focused group instruction.

- Show how to use modeling as a scaffolding technique.

- Describe how to encourage collaboration and cooperation among peers as More Knowledgeable Others (MKOs).

- Explain how to facilitate and guide learning with computers as MKOs.

Classroom Snapshot

Robert Szabo's fifth graders have been studying the oil industry and are about to learn how oil is pumped from the ground. Mr. Szabo begins today's lesson by helping children connect to previous lessons. The children talked about how oil is a source of nonrenewable energy that formed more than 300 million years ago, long before dinosaurs roamed Earth. They recalled that fossil fuels are made up of decomposed plant and animal matter that was buried under layers of silt and sand. The students then located on a map the major oil-producing regions of the United States—Texas, Alaska, California, and North Dakota.

"Yesterday, we discovered how oil was formed and where the major oil fields of the United States are located," Mr. Szabo said. "Today, we will find out how oil is drawn out from under the ground in those fields."

Instead of giving a definition of the kind of oil pump they were going to be learning about, Mr. Szabo asked the students to think about a seemingly unrelated question: "How would you describe a grasshopper to someone who had never seen one before?" Immediately, the students began to talk about the familiar insect they all knew as denizens of the lush fields in and about their rural community. Some talked about its thin, powerful back legs and how far grasshoppers are able to leap; others mentioned the antennae, the oddly shaped head, the long, thin body, and the wings. Most children volunteered something, whether they merely watched the grasshoppers jump and fly around in the barren fields or used them for something rather practical—fishing bait! Mr. Szabo displayed a large illustration of the insect and asked if the students would agree that this was the "bug" they were all speaking of. The students agreed that it was and went on to talk more about its unique characteristics. Next, Mr. Szabo asked a question that raised a few eyebrows: "Here's a question I'd like you to think about: How do you suppose grasshoppers are used in the oil industry?" The students glanced silently at one another and in due course giggled in disbelief. "Are you serious, Mr. Szabo?" they asked. "Of course I'm serious," countered Mr. Szabo. "I know it's hard to believe, but grasshoppers actually are used in the oil industry. Turn to a partner and talk about how you think that could be."

After a few minutes, Mr. Szabo invited the students to list their hunches: "The oil workers put them in small cages and walk around a field that might have oil in it. The grasshoppers have a special sense that causes them to jump around real fast if oil is underground."

"The brown 'tobacco' that they spit on your hand when you hold them can be collected and used to lubricate the machinery until the well begins to produce oil."

"You'll find that more grasshoppers live in fields where there is oil underground."

"Grasshoppers don't live where oil is underground."

After writing each idea on the whiteboard, Mr. Szabo made a direct connection to the forthcoming learning experience: "Your ideas are very interesting. Please search through the resources I have arranged for you to determine which, if any, of your thoughts explain how grasshoppers are actually used in the oil industry." The students quickly gathered at the center, using various books as well as websites to search for data to test their claims. Shortly, they returned to the discussion area and bellowed incredulously: "You tricked us, Mr. Szabo! The oil industry doesn't use the grasshopper insects, they use grasshopper pumps!" The students discovered that oil industry "grasshoppers" were large low-pressure pumps having a component that resembles the head of the actual insect. Mr. Szabo displayed a large illustration of a grasshopper pump, as well as a model pump, next to the insect illustration and invited the students to discuss the similarities and differences. Although the oil "grasshoppers" weren't of the insect variety, signs of learning were obvious as the students continued to talk about the oil industry grasshoppers during a spirited and informative discussion.

To complete the day's activity, Mr. Szabo divided the students into work groups and told them that since they now have learned a great deal about the oil industry and oil pumps, they have a mission to share their knowledge with others. One way of doing this was to make a set of posters and put them in places where they could be seen. Each poster was to feature a catchy title, a brief reminder of how the grasshopper pump works, and an instructive illustration. One group, for example, labeled its poster "We Want to Pump You Up!" and wrote the following description below an illustration: "Pumping oil out of the ground is like drinking with a straw. At first, there is usually enough pressure to bring the oil to the surface. In time, the pressure weakens, and a grasshopper is needed to bring the oil to the surface."

Mr. Szabo had struggled for years when it came to teaching about the oil industry. It was apparent that his students were bored with the textbook coverage, and any attempts to enrich the text with supplementary materials only prolonged complaints that the material was just too hard to understand. "I think part of the problem was that social studies class was deeply teacher-centered and my responsibility was basically that of a transmitter of knowledge," reflected Mr. Szabo. "My students didn't exactly cherish their role as information sponges whose main job was to soak up as many facts as they could. It was surprising to see how much they could squeeze out for tests, however, but fact-based tests don't come close to measuring a student's true understanding. The unfortunate part was that whenever I asked them to apply what they had learned in real-life settings, they showed they really didn't understand much. It seemed that information unconnected to their immediate lives was either rejected or quickly forgotten."

Desperate to breathe new life into his spiritless social studies classroom, Mr. Szabo searched for a model that focused on thinking and understanding rather than memorization of facts. "I found what I was looking for in constructivism," explained Mr. Szabo. "It's based on the idea that knowledge is *constructed* by students through an active process that builds new understandings on a framework of established knowledge. The days of considering students as information sponges are over in my classroom! From now on, my students will have the freedom to think, to question, and to interact with ideas, objects, and their peers. There are many ways to carry out this constructivist process; one of my favorites is to begin a lesson by tossing out provocative statements to tap into the students' preexisting knowledge, as in the grasshopper example. I find that an intriguing initial prompt that challenges what they already know sets off a spark in my students that whets their appetite for more to come. Once I hook them like this, they can't help but become active participants in the learning process . . . curiosity is a natural part of every elementary schooler's life."

Of course, there are ways other than Mr. Szabo's to tap into a student's current understandings of the world, but the whole idea of constructivism is based on the notion that when students encounter something new, we have capitalize on their natural inner drive to bring it into harmony with what they already know. What do constructivist practices look like? How does constructivism influence your responsibility as a facilitator of learning? The rest of this chapter is designed to help you understand what constructivism is and what it means for your social studies classroom.

Reflection on Learning

You may simply scribble rough notes or jot down something more polished and complete. The point is to simply start recording your ideas spontaneously and candidly.

Describe how you would respond to a fellow teacher who made the following comment at a faculty meeting: "I can't buy all this criticism of standards testing. Teaching to a test is important. I love taking tests. Tests are a breeze for me because I absorb knowledge like a sponge and can recall it at any time. Students must be taught to memorize facts if they ever expect to be successful in life!"

Constructivism as a Way of Thinking and Learning

When we talk about constructivism, we refer not only to *what* the children know but also to *how* they acquire and organize what they know—the process by which they think and reason. We have learned a great deal about how this happens from the work of Jean Piaget (1972), who informs us that the understandings children construct as they mature from infancy through the elementary school years are generally governed by intuition rather than logical thought. That is, if you ask young children how airplanes fly, they will invariably compare airplanes to other flying things they know about and explain that airplanes flap their wings like a bird. It is highly unlikely that anyone told them that airplane wings work that way, but their limited life experiences often lead to conclusions that defy logic. That is why a young child's explanations of the world are characterized as *naïve theories*, or *primitive concepts* that, through a combination of maturity and experience, will gradually evolve into more fully developed interpretations of the world.

Despite the fact that naïve theories frequently bypass logic, they actually have an important role to play in the process of constructivist learning. To explain, children's perceptions of the world are taken in, sorted, and stored in their brains as what Piaget referred to as *schemata* (plural of *schema*), which we more commonly call *concepts*. Concepts can be thought of as the basic building blocks of intelligence—mental "file boxes" in the brain, each ready to sort and accept new information. Any new experience either fits into or conflicts with these existing concepts. For example, let us assume a young child has developed a basic concept of *cow*. She knows that a *cow* is large, eats grass, and has brown eyes, four legs, and a tail. When this same little girl encounters a *horse* for the first time, however, she will most likely point to it and excitedly blurt out, "Cow!" After all, the animal fits her existing concept of *cow*—it is large, eats grass, and has brown eyes, four legs, and a tail. As new experiences become part of her life, however, new information will change or modify these concepts and, in all likelihood, form new concepts (such as *horse*). Cognitive development, then, is considered a progressive reorganization of mental structures that results from environmental experiences that challenge what children already know. We cannot get through a day without hearing some reference to concepts, or one of its synonyms:

"He has no idea what a deltiologist does."

"The candidate offered a new view of city government."

The explorer's understanding of dengue was vague until she visited a tropical rain forest in Africa."

Can you pick out the major concepts in the sentences above? Among the most significant are *deltiologist, candidate, city government, dengue, explorer,* and *tropical rain forest.* You may have a very clear picture in your mind of a few—*candidate* and *explorer*, for example. Through the years, you acquired a comprehensible picture (concept) of them by filing away an accumulation of pertinent information into steadily expanding mental "file boxes." However, you may have found out that a couple of other concepts above, such as *deltiologist* and *dengue* were either vague or nonexistent; a quick search of your mind to access those "file boxes" probably turned up empty. Now suppose you were responsible for knowing the meaning of *deltiologist* and *dengue* for an upcoming test. What choice would you have other than memorizing their meanings? Let us say that you successfully did that and passed the test, but would you have developed deep understandings of those terms? As a teacher, will you be satisfied if your students can name three explorers but are not able to explain what an explorer is? Without the ability to categorize information into meaningful concepts, our students' minds would be cluttered with a confusing mixture of unrelated gibberish—nothing would seem to make sense and they will stand in line complaining that, "Social studies is boring!" This is not meant to convince you that facts are unimportant. On the contrary, facts are indeed important. They help learners distinguish countries from continents, Anasazi from Iroquois, and law from anarchy. Facts are the building blocks of concepts.

How does the constructivist approach use facts to help build concepts? To explain, read the following paragraph describing a day in 1621 when Samoset first walked into a Pilgrim settlement at Plymouth:

The Pilgrims arrived in Plymouth, Massachusetts in 1620, after fleeing religious persecution in England. Many died due to the insufferable first winter and the survivors were too weak to defend themselves against any suspected attack by Indians.

Astonishingly, any plans to defend their compound were brought to a brief delay on March 16, 1621 when an unpretentious Indian walked directly into Plymouth, saluted the Pilgrims, and uttered the words, "Welcome! Welcome, Englishmen!" His name was Samoset and the friendly Indian was able to speak English!

The Pilgrims gave Samoset some food and water, a coat for his nearly naked body, and invited him to stay the night. During the afternoon and evening, Samoset shared much useful information about the land and its people with the Pilgrims.

The next day, Samoset returned and brought along a special companion, Squanto, who also was able to speak English.

To attach meaning to this paragraph, you must already know something about the adventure of the Pilgrims when they came to America on the Mayflower in 1620. However, if you had little or no knowledge of the event, the paragraph would be little more than "mumbo jumbo" and you would either lose interest in it or reject it. Let us say, though, that you knew enough about the Pilgrims during the early 1620s that the content of the paragraph was easily incorporated into your conceptual framework. You quickly applied what you already knew about this event and experienced no problems making sense of it. In that case, your mind felt at ease and you are now ready to move on to bigger and better academic challenges! However, if your existing conceptual framework was not helping you comprehend the material, resulting uncertainty may have prompted you to say, "I've just got to find out how Samoset and Squanto learned to speak English before the first Pilgrims came to Plymouth!" Cognitive growth, then, is seen as a constant process of modifying existing concepts or creating new concepts to account for new information.

When I presented the Plymouth challenge to a group of fourth graders, they immediately blurted out: "How did the Indians learn to speak English if this was the first time they ever saw the Pilgrims?" The students were genuinely perplexed! We had a great time hypothesizing about how things happened and reshuffling and adding to their existing conceptual framework with new and meaningful information. Did *you* know that Samoset and Squanto spoke English before they met the Pilgrims at Plymouth? How *did* they learn to speak English if this was their first contact with outsiders? Are you the least bit interested in finding out? If so, you are experiencing a constructivist moment—legitimately motivated to uncover real meaning about your world rather than simply receiving and storing unattached facts and details. (FYI: Samoset had learned English from several contacts with English fishermen and traders who visited the region prior to the Pilgrims' arrival. Squanto had been kidnapped and taken to England where he learned to speak English quite well, and returned to America before the Pilgrims arrived.) Congratulations! You have now experienced the "aha" moment when cognitive balance has been restored and you are primed to conquer a whole new world of understandings.

Many social studies concepts, such as *hogan, coin, flag, sarape, fjord, wok,* and *safari* are called *concrete concepts* because they refer to objects or events that are accessible to our senses. Others, such as *democracy, peace, freedom, justice, equal opportunity, liberty,* and *war* are not accessible to our senses; these are called *abstract concepts*. Concrete concepts are generally easier to understand than abstract concepts because they are rooted in the "here and now"; that is why you will find concrete concepts like *family* or *home* or *firefighter* taught at the first-grade level while *democracy* or *freedom* are held off until the upper elementary school grades or even middle school. Not only are abstract concepts harder for students to grasp, but they are also harder for teachers to teach. Whether the concept is concrete or abstract, however, if children actively seek out information and connect it to their current conception of the world, they will learn. If not, they will struggle.

Principles of Social Constructivism

Constructivism can point toward a wide array of teaching practices. If you think of all the possibilities as points on a constructivist teaching continuum, you will discover countless intermediate points, each emerging from distinct interpretations: at one end, we find *cognitive constructivism,* an interpretation based primarily on Jean Piaget's conception of learning, and at the

Each student's individual background and experiences will influence the meaning-making process in your social studies classroom.

other end, *social constructivism,* an option based on Lev Vygotsky's work (see Figure 3.1). Both share the conviction that students construct relevant and meaningful concepts on a framework of existing knowledge. This approach is consistent with the National Curriculum Standards for Social Studies (NCSS, 2010): "Learners build knowledge as they work to integrate new information into existing cognitive constructs, and engage in processes that develop their abilities to think, reason, conduct research, and attain understanding as they encounter new concepts, principles, and issues" (p. 10).

Cognitive constructivism and social constructivism are two similar approaches to learning that share a number of underlying assumptions, but a major departure is the social constructivist view of the collaborative nature of learning and the importance of cultural and social contexts. That is, social constructivism emphasizes that learning is a social process influenced either by adult guidance or by the collaboration of peers while the cognitive constructivist perspective emphasizes that learners must be provided with a variety of independent problem-solving opportunities, through which they discover new ideas and construct their own knowledge (that is, primarily individual, internal forces). The view of constructivist teaching in this book is that teachers must be able to mix social and cognitive constructivism, combining active learning strategies as disparate as "socially-mediated instruction" with "self-directed inquiry and problem solving," as well as various other viable options that fall between these contrasting points. In support of this viewpoint, Bybee (2002) pointed out, "Teachers will blend [socially-mediated] instruction and inquiry-learning activities to foster the construction

FIGURE 3.1 Continuum of Constructivist Practices

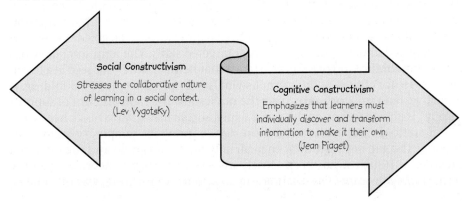

of knowledge. Both are effective strategies for teaching. . . . However, when used exclusively, each strategy ignores individual differences and leaves instructional gaps" (pp. 58–59). Because the educational outcomes for social studies are both deep and wide-ranging, good social studies instruction requires such diverse approaches. That view coincides with Joyce, Weil, and Calhoun (2009), who say, "There is no *one* overriding model at this time in our knowledge about teaching. But we have a *storehouse of models. We are rich!*" (p. xv). What is the advantage of using several instructional approaches in your teaching? Joyce et al. (2009) go on to explain: "If you develop a repertoire of effective approaches to teaching, you can confidently try them with your students to help them achieve a variety of goals; moreover, you can help students with different learning styles to find ways of learning. The larger our repertoire, the less we and our students are trapped in a few ways of learning" (p. xiv).

Leila Christenbury (2010/2011) is a strong advocate of this viewpoint on variable instruction. She claims that although there is no simple list of do's and don'ts, no precise recipe to ensure effective teaching, we can recognize effective teaching by a number of characteristics, each of which involves a degree of flexibility:

- *Effective teaching is variable.* Effective teachers use a variety of strategies and a range of methods. Good teaching comes not from following a formula but from putting students' needs first.

- *Effective teaching is contextual.* Effective teachers alter, adjust, and change their instruction based on the individual interests and needs of their students and the degree to which their students are achieving targeted standards.

- *Effective teaching is premised on students' intellectual curiosity.* Effective teachers begin with the belief that students are eager learners and can be appropriately "hooked" into classroom learning.

- *Effective teaching must be somewhat autonomous.* Effective teachers should not be overly controlled and managed, but must be empowered to use their judgment to make instructional decisions.

- *Ultimately, effective teaching is fearless.* Effective teachers place student needs above the strictly interpreted demands of the school district curriculum guide or the year-end test. To do this, they must have a great deal of courage and determination.

The principles of social constructivism will be the focus of this chapter.

Social Constructivist Instructional Practices

An important principle that underlies all aspects of *social constructivist instruction* is Vygotsky's (1978) idea of a zone of proximal development, commonly referred to as ZPD. Although it has been several decades since Vygotsky initially introduced his concept of the ZPD, it has become a classic idea in education—widely cited and having a time-tested, significant overall impact on the field. Vygotsky defined the ZPD as the distance between what a child can do with assistance and what he or she can accomplish without assistance. Similar in many ways to Piaget's twin processes of assimilation and accommodation, the ZPD can be thought of as a "construction zone" where just the right amount of assisted support from a more knowledgeable other (MKO) helps students build targeted understandings or master targeted skills. The term *scaffolding* has become the accepted term for the kind of MKO assistance that helps children succeed at a learning task. A flotation device for children who cannot swim is a simple example of scaffolding. It is facilitative, supportive, but transitory, providing the novice just the right amount of support until the "little guppy" is able to toss aside the water wings and swim away on his or her own.

An educational scaffold, much like a flotation device, provides temporary support as students work to bridge the gap between what they already know or can do and the intended instructional outcome. Although it has been closely associated with his theories, Vygotsky never used the term *scaffold* or *scaffolding*. Scaffolding, as applied to learning, was introduced by Wood, Bruner, and Ross (1976), who defined it as a process " . . . that enables a . . . novice to solve a task or achieve a goal that would be beyond his unassisted efforts" (p. 90). The authors went on to explain that scaffolds required an MKO to control " . . . those elements of the task that are initially beyond the learner's capability, thus permitting him to concentrate upon and complete only those elements that are within his range of competence" (p. 90). As students demonstrate increasing awareness of a learning task, the MKO gradually relinquishes the supportive role and eventually turns over full responsibility to the student.

In social studies classrooms the MKO is someone who has a better understanding or a higher ability level than the learner. Obviously, the kinds of MKOs found in most elementary school classrooms are adults—teachers and support staff. But they also include resources you may not at first expect; many times a child's peers assume the role. Actually, the MKO need not be a person. Computer tutors are gaining widespread use in educational settings as MKOs that facilitate and guide students through the learning process. For example, new online tools such as Google Docs and wikis allow for synchronous authoring of documents, a process that provides scaffolding, reciprocal teaching, and facilitated instruction. Anything or anyone can be the MKO; all that is needed to be the MKO is to have more knowledge or be more skilled than the learner. Because the essence of social constructivism is that cognitive processes develop through social interaction with MKOs, this chapter focuses on the three major types of MKOs typically associated with social studies instruction: *teachers*, *peers*, and *computers*.

We will consider how to apply socially mediated strategies for a different purpose—to help build increasingly complex and abstract concepts on a framework of prior knowledge. In the social studies classroom, scaffolding can be applied to almost any learning task, but regardless of when and how it is used, a teacher MKO's major responsibility is providing solid support until the students can move through the learning tasks independently. That scaffolding support encompasses eight major professional tasks:

1. providing a meaningful and purposeful learning context;
2. engaging students with a wide variety of instructional resources;
3. using language to promote learning—especially discussing, questioning, and explaining;
4. organizing and communicating ideas with graphic organizers;
5. breaking down concepts into explicit, focused group instruction;
6. using modeling as a scaffolding technique;
7. collaborating and cooperating with peers as MKOs; and
8. facilitating and guiding learning with computers as MKOs.

 CHECK YOUR UNDERSTANDING 3.1 **Click here** to check your understanding of this section of the chapter.

Task 1: A Meaningful and Purposeful Learning Context

Because learning takes place within individual ZPDs, a student's current level of understanding and interest must be assessed and addressed before students can be expected to develop new understandings and interests. So your first major task before any learning experience is to take 5 to 10 minutes to inspire, challenge, and stimulate your students. Getting students ready and motivated involves three major responsibilities: (1) *developing curiosity and interest*, (2) *accessing prior knowledge*, and (3) *establishing a clear purpose for learning*. Successful engagement culminates in students being puzzled by, focused on, and actively motivated to pursue the forthcoming learning activities.

Developing Curiosity and Interest

Constructivists refer to "interest" as the energy required to drive the learning process. To make constructivism work in social studies classrooms, you must be able to create and present *intriguing situations* (challenging tasks, questions, or problems) that inspire students to want to figure something out. The interest may come entirely from the children as they investigate an intriguing situation for its own sake, or the children might be challenged by a contrived interest and accept it as their own. Whatever the source, if children find a learning situation meaningful and worthwhile, and become energized to apply significant effort to unlock its mysteries, we say they are *motivated* to learn. You can think of motivation as a strong internal desire that rouses us to action or keeps us absorbed in certain activities until we accomplish our goals. For example, in recent years I have learned to play fantasy sports on the Internet. I am not addicted to the game as I understand many are, but I love drafting teams, trading players, and fighting for league championships (yes, I've won a few). I take part in fantasy sports not because someone has told me I must, but because I enjoy it. Certainly, the prizes that come with league championships are a special reward for doing well, but I enjoy the competition whether or not it results in a championship or a prize. To me, the activity is pleasurable and worthwhile in and of itself. What activities do you engage in on a regular basis simply because you enjoy doing them? Intrinsic motivation is what leads you to action and keeps you engaged in those activities.

There are some activities I engage in that are not so enjoyable, but I do them anyway because they bring me things I do enjoy. Mowing my lawn is an example. It's not something I just can't wait to do during my free time; I don't particularly like doing it. However, my neighbors and my community expect a clean, well-groomed yard. The motivation to mow the lawn is the same as shoveling the snow from my driveway and sidewalk. The drive to do these tasks is called extrinsic motivation because the desire to complete these chores does not come from within; the activities themselves are not enjoyable, but the rewards are—a clean yard and a clear driveway and sidewalk. Likewise, a child who searches a number of trade books to find out how it might have felt to leave home at the age of 12 to work as an apprentice in Colonial America because he or she is genuinely interested in finding out is intrinsically motivated, while the child who researches the topic just to get a good grade or a teacher's praise is extrinsically motivated. The interest, enjoyment, and satisfaction is in the work itself when one is intrinsically motivated; when one is extrinsically motivated, the driving force is outside pressure or reward. The tricky part about motivation, however, is that no activity in itself is intrinsically motivating for everyone. Fantasy sports are fun for me, but I'm sure there are some of you who would rather watch paint dry than play fantasy sports on the Internet. The same is true for any activity; it can be motivating only to a particular person at a particular time.

What are some of the factors that motivate learning? First, the social climate of the classroom is significant. If students can think of the classroom as a caring, supportive place where learning is considered to be important, they will tend to become more fully involved in the learning process. Eager learners are nurtured by wholesome encouragement and support. Second, the demands of a learning situation also influence a student's motivation to learn. For intriguing situations to work properly, teachers must be clearly aware of what their students already know and what they are able to do. If students are confronted with something far removed from their current ZPDs, for example, they will become frustrated and bewildered. Obviously, they will be unable to successfully participate in the learning task. Conversely, if the intriguing situation lies comfortably within their ZPDs, they will be unchallenged and uninspired to explore the situation any further. The key to effective instruction is to gear the intriguing situation slightly in advance of the children's existing level of cognitive development—challenging but achievable. It is within this region that children are inspired to learn and teachers are confident that children are experiencing challenges that are neither too easy nor too difficult. Third, the significance of a learning task also promotes motivation. Students must understand how any particular learning can be applied in the real world. They are more motivated by something they know has meaning in their own lives than by something with no perceived value. Fourth, the learning task must be pleasurable. Youngsters tend to become more engaged in the experience when they are upbeat about and thrilled with the subject matter content or learning task. And, just as important, be sure to model the idea that you have curiosities and varied interests in social studies content, too. When children see their role models are curious, eager learners, they will be more likely to follow suit.

Accessing Prior Knowledge

As with a space mission, the launch phase is one of the most critical phases of an educational mission. The launch phase of a spacecraft provides the propulsive energy to successfully set in motion a spacecraft from the launch pad up to the time when the payload (activity) is safely positioned. Likewise, the most crucial part of a lesson occurs during the first 5 minutes—the launch phase—when you will need to supply the energy to set a lesson in motion. The launch phase of a social constructivist learning experience establishes a connection between what the students already know or can do and the new content or skill to be learned. This principle has been considered such an important piece of advice over the years that a statement made by Ausubel in 1961 continues to hold a place as one of the most often quoted and most highly regarded statements associated with constructivist teaching methods: "If I had to reduce educational psychology to just one principle," wrote Ausubel, "I would say this: The most important single factor influencing learning is what the learner already knows" (1961, p. 16). Ausubel used the term *advance organizer* to label the techniques used to help students retrieve past knowledge; you may have heard different terms used in other methods classes.

Regardless of the term, think of this initial phase of instruction as providing a prompt, task, or activity that connects the new content to what the child already knows. This can be done in a variety of ways, but three of the most conventional are *open-ended questions and prompts*, *stimulating materials*, and *graphic organizers*.

OPEN-ENDED QUESTIONS AND PROMPTS

Perhaps the most common strategy for helping students access their prior knowledge is to offer introductory *open-ended questions and prompts* related to the content to be learned, followed by a general conversation that helps connect the students' existing knowledge to the new material. Open-ended questions and prompts typically include *questions* that begin with words such as "Why" and "Do you agree with" or *prompts* that begin with words such as "Tell me about." (Prompts are not technically questions but statements that suggest responses.) To start the conversation rolling, ask students to brainstorm anything that comes to their minds related to the learning experience by using an open-ended question or prompt like this: "What comes to your mind when you (see this picture, read this title, observe this object, hear this word, etc.)?" This process is designed to encourage full, meaningful responses related to the students' background knowledge and experiences.

In Chapter 7, you will read that there are three main ways to connect prior knowledge to any new social studies learning encounter: *experience-to-self* ("*What does this remind you of?*"), *experience-to-experience* ("*How is this experience like or different from other experiences you have had?*"), and *experience-to-world* ("*What does this remind you of in the real world?*"). Constructivists believe that as students learn to make these connections on their own, they become fully engaged in the learning process and increasingly skilled at extracting deeper meaning.

STIMULATING MATERIALS

Discussions and conversations enable students to connect new social studies content to established ideas, but students would ultimately tune out if that were the only approach you ever used. A young learner, like anyone else, needs to be drawn into experiences through variety. Therefore, you could periodically select hands-on experiences to create interest and help make connections. Referred to as *realia,* these are real items found in everyday life and used as aids to introduce almost any social studies topic. When teaching about ancient Egypt, for example, bring the culture directly into your classroom by collecting a basket full of replicas—a model pyramid, a sheet of papyrus, hieroglyphics, a miniature cartouche, an amulet, a jar, coins. Encourage your students to explore them and tell what the items bring to mind. You will want to model exploratory talk with prompts such as, "I wonder what this is," or "The _____ really caught my eye. It's amazing!" Be sure to leave plenty of gaps for the students to join in the commentary. I can assure you that students will be both surprised and thrilled, and they will be eager to sink their teeth into the topic. In social studies, realia is a must.

GRAPHIC DISPLAYS AND ORGANIZERS

In addition to arousing interest in new content through carefully planned discussions and stimulating materials, teachers often find it helpful to use graphic organizers such as diagrams, charts, drawings, and other visual displays. Graphic displays of information help students consciously connect their past experiences to the targeted skills or concepts under study. Given to students before they begin the learning activity, graphic organizers function as a mental framework that provides a springboard for discussions that will later give rise to additional knowledge on the topic.

There are many kinds of graphic organizers, but concept webs are a quick and easy-to-use option. Simply write the main idea or topic of the learning experience in the center. Your students then fill in the radiating categories with information that they know (or think they know) about the topic (Figure 3.2). After the learning activity, ask your students to react to the chart and to add new information or determine if they have changed their minds about any of the information that was listed earlier. Lines or arrows can be added to show relationships among the data.

Establishing a Purpose for Learning

During a visit to one of my field students one day, I was feeling a bit adventurous so I asked a third grader why she was reading a particular selection. I was not terribly surprised when she responded, "Because my teacher said I have to." Curious, I persisted: "Is that the only reason?" Looking a bit uneasy because of my questions, the little girl added, "I don't want to get a bad grade." Although her comments should not be considered improper, students should become more involved in their learning if they have a clearer, more genuine purpose for learning. A genuine purpose sets learning in motion. It informs your students why a selected learning activity is about to be shared with them. Challenging your students to watch a video to, "Learn why banana farmers cut the stalks while the fruit is still green," will be a much more meaningful and productive "launching pad" than instructing your students that "Our assignment today is to read about how bananas are grown in India on pages 78–79." Establishing a purpose for learning basically involves clearly communicating a learning activity's objective (or standard) to your students, informing them of the expected learning outcome. A clearly stated and understood purpose lays the foundation for meaningful concept construction.

FIGURE 3.2   Prior Knowledge Map

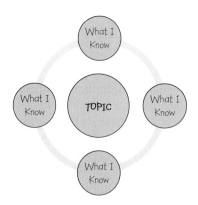

One of the hardest things for new teachers to understand about Task 1 is how much time to spend on it. I once observed a preservice teacher spend 20 minutes on an introduction to an activity, using up so much time that he had only 10 minutes left for the main instructional task! Think about introducing students to a learning activity much as you would introduce two friends. You might say, "Hannah, I'd like you to meet Clay. He loves bike riding as much as you do." Such a brief, clear statement establishes a common bond between the two and provides a conversation starter that entices them to explore their interests more fully. A lesson introduction, too, is meant to be a brief and lively discussion lasting no more than 4 to 7 minutes, depending on the situation. You do not want to cut students off when they are offering ideas, but you want to be careful not to repeat things over and over again. However, an extremely brief introduction such as, "Hannah, I'd like you to meet Clay," leaves both feeling awkward and wondering where to go from there. At the other extreme, if your introduction goes on forever, it will seem too pushy and impolite, prompting both parties to think: "Hurry up and get this over with!" If your introduction sparks mutual interests, your friends may choose to explore common interests more deeply and learn more about each other. The same is true for a lesson introduction; knowing how to introduce a lesson is an important instructional skill that you cannot overlook. Notice how the following suggestions function as a short springboard to launch the students into a main instructional task:

1. *Identify the major concept that will serve as the focus of the lesson.* For example, *glaciers*.

2. *Select a stimulus word, picture, or object to focus the children's attention on the topic and elicit their background knowledge.* For example, show the front cover of a book you will be reading to the class, such as *The Glaciers Are Melting!* by Donna Love and Shennen Bersani (Sylvan Dell Publishing). The illustration on the cover of this book shows a pika in distress, sitting on a huge sheet of ice and snow. (Pikas are little mammals that live in rock piles high in the mountains of western North America and Asia. They are related to rabbits and are about the size of large hamsters.)

3. *Prepare a stimulus question or prompt.* "What comes to your mind as you look at this picture?" "What do you think of when . . . ?" "What do you know about . . . ?"

4. *Record the children's responses to the stimulus question or prompt on a chalkboard or a graphic organizer.*

5. *As the children respond, ask them to justify their remarks.* "What made you think of . . . ?"

6. *Establish a purpose.* Guide students into the learning activity with a statement of purpose: "Today, our story contains information about a huge and serious problem we're all facing on Earth. Listen as I read to see how humans are playing an increasing role in the melting of glaciers."

Students like to know why they are learning something and that it has real-life meaning.

Aletia2011/Fotolia

Reflection on Learning

You may simply scribble rough notes or jot down something more polished and complete. The point is to simply start recording your ideas spontaneously and candidly.

Many factors determine whether your students will or will not be motivated to learn, and no single explanation of motivation explains every aspect of student interest or lack of it. What factors do you feel would spur some to say, "Yes, I will!" or "Sorry, try again!"

 CHECK YOUR UNDERSTANDING 3.2 **Click here** to check your understanding of this section of the chapter.

Task 2: Engaging Students with Quality Instructional Resources

Some people will tell you that traveling to a foreign country is the best way to learn about it . . . walking its streets, observing its people, eating its foods, visiting its sights, and so on. Those who cannot travel to another country may deepen their knowledge by searching the Internet or reading the country's newspapers and magazines. Movies may enable others to understand a country's standard habits, behaviors, and moral values. There are also those who learn much about a country by watching a movie or listening to someone tell them about it. We deepen our understanding of a country (or any concept) through multiple resources. The same is true for elementary school students; it is impossible to overemphasize the importance of providing multiple instructional resources that are clearly aligned with curriculum goals and standards as well as with the needs and strengths of your students. An important aspect of Vygotsky's ZPD is the idea that teaching must take place with authentic activities and quality instructional materials that mimic real life. That is, a student should not be taught to read a map as an abstract skill, but through purposeful tasks such as using a digital map to locate a friend or relative.

Many schools continue to consider textbooks as the single most important instructional tool, but today's classrooms demand that we make available a more comprehensive set of instructional materials, including technology resources, supplementary reading materials, hands-on materials, charts, community resource people, agencies and organizations, games, globes, kits, maps, models, periodicals, pictures, realia, sound recordings, and videos. Because students learn primarily through interactive activities involving their teacher and multiple resources, the selection of instructional resources supplies limitless power for student learning. Here is a basic summary of critical criteria for selection of instructional resources:

- Learning resources should be consistent with the general and subject-specific goals and standards.
- Learning resources should reflect the varied interests, abilities, learning styles, and needs of your students.
- Learning resources should be representative of our nation's varied religious, ethnic, minority, and cultural groups, as well as their contributions to our pluralistic society and the world community.
- Learning resources should meet high standards of quality in the presentation of key social studies concepts, especially those targeted by specific content standards.
- Learning resources should offer opportunities for students to think critically about the information and perceive its relevance to the real world.

- Learning resources should include abundant technology-based elements that support purposeful learning.
- Learning resources should provide students with alternative representations of concepts, multiple means of becoming involved with the concepts, and a variety of ways for students to demonstrate and communicate what they have learned.

 CHECK YOUR UNDERSTANDING 3.3 **Click here** to check your understanding of this section of the chapter.

Task 3: Using Language Processes to Scaffold Learning

When carried out properly, Task 1 will provoke a desire and establish direction for investigating and learning; Task 2 will furnish the multiple instructional resources necessary to engage students in the subject matter. Now, with Task 3, you will be asked to apply your pedagogical knowledge to take on the role of coach and guide as your students interact with the various instructional resources—to target the specific goals of instruction and offer just the right kinds of scaffolded assistance that help your students "get it."

According to social constructivists, the act of "getting it" cannot happen simply by handing students an assortment of instructional resources and directing them to get to work. Teachers do not simply stand around and watch students explore and discover, but they collaborate with and guide them as they approach problems and think about issues and questions. Opportunities for discussion as well as interactions with teacher and peers will play a vital role in building deep understandings. Your social studies classroom now becomes a community of learners working together to construct meaning, and this cannot be accomplished unless there is ample opportunity for conversation. A teacher and other MKOs model behaviors and/or convey understandings to children through collaborative dialogues that communicate the meanings their culture attaches to objects, events, and experiences.

General Instructional Conversations

Instructional conversations are occasions during which students participate in thoughtful discussions with their teacher and their peers. Instructional conversations are considered *instructional* because they assist learning; they are *conversations* because they are informal and interactive. The course of dialogue flows naturally from teacher to students, from students to teacher, and among students—the way true conversations take place. Instructional conversations are important because, to social constructivists, language is the primary conduit for scaffolding. Language is used to introduce and fortify understandings, clarify problems, explore and clarify difficulties, assess progress, and interpret various learning resources such as realia, pictures, videos, and charts and graphs.

Instructional conversations occur in a classroom environment where students can talk freely, presenting their ideas and opinions in whole-class or small-group situations. You may set off instructional conversations with well-planned questions and prompts that provoke students to think and reason about the content. Then, as the students respond, you listen and react to their ideas in a supportive, considerate manner. Sometimes you will invite students to expand ideas through prompts such as, "Tell me more about this," or "What do you mean by . . . ?" At other times, you will challenge them to support their arguments with sound evidence: "How do you know that?" "What makes you think that?" In order for instructional conversations to be productive, you must dismiss from your mind any notion of traditional classroom dialogue where teachers use questions as tools of "interrogation" rather than as prompts to help students search for meaning. "Interrogations" can best be described as peppering students with closed-ended questions that require them to simply retrieve unconnected bits of information from memory. For example, a question such as, "In what year did a German submarine sink the Lusitania?" is considered closed-ended because there is only one possible answer. And once a student responds, all further dialogue stops—the discussion is closed. One closed-ended question after another flows monotonously in a steady stream until all the facts are recited: "Where did the ship begin its voyage?" "Where was it sailing to?" "In addition to passengers, what was the ship carrying?" "What nation fired the torpedo that sunk the Lusitania?" Through this type of factual exchange, students learn very early in their schooling that their role in classroom discussions is to send back the facts that the teacher wants to hear rather than talk about what is truly important to them.

A TEACHER'S QUESTIONS AND PROMPTS

Instructional conversations are an alternative to classroom interrogations. The teacher is more of a facilitator who helps students think deeply about the content. Although teachers may use fact-centered, closed-ended questions during instructional conversations, the purpose of these questions is to ensure that students have adequate knowledge about a topic to discuss it wisely. Conversely, open-ended questions lead to more complex thinking: "Do you agree or disagree with the German people who claimed that the British deliberately tried to get the Lusitania sunk so the Americans would join the war on their side?" They challenge students to go beyond the content by engaging higher-order thought processes such as critical and analytical thinking. Students are usually more involved in class discussions when open-ended questions are asked because those kinds of questions are much more thought provoking.

Asking good questions, as important as the process is, represents only one critical concern in leading constructivist-oriented instructional conversations. Teacher MKOs must also be skilled at sequencing or patterning the questions so that students can be systematically guided toward intended learning outcomes. Questions should never be randomly selected; it is important that they have a focus because discussions happen for different reasons. Perhaps you want your students to organize and elaborate on what they've learned. Maybe you would like them to critique a controversial issue. Whatever the reason for designing a questioning plan, the purpose must be kept foremost in mind so that you can maintain focus throughout the instructional conversation. So as you begin to think about the kinds of questions to ask during this phase of a learning episode, ask yourself these questions: "What do I want my students to gain from this discussion?" "How will the questions contribute to the overall purpose of the lesson?" Your answers will help you design worthwhile questions and help guide your students to deeper understanding of the targeted concept or skill.

To illustrate, let's examine the questioning patterns of two teachers, both of whom shared the same instructional purpose: to help students understand how the migration of White settlers changed the lives of the Plains Indians. Paul Hansen decided to launch his instructional conversation by asking an open-ended question intended to draw out personal feelings: "The Plains Indians had deep respect for nature and the land. Do you think the settlers shared this point of view?" The students eagerly offered several different viewpoints, and Mr. Hansen challenged them to support each of their beliefs with appropriate details: "What evidence do you have to support your position?" So even though Mr. Hansen began the instructional conversation with an open-ended question, students were required to use relevant information to back up their arguments.

Grace Moore, by contrast, preferred to set her instructional conversation in motion with a question that called for her students to summarize the content: "In what ways did the settlers upset the Plains Indians' way of life?" As the students volunteered a number of details, Miss Moore transcribed each fact onto an information summary chart. At the point when her students exhausted their information, Miss Moore suggested, "Let's examine what you've come up with. What does this information tell you about how the Plains Indians and the settlers felt about the land? Do you think Americans of today have attitudes similar to the settlers at that time?"

Neither teacher asked questions randomly, nor simply to test the number of accurate facts the students took from the learning experience. Mr. Hansen asked an open-ended question to start the instructional conversation and then challenged the students to support their views with relevant details. Miss Moore did just the opposite: She started by asking the students to recall details with closed-ended questions and then encouraged them to draw their own conclusions from the data. Which approach is best for elementary school social studies instruction? Both are acceptable; each sequence was driven by a logical purpose, was patterned to address that purpose, and helped students engage in different levels of thinking. Rather than worry about whether your sequence begins with an open- or closed-ended question, it is more important to become skilled at applying John Dewey's (1933) helpful "art of questioning," which he proposed over 80 years ago:

- Questions should not elicit fact upon fact but should be asked in such a way as to delve deeply into the subject—that is, to develop an overall concept of the selection.
- Questions should emphasize personal interpretations rather than literal and direct responses.
- Questions should not be asked randomly so that each is an end in itself but should be planned so that one leads into the next throughout a continuous discussion.
- Teachers should periodically review important points so that old, previously discussed material can be placed into perspective with that which is presently being studied.
- The end of the question-asking sequence should leave the children with a sense of accomplishment and build a desire for what is yet to come.

In addition to understanding how to *pattern* questions, it is also important to know how to *frame* questions—that is, to provide students enough time to think of a response and to transform their thoughts into comments that they can share with their classmates. In many classrooms, teachers seem to become extremely uncomfortable with the deadly silence when students do not join in immediately after the teacher has asked a question. After about 1 second, teachers cannot resist the temptation to break the silence by either cold calling a student, reframing the question, or, in desperation, providing the answer. The fundamental system for framing questions is as follows: (1) ask the question; (2) pause for 3 to 5 seconds (wait time 1); (3) call on a volunteer to respond; and (4) pause again for 3 to 5 seconds to give the students some time to think about the response (wait time 2). There are a number of benefits associated with giving students ample time to think. First, a larger number of students will respond. Second, their responses tend to be longer, more complex, and more precise. Third, a pause provides the teacher with time to study students' body language. With experience, you will be able to pick up their satisfaction, delight, concern, or boredom. Fourth, teachers who pause after asking questions become more patient while waiting for answers and the students become more comfortable while sharing their thoughts.

 Video Exploration 3.1

STUDENT-GENERATED QUESTIONS

There is no doubt that teacher-led classroom conversations are fundamental to learning, but student-generated questions are of equal importance. Formulating their own questions helps students take ownership of their own learning and view the learning process through a fresh, unconventional perspective. Social scientists will emphasize that the ability to ask good questions is the heart of inquiry and the basis for real learning in social studies. Therefore, the most important classroom questions may be the ones your students ask as they struggle to find purpose and understanding associated with any topic of study. For that reason, a most important responsibility in teaching social studies is to plan strategies that promote and extend student-generated questions. Scaffolds in the form of teacher modeling are especially valuable in this regard. Although there are a number of ways to scaffold instruction for this purpose, it is important to note that there are two critical elements to keep in mind:

- *Modeling.* Students must be able to observe you modeling, or demonstrating, effective questioning strategies many times during the learning activity.
- *Practice.* Students, either individually or as a group, must have ample opportunity to practice the question-asking strategy.

One commonly suggested modeling strategy is *reciprocal teaching*, a process that invites students and teachers to share the roles of learner and teacher during episodes that promote collaborative meaning making; a traditional reciprocal teaching scheme is *reciprocal questioning*, or *ReQuest* (Manzo, 1969). In true social constructivist fashion, the teacher models the ReQuest questioning strategy and helps students develop their own questions about print, but can be easily adapted for most instructional resources. To implement the ReQuest strategy, follow the steps outlined below:

Step 1: Work with small groups. Give each student a copy of the reading material. Be sure it is on the students' reading level and that it contains enough detail that questions will be easy to generate.

Step 2: Introduce ReQuest. Inform students that the purpose of the activity is to improve their understanding of what they read by learning how to ask good questions.

Step 3: Silently read the first paragraph of the text with the students. Explain that, as they read, the students should be thinking of questions they could ask you.

Step 4: Direct students to ask questions. Close your book, keeping your place with a paper marker, and invite the students to ask as many questions as they want about the first paragraph (students' books remain open). The object is to "stump" the teacher. Make sure you establish basic rules that the questions must be about the text and should be appropriate to the topic. Answer the questions; you can check your responses by referring to the text. The students' initial questions will be primarily factual, but that will change as you model higher-level questions later in the ReQuest strategy: "When was Mesopotamia developed?" "Where was Mesopotamia located?" "What does Mesopotamia mean?" "How do you spell Mesopotamia?"

Step 5: Reverse the roles. Students close their books, using a paper marker, and you ask the questions. Students can request clarification if they don't understand a question. They are expected to give evidence for their ideas. As students asked only the simplest questions (factual), you must model questions that require deeper thought: "Why is Mesopotamia nicknamed 'The Fertile Crescent'?" "Why would anyone want to build a civilization in the middle of the desert?" "Why do great civilizations eventually collapse?"

Step 6: Repeat the pattern. Go to the next paragraph. Continue to model by silently reading it and following the pattern in Steps 4 and 5. The accumulated questioning time to this point should not exceed 10 minutes.

Step 7: Establish a purpose for reading. By now, the students should have developed a clear enough idea of the written text that they are ready to make a prediction about the remainder. Then the prediction statements are turned into questions. For example, "I think war played the most important role in Mesopotamia's collapse" would be restated as "What was the most important factor contributing to Mesopotamia's collapse?" There may be several different predictions; each should be written down on the chalkboard or on student papers to be used for later reflection. If predictions are not appropriate, repeat Steps 3 through 6 with the next segment of the selection before having students read independently.

Step 8: Read silently. Students silently read the remainder of the selection and complete a response activity.

Step 9: Discuss the selection. You should initiate the student discussion by asking the purpose-setting question: "What was the most important factor contributing to Meso-potamia's collapse?" This demonstrates that the purpose-setting question was important, and it is the first issue to be discussed after the silent reading. This process helps students to eventually establish individual purposes for reading as they encounter subsequent social studies texts.

With experience, students will learn to imitate the teacher's questioning behavior. Then they can work in pairs or small groups to collaboratively use the ReQuest technique. Receptive students will then find themselves asking good questions at different stages—before, during, and after they read.

Providing Explanations

Because you must communicate accurate concepts while using appropriate learning materials, it is important to step in to provide direct, clear explanations when your students need help grasping key ideas. Therefore, your explanation should be neither so complex as to be confusing nor so shallow or unchallenging as to be dry and uninteresting. By knowing your students, you can adapt your language to draw on their prior knowledge while activating prior understandings according to the demands of the current learning situation. For example, one group, after exploring a series of pictures depicting Civil War battles, commented that they saw, "Union soldiers hiding behind a pile of rocks." The teacher at this point introduced the term "rampart" as a rock, earth, or debris fortification used for protection. Introducing new vocabulary as students are immersed in learning experiences is far more meaningful than presenting new words in a list prior to the experience. The established learning base offers students a meaningful attachment place for the new language label.

At other times, you may know the answer to a question or the solution to a problem, but will find it more advantageous to prompt students to reflect on and examine their current knowledge and come up with the relevant concept themselves. As a student approaches an answer, take advantage of the situation by suggesting to the group that this might be a productive path for further exploration. The students should then discuss their ideas and bolster them with additional, relevant information. Afterward, you and the students should talk about what

Collaborative dialogue between teachers and students leads to deeper learning.

Pavla Zakova/Fotolia

they have learned, and how their own ideas and information search helped (or did not help) them to better understand the concept.

To see how instructional conversations and explanations are incorporated into a social constructivist learning experience, let's visit Myra Stanley's classroom to witness the creativity, passion, and intrigue that resulted after a group of students asked, "What is the Universe, anyway?" "Where did it come from?" "Is Earth part of the Universe?" To initiate an investigation into the mysteries of the Universe, Mrs. Stanley felt it was important to strengthen the students' personal connection to the cosmos by reading a book that approached their questions in a satisfying, entertaining way.

> *Today, Mrs. Stanley has decided to use a highly enjoyable and appropriate picture book, an instructional resource fundamental to all of her teaching plans. For the engagement phase, Mrs. Stanley printed address labels for each child in her classroom and attached them to business-size envelopes. She put the envelopes into a cloth shoulder bag that she sewed together to resemble a mail carrier's sack. Mrs. Stanley then randomly selected one child to act as a mail carrier and deliver the contents of the bag. The children each received envelopes with their names and addresses on them. Mrs. Stanley asked, "How did the mail carrier know where to deliver the letters?" The children had no difficulty responding, "Our names are on the envelopes. He looked at our names."*
>
> *"Yes," Mrs. Stanley concurred. "What question, then, does the first line of the address answer?"*
>
> *"Who gets the letter," the children responded nearly in unison.*
>
> *"What's on the next line?" Mrs. Stanley continued.*
>
> *"It's my house number and street," countered Sanjay in an instant.*
>
> *"Yeah, ours, too," the children agreed.*
>
> *"What question does the second line answer?" asked Mrs. Stanley.*
>
> *"Where we live," answered Jason.*
>
> *"It tells where our houses are. The street address," added Damares.*
>
> *"What about the next line?" continued Mrs. Stanley.*
>
> *"It tells the town and state we live in. The third line tells where we live, too," offered Elsa.*
>
> *"What do you think would be on the next line of the address if we moved on from our state?" challenged Mrs. Stanley. "If you think you know, write it in the space below your city, state, and zip code."*
>
> *Offering hints along the way, Mrs. Stanley continued to challenge the children to add lines to their envelope. Many added country and continent, a few added the hemisphere, and only one or two included our planet, Earth, the solar system, or the galaxy in the address.*
>
> *Next Mrs. Stanley introduced the book of the day to the children:* My Place in Space *by Robin Hirst, Sally Hirst, and Roland Harvey (Orchard Books). In the book, Henry Wilson and his sister Rosie ask the bus driver to take them home. The bus driver inquires where they live, teasing that they probably don't know the address. Henry shrewdly tells the driver exactly where he lives and offers a brief description of each part of his growing address: 12 Main Street, Gumbridge, Australia, Southern Hemisphere, Earth, solar system, solar neighborhood, Orion Arm, Milky Way Galaxy, local group of galaxies, Virgo Supercluster, the universe. As darkness descends during Henry's humorous explanation, we are offered a glimpse of several interesting astronomical phenomena. The book offers a richly illustrated and entertaining description of "where we are" as well as an indication of the incredible distances involved.*
>
> *Moving on, Mrs. Stanley helped the children chart their expanding universe on a large wall exhibit and directed them to add the relevant information underneath their addresses on the envelopes. The students were enthralled with the length of their final addresses and couldn't wait to get home and share it with their families.*

Instructional conversations offer students authentic opportunities to talk about what they are learning. As with Mrs. Stanley's classroom, social constructivist classrooms are considered communities of learners where both student and teacher comments are respected and encouraged. Students participate actively in instructional conversations and offer responses that often build on and enlarge those of their classmates. Teachers use carefully worded questions and prompts that help students unlock meaning from the mysteries that confront them:

- "What do you see here?"
- "How do you suppose it is used?"
- "I wonder what would happen if . . . ?"
- "If we try it again, do you think the same thing will happen?"
- "Is this like anything you've ever (used, seen, tried out) before?"
- "How can we find out more about . . . ?"
- "Can we find out if we watch it carefully?"
- "What makes you think so?"
- "Who do you think might use this?"
- "Where do they live? What makes you think so?"
- "What can you tell about the people who use this?"
- "What do you think of the people who use this?"

Some of these questions and comments help children look for specific things; others are more open and encourage higher thought processes, such as predicting and discovering relationships. Through such thought-provoking observational and conversational experiences, you are able to model the basic questioning and thinking strategies that form the framework of social constructivist learning. But, it is important to remember that, in addition to asking good questions, you must encourage your children to ask questions, too. Do not be concerned if you are not able to answer some of their questions; no one has *all* the answers. The most important thing is that your students know it is okay to ask questions and to look at things in new ways. Knowing that you are willing to listen will help your students gain confidence in their own thinking and encourage further interest in social studies content. And listening to what they say will help them understand that you care—an important emotional component that will encourage students to figure out what they know and how they know it. In a social constructivist–oriented classroom, questions may be posed by the teacher *or* suggested by the children.

 CHECK YOUR UNDERSTANDING 3.4   Click here to check your understanding of this section of the chapter.

Task 4: Organizing and Communicating Ideas with Graphic Organizers

Graphic organizers are visual models that assist students in actively organizing information and communicating clearly and effectively. The job of graphic organizers is to connect and organize knowledge to make it more meaningful. You may hear graphic organizers called *concept maps*; this is because they help teachers and students "map out" their ideas graphically. A concept map is a graphic representation of a network of concepts with links revealing patterns and relationships between the concepts. Graphic organizers help students detect helpful patterns and relationships within the content. Students are able to see how ideas are connected and how information can be stored in an orderly fashion.

Graphic organizers, like instructional conversations, are considered to be language-based scaffolding experiences because students need not only draw and write in order to complete an organizer; they must also talk, listen, and think. In fact, graphic organizers help teachers enhance instructional conversations with visible organizers that can be displayed and referred to throughout the day, or throughout the duration of the instructional unit. Let's consider some of the most well-known varieties of graphic organizers. There are five basic patterns, with endless variations, that appear to have the greatest utility in social studies classrooms: *conceptual*, *cyclical*, *hierarchical*, *sequential,* and *decision-making*.

Conceptual Organizers

Conceptual graphic organizers (also known as *concept maps*) are simple diagrams that spotlight a central topic or concept in the center oval and show the details in the outer ovals. Additional ovals can be added as necessary. Concept webs are graphic organizers that look much like a spider's web when complete—hence their name (see Figure 3.3).

Cyclical Organizers

Cyclical graphic organizers help students visualize a series of connected events that occur in sequence but produce a repeated result. The months and seasons of a year, for example, demonstrate a cyclical process, as does the water cycle and the metamorphosis of a caterpillar. One cyclical process taught in most dynamic social studies classrooms is the practice of recycling. Help your students understand this process by first writing the word "recycling" on the chalkboard. Then have the students complete a cyclic graphic organizer as they learn about recycling (see Figure 3.4).

Hierarchical Organizers

Hierarchical graphic organizers focus on a main concept or process and the subcategories under it. For example, students in one fifth-grade classroom were learning about the three branches of the U.S. government. Their hierarchical diagram of the branches is shown in Figure 3.5.

Sequential Organizers

When introducing students to any graphic organizer, be sure to describe its purpose, model its use, and provide students with opportunities for guided practice. Then, when students become comfortable with the organizer, independent practice is suitable. In the end, you should encourage and assist students to design their own organizers. Figure 3.6 shows a variation of a sequential graphic organizer Jean Linton came up with when she and her fifth-grade classmates were given the assignment to write about a special talent or skill that makes them an "expert." Instead of using a single sheet of paper to build her sequential graphic organizer, Jean recalled a hula she had created, jotted the major elements of the process on a number of index cards, and arranged the index cards in order. Using the cards as "organizational handles," Jean then expanded on each and wrote her story. You can easily see how the graphic organizer helped Jean write a clear, descriptive account of the steps involved in creating her new hula.

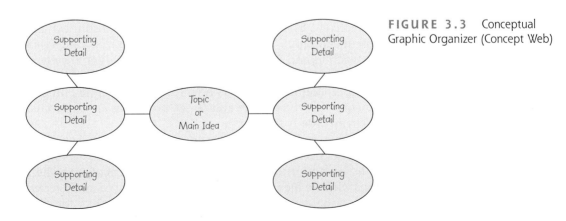

FIGURE 3.3 Conceptual Graphic Organizer (Concept Web)

FIGURE 3.4   Cyclical Graphic Organizer

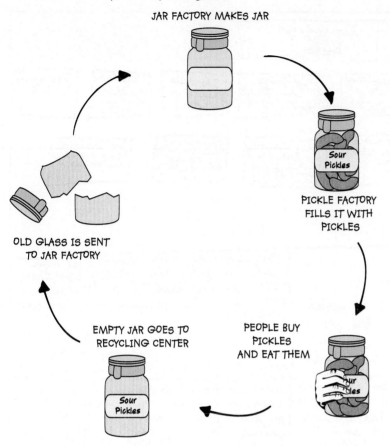

JAR FACTORY MAKES JAR

PICKLE FACTORY
FILLS IT WITH
PICKLES

OLD GLASS IS SENT
TO JAR FACTORY

EMPTY JAR GOES TO
RECYCLING CENTER

PEOPLE BUY
PICKLES
AND EAT THEM

▶ **Video Exploration 3.2**

FIGURE 3.5   Hierarchical Graphic Organizer

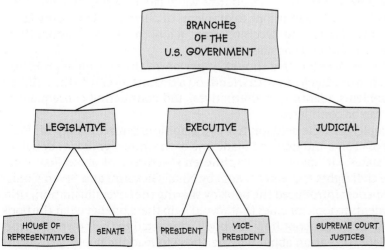

FIGURE 3.6   Using Cards to Organize a Sequential Graphic Organizer

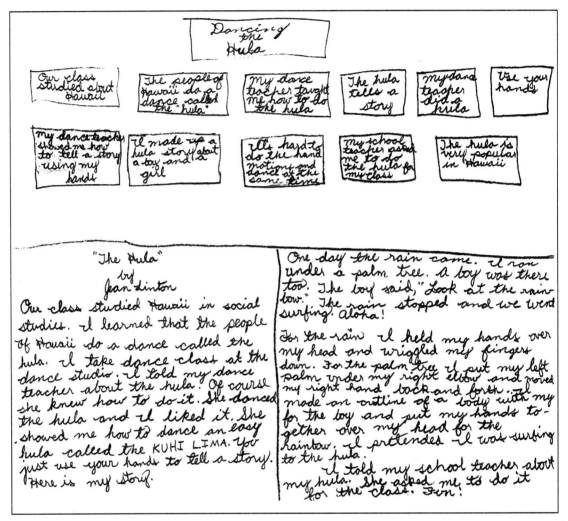

Decision-Making Organizers

Decision-making graphic organizers help students address value-laden issues; they provide a clear, visual layout for organizing possible solutions to problems or dilemmas. One of my favorite decision-making graphic organizers is the "Decision Tree," a tool that helps children think through their options and act with careful consideration.

Initial experiences with the decision tree should center on relatively simple problems, such as where to go on a field trip or what to do with friends on a free afternoon. As the children become used to defining problems, identifying alternatives, and considering consequences, increasingly complex issues can be considered.

Myles Spencer, for example, used the decision tree as a graphic organizer to help his fifth-grade students learn about Rosa Parks and how she made one of the most significant decisions in the history of the United States. Mr. Spencer read a children's picture book about Rosa Parks and her struggles during the civil rights movement: *Rosa* by Nikki Giovanni and Bryan Collier (Square Fish). To begin, Mr. Spencer introduced the book by sharing the cover illustration, title, and author. He asked the students to look for clues that would help them predict what the book would be about, and talked with them about how the book connected to their own life experiences. He also offered a brief explanation about why he chose to read the book: "This is the story of a courageous woman who became one of the most important figures in the American civil rights movement. I chose it because today is the 60th anniversary of the day she changed America's history." Mr. Spencer then asked: "Was there ever a time in your life that you took a big risk to stand up for what you thought was right?" "Why did you decide to take that action?" Then Mr. Spencer read the story of Rosa Parks' famous act of disobedience on a bus in Montgomery, Alabama, stopping the story at the point when she was confronted by the bus driver and directed to give up her seat. He divided the class into small discussion groups and introduced the decision tree by comparing the process of making difficult personal decisions to the childhood pastime of climbing a tree. "Tree climbing doesn't always come naturally," Mr. Spencer commented, "especially for those with a fear of heights or concerns about the tree's safety. So there are many decisions you must make before you start: 'Is the tree healthy?' 'Does it have stable limbs and branches that provide safe *alternative* routes?' 'What are the *consequences* of selecting a branch that won't support you?' " Mr. Spencer then informed the children that they were going to see how the decisions involved in climbing a tree are similar to the decisions Rosa Parks had to make (see Figure 3.7).

Mr. Spencer pointed to the empty "Occasion for Decision" box on its trunk. The first thing the students needed to do was carefully define Rosa Parks' decision. The class easily agreed that the decision was: "What should Rosa Parks do?" He directed the scribe for each group to write

FIGURE 3.7 A Decision Tree

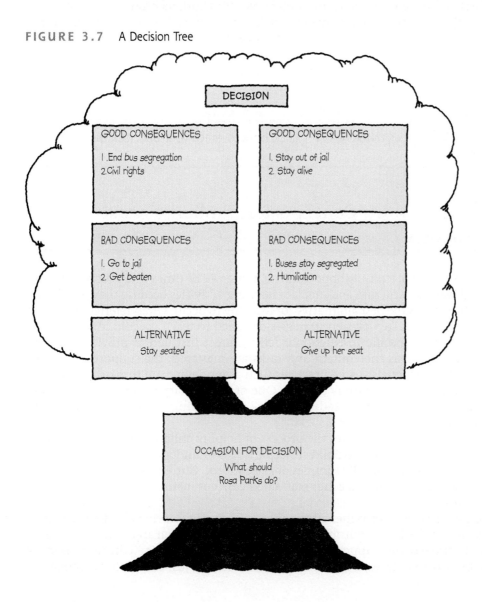

the question on the "Occasion for Decision" box. He pointed to the two empty "Alternative" boxes on the tree and advised the students that, in order to climb the tree, they had to think of Rosa Parks' alternatives. After some thought, the students decided that Rosa had two very clear choices: she could either stay in her seat or she could give up her seat. The scribes wrote their responses on the two "Alternative" branches.

Mr. Spencer then challenged the students to climb higher into the tree by looking at the consequences of Rosa Parks' decision. He asked, "What would be a good (or positive) consequence of staying in her seat? What would be a bad (or negative) consequence of staying in her seat?" He used the same pattern to elicit consequences for the second alternative, giving up her seat.

As the students deliberated, Mr. Spencer moved from group to group and offered prompts to guide their thinking. When they finished deliberating and listed their responses, each group shared its decision tree with the class.

The students were naturally curious about the real outcome of this event, and their questions flowed spontaneously: "What did Rosa Parks really do? What happened to her?" Mr. Spencer read the rest of the story to explain what happened. The questions made a perfect starting point for investigations into other struggles of the African American community against Jim Crow laws.

Traditionally, graphic organizers like the ones described in this section have been drawn as large wall charts or illustrated in a student's notebook. With both techniques, however, revisions are often difficult; changes can be made only by crossing out, erasing, or even redrawing the graphic organizer. Now, with computer resources such as Kidspiration and Microsoft Word, graphic organizers are no longer hampered by space and editing problems. What's more, a number of websites also offer teachers and students a variety of graphic organizer generators. You might be interested in checking out the possibilities.

 CHECK YOUR UNDERSTANDING 3.5 **Click here** to check your understanding of this section of the chapter.

Task 5: Breaking Down Concepts for Explicit, Focused Group Instruction

In addition to many informal learning opportunities, there will be times when social constructivist teachers will want to structure and mediate learning activities because they feel closely regulated instruction offers the best alternative for learning to occur. Often referred to as *direct instruction*, these are explicit step-by-step strategies designed to teach specific cognitive tasks or skills. In addition to a specific instructional script, direct instruction provides students with scaffolding assistance; as the content and tasks are mastered, the supports are gradually removed. Other constructivist-based practices such as modeling and thinking aloud help enhance learning and aid in the mastery of tasks. One of the primary reasons for using direct instruction in social studies is to help students unlock the meaning of concepts and perceive their interrelationships.

Concept-based instruction involves the process of helping children take in new content in such a manner that they are able to build concepts (ideas or understandings) after examining the critical attributes shared by all examples of the concept. Currently, there are two major approaches to socially mediated, or teacher-scaffolded concept instruction: *concept formation* and *concept attainment*.

Considering alternative approaches often confuses beginning teachers (and, to be honest, experienced teachers, as well). The burning question always is, "Which approach works best?" The answer is that neither of these approaches works "best" for all students all the time. Each has its own advantages, disadvantages, and controversies. Mastering just one of these approaches will not make you a successful teacher; you need to be able to use various approaches with confidence, and know when to use them.

Concept Formation

Concept formation is an inductive strategy developed by Hilda Taba and her colleagues (1971). Taba proposed that students are best able to construct new concepts only after being directly involved in collecting, examining, and organizing the information, so the first step in Taba's concept formation strategy is data collection from a variety of sources, ranging from direct experiences to print and electronic resources. The data can be generated by, discovered by, or given to the students, but regardless of the source, it should be chosen on the basis of clearly identified criteria: *validity* (up-to-date), *significance* (fundamental information), *relevance* (to the students and to the realities of today's world), *relationship* (to student needs and developmental levels), *depth* (richness), and *breadth* (applicability). Once the data has been collected, students construct concepts and generalizations as the teacher leads them through a number of carefully planned, sequential instructional steps during a unit on life in ancient Rome:

1. *List items.* "What did you learn (see, find, notice) here?" Students offer items; the teacher lists the items on a chalkboard or chart as unorganized details. A sample opening question is, "What do you now know about ancient Rome?"

2. *Group similar items.* "Do any of these items seem to belong together?" Students look for patterns and form categories by circling or underlining similar items—such as clothing, food, houses, art, sports, military, or government.

3. *Identify common characteristics of items in a group.* "Why did you group these together?" Students identify and verbalize common characteristics; the teacher seeks clarification when necessary.

4. *Label the groups.* "What would you call these groups?" "What title could you give this collection?" Students come up with a name that encompasses all items—the teacher records responses.

5. *Regroup and relabel items.* "Could some of these belong in more than one group?" "Did you notice any connections?" Students discover different relationships; the teacher records their findings.

6. *Summarize information.* "Now, looking at the groups we have just made, what can we conclude?"

Once the students have connected the name of the concept with its defining characteristics, you have several options for deepening and extending learning. The students can illustrate major ideas or perform a skit to highlight important points, for example. In this instance, students composed a summary statement for each grouping. For the "government" grouping they wrote: "Rome was first ruled by kings, then by a mixture of officials, and, until the fall of Rome, by emperors."

Taba first introduced her concept formation strategy over 45 years ago as a model for social studies instruction; since that time, it has been widely adapted and continues to be used as a popular approach to social studies instruction. Taba's philosophy is quite compatible with Vygotsky's. She suggests that if students repeatedly participate in her logical sequence of constructing concepts with temporary scaffolded assistance from a model, they will eventually internalize the procedure and develop their own ways of forming concepts and establishing conceptual relationships.

Concept Attainment

We see, then, that in Taba's concept formation strategy, the students generate the data, group items in the most appropriate way they can contrive, and assign each group a label in the most appropriate way they can devise. By contrast, in the concept attainment strategy developed by Jerome Bruner and his associates (1956), the data is neither generated nor grouped by the students. The students form concepts by differentiating the characteristics and relationships within a wide range of examples and nonexamples of the concepts that you have arranged beforehand. The major difference between concept formation and concept attainment is in the degree of control utilized in the production of data and the labeling of the concepts.

In the broadest sense, concept attainment can be thought of as a detective game where students try to discover patterns from a series of clues. The teacher offers examples and non-examples (verbal or picture clues) of a concept and prompts the students to detect what the concept is by unlocking the attributes of groupings. The basic concept analysis format follows:

- *Select the concept targeted for instruction.* For the sake of illustration, let us work with the geographic concept *port city*.
- *Establish your definition of the concept.* A definition might look like this: "A port city is a city or town on a waterway with facilities for loading and unloading ships."
- *Identify the critical attributes of the concept.* Critical attributes are what give concepts their defining features. Critical attributes help students distinguish continents from countries, glaciers from icebergs, and rivers from drainage ditches. The critical attributes that provide the concept *port city* with its defining features include:
  - Port cities are places where goods and passengers are transferred between ship and shore.
  - *Seaports* handle oceangoing vessels.
  - *River ports* are used for river traffic, such as barges and other shallow-draft vessels.
  - *Inland ports* are on a lake, river, or canal, and have access to a sea or an ocean.
  - Port cities are regional and global trading hubs.
  - Cultures and ideas mix readily and enrich each other in the life of port cities.

A word of caution about the defining characteristics of concepts must be given here, however, for although facts provide the defining features that make a concept what it is, they must be selected carefully. For example, details of George Washington's $60-a-set dentures (made from ivory, wild animal teeth, or lead covered with gold), as interesting as they may be, would not contribute much to enriching the concept of the presidency. However, they could provide interesting content to help construct an understanding of health care during colonial times. Concepts are superb organizational devices, but they can be formed accurately only when learners gather meaningful information through sound, developmentally appropriate activities. Concept attainment is a process of understanding what key features (defining characteristics) are essential components of a concept and what other features (irrelevant characteristics) are nonessential. Learning to differentiate defining features from irrelevant features takes time and experience; this process takes longer and becomes more difficult to master when teachers present students with confusing examples.

- *Select meaningful examples of the concept.* Some major port cities in the United States are New Orleans, LA; Los Angeles, CA; Chicago, IL; Baltimore, MD; Detroit, MI; New York, NY; Honolulu, HI; Pittsburgh, PA; Seattle, WA; St. Louis, MO; and Miami, FL.
- *Identify clear nonexamples of the concept.* Examples must include cities that do not function as major ports, such as Atlanta, GA; Las Vegas, NV; Denver, CO; Phoenix, AZ; Indianapolis, IN; Dallas, TX; Oklahoma City, OK; and Columbus, OH.
- *Select efficient, interesting, and thought-provoking techniques by which to present examples and nonexamples.* The following procedure is a common pattern of instruction:
  - Present a number of city cards, one at a time, to the students. These should include both examples and nonexamples of port cities. The cards can be displayed on the chalkboard or another flat surface.
  - Designate one area of the chalkboard for examples and one area for nonexamples. Or, set up a chart in the front of the room with two columns, one marked "Yes" and the

other marked "No." Present the first card (Seattle, WA, for example) by saying, "This is a 'Yes,'" and place it in the appropriate column. Show the next card (Las Vegas, NV, for example) and say, "This is a 'No.'" Place it under the appropriate column. Repeat the process until there are three cards in each column (see Figure 3.8).

- Randomly present a few more (two or three) examples. Ask the students to decide whether the examples should be placed in the "Yes" column or the "No" column. Students duplicate the chart on individual data sheets. Ask the students to examine each column and discuss how they are alike: "What do these cities have in common?" Students who know the concept should remain silent and write the answer on the data sheet; then they can add their own examples to the "Yes" category. Almost all students, however, will be either unsure or incorrect at this early point of the activity. To move on, you may have the students work together in pairs. Place the city cards in the appropriate columns. Each student works with a partner to list and discuss the common attributes of the "Yes" items. They combine their efforts to come up with a hypothesis about the concept.

- The hypotheses should be listed and tested by analyzing the examples. The attributes of the "Yes" column are discussed with the entire class and contrasted with the "No" column. If students are still stumped, continue to add examples to both columns.

- The teams then place the remaining items in the appropriate category and generate examples of their own. Each team should state and define the concept.

- Students examine their thought processes used to solve the problem: "How many times did you change your mind?" "How did the concept finally become clear to you?"

The following is an early grade example of the concept attainment strategy:

- The teacher gives the students a concept label: "Say these words after me: *dairy product*."
- Students repeat the words.
- Teacher shows students a number of examples, such as a carton of milk or carton of cottage cheese: "This is a *dairy product*."
- Students look at the items and listen to the descriptions.
- Teacher shares a number of nonexamples, such as a cucumber or bottle of water: "This is not a *dairy product*."
- Students look at the items and listen to the descriptions.
- The teacher asks the students to point out an example of the concept from a group of three—two examples and one nonexample: "Show me a *dairy product*."
- Students select an item.
- The teacher presents students with examples of the concept: "What is this? How do you know?"
- Students generate the concept label and give a description.

FIGURE 3.8 Concept Attainment Chart

YES	NO
New Orleans, LA	Las Vegas, NV
Baltimore, MD	Denver, CO
New York, NY	Dallas, TX

Based on student needs and interests, social constructivist instruction may include prompting, questioning, modeling, telling, and explicit, whole-class concept instruction.

WavebreakMediaMicro/Fotolia

 CHECK YOUR UNDERSTANDING 3.6 **Click here** to check your understanding of this section of the chapter.

Reflection on Learning

You may simply scribble rough notes or jot down something more polished and complete. The point is to simply start recording your ideas spontaneously and candidly.

In cognitive constructivism, *explicit instruction* is the general term that refers to direct teaching with teacher-led demonstrations. Many consider it to be the most effective method for coaching and facilitating the learning of basic concepts and fundamental skills. Others believe that students should accept responsibility for making decisions about their learning. What instructional methods and strategies do you favor at this point in your professional education? Do you prefer direct teaching or student-centered learning? Or do you see yourself using a combination of those methods?

Task 6: Modeling as a Scaffolding Technique

From their earliest years, children are surrounded by influential models who furnish innumerable behaviors for them to imitate—family, friends, media, and, of course, teachers. Children learn by observing others' behaviors and detecting the consequences of those behaviors. Social constructivists believe that social studies skills, too, can best be acquired through the process of *modeling*; they emphasize, for example, that it is no coincidence that better readers come from homes where parents read frequently. If children see their parents reading the morning newspaper or a book, they will be inspired to read. The principle of imitating an MKO undergirds the use of modeling in the classroom—students learn by watching teachers execute a process or activity, a strategy that involves a few important considerations:

- students must focus direct attention on the modeled activity;
- students must be motivated to imitate the behavior;

- students must assimilate what they observe into their internal world—the behavior must be understandable before it can be reproduced;
- students must be given many opportunities to try out and practice the modeled behavior; and
- students will be more likely to imitate a behavior if the model is held in high regard and if the outcome is perceived as useful, practical, and functional.

Although modeling is more closely associated with motor skills such as printing or using scissors and self-care tasks such as eating, dressing, or brushing one's teeth, teachers also use modeling as a strategy to demonstrate cognitive processes. Teacher modeling in social studies, then, will be considered a form of as scaffolding to help students approach both *cognitive* and *motor* processes.

Modeling Cognitive Processes (Think Alouds)

Most appropriately used when your students read or view any social studies content, the modeling process demonstrates the kind of thought processes effective learners employ as they encounter new concepts. Called *think alouds*, the strategy may begin, for example, when you read aloud a selected passage as the students follow along silently. As you read, you will make frequent stops to orally describe what you are thinking while using strategies such as making predictions, rereading a sentence, or searching for context clues ("thinking aloud"). As students become familiar with the process, they will respond to your questions and prompts and begin to imitate your questions and prompts. For example, fifth-grade teacher Valeria Castillo planned to read aloud a story about the voyage of the Mayflower for social studies class today, but first she planned to model prereading strategies while examining the book's cover:

"I can't believe what the Pilgrims had to go through on the Mayflower. As I look at the picture on the cover, I can't help but ask myself what the Mayflower voyage was like."

"I know," added Sofia. "I would be so scared to leave home."

"Did the Pilgrims ever see their families again?" asked Edwin.

"Look at that small old ship," chimed in Freddie. "The trip couldn't have been easy!"

"It makes me wonder what the trip was like . . . what food did they eat on the Mayflower?" "Where did they sleep?" probed Mrs. Castillo.

"Yeah," contributed Rene, "I wonder if they had to go to school on the ship."

"This may sound silly," Harold added, "but where did they go to the bathroom?"

"As I look at the drawing on the first page, it's hard to imagine what could have been so bad in England to cause these people to set out on the journey from their homes to an unknown land," remarked Mrs. Castillo.

"I don't think it could have been all bad," countered Emma. "I think it would be exciting to come to a New World and start a new life in a new place."

For the next minute or two, Mrs. Castillo modeled effective prereading thinking strategies while at the same time encouraging the students to ask their own questions, make comments, and offer their own predictions.

Mrs. Castillo then read the text aloud while the students followed along with their own copies. She stopped periodically to think out loud and ask and answer more questions: "So far, I have learned . . . ." "I think the most interesting part was . . . ." "I think _____ will happen next." Mrs. Castillo modeled how skilled learners may reread sentences for clarification or for context clues that help them figure out something. Since Mrs. Castillo's students have had previous exposure to think alouds, she allowed time for them to practice asking questions aloud to themselves individually, with a partner, or as members of a small group.

Mrs. Castillo, along with many teachers, is sold on the value of providing students with a clear model of a skill or concept before, during, and after a learning experience, especially text-based experiences. The critical elements of a think-aloud strategy follow:

BEFORE READING

Before I start to read, I ask myself: What does the title mean? How do the photos, illustrations, and headings help me figure out what the passage might be about? What other book or story does this remind me of? What will this help me learn more about? What do I predict that this story will be about?

DURING READING

As I read the story, I have the following thoughts: Since I don't understand this word, I could _____ and try to figure it out. I'm confused by this, so I'll reread the section to see if I can clear it up. Something like this once happened to me. This isn't anything like I expected. When I close my eyes, I can imagine _____. I would not want to be in that person's shoes because . . . . I'm guessing that _____ will happen next.

AFTER READING

After I complete the passage, I consider _____. From this story I learned _____. I originally thought _____, but now I think _____. Some ideas I still don't understand are _____. Here is a question I would like to discuss. This story made me think more deeply about _____. I will use what I learned to _____. How does this relate to my life? My opinion of the story is _____.

Modeling Skills Processes (I Do It, We Do It, You Do It)

In addition to concepts, a second major goal of social studies instruction is helping children to develop specific skills such as constructing and interpreting charts and graphs, using the computer, composing a meaningful written research report, making a time line, reading a map, creating a model, outlining information from reference books, planning an interview, making a mural, learning the steps of an ethnic dance, comprehending textbook material, collecting data, or testing hypotheses. Skills are mental or physical operations having a specific set of actions that are developed through practice. Those who employ instructional strategies based on the social constructivist philosophy are convinced that students acquire skills most advantageously with clear assistance from an MKO followed by numerous opportunities for practice. This process begins by carefully breaking down the skill down into its smaller, specific sub-behaviors—the sequential chain of distinct behaviors that must be carried out to perform a specific task. This process is referred to as *task analysis*.

Kindergarten and early grade teachers use a task analysis strategy called *forward chaining* when they teach children to accomplish skills such as tying their shoes or washing their hands. Forward chaining involves teaching the sequence beginning with the initial step and not moving to the second step until the first step has been mastered: Turn on water, get soap, rub hands, rinse hands, turn off water, get paper towel, dry hands, throw away towel. Social studies students will find forward chaining helpful when learning how to use a map grid system or prepare a PowerPoint presentation. Here is the strategy one teacher used to guide her students through the process of preparing a PowerPoint presentation. It is patterned after a useful and easy-to-remember approach to skills instruction created by Anita Archer (Archer & Hughes, 2011). Archer and Hughes refer to the first step as "I do it" because this is the point in the instructional sequence where a teacher models the skill by clearly demonstrating and verbalizing each step. For example, you would say: "Watch and listen to me as I open the PowerPoint program."

After modeling the skill, you would guide the students in performing the skill for themselves. Since this step involves performing the skill along with the students, Archer and Hughes call this step "We do it." For example, you would say: "Open the PowerPoint program with me. The PowerPoint dialog box will appear on your computer screen. Watch as I open the program. What will you need to do first?" You should monitor each student's efforts and provide corrective feedback when necessary.

Next, the students move on to performing the targeted skill by themselves; this is called the "You do it" phase. Depending on the students' skill, you might say, "Watch again as I click the Blank Presentation option button. The New Slide dialog box will appear. It asks me to choose an AutoLayout format. I click the Title Slide layout. When you have done that, look up." The assistance will continue directly and indirectly as students learn how to add text to blank slides: "Let me show you how to add text to those blank slides." When completed, it is important to close the session with a discussion: "Let us talk about what we just learned."

In closing, you may want to connect the current lesson to the following lesson by previewing the skill that will be introduced in the next lesson: "Today, we learned how to make PowerPoint slides. Tomorrow, you will learn how to move from slide to slide in Slide View."

To conclude, you will need to offer independent practice that focuses *on skills that the students have been taught during instruction:* "Please continue making the rest of the slides you will need for your presentation."

 Video Exploration 3.3

Although modeling is recognized as a highly effective and efficient method of helping students learn a specific skill or behavior, it must be emphasized that not just any model will do. Students have a greater tendency to accept their teachers as high-quality models if they perceive them as competent and capable professionals. I'm sure, for example, that you would have much more faith in a golf pro teaching you the nuances of the game than in a friend whose experiences consisted of watching the PGA Championship on television. Likewise, children learning how to use the Internet as a research tool are more likely to place their faith in a teacher who exhibits technological savvy rather than one who calls in sick with a computer virus!

 CHECK YOUR UNDERSTANDING 3.7   Click here to check your understanding of this section of the chapter.

Task 7: Collaborating and Cooperating with Peers as MKOs

Working in groups gives students an opportunity to learn from and teach each other. Various names have been given to this type of teaching and learning; the two most popular are *cooperative learning* and *collaborative learning*. Although many people have trouble differentiating between the two, you should think of collaborative learning as a natural, informal social act in which the participants talk, share, plan together, and work together. A team of students constructing a topographic map of their state, sets of students from schools in different parts of the country communicating over the Internet to compare prices of gasoline, or even two students helping each other with homework are examples of collaborative learning. Collaborative learning takes place any time students work productively together, whether they are practicing a basic skill or solving a complex problem. Cooperative learning, on the other hand, is a type of collaborative learning where students work together in small teams to achieve a common goal; the goal is reached through interdependence among all group members rather than working alone. That is, individuals are responsible for each teammate's success as well as their own.

Sometimes the transition from traditional to group-oriented learning goes smoothly, but it can easily turn out to be chaotic. One of my favorite stories was told by Selma Wasserman (1989), as she recalled her frustrating first weeks of attempting to put her ideas about student-centered cooperative learning into operation—a system completely outside the realm of their previous school experiences. Her students' ability to comprehend what Wasserman was proposing was 0 on a scale of 10. As Wasserman told her students about the joys of her new teaching approach, her words rang few bells, and no eyes lit up with interest or understanding. Increasingly, uncooperative and disruptive behavior took over the classroom; the children did not focus on assigned tasks, they were disrespectful to each other, and they didn't understand their place in the group. Without the familiar commands "Do it right now" and "Do it this way," they were bewildered and frustrated. Wasserman's dreams of a productive and engaged group of learners slowly began to fade.

Wasserman went on to describe her biggest disappointment: "My biggest disappointment was not that the children were unable to function in . . . sophisticated, mature and self-disciplined ways. . . . The killing blow was that the children wanted, asked, begged for a return to 'the way we did it in Grade 5'" (p. 204). At that point Wasserman realized that she needed to help the children learn the skills required to function as thoughtful, responsible, supportive learners. She needed to *teach* those skills. This was not an easy task either, for as she admits, "It may be a lot easier to teach children to read and spell than it is to teach them to behave cooperatively . . . with each other" (p. 204).

If your goal is to engage students in collaborative or cooperative group work, then you must help them gain an understanding of what it takes to function effectively as team members. This is good news: Group work skills can be taught and learned just like any other skill. And, like any other skill, you will need to be patient while offering meaningful opportunities to help children learn it. It may be November before you are able to recognize any major shift in the way your students approach group work, but you must follow the children's lead, never moving so fast that students are overwhelmed by your efforts.

Peers as MKOs

When a competent peer, with help and guidance from a teacher, provides a novice with support, encouragement, and assistance in completing tasks and assignments, this is drawing on a special collaborative process referred to as *peer tutoring*. In peer tutoring, the "expert" gives just the right amount of assistance for the novice to master the information or skill without doing the work for them. Because both students are at the same grade level, advice is often more openly accepted from the novice through a type of peer rapport that a teacher often finds difficult to establish. Suppose that the teacher who modeled the PowerPoint slide preparation process described earlier observed that Doreen continued to struggle with the process:

> *Ms. Gridley noticed that Doreen was having trouble adding the hyperlinks, so she asked Shirley, the "class computer expert," to help. Shirley's job was not to carry out the task for Doreen, but rather to explain the process and offer encouragement until Doreen was able to do it herself.*
>   *"Here's what I do," explained Shirley. "First, I bring up the slide that I want to add the buttons to. Then I select Action Buttons from the Slide Show menu. Now, see the blue bar above the action buttons? You do the next job. . . . Ready? Now, click the blue bar and drag the box." Shirley guided Doreen through the next few steps of the process and then stood by for support as Doreen confidently went through the process by herself and added hyperlinks to the next two slides. With her tutoring help and individualized support, Shirley helped Doreen acquire a skill through carefully designed instruction called peer tutoring, or peer scaffolding. In other words, Shirley provided the necessary support for Doreen until she was able to master the task by herself.*

It is recommended that every child have an opportunity to be a peer tutor. In that regard, teachers should think of themselves as talent scouts, searching for the special abilities hidden within each child. Speaking? Planning? Writing? Singing? Human relations? Discover the many gifts concealed within the children in your classroom and give each a chance to shine!

Video Exploration 3.4

Collaborative Groups

Collaborative learning can be carried out within a wide assortment of alternative structures; some are short in duration while others can last for weeks. A large number of different grouping configurations are associated with *collaborative learning*, for the term generally covers a wide assortment of strategies that employ shared efforts among students to achieve a common goal. Some collaborative groups are informal in nature while others are quite formal in scope and objectives. *Informal learning groups* are temporary collections of students within a single class period. For example, *buzz groups* consisting of two or three students may meet for just a few minutes to quickly pool their knowledge or ideas related to a topic or problem. To start, a teacher gives specific directions, such as, "Turn to a person sitting next to you and take two minutes to talk about this question: 'Is it ever okay to break the law?'" The teacher makes sure everyone understands the question or challenge and then signals the groups to start "buzzing." It is helpful to write the question on the chalkboard or chart paper, for groups will frequently refer to it to stay on track. One child should serve as a recorder who is responsible for keeping accurate notes of the key items discussed, as well as recording the group's final proposal. Because the recorders are most closely linked with the written record, they should stand up one by one and report the group's information to the whole class.

Formal learning groups are groups established to complete a specific task, such as write a report, carry out a learning project, or prepare a mural. These groups may complete their work in a single class session or over several weeks. Typically, students work together until the task is finished, and their project is assessed. Bill Pancoast, for example, has experimented with collaborative group work in his social studies classroom for some time. He feels that well-run group instruction tends to keep students motivated and more fully engaged in the learning process. Today, he has worked out a carefully planned, active learning episode that offers meaningful opportunities to learn about the civil rights movement. This is his outline:

1. *Read Paula Young Shelton's memoir of her family's participation in the civil rights movement,* Child of the Civil Rights Movement *(Schwartz & Wade). Bring in a number of artifacts related to the civil rights movement: a photo of Rosa Parks being fingerprinted, a reproduction of a sign reading "Colored Section in Rear," a reproduction civil rights button featuring an illustration of clasping black and white hands above the date 1965, a short video clip of Martin Luther King's "I Have a Dream" speech, and a duplicate of the Voting Rights Act of 1965. Display one item at each of five tables spread around the room. Tape two large sheets of chart paper near each table.*

2. *Divide the class into groups of four students each. Explain that the artifacts are to be used for an activity that will take place in stages, each lasting for about 5 minutes. One group starts out at each of the tables, brainstorming ideas and words associated with the artifact on the table and writing them down on one of the sheets of chart paper: What does this artifact bring to mind for you? What do you think the person or people pictured were thinking at the time? What does this image tell you about the event or time it was taken?*

3. *Rotate each group to the next table. Each group will now have a different object than the one it had previously brainstormed. The Rosa Parks group, for example, now moves to the "Colored Section in Rear" sign, the "Colored Section in Rear" sign group now moves to the civil rights button table, and so on. The groups must now write a short story about their object on the second sheet of chart paper, using the brainstormed words of the previous group.*

4. *Rotate again in progression. This time, each group revises the story written by the previous group—adding to, deleting, or revising ideas.*

Collaborative learning may include students teaching one another, students teaching the teacher, and the teacher teaching the students.

WavebreakMediaMicro/Fotolia

5. *Rotate once again. Now each group edits the work of the previous groups, checking for mechanics such as spelling, punctuation, and grammar.*

6. *On this fourth rotation, students examine the edited piece and compose a final copy on a clean sheet of chart paper (leaving room for an illustration).*

7. *On the last rotation, each group returns to its original table, examining the story written for its object and sharing their reactions. The separate pages are then read aloud to the whole class and finally bound together as a chapter in a class-generated book on major events in the civil rights movement.*

Cooperative Groups

Cooperative learning is the instructional use of small teams, consisting of students of various ability levels, working together to accomplish an instructional goal. Group members are responsible not only for their own learning, but for contributing to team success as well. The cooperative learning concept is rather straightforward. Class members are organized heterogeneously into small teams whose members work together until all group members successfully understand a concept, solve a problem, or complete a task. Students must believe they are connected with teammates in such a way that the group cannot succeed unless everybody succeeds—they "sink or swim together."

Cooperative learning groups vary in duration, depending on the task to be accomplished. Some groups remain together for only a short time—until they complete a special project, study new material, or solve a problem. Others change frequently throughout the day (e.g., dyads), especially those formed quickly when teachers ask questions that have numerous possible answers. And others, called *base groups*, stay together for an entire year or semester, thus providing a means by which students can offer stability and support.

Teachers interested in using cooperative learning in their classrooms are free to select from among a wide variety of strategies. The following are three of the more successful alternatives. They are examples of specific, tried-and-true strategies that you might find useful.

THINK-PAIR-SHARE

Think-pair-share is one of the simplest cooperative learning techniques. The teacher stops at natural "break" points during a lesson and poses a question. The students are given a short time to *think* about the question silently. The teacher then tells the students to *pair* up: "Turn to your partner and . . ." (think about what makes the San Joaquin Valley a good place for farming; predict where the Mississippi River begins; tell why the Cheyenne held Medicine Dances). The teacher gives the students a minute or two to talk together and discuss their ideas. The teacher may ask a few groups to *share* their ideas with the whole class or another group, but not all groups are required to share each time.

NUMBERED HEADS TOGETHER

Numbered heads together entails a simple four-step course of action:

1. The teacher divides the class into groups of four and assigns a number to each student: 1, 2, 3, or 4.
2. The teacher asks a question related to a topic under study. For example, while studying medieval England, one teacher asked, "What were some of the responsibilities of the women inside a castle?"
3. The teacher tells the students to "put their heads together" and work until she gives them a signal to stop.
4. The teacher calls a number (1, 2, 3, or 4). The students with that number raise their hands, become the groups' representatives, and can be called on by the teacher to respond.

JIGSAW

Just as in a jigsaw puzzle, each piece—each group member's part—is critical for the completion and full understanding of the final product. The jigsaw process starts when a teacher assigns students heterogeneously to groups of four, called their *home group*. Each home group works on content material that the teacher has broken down into sections. Each home group member is responsible for one of the sections. Members of the different home groups who are responsible for the same sections leave their home groups and meet in *expert groups* to study and discuss their specialized sections. These students then return to their original home groups and take turns sharing with their teammates about their respective sections. The following scenario illustrates how the jigsaw strategy has been used in Jack Cosgrove's social studies classroom.

> To introduce the activity, Mr. Cosgrove divided his students into home groups of four members each. The home groups followed this routine while learning about the life of Helen Keller:
>
> 1. The class started out with five home groups, each consisting of four team members.
> 2. Mr. Cosgrove randomly distributed to each member of a home group one sheet of writing paper with a different-colored adhesive dot (red, yellow, blue, green) at the top. The dots signified forthcoming membership in different expert groups (each expert will become a piece of the topic's puzzle).
> 3. The students joined the other members of their expert groups by moving to a section of the room having sheets of colored construction paper that matched their dots. Mr. Cosgrove had four expert groups, each focused on a different aspect of Helen Keller's life: Helen's childhood, Helen's early accomplishments, Helen's adult life, and Helen's influence on history.
> 4. While in their expert groups, the students studied the contents of several resources and selected important information, becoming "experts" on that part of Helen Keller's life. They summarized the information so it could be used to teach the members of their original home groups about what they had learned. The experts returned to their home groups; now each home group had an expert on each aspect of Helen Keller's life.
> 5. Each expert shared information about her or his segment of Helen Keller's life with other members of the home group. Others in the group were encouraged to ask questions for clarification. Once all experts shared their ideas, their jigsaw puzzle was complete.
> 6. Each home group planned a special presentation to share its collective learning about Helen Keller.

Group learning may be broadly defined as any classroom learning situation in which students work together toward a joint or common goal. Of all the student-centered instructional options available for social constructivist classrooms, teachers seem to prefer group instruction to any other. Collaborative and cooperative learning comprise an ideal partnership with social constructivism primarily because they require students to work together to achieve goals in ways they could not attain individually. Instead of working in competition with other students in the classroom, children are assigned the task of building a learning community where everyone contributes in important and meaningful ways.

 CHECK YOUR UNDERSTANDING 3.8 **Click here** to check your understanding of this section of the chapter.

Task 8: Scaffolding Learning with Computers as MKOs

Central to social constructivism is Vygotsky's (1978) idea that we humans are fundamentally different from animals because we have learned to make and use tools. Tools can be classified as *physical tools* that help us act on and master the environment (e.g., hammers and rakes) or *tools of the mind* that help us think and reason (e.g., language and counting systems). Similar to the way physical tools extend our physical capabilities by acting as enhancements of the body, mental tools extend our mental abilities by acting as enhancements of the mind. Throughout this chapter, you have learned that MKOs use various tools to scaffold learning in a number of ways to bridge the gap (ZPD) between what a learner has already mastered and what he or she can achieve when provided with educational support—from giving hints and prompts, to modeling, to direct, specific instruction. Recently, particular interest has emerged in adding a tool to the scaffolding toolbox: computer-enhanced environments. MKOs can be anyone or anything that is more knowledgeable or more skilled than a novice; computers fulfill that criterion. When computers were gaining popularity in elementary schools during the 1980s, they were used primarily as "interactive taskmasters," providing drill and practice exercises much as an electronic workbook would. This singular use clearly concerned many, for they feared that computers would operate exclusively as "busywork" stations rather than as conceptual, exploratory, or creative tools. Today's computers, however, can do almost anything, and many have evolved into MKOs that scaffold learning for students of all ages and developmental levels. Experiences with computers and other technology can support unparalleled learning opportunities. However, without a strong pedagogical component, technology will be unable to achieve its full potential. In order to capitalize on the power of computers as MKOs, you must gain the knowledge and skills to select and use computers and other technology in appropriate ways with elementary school children: What are you attempting to achieve (goals and standards)? How may computers help you achieve those outcomes? Is technology the *best choice* for achieving the intended outcomes?

 Video Exploration 3.5

 CHECK YOUR UNDERSTANDING 3.9 **Click here** to check your understanding of this section of the chapter.

A Final Thought

Becoming an MKO is a complex professional responsibility that involves a great deal of knowledge, hard work, and skill. As a new teacher, you may wonder whether the results are worth the effort. You may ask, "Why bother? After all, the textbook and teacher's manual were written by experts in the field who really know the social studies." Admittedly, you are correct to a degree. Manuals can be very helpful, especially for student teachers or beginning teachers. You will probably start your career by using the teacher's manual closely, but as you gain experience, you will adapt it to the changing needs of the different groups of children you will teach each year. Will you emerge as a student-centered or a direct instruction teacher? My philosophy is that the best teaching is not one or the other, but a combination of both. In making your decision, I challenge you with these questions: If I were to step into your social studies classroom tomorrow and observe you teaching, what would I see? If students were not required to attend your class, what kinds of instructional practices would you employ to entice them to stay?

References

Archer, A. L., & Hughes, C. A. (2011). *Explicit instruction: Effective and efficient teaching*. New York, NY: Guilford Press.

Ausubel, D. P. (1961). In defense of verbal learning. *Educational Theory, 2,* 16.

Bruner, J. S., Goodnow, J. J., & Austin, G. A. (1956). *A study of thinking*. London, England: Chapman & Hall.

Bybee, R. W. (2002). *Learning science and the science of learning*. Arlington, VA: NSTA Press.

Christenbury, L. (2010/2011). The flexible teacher. *Educational Leadership, 68,* 46–50.

Dewey, J. (1933). *How we think*. Boston, MA: D.C. Heath.

Joyce, B., Weil, M., & Calhoun, E. (2009). *Models of teaching*. Boston, MA: Pearson.

Manzo, A. V. (1969). The ReQuest procedure. *Journal of Reading, 13,* 123–126.

National Council for the Social Studies. (2010). *National curriculum standards for social studies: A framework for teaching, learning, and assessment*. Silver Spring, MD: Author.

Piaget, J. (1972). *The child and reality*. Harmondsworth, UK: Penguin Books.

Taba, H., Durkin, M. C., Fraenkel, J. R., & McNaughton, A. H. (1971). *A teacher's handbook to elementary social studies* (2nd ed.). Reading, MA: Addison-Wesley.

Vygotsky, L. S. (1978). *Mind in society*. Cambridge, MA: Harvard University Press.

Wasserman, S. (1989). Children working in groups? It doesn't work! *Childhood Education, 5,* 204.

Wood, D. J., Bruner, J., & Ross, S. (1976). The role of tutoring in problem-solving. *Journal of Child Psychology and Psychiatry, 17,* 89–100.

Cognitive Constructivism:
A Spotlight on Project-Based Learning

Learning Outcomes

Today, many feel that teaching and learning social studies are more effective when students acquire knowledge and skills by working for an extended period of time responding to and investigating a driving question or challenging problem. Students are expected to develop authentic projects or presentations that establish connections to real-world life outside the classroom as they answer those questions or solve those problems. Such an approach can work only if the teacher is able to provide just the right amount of support and guidance. After completing this chapter, you will be able to:

- Define the nature and instructional implications of cognitive constructivism.

- Describe how to incorporate project-based teaching methods, strategies, and tools into an elementary school social studies classroom.

- Design and utilize appropriate inquiry strategies.

- Explain and illustrate the use of creative problem-solving and its impact on learners.

Classroom Snapshot

Students in George Hutter's fifth-grade social studies class have spent the past week learning about unique customs of diverse cultures around the world. Today, their attention is focused on various cultural greetings. The students talked freely about the unique ways people from diverse cultures greet one another.

Sean suggested, "In Japan, it's polite for men and women to bow when they greet someone. But the Japanese now use the handshake, too."

Christine focused on the formal Muslim greeting from the past—keeping the palm of one's hand open and touching the breast, forehead, and lips, signifying endearment in heart, thoughts, and words. "It was like saying, 'You are in my heart and my mind,'" explained Tara.

"People from Italy sometimes greet friends by kissing on both cheeks," added Patrick.

"My family is from India," volunteered Tanya. "We use a greeting called Namaste. You press both palms together in front of your heart. Then you bow your head."

"I'm a Boy Scout," said Warren. "We shake left-handed—the hand nearest the heart."

The most important questions in Mr. Hutter's classroom are those asked by students as they try to make sense of interesting topics; one absorbing question emerged when some students began to describe and demonstrate the handshaking styles of present-day athletes. Their main questions were: "Where did these handshake routines come from?" and "What do they all mean?" Mr. Hutter is convinced that children have a natural tendency to seek information whenever they are confused or curious about something, so he is always receptive to their inquiries: "That's a splendid question, Sofia, and it has a number of possible answers. Let's talk about some possible ways to approach this problem." Mr. Hutter knows that curiosity is the heart of inquiry and realizes that he has a significant responsibility in helping his students seek answers to and gain meaning from their questions.

Some students searched the web and other computer resources. Others looked through pertinent books and magazines. A few students interviewed siblings, parents, teachers, and other adults. Their investigation uncovered some fascinating information. Although the students found that modern "shaking" variations of today's athletes are rooted in African American culture, the evidence was inconclusive: Basketball player Magic Johnson claimed to have originated the "high five" at Michigan State in 1980, but long jumper Ralph Boston argued that the "slap five" began among African American track athletes on the international track circuit prior to 1968. Some insist that revolutionary handshakes started as far back as the 1940s, when African American musicians greeted each other with a special shake accompanied by the jive phrase "Gimme a little skin, man." Regardless of the origin of the handshakes, Mr. Hutter's students became convinced that these handshakes were not just a passing trend. They pointed out that some sports teams have a pregame handshaking routine that is more carefully orchestrated than a classical ballet.

"They're not just a fad," argues Darius. "I've high-fived a million times! No contest."

"People will keep inventing new handshakes forever," added Lillian in support.

"I agree," said Nicole. "But by the time you learn all the handshakes, the season is over!"

Mr. Hutter supported the efforts of his students throughout this thought-provoking classroom episode because he believes that the most worthwhile social studies learning takes place when children work at what they want to know. His viewpoint is based on a conviction that elementary school students are naturally inclined to dive headlong into whatever excites their interests, and social studies teachers should be a little more flexible, a little more spontaneous, and a little more willing to help children investigate their social world. Certainly, in his balanced approach to instruction, there are times when Mr. Hutter directs his students to read for specific purposes from their social studies textbook or points out what to watch and listen for as he explains something through modeled instruction. However, Mr. Hutter knows it is crucial to also provide many opportunities where the focus of activity shifts away from the teacher to the students.

A powerful instructional conversation had touched off an unanticipated spark; Mr. Hutter's students had acquired a deep passion for and made an emotional commitment to an idea that had captured their attention and curiosity. Realizing that genuine interest like this does not flare up every day (or week), Mr. Hutter faced a puzzling dilemma: "Should I capitalize on their burning curiosity and encourage my students to explore their obvious and deep interests or leave it alone and return to the lesson plan I wrote yesterday?" Obviously, Mr. Hutter chose to grasp the moment; he concluded that pulling the plug on his prepared lesson plan was a small price to pay for a quality learning experience. Because he supports the idea of flexible teaching, Mr. Hutter does not always rely on the teacher's manual to know what to do next; he goes where the action is. Only one thing matters to Mr. Hutter: being tuned in to and encouraging the curiosities of his students. "Children have an instinctive curiosity that compels them to probe their world," Mr. Hutter says. "The very nature of childhood drives them to explore, and this need must be taken advantage of through inquiry-driven investigations in social studies classrooms. What's interesting is that the students don't even know they're in social studies class. They think they're just having fun!"

Because their curiosities are such an innate part of their development, many children clearly agree with the comment I once overheard Miles, a second grader, make after his teacher asked the class, "What would it be like to know *everything*?"

"Awful!" Miles exclaimed without hesitation.

"Awful?" probed the teacher in disbelief. "Why do you think that knowing *everything* would be awful?"

"'Cause then there'd be nothin' left to wonder 'bout!" countered Miles.

Rachel Carson (1965) believed that the innate sense of wonder displayed by children like Miles was an exciting and fresh part of childhood: "A child's world is fresh and new and beautiful, full of wonder and excitement. It is our misfortune that for most of us that clear-eyed vision, that true instinct for what is beautiful and awe-inspiring, is dimmed and even lost before we reach adulthood" (p. 42). Carson believed that to keep from losing this inborn sense of wonder, children must have the support and encouragement of adults who can both nurture and share the mystery and excitement of the world; teachers must keep the children's and their own sense

Curiosity is a basic childhood trait—an intense desire to know and find out. If a classroom values curiosity, children will continue to explore and discover.

Jason Hammond

of wonder alive. "If teachers are reluctant to wonder, will they ever keep curiosity alive in their students?" Mr. Hutter asks. "It is the job of social studies teachers to arouse, not suppress, the natural wonder their students carry to school." In that single persuasive statement, Mr. Hutter summed up the beliefs of those who contend that social studies education must keep the spark of wonder burning in our children's lives.

Cognitive Constructivism

Social and cognitive constructivists each fundamentally agree that learning can be explained as a path of action by which students attempt to make sense of their world by building new knowledge on a foundation of previous learning. In the last chapter, you read about Lev Vygotsky (1978) who portrayed the region of the mind where this process occurs as the zone of proximal development (ZPD), which is the gap between what a learner has already mastered and what he or she can achieve when provided with educational support. Vygotsky's supporters stress that this ZPD mechanism operates to the highest degree within "communities of learners" where more knowledgeable others (MKOs; usually the teacher or a peer) provide assistance to less-skilled learners. Proponents of this view are called *social constructivists* because they emphasize the social impact on the process of cognitive development. *Cognitive constructivism*, on the other hand, is based on the work of Swiss developmental psychologist Jean Piaget. In many ways similar to Vygotsky's concept of a ZPD, cognitive constructivists explain the learning process through Piaget's concept of *equilibration*, a path of action by which learners try to make sense of their world either by fitting new experiences into existing schemata (*assimilation*) or revising an existing schema as a result of a new experience (*accommodation*). Both Piaget and Vygotsky agree, in their own way and with unique jargon, that individuals learn by connecting, or attempting to connect, new knowledge to what they already know. Cognitive constructivists and social constructivists, therefore, have much in common, but they differ noticeably in one key area—the extent and type of involvement of both students and teachers. Although each model requires effort and responsibility on the part of both, cognitive constructivists favor a learner-centered environment where knowledge construction is primarily carried out by individual students in a fashion that supports their interests and needs. For cognitive constructivists, learning is an individualistic venture; substantial understandings are best brought about when students uncover information for themselves.

At this point, it is important to point out a common misunderstanding among preservice teachers. In articulating their philosophy of teaching, they often feel that they must eventually select either a social constructivist or a cognitive constructivist approach for their social studies classrooms. However, we oversimplify philosophies of teaching when we ask people to make straightforward either/or philosophical decisions. Sometimes it is helpful to facilitate learning as a social process—students connecting with their peers, teacher, and other MKOs. At other times it is productive to facilitate learning by encouraging students to create new understandings for themselves as they ask questions, search for answers, experiment, and try things out. In both approaches, instructional activities require the students' full and active participation. Therefore, in this chapter, I will build on the social constructivist approach by describing the ways cognitive constructivism assists learners in uncovering knowledge and building new understandings through a process referred to as *project-based learning*.

 CHECK YOUR UNDERSTANDING 4.1 **Click here** to check your understanding of this section of the chapter.

Project-Based Learning (PBL)

"It's time to go fishing for your group!" When their teacher gave his students that cue, they fully understood what was about to take place—they would soon be working with a few classmates for one day, or several days, on a "project." The teacher shuffled a stack of "Go Fish!" cards and passed them out randomly; the students were to gather into groups of four by finding the matching cards—4 blowfish, 4 sea horses, and so on. (Besides the attractive storybook style art, the teacher especially liked the fact that the matching card sets consisted of four different colors which will help in assigning roles within the group.) The teacher walked around the classroom, ceremoniously depositing four sheets of paper on each group's desk and announcing that they would be working on a "project" connected to their unit about the native people who lived in the Far North and were commonly referred to as Eskimos: "The Eskimos of Alaska." The students had already explored several related topics; the purpose of today's lesson is to help them understand the kind of homes the Eskimos of long ago lived in. A pretty good start, isn't it?

Focus for a minute on the first mental image of an *Eskimo* home that develops in *your* mind. Much as the informational paragraph on the sheets of paper passed out by the teacher, chances are that your mental picture of an *igloo* is a dome-shaped snow house sitting on a frigid, treeless, barren blanket of snow and ice. And perhaps the image may contain spear-wielding whale hunters dressed in heavy fur clothing standing near a sled ready to be pulled by a team of huskies. With such a clear-cut concept of *Eskimos* and their *igloos*, there wouldn't be any need to dig up much additional information, would there? You bet there would! If the teacher had been thorough enough to do an information search, he would have found that the people from the Far North he had been referring to as *Eskimos* do not use the word *Eskimo* when speaking of themselves. They are offended by that expression, primarily because it was an objectionable word anthropologists borrowed from American Indians meaning *eaters of raw meat*. Instead, the people of the Far North prefer to use a name that simply means *the people*. In Canada, that name is *Inuit*. In Alaska it could be either *Inupiat* or *Yupik*. The name *Yuit* is used in Mongolia. With his prevailing image as a guide for planning, the teacher's handout included an informational paragraph on *Eskimo igloos* with a choice of construction "projects": (1) a tabletop model made from sugar cubes and glue, (2) a tabletop model made from marshmallows and toothpicks, or (3) a floor model made with blocks. As the students made their selections, the teacher distributed an assignment sheet with due dates and grading policy, a rubric, and a guide for designing the "igloos." When everyone was done, the teacher would display the "best igloos."

Can you recall similar classroom "projects" from your elementary school days? Did you make posters, dioramas, crafts, and models of buildings or volcanoes? Some social studies "projects" surely involved productive inquiry that resulted in tangible, useful products that were shared with others. By contrast, a few may have been considered more as "busywork" than as meaningful learning. And, unfortunately, one or two may be considered culturally insensitive. A classroom filled with sugar cube or marshmallow igloos, for example, may suggest that students have been engaged in profitable learning, but was the activity relevant to what the students were expected to learn?

In our example, focusing solely on the dome-shaped snow houses many people picture as the primary shelter of the people of the Far North and creating a marshmallow, block, or sugar cube model would have been both incorrect and culturally insensitive. In the past, the people of the Far North lived in various types of shelters. Tents made of skin (seal or caribou) provided shelter during the summer months while in winter, most built semi-subterranean sod houses. And some permanent shelters were built from logs. Yes, a dome-shaped snow house consisting of blocks cut from snow and stacked upward in a spiral shape was built by some groups, but only as temporary shelter while traveling or hunting. Many people mistakenly think of these temporary dome-shaped snow structures as the *"Eskimo's"* primary *igloos*; actually, the people of the Far North call any place for living by that name, including the dormitory room, house, or apartment you are sitting in right now. In point of fact, *iglu* is the Inuit word for *house*, and *Inuit* now live in modern houses, or split-level, colonial, condo, or apartment *iglus*, just like the ones you and I live in. And, like you and me, they live in towns and villages, work at contemporary jobs, wear modern clothing, eat food purchased in stores; and instead of kayaks and dogsleds, they use motorboats and snowmobiles.

What would children have learned about the *Inuit* if they were offered what we *thought* we knew about this fascinating culture? In this case, the result would certainly be unjust, stereotypical, and incorrect, abusing all the major responsibilities of a contemporary multicultural society. In any lesson, our instructional resources must be supported by considerable information so that students acquire a genuine concept of the culture, period of time, or phenomenon being studied. You must be tuned in to the subject matter; you must have a deep background of information, for each concept targeted for instruction has its own body of subordinate facts; each has a precise set of data. You must be in command of this knowledge and able to use it to help your students process and organize the information. If you don't know the content, how can you hope to assist students in their efforts to construct new, accurate understandings from the instructional resources?

Instead of thinking of a project as a "product," we must start with an understanding of what distinguishes project-based learning from busywork. Project-based learning (PBL) exposes students to a broad range of opportunities for problem solving and inquiry; students design, plan, and carry out an extended investigation to uncover information that concludes with a useful product, publication, or presentation. PBL is neither a present-day sensation nor a new kid on the block. It has been around for decades. Its initial popularity was spurred at the start of the 20th century at John Dewey's Laboratory School at the University of Chicago. In his school, known as the "Dewey School," the curriculum was centered on activities called "occupations" because they reproduced, or ran parallel to, the work carried out in everyday life. Dewey (1896) explained that "... the child comes to school to *do*; to cook, to sew, to work with wood and tools in simple constructive acts; within and about these acts cluster the studies—writing, reading, and arithmetic" (p. 245). Subject matter content was addressed when students needed it to solve problems and inquire into questions that confronted them during their occupations. Although a few remnants remain active today, Dewey's PBL approach (known as "progressive education") was short lived; it virtually disappeared by the 1930s and 1940s. Progressivism did experience a rebirth, however, straddling the 1960s and 1970s. Known then as "open education," its proponents lauded the active, child-centered classrooms that unchained students from the shackles of the more formal classrooms of its day. Multiage groups of students moved from learning center to learning center in nongraded "open space" elementary schools, taking pleasure in "learning by doing." However, just as with the pet rocks, polyester leisure suits, and disco music of its time, the open education fad was quickly retired after its short-lived appearance as the rage on the educational scene. It seems that a public outcry to raise academic standards through increased rigor in the curriculum prompted a powerful "back-to-basics" movement. Competency-based education restored teachers to their traditional role of delivering instruction straightforwardly to students; walls were brusquely rebuilt in open space schools.

At present, in an educational climate heavy with standards-based curricula and test score obsession, it is surprising to see that elementary school teachers have begun to breathe new life into project-based learning. With progressive education and open education essentially out of chances to recapture a prominent place in American education, teachers have latched onto another variation of student-centered learning: project-based learning. With two failed attempts during the 1900s, however, it makes one wonder what has triggered renewed interest in yet another mutation of student-centered learning. Far and away, the most influential factor has been digital technology. Now it is easier than ever for students to conduct quality research and share their results widely. In addition, we now know much more about how to carry out productive, challenging project-based learning. Lack of such knowledge is often cited as a major contributor for the quick demise of both progressive and open education, as many attempts to apply both philosophies resulted in students running amok or aimlessly drifting from one activity to another . . . far from what was intended.

Some teachers choose to use variations of PBL as their sole instructional method, and others take advantage of PBL sporadically during the school year. Projects vary in length; the most common time frames are from several days to several weeks. While student input is invited, project-based learning is most often planned, managed, and assessed by the teacher. Think of the teacher's role during PBL as that of facilitator, working with students to frame worthwhile questions, structure meaningful tasks, and coach and scaffold the acquisition and application of knowledge and skills. PBL does *not* mean copying information from the web followed by an illustrated written report attached to the classroom wall to impress visitors. More than just a day of research in the library, PBL is an extended educational episode during which students investigate a meaningful problem or inquire into a driving question, mirroring the types of learning and work people do in the everyday world. A major strength of PBL is that it helps students acquire 21st-century skills, including creativity and innovation, critical thinking and problem solving, communication and collaboration, information literacy, and media literacy.

Students are the center of activity in PBL; they learn about their world by attempting to solve a problem or find an answer to a *driving question* that provides a focus for an investigation and guides the project work. Driving questions pose a difficulty or uncertainty that students find captivating and absorbing; they are "driven" to find an answer or solution. (As with other educational jargon, you will come across many different names for the kinds of questions that incite students to think and wonder: "driving" questions, "compelling" questions, "essential" questions. Regardless of what they are called, the purpose of these questions is to promote curiosity, interest, and enthusiasm.) The resulting real-world projects develop academic, research, and social skills, as well as creative-thinking and problem-solving talents. In social studies, two major models drive PBL: *inquiry* and *creative problem solving*. Neither is a simple strategy, but success in using both depends on addressing a number of features common to all variations of PBL:

- creating a need to know with a good introduction that "hooks" the learner and establishes a purpose to investigate;
- establishing curiosity, interest, and enthusiasm with a high-level driving question;
- exploring what is already known about the question or problem;
- determining how to approach the question or problem;
- using a variety of research tools, including print and electronic, that focus thinking on the problem or question;
- stating and defending an argument, plan, or conclusion with evidence and sound reasoning;
- utilizing collaboration and teamwork; and
- sharing results in authentic, real-world settings beyond the classroom.

For social studies purposes, think of inquiry and creative problem solving as the two major components of project-based learning—that is, you may initiate a project either "investigating a question" (inquiry) or "solving a problem" (creative problem solving). *Inquiry* is an instructional process that mirrors how social scientists study our world—by posing, investigating, and answering questions. The overall goal of their inquiry is to come up with rational (logical) answers to answer a meaningful question or uncover vital information—for example, "I wonder what important geographic factors influenced the development of the ancient River Valley civilizations." The term *creative problem solving*, on the other hand, has been used to cover a number of things we do in social studies, from fitting together puzzle pieces to creating solutions to poverty and pollution. One of my favorite definitions of creative problem solving, however, came from a speaker who once said, "Problem solving is what you do when you don't know what to do!" Creative problem solving is a process we employ when facing a problem, an uncertainty, or difficulty requiring a unique solution: for example, "If you were making recommendations to your school principal to address bullying, what would be the three most important actions you would suggest?" To solve the problem, you must generate several original, inventive, and useful solutions, eventually selecting the most reasonable alternative(s). We confront creative problem-solving situations, then, by devising a number of original solutions, but we resolve inquiry questions with rational, persuasive claims or conclusions. Each component of PBL has a set of characteristic procedures that will be explained throughout the remainder of this chapter (see Figure 4.1).

 Video Exploration 4.1

 CHECK YOUR UNDERSTANDING 4.2 **Click here** to check your understanding of this section of the chapter.

Inquiry-Based Learning

Inquiry-based learning and teaching are powerful approaches designed to engage students in meaningful investigative processes. Inquiry is found in many forms, but for all practical purposes, students in inquiry-oriented classrooms are portrayed as *mini-social scientists* making their own discoveries. By no means will they be expected to reinvent the wheel or join the ranks of Einstein or Galileo, but when engaged in inquiry, students are counted on to dig up information that is new to them. Despite the fact that their investigative processes are not as refined as those of a professional social scientist, both share a thirst to poke, prod, inspect, inquire, discover, and explore all the wonders of our world.

Do you remember learning about or using inquiry in elementary school, middle school, or high school? Those who do often tell me that the way to conduct inquiry is to figuratively slap on your horn-rimmed glasses, grab a clipboard, sharpen your no. 2 pencil, and carefully check off each step of the inquiry process as it is completed. Perhaps they developed these

FIGURE 4.1 The Components of Project-Based Learning in Social Studies

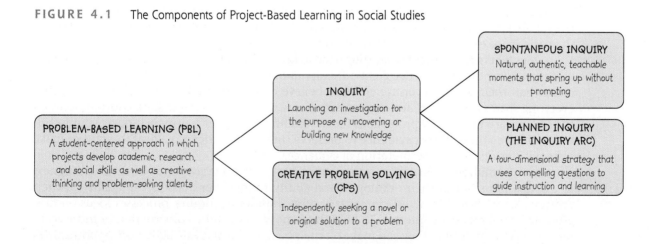

impressions because inquiry often tends to be taught as a series of linear steps—a fixed, chain of actions mirroring the ways social scientists approach a question or problem through the scientific method:

- Identify a question that can be investigated.
- Generate a hypothesis.
- Collect data or construct an experiment.
- Analyze the data and draw conclusions.
- Share your results.

However, most elementary school inquiry is not a rule-dominated scheme consisting of a fixed series of stages and responsibilities. Instead, think of inquiry as a probing, prying spirit of wonder and curiosity about every aspect of our world. As such, it pervades all aspects of life and is essential to the way we search for answers to our daily questions and problems: "What will be the impact of building a new highway through our county's native forest land?" "I'm a penniless college student. What can I do to pick up extra cash?" Some decisions will make you happy, some will make you unhappy, and chances are that you will keep trying to adjust your plans and correct any negative consequences. In the real world, we rarely pull out an inquiry guide to seek a solution for such concerns. Does a flexible, unsystematic approach remind you of the way children tackle problems, too? It is. Children, by their very nature, are curious about their world and love to dig in, explore, and investigate until they resolve their "mysteries of the mind"—sometimes unsystematically and sometimes in a more organized manner, just like certified social scientists. In our classrooms, then, *sometimes* students will employ a somewhat scientific approach, *sometimes* they will mix up the order, and *sometimes* they will ignore the steps altogether while digging around and prying for answers. *Sometimes* adult social scientists follow the scientific method to the letter, too, but more often they work in a slightly more informal manner. They have found that there is no single way to explore all questions, so they use a variety of approaches, techniques, and processes in their work.

Sparking the Spirit of Inquiry

Although children possess strong natural curiosities, some teachers are concerned that the youngest elementary school children (up to second grade) are not quite capable of the kind of thinking required to carry out authentic investigations; limitations in reasoning affect the kinds of inquiry they can perform. Piaget has described the thinking of these preoperational-stage youngsters (ages 2 to 7 years) as marked by fascinating errors in logic; their thought is dominated more by perception than by logic. They look outside, for example, and see a flat world. They may have heard from adults or television that Earth is round, so, when asked, they often say, "Yes, Earth is round." But their minds picture the roundness of a pancake rather than the sphere perceived by adults. So the children's thinking is at a point where they struggle with the basic shape of Earth, yet we insist on teaching them about the solar system!

Does it help to tell them what they need to know? Not much. Preoperational children are quite *egocentric*; they experience great difficulty understanding our world from any perspective other than their own. Egocentric children believe that everyone thinks as they do and that everyone shares their views, feelings, and desires. Critics point out the stark contrast between the reasoning employed by professional social scientists and that routinely used by young children: Children often distort evidence to preserve their egocentric or magical thought or make systematic errors in the interpretation of evidence.

Young children, then, differ from professional social scientists not in their willingness to ask questions but in their developmental ability to locate and assess the quality of their answers. So, with our youngest elementary school students, inquiry processes focus on tangible items of immediate interest. To help them move toward the construction of more accurate understandings than they can make on their own, we must create classroom opportunities that help children explore phenomena and materials much as they would do on their own, but enriched with a focus and structure provided by the teacher. Children's first experiences with classroom inquiry, then, should serve as a bridge between their free, natural, childhood play-oriented explorations and the organized processes and skills that children will need as they methodically question, explore, and investigate their social world. You must provide your students with new experiences that challenge their existing ideas and help build new concepts. Then, as children grow through the upper elementary grades, they will progress from giving the naïve explanations of their early years to processing their own ideas, proposing hypotheses, rethinking their ideas, and coming up with sound conclusions.

OBSERVATIONAL EXPERIENCES

The first step in helping students support informal inquiry skills is to arrange a self-contained section of your classroom where students can learn through interactive experiences with real objects of interest. These classroom sections, or what I like to call "mini-museums," when they are arranged for social studies purposes (others have variously called them *interest areas*, *curiosity centers*, and *theme tables*), are essentially exhibit areas designed to encourage children to explore, question, think, and talk. Today's exhibit might be origami, a Chilean rain stick, foreign coins, a butter churn, a powder horn, shark's teeth, campaign buttons, a tape recording of city sounds, or a sombrero. Whatever you select for the mini-museum should be treated like an exhibit in the best public children's museums—not with a "hands-off" warning but with a policy that invites touching, exploration, and investigation.

Todd Lewis, a fourth-grade teacher, modeled a curator's responsibilities by placing a seemingly odd object on a table—a cornhusk doll. On the wall above the table was a sign that read "Classroom Mini-Museum."

"I've brought something interesting to our classroom museum today," he told the children. "Look at it carefully, and we'll talk about what you see." Almost instantly, the children began looking at the doll, touching it, and talking about what it might be. Mr. Lewis watched and listened, occasionally asking open-ended questions and making comments to stimulate the children to think more about the object. Jaime suggested that it looked like a like a toy " . . . from olden times . . . a doll, maybe?"

Mr. Lewis inquired, "What makes you think it's a doll, Jaime?"

"It looks like it has arms and legs and a body. It doesn't have a face, but the top looks like it might be a head," replied Jaime.

"I agree, it is shaped like a doll, Jaime," continued Mr. Lewis. "What do you notice, Rita?"

"It looks like a doll, but I think it might be made out of corn plants," suggested Rita. "It looks like the dried corn plants we have at Halloween. I never, ever saw a doll made from corn leaves, though."

"You're right; that doll was made from part of a corn plant, Rita," affirmed Mr. Lewis. "It's made from the part called the husk. Here, look at this. It is a cornhusk before it is made into a doll."

"How do people make dolls out of cornhusks?" the children asked spontaneously.

Mr. Lewis took a few minutes to demonstrate how to make a cornhusk doll. (He found the directions on the Internet.) Mr. Lewis asked the students to follow his lead to make their own. The craft activity continued for several minutes.

Mr. Lewis emphasized the importance of checking other sources, too, calling the children's attention to the classroom computer station, where he used a kid-safe directory to handpick several websites that provided appropriate information about cornhusk dolls. "What does the doll tell you about the people who used it?" he asked after the children explored the sites.

During their instructional conversation, the children brought out some very interesting information: Cornhusk dolls have been made by American Indians for hundreds of years; brittle dried cornhusks become soft if soaked in water; they were used to produce other children's toys, too; some cornhusk dolls were used in sacred ceremonies; and children in the American colonies often learned how to make toys from the American Indian children who lived nearby.

FIGURE 4.2   Completed Observation Sheet

"We must keep careful records of everything we discover so we can share our findings with other people. We will use a special way of keeping a record of our discoveries, just like real social scientists—observation sheets." Mr. Lewis passed out a sheet to each student: There's a place for your name and date, and then the sheet asks you, 'What I Know About,' but it's followed by a long blank. What words should you put in the blank?"

"Cornhusk dolls!" shouted most of the children in unison.

Mr. Lewis continued, "That's a wonderful suggestion. What are some things we might write about this cornhusk doll?"

Denise suggested, "American Indian children made them from cornhusks." Other suggestions kept coming for several minutes. Then, Mr. Lewis directed the students to write a sentence or two on their sheets and make a careful drawing of their observation (see Figure 4.2).

Mr. Lewis planned to display something new that would be directly tied in to the social studies topic under study in the mini-museum every few days. The children were told that they would be using their skills of observing and investigating to uncover relevant information.

As important as they are, observational experiences by themselves do not guarantee the acquisition of inquiry skills. Mr. Lewis also used carefully worded probes and prompts to help the children unlock meaning from the mysteries that confronted them:

- "What do you see here?"
- "How do you suppose it is used?"

What questions or prompts might a social studies teacher use to focus exploration of this vintage postage stamp located at today's classroom display?

Sylvana Rega/Shutterstock

- "I wonder what would happen if . . . ?"
- "If we try it again, do you think the same thing will happen?"
- "Is this like anything you've ever (used, seen, tried out) before?"
- "How can we find out more about . . . ?"
- "Can we find out if we watch it carefully?"
- "What makes you think so?"
- "Who do you think might use this?"
- "Where do they live? What makes you think so?"
- "What can you tell about the people who use this?"
- "What do you think of the people who use this?"

Some of these questions and comments help children look for specific things; others are more open-ended and encourage higher thought processes, such as predicting and discovering relationships. Through such thought-provoking observational experiences, you are able to model the basic questioning and research skills required for sophisticated scientific investigations. In that light, in addition to asking good questions, you must encourage your children to ask questions, too. Do not be concerned if you are not able to answer some of their questions; no one has *all* the answers. The most important thing is that your students know it is okay to ask questions and to look at things in new ways. Knowing that you are willing to listen will help your students gain confidence in their own thinking and encourage further interest in social studies content. And listening to what they say will help them understand that you care—an important emotional component that will encourage students to figure out what they know and how they know it. In an inquiry-oriented classroom, questions may be posed by the teacher *or* by the children. Regardless of the curiosity source, the defining characteristic of inquiry is not only that a question has been asked but that the children are also directly involved in coming up with answers.

 Video Exploration 4.2

SPONTANEOUS INQUIRY

Very young or inexperienced students must be given numerous opportunities to develop inquiry skills through authentic, informal classroom experiences. Keep in mind that scientific inquiry is a developing process; students must progress along a continuum of movement from undeveloped to mature inquiry skills. Therefore, you will not follow the scientific process during your students' initial encounters with inquiry, but informally practice some of the skills that mimic the thinking and doing processes involved. I like to call these experiences *spontaneous inquiries*. Not necessarily connected to a "driving question," "compelling question," or "essential question," *spontaneous inquiries* are unplanned classroom incidents that are taken advantage of as they happen—priceless informal learning openings that may be gone forever if not immediately seized and acted upon.

"Why shouldn't elementary school children freely explore, inquire, solve problems, and discover?" asks fourth-grade teacher Wendy Fowler. "Perhaps a formal curriculum can help children acquire specific facts and designated skills, but what about curiosity and creativity—21st-century attributes that are even more important for learning throughout life?" Miss Fowler feels it is important to give childhood's natural learning free rein within a rich, supportive, and safe classroom; with devoted and caring teachers; and with plenty of opportunities for exploration and investigation. One day Miss Fowler's students returned from lunch upset about watching their peers unload huge amounts of food from their trays into the trash containers. The subsequent *inquiry dialogue* inspired a searching "why" from the students. (An inquiry dialogue is classroom talk that mirrors, but does not duplicate, formal inquiry processes.)

> *Antonio suggested that most children didn't like greasy pizza—the meal served that day. There were a number of contrasting views, but most expressed an opinion that the overall quality and nutritional value of the food needed to be improved: "Turkey chili with cornbread is the favorite of most kids. They hardly throw any away," "Tacos are number one! Everybody likes tacos," "No one likes meat loaf. It ends up in the trash every time," and "Chicken fingers are yucky. The stuff inside doesn't even look like chicken!" Miss Fowler sensed that student interest in this situation was deep and that their concerns centered on two fundamental questions: "What is the least favorite food served for lunch?" and "What is the most favorite food served for lunch?"*
>
> *Miss Fowler now had two choices: She could extend the impassioned class discussion a few more minutes and then move on to spelling class, or she could seize the opportunity and use her students' deep interest in the situation as a springboard for spontaneous inquiry. Rather than limit the experience to a short, heated exchange about why so many lunches ended up in the trash, Miss Fowler decided to help her students substantiate their claims about what the children "really liked" by turning their problem into a spontaneous inquiry project.*
>
> *The students decided to find out exactly what their peers preferred for lunch, and they planned to conduct a quick survey. They selected clear-cut survey questions and designed an authentic survey instrument: Should the students poll their peers orally and keep a running record of the results, or should they distribute written questionnaires? Could voting be arranged on classroom computers? The students settled on a written questionnaire and subsequently settled on a population for their investigation. Should they question every child who eats lunch in the cafeteria? Should only a small portion of the student body be surveyed? Should they randomly select 50 fourth graders by drawing names out of a hat? They made up their minds to poll every third boy and every third girl in lunch line until they reached the end of the line.*
>
> *Once the students gathered the data, Miss Fowler helped them examine and analyze the results. They didn't perform a complex chi-square analysis, but they did interpret the numbers simply and accurately. They constructed a graph that showed most of the children preferred tacos; turkey wraps were a close second; chicken fingers with "limp, salty" fries were not very popular and, as predicted, "mystery meat" meatloaf was comfortably in last place.*
>
> *"Look," exclaimed Alex, "we were right about the meatloaf. Nobody likes it!" "Yeah," added Laura, "and most of the kids liked tacos . . . just like we thought!" "You guys are right,"*

interrupted Caesar. "But before you get too carried away, take a look at the turkey wraps. We said they were awful, but a lot of kids like them." Discussing the data was a valuable experience for Miss Fowler's students; they were encouraged to examine and argue the results at length.

While considering how to share the results of their lunchroom survey with others, it was necessary for Miss Fowler's students to determine who would benefit most from seeing their results. Should they compose an oral response and deliver it to the cafeteria manager? Should they write an article for the school newspaper so that everyone could see the results? Perhaps a letter to the school principal would be most appropriate? Miss Fowler's students deliberated several possibilities before choosing to orally present the cafeteria manager and school principal their findings, supplemented with large charts displaying their data.

A valuable outgrowth of Miss Fowler's students' work was the recognition of a deep concern suggested by Beatrice: "We've been talking about what food is our favorite, but shouldn't we think about how good the food is for us, too?" This propelled the students into an analysis of the nutritional value of foods served in the lunchroom: "How does eating the food usually served in the lunchroom affect our health and growth?" They were particularly interested in the Healthy School Lunch Campaign, which advocates for healthier school lunches, and the Farm to School program, which connects farms with nearby schools to produce healthier lunches with more fresh produce.

The school principal and cafeteria manager were especially interested in the students' research into the topic and their results. Working together with Miss Fowler's class, they examined options that might become new lunchroom favorites. After considering Yadier's claim that his classmates were "programmed to like fried stuff," the school changed from fried to baked chicken with whole-grain breading that the children agreed "tasted real good." The students also approved "greaseless" pizza with whole wheat crust, but they rejected breaded baked fish. They ditched hotdogs as being too unhealthy and added more fruits and vegetables, more whole grains, reduced-fat instead of high-fat milk, and sensible reductions on calories, unhealthy fats, and salt. Their investigation into the nutritious benefits of lunchtime favorites led to a major overhaul of the lunchroom menu. In addition to encouraging children to collaborate for a variety of purposes and use an assortment of skills, the educational benefits of this spontaneous inquiry episode included empowering youngsters to change their behaviors in matters that affect their lives.

Student inquiry was the force that persuaded this student's cafeteria to switch from deep-fried mystery meat to nourishing, delicious meals.

Monkey Business Images/Shutterstock

None of these outcomes were planned in advance; they were prompted mainly by a natural childhood tendency to find out about things. Based on a belief that children should be allowed to explore, inquire, and discover, Miss Fowler's instructional style is designed to encourage students to discover new information on their own in addition to constructing specific concepts and skills through a planned curriculum.

Although spontaneous inquiry works for some teachers, most are not completely sold on the approach. They insist that spontaneous inquiry is too difficult to manage; those who need more structure in their professional lives worry about not knowing in advance where the study will take the class or how long it will go on. They argue, in frustration, "I have so many other curriculum requirements to be concerned about that I don't have time for spontaneous inquiry." They believe that it is unreasonable to expect teachers to have a "bagful of tricks" on hand every time a new interest emerges. In addition to these complaints, a large majority of school districts supply curriculum guides for teachers that specify the topics for instruction. Teachers are permitted to extend and enrich those topics, but the basic subject matter and sequence must be closely followed. "I prefer that kind of curriculum," explains one teacher. "What happens if my students never develop a natural interest in the Great Sphinx at Giza? Does that mean they will miss out on all the interesting mysteries and discoveries associated with this immense stone structure?" Certainly not, mediators maintain; the motivation might not be as high as when children discover something by themselves, but if they are allowed to actively pursue what the teacher brings to them, students will become interested in it and become eager to learn. The idea is that concepts worth knowing about should be developed in a variety of ways; children need a mixture of direction and freedom. A learner's spontaneity should be encouraged and exploited, but teachers must also organize materials and situations to provide well-designed learning opportunities for their students. When something comes up unexpectedly and does not fit into your curriculum, you should not totally ignore the teachable moment; unfortunately, if you do, it may be gone forever.

There are clear differences between planned inquiry and spontaneous inquiry, but these two approaches are not completely unrelated to each other. Vygotsky (1962) clarified the relationship by explaining that children acquire two major types of concepts during the elementary school years—spontaneous and scientific. *Spontaneous concepts* are acquired through self-initiated activity, informal experience, and, of course, spontaneous inquiry. Spontaneous concepts form the necessary building blocks for *scientific concepts*, or deep, more abstract concepts. The development of scientific concepts in children is possible only when the development of spontaneous concepts reaches a certain level of maturation; therefore, spontaneous concepts provide the prerequisite structures necessary for the development of scientific concepts. Likewise, Piaget (1969/1970) was so impressed with childhood tendencies for spontaneous inquiry that he used them to characterize his idea of *active learning*: "Active methods . . . give broad scope to the *spontaneous research of the child* [italics mine] . . . and require that every new truth to be learned be rediscovered or at least reconstructed by the student and not simply imparted to him" (p. 21). In contrast, however, Vygotsky theorized that scientific concepts can be acquired only through the systematic assistance of a teacher in an educational setting while Piaget suggested that students must be given opportunities to construct knowledge through their own experiences.

Young learners radiate exceptional curiosity about the world around them and look at life as a mystery to be searched and solved. Nothing is too small for their eager minds; nothing is so insignificant that it passes them by. Children's observations of "their world" lead almost everyone to conclude that they are doers, thinkers, and natural inquirers. For this reason, social studies classrooms must provide a wide range of instructional practices that offer children both the informal, self-initiated experiences required to form spontaneous concepts as well as the scaffolded assistance that helps produce deeper understandings.

Planned Inquiry (The Inquiry Arc)

Inquiry-based instruction can be quite varied; the process can be thought of as a continuum: *spontaneous inquiry* (informal) to *planned inquiry* (formal). *Spontaneous inquiry*, as the name implies, resembles the natural, intuitive style we have just examined—fueled by natural childhood wonder and curiosity. Students act on their own observations, questions, or problems and plan and carry out all phases of investigation. Self-determination, active participation, and collaboration embody the classroom climate. Teachers facilitate the process, often by furnishing materials for the students or by taking on the role of co-learner. *Planned inquiry* is more systematic; students are expected to employ increasingly formal methods of investigation. These methods prompt and guide students throughout the process, providing the structure and support they need to be successful throughout the inquiry process.

It may take several weeks or months of informal, spontaneous inquiry to reach the point where you and your students are able use planned inquiry productively, but I have heard teachers give up after only one unsuccessful attempt, saying, "I knew it! These kids just can't think for themselves!" and go through the rest of the year doing their thinking for them. But I doubt that the same teachers would say, "These kids just can't add and subtract by themselves or understand what they read," and remove any further opportunity to learn how to compute or comprehend text. Before you make the same mistake and end up shrieking, "Bring back the textbook! Give me back my worksheets! This business of inquiry-centered learning just doesn't work!" you must know that children change direction slowly; the processes of inquiry will not magically emerge after a single exposure to the process. Introducing new expectations all at once can produce a condition in which the children's cognitive systems collapse under an overload of input. Time, patience, and your belief in the importance of student-centered learning are the key elements of a successful transition.

Regardless of its form, inquiry has received growing recognition as an important learning strategy in dynamic social studies classrooms. For example, the influential *College, Career, and Civic Life Framework*, dubbed the C3 Framework (NCSS, 2013), has defined a set of four interlocking and mutually reinforcing elements, the four dimensions of the "Inquiry Arc," which should drive planned inquiry instruction in elementary schools today (see Figure 4.3).

FIGURE 4.3   The Four Dimensions of the Inquiry Arc

DIMENSION 1

Developing Questions and Planning Inquiries

- Compelling Questions
- Supporting Questions
- Sources and Evidence

DIMENSION 2

Applying Disciplinary Concepts and Tools

- Civics
- Economics
- Geography
- History
- Standards from State and National Sources

DIMENSION 3

Evaluating Sources and Using Evidence

- Analyze Information
- Make Evidence-Based Claims
- Form Conclusions

DIMENSION 4

Communicating Conclusions and Taking Informed Action

- Collaborate with Others
- Communicate Conclusions Publicly
- Critique Conclusions Publicly

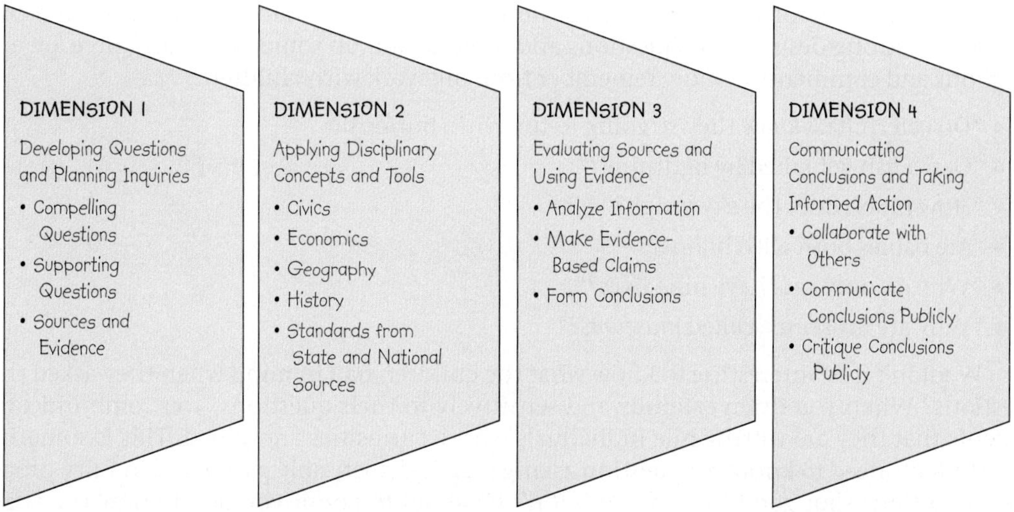

Those four Inquiry Arc dimensions are:

1. *Developing questions and planning investigations:* Students and teachers create questions as they investigate societal issues, trends, and events. *Planned inquiry* starts with a good question; good questions are the heart of any inquiry.

2. *Applying disciplinary concepts and tools:* Students analyze societal issues, trends, and events by applying concepts and tools from civics, economics, geography, and history.

3. *Gathering, evaluating, and using evidence:* Students work toward conclusions about societal issues, trends, and events by collecting evidence and evaluating its usefulness in developing causal explanations.

4. *Working collaboratively and communicating conclusions:* Students draw on knowledge and skills to work individually and collaboratively to conclude their investigations into societal issues, trends, and events.

Reflection on Learning

You may simply scribble rough notes or jot down something more polished and complete. The point is to simply start recording your ideas spontaneously and candidly.

The C3 Framework as well as the *Common Core State Standards* intentionally envision social studies instruction as an Inquiry Arc with its use of questions to spark curiosity, guide instruction, deepen investigations, and acquire rigorous content. Does this imply that teachers should use inquiry for every social studies lesson?

DIMENSION 1: DEVELOPING QUESTIONS AND PLANNING INVESTIGATIONS

Young children come to school with a lot of questions, but teachers sometimes respond in ways that are not always encouraging. For example, Thomas Edison's last day in school came when he asked, "How can water run uphill?" after he noticed that a river in Ohio did just that. Young Tom was very curious about his world, and he tried to learn all about it by asking a constant stream of questions. His first-grade teacher became so annoyed at Tom's incessant questioning that he angrily labeled Edison "slow witted." This infuriated Mrs. Edison to the point that she took Tom out of school and taught him at home. Like young Thomas Edison, children come to us with a strong desire to ask questions and often dream up some "winners." Here are a few questions and comments I fondly remember from my work with children:

- "Do caterpillars *know* they're going to turn into butterflies?"
- "Can a fish get killed by lightning?"
- "How much does the sky weigh?"
- "Are babies born with brains?"
- "Why do only cats have nine lives?"
- "Why are museums called *museums*?"

Wouldn't it be interesting to know what the children had in mind when they asked those questions? When you listen carefully and sensitively to their questions, you communicate to students that they are worthwhile individuals whose curiosities are valued. This is something your students need to know, for question asking is an indispensable part of the inquiry process. Good questions spur good inquiry. And don't be afraid to admit you don't know the answer when children ask questions: "I don't know the answer, but that's a very good question." Then find the answers together: "Let's look that up on the web." "Let's look that up in the library." "Do we know anyone who might have the answer to that?" If we want to encourage children's natural curiosity, we must model the joy of inquiry by wondering, being curious, posing questions, and exploring.

 Video Exploration 4.3

Asking Compelling and Supporting Questions As students accumulate spontaneous inquiry experiences, their curiosities will begin to inspire the kinds of questions that often lead to deeper subject matter investigations. Herein lies one of the most sensitive decisions for Dimension 1. Some take the position that if teachers propose the question, students have little or no personal stake in the investigation; therefore, they are not taking part in "real" inquiry. The opposing argument is that, because of today's passionate attention to standards testing, inquiry topics must be selected by teachers so that they fit into their district's standards and curriculum structure. In planned inquiry, it is hard to tell when either source is most powerful, but an interesting parallel can be drawn between students' earliest attempts at planned inquiry and the responsibilities assigned to professional social scientists when they take a new job. Many report that their first inquiry questions had been assigned to them by supervisors or by more advanced coworkers. Their job was to assemble and assess information for that question in a competent way until they demonstrated an ability to design and carry out their own inquiry investigations. Might we consider teacher-sparked questions, then, as a similar approach to introducing planned inquiry in your social studies classroom?

While using the Inquiry Arc, you will rarely saunter into the classroom, ask your students what they want to learn that day, and go on from there. What is to be learned must fit into your social studies curriculum framework—its goals, objectives, and standards. For that reason, you will find it necessary to search your school district's social studies standards to determine whether a compelling question can be answered with the targeted content of your grade level social studies program. Suppose, for example, that your students are fascinated by a question such as, "Should immigration be regulated?" but the related content does not match what is specified in your school's social studies standards. You may be forced to set it aside and select a question that is more compatible with your standards. The end result can be problematic, especially if the process is so transparent that students perceive it as a type of bait-and-switch maneuver. Bait-and-switch advertising is a type of fraudulent business practice that is a violation of consumer laws; the maneuver can be equally deceitful when teachers "bait" students with an apparent interest in their questions but, when it comes to "crunch time," require them to "switch" to the teacher's preference. To stave off such a damaging predicament in your social studies classroom, help your students select good compelling questions by combining assistive modeling with skillful questioning and discussion strategies. Grant (2013) advises: "This process is an artful balancing act; teachers must preload some disciplinary content when developing questions with their students. At the same time, teachers must provide students with enough content to propel their inquiries without quashing their curiosity or, worse yet, doing their work for them" (p. 322).

What specifically can you do to help students reconcile the gap between what the district standards say that they must learn and what they really want to learn? A few of my favorite ways to prompt student questions is to show them an intriguing picture or photo and ask your students to write their own questions about it. Another is to have them react to a mind-challenging or discrepant event (as in the chapter-opening scenario). If your classroom is wired for the Internet, there are few other "hooks" more impressive than computer-aided anecdotes or stories. Reading something from a newspaper or communicating a real-world problem that your students find relevant usually works very well. Food is always a good instigator of questions, as are hands-on items or artifacts. Each option will help kick-start thinking about a topic, spur students to take "psychological ownership" of the question, and arouse them to explore possible answers with their peers.

What about the place of teacher-initiated compelling questions . . . those times when it is more appropriate that you light the way for your students with a compelling question that grabs their attention and helps them focus on the topic at hand? First, it should be obvious to all but the uninitiated that a feeble statement such as, "Today we're going to learn about . . . " will not work. What does work in getting inquiry off to an effective start is to ask the right compelling questions and then go to work facilitating student discoveries. Ignite your students' curiosities and inspire them to learn more about the topic with compelling questions designed to initiate student inquiry (NCSS, 2013):

- *Most importantly, the question should be something the children are sincerely interested in.* Tackling good questions about issues of interest is the heart of effective lifelong thinking and learning. Students will develop interest if they can connect themselves to the question; they must be convinced that the question is worth thinking about. A proper question must be clear, understandable, and meaningful, and it must involve a high degree of mystery. In addition, the question must lie within the students' zones of proximal development (ZPDs)—offering just the right amount of intrigue to challenge previously established ideas but not so much that it is either too easy or too difficult to understand. If the question is too difficult, students will be intimidated by it; they will have too little or no background knowledge to help them make sense of it. By contrast, if it can be easily unraveled with information the students already have, it is obviously not a challenge, and the students will quickly discard it.

- *The question should hold a high degree of mystery and intrigue.* Children find it difficult to attach themselves to anything they care little about. I clearly recall one youngster's reaction to a teacher who passed out a list of 12 topics related to the Civil War and directed the students to select one for a written research report (and called this an inquiry lesson). The student's comment regarding the assignment was quite memorable and insightful: "Social studies can be so boring when the teacher makes you research stuff you don't even care about!"

 Some teachers have found it helpful to select an appropriate goal/objective/standard and rewrite it as a compelling question. For example, suppose a social studies goal/objective/standard for your social studies program reads: "The students shall understand that major ideas and events from the past have shaped the United States into what it is today." You can turn that statement into an effective compelling question: "What major ideas and events from the past have shaped the United States into what it is today?"

- *Compelling and supporting questions must be used in combination.* Compelling questions are broad questions that shape the direction of the investigation; they are not convergent questions intended to acquire a simple fact, such as, "Who designed the first American flag?" A good *compelling question* has no simple "correct" answer. It is considered divergent because it encourages a number of alternative answers and requires students to take risks in their thinking without the fear of being "wrong." A sample compelling question is, "If America were to redesign the American flag, what would it look like?" The question is *multidimensional, intriguing,* and *intellectually honest.* That is, it raises additional questions and challenges learners to explore the disciplines for answers. *Supporting questions* reinforce and deepen compelling questions; they help students answer the compelling question by contributing specific knowledge and insight. For example, the compelling question, "If America were to redesign the American flag, what would it look like?" could pull the students in a number of directions if it is not more expressly defined. However, supporting questions serve to provide focus and establish a direction for the subsequent inquiry investigation: "How many different American flags have there been?" "How has the flag changed over the years?" "What factors caused those changes to happen?" "What does the current American flag represent?" and "What current factors warrant a change?"

● ***The students will develop their own questions, when appropriate and necessary.*** Although most classroom questions tend to come from a teacher, students must learn how to generate their own compelling questions, refine them, and respond to them. The ability to learn constructively is based on the ability to ask and respond to important questions. Elementary school students will experience great difficulty constructing compelling and supporting questions, so they will require a great amount of assistance in constructing original versions. (How can we expect students to come up with compelling questions when they don't know what compelling questions are?) That is why compelling and supporting questions are recommended for planned, formal inquiry episodes and not considered appropriate for spontaneous inquiry.

Reflection on Learning

You may simply scribble rough notes or jot down something more polished and complete. The point is to simply start recording your ideas spontaneously and candidly.

The C3 Framework's Inquiry Arc (NCSS, 2013) is based on the idea that inquiry must be initiated by a compelling question that requires the use of higher-order thinking skills. Do we take this to mean that a student's deep inner drive to find answers to an intriguing, engaging factual question such as, "Who *really* invented the lightbulb?" is so low level that the process of resolving it cannot be considered inquiry? Should there be a hierarchy of questions considered worthy as inquiry starters, or must we limit all inquiry to compelling questions such as, "How has the invention of the lightbulb changed the world?"

You have a critical role in creating the spirit of exploration students need to become engaged in a compelling question. One of the most effective ways to do this is to serve as a worthwhile model, thinking aloud about fascinating things and exhibiting the behaviors you would like your students to use. You frequently ask questions: "What's going on here?" "What do we need to know more about?" You encourage students to ask questions, too. Demonstrate that you are open to new ideas and experiences. Students welcome teachers reaching out for the different and unusual—teachers looking at life with passion. You must stop, look, and listen; feel, taste, and smell. Ask, "What is it? Where does it come from? What is it for?" Perform your own classroom inquiries and, through your passion for new discoveries, you will offer the greatest source of encouragement to your students. You must do your best to nurture curiosity for life; one of the best ways to do this is to respond to the world with a probing, wondering mind and regularly propose, "What do you think? Let's find out! What should we try?" Discovering something new is usually accompanied by a strong feeling of pleasure and satisfaction; this is what drives people to explore and investigate—it feels good!

Now that you have stirred your students' curiosity and created a passion for exploration, the actual investigation can now effectively take over.

Planning Investigations   Once students have accepted the question as interesting and worthwhile, they are ready for the next big step—the investigation. They begin their quest to answer compelling and supporting questions by proposing a tentative explanation—a *hypothesis*. A concern with proposing a hypothesis is that a true *hypothesis* has a very precise and intricate meaning when it is used as part of the scientific method. Putting forward a true hypothesis would be fine for a high school or college statistics course, but constructing a true scientific hypotheses is beyond the ability of elementary school students. Instead, consider an elementary school hypothesis to simply be "an educated guess" or a "prediction." You may often hear the terms *prediction* and *hypothesis* used interchangeably. That is because predictions, like hypotheses, are proposed answers to the research question that are based on a pattern of past experience and prior knowledge (but less scientific).

Did you ever go to a movie and just simply know how it would end? If you did, you made a hypothesis, or prediction. How did you do that? You used clues from past experiences and prior knowledge to figure out what was going to happen. Students regularly make predictions based on prior experience or on information they already have. In a short time, they will be able to activate their prior knowledge and past experiences to come up with predictions for inquiry questions, too. Students should not make wild guesses; hypotheses must be supported by sound reasoning.

You can help your students suggest a hypothesis by asking questions such as these: "What do you already know about this situation?" "What have you already learned that we might be able to use now?" "How could this information help us come up with a preliminary answer to our problem?" "What ideas can you suggest as a solution based on what we've just discussed?" The purpose of these questions is to help students attach information they already know to the problem.

Proposing hypotheses involves risk for students, so be especially careful to attach importance to each individual's input. It is easy for teachers to acknowledge hypotheses they might agree with or those that they think might be "sensible." But responding to incomplete or unusual suggestions is not quite as easy. Remember that students' ideas are nothing more than predictions, so dignify all responses by offering comments and/or questions such as these:

- "I heard you say . . ."
- "What I believe you are telling me is . . ."
- "That is a very interesting idea. I never thought of it that way."
- "You have an intriguing idea, but I'm a bit confused. Could you enlarge on it a bit?"
- "What if I told you (add some information)? How would that change your prediction?"
- "What clues did you use to make your prediction?"

After your students have addressed the compelling question and made their predictions, you are in business. Your eager learners will be ready to move on with a spirited, "I can't wait to find out . . . !" The portion of the Inquiry Arc that comes between the question and the answer requires consideration of informational sources available for *researching* an answer.

Survey research helps students to develop their own questions and to seek answers for those questions.

Miguel DomÃnguez MuÃ±oz/Pearson Education Ltd

Informational sources come in many forms, including all those discussed in Chapters 5–13. One resource category can be thought of as *quantitative research*, which uses *measurable data*—that is, numbers. Quantitative research tools include polls and surveys—using either questionnaires or interviews. Quantitative results are most often represented as tables, graphs, and charts. A second source for uncovering answers to compelling and supporting questions is called *qualitative research*, a technique that involves *verbal data*—that is, words. Verbal resources may include a variety of print texts, electronic text, direct observations, field notes, pictures, and other language or literacy resources. If a compelling question is designed to find out something through numerical evidence ("How many fifth graders think the tropical rain forest is important to our everyday lives?"), then you should make use of quantitative sources, such as a survey. However, if you wish to explain why a particular event happened ("What caused the extinction of the dodo bird?"), to report why a certain phenomenon exists ("What is homelessness really like?"), or to describe a societal condition ("Does the American government really care about climate change?"), then you should make use of various qualitative sources.

DIMENSION 2: APPLYING DISCIPLINARY CONCEPTS AND TOOLS

Disciplinary literacy has quickly and convincingly risen to prominence in all influential 21st-century professional and state standards. As a result, the C3 Framework and its Inquiry Arc are built on the strengths of the *Common Core State Standards* (2010) to establish the context for teaching literacy in social studies. Because of that partnership, the C3 Framework is built on two broad literacy categories. First, the anchor standards of CCSS incorporate a wide range of English language *literacy standards* (reading, writing, speaking, and listening) that are uniquely supportive of social studies inquiry. For example, the Reading Standards include the importance of reading informational text; the Writing Standards include expectations for conveying ideas and information through written text; and the Speaking and Listening Standards draw attention to skills students need to present their ideas clearly and effectively in speech and to analyze and evaluate information presented verbally. Second, the C3 Framework details *disciplinary literacies*—skills that are needed for inquiry, such as questioning, evaluating evidence, and communicating conclusions. Disciplinary literacies also are grounded in the ability to organize and make sense of academic concepts.

Applying Disciplinary Concepts   Throughout Dimension 2 you will be challenged to integrate concepts and tools from the following four social sciences to deepen your students' inquiry investigations: civics, economics, geography, and history. (The C3 Framework includes companion documents for anthropology and sociology as appendices.) Each of the four social science disciplines was selected for its ability to provide students with a crystal clear lens to facilitate and influence their perception, comprehension, and evaluation of the content related to their compelling question. Sometimes a compelling question may demand that they filter content through a single lens; for example, civics is the obvious social science to address the question, "Is anyone ever justified in breaking the law?" Additional single-discipline samples are shown in Figure 4.4. At other times, compelling questions will require students to integrate content from multiple disciplines. For example, the question "How did European exploration and colonization affect the rest of the world?" demands the implementation of economic, geographical, historical, and political lenses.

Although Dimension 2 does not spell out specific disciplinary content, it does lay out an array of "conceptual umbrellas" (big sets of ideas) that cover specific content associated with the four social sciences. A "conceptual umbrella" for fifth-grade geography, for example, reads that, by the end of Grade 5, students should be able to "Explain how cultural and environmental characteristics affect the distribution and movement of people, goods, and ideas" (NCSS, 2013, p. 43). The Inquiry Arc developers outline conceptual umbrellas rather than more highly detailed content because there are so many differences among states as to what specific content is taught and when. For example, the standard, "Identify the early civilizations that developed into empires in Central and South America" may indicate exactly what you are expected to teach and when your students are expected to learn it in your school district, but it may not be

FIGURE 4.4   The Four Core Disciplines within Social Studies

CIVICS: How governments address the rights, duties, and responsibilities of citizens

• What would happen if there were no governments?
• Should the majority always rule?

ECONOMICS: Describes and analyzes choices about the way goods and services are produced, distributed, and consumed

• Why do people work? Should everyone in our society be expected to work?
• Does it really help when richer nations give poorer nations money each year?

GEOGRAPHY: The study of the Earth's surface features and of their relationships to each other and to people

• How has Earth been transformed by human actions?
• What role has geography played in the evolution of human beings?

HISTORY: Analyzing change and continuity over time

• How am I connected to the past? the future?
• What event most influenced the course of history in the United States?

found in the standards of a neighboring state. You will find the specific disciplinary content required for Dimension 2 in your school district's standards for social studies (often based on the *Common Core State Standards in English Language Arts and Literacy* [2010]). *The National Curriculum Standards for Social Studies: A Framework for Teaching, Learning, and Assessment* (NCSS, 2010), is another influential professional guide that states have used to identify content standards. Its "Snapshots of Practice" offers specific ideas to help you envision what the standards-based approach looks like in elementary school classrooms.

Applying Disciplinary Tools   You have approached Dimension 2 with a compelling question in hand and an idea of the investigative tools your students plan to employ. Your students will now be ready to begin their investigation by activating the sources of information as selected in Dimension 1: historical and contemporary documents, data from direct observation, print texts, computers and other technology, guest speakers, the arts, and so on. Although both quantitative and qualitative sources hold important places in planned inquiry, qualitative research has been receiving the greatest attention in today's standards-focused classrooms. The C3 Framework (NCSS, 2013) connects questioning and information gathering by emphasizing " . . . questioning as a mechanism for supporting reading and as a tool to prompt research" (p. 27). Such research is typically conducted in one of four major ways: *library research, observational research, survey research,* or *historical research.*

Library research, perhaps the most common source of information for inquiry-based questions, involves materials such as encyclopedias, informational books, computers, magazines, newspapers, pamphlets, almanacs, catalogs, dictionaries, travel brochures, atlases, guides and timetables, posters, films, videos, photographs, and even the phone book. Library research also embraces Internet research, especially the World Wide Web. The Internet very quickly provides information on almost every topic a child might study. Surfing through the wealth of educational sites on the web is fun and can be instructive, as students follow links from page to page, hoping to uncover useful information. But surfing can also be overwhelming when young children seek out focused information. Therefore, it would be wise to encourage appropriate use of "child-specific" search engines, such as *Ask Kids,* which allows students to search for information by asking broad questions. Or you might furnish reference links on the Internet start page to get the young researchers moving in the right direction. School librarians know the web well, and a librarian can help find excellent results.

Observational research can include all the experiences through which students look at, handle, participate in, or try out genuine objects or events. For example, while investigating significant American Indian cultural traditions, one class visited a display of authentic arrowheads, beaded items, pottery, stone artifacts, and other items from the past. Likewise, an outing to the commuter train station to observe the "crunch" of rush hour is considered observational research, as is a field trip to the water-powered grist mill where grain was ground to the customer's order or a classroom visit by a Civil War reenactor.

Survey research is one of the most satisfying investigation approaches for elementary school students as it actively engages students in uncovering their own data. This area of student research incorporates two major fact-finding strategies that involve asking questions of a target population: paper-and-pencil *questionnaires* and in-depth one-on-one *interviews*. Questionnaires are most commonly administered to a large group when there is a need for a quick rating or ranking of opinions or experiences. They present a predetermined set of questions that provide information from responders. Face-to-face interviews are more personal than questionnaires as the interviewer interacts directly with the respondent and has the opportunity to explore responses more deeply with follow-up questions.

Survey questions can take either of two forms: *structured* (fixed-choice) and *unstructured* (open-ended). Structured questions are most often used for questionnaires while unstructured questions are more suitable for interviews. Structured questions lock responders into making a choice from a series of alternatives as shown in the example below:

Which school subject do you enjoy most?
- Math
- Reading and language arts
- Social studies
- Science

Unstructured questions do not use predetermined response choices from which to select, but allow responders to express their ideas freely and openly in answer to a question. Because their responses are not limited, responders tend to provide richer, deeper responses. Here is an example:

What do you enjoy most about social studies?

When children delve into conditions of "long ago," they must gather and evaluate relevant traces of the past. *Historical research* is the process of searching for answers to questions about the past by examining and interpreting evidence such as artifacts, diaries, newspapers, pictures, letters, music, oral history, advertisements, or speeches. The student's job is to find evidence, analyze it, and use it to create an explanation of past events. Disappointingly, however, student explanations often end up as pointless outlines of dates, names, and events. Social studies teachers expect more than this; they want their students to carry out research in such a way that historical facts come to life and gain personal meaning through the construction of new ideas. Students should think about using historical research when they have these kinds of questions for inquiry:

- "What happened?"
- "When did it happen?"
- "Why did it happen?"
- "To whom did it happen?"
- "What did it mean to the people at that time?"
- "What does it mean to people today?"
- "What do historians have to say about what happened?"

With elementary school students, research is mostly a guided process—for example, let's turn to our *compelling question*, "If America were to redesign the American flag, what would it look like?" You can help students learn how to dig more deeply into the compelling question by asking questions that call for more precise information; these are called *supporting questions*. Their supporting questions will provide clearer focus and establish a direction for research: "How many different American flags have there been?" "How has the flag changed over the years?" "What factors caused those changes to happen?" "What does the current American flag represent?" and "What current factors warrant a change?" You may want to facilitate the research process by establishing collaborative work groups. For example, the supporting question, "How many different American flags have there been?" may be selected by a collaborative group with individual students exploring notable flags such as Don't Tread on Me, the Grand Union Flag, the "Betsy Ross" flag, and our current flag. This way, the students can support each other during their research by sharing sources and placing their information in a historical context. It is important to consistently reinforce successful research efforts by highlighting small and large achievements along the way. As an example, one teacher designed a small bulletin board space that highlighted a research "Discovery of the Day"—a fascinating piece of information or impressive source of data that significantly influenced individual or group research objectives.

As your students uncover and collect their information, they will find it helpful to organize and make sense of it, most typically with charts or graphs: "What does this information mean as it relates to the hypothesis, or prediction?" Hoffman (1992) suggests a helpful aid to guide and organize research during this dimension of the Inquiry Arc—an *Information Chart* or *I-Chart*. I-Charts are particularly helpful during the first few attempts at using the Inquiry Arc, especially when you model the process for the students. Hoffman (1992) suggests that the I-Chart should be constructed from a long sheet of butcher paper that can be attached to a wall of the classroom so all can see. (As students become more familiar with the strategy, individual-size I-Charts can be supplied for independent use.) An I-Chart should reveal the compelling question, supporting questions, and research sources, including trade books, textbooks, journal articles, realia, encyclopedias, Internet searches, and even real people who shared knowledge about the compelling question (see Figure 4.5).

The first step is to question students about what they already know about the compelling and the supporting questions. Record each contribution on the I-Chart even if it seems off-base or inaccurate. The next step, researching and recording, provides the opportunity to scrutinize the selected informational sources and assess the applicability of the information. This process can extend over several days. Any useful information should be recorded in the appropriate sections. The final phase of the I-Chart strategy begins with summarizing. Students should produce a short summary for each of the questions by blending the information found in the individual sections and transcribe the summary onto the chart. The summaries are also compared to the prior knowledge listed for each question. The students should also identify any questions that were left unanswered and then initiate individual or small-group research to learn more about their uncertainties. The last step in this strategy, and the focus of the next dimension of the Inquiry Arc, is to engage the students in reporting on what they have learned—a culminating activity where findings of the research are purposefully presented in a meaningful, real-world context.

DIMENSION 3: EVALUATING SOURCES AND USING EVIDENCE

This stage of the inquiry process is a time for reflection—looking back at the question, revisiting the predictions or hypotheses, summarizing the data, and drawing conclusions: "Has a solution, a conclusion, or an answer been found?" "Have new questions come to light?" This is the point at which students make a final statement that summarizes the investigation; it is called the *claim* or *conclusion*. To fulfill the responsibilities of Dimension 3, students must apply literacy skills such as selecting the most accurate, relevant, or important information; organizing their ideas; making inferences; and forming reasoned claims or conclusions. Students cannot expect to extract suitable

FIGURE 4.5   An I-Chart

COMPELLING QUESTION: If America were to redesign the American flag, what would it look like?				
	How many different American flags have there been?	How has the flag changed over the years?	What factors caused the changes?	What does the current flag represent?	What current cultural/social factors warrant a change?
WHAT I (WE) KNOW				
SOURCE 1				
SOURCE 2				
SOURCE 3				
SUMMARY				

information for their compelling question from every resource they look at, so you will need to help them assess the content from several sources of information. This responsibility may be the most difficult for both teachers and students:

- Is the source applicable to the inquiry question?
- Who is the author? What are his or her qualifications?
- Is the source informational or does it express an opinion? Is it balanced?
- Is the source clear and understandable?
- Is the source recent and up to date?
- Does the source provide enough information to answer the compelling and supporting questions?
- Is any important information left out?
- Is the information supported by evidence?
- Can the information be verified or contradicted by another source?
- If electronic, does the source provide links to other sources?
- If a print text, does it contain a complete bibliography?

This is the portion of the Inquiry Arc where you most thoroughly integrate literacy skills instruction with social studies, thereby carrying out the intended partnership of the C3 Framework and the Common Core State Standards: *applying reading and writing for the purpose of acquiring and communicating new social studies content.* After your students have accessed and assessed several primary and secondary sources, you have reached the summit of the Inquiry Arc process—proposing an argument. The type of argument referred to here is not a dispute or disagreement, but an evidence-based, reasoned, logical justification for a proposed conclusion or claim. Elementary school students often have difficulty drawing valid conclusions or shaping evidence-based arguments, so they will require explicit instruction and modeling of the processes involved. As with all other forms of writing in your classroom, then, your students will need a good idea of what an argument looks like before they are asked to write one. Be sure to start out by showing them or modeling examples of a writer's conclusions or claims that are supported by sound evidence. You will want to demonstrate what goes on in your mind while forming a conclusion or making a claim about the compelling question, describe the information or other data that you used to support your conclusion/claim, and disclose any new questions that have sprung up as a result of coming up with your conclusion/claim. Some guiding questions that may be helpful in directing your students include: (1) What is my answer/ decision/opinion regarding the compelling question? (2) How can I defend my answer/decision/ opinion? (3) What new questions do I now have as a result of my research? Throughout the evolution of their written arguments, you will find it useful to provide plenty of scaffolding help through formal conferences and informal assistance, as well as to encourage students to thrash out their ideas with their peers through academic conversations. One good source of argumentative writing samples is Appendix C of the *Common Core State Standards* (National Governors Association, 2010). They will help you understand the key developmental characteristics of argumentative writing.

If you inform your students when you begin the Inquiry Arc that they will publicly present their final conclusions to their peers or others or other audiences heightens the significance they will place on their inquiry efforts and helps prolong motivation throughout the course of action. Now, after working both independently and collaboratively through the first three dimensions of the Inquiry Arc, students will be ready for the fourth, and final, dimension—*communicating and critiquing conclusions*.

DIMENSION 4: COMMUNICATING AND CRITIQUING CONCLUSIONS

When you offer your students the opportunity to share their claims/conclusions in an authentic forum, you send them a powerful message that their efforts and ideas are important enough to share with audiences outside the classroom doors. In the adult world, much of the reward gained from inquiry comes from having an impact on desired audiences; your professor, for example, experiences great pleasure after receiving approval from his or her peers while presenting information about research into a revolutionary new instructional approach, and social scientists appreciate the recognition they receive from others in their field after publishing a paper describing how a person's education level influences civic participation. Each of these individuals values and respects the attention given to their efforts and experiences an immeasurable amount of inner satisfaction for the accomplishments. Likewise, young learners take pleasure and pride in the recognition they receive after sharing the results of their research

The Internet has had a profound impact on social studies inquiry. Whether used daily or occasionally, the ways to integrate the web into your classroom are limited only by your imagination.

Monkey Business Images/Shutterstock

with an authentic audience. Sincere recognition helps legitimize what your students are thinking and learning. For the process to work to its fullest potential, however, students must not be ordered what to do, but given opportunities to select from various print and oral technologies, for example: Internet, social media, digital documentaries, exhibit, poster, essay or report, map, speech, display, letter, mock interview, feature article for class newspaper, political ad campaign, or performance.

As an example of how the four dimensions fit together, let us visit Tommy Page's fifth-grade classroom. As Mr. Page's students came back to their classroom after recess, he had begun playing a tape of the sounds of a rain forest. He asked the students to describe the environment where these sounds might be coming from. Then he asked, "What does the tropical rain forest look like in your mind?" As they shared their ideas, Mr. Page recorded what they already knew about the rain forest on chart paper. Using a wall map, Mr. Page helped the students locate the world's largest tropical rain forests. He then introduced the poetic book *Welcome to the Green House* by Jane Yolen (G.P. Putnam's Sons), in which the author explores the sights and sounds of exotic animals and other features of a tropical rain forest. Following the reading, Mr. Page led a group discussion of the new information presented in the book and helped the students compare it to their initial list. The students enjoyed the book and follow-up discussion; they appeared particularly interested in the richness of animal life in the rain forests. Because "the interdependence of animals and plants in an ecosystem" was an expectation in his district's science and geography standards, Mr. Page seized the opportunity to capitalize on the students' interest and introduce a question that the students would research through scientific inquiry. Mr. Page's sequence of instruction is outlined in Figure 4.6.

The students concluded that rain forests are very important to the world for many reasons, one of which is that the canopy structure of the rain forest provides an abundance of places for animals to live. The canopy offers sources of food, shelter, and hiding places, providing for interaction between different species.

Contrary to what some may believe, the Inquiry Arc is relevant even for early-grade children. Young children need to have a chance to ask questions, do investigations, and apply investigation skills, too. The natural events of a classroom, happenings in the children's own lives, and events in children's books appear to be the richest sources of compelling questions to inspire inquiry. Consider this example from Doris Howard's first-grade classroom:

Today, Mrs. Howard read The Little Red Hen *by Paul Galdone (Seabury Press) to her eager group of first graders. She knew that the book satisfied several instructional purposes, not the least of which was critical thinking. Therefore, as she finished reading, Mrs. Howard encouraged the class to think about the story's ending and the hen's decision not to share her bread with the animals refusing to help her: "May the animals who refused to help have had good reasons?" The compelling question was: "Did the Little Red Hen do the right thing?" The more they thought about it, the more the students questioned whether the Little Red Hen did the right thing. The students were animated in their discussion of the hen's decision and suggested other actions she could have taken. Eventually, Mrs. Howard displayed a large wall chart divided into three columns: (1) each child's name, (2) a "YES" column, and (3) a "NO" column. Mrs. Howard explained the chart to her students and asked them to make predictions about whether there would be more "yes" or more "no" votes to the compelling question, "Did the Little Red Hen do the right thing?" The students came to the chart one by one to register their votes (see Figure 4.7). Afterward, their results were published on their class website.*

Because there is no consensus in the educational literature about a single best approach to social studies inquiry, teachers are often unsure about the nature of inquiry-based instruction. Some think that what they are doing is not inquiry unless they allow their students to investigate their own questions through self-selected research strategies. At the other extreme are teachers who believe that inquiry happens only when they pose questions to their students and guide them toward seeking answers using the scientific method. Given these two extremes, it is not surprising that frustrations about using inquiry-based instruction abound. However, the

FIGURE 4.6   Using the Inquiry Arc

Step	Description	Example
Observe and question	Students observe something that they want to know more about and ask a question. Or the teacher may ask a question.	After listening to *Welcome to the Green House*, the children were intrigued that rain forests were tremendously rich in animal life. They were assigned to small teams to research this compelling question: "How do the plant and animal relationships within a tropical forest affect the forest community?"
Form a prediction or hypothesis	A prediction or hypothesis is a statement of what the students think will happen, or what the result will be. The hypothesis must be observable and testable, but the prediction can be a general statement.	The students agreed that, "Because of what we read in the book, we predict that the reason for the great number and variety of animals in the rain forest is the steady warmth, constant supply of water, and wide variety of food for the animals."
Collect and analyze data	An important part of the scientific method is collecting data. Students must be able to gather evidence from reliable resources to construct explanations. After the data are collected, they are analyzed. This step often involves organizing data in charts and graphing the information.	In this investigation, students considered a number of possibilities, including library and Internet resources. They decided on a combination of both sources. The students found that rain forests are tremendously rich in animal life. They classified the animals according to where they lived in the different strata of the rain forest: eagles, monkeys, bats, birds, and butterflies in the emergent layer; insects, arachnids, many birds (like the toucan and the macaw), mammals (like the howler monkey and orangutan), reptiles (like snakes and lizards) in the canopy; a large concentration of insects (like beetles and bees), arachnids (spiders), snakes, lizards, and small mammals (like the kinkajou) on and in tree bark in the understory; and insects and arachnids (like tarantulas), the largest animals in the rain forest (gorillas, anteaters, wild boars, tapirs, jaguars, and people), and decomposers like termites, earthworms, and fungi on the forest floor.
Make claims/ Draw conclusions	After they assessed and analyzed the data, the students checked to see if the results supported their prediction. They also considered a way to share their results with others.	To create schoolwide awareness of the wonders of the rain forest, each group created a mural on which they painted or drew the different layers of the rainforest and then added small cutouts of the animals living in the different layers. Each group prepared a written script about its mural. The script included one or more sentences about each animal (for example, "Soaring high above the emergent layer, 200 feet above the forest floor, you see animal number one. It is a harpy eagle, one of the world's largest and most powerful eagles."). Each group recorded its script on cassette tape, taking turns reading a portion of the script. They placed a tape recorder near each mounted mural and posted signs inviting students and teachers to visit the talking mural display.

FIGURE 4.7 *Little Red Hen* Graph

DID THE LITTLE RED HEN DO THE RIGHT THING?

NAME	YES	NO
Connie	X	
Robert		X
MarthA		X
Jed		X
DarriN	X	
Anita	X	
Arriram	X	

Reflection on Learning

You may simply scribble rough notes or jot down something more polished and complete. The point is to simply start recording your ideas spontaneously and candidly.

In carrying out the Inquiry Arc, a teacher has two major options: (1) the students may investigate a teacher-presented question and receive explicit step-by-step guidelines at each stage of the investigation leading to a predetermined content outcome, or (2) teachers may define the content framework in which the inquiry will take place but allow the students to select the inquiry question; the investigative results are unknown in advance. What do you suppose are the advantages and disadvantages of both options? Which most appeals to you at this stage of your professional development?

Inquiry Arc should now help you understand the basic features of inquiry as a multifaceted process, its flexibility in the classroom, how willing students are to take part in it, and its essential part in your teaching repertoire.

Despite the many advantages of inquiry, social studies teachers must be careful not use inquiry as the only tool to meet every instructional goal; social studies demands the use of varied techniques and strategies. Any single instructional method, regardless of its effectiveness, eventually becomes tiresome and monotonous if it is used exclusively.

 Video Exploration 4.4

 CHECK YOUR UNDERSTANDING 4.3 **Click here** to check your understanding of this section of the chapter.

Creative Problem Solving (CPS)

We once saw a tyrannosaurus.

And we feared he'd end our lives faurus.

But, "Look!" said my friend,

"He's rubber, can bend!"

Then we realized we were in Toysaurus. *

My son Jeff wrote this limerick in elementary school, as part of an integrated thematic unit on dinosaurs. His teacher sent the poem home along with a note telling us that she felt the limerick was remarkably creative. Of course, Jeff's "impartial" parents thought likewise and displayed it proudly on the refrigerator door. What do you think of Jeff's limerick? Would you say it is creative? If so, what makes it creative? If not, you've just failed this course (only kidding)!

Creative Thinking

What do we mean by *creativity*? As with love or intelligence, not even the wisest person among us can truly grasp or explain the full meaning of this complex concept. Creativity comes to all of us in various ways; it is a subjective experience that is expressed differently by each person. Despite this ambiguity, experts have highlighted various aspects and dimensions of creativity, and there appear to be some common threads in their theories. For example, most definitions of creativity include two major components:

- *Novel or original behavior:* Behavior that has not been learned from anyone else; it is fresh, new, and unique.
- *An appropriate and productive result:* A socially useful or worthwhile product or an effective solution to a problem.

* Reprinted by permission of Jeffrey G. Maxim.

Does Jeff's poem reflect these two components? Is it fresh and original, or did he get the idea from somewhere else? Is it an appropriate response to the teacher's assignment to write a limerick about the dinosaurs they had been studying?

What enables some children to create in such fascinating ways, while others struggle to move beyond the ordinary? Although a certain degree of intelligence is helpful, something more is required. In Jeff's case, that "something more" was the ability to "play" with ideas—to see things in a new way. Identifying what that "something more" might be has been debated over the years, but the consensus seems to be that an individual's creativity is influenced by the intermingling of four intellectual traits:

- *Fluency.* Fluency is the ability to produce a large number of ideas. A child who responds to the question, "What things are crops?" with "Wheat, corn, beans, peas, and tomatoes" is more fluent than a child who responds with "Wheat and corn."

- *Flexibility.* Flexibility is the ability to produce a number of different categories of responses. A child who responds to the question, "What things are crops?" with "Wheat, tomatoes, apples, peanuts, and tobacco" is a more flexible thinker than a child who responds "Wheat, rye, oats, and barley" (which are all grains).

- *Originality.* Originality is the ability to produce unusual or clever responses. A child who responds to the question, "What can you do with an empty cereal box?" with "Make a snowshoe out of it" is more original than a child who says "Store things in it." Originality is usually determined statistically; the response is considered original if it is offered by fewer than 10% of those responding.

- *Elaboration.* Elaboration is the ability to expand on a simple idea to make it richer. A child who responds to a teacher's request to draw a picture of the geographical area where the Sioux lived with a simple landscape drawing shows less elaboration than a child who includes buffalo, tepees, and Sioux farmers working in the fields.

Creative individuals also tend to display four unique emotional characteristics:

- *Risk taking.* Risk takers have the courage to take wild guesses and expose themselves to criticism or failure. They are strong willed and eager to defend their ideas. They have the spirit to try new things, fail, and get up to try again.

- *Complexity.* Students who demonstrate complexity enjoy delving into intricate problems and bringing order from chaos. They like to learn new things, are willing to examine the unusual, and are highly inquisitive. They tackle tasks and problems in a well-organized, goal-directed, and efficient manner.

- *Curiosity.* A curious child is inquisitive and full of wonder, always asking questions and seeking answers. A curious child has the drive to seek out mysteries and the creativity to solve them.

- *Imagination.* An imaginative child dreams, often straddling the fine line between fantasy and reality. Imaginative children explore in ways the logical mind finds difficult to understand.

Creativity helps children grow into independent and productive citizens of our society. To help students strengthen their creative thinking abilities, we must know about and apply the kinds of classroom practices that are supportive of creativity. The remainder of this chapter addresses that responsibility, for encouraging creativity in children demands a great deal of creativity from their teachers.

The Creative Problem-Solving Process

Perhaps the most traditional and most favored strategy to support creative thinking in social studies classrooms is the *creative problem-solving (CPS)* model developed by Alex Osborn (1963) and Sidney J. Parnes (1981). To understand CPS, it would be instructive to contrast it with what you have learned about inquiry. Remember that the goal of inquiry is to systematically search for solutions to compelling questions. Some students do this well; they sort out the clues, pull them together, look for logical patterns, and deliberately arrive at valid conclusions. Others, however, attack problems in quite different ways. This variation of a well-known story helps illustrate the difference between the two:

> *An engineering major and an elementary education major were hiking in the woods when they came across a grizzly bear. Both were terrified and quickly began to search for an escape route, each in his or her own way.*
>
> *The engineering major took out his smartphone and quickly computed the mathematical differential between his speed and the bear's. His face turned ashen as he stared at the results.*
>
> *The elementary education major simply took off her hiking boots, opened her backpack, slipped on a pair of jogging shoes, and took off.*
>
> *"Boy, you are STUPID," the engineering major yelled to the elementary education major as she sprinted down the trail. "My calculations show you can't outrun a grizzly bear!"*
>
> *"I don't have to," the elementary education major shouted back. "I only have to outrun YOU!"*

This story demonstrates how two people can respond very differently to the same problem. The two response categories in this example are generally referred to as *systematic* (the engineering major who relied on facts and logical thought) and *intuitive* (the elementary education major who relied on gut feelings and intuition). Original, intuitive solutions to problems come from an ability to shift directions in thought—to move beyond the obvious to the subtle. Some would say that the elementary education major's solution was more creative than the engineering major's. Do you agree? What made it so? Regardless of whether you are trying to figure out how to study for an exam when your friends want you to go to a movie or where to get money for next year's tuition hike, you are likely to rely on either logical inquiry or creative problem-solving strategies.

Traditionally, most schoolwork has called for systematic rather than intuitive thinking, and we find that schools tend to overemphasize logic-related skills at the expense of intuitive-related skills, giving our children an apparently "lopsided" education. Teaching for creativity, however, does not minimize the importance of a *solid background of information*; creativity in social studies is more likely to occur when students have mastered the content. Creative ideas do not spring forth in a vacuum. Knowledge is one component of creative thinking, but it is not sufficient by itself; there is that "something extra" that contributes to a creative personality.

The CPS model is a designed plan for creative thinking—a process for solving problems when you want to go beyond conventional thinking and arrive at novel and useful solutions. The original CPS model has six steps. That model works well with high school students and adults, but I prefer a simplified four-step model for elementary school students:

- *Problem finding (clarify the mess):* What is the problem that needs to be focused on? What do you want to accomplish?
- *Idea finding (brainstorm solutions):* What are all the possibilities for solving the problem?
- *Solution finding (select and strengthen solutions):* What idea will work best?
- *Acceptance finding (plan for action):* How will the solution be implemented?

PROBLEM FINDING (THE MESS)

The problem definition/redefinition stage is the most important step of the CPS process. Establishing a clear question or problem provides a focus that facilitates the investigation of potential solutions. A question such as, "How many uses can you think of for an automobile tire other than for moving a car?" presents a situation that forces students to generate a variety and quantity of ideas rather than "converge" on a single correct response.

IDEA FINDING

This is the step where divergent, creative thinking is most important. It begins with students brainstorming dozens of possible remedies for the problem. *Brainstorming* works best when groups are small and manageable (e.g., four to six students) and when you allocate sufficient time (e.g., 15–20 minutes). The problem, or mess, should be worded clearly and concisely: "In what ways might our modern society become 'more civilized'?" The students then take a few moments to think silently about the mess and, once the brainstorming starts, propose their ideas freely and openly while a recorder jots them down. The guidelines for brainstorming are:

- *Generate a large number of ideas.* The goal of brainstorming is quantity because producing a large number of ideas results in a better chance of coming up with a top-notch idea. It helps when children experience "brain drain," or getting all the common responses out of the way before the really creative ideas emerge. Each idea should be written down on a large sheet of paper or a whiteboard by a group recorder; a simple list is fine, but a web or map format works well, too. One teacher referred to this phase of brainstorming as "popcorn thinking" and encouraged her students to "just keep the ideas popping out of your head." Think about quantity as being much more important than quality during this phase; students will examine their responses later and determine which ideas are worth further exploration.

- *No criticism.* Criticism has no place during this stage of the brainstorming process; it inhibits the free flow of thought. All types of verbal and nonverbal feedback (eye rolling, making faces, groaning, and cynical smiles) must be avoided. Accept every idea that is offered, no matter how outlandish or bizarre it may appear to be at first; everyone must be assured that their ideas are valued and respected. I once heard it said that creativity could be compared to a flower; encouragement makes it bloom while discouragement nips it in the bud.

- *Encourage "hitchhiking."* The children should feel free to latch on to and improve other students' ideas or to use other ideas as a base from which to dream up their own. Combining ideas often results in one idea that is more novel and useful than either idea by itself.

- *Encourage freewheeling.* The energy of elementary school brainstorming sessions tends to peak and wane. Sometimes, during slow periods, students may exert only nominal effort before announcing, "We're done; we just can't think of anything else." When the momentum begins to plateau or diminish like this, it is tempting to move on to something else. However, children should display the courage to stay in the battle beyond this point of "idea exhaustion." The most original ideas seem to pop out after students think they don't have anything left. I like to challenge students to "give me three more ideas" after they say they cannot think of anything more. Rather than always equating silence with diminished interest, noninvolvement, or a lack of production, I have found that children often do their deepest thinking about or incubating of ideas during periods of silence. If undisturbed, some of the best ideas surface after a period of silence.

As effective as brainstorming can be during this stage of CPS, it is important to know there are other useful techniques that stimulate creative idea finding. Here are just a few:

- *Mind mapping.* This webbing technique can be very useful in helping children organize their thoughts and discover new relationships. Just write the brainstorming topic in the center circle and then jot down brainstormed words or phrases in the outer smaller circles surrounding the central circle. Any diagram, such as those shared in Chapter 3, used to visually organize ideas generated while brainstorming complex problems can be applied here.

● *SCAMPER.* This is a strategy in the form of a checklist that helps students think of changes they can make to an existing product to create a new one. Bob Eberle (1997) developed SCAMPER, which stands for:

Substitute: "Can I replace something or someone with something or someone else?"

Combine: "What parts or features can be put together to achieve a significantly different product or process?"

Adapt: "What else is already out there that I could use to model, copy, or borrow?"

Modify (or Magnify): "Can the item be changed in some way by increasing or decreasing features, adding or removing . . . ?"

Put to Other Uses: "What else could this be used for (other than originally intended)?"

Eliminate: "What features or parts can be removed or simplified?"

Rearrange (or Reverse): "Can I reverse or reorder sequences?"

● *Analogies.* Analogies offers an approach to creative idea finding that examines what appears on the surface as unrelated phenomena and draws connections. For example, say that students need to solve the problem of limited parking space in the downtown area of a large city. Instead of stating the problem that way, the students could be told that the problem is one of storing things. Then they would be asked to brainstorm: "How many ways can you think of to store things?" They may come up with ideas such as "Put them in boxes," "Can them," "Pile them up," "Put them on shelves," "Put them in bags," and "Hang them on hangers." After the students complete their list, the teacher gives the actual problem to the class. The students examine items from their list to come up with solutions they may never have considered if presented only with the actual problem. For example, I once presented the parking problem to a group of fifth graders and was amazed by the interesting parking garage proposed by one group, who elaborated on the idea of "putting things on hangers." Their parking garage was an elaborate system of motorized rails and hangers that picked up cars and stacked them neatly and safely until claimed by their owners.

● *Morphological synthesis.* To use morphological synthesis, students combine attributes of two categories in the form of a grid. For example, say that you want to use this technique on *animal bodies* and *animal heads.* Draw up a table listing the animal bodies along the left vertical axis and animal heads along the top horizontal axis (see Figure 4.8). Morphological synthesis will force you to look at many surprising combinations. Idea combinations, or syntheses, will appear in the intersections, or cells, of the table. Either do this randomly (pointing to the paper with eyes shut) or select interesting combinations. By mixing an item from each column and row, you will create a new combination of animal parts. For example, I combined a horse with an alligator to invent a new animal that will be used as the central character of a political cartoon. Consider how a political cartoonist might create a cartoon about soil conservation with my "horsigator" as the central character.

SOLUTION FINDING

At this point, students establish criteria for evaluating the proposed ideas, selecting the most workable. One strategy is to have the children examine their lists and agree on the three to five ideas they like best. The children should chat about the pros and cons of each, and then individual group members can assign each of the ideas a score of 0 to 5 points. The scores for each idea are added up, and the one with the highest score becomes the workable idea—the one that will be more fully explored and presented to the whole class as a solution.

FIGURE 4.8   Morphological Synthesis Grid

	giraffe	ape	elephant	boa	alligator	kangaroo	tiger	toucan	iguana
cow									
pig									
chicken									
sheep									
horse									
mouse									
dog									

During their deliberations, students should address considerations such as, "Will this idea actually solve the problem? Will it create new problems? What are the chances it will work? Is it practical? Will we be able to use it in the near future? What are the strengths and weaknesses? Can any of the ideas be combined into one useful solution?" After narrowing their lists, each group works toward an agreed-upon decision. The ultimate choice might contain one idea or a combination of ideas.

ACTION PLANNING

This step involves expanding the interesting idea or combining interesting ideas into a statement that outlines an action plan that details the steps necessary to implement the solution: "What course of action will we take?" "Does this plan depend on someone else's approval or support?" "What steps are needed?" "Who will do what?" "When must the steps be completed?"

Solving problems is one of the most fundamental skills required throughout one's lifetime; children must practice testing alternative paths and possibilities each day.

Zurijeta/Shutterstock

Reflection on Learning

You may simply scribble rough notes or jot down something more polished and complete. The point is to simply start recording your ideas spontaneously and candidly.

Try the following challenge to see whether the manner in which you choose to approach a problem is rational/logical or creative/innovative. Although the problem appears simple at first, it is actually quite difficult.

PROBLEM

There are four volumes of Shakespeare's collected works sitting on a shelf. Each volume is exactly 3" thick (pages only); the covers are each ¼" thick. A hungry bookworm starts eating at page 1 of volume I and eats all the way through to the last page of volume IV. How far did the bookworm crawl during its feast? Try to work the problem before you look at the solution!

SOLUTION

Only about one person in a hundred solves it the first time around; the answer is 7½ inches. Surprised? Most of the time, students tell me the bookworm crawled between 10 and 14 inches. Remember that the bookworm started at page 1 of volume I. Put your pencil at that point; do not count the back cover of volume I or all the pages between. Are you catching on? Similarly, the bookworm ate only to the last page of volume IV. Put your pencil point on that spot. Do not count the front cover and all the pages of volume IV.

What causes so many of us to look only at "obvious" solutions to problems?

FIGURE 4.9   How many inches did the bookworm travel?

Three major benefits result when students are involved in CPS in dynamic social studies classrooms:

1. students have greater feelings of self-confidence, self-esteem, and compassion;
2. students undertake wider exploration of traditional content subjects and skills; and
3. students use higher levels of creative invention in content and skills.

Therefore, our classrooms must encourage not only the systematic efforts associated with inquiry but also the inventive, intuitive thinking associated with creative problem solving.

Creative problems differ from inquiry problems in that they call for divergent thinking as opposed to convergent thinking, as students search for solutions to problems. Both types of problems, however, are crucial to today's dynamic social studies classrooms in that they encourage children to dig into things, turn over ideas in their minds, try out alternative solutions, search for new relationships, and struggle for new knowledge.

To recognize what problem-based learning looks like in classroom practice, examine the following classroom scenario, which employs features of both inquiry and creative problem solving. The sample is not meant to be prescriptive, but to inspire your own creative application of the principles offered in this chapter. The learning experience takes place on a clear, crisp day just before Halloween when students from Sharon Reilly's fifth-grade class learned that there's more to cemeteries than cold gravestones and chilling ghost stories. The scene is Oaklands Cemetery, a venerable setting where young imaginations seem to reach a peak during this spooky season. To prepare her students for what they would experience on their trip to the cemetery, Ms. Reilly shared what she begins most social studies lessons with—novel objects she calls "interest-grabbers."

In this instance, Mrs. Reilly's "interest grabber" was a bronze metal star with an American flag attached, the kind used to decorate the graves of soldiers who had died in battle. The star had the letters GAR (Grand Army of the Republic) on it. Along with the star and flag, Mrs. Reilly showed the students a crayon rubbing of a grave marker she had made from a local cemetery. The worn, very simple stone had only the name of the deceased: J. R. McTavish, Co. B. 9th Pa. Inf. Nothing else was written. The students were prompted to examine the flag and marker and to make comments or ask questions to see what they might know about those objects or what questions they might have. Initially, they had no idea what those items were until Richard, a budding Civil War buff, finally spoke up: "Grand Army of the Republic! That was what they called the Union Army during the Civil War. I bet this is a soldier who died in the Civil War."

"Yeah!" added Molly. "Look at the grave rubbing. It says the soldier was from the 9th Pa. Inf. He must have been a Union soldier from Pennsylvania."

Persistent observations eventually led them to the conclusion that the items on display had something to do with the Civil War, the current social studies unit under study. Mrs. Reilly knows it is important to lay a foundation for their visit by talking about things students can look for and eliciting questions that they hope to answer. Next, she read words written by Frederick Douglass in 1894, years after the Civil War ended:

"Though the rebellion is dead, though slavery is dead, both rebellion and slavery have left behind influences that will remain with us, it may be, for generations to come."

—*Frederick Douglass, 1894*

Mrs. Reilly asked a compelling question intended to capture student interest and guide her students to examine and reflect on Douglass' prophetic words: "How does the Civil War conflict relate to us today?"

When the class arrived at the cemetery, they were greeted by Fred Hubbert, a caretaker who led them on a walking tour past obelisks, shrines, sarcophagi, and ornate gravestones. "Look at the names; they're sure different than our names today!" commented Herschel. Mr. Hubbert picked up on Herschel's comment and explained how several of these people had helped shape their community's history. "That big old shrine over there belongs to Cyrus Hadfield. When he returned from fighting in the Civil War, he opened a carriage factory on Front Street. It became one of the country's largest carriage manufacturers. Hadfield Street is named in honor of Cyrus Hadfield." As they walked, Mr. Hubbert pointed out more of the cemetery's interesting features: At one rather plain gravestone, Mr. Hubbert explained: "Ebenezer Taylor was the village physician in the mid-1800s. He stopped riding his bicycle after he turned 90. He said the streets were getting too busy."

"Some of the earliest monuments date back to before the Civil War," Mr. Hubbert explained. A bronze statue of a Union soldier sitting on his horse guarded the cemetery's fenced-in Civil War section. The students counted 24 soldiers buried there. "Here's a Union soldier who was only 14 years old when he was shot," commented Kendra sadly. "That's how old my big brother is . . . and he's only in eighth grade!"

"We used to plant tulips at the base of the statue guarding this section of the cemetery, but the deer and squirrels ate them all," explained Mr. Hubbert. "We're looking into something safer that could be planted."

After this interesting introduction by Mr. Hubbert, each young historian was assigned a partner, and the dyads were sent off to assigned portions of the Civil War section to carry out their investigation. The students carefully filled out their observation sheets with responses to the tasks they had talked about in the classroom, made gravestone rubbings by placing large sheets of newsprint against the gravestones and carefully rubbing crayons over the paper, and mapped each location. Everything on the gravestone (names, dates, epitaphs) transferred to the paper and provided excellent research material the students could take back to the classroom. For example, one pair found a marker that read: "Sibyl—A little refugee from N.C. who died in 1865."

"What's a refugee?" they asked Mr. Hubbert. After he explained that a refugee is someone who seeks protection from something harmful, the young historians inquired further: "What kind of refugee would come to Pennsylvania from North Carolina in 1865? What kind of harm would this person face in North Carolina?" Mr. Hubbert explained that Sibyl was a slave who was brought to southeastern Pennsylvania and given her freedom by the Hastings family, members of the Society of Friends (a religious group strongly opposed to slavery). Throughout their tour, Mr. Hubbert was an impressive source of dates, facts, troop details, and interesting personal stories.

Returning to the classroom, Mrs. Reilly's young researchers analyzed their data and shared their findings. It was very interesting to learn of the generals, officers, and enlisted men buried at the cemetery. They found that the soldiers were buried in order of rank, from privates to generals. Also, they found that there were White soldiers, Black soldiers, unknown soldiers, foreign soldiers, and women and children—all victims of the war. The students were overwhelmed with the significance of the ground that had been the final resting place of those who made the ultimate sacrifice during the Civil War. The solemnity of their experience inspired them to action: How might they actively demonstrate their respect and concern for the individuals buried at Oaklands Cemetery? "I have an idea," suggested Rita. "Maybe we can help do something about those tulip bulbs that the deer and squirrels keep eating."

"Yeah, great idea," offered Colleen. "Maybe we can check the Internet to see if there's something the animals won't bother."

The class checked the Internet and learned that deer, squirrels, and other wildlife love tulip bulbs, but they have a strong dislike for daffodil bulbs. "In what ways might we provide daffodil bulbs for the monument?" questioned Taylor. Knowing that a solution would be difficult, the students agreed that their effort required a team approach. They addressed the challenge in a creative manner by brainstorming a list of innovative and novel solutions. They combined and evaluated ideas until a winning idea came forth. They drew up an action plan to implement their winning idea—selling flower bulbs to their families and community. The students eventually earned enough money to buy 300 daffodil bulbs and five Civil War grave markers. Each member of the class planted 15 bulbs that autumn and helped place the grave markers; now, each spring, the base of the Civil War monument is awash in a glorious blanket of brilliant yellow flowers.

Ms. Reilly didn't bother to quiz her children on their cemetery adventures. "That's one story they'll always remember," she proudly declares.

 CHECK YOUR UNDERSTANDING 4.4 **Click here** to check your understanding of this section of the chapter.

A Final Thought

It often happens that when the word *research,* is mentioned to college students, groans and steely glares accompany the predictable questions: "How long does the paper have to be?" "How many references do we need?" "What's the topic?" Exposing students exclusively to this type of forced research often builds negative attitudes toward the processes of problem solving and inquiry. Written reports on teacher-determined topics using secondary sources not only produce downbeat attitudes in students but also present an unrealistic view of research in the real world. While this kind of research has a place, to present it as the only form of research does students a disservice. We cannot limit elementary school research to such practices either; remember that most elementary school youngsters are natural problem finders. They take pleasure in investigating the mysteries of their world. On their own, they deftly uncover problems of interest—the important first step of research: "Why do farmers cut off the corn and leave behind the lower part of the plants?" "How many ears of corn grow on each corn plant?" What students need at school is to learn the methods through which these questions can be explored. While not all the particular problems children bring to school may be particularly significant, the processes they go through and the feelings they gain about themselves as capable researchers *are* significant. Therefore, authentic research associated with creative problem solving and inquiry processes teaches students that they have the skill and ability to pursue knowledge in a meaningful way and that their efforts have real value now and in the future.

Lifelong learners get their start in elementary school social studies classrooms as teachers arouse curiosity for stimulating questions or problems and propel their students into research to obtain answers. The resulting outcomes lead to the intellectual independence we so often find in self-motivated, lifelong learners. Despite their usefulness, inquiry and problem solving are not the only tools suggested for every social studies instructional situation. Teaching social studies requires varied approaches. Eventually, using a single method becomes boring for eager young learners.

References

Carson, R. (1965). *The sense of wonder.* New York, NY: Harper & Row.

Dewey, J. (1971). A pedagogical experiment. In *Early Works of John Dewey* (Vol. 5, pp. 244–246). Carbondale, IL: Southern Illinois University Press. (Original work published 1896)

Eberle, B. (1997). *SCAMPER: Creative games and activities for imagination.* Waco, TX: Prufrock Press.

Grant, S. G. (2013). From inquiry arc to instructional practice: The potential of the C3 framework. *Social Education, 77,* 322–326, 351.

Hoffman, J. V. (1992). Critical reading/thinking across the curriculum: Using I-Charts to support learning. *Language Arts, 69,* 121–127.

National Council for the Social Studies. (2010). *National curriculum standards for social studies: A framework for teaching, learning, and assessment.* Washington, DC: Author.

National Council for the Social Studies (2013). *The college, career, and civic life (C3) framework for social studies state standards: Guidance for enhancing the rigor of K–12 civics, economics, geography, and history.* Washington, DC: Author.

National Governors Association Center for Best Practices & Council of Chief State School Officers. (2010). *Common core state standards for English language arts and literacy in history/social studies, science, and technical subjects*. Washington, DC: Authors.

Osborn, A. F. (1963). *Applied imagination: Principles and procedures of creative problem-solving.* New York, NY: Scribner's.

Parnes, S. J. (1981). *The magic of your mind*. Buffalo, NY: Creative Education Foundation and Bearly Limited.

Piaget, J. (1969/1970). *Science of education and psychology of the child.* New York, NY: Viking Compass.

Vygotsky, L. S. (1962). *Thought and language.* Cambridge, MA: MIT Press.

Vygotsky, L. S. (1978). *Mind in society*. Cambridge, MA: Harvard University Press.

SECTION THREE

Instructional Resources

A key component of effective social studies instruction is the selection of instructional resources that meet the diverse needs and interests of all students. It is not uncommon for the public and many educators to consider the textbook to be the social studies "curriculum"- the single and most important learning tool in the social studies toolbox. But, in this book, instructional resources refer to all the essential tools used to support and enrich the social studies curriculum- print, non-print, digital, or any combination thereof. The selection of instructional resources is a complex professional responsibility that must support rather than hinder or frustrate learning. What should you consider in selecting social studies learning materials? What should you avoid? This section offers insights into the selection of instructional resources that enrich and support the social studies curriculum in 21st century classrooms.

dglimages/Fotolia

Beyond the Ordinary:
Teaching and Learning with Concrete Instructional Resources

Learning Outcomes

Don't we learn most of what we know by purposefully doing something—driving a car by driving, learning to swim by swimming, or driving a nail by hammering? Likewise, few social studies textbooks ever published or lectures ever delivered can hope to engage students more thoroughly or purposefully in the learning process than concrete experiences. Of course, students cannot directly experience everything they learn in social studies; there are many times they must rely on language and other indirect sources of information. However, social studies has many built-in opportunities for direct engagement in learning, especially when students have little knowledge of a topic, or when something real is required to gain deeper or more precise understandings of a complex concept.

After completing this chapter, you will be able to:

- Describe what is meant by *authentic learning.*

- Defend the use of field trips as meaningful social studies learning experiences.

- Acknowledge the contributions of classroom visitors.

- Explain how interacting with artifacts contributes to learning.

- Offer a rationale and provide a framework for integrating the arts and social studies.

- Describe how sharing games of other cultures contributes to learning in social studies.

Classroom Snapshot

Stephen Shudlick teaches in a culturally diverse school located in a large urban school district. He planned to create a fair balance among different December holidays celebrated by the children and their families, including Kwanzaa. Kwanzaa is a festival honoring one's African American heritage and is celebrated for seven days, beginning December 26. Mr. Shudlick prearranged a number of attention-grabbing items on a large table at a classroom interest center, above which was draped a large banner bearing the word Kwanzaa (a Swahili term meaning "First Fruits"). A number of symbols commonly used in Kwanzaa celebrations were displayed on a large table. The first symbol of Kwanzaa was an arrangement of mkeke (m-KAY-kah), or handmade mats, on which the other six symbols were arranged. On the first mkeke was a kikombe cha umoja (kee-KOOM-bay CHAH oo-MO-jah), a unity cup that everyone drinks from to show that African Americans are a united people. On the second were ears of corn, called muhindi (moo-HEEN-dee); one ear is put out for each child in the family to remind everyone that children are the promise of the future. On the third was the kinara (ki-NAH-rah), a wooden candleholder. It holds the fourth symbol—seven candles, or mishumaa saba (mee-shoo-MAH-ah SAH-bah). One candle is black, three candles are red, and three candles are green to symbolize hope—symbolic of African Americans and their struggles. The fifth held mazao (mah-ZAH-oh), or fruits of the harvest—corn, grapes, bananas, and apples. The last mkeka on the table held gifts. They are called zawadi (zah-WAH-dee) and are handmade educational or cultural gifts. There was a dashiki (de-SHE-ke), or traditional shirt for African men and a gele (GAY-lay), or woman's traditional headwrap.

After the children had an opportunity to explore the items, Mr. Shudlick brought the class together and read the book The Gifts of Kwanzaa by Synthia Saint James (Albert Whitman). The book clearly and interestingly explains each of the items on display. Afterward, Mr. Shudlick led a discussion of the story, focusing on the relationship between the items on the table and the experiences of the people in the book, as well as on similarities and differences between Kwanzaa and other traditional December celebrations.

On succeeding days, Mr. Shudlick offered these learning experiences:

- He arranged candles on a kinara (a candleholder supporting the seven candles representing the Kwanzaa principles) so that a black candle was in the middle, red candles on the left, and green on the right. Each day, a candle was lit and Mr. Shudlick and the children talked about the associated principle of Kwanzaa.

- He invited parents, grandparents, and members of the community into the classroom to share a family photo album or some valued articles that had been passed down through generations. And since music, song, and dance are important to the celebration of Kwanzaa, some guests were able to demonstrate musical instruments with African or African American roots.

- He showed the children examples of beads that were worn by some Africans for adornment, ceremonies, and religious purposes. The children learned that in some tribes, the patterns or colors of strings of beads could carry special meanings. The children strung their own colored wooden beads, which they wore during Kwanzaa week, and others that were to be given as gifts during the classroom's planned Kwanzaa festival.

- The class tried the traditional African art of tie-dyeing as they fashioned their own dashiki ("de-SHE-ke"), or traditional shirt for African men and gele ("GAY-lay"), or women's traditional headwrap.

- In keeping with the spirit of Kwanzaa, the children created a simple but natural "gift of the heart" for the animals near their school. They threaded popcorn and fresh cranberries on long strands of string. Later, they would drape the food-covered strings on trees or bushes as a holiday treat for the animals.

Mr. Shudlick and the class were so pleased by what they had learned about Kwanzaa that they decided to invite the students' families to a classroom Kwanzaa celebration, or karamu (kah-RAH-mu). The karamu would serve not only as an excellent review of all the learning experiences that had taken place, but it also would provide an interesting and authentic way to share what they had learned with others. To begin, the students placed two large tables in the center of the room. They positioned an unlighted kinara at the center of each table and spread 20 ears of corn (1 for each child in the home or, in this case, the classroom) on each. Since the mazao (fruits of the harvest—usually corn, grapes, bananas, apples, and pears) is an important element of the Kwanzaa table, each child brought to school two pieces of fresh fruit and worked together with their classmates to put together a nutritious "First Fruits" salad. On a smaller table, the children *arranged their Kwanzaa gifts—beads for family members in attendance and the popcorn and cranberry string for the birds. Using red, green, and black construction paper strips, students wove their own mkekas on which to place the items.*

The celebration began with a welcome to all and a brief explanation of Kwanzaa. The boys were elegantly clad in their dashikis; the girls were attractively adorned in their geles as they told the story of Kwanzaa. Each family member in attendance received a student-constructed booklet explaining the seven Kwanzaa principles; the class and the adults in attendance joined together to read aloud the principles and meanings. Then, the "First Fruits" salad and other nutritious treats were enjoyed by all. Finally, the children presented their parents with the gift of beads and, together, the children and their parents took the popcorn and cranberry strings outdoors and placed them in trees and on bushes for the animals to enjoy.

At the end of the Kwanzaa experience, Mr. Shudlick separated the class into groups of two or three students, each of which developed an iMovie script by discussing and summarizing what they had learned about the different aspects of Kwanzaa. After completing their scripts, creating a video storyboard, selecting appropriate props and music, and practicing what they wanted to say, the students used iMovie software to produce a movie highlighting the main features of Kwanzaa. They clicked on the "share" tab at the top of the screen and chose to share it with others via Facebook and YouTube.

Sometimes a classroom adventure like Mr. Shudlick's Kwanzaa project can bring about very unexpected and prized outcomes. In this case, just after the classroom celebration had ended and guests were leaving the school, one child's parents approached Mr. Shudlick and thanked him for the opportunity to participate in the *karamu*. They admitted knowing very little about Kwanzaa before this experience but said that having the opportunity to join together with their children and other families in such a meaningful way convinced them that celebrating Kwanzaa in their own home would be a tradition they would like to start. Since the school calendar made it necessary for the class to celebrate Kwanzaa prior its normal dates in late December, the parents had plenty of time to prepare for their own celebration at home. Certainly, the major goal of this learning experience was to help children understand holiday traditions and be respectful of diverse customs and beliefs, but it also encouraged quality lifelong practices. Meaningful social studies activities often extend far beyond the limits imposed by classroom time and space.

Authentic Learning

Mr. Shudlick's social studies program incorporates assorted opportunities for authentic learning where students ask questions, do research, and take on real challenges that fascinate them. How is he able to do that in today's standards-driven atmosphere? "It's tough to manage and implement," admits Mr. Shudlick, "but I think that bringing about learning in realistic and meaningful contexts is perhaps the best way to nurture the higher-order thinking fundamental to today's standards movement."

A relatively new addition to the overload of educational jargon, the basic idea behind *authentic learning* is that students are more motivated to learn new concepts and skills when they get a chance to use what they have learned in real-life contexts and situations—when they produce a tangible, useful outcome that can be shared with others in a meaningful context. "It seems that students are more likely to display a high level of motivation when they find the subject matter they are studying to be interesting, when they like what they're doing, when they feel they are capable of accomplishing a task, and when they believe what they are doing is useful," suggests Mr. Shudlick. "My role during authentic learning is that of a guide or facilitator who arranges real-life tasks, or simulated tasks, that provide the students with opportunities to conduct sustained investigations into real-world problems." Some teachers in today's standards-driven world have shied away from authentic learning because they think it takes too much time and effort to plan and execute such elaborate and stimulating instructional tasks. But, just ask yourself: "Aren't our students worthy of elaborate and stimulating classroom experiences?" In any case, what many skeptics don't fully understand is that much of authentic learning is fairly routine, not elaborate. Any teacher who has asked her students to write a letter to the principal requesting an extra iPad for their classroom is using authentic learning. Any teacher who has asked his students to use web-based functions and tools to research, create, and publish original products is also using authentic learning . . . it's not that complicated.

The instructional resources and activities you provide for your students merge together with the instructional strategies you read about in Chapters 3 and 4 to shape successful authentic learning classrooms, so one of the most important decisions you will face as a teacher is selecting relevant instructional resources. While dealing with your decisions, you must be sure that whatever you choose will be (1) aligned with the general philosophy of your school district, (2) based on suitable assessment evidence (student backgrounds, needs, and interests), (3) coordinated with the goals and objectives of the social studies program, and (4) consistent with school district learning outcomes as presented in its content standards.

Historically, textbooks have been the primary instructional resource used in social studies classrooms at all grade levels. If we think of placing the many possible forms of instructional resources on a continuum, *textbook alone* instruction would be positioned at one end (See Figure 5.1.). The current standards movement has accorded much attention to comprehension of complex texts, so pressure to return to the dominance of textbook-based instruction has been widespread. If this is true in your school district, *textbook alone* instruction must be enriched, at least by using suggested activities, learning experiences, and instructional resources that are found in the textbook's Teacher's Edition. To experience success in today's social studies classrooms, however, you must provide a broader set of instructional resources than *textbook alone* instruction. Therefore, around the middle of the continuum you can expect to encounter *expanded textbook* instruction; this strategy is also centered on social studies textbook usage, but incorporates a variety of audio and visual resources such as computer applications, pictures, study prints, videos, literature, and documents. However, direct multisensory experiences such as cooking, dancing, skits, examining artifacts, interacting with guest speakers, and going on field trips seem to serve more as "icing on the cake" than as integral tools for instruction. On the opposite end of the instructional resources continuum we place programs that use *multiple instructional resources,* ranging widely from field trips to technology sources to information books that relate to student interests and needs. These programs have built an extensive collection of varied resources that create balance in the social studies curriculum and encourage students to take responsibility for their own learning. Although direct experiences and hands-on materials help their children make solid connections to new concepts, teachers also use a variety of other stimulating materials: *three-dimensional models* such as a globe or architectural models

FIGURE 5.1   Continuum of Instructional Resources

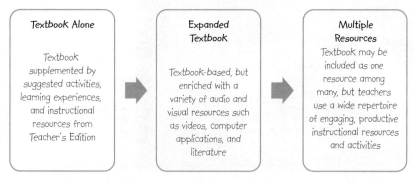

Textbook Alone

Textbook supplemented by suggested activities, learning experiences, and instructional resources from Teacher's Edition

Expanded Textbook

Textbook-based, but enriched with a variety of audio and visual resources such as videos, computer applications, and literature

Multiple Resources

Textbook may be included as one resource among many, but teachers use a wide repertoire of engaging, productive instructional resources and activities such as a plastic castle or pyramid; *graphic materials* such as charts, pictures, photographs, maps, diagrams, and drawings; *audiovisual materials* such as video clips, transparencies, tape recordings, and radio and television presentations; and a wide variety of *text resources* such as picture books, poetry, nonfiction, biography, folktales, written documents, and textbooks.

Instructional Resources

Successful social studies instruction demands teachers who are able to select instructional resources appropriate for teaching targeted concepts and skills. Is there major role for students' use of textbooks? How important is it to provide for well-prepared teacher presentations, trade books, demonstrations, videos, slides, artifact kits, charts, cards, games, field trips, and guest speakers? In what ways is it possible to take advantage of television, computers, the Internet, and a range of other electronic technologies? So a very important decision successful teachers face while selecting instructional resources is how to arrange opportunities for students to interact with the content: with concrete materials (e.g., a set of castanets or the flag of Canada), with abstract materials (e.g., the textbook or a map), or with a combination of abstract and concrete. Conducting research to address this dilemma, Pashler et al. (2007) found that presenting content in a combination of concrete and abstract terms is far more powerful than using either one in isolation. Huebner (2008) claims that a teacher's most essential job, therefore, is to initially present concepts as concretely as possible and then, over time, enlarge and reinforce that initial presentation with progressively more abstract representations: "By moving between concrete and abstract examples, teachers enable students to gain deep understanding of the core concept, apply their new knowledge in different situations, and acquire true ownership of what they have learned" (p. 87). Make sure to recognize the need for balance among instructional resources; be careful that there is not too much abstraction (textbook selections, workbooks, practice sheets, talking, reading) and too little realia (hands-on items)—or vice versa—in your program. As a rule of thumb, remember that all students thrive on a balance of solid learning experiences, but that younger students need direct contact and real experiences (e.g., a visit to an orchard) and visual representations (e.g., a videotape of apple-growing procedures). Older students still require concrete experiences but are better

Interacting real things entices children to touch, smell, hear, and look (and taste, when appropriate). These firsthand experiences make learning meaningful and memorable.

Miguel Montero/Fotolia

able to obtain knowledge from abstract sources (even periodically listening to a well-planned, interesting lecture).

Figure 5.2 illustrates a useful model you might consult while considering instructional resources by level of abstraction: a *concrete* to *representational* to *print-based* sequence.

The *concrete level* involves learning about some aspect of our world through direct interactions with the environment. This mode is highly sensory and manipulative; it includes objects, people, places, and real-life classroom experiences. Within this mode, children come to understand the world through firsthand involvement and their interactions with objects. For example, suppose your goal for today is to help students learn about the hardships endured by slaves in the pre–Civil War South as they picked cotton from sunrise to sunset and then joined the elderly, infirmed, and even the young children to gin the cotton by hand (remove the lint, or fiber, from the seed). Your concrete experience possibilities include bringing in cotton bolls for the children to handle as they examine the soft fibers, observe the tiny seeds, and touch the prickly shell. By handling the real item, students can appreciate the agony slaves experienced as they were forced to spend immeasurable hours picking out the little seeds from within the boll in order to free the attached fibers.

The *representational level* is made up of likenesses of real objects to communicate knowledge and increase students' understandings of the world, such as pictures, videos, and computer applications. For example, it is impossible for your students to directly observe slaves of the 1800s picking cotton in the hot fields all day, or to directly observe the hours of agony when the slaves would clean the fiber out of the cotton bolls after returning from the fields.

FIGURE 5.2   Model Representing Three Levels of Abstraction

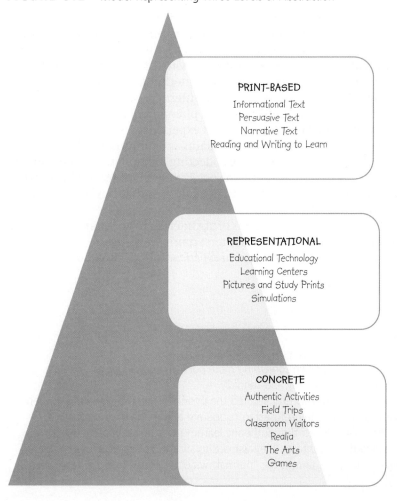

PRINT-BASED
Informational Text
Persuasive Text
Narrative Text
Reading and Writing to Learn

REPRESENTATIONAL
Educational Technology
Learning Centers
Pictures and Study Prints
Simulations

CONCRETE
Authentic Activities
Field Trips
Classroom Visitors
Realia
The Arts
Games

Moment-in-time limitations make this impossible. A well-produced video documentary, a website that contains links to past cotton production processes, or possibly a set of study prints or pictures with clear explanations would then be a useful substitute for the real experience. Representations of reality help children construct new understandings when real actions or objects are not available for them to sample.

The *print-based level* uses verbal or written symbols (language) to communicate information when it is not feasible to use more concrete instructional sources; learning is carried out through an abstract and arbitrary system of communication. Knowing that print material is beneficial in many ways, you will want to find meaningful texts that tell the harrowing tales of slavery, such as the writings by and interviews with slaves in Julius Lester's *To Be a Slave* (Puffin). And Jeanette Winter's picture book *Follow the Drinking Gourd* (Dragonfly) relates the story of an old white sailor called "Peg Leg Joe" who went from plantation to plantation in the pre–Civil War South, teaching enslaved blacks a folksong that he wrote, the lyrics of which held directions for following the Underground Railroad to freedom.

As you may surmise, the three levels of abstraction make it clear that, in some situations, a concrete experience is the best (or only) way to learn something. Regardless of how many books you read about something or how many videos you watch, there is no substitute for the real thing. It is much like making sense of a new device such as an Android or iPhone. If you're like most people, you will probably want to pick it up, turn it on, unlock the device, and see your home screen, which you simply swipe left to right to access. You may be able to place a whole variety of app shortcuts, app groups, and widgets on your home screen. So far, you have operated at the *concrete* level of abstraction; you initially took in information through direct experience, by doing, acting, sensing, and feeling. Now, however, you realize that your device has a lot of features you have no idea how to use and you are excited to make the most of them. In this instance, "concrete" was able to take you only so far; now you have to gather information through drawings, diagrams, and pictures that *represent* how your device works, as well as through the *print-based* letters, words, and numbers that bring deeper meaning to the concrete and representational levels. Likewise, in your classroom, involvement with real things may provide students with a general perception of something, but the details can be lost. Therefore, students will find it instructive to initiate an Internet search or consult a good information book to acquire a deeper understanding of the phenomenon. In addition, there are some concepts that simply cannot be taught using direct experiences, such as Paul Revere's famous ride to Lexington, Massachusetts to warn Samuel Adams and John Hancock that British troops were marching to arrest them, or Neil Armstrong collecting lunar material following his first step onto the moon. A key to successful teaching in social studies is to use a wide range of instructional resources that will enrich and support the curriculum and address the individual needs and varied interests of your students.

Because there is a place for each of the three levels of abstraction in authentic social studies instruction, each will be discussed in separate chapters: *concrete experiences* in Chapter 5, *representational experiences* in Chapter 6, and *print-based experiences* in Chapters 7 and 8.

Reflection on Learning

You may simply scribble rough notes or jot down something more polished and complete. The point is to simply start recording your ideas spontaneously and candidly.

One teacher commented, "When our faculty studied the possibility of implementing authentic learning strategies for social studies, many refused to cooperate and made their opposition to the approach very clear. They complained that authentic learning was not advantageous for preparing students to take standards-based tests; they wanted to stick to *normal practices*." Do you agree that students learn more if they are taught the "normal" way?

CHECK YOUR UNDERSTANDING 5.1 **Click here** to check your understanding of this section of the chapter.

Field Trips

Do you remember the times you and your elementary school classmates broke into spontaneous bursts of applause as you were told you were going on a field trip? Something other than the daily grind . . . the bus ride, with miscellaneous versions of childhood's ever-popular song "99 bottles of milk on the wall, 99 bottles of milk" (have you ever made it all the way through the 100 verses of that song?) . . . the magic of opening your minds to new interests or new ideas or new ways of thinking . . . there was simply nothing like it. That was the life! Unfortunately, those memorable childhood adventures seem to be joining the inkwell and nib pen in the murky world of educational obscurity; school field trips are experiencing a dramatic decline in popularity. What has caused this dramatic turnaround in the appeal of field trips? One frequent explanation is the perceived pressure to have students perform well on standards-based tests; taking time away from the prescribed classroom routine is often considered a waste of time. Field trips have been a hard to sell to administrators focused on raising test scores. It is difficult to understand such reasoning, though, especially since standards are meant only to describe desired outcomes; they do not explicitly spell out the instructional resources and methods that are likely to lead to those outcomes. Even for those teachers who are successful in gaining approval, their trips generally get tacked on to the end of the school year as a type of reward for all the hard work that went into preparing for and weathering the standards-based tests.

All is not lost, however. Some teachers are fortunate to work in school districts where field trips remain a valued component of a balanced social studies experience—districts that sense their students' excitement about participating in shared opportunities to encounter and explore new things in authentic settings. Who doesn't learn best when taken to a firsthand source of information? Children's museums, for example, often have displays and exhibits that children can touch and explore. Zoos can be interactive for students and animals. Children can pick strawberries while on a trip to the orchard in springtime or visit the pumpkin patch or corn maze in the fall. A trip to the farm can help children learn how milk or veggies get from the farm to their dinner table. And nature comes alive during trips to parks and nature preserves. Think about the possibilities as you take your students to a local hospital, post office, television station, newspaper, aquarium, train station, soup kitchen, nursing home, local historical monument, theater, local festival, police department, fire station, or museum.

Wherever you go, good field trips for elementary school youngsters must involve them as active participants. A trip to the automobile museum during which children are lectured to by a guide or required to be silent observers is not as good as a trip that allows them to get into an automobile, sit in the driver's seat, talk to the owner, listen to the engine's roar, and possibly be taken on a short ride on a protected course. A trip to the bakery where the children merely look at something being prepared is not as good as a trip that allows them to measure and mix the ingredients for a batch of healthy muffins that they will devour later. A good field trip must envelop elementary school children in opportunities for direct, meaningful involvement.

The following scenarios provide examples of how two different field trips provided fresh and original learning experiences that involved students as active learners and creative problem solvers. The first scenario describes a visit to a living history museum followed by a project through which the students created their own classroom museum. The second scenario is a little less traditional; it recounts the time fifth-grade students took a field trip to a senior center to visit, play games, give gifts, and eat lunch with the seniors. The trip ended up with a productive service-learning project that added a new dimension to their curriculum.

Living History Museum

There is no shortage of benefits associated with taking your students on a museum field trip. Museums provide memorable learning experiences, spark imagination, and introduce or reinforce concepts. Through interactive exhibits and hands-on involvement, children can take ownership of their own learning and develop and explore their own curiosities. At no time was this point clearer than when Kylie Brennan and her students took a field trip to a "living history museum" to observe the clothing, houses, furnishings, tools, and other artifacts that both enlightened and enriched their understandings of the colonial period of United States history.

A fifth-grade teacher, Kylie Brennan, who was teaching a unit titled "Colonial Life in America," makes the value of field trips crystal clear. She realized that her students' failure to comprehend concepts of time and place might stifle their curiosity and interest in studying Colonial America, so she arranged a trip to an authentic living museum in Cooperstown, New York. Authentic in every detail, the "Farmer's Museum" village was an actual working farm in which people dressed in period garb and used authentic implements to perform the duties of colonial farmers. About halfway up the path, the class fixed their eyes in horror as a farmer led a huge ox hauling a cart directly toward them. None of the children had ever seen a real ox before; few knew exactly what an ox was. "Get it away from me!" shrieked Frank as the snorting animal, covered with flies and slobber, ambled up and stopped next to him. The farmer invited Frank to pat the ox, but Frank was too scared to try.

"I never knew an ox was so big," Lois marveled as she reached up and patted its wet nose.

Following Lois's lead, several classmates approached the ox, some patting it and others commenting on its size, smell, and power for drawing flies. Some children were satisfied to simply look at the ox, while others ran away from it when it made the slightest movement; one or two even made faces at it—they did all sorts of things. The farmer told the class about the importance of oxen to colonial life and they were enthralled with his story. He thanked them for stopping and told them that his tired animal needed to go to the barn for a rest.

From that day on, the children all knew exactly what an ox was. Pictures of oxen, stories of oxen, or a video of oxen could never hope to approach the sounds, smells, sights, and tactile sensations of the real animal.

The ox experience seemed to transform the students from audience to actors. "That was awesome," shouted Eugene in anticipation. "I feel like our school bus was a time machine that took us back to the old days! What else is there?"

The first building the students came to was a school, where a "school marm" taught them about the ABCs exactly as a teacher would have done in colonial times. Spirits soared as the children went to the barn, where workers involved them in the entire process of making linen from flax. (Ms. Brennan was as fascinated by the process as the children. She, too, had never before seen linen made from flax, even though she had taught the concept from textbook diagrams for years.) By now, it was getting late, and Ms. Brennan tried to get the class to move on to the tanner, wigmaker, blacksmith, gunsmith, cooper (barrel maker), and glass blower, but the children insisted on staying at the barn for the corn husking bee and gunnysack race. At every stop, the children had an opportunity to touch, handle, and use; Ms. Brennan had a tough time pulling them away from each stop so they could visit the next exhibit.

It was amazing to see how much the field trip helped students broaden their understanding of colonial America with experiences that went far beyond what they found in books, videos, the Internet, or other multimedia presentations.

 Video Exploration 5.1

To improve your prospects of carrying out an enjoyable and productive field trip, you will find it useful and necessary to follow a set of specific guidelines. Such guidelines include the considerations shown in Figure 5.3.

A field trip to the museum provides a shared social experience during which students encounter and explore items that bring life to curricular content.

Pavel Losevsky/Fotolia

FIGURE 5.3   Planning a Field Trip

_____ 1. Contact the field trip location to arrange for your class visit.

_____ 2. Familiarize yourself with the trip location by visiting the site beforehand.

_____ 3. Prepare students with the purpose for the field trip. Read books, share brochures or posters, and talk about what to expect. Be sure students understand why they are going: "What are we looking for?" "What do we want to find out?" "How does the trip relate to what we are doing in class?"

_____ 4. Remind students that while this trip will be fun, school rules still apply. Be sure to clearly communicate behavioral expectations and any special rules or regulations. Consider how you will handle students who may present special behavioral challenges.

_____ 5. Plan for a safe trip. Consider student allergies and other medical needs. Bring a first aid kit.

_____ 6. Arrange transportation. (For liability concerns, a school bus is a better option than private cars.)

_____ 7. Plan for proper supervision. A good ratio of adults to students is 1:4. Be sure to inform volunteers of your field trip plans, behavioral expectations, and what you expect of them before the day of the trip.

_____ 8. Remind students and volunteers to dress for the weather.

_____ 9. Don't forget the basics! Be sure you know where the students are required to eat their snacks, where restrooms are located, and what accommodations are available for children with special needs.

_____ 10. Have a clear signal for getting everyone's attention and gathering students together. Practice before you go on the trip.

_____ 12. Assign a partner, or buddy, for each student. Explain why it is important to stick together. Remind the students that if they get separated from the group, they should sit and wait. Someone will come for them.

_____ 13. After the trip, students should write thank you notes expressing their appreciation to volunteers and field site personnel.

_____ 14. Discuss, draw pictures, prepare a chart, write first hand accounts, make a map, create a dramatic skit, or plan any suitable information summary activity.

Classroom Museum

Trips to one kind of museum or another often inspire students to plan, design, and build their own classroom museum. To carry out this project with your students, review what a museum is—a place where interesting objects are displayed; often, the objects are of historical or cultural significance. Talk about what students saw at the museum: "What exhibit do you remember most?" "What made that exhibit stand out?" "How might we arrange items in a classroom museum?" Even upper-grade students enjoy designing exhibits and sharing interesting collections of objects. For example, the New York State Social Studies Standards includes a requirement that elementary school children learn about themselves and their place in history through resources such as family artifacts and children's literature. Nicholas Grego decided to address this standard by integrating family artifacts and children's literature into a history project called the "Family Heritage Museum."

> Mr. Grego launched the project by reading aloud Bonnie Pryor's picture book The House on Maple Street (HarperTrophy). In the story, a Native American Indian child loses an arrowhead, a pioneer child loses a china cup, and then time travels forward past a forest fire, buffalo, Indians, wagon trains, settlers, farmers . . . all the way to a contemporary family who live in a house on Maple Street. That is where the arrowhead and china cup are both unearthed in a young child's garden. The story exemplifies the idea that historical artifacts are tactile, visual reminders of an earlier time or culture. During a follow-up discussion, Mr. Grego's students agreed that artifacts are key sources of historical evidence and that a good working definition for "artifact" would be "something important from long ago that is very special to you or your family."
>
> Mr. Grego then introduced the "Family Artifact Museum" project by sharing his own family artifact: a handmade wooden rake (circa 1910) that his Italian immigrant great-great-grandpa had used while cultivating a vegetable garden on a small plot of land in Michigan. The rake had been passed down through the generations because it was a potent reminder that many immigrants, including Great-Great-Grandpa Domenic Grego, had very little when they came to the United States. The story Mr. Grego told helped make the children aware of how cultural practices can be embedded in an artifact.
>
> After Mr. Grego explained the classroom artifact project to the children, they took home letters, asking their parents to help them select a meaningful family artifact—a photograph, a letter, a toy, food, a religious object—anything significant that would bring a touch of their past to school. The children were to prepare a short oral presentation during which they described their artifact, told how old it was, described what it was used for and who it belonged to, and told a short story about its importance to the child, family, or culture.
>
> The next day, Enrique shared his interesting family artifact—a photo of a "Welcome to Arizona" sign. He explained that it had been taken by his Grandpa Erubiel when he emigrated from Mexico and was searching for a piece of land near Tucson. Grandpa Erubiel eventually found suitable ground, and part of the Chavez family still lives in the little adobe farmhouse he built on it.
>
> "My grandmother made this clay storyteller doll for my father," reported Luz. (Navajo storyteller dolls are a rather contemporary addition to traditional Navajo pottery. These handmade clay figurines depict a Navajo storyteller with little children gathered tenderly in his or her arms telling stories that serve to pass on knowledge and cultural values from one generation to the next.) "The storyteller is telling stories of our Hopi people to the little babies in her arms," explained Luz. "Our Navajo people mixed their craft skills with their love of storytelling to make these storyteller dolls. The dolls are very popular and are becoming more valuable every day."
>
> Alicia struggled to hoist an old manual typewriter onto the sharing table. (For those who don't remember, a typewriter is a mechanical device with a set of keys that, when pressed, prints characters and words on paper!) "My grandma used this typewriter in a business office when she was a secretary," Alicia reported. Alicia went on to provide a short demonstration of how typewriters work. "Now computers and printers have taken the place of these old typewriters," Alicia explained.
>
> Other technological phenomena seemed to capture the children's interest: Sammy shared a handheld console that created quite a buzz: "Here's a Nintendo Game Boy with a Tetris game cartridge. My dad got this one in 1989, when he was just a little boy. I think it was the first year they made the Game Boy, and he said they were very popular."

The children located their artifacts in time and space by arranging them on a time line and pin-pointing where they came from on a map of the world. Some of the artifacts were much too prized by the families for them to remain on display in school beyond the day of the presentation, so Mr. Grego took digital photographs of each student holding her or his artifact and mounted the photos on the museum display. The children filled out "museum information cards" that described the artifacts—where they came from, how old they were, who they belonged to, and what they were used for—and placed them next to the artifacts and/or photos. The exhibit proudly became known as the classroom "Family Heritage Museum." The children were surprised to see how much they had in common; they remarked time after time that these artifact presentations really helped them get to know each other. The artifacts, along with their explanations, effectively generated great interest in the cultural heritage of the class.

Mr. Grego bases his overall approach to building a classroom museum on a conviction that social studies instruction cannot be confined to memorizing "who did what to whom, when, and where." He firmly believes that instructional resources can be found everywhere—not only in actual museums, but also in the students' own homes. They can be uncovered in a box of old receipts; in games children play; in stories people tell; in clothes, tools, furniture, books, letters, and diaries; wherever we look, we can find objects we can learn from. While social studies textbooks are often used to provide a good overview of topics under investigation, Mr. Grego has found that they are not as effective if not accompanied by hands-on, authentic resources that invite students to explore, analyze, and interpret firsthand evidence.

Community-Based Field Trips

Oftentimes, field trips to community locations can help students successfully contribute to their community and connect to local issues. Feeding the hungry and helping senior citizens are just two constructive ways students can donate time and effort toward bettering their community. For example, a field trip to a local senior center resulted in a community action project supported by an alert and sensitive teacher, Debra Wood.

At present, The Clarksville Senior Center has a serene new flower garden—thanks to Debra Wood's fifth graders. While visiting the center in early autumn to bring a gift of potted chrysanthemums, the students noticed that an area between the main building and a shed looked desolate and depressing. After returning to the classroom, the students asked Ms. Wood if they could do something to improve the area. After brainstorming several suggestions, the class eventually decided on a flower garden. "A garden is so restful and peaceful," explained Jana. "Yeah," added Vance, "a garden could even bring back memories of World War II victory gardens."

Ms. Wood is an avid gardener and the president of the largest local garden club. She invited several members of the club to visit the class to recommend plants that would need minimal upkeep in their hot and dry climate. The garden club donated the flowers for the children's project and offered advice to the children as they cleaned up the area and planted the flowers. A parent who owned a landscaping company wanted to help, too, and the students dressed the flower area with his donated mulch. The class then solicited other local businesses for help; several chipped in to help as the garden expanded beyond the children's wildest dreams. A retired carpenter volunteered his time and expertise to make benches. A local lumberyard supplied the gravel and decorative block for a patio where the beautiful wooden benches now rest. An individual donor contributed a birdbath and feeder. In addition, the students took up a collection for a butterfly bush that added to the overall ambiance of the garden.

The garden is wheelchair accessible, a definite plus for seniors with restricted mobility. The senior adults are now responsible for the general upkeep of the garden and have passionately accepted that responsibility. "It gives them something to take pride in," explains Ms. Wood. "Some senior adults like the tranquility of the garden and will sit on the benches reminiscing. Others find the garden a great place to socialize. I'm so glad the students thought of this wonderful idea."

Billy's response to the project is shown in Figure 5.4.

FIGURE 5.4 Student's Response Letter

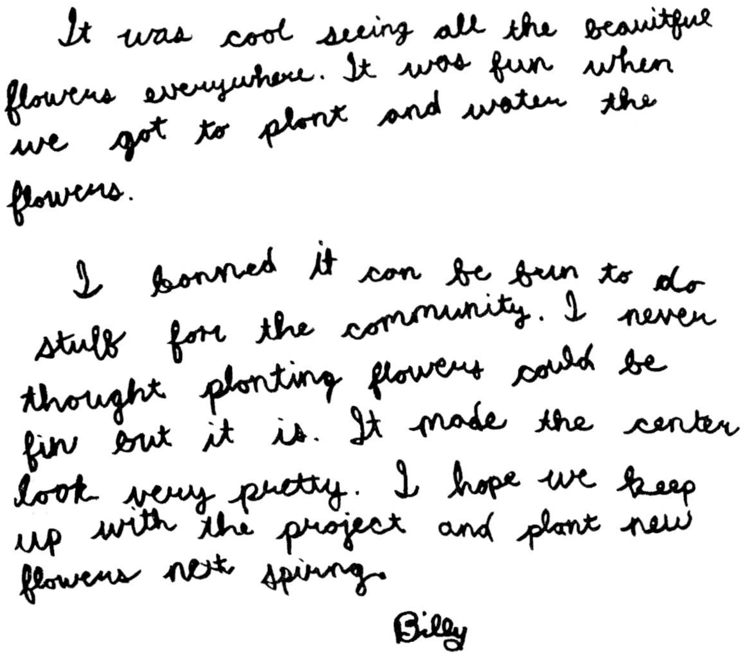

It was cool seeing all the beautiful flowers everywhere. It was fun when we got to plant and water the flowers.

I learned it can be fun to do stuff for the community. I never thought planting flowers could be fun but it is. It made the center look very pretty. I hope we keep up with the project and plant new flowers next spring.

Billy

✓ **CHECK YOUR UNDERSTANDING 5.2** **Click here** to check your understanding of this section of the chapter.

Classroom Visitors

Classroom visitors are people from the world outside of school who come into your classroom to share some specialized skill or knowledge with your students. They fulfill essentially the same educational purposes as field trips, but instead of the children leaving school, visitors bring the action to the children. As with field trips, though, the classroom visitor should not be a lecturer and the children a captive audience; the children must be involved in the action. Your students can meet veterinarians, bankers, tradespeople, construction workers, lawyers, mechanics, police officers, nurses, businesspeople, entrepreneurs, Zydeco musicians, dentists, architects, politicians, firefighters, artists, tailors, and a host of others. Your students will become fascinated as various speakers share props like a stethoscope, badge, tailor's clapper, old-world accordion, search-and-rescue helmet, or microphone to support their explanations of what their profession entails. None of us is an expert on everything, so bringing in speakers with proven expertise provides an added dimension to any dynamic social studies classroom. Also, don't ignore the potential gold mine of talent in your classroom: Mom's background as a news reporter, Dad's carpentry business, Grandma's expertise as an amateur magician, Grandpa's skill playing the vihuela (five-string guitars). And, importantly, remember that the students in your classroom will have expertise in an area relevant to what you are teaching and would be thrilled to offer a perspective otherwise difficult to provide.

Although not as patently irresistible as leaving school for part of the day, children do enjoy contact with outside visitors and their interesting ideas and materials. You must exercise care in the way classroom visitors are selected, however. The safest approach seems to be asking for recommendations from other teachers, informed parents, and other school personnel.

Jamiyah Bey, for example, wanted to introduce her fifth-grade students to American history in a new way. "If you eat soup for lunch each day, you never get to try anything new," she maintains. So, when it came time to study the accomplishments of Teddy Roosevelt, Ms. Bey contacted the local history museum for suggestions of a guest speaker who might present the major highlights of Roosevelt's life in a fresh, attention-grabbing way. The question barely cleared Ms. Bey's lips before the museum director blurted, "Ed Crocheron! Call Ed Crocheron!" The director went on to explain that Ed was a local resident and amateur historian who had become fascinated with the life of Teddy Roosevelt. After completing years of research, Crocheron now brings Roosevelt to life as a realistic, attention-grabbing recreator. He looks like Roosevelt, complete with the droopy mustache and undersized spectacles that make Teddy Roosevelt instantly recognizable. Ed even dresses in the cowboy image of Teddy Roosevelt, complete with vest and weather-beaten hat.

When Ed Crocheron entered Ms. Bey's classroom, he became instantly transformed into Teddy Roosevelt. He began by holding up a large, old, grainy photo and explaining: "My earliest recollections were as a young boy. My most noteworthy early memory was viewing the funeral procession of Abraham Lincoln from the upstairs window of our family home in New York City." Crocheron, complete with illustrative props, continued telling about the early life of Roosevelt, until his voice suddenly turned somber. "On Valentine's Day in 1884, when I was only 22 years old, I was at the center of one of the cruelest twists of fate ever. On that day—on Valentine's Day, no less—my wife Alice died during childbirth. On the same day, in the same house, my mother died of typhoid fever." Displaying a reproduction of the actual document, Crocheron sadly went on to exhibit a facsimile of a page from Roosevelt's diary of that day. Covering the page was a black X, two lines high. Then "Roosevelt" went on to read the few words that were entered on that page: "The light has gone out of my life." "Roosevelt" paused for a second or two, regained his composure, and explained that he spent much of the next two years on his ranch in the Badlands of Dakota Territory. There, he overcame his sadness as he learned to ride horses, rope, drive cattle, and hunt big game. "The other cowboys called me a dude," the re-energized speaker joked.

"Some of my proudest achievements were my conservation projects," "Roosevelt" disclosed as he displayed large picture prints of national parks in the United States. "In 1908, I set aside 800,000 acres in Arizona as Grand Canyon National Monument to protect it from developers."

In much the same way, "Roosevelt" moved on to shed light on his career in politics and describe an African safari (decked out in a yellow pith helmet). He concluded his riveting presentation by describing an event that occurred in 1912, when he ran for President on the Progressive ticket: "When I was campaigning in Milwaukee, I was shot in the chest by a fanatical saloonkeeper. The bullet didn't kill me, but it did become lodged in my chest. I was saved only because the bullet hit both a steel eyeglass case I was carrying and a copy of the speech I had in my jacket. (Crocheron displayed facsimiles of both.) I went on to deliver the speech and, afterwards, a doctor's exam confirmed that I was not badly wounded. They felt that it would be more risky to remove the bullet than to let it stay in my chest." "Roosevelt" explained that he soon recovered, but the words he spoke at that time would have been appropriate at the time of his death in 1919: "No man has had a happier life than I have led; a happier life in every way."

Ed Crocheron stopped at this point and asked the children if they had questions. Without hesitation, the children fired out questions on a number of topics: "How much did your asthma bother you as a child? I have asthma, too!" "Are teddy bears really named after you?" "Would you like to be president today?" "Are you related to Franklin or Eleanor Roosevelt?" Of course, Crocheron's responses were conveyed in the manner of "Teddy Roosevelt."

Other than role-playing historical figures from the past, inviting guests from the community to recount their personal experiences is an idea with exciting possibilities for any social studies program. Take the time Jim Mosteller, a sprightly 93-year-old, visited a fifth-grade classroom and mesmerized the children with firsthand accounts of life during the early years of the 20th century: "When we got automobiles around here, you couldn't use them in the winter. There weren't any paved roads in town!" Mr. Mosteller chuckled. "My father had one of the first cars in town. It was one of those open cars with leather seats and brass lamps. I'll never forget one Sunday; we had 11 flat tires!"

Mr. Mosteller had the children's undivided attention when he told what a dollar would buy: one dozen eggs, a loaf of bread, a pound of butter, and a half-pound of bacon. He also told the children about a whistle-stop campaign during which Teddy Roosevelt visited town in 1912 ("I can see him to this day") and the transfer of the Liberty Bell on a flatbed car from Philadelphia to San Francisco for safekeeping during World War I. Mr. Mosteller went on to capture the children's interest with other enchanting anecdotes about his early years: the average wage was $.22 per hour, there was no Mother's Day or Father's Day, and most women washed their hair only once a month. The stories stimulated the children's curiosities about the past to such a degree that their teacher decided to launch a "One Hundred Years Ago" investigation. The children were assigned to research separate topics (such as clothing, games, songs, lifestyle, or school) and used library and Internet resources to uncover attention-grabbing information about the world of 100 years ago. They composed short illustrated stories that were bound together into a book titled *If You Lived 100 Years Ago*.

 Video Exploration 5.2

Careful planning and organization are required if you expect fruitful classroom visits such as these. The following questions can assist you in establishing a productive course of action.

- Is the speaker really necessary? Does she or he address standards or educational objectives in ways in which other sources fall short?

- What would you like to have addressed in the presentation? Inform the speaker about the topic of study and how she or he can contribute to it.

- Have you offered the speaker suggestions on what it takes to involve your students in an appropriate and enthusiastic presentation? In order to make these experiences valuable for your students, prepare the speaker ahead of time. Advise the speaker to bring real, touchable items or visual aids. Let her or him know how important it is to include students in demonstrations or other activities. Also, suggest that the speaker move around the classroom so the children will feel personally involved. And let the speaker know that it helps to ask students questions once in a while, too.

- What is the date, time, and location of the visit? How long do you want the visitor to talk? (The speaker will want to match the presentation to the attention level of the children—about 20 minutes for K–2 children and 30 minutes for Grades 3 and up.) Contact the classroom visitor and clarify, well in advance, the details of the presentation.

- Have the students been prepared for the classroom visitor? Clarify precisely who the guest is and why she or he will be visiting. Include student involvement in all phases of planning, including setting up desired behavioral expectations.

- Does the speaker welcome student-generated questions? Questions regularly arise during a presentation, so the guest speaker should be willing to answer them. At times, it is useful to help students prepare appropriate questions in advance. Questions are always a great way to initiate an open, honest dialogue between a guest speaker and your students. Remember, however, that young children have no filters, so never be surprised at what they may ask. While some questions may be light and humorous, others may truly make the speaker pause before answering. For example, take the time a kindergartener asked a police officer if he knew the child's father because "he goes to jail a lot."

- Is *your* attention focused on the speaker? It is important for you as the teacher to model appropriate behavior during the presentation.

- What is the teacher's role at the conclusion of the presentation? Discuss the visit with the students, making sure to associate new understandings with the established purposes for the visit. Help students compose a thank you note for the visitor; you must promptly mail the speaker a professionally suitable letter of thanks, too. Plan a follow-up experience with activities that summarize, reinforce, or highlight key outcomes. These might include an art activity, dramatic skit, or other suitable experience.

You can uncover helpful concrete instructional resources by seeking input from your students, parents, and the local community. Invite various people from the community who are willing to come to your classroom. Resource people can demonstrate a special craft or talent, read or tell a story, display and talk about an interesting artifact or process, share a special food or recipe, teach a simple song or dance, or help children count or speak in another language. Invite parents and elders to share stories, wisdom, and cultural traditions. Plan special activities that will naturally invite family participation, such as multicultural holidays, festivals, and celebrations.

Reflection on Learning

You may simply scribble rough notes or jot down something more polished and complete. The point is to simply start recording your ideas spontaneously and candidly.

Taking field trips and inviting classroom visitors are established practices in many schools. Students clearly look forward to both—field trips give them a chance to get out of the classroom and experience something new and classroom visitors clearly personalize the subject matter content. There are advantages and disadvantages of field trips and classroom visitors, however, that must be considered before you decide to use either. What do you suppose some of those advantages and disadvantages are?

 CHECK YOUR UNDERSTANDING 5.3 **Click here** to check your understanding of this section of the chapter.

Guest speakers provide current, realistic information and offer perspectives on a subject that cannot be matched by other instructional resources.

Daniel Korzeniewski/Shutterstock

early 20th century? What can be learned about the clothing or hairstyles of the people during this time? Any idea what the woman is holding to her ear? What is that strange object? Is that some sort of USB cable attached to it? Photographs can, with careful teaching, present children with a wealth of useful historical data that could otherwise take written resources pages upon pages to convey.

Realia can be used singly (such as a colonial saltcellar), or they can be placed together into special collections, boxes, or kits related to historical topics or themes; one teacher, for example, assembled an artifact kit on colonial kitchens to demonstrate that early colonial homes were very simple places. The kit consisted primarily of woodenware—bowl, trencher, tankard, spoon, saltcellar, and candle box. Other than the iron cooking pot, these were among the most important items in a colonial kitchen. A pewter tankard was added, but just to illustrate that metal was valuable and rarely found in ordinary homes. Creating a collection to represent something being taught authenticates the experience for children and helps them deal with abstract concepts.

DURING INTRODUCTORY EXPERIENCES

Teachers find tangible items to be extremely useful during the introductory phase of lesson plans (see Chapter 2 and 3) or the pre-reading phase of guided reading in the content areas (see Chapter 7). During this time, you will be expected to help your students acquire interest in and motivation for what will follow. And if the concept is challenging or the students have limited experiential backgrounds, you may find it most appropriate to introduce real objects. Unless the objects are unusually fragile or valuable, encourage students to handle them. Help students understand the object and the conditions in which it exists in the world. Discuss the objects in a way that stimulates interest and paves the way for learning. For example, Orpha Diller, a student in one of my social studies methods classes, was assigned by her field experience teacher to introduce her fifth graders to Chinese tangrams by reading aloud Ann Tompert's picture book, *Grandfather Tang's Story* (Dragonfly). This is a folktale in which the illustrator, Robert Andrew Parker, uses watercolor washes and novel tangram patterns to help the author retell a traditional Chinese tale about two shape-changing fox fairies. The fox fairies match wits while trying to outdo each other by arranging and rearranging seven "tans" to represent various characters in the story.

After considering several options, Orpha decided to help her students make a strong connection to Tompert's narrative by using an antique-like trunk that she called "Grandma's Trunk." She told the students that she comes from a very close family in which everyone felt duty-bound to help get her ready for her first teaching assignment. She went on to explain that the trunk was a gift from her grandmother, who was so very proud that Orpha was about to become a teacher. It was a special trunk, her grandmother explained, because whenever Orpha needed something special to use in her classroom, all she had to do was wish really hard, say the magic word (the students suggested "Shazam!"), open up the trunk, and look inside. In anticipation, the students and Orpha chanted "Shazam!" together, Orpha slowly opened up grandma's trunk, and inside they found two stuffed toy foxes and seven flat shapes Orpha called "tans." She explained that the tans were part of an ancient game that originated in China. To play, one must put together a recognizable shape (called a tangram) using all seven pieces. She then invited the students to examine and to touch, move, and rotate the pieces as she fielded comments and questions. "Hey, these are all like puzzle pieces. Here's a triangle!" shouted Giselle. "I can make a square out of two triangles, watch!" asserted Rita." "Can anyone make another shape?" challenged Orpha. After a few minutes of exploration, Orpha asked the students to venture guesses about the connection between the foxes and the tans. Then she asked the students to listen to the story to test their predictions.

The story opens with Grandfather Tang and Little Soo sitting under a peach tree in their backyard. Grandfather Tang tells Little Soo a story about two friendly foxes, Chou and Wu Ling, who were always trying to outdo each other. Wu Ling transforms into a rabbit, Chou morphs into a dog who chases Wu Ling, and the contest is on. Parker uses seven tans to form tangrams representing

FIGURE 5.5   Seven Tans Used in Forming Tangrams

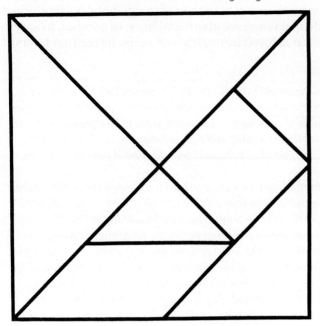

the various characters in the story. As Orpha read the story aloud, she manipulated her own set of tangram pieces on an overhead projector to show the students how each animal was formed in the story. (See Figure 5.5.) After the story was read and discussed, Orpha challenged the students to search the web for information regarding the origin of tangrams in Chinese society. The students uncovered several accounts and legends, but the one they liked the best told of a tiny village that wished to honor its emperor. The finest craftspeople set about to fashion a beautiful glazed tile. As a servant of the emperor was carrying the ceramic tile, he tripped over a stone in his path and fell, shattering the extraordinary tile into seven pieces. In a panic, the servant and the villagers desperately tried to reassemble the tile into a square, but could not. Dejectedly, they went before their emperor. But before they could explain what happened to the tile, the emperor discovered that many other shapes could be formed from the pieces. Absorbed in arranging and rearranging the pieces, he thought the villagers had made him a magnificent puzzle!

After their research was completed, Orpha gave small groups a set of seven-piece tangrams and challenged them to use their pieces like the fox fairies. They formed trains, cars, houses, birds, balloons, rockets, sailboats, monsters, crab claws . . . the list is almost endless. Then, using Grandfather Tang's Story *as a model, the students wrote a collaborative story based on one of their tangram creations.*

DURING DEVELOPMENTAL EXPERIENCES

In addition to using tangible items during a lesson's introductory phase, realia can also help knit strong and powerful links to learning within a lesson's developmental phase. Simply watching a video or observing a teacher perform a physical demonstration doesn't seem to sow the seeds for learning nor to engender a passion for learning as deeply as direct, hands-on experiences that require the use of multiple senses. Sam Brown, for example, was about to initiate a thematic unit on the arts of various African cultures. The essential question that served to guide instruction was, "What can we learn about a culture through its artifacts?" Mr. Brown introduced his students to the Igbo (or Ibo) people of southeastern Nigeria by reading Ifeoma Onyefulu's award-winning book *My Grandfather Is a Magician: Work and Wisdom in an African Village* (Frances Lincoln). This is the story of a little Nigerian boy who is confused about what kind of job he would like to do when he grows up. He is exposed to several role models—his father is a teacher, his mother owns a bakery, his aunt is a doctor, and his uncle is a blacksmith. But his grandfather seems wiser and stronger than any of the rest of them, for he is a traditional healer who knows about the special medicinal powers of plants and trees. In addition to anticipating the little boy's decision, the children enjoyed learning about many interesting facets of Igbo village life.

To encourage his students' newfound interest in African village life, Mr. Brown took his fifth-grade students on a field trip to an Igbo arts exhibit at a local cultural museum. The exhibit displayed more than 100 objects produced by Igbo artists and craftspeople. The items at the exhibit included wooden totemic sculptures, pottery, textiles, examples of painting and body adornment, and a variety of masks. Though wood predominated, the exhibit also included objects fashioned from bronze, iron, and ivory.

The purpose of the visit was to stimulate further interest in the Igbo through the beauty of their arts and artifacts. Mr. Brown's goal appeared to have been achieved as the students returned full of questions ripe for investigation: "Why are the small totemic figures important to the Igbo?" "What was the

in the students' spontaneous interests by establishing world of the Igbo through open-ended, individualized books, newspapers, and other references, such the end of their investigations, the students orga- what they had learned with their peers. Students each day. A whole new world opened up to rms and artifacts were a direct expression of their ures (ikenga) symbolized traditionally masculine eness. These carved figures were kept in the men's ivory and brass anklets symbolized prestige and he Igbo's masquerades, in which male performers

ormation to satisfy their curiosities, they consid- hey had uncovered. One group created jewelry for ask; a third designed calabashes with intricate ga. Each group described its project by writing a investigative adventure. Each student published his or her paragraph on a hyperlinked website that the class developed (using Google Pages). Each paragraph included the following information:

- *What is the item?*
- *What is it made of?*
- *How is it used?*
- *What do we have in our culture that compares to this item?*

Whenever teachers use realia in their classrooms, they do not simply display the items and turn the students loose. They understand that learning to "read" an object is not much different than learning to read a book. Therefore, after you select an object that may be unfamiliar to students, the important thing is to teach them how to really look at it and to use observational strategies to sort out information about it. There is no correct order for the following questions, nor do you need to use all of them.

1. ***Introduce the experience.*** Select an artifact that may be unfamiliar to students; teach the students how to look at it carefully and how to use their investigative skills by associating it to their past experiences with questions such as, "What do suppose this is?" "What do you already know about this?" "Have you ever seen anything like this?" "What do you want to find out about it?" Then have the students interact with and explore the items.

2. *Reflect on the experience.* Check to see if the students have a clear grasp of the targeted concept. Guide students with the sample questions as they respond to the object: "What do you notice first?" "What does it look like, feel like, sound like?" "How was it made?" "Who made the item?" "What was it made of?" "How do you think this item was used?" "Why do you think this item is important to the people who made it?" "What does this item tell you about the people who made/used it?" "If you could talk to the person who made or owned this artifact, what questions would you ask?" Based on the results of the class discussion, decide what additional resources or experiences you will need to help students get a clear idea of the subject matter content related to the artifact.

3. *Apply what was learned.* Students use the new subject matter and skills in other parts of their lives. Ask students how the experience relates to their own lives or to the real world: "What did you learn from the experience?" "Where is the item, or a similar one, used today?" "Has something new taken its place?" "How might use this new item solve the problems we discussed at the start of class today?" "Can you use the item for some need of your own?" "What more do you want to learn?" "How can you find out?"

CHECK YOUR UNDERSTANDING 5.4 **Click here** to check your understanding of this section of the chapter.

The Arts

What would the world be like if there were no arts? Stop for a moment and think: no Elvis Presley or Marian Anderson, no chicken dance or classical ballet, no *Anna Karenina* or "It was a dark and stormy night . . . ," no Mickey Mouse, no Lorax, no Mona Lisa's smile, no *Better Homes and Gardens*, no graffiti, no tattoos, no Howdy Doody, no stirring band performance at halftime, no *Gone with the Wind*, no Michelangelo's Sistine Chapel ceiling. As a matter of fact, you wouldn't even be reading this text if the arts did not exist—literary, visual, graphic, and digital arts. There is no doubt that our pleasurable, colorful, and vibrant world would be reduced to a gray, flat, and lifeless place. Likewise, you can be assured that social studies would mutate into a colorless, spiritless, and meaningless elementary school experience if deprived of the arts.

Certainly, a great deal of what we take from the arts is intrinsic; the arts invigorate our inner lives and enhance our emotional well-being. But the advantages of incorporating the arts in social studies go far beyond intrinsic value; the arts help students understand the real world by experiencing ideas and emotions in ways that words cannot hope to equal. Can you think of a better way to understand and appreciate ancient Japanese culture than through its magnificent kabuki theater, kana characters (writing), kites, folktales and folk songs, origami (paper folding), men's and women's kimonos, temples, statues, and pottery? Isadora Duncan, a renowned dancer, is said to have once commented: "If I could tell you what I mean there would be no point in dancing." The arts reflect cultures to such a degree that they, more than words and numbers, may well tell the most complete story of any civilization.

Neither the social sciences nor the arts, by themselves, offer a complete picture of the world, but a combination of both provides a more complete picture and a more comprehensive understanding that is difficult to duplicate. Standardized test scores improve in non-arts subjects, truancy rates decline, and critical and creative skills increase. The arts have been assigned a range of meanings throughout the years, but in this text "the arts" will include *music, dance, drama,* and the *visual arts.* As you explore opportunities to include the arts as instructional

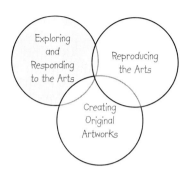

FIGURE 5.6 Techniques for Integrating the Arts and Social Studies

resources in your social studies program, consider that students should experience the arts in three viable ways: (1) *exploring and responding to* the arts (2) *reproducing* the arts, and (3) *creating* original artworks (see Figure 5.6).

Exploring and Responding

There are plenty of wonderful ways to connect students to art and culture through social studies content, but to have the greatest impact on learning, we must expand our ideas of what the arts encompass. Certainly, many examples of the arts must be included in your social studies class, not just those found in galleries, museums, concert halls, or theaters. Help students notice the arts all around them by informally experiencing the arts in the classroom and in public spaces such as parks or safe neighborhood streets. Look for interesting events and experiences; for example, there is something fascinating about busking, or street performing. From double dutch rope jumpers, to magicians, to musicians, to face painters, there is enormous talent to be found in the neighborhood. Street arts and popular arts also provide rich experiences—advertising posters, paintings on buildings and sidewalks, housing design, comic books, advertising jingles, rock songs, patriotic tunes, television shows, and holiday rituals. What is initially meaningful to your students may not be the same as "great arts," but students must gain a sense of art in their own lives before they can be expected to value the arts in expanded contexts. Naturally, interactive, child-friendly museum exhibits, galleries, and performances or festivals are wonderful places for children to learn about arts and culture. While most galleries and museums are designed for older children and adults, "Children's Museums" stand out with interactive exhibits where younger children are welcome to learn and explore. You need not be a professional musician, actor, dancer, or artist to present the arts to your students; you need only to be tuned into the beauty and excitement of the arts and be willing to bring that world into your social studies classroom.

Whether they experience the arts in the neighborhood, on the Internet, in the classroom, in books, on television, or in galleries or theaters, students need to do much more than observe the product or performance and offer a quick opinion about it. Learning to explore requires students to carry out careful examinations, construct new or deeper understandings, and respond meaningfully to the arts. Children often come up with insightful and interesting comments as you guide them in exploring an arts experience through open-ended class discussions:

- What do you see here? What's going on?
- What story do you think the artist/performer is trying to tell?
- How do you think the artist/performer does this?
- Does the product/performance remind you of something you already know about or have done before?

Exploring and responding to arts objects such as these ancient amphores (large two-handled storage jars from Greek and Roman antiquity) creates a direct, sensory connection between students and concepts that results in increased levels of interest and understanding.

JackF/Fotolia

- What is the purpose of the product/performance?
- How has the product/performance made important contributions to the culture?
- Do you like this? What is the most interesting part of this product or performance?
- Would you like to meet the artist, musician, dancer, or actor?

Reproducing

Exposure to the arts does not stop with exploring and discussing. Students must have many opportunities to try their hand at *reproducing the arts*. As they reproduce the music, drawings, songs, dance movements, or other nonverbal expressions of people they are learning about, students are also personalizing the information. Because the process of reproducing art is intended to reinforce specific understandings, authenticity and accuracy must be primary considerations; otherwise, you run the risk of being personally or culturally insensitive. To understand what it means to be personally or culturally insensitive, imagine for a moment that you are observing a classroom where a teacher is preparing to use arts resources to help his students learn about rituals and ceremonies of the Hopi Indians, natives of northwestern Arizona. Hopi rituals and ceremonies often included special headdresses and clothing; symbolic chanting, singing, and dancing were done to the rhythm of drums, rattles, and flutes or whistles. For today's lesson, the teacher, with all good intentions, wanted his students to understand that in August, when it is particularly dry in the Southwest, the Hopis performed a ceremonial rain dance as a way to ask the spirits to send them the rain they desperately needed for their crops. To help his students understand this unique ritual, the teacher selected a "Native American Rain Dance" activity that he found in a widely used commercial teaching resource. Following the clear instructions, the teacher directed his students to form a circle and sit quietly in their chairs until he modeled the actions they were to mimic. The teacher started by rubbing his palms back and forth to imitate the sounds of a "mist." He turned toward the child on his right and passed the action to that child. He explained that when the action went around the circle and returned to him, he would switch to a new action and pass it back around. The child dutifully mimicked the teacher's action; the "mist" was passed, one by one, until all the children around the circle were rubbing their palms. When the action returned to him, the teacher changed the motion by snapping his fingers to imitate the sound of a "drizzle" and passed the "drizzle" to the child on his right. That student passed it to the next student until the "drizzle" made its way around the circle and back to the teacher. Soon, everyone would be doing the same action. Next, the teacher patted his thighs to indicate "rain" and passed it on around the circle. Finally, the group stomped its feet to indicate a "downpour." The process was reversed to end the rainstorm. Thus, the class participated in what the resource called a "Native American Rain Dance." Although there are various descriptions of "rain dances" online and in print resources, I have yet to find one quite like that! This classroom experience paints a clear picture of how culturally disrespectful uninformed teaching can be. It has no place in today's social studies classrooms.

Unfortunately, the students did not learn that the Native American tribes who live in dry southwestern regions are a very spiritual people, and a large part of their time was devoted to rituals to help bring rain for the growth of crops on their dry land. The Pueblo, for instance, had particularly intricate rain dances. Their dances were not "circle dances" but complex rituals during which men and women wearing special headdresses, masks, and clothing stood in separate lines and moved in multiple patterns to steady drum beats and solo and choral vocalizations. The Pueblo keep these rituals alive even today; they can be viewed on various websites.

The "rain dance" learning experience is similar to that of a teacher who asked his students to construct model colonial log cabins with pretzel sticks and peanut butter or another teacher whose students constructed tepees (conical structures intricately made of animal skins or birch bark by Native Americans of the Great Plains) with painted construction paper cones and the one whose students made them from soft corn tortilla shells! How could these "learning activities" possibly help students gain an understanding of how log cabins were built from logs laid horizontally and interlocked on the ends with notches, the gaps plastered over with mud and grass mixtures to keep most of the weather outside? How would students understand that, despite their appearance, tepees were not just simple conical tents; the way the shelters were constructed communicated important expressions of spiritual beliefs and cultural values? These kinds of activities commonly appear in idea resource books, but they establish a weak connection between the experience and the culture. This word of caution is not meant to stifle your eagerness for a "hands-on" arts component of social studies instruction, but rather to point out your responsibility to organize and coordinate meaningful knowledge through the arts.

While studying Native American Indians of the Southwest, for example, Ethel Carter carried out an arts experience that can be considered culturally responsive as opposed to culturally insensitive. Ms. Carter began the lesson by showing her fourth graders an authentic reproduction that she picked up at the American Museum of Natural History in New York City.

Ms. Carter explained that, according to Native American tradition, the "talking stick" was used for centuries by many American Indian tribes in council circles to designate who had the right to speak (see Figure 5.7). When matters of great concern came before the council, the chief would hold the talking stick and begin a discussion. When he finished what he had to say, the chief would hold out the talking stick, and whoever wished to speak after him would take it. Only the person holding the stick was allowed to speak. The stick was passed from one person to another until all who wished to speak had had an opportunity. After everyone had had a chance to speak, the stick was passed back to the chief.

FIGURE 5.7   Native American Talking Stick

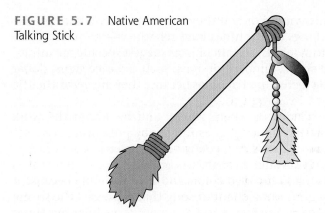

Some tribes used a peace pipe, feather, wampum belt, sacred shell, or some other object instead of a talking stick. Regardless of its form, the purpose of the talking stick was to keep order during a council meeting. The students decided that this would be a useful and appropriate technique to guide small-group discussions during their unit and, throughout the year, class meetings in their classroom. The students wanted to make their own talking sticks to take home, so Ms. Carter found online directions for making talking sticks. The students were careful to select the appropriate ornamentation, for each item used on a talking stick has special meaning. In the Lakota tradition, for example, red is for life, yellow is for knowledge, blue is for prayer and wisdom, white is for spirit, purple is for healing, orange is for feeling kinship with all living things, and black is for clarity and focus. The types of feathers, skins, hair, or hide used on a talking stick are very important as well.

The students took their talking sticks home and introduced the process to their families. Surprisingly, several households decided to use the talking sticks to guide important family discussions.

Ms. Carter's activity is considered an example of authentic learning because the learning resources she employed engaged the students in a bona fide task that was *real to them* and could be used either by themselves or by others *in the real world*. Ms. Carter could have taken her students on a field trip to the museum, invited a guest speaker, shown a video, or displayed a series of pictures that gave students enough background information about talking sticks. Maybe next time . . . this time, Ms. Carter decided that the real item would be the best arts resource to use.

Creating

One of the primary goals of integrating the visual and performing arts in your social studies program is to engage students in learning social studies content and concepts while having fun participating in the learning process. The arts also serve as a catalyst for maximizing students' creative potential, so they should not only examine and reproduce art, but also experience the thrill of *creating* art using specified artistic techniques. Because the processes of examining, recreating, and personally creating artistic expressions are all intended to strengthen social studies concepts, authenticity and accuracy once again must be considered extremely important. If the primary purpose of accurately reproducing a Kachina, for example, is to "expand children's understandings of Kachina dolls as religious items of the Hopi people of the American Southwest," then your students must use precise detail in creating their own versions of the dolls. For example, a depiction of a rain cloud on the face of a Kachina is a significant Hopi symbol—its purpose is to seek out spiritual help to provide rain for fertile crops. The children, then, should use this symbol only if they intend to convey that precise meaning. Likewise, all symbols and markings on Kachinas have relevance—the sun, clouds, moon, stars, and lightning. In addition to symbols, certain objects suggest specific meanings, too—feathers, bells, boughs, beads, and shells. Flippant designs, such as peace signs, dollar signs, or smiley faces, have no place while recreating Kachinas because they are *not* authentic symbols of the Hopi culture.

Understandings broaden with knowledge of when, where, and by whom the work was made, but a quality interdisciplinary arts program goes further by presenting students opportunities to express their own creativity, too. When you were of elementary school age, did you enjoy expressing yourself creatively through favorite arts activities? Were there times you sat down with a crayon or paintbrush and blended colors and figures simply because it was fun? Or did you ever spontaneously blurt out a chant or song that expressed the strong emotion you were feeling at the moment? I'm sure you must have spent some hilarious times making up new dance moves with your best friends. It isn't surprising that the preschool and elementary school years can be the most creative period in an individual's life. That is why this third (creative) dimension of interdisciplinary arts is important, for just as nature and nurture combine to help children grow intellectually, physically, socially, and emotionally, those two factors also work together to help children grow progressively more creative. In social studies, process-based arts activities are deliberately centered more on what the students do than on what they produce, although the overall goal is to link the artistic process with an end product; that is, although a product will most often be the end result of an arts project in social studies, students should have the opportunity to explore, create, and discover during the process. To illustrate, let us return to the Kachina doll example. Suppose that you have carried out instruction as recommended in the preceding paragraphs—(1) your students learned about the "who, what, where, why, and how" of real Kachinas, and then (2) they made accurate reproductions, or models, to communicate what they had learned. Now, your instructional goal is to have your students create original symbols for Kachina dolls. Would a baseball or musical note symbol be appropriate in this case? This is an appropriate activity only if the artifact lends itself to original interpretation. In the case of the Hopi, there are over 1,000 documented Kachinas, and new ones are regularly invented or created by Hopi people. Because of this spirit of continuous originality, it is considered proper to encourage your students to design new Kachinas. If the object does not lend itself to original expression, however, creating new symbols would not only be an incorrect interpretation of these highly creative and resourceful people, but would also disrespect and trivialize their cultural values and beliefs.

Visual Arts

Dynamic social studies teachers operate with a conviction that the visual arts must play a significant instructional role if students are to truly understand and appreciate any culture. As students explore the visual arts of various peoples of Africa, for example, they are eager to try their hand at tie-dyeing, weaving, mask construction, or sculpture. You help enhance the study of Greece by having students experience its architecture, sculptures, paintings, and pottery. Enliven a unit on medieval Europe by having children study and recreate coats of arms, stained glass, and castle designs. You can use the arts of gyotaku (fish printing), block printing, kite making, batik, and folded-paper design to introduce students to Asian cultures. Native American sand paintings, blankets, bead-working techniques, textiles, pottery, and basketry help students learn about the earliest cultures in North America. Pysanky (intricately designed Easter eggs) and flax (straw) dolls bring to life important aspects of Ukrainian culture. The potential is unlimited for integrating the visual arts and social studies. Much of what is known of cultures comes from visual art and architectural evidence, and when students have the opportunity to study visual art from the past, they begin to understand how art reflects the values of a culture. Artworks are primary resources in the study of cultures, so context is extremely important to their understanding.

The discovery of the Lascaux Cave paintings in France, for example, conveyed insights into daily life in the Paleolithic Age. Accidentally discovered in 1940 by four boys near a small French village, Lascaux, the cave contains nearly 2,000 figures on its walls. There are more than 600 animals depicted including horses, bison, ibex, aurochs (an extinct type of ox), mammoths, reindeer, and bears. The paintings were created over 17,000 years ago; the figures provide concrete clues about life at that time. But were these paintings meant to be enjoyable decorations, a way of recording information, or a way to carry out a religious ceremony? Who were these artists and why did they depict their surroundings like this?

Mildred Tanner enriched her fifth graders' unit on prehistoric life by involving the children in a study of the ancient French cave paintings. The lesson required her to access Cave of Lascaux websites (http://www.culture.gouv.fr/culture/arcnat/lascaux/en/ and http://www.mazzaroth.com/ChapterOne/LascauxCave.htm). Ms. Tanner's overall instructional goal was to have the students discover what was important to a prehistoric culture as depicted by its art. Itching to try something new to enhance the study of this facet of early human life and employ a novel approach to draw her students into the topic, Ms. Tanner assembled a low cave in the classroom by stuffing wrinkled paper bags loosely with newspaper, taping the bags closed, and attaching a number of bags together on a stationary classroom wall to simulate rock walls. She then fashioned two side walls by turning some worktables on their sides and covering the tops with crumpled brown craft paper that gave the appearance of jagged rock. Ms. Tanner completed the cave by forming a roof from long sheets of crumpled brown craft paper. She pasted print images from the caves in Lascaux as well as photocopies from three books she found particularly useful onto the walls:

> Cave of Lascaux: The Cave of Prehistoric Wall Paintings *by Brad Burnham*
> *(Powerkids Press)*
> The Cave Painter of Lascaux *by Roberta Angeletti (Crystal Productions)*
> Mystery of the Lascaux Cave *by Dorothy Hinshaw (Benchmark)*

As the students entered the classroom, Ms. Tanner told them that they were about to embark on an adventure to a deep, dark underground cave. She drew them into a series of imaging tasks as they came upon the cave—"walking" into the dark passage, "touching" the damp walls, "listening" to the water as it dripped from the ceiling, and "smelling" the damp, stale air. As they looked around, the children were dazzled by the primitive yet lifelike images of horses, deer, and bison. They were asked to speculate about how the paintings got there, who might have painted them, how long ago they were painted, what art media were used for the paintings, and why they were there. Ms. Tanner wrote their guesses on a large sheet of chart paper taped to one of the walls so they could be reviewed after Ms. Tanner read the book The Cave Painter of Lascaux.

When the story was finished, the children re-examined the pictures stuck on the walls of the virtual cave with increased knowledge and insight. They discussed the ways that people made pictures, looking once more at their hypotheses and collecting information to support or revise each one. Then, as the children remained "huddled" in the cave, they went on to discuss possible reasons why the paintings were rendered on the cave walls: Some were convinced that they may have been a way of passing on information, others felt that they had religious or ceremonial functions, a few thought the paintings were part of a hunting ritual, and one or two argued that the paintings existed simply because the people enjoyed the painting experience itself.

The children's interest in creating their own rock paintings grew as they digested all this information. They were particularly impressed with the ability of the Cro-Magnons to create the images without paintbrushes or paint. After a great deal of research and planning, they decided to reproduce the paintings by fashioning brushes from sticks, reeds, and grass and paint from natural sources such as berries. Then, using homemade brushes and paint, the students recreated several designs as a mural on the remaining blank "cave" walls.

The benefits of such a visual art experience can best be summarized through the words of Wylam who, when asked how he liked the ancient cave painting experience, responded: "I learned all about the Cro-Magnon people, the animals that lived then, and how important hunting was to the Cro-Magnons. Cave painting is not as easy as it looks. The part I liked best was doing our own cave painting. The part I didn't like so much was writing about it in our journals. It was fun making the rock painting. It was COOL!"

You don't have to wait until art class for students to experience great art. Bring the excitement to your social studies program by welcoming into your classroom some of the great artists of the past. It's not necessary to build a mock art museum to house copies of their works, but when you're studying the Civil War, why not set aside a little alcove to display the works of Thomas Nast (call it "Nast's Nook") or Winslow Homer ("Homer's Homestead")? If you're carrying out a unit on Colonial America, think about turning a small corner of your classroom into a Benjamin West display. (West was a painter of historical scenes, mostly portraits, around and after the time of the Revolutionary War.) Whether or not you like these specific suggestions, convert a small corner of your classroom into *something* at least twice a year so your children can step back, look at, and explore great historical art. Setting up a mini-gallery doesn't need to be expensive. You can purchase prints with funds from your principal's petty cash account or buy them online or at local bookstores very reasonably. If that's not possible, try to borrow prints from your local library. You will find that a love for social studies will grow as children experience the greatness of art.

Music

Music is a widely enjoyed art form that can be found in cultures all over the world; it has had an impact on society for as long as people have lived together in groups. Music had its beginnings not in an early human desire to display talent or entertain an audience but to use repetition and tonality to reproduce naturally occurring sounds—possibly as a way to lure animals during a hunt. From this utilitarian start, early humans used music to appease nature and the gods, and music became an essential part of indigenous rituals and ceremonies. Through the years, people have sent messages across distances by pounding on drums; military songs have inspired troops and love of country; millions have received their diplomas while marching onstage to the joyful strains of "Pomp and Circumstance"; people have raised their voices in national anthems to experience patriotism; songs or chants have been sung to keep a rhythm as workers have pulled in nets or pried rails back into line; people have derived inspiration through songs of worship; and cultures have communicated their grief with tender ballads and rocked their babies to sleep with gentle lullabies. Wherever and whenever possible, people have expressed patriotism, grief, love, fear, pleasure, and joy in making music for themselves and for others. Music, without question, has the power to bring forth and communicate powerful messages of cultures across the curriculum.

Music is a very important part of all cultures; it tells us a great deal about people—about when, how, and where to escape. These coded spirituals were of two types: a warning signal or a map to freedom. At face value, for instance, the famous spiritual, "Wade in the Water," seemingly was meant to encourage people to be baptized in order to find religious purification. However, it is actually an ingeniously coded *warning song* that advised slaves to travel along the riverbank so the chase dogs would be thrown off their scent. In a *map song*, the lyrics actually contained elements of a map that directed escaped slaves along a series of routes and safe houses, often run by Quakers, known as the Underground Railroad. For example, "The Drinking Gourd" is a map song closely associated with the Underground Railroad. Taken at face value, a "drinking gourd" refers to the hollowed out gourd used by slaves as a water dipper. However, the song is actually a code intended to guide fugitive slaves. The song is said to have been written by an

Connecting music with social studies is an excellent way to motivate learning and facilitate creative thinking.

Micromonkey/Fotolia

itinerant handyman known as Peg Leg Joe, who spent his winters in the South teaching slaves to interpret its meaning. The first verse is below:

When the sun comes back and the first quail calls,
Follow the Drinking Gourd.
For the old man is waiting to carry you to freedom,
If you follow the Drinking Gourd.

The first verse instructs slaves to leave in the winter or spring. "When the sun comes back" refers to the time from the beginning of winter through spring when the days are getting longer, and the angle of the sun is higher each day at noon. In late winter, the call of migratory quail echoes across southern fields. And, since their breeding season starts in early to mid-April, the quail start calling to each other in early spring. The "drinking gourd" is the Big Dipper. By finding the "drinking gourd" in the sky, people traveling at night could always find the North Star and follow it north to freedom. The old man is Peg Leg Joe (or a guide who will be waiting along the line). So, Peg Leg Joe's ingenious song directed slaves to escape in winter and head north toward the Big Dipper—code name, drinking gourd. A guide will be waiting at the end of the line.

Dance

Music has always had the unique power to stir people to move or dance along to it. "It's exciting to see the kids' faces while they are learning how to do the European Maypole dance," related one satisfied teacher during a "Welcome Springtime" celebration that included music and dance. "You can see a sense of cultural acceptance and pride as they weave the colorful ribbons over, under, over, under, all around the pole!" Dance, usually with the accompaniment of music, is an art form in which the human body is used as a vehicle of expression. In most cultures, dance has been regarded as an integral part of religious, community, and family celebrations, and movement is regarded as an important mode of communication.

Cultural dance has developed in two major directions: folk dance and ritual (ceremonial) dance. *Folk dances* have, perhaps, the deepest cultural roots of any form. Folk dances are traditional dances that originated among the "common people" of a culture; many groups perform folk dances onstage today. Popular folk dances include Western square dancing, Appalachian clogging, African American and Hispanic American hip hop, Jewish hora, Cajun zydeco, Chinese Dragon Dance, Eastern European polka, Mexican La Bamba, English country dance, and the Hawaiian hula. *Ritual dances* are ceremonial dances that are part of a religious ritual. They include dance forms such as the Native American rain dances and the "coming of age" dances of Africa. Ritual dances are usually performed to call on the gods to drive out evil spirits, help in farming or hunting, increase the fertility of humans and animals, or take care of many other pressing group concerns.

One teacher, Verna Oakley, structured the learning environment to incorporate music and dance into the study of the Chinese Dragon Dance.

New Year, the most important of the traditional Chinese holidays, begins each year on the first day of the first lunar month. In 2012, that day fell on January 23, a time when Mrs. Oakley introduced a meaningful, integrated, arts-based learning experience to help her students deepen their understanding and appreciation of Chinese culture. To help them acquire a basic background of information, Mrs. Oakley read aloud the beautifully illustrated book Chin Chiang and the Dragon's Dance *by Ian Wallace (Groundwood). The book tells the story of young Chin Chiang, who had dreamed of dancing the Dragon's Dance on New Year since he was as high as his grandfather's knees. But, now that the holiday is approaching, the young boy worries that he might not be able to dance well enough to make his grandfather proud of him. Eventually, though, a friend helps Chin Chiang discover the confidence he needs to perform the dance with skill and pride.*

The book is a fascinating story that highlights the importance of the holiday as well as the meaning of the Dragon's Dance, a dance that is believed to bring Chinese people strength, wisdom, and good fortune. The children learned that the Dragon's Dance is performed at New Year to scare away evil spirits. They watched an actual Dragon's Dance on their computers after Mrs. Oakley

Dance can be integrated nearly everywhere in social studies, but the cultural aspect is especially valuable.

Elizabeth A. Maxim

found an appropriate Internet site. They loved seeing the Dragon's Dance dancers raise and lower the ornate dragon rhythmically as nearby musicians supplied the pulsating accompaniment. The class learned that dragons used in the Dragon's Dance vary in length and that longer dragons are thought to be luckier than shorter ones.

The children were enthralled with the story and video and begged Mrs. Oakley to let them make their own moving dragon to celebrate the holiday. She welcomed their enthusiasm and guided their initial efforts to construct a sturdy frame for their dragon. The children covered the frame with cloth that was painted and decorated to resemble a dragon's head and body. Because the length of the dragon is associated with the luck it brings, the children decided that they wanted a very long dragon.

To perform the Dragon's Dance, the young dancers carried the dragon's representation on poles. The lead dancers lifted, dipped, and shook the dragon's head while those who followed imitated the rhythmic movements of the dragon in a rising and falling manner. Accompaniment was supplied by a number of student "musicians" using traditional drums, cymbals, and gongs.

To add some festive pizzazz to the classroom in recognition of the Chinese New Year, the children made colorful hanging paper lanterns and suspended them throughout the classroom.

Theater/Drama

As we have discovered with the other arts forms discussed to this point, people since the dawn of civilization have used drama to reveal their innermost feelings. Drama is a universal form of human expression found in cultures all over the world and throughout history; it brings out the heart of a culture. During ceremonial rituals, while dressed in masks and animal skins, primitive humans attempted to communicate through drama with magical spirits for their control of certain events (e.g., a good hunt, weather, fertility). As humans settled into communities and began to rely on agriculture, their greatest fear was of a failed harvest. Special dances and rituals were created to appeal to the spirits controlling those events. From these early forms, drama developed into a stylized form of communication with intricate dialogue, costumes, and symbolism that expressed and reinforced the shared values and beliefs of a culture. Examples include the comedies and tragedies of ancient Greece, the temple drama of early India, the kabuki dance drama of Japan, the religious mystery cycles of medieval Europe, Italian commedia dell'arte, Balinese shadow puppet theater, Native American and African mask rituals, and French farce comedies. Although they took place in different places and at different times, all these forms of drama have one thing in common—they dig down to the essence of a culture. While dramatic performances can introduce students to ideas or values that are particular to cultures, finding dramatic forms that can be understood and appreciated by elementary school children can require great effort. Children's theater performances and programs especially designed for young audiences are a good place to start. You can also seek help through social and cultural organizations; websites, including YouTube; community centers; city or county recreational departments; libraries; museums; or local performing arts centers.

Drama is a versatile teaching tool that reaches multiple learning styles, content areas, age groups, and levels of language and experience. However, do not think of classroom drama as presenting plays for an audience or teaching acting and performance skills. The goal is to enhance learning in social studies through improvisational role-playing or lightly scripted performances. In cultural play-building, students develop scenes, through dialogue and action, which are focused on the interactions of characters. To be successful, the students must not only research their characters but must also become familiar with a lot of cultural information, such as the clothing they should wear, food-related beliefs and taboos, or samples of the language they should speak. Consequently, play-building truly ignites the interests of children and enhances their personal drive to unearth information about people, places, and things.

Classroom drama, then, should emerge from cultural content. However, the students' concern for elaborate scenery and costumes should not take precedence over the concepts or ideas the play is designed to convey. Simple objects can effectively represent more intricate items; for example, a mural or bulletin board can serve as a backdrop; a branch in a big can filled with dirt makes an excellent tree or bush; a large box becomes a boat; chairs placed in a straight line can indicate seats on a train or airplane; and a wooden spoon can serve as a handheld microphone.

The following example describes a highly interesting and culturally relevant learning experience that took place in Chandra Venna's fifth-grade classroom after her students listened to the reading of a popular African folktale, *Mufaro's Beautiful Daughters* (Lothrop). (Yes, well-written picture books, like *Mufaro's Beautiful Daughters*, can work very well with upper-grade elementary school students and teach them a lot.) A Cinderella variant retold by John Steptoe, the tale tells of Mufaro, a proud and happy man, who lived long ago in a small village in Zimbabwe with two beautiful daughters, Nyasha and Manyara. Nyasha was kind and considerate, while Manyara was selfish and always ill tempered. When a call went out from the king seeking the most beautiful and worthy queen, Mufaro sent his two daughters. After a series of magical events tested the goodness of both daughters, the king, of course, selected Nyasha. Manyara ended up as a servant in the royal household.

The students talked about the events of the story and the cultural norms of the village. They eventually wanted to learn more about village life in early Zimbabwe. Of all the interesting information they uncovered, the students seemed to be particularly captivated by the importance of babies to African village life and were convinced that the king (Nyoka) and Nyasha should now be planning their first child. Therefore, they thought it would be interesting to continue the Mufaro story by writing their own authentic naming ceremony for the couple's imaginary first baby. Ms. Venna helped her students obtain useful information about traditional African naming ceremonies from a local African American cultural organization. After reading the information, several students noted a connection to the opening scenes of the movie *The Lion King*, when Rafiki presents Simba, the newborn cub of King Mufasa and Queen Sarabi, to a gathering of animals at Pride Rock. The students used all this information to write and perform the following skit:

> *Narrator: African villagers celebrate the birth of babies with great pride. Babies are an important part of African life; the African baby belongs not only to its mother and father but rather to everyone in the village. Everyone in the village loves the baby and is responsible for giving it protection and direction in life.*

SCENE 1

People are milling about the village. Nyoka (the king) and Nyasha are sitting on benches and holding their baby. Soundtrack music from The Lion King *is playing softly in the background.*

Nyoka: With pride and joy, we announce that on this special day our child is to be named.

Nyasha: Come be our guests at this joyous celebration.

SCENE 2

Narrator: Everyone comes together. All guests sit in a circle with Nyoka and Nyasha. The ceremony begins when the oldest living member of the family recites the family history.

Elder: Welcome to all who join us to bless and honor the child of Nyoka and Nyasha. Out of deep respect for their ancestors, we begin the ceremony with a short family history. (A brief history is recounted.) Now, everyone will join together to introduce this child to the nature of life.

Friend 1: I offer a few drops of wine to the baby because the wine ensures the child a full and fruitful life.

Friend 2: I splash a few drops of water on the baby's forehead and put a drop or two into its mouth when it cries. This is a way of showing that water is important for all living things. It also tells me if the baby is alert.

Friend 3: I drop a bit of honey onto the baby's tongue. This is to show the child that life is sweet.

Friend 4: I place a pinch of pepper on the baby's lips to represent the spice of life. Although we have learned that life is sweet, we must also know that life is exciting.

Friend 5: I lay a dab of salt on the baby's lips. The salt stands for the liveliness and zest of life.

Elder: The baby of Nyoka and Nyasha will be rich in its pursuit of life.

SCENE 3

Narrator: Everyone, including Nyoka and Nyasha, must give the baby a name. Girls are named on the seventh day after birth; boys are named on the eighth.

Elder: On this joyful ___th day after birth, all who are present are invited to offer a chosen name for the baby of Nyoka and Nyasha. (Each member of the group uses the sentence pattern spoken by the child below to offer a name for the baby.)

Child: I have picked the name Nayo because it means we have joy. This child brings much happiness to Nyoka and Nyasha.

Elder: The ceremony is now complete. May Nyoka and Nyasha have many grand days with their beautiful new child.

On the day of the performance, it was stunning to see how seriously the students took on their roles. They dressed to look like the characters and brought simple items from home to serve as props. Many of them did extra research on their own to carry out their roles realistically. They took themselves back in time and place as they carried out the naming ceremony. While they went through the skit, it was apparent that the class had become "experts" on African naming ceremonies.

 Video Exploration 5.3

Reflection on Learning

You may simply scribble rough notes or jot down something more polished and complete. The point is to simply start recording your ideas spontaneously and candidly.

As a result of tight budgets, standards-based education reform, and a public perception that the arts are enjoyable but not vital, the study of high-quality arts, either as stand-alone subjects or integrated into the curriculum, has been dwindling in recent years. What arguments would you use to convince others that it is important to keep the arts strong in social studies?

 CHECK YOUR UNDERSTANDING 5.5   Click here to check your understanding of this section of the chapter.

Games

It seems that children around the world and throughout time have one thing in common—they enjoy playing games. In order to get a realistic picture of people, places, and the times in which they lived, games can be one of the most enjoyable and effective resources to add to your instructional resources repertoire. Help your students discover how children from Brazil, Mexico, Canada, Korea, China, Germany, Russia, and many other countries play unique games. Students also enjoy playing different versions of the same games enjoyed by children in the United States, just under a different name. It is fun and instructive to teach your children the

Mexican or Japanese version of *Rock, Paper, Scissors* ("Piedra, Papel o Tijeras" from Mexico and "Jan-Kem-Po" from Japan) or, as we see with Theresa Garza, a cultural variation of a game you should remember from your childhood. Mrs. Garza believes that games can be used as a vehicle to promote multicultural knowledge and values, so she makes certain games will always be part of an annual week-long "Multicultural Children's Jubilee," an event in which students enjoy and participate in games, crafts, music, folk dancing, and art activities from cultures represented in their classroom. As part of the jubilee, parents and other family members show students, other families, and Mrs. Garza how to play games enjoyed by children in their home countries.

Mrs. Garza and her parents, who are originally from Mexico, opened this year's Children's Jubilee with all the essentials of a Mexican Fiesta—piñatas, arts and crafts projects, mariachi music, a brief hat dance, and nachos and salsa. And several Mexican parents taught a game popular among Spanish-speaking children called Los Colores *(Colors). The game is a lot like the popular childhood game you may have played as a child,* Red Rover.

In this game, one child is chosen to be St. Guadalupe and another is chosen to be Mother-of-Color, or Rainbow. All of the other children are assigned color names, each one assigned by Rainbow. (Spanish color names: rojo = red, verde = green, azul = blue, amarillo = yellow, negro = black, or blanco = white.) All the colors belong to Rainbow, and they line up behind her, across the play space from St. Guadalupe. St. Guadalupe's area is designated as "Home Base." St. Guadalupe then initiates the dialogue depicted below. When St. Guadalupe calls out a color, all the children assigned that color name must attempt to reach "Home Base" without being tagged by St. Guadalupe. If they reach "Home Base" safely, they get ready to go again. Those who are caught help St. Guadalupe tag other players until everyone (including Rainbow) is captured. Then the game is over.

St. Guadalupe: "Knock, knock!" (Child pretends to knock on a door.)
Rainbow: "Who's there?"
St. Guadalupe: "St. Guadalupe."
Rainbow: "What do you want?"
St. Guadalupe: "I want a color."
Rainbow: "What color?"
St. Guadalupe: "Verde!"

As the children played these games and learned about their classmates' cultural backgrounds, Mrs. Garza displayed a world map to show the class their home countries: "Where in the World Are We From?" The Internet contains a range of multicultural games that will engage and enlighten your students as they explore cultures in their classroom or around the world. As a bonus, these games also help develop awareness and acceptance of other languages as well as basic skills such as counting, word recognition, matching, turn-taking, and color and shape identification.

 CHECK YOUR UNDERSTANDING 5.6   **Click here** to check your understanding of this section of the chapter.

Reflection on Learning

You may simply scribble rough notes or jot down something more polished and complete. The point is to simply start recording your ideas spontaneously and candidly.

Study your state's social studies standards for a grade level of your choice. Identify two or three targeted outcomes that lend themselves to being taught with varying instructional resources from the *direct experiences* realm. Brainstorm ideas for activities that you might use to help students of various abilities and interests acquire or strengthen your selected outcomes.

Video Exploration 5.4

A Final Thought

Among the many standout qualities of successful social studies teachers is their ability to establish connections across the school subjects and engage their students in the kinds of instructional resources that ensure the participation of all. Would you like to stand out one day? To become a memorable teacher, you must learn to offer classroom experiences like no other. You cannot continually do the things all other teachers are doing because you will end up being just another face in the crowd. Standout teachers can do it all—motivate, inspire, and lead children through creative learning experiences that blur traditional subject matter lines and engage them in things they love doing.

The heart of standout social studies teaching is balance and proportion. These elements do not normally emerge as part of a teaching personality during a student's undergraduate certification program, during student teaching, or even after a year on the job. They often emerge after repeated successes that start with textbook-based instruction. But you will not rely on textbooks to guide you throughout your entire teaching career; a feeling of unrest and a strong desire to "spread your wings" will begin to entice you to expand your repertoire and experiment with varied instructional materials and activities during your earliest years of teaching. Years ago, Katz (1972) described this professional evolution as a stage-related process. It holds much meaning today:

- *Stage 1 (first year): You are preoccupied with survival.* You ask yourself questions such questions as, "Can I get through the day in one piece? Without losing a child? Can I make it until the end of the week? Until the next vacation? Can I really do this kind of work day after day? Will I be accepted by my colleagues?" Textbooks are useful tools that help teachers gain the confidence necessary to manage the routines causing most of the anxiety during this stage.

- *Stage 2 (second year): You decide you can survive.* You begin to focus on individual children who pose problems and on troublesome situations, and you ask yourself these kinds of questions: "How can I help the shy child? How can I help a child who does not seem to be learning? What more can I do for children with special needs?"

- *Stage 3 (third and fourth years): You begin to tire of doing the same things with the children.* You like to meet with other teachers, scan magazines, and search through other sources of information to discover new projects and activities for the children. You ask questions about new developments in the field: "Who is doing what? Where? What are some of the new materials, techniques, approaches, and ideas? How can I make social studies (or any other subject) more powerful?"

According to Katz's developmental theory, then, you should not expect to move away from a deliberate textbook-based routine until sometime during the third year of teaching. At first, you will feel more comfortable teaching with the help of textbooks and with ideas taken from others. The need to grow and learn will become evident as an inner drive gives you no other choice but to branch out. You should then begin to formulate and refine a personal philosophy of instruction that will serve as a foundation for all of you future professional decisions. The difference between teachers who are good "technicians" and those who are educational leaders appears to be their willingness to constantly think about and work toward methods based on a sound personalized philosophy of teaching and learning. Take every opportunity to aim for a professional life as an educational leader; just imagine how you will feel when you succeed!

References

Chu, J. (2015, March 18). A perfect place to start: Arts in education [Web log post]. Retrieved from http://arts.gov/art-works/2015/perfect-place-start-arts-education

Huebner, T. (2008). What research says about . . . / balancing the concrete and abstract. *Educational Leadership, 66*(3), 86–87.

Katz, L. G., Developmental stages of preschool teachers. *Elementary School Journal, 73,* 50–54.

Pashler, H., Bain, P., Bottge, B., Graesser, A., Koedinger, K., McDaniel, M., & Metcalfe, J. (2007). *Organizing instruction and study to improve student learning* (NCER 2007–2004). Washington, DC: National Center for Education Research. Retrieved from http://ies.ed.gov/ncee/wwc/pdf/practiceguides/20072004.pdf

Potter, L. A. (2003). Connecting with the past. *Social Education, 67,* 372–377.

Beyond the Ordinary:
Teaching and Learning with Representational Instructional Resources

Learning Outcomes

According to constructivist theory, experiential learning can be divided into two major categories: (a) direct involvement in *concrete experiences* as well as (b) exploring a variety of *representations* that are used to depict or mimic the real world (for example, storytelling, looking at pictures, watching television, and using various forms of technology). In social studies education, using a variety of instructional sources from each category is essential; experiencing multiple perspectives of a particular phenomenon provides students with various contexts from which to access knowledge and develop progressively more complex concepts. Determine your instructional goals, decide how you will assess progress toward those goals, and then employ the instructional resources that are most likely to achieve the intended outcomes. Selecting the right option is crucial and must be made purposefully; there is no "best" form of representation that will satisfy *all* instructional purposes. As your decision-making skills will influence student progress, students must also learn to select and use multiple forms of representation when communicating information to others.

After completing this chapter, you will be able to:

- Identify the key ways technology can help promote and enhance powerful social studies teaching and learning.

- Explain how to organize self-instructional learning centers that are set aside for independent review or investigation of a particular skill, understanding, or interest.

- Describe how to facilitate the process of understanding and appreciating information presented through pictures and study prints.

- Describe the use of staged simulations that recreate, as realistically as possible, an event, process, role, or understanding from the real world.

Classroom Snapshot

The focus of Joe Drozd's unit was the Sioux Nation, made up of three subdivisions based on the language dialects spoken: the Lakota, the Dakota, and the Nakota. The students had previously learned that the Sioux maintained many separate tribal governments scattered across several reservations and communities in the Dakotas, Minnesota, and Nebraska. Students explored the life basics of the Sioux—including food, clothing, and shelter (but they did NOT make tortilla tepees!). They also learned about the importance of the buffalo to the Sioux and that the Sioux were a deeply spiritual people who communed with the spirit world through music and dance.

The goal of today's lesson was to understand that the Sioux, like all North American Indians, had no written language and that, in the past, storytellers (oral historians) passed down history and morals to younger generations through the oral tradition. To begin today's lesson, Mr. Drozd and his students gathered at the rug area where informal discussions frequently took place. He showed the children a parfleche, a rawhide bag decorated with geometric designs that the Sioux used to hold many things—clothing, valuables, food, and tools. (The word "parfleche" was adapted from the early French fur traders; it is not an original Sioux word.) Because Mr. Drozd liked to use realia whenever possible, he searched online sites and other sources to buy a real parfleche. Unfortunately, an authentic parfleche would cost him hundreds of dollars, so Mr. Drozd crafted an authentic-looking parfleche from a kit that he purchased much more reasonably online. After explaining the significance of the parfleche to his students, Mr. Drozd informed them that his contained something special related to today's lesson. He opened the pouch and revealed a chamois cloth he had previously decorated with colored markers to replicate the pictographic symbols that a Sioux historian, or storyteller, would have drawn on cured buffalo hide to document important events. Mr. Drozd gave the children an opportunity to examine the hide carefully, recording their thoughts about what the object of intrigue might be: "It looks like maybe something the Sioux might wear," suggested Myron. "I think it tells a story . . . maybe about hunting or something to do with nature. The Sioux had a strong connection to nature," claimed Reggie. Mr. Drozd used timely prompts and questions to promote deeper thought about the predictions: "What makes you think that?" "What clues helped you come up with that idea?" "How do you know that?" "Does it remind you of something else?" The students then discussed their observations and compiled a list of several predictions from their discussion.

Mr. Drozd slowly looked into the parfleche once again and revealed a book—The Year the Stars Fell: Lakota Winter Counts at the Smithsonian by Candace S. Greene and Russell Thornton (University of Nebraska Press). The book was a detailed reference source on Lakota winter counts. As Mr. Drozd read it aloud, the children learned how wise storytellers kept track of major events that took place in years past by doing a "winter count." Since he had a high-speed Internet connection with a projector, Mr. Drozd and his class visited a website and uncovered more information about how a year's events (from first snowfall of one year to first snowfall of the next) were recorded in pictographs. Through both experiences, Mr. Drozd's students learned that the Lakota Sioux had community historians called winter count keepers. Each year, the keeper drew a pictograph depicting a memorable event that took place that year on tanned animal hide, bark, or cloth. The pictographs, each representing a single year, were organized in chronological order, either in spirals or in horizontal rows, so that the winter count as a whole served to spur the storyteller's memory whenever tribal elders passed on the history through songs and stories geared to teaching the "little ones." The Lakota call the winter counts "waniyetu (year) wowapi (drawing)." A particularly memorable event would become the year's name; a year of a great meteor shower, for example, was actually called "The Year the Stars Fell."

The next day, Mr. Drozd helped the students create a class winter count using a brown paper bag. He made one ahead of time as a model. To begin, the class discussed the major events of the school year and decided which events were the most unique and memorable. Then they were directed to lightly dab a brown paper grocery bag with a damp sponge to soften the paper and crumple the paper into a large ball a few times to give it the look of animal hide. Next, they tore an animal outline around the border, keeping in mind its four legs, tail, and neck. The children drew their own school year winter counts (in chronological order) using symbols found on websites or from an informational book. Each winter count was shared orally and placed in a classroom display.

All unit projects were shared at an end-of-unit "powwow" (Native American Indian gathering focused on dance, song, and family), to which all the "little ones" (third graders) of their school were invited. The wacipi (powwow) was an opportunity for Mr. Drozd's students to share what they had learned about the Sioux language, history, food, clothing, dance, song, family celebrations, and other cultural elements.

As we extend our search for potential instructional resources that help make knowledge communicable in our social studies classrooms, we must think about the many representational sources (a likeness of the real world) that may be used when the richness of concrete experience is unavailable or impractical for classroom use. In essence, we must ask how to mimic a real-world experience without actually being there: instrumental music? singing? dancing? visual art? photos? technology? blogs? email? Internet? mass media? learning centers? I could go on and on. These days, we have many excellent resources available for learning, either actually being there or experiencing representations of real things. Did you notice how Mr. Drozd used representational resources with his students (parfleche and Internet site) when he was unable to obtain concrete ones?

In the opening scenario, Mr. Drozd obviously involved his students in doing several things and in thinking about what they were doing. "I find that learning is most fruitful when I assemble a reasonable combination of instructional resources," he explains. "Throughout my career, I've learned that success can rarely be achieved when I limit instruction to a single resource, regardless of whether that source is as abstract as a textbook reading selection or as concrete as a well-planned field trip." Despite its advantages, however, selecting multiple instructional resources for social studies can be difficult and confusing. But at the same time, no other elementary school subject has as many built-in opportunities for the creative use of multiple instructional resources as social studies. "That's why I love teaching social studies . . . it's by far my favorite subject to teach!" beamed Mr. Drozd. "Reading class, by its nature, is primarily dominated by print material or digital text; math often includes manipulatives and games, but students are most frequently involved in paper-and-pencil exercises; science is more hands-on with its interesting experiments that challenge and guide students through topical investigations; but social studies contains all of those possibilities along with a wealth of other resources to support your instructional planning: books, periodicals, documents, pamphlets, field trips, resource people, music, visual arts, dance, drama, cultural games, study prints and pictures, photos, videos, globes and maps, models, compasses, concrete objects, technological media. I can go on and on and on. Of all the resources at our fingertips, though, I've never understood the attraction some teachers have to the mishmash of 'cutesy' Internet resources for coloring pages, connecting the dots, fill in the blanks, or other worksheet activities. Why waste your time searching for those low-level, *hands-off* instructional resources when you could be planning to use some of the wonderful social studies instructional resources that have the potential to really open up your students' minds. Sure, I understand how worksheets can be a valid means to practice and reinforce some concepts and skills, but they should never be used, as they often are, as a time filler or as a substitute for real teaching. For true understanding in social studies, I propose a different tactic—use instructional resources that engage students, foster deep thinking and understanding, and build a true appreciation for the joy and satisfaction of learning social studies!"

What factors should you consider when beginning to select multiple instructional resources? Generally, your school district will have developed its own criteria for selecting instructional resources, but virtually all criteria will relate to two general requirements: (1) "Do the instructional resources match the goals and standards of the studies curriculum?" and (2)

"Do the instructional resources address the assessed individual needs and varied interests, abilities, socioeconomic backgrounds, learning styles, and developmental levels of your students?" Once those two requirements have been addressed, you are free to access a variety of materials for your toolbox of instructional resources by collaborating with colleagues, searching the Internet, perusing professional journals, examining good resource books, and trying out many other reference sources. These resources may be versions of the concrete experiences described in Chapter 5, or they may be drawn from the representational experiences (portrayals or depictions of something real) described here in Chapter 6: *educational technology, learning centers, pictures and study prints*, and *simulations*.

Educational Technology in the Classroom

Hornbooks—wooden paddles protected by a thin sheet of transparent horn and containing the alphabet, vowel and consonant combinations, the Lord's Prayer, and a cross—were the rage in colonial classrooms. The slate chalkboard and wooden pencil were introduced as powerful tools that enlivened learning in elementary school classrooms by the late 19th century. Today, technology touches every part of our daily lives; it is a bit of a no-brainer to proclaim that young people in particular have become inseparably attached to technology. Much more than with the older crowd, it is rare to catch a glimpse of our youth without some form of technology, especially smartphones and tablets. They appear to accept and adopt new forms of communication seamlessly and effortlessly, receiving and sharing information through a range of new and improved formats without a hitch. Today, the classroom is an interactive world where teachers as well as students are engaged with technology.

This section provides a basic introduction to educational technology (instructional technology) and describes how it can be used to support student learning in social studies. The technology we are talking about is not, as many are inclined to think, exclusively limited to computers. Computers are undeniably important; they deserve major credit for enhancing learning in our schools. But they have been in our schools for decades now; new technological tools are expanding the ways in which students can interact with the world. We can only guess about how their power will affect education in the coming years. For social studies teachers especially, many aspects of instruction are ideal for technology integration. Whether they engage students in tasks such as social networking, online research, podcasts, PowerPoint presentations, or WebQuests and web scavenger hunts, ideas abound for integrating technology into social studies instruction today.

If we hope to make learning relevant and meaningful for students in the 21st century, social studies classrooms must reflect new information and communication technologies to better enable young people to interact with ideas, information, and other people. Thus, the NCSS "Technology Position Statement and Guidelines" (NCSS, 2006) states, "In an age of standards and accountability, teachers need to include the realities of students' lives, technology use in students' everyday lives, and the role and use of technology when planning for instruction. . . . We need to capitalize on many students' ubiquitous, yet social, use of . . . technology and demonstrate . . . technology's power as a tool for learning" (p. 330). To that end, NCSS recommends that teachers demonstrate understanding of technology operations and concepts, plan and support technology-based learning environments and experiences, apply technology to assess and evaluate student learning, and apply technology resources to empower learners with diverse backgrounds and needs. Technology offers no educational advantage however, if you include it only as trendy "window dressing" or as "technology for technology's sake."

Computers

"I see the computer as an irreplaceable tool in my classroom," declares Kathy Nell, a fourth-grade teacher in Philadelphia. She went on to explain:

> *Today's elementary school kids grew up in the digital age, and they love computer-based activities and learn from them easily. Whether students are using computers for research or as a device to communicate with others, they are having fun while they're learning. Computers, especially computer games, are much more enjoyable than traditional teaching. And one of the most important outcomes of computers in my classroom is that children who show little initiative for routine classroom activities become driven when working at the computer. Motivation to use computers is really high for both me and my students! I'm not so naïve as to think that technology can remake a poor teacher into a good one, but I am convinced that it can make a good teacher even better.*

INTERNET RESEARCH

Mrs. Nell went on to explain how Internet research is a main computer activity in their classroom:

> *I have found many sites that easily lend themselves to social studies integration. Of course, I don't just turn my students loose to randomly search through Internet sites; obviously, that's risky. However, I think it's important for my students to develop an interest in what the Internet has to offer before I ask them to become involved in carrying out formal research. Some of my students come to school with limited use of the Internet, so I like to introduce them to the World Wide Web by reading aloud Vuthy Kuon's picture book* Willie and the World Wide Web *(Geissen). The book tells the story of Willie McBee who, on his birthday, receives a mysterious present— a magic CD-ROM that offers Willie the opportunity to enter his computer, fly through the Internet, and explore different websites on the World Wide Web. I find that those students who are computer savvy and those who have no experience with the web take away different levels of meaning from the story. The book does a great job introducing the Internet through Willie's adventures. After I finish reading the book, the students are primed to discuss questions such as, "Where would you like to go on the World Wide Web?"*
>
> *One of the sites the students have learned to love is Refdesk. It's a goldmine of useful and interesting websites all in one place. We look forward to daily sections of the site. They include the Fact of the Day, Word of the Day, This Day in History, Site of the Day, and a bunch of other interesting features. There are also links to YouTube, popular search engines, social networks, free dictionaries and encyclopedias, translation sites, a ton of news features, weather resources, MapQuest . . . there are so many more useful sections for research and discussion, and they're all in one place . . . on one page! We also like Wonderopolis, which answers questions on subjects my students are curious about. They can submit a question about almost anything and it will be answered, sometimes with a video. It's a great introduction to Internet research. And my students love to spend time navigating the animal videos and photo gallery of National Geographic Kids.*
>
> *After my students have an opportunity to explore safe sites like these, we discuss what research is, why we carry out research, and how we carry out research. I involve them in a process that involves coming up with a good question, gathering information, analyzing and evaluating the information, drawing conclusions, and sharing the results with others. The research question is very important, so I don't start out asking a question that results in simply locating facts about a topic, such as, "What can you find out about our world's oceans?" I model a larger question, such as, "What makes the oceans a unique part of our living Earth?" I then have a sequence of activities to help students locate information on the Internet using an effective and precise selection of keywords. They use their keyword pool to explore kid-friendly search engines such as KidRex, KidzSearch, or Safe Search Kids. The safe search engines do a good job of weeding out the junk they can find on unfiltered search sites.*

As the students collect information, I make sure they evaluate it: "Is the information useful?" "Was the information published by a qualified expert, organization, or agency?" and "Can the accuracy and truthfulness of the information be checked by examining other websites or library resources?" Once that is done, we put together the useful data to create a worthwhile response. The final step is to develop an interactive presentation to communicate the results of their research.

WEBQUESTS

Mrs. Nell says that it doesn't take much for her students to immerse themselves in Internet research; she feels her online connection has revitalized her teaching and re-energized her students. She particularly enjoys using WebQuests. Bernie Dodge (1995) and Tom March (2003) have been working since early 1995 to develop the WebQuest as a strategy for effectively integrating the web into classroom instruction. They describe a WebQuest as an inquiry-oriented activity in which some or all of the information that learners work with comes from preselected resources on the Internet. Because the developers felt that there was questionable educational benefit in having students surf the web without a clear task in mind, they created WebQuests to help achieve efficiency and clarity of purpose. According to Dodge (1995), the six building blocks of a WebQuest are:

- **The introduction.** The introduction engages and excites students and captures their interest. The goal of the motivational component is to "hook" the students and connect the topic to their existing knowledge and past experiences.

- **The task.** The task clarifies the main research question and describes the activity's end product. Considered by Dodge to be the single most important element of a WebQuest, the task must be doable and interesting. First, the teacher finds resources on the web and then describes the end product that will incorporate the information from the various sites, such as publishing their findings on a website, collaborating in an online research initiative with another site or school, or creating a multimedia presentation.

- **The process.** The process explains strategies students should use and the steps they will be expected to follow to complete the task or activity. The process should be detailed as clearly described steps.

- **The resources.** Resources are the research materials students will use to complete the task. The list of resources includes bookmarked websites and books and other documents physically available in the classroom or library. Because teacher-selected websites are included, the students are not left roaming off course throughout any portion of the research process.

- **The evaluation.** The assessments should be fair, clear, consistent, and specific to the tasks set. Traditional techniques such as tests and quizzes are not the most effective tools for assessing WebQuests, since students researching different components of the overall question will be involved with dissimilar subject matter. Individual evaluation strategies such as portfolios and rubrics are recommended.

- **The conclusion.** The conclusion brings closure to the experience; it sums up the activity and encourages students to reflect on the process and results.

You do not need be a computer genius to carry out WebQuests in your classroom. Mrs. Nell has created a number of WebQuests for her social studies classes and often urges others to follow her lead: "It's easier than you might think!" she points out passionately. Although the quality of what you may find varies widely from site to site, many good sites help walk you through the process. And innumerable web sources offer premade WebQuests on many topics and advice to help build your own WebQuests; two of the most convenient are the WebQuest pages of both Dodge and March. Their databases are kept up to date, with dead links being weeded out as needed (a big problem with a number of sites).

To illustrate how a WebQuest works, let us peek into Mrs. Nell's classroom to see how the process helps her students investigate tropical rain forests. She started out by having her students read Tim Knight's fascinating book, *Journey into the Rainforest* (Oxford University Press). Whether paddling upstream in a canoe or flying above the treetops in a small plane, Knight helps young readers explore the rain forest from its floor up to the canopy and beyond. After they discussed the book, Ms. Nell pulled out an official-looking letter from the "director of a zoo" and read it aloud to the class. (The letter was actually written by Mrs. Nell.) It explained that the zoo was planning to redesign its rain forest exhibit and was looking for input about how the lives of the plants and animals of the rain forest are entwined. Could the class please consider developing a guidebook that would be used by visitors to the zoo describing the immense biodiversity of the tropical rain forest? This was all it took to launch Mrs. Nell's students into something they really wanted to learn about. In this case, the students' motivation to use a WebQuest for the rain forest task was very high, and Mrs. Nell wanted to strike while "the iron was hot."

The first of Dodge's six building blocks (*introduction* activity) had already taken place with the book reading and letter from the zoo director. Mrs. Nell addressed the *task* responsibility by explaining these WebQuest directions: "You will work with a group to develop a guidebook that will be used by visitors to the zoo describing the immense biodiversity of the tropical rain forest. Your group will use a multimedia application such as HyperStudio or KidPix to prepare the guidebook." Next, Ms. Nell asked the students to examine the *process*. She directed the students, "You will work in teams of four people:

- The *geographer* will be responsible for finding out about the location and physical characteristics of tropical rain forests.
- The *botanist* will be responsible for finding out about the species of plants in a rain forest.
- The *biologist* will be responsible for finding out about the animal species living in a rain forest.
- The *demographer* will be responsible for finding out about the people who live in rain forests."

Despite the fact that some of your students will know a lot about computers, it is still necessary to teach strategic research skills through techniques such as WebQuests.

WavebreakMediaMicro/Fotolia

Mrs. Nell continued by clarifying the WebQuest *resources* the students were to use: "Almost all of your information will be collected from Internet sites, but you are also encouraged to use additional information books and other print materials. And you will be doing a multimedia presentation. Be sure to collect pictures as you make your journey through Internet and print sources." Mrs. Nell then listed the preselected links.

For the *evaluation*, Mrs. Nell informed the students: "Your guidebooks will be judged for creativity, effectiveness, accuracy, and neatness. Based on the rubric you received, each of you will receive a group grade as well as an individual grade for the separate guidebook responsibilities."

Finally, after the one-week WebQuest was completed, a discussion during the *conclusion* revealed that the students acquired information and built concepts associated not only with their own group responsibility but also about many more rain forest issues. They indicated a much stronger appreciation for the many creatures that rely on this tropical ecosystem and why rain forests need to be saved.

As fascinating as the Internet world can be, it can also present some serious problems. Perhaps the greatest issue is the availability of material that is not suitable for children. The Children's Internet Protection Act (CIPA) is a federal law enacted by Congress to address concerns about access to offensive content over the Internet on school and library computers. Be assured that your students will be protected with the convenience and protection of filter software such as Net Nanny or CYBERsitter.

 Video Exploration 6.1

VIRTUAL FIELD TRIPS

Just imagine that your class is learning about the penguins of Antarctica or about Jamestown, the first permanent English settlement in the Americas. Surely, having the students see them firsthand would be a breathtaking learning opportunity, but how realistic would it be to jump on a school bus and embark on such once-in-a-lifetime expeditions? Take heart, however, because virtual field trips on the Internet are here to save the day . . . just buckle up your seat belts, access your browser, and hold on for an educational sightseeing excursion!

Going on virtual field trips is wonderful way to inform youngsters about our world. They won't cost you a penny and are less time-consuming and complex than a real trip. You and your students are free to enjoy guided expeditions to Alcatraz, the Great Pyramid of Giza, the Grand Canyon, the Panama Canal, the Empire State Building, or even travel to the moon and back. You will find more virtual field trips on the web than you can ever expect to use; there is no shortage of people, places, and things not normally approachable with run-of-the-mill classroom experiences: the Smithsonian Museum, Colonial Williamsburg, the U.S. Capitol Virtual Tour, the Civil War Virtual Tour, and Virtual Farm are but a few of the hundreds of thousands of available sites. When you judge that a virtual field trip is perfectly connected to your social studies program, it is important to identify a structure that will make it successful. I like to think of the structure required to navigate virtual field trips as having three essential elements, just like the structure of all good lessons: a good *beginning* to "hook" the learners, a captivating *middle* that holds their attention as the events unfold, and a satisfying *ending* where the conclusion ties up the loose ends and encourages reflection.

Beginning Where are we going, and what do we hope to learn? What kind of a "hook" (attention-getter) will help capture the students' attention and introduce the trip? Is there a question or activity that can help tie in what students already know about the topic or what their preconceived notions are? Is there a question or comment that creates a compelling purpose for taking the virtual field trip?

Middle   Facilitate students' efforts to sketch, describe, take notes, or ask and answer questions in their "field trip notebooks."

End   "Debrief" students to maximize the virtual field trip's impact. What did we set out to learn? What did we learn? What do we still need to know? How can we find out? Ask students to summarize their experience and have them rate the field trip. You should also have a culminating activity that allows them to apply what they learned on the virtual field trip and demonstrate this knowledge in some way.

WORD PROCESSING

The great majority of student time working with classroom computers involves Internet activities and word processing. But although even the youngest students come to school with fairly sophisticated web surfing skills, a large number will have limited word-processing know-how. Consequently, you will most likely need to work with your students on word processing basics. It will not be long before your students are preparing neat, well-edited written pieces with graphics and text or printing out other products such as signs, banners, greeting cards, newsletters, letterheads, travel brochures, and newspapers.

There are a number of popular word-processing programs available today for classroom use. Some are free, and others will require an initial software purchase. Microsoft Word is by far the most popular word-processing application used in schools, although Apple's OK-Writer is among a few of the other products available for use in schools.

In addition to word-processing packages, online collaborative writing tools are growing in popularity and are readily available free of charge. Google Docs, for example, is an easy-to-use online word processor, spreadsheet, and presentation program that empowers students to create, store, and share instantly and securely, as well as collaborate online while sharing documents among multiple users (thereby assisting group work and peer editing skills). Students can create new documents from scratch or upload existing documents, spreadsheets, and presentations. All this work is stored securely online and can be accessed from any computer. A similar web publishing tool is a *wiki*. Wikis can be used for collaborative Internet research in which students work together in teams, freely editing each other's work, to research a topic and publish their findings on a website for their classmates or for students anywhere around the world.

HYPERMEDIA (PRESENTATION SOFTWARE)

A special computer application that has contributed greatly to curriculum integration today is *hypermedia* (also known as "linked media" or "interactive media"), a communications tool that combines video, graphics, animation, and text. Known as "presentation software," hypermedia authoring programs enable students to organize and communicate information in innovative and thought-provoking ways, accessing and integrating information from such diverse sources as the Internet, sounds or clip art pulled from public domain software, photographs from a digital camera or scanner, and clips from a video camera or CD-ROM. Three widely used presentation programs, HyperStudio, KidPix, and Microsoft PowerPoint include hypermedia authoring as a function of their software packages. These are not the only hypermedia tools available to teachers and students, but they are excellent examples.

I once heard a computer expert say, "To be truly literate, one must learn to communicate in the dominant system of a culture." At no other time was this truism clearer to me than when I was invited to visit an elementary school "History Fair" and examined all the wonderful projects. Every display attracted a great deal of attention, but one stood out above all the others.

I was made aware of this special display by another guest, who turned to me and asked in admiration, "Can you believe what Michael did on the computer?"

> *I walked over to Michael's space and was met with eye-popping graphics, clear text, dazzling animation, and breathtaking audio. Telling about the life of Harriet Tubman, Michael's project gave every impression of a professional presentation. Scanned photos from literature sources, spoken text that highlighted the key events in Harriet Tubman's life, recorded spirituals, and the culminating video clip of Martin Luther King, Jr.'s "I Have a Dream" speech made the presentation a special occurrence. Michael's presentation included a button at the point in Harriet Tubman's life when she gave slaves secret directions on how to flee to the North. By using the mouse to click the button, the user could listen to the song "Follow the Drinking Gourd" while looking at an illustration of the Big Dipper. The "flash" was not the priority in Michael's presentation; the message was certainly the important element. However, the presentation software added much more to Michael's research than if he had simply put together an oral or written report.*

If students find learning more interesting and engaging as a result of creating an interactive project, then computers have served their purpose. Presentation software creates increased excitement about doing research because students know that their final report is going to look good and be fully interactive. Presentation software is readily available, relatively inexpensive, and not difficult to use. Teachers should use this practical technology application and demonstrate modern, effective communication techniques to their students.

EMAIL

Electronic mail (email) enables students and teachers to communicate with each other and with people all over the world. "But my concern is safety," says Mrs. Nell, "so I want to be able to monitor outgoing and incoming emails. I want the emails to go through *me* first." Mrs. Nell's concerns were alleviated to a great degree by Google. Gmail allows teachers to create subsidiary student accounts linked to a primary Gmail account. This means that a teacher can have

Technology has had a profound impact on social studies instruction. The ways to integrate it into your classroom are limited only by your imagination.

Monkey Business/Fotolia

student email accounts that are all delivered into their teacher's account. Therefore, if Mrs. Nell's account is nell4th@gmail.com, then all she has to do is add a "+studentname" before the @ symbol to establish a linked account: for example, nell4th+tommysmith@gmail.com. Now, any email sent to Tommy Smith will go straight to nell4th@gmail.com. "Importantly, because Gmail terms and conditions require users to be at least 13 years old, I thought it was important to send permission slips to all parents to get their authorization for these linked accounts," advises Mrs. Nell. "Now I can establish an email dialogue among my students or students from different schools who are studying the same topic; it is so easy to create and collaborate using email in my classroom."

BLOGS AND PODCASTS

The present-day blog evolved from online diaries, where individuals would keep a written account of their personal lives. Blogs (short for **web logs**) have now expanded into websites where people contribute written observations or news on any particular topic, such as American history, politics, or local news. A typical blog blends text and images, as well as links to other blogs, web pages, or media related to its topic. The ability for readers to leave comments or additions in an interactive format on free online blog sites is a vital part of many blogs. Students can discuss important topics, ask questions, and receive feedback from other students. Most blogs are primarily textual and can be created and updated with minimal technological expertise. If you've never created a blog site before, a great deal of helpful advice for setting up blogs and examples of how blogs can be used productively in the social studies classroom can be found throughout the web.

Podcasts are becoming progressively more accepted in social studies education. In addition to listening to and viewing podcasts on boundless topics, social studies teachers and students can create podcasts as a way to communicate information with anyone at any time. An absent student can download the podcast of the recorded lesson. Students can listen to a teacher's podcast as they review an assignment or study for a test. Perhaps the most popular use of podcasting in schools is for student presentations. All you need is a microphone and a script; then you can just download free, easy-to-learn software, such as Audacity, and use it to produce and edit audio files. You can easily insert sound effects and music. The simplest way to make the podcast available is to link from a web page to your audio file.

DIGITAL STORYTELLING

Digital storytelling, as the name implies, involves the use of computer-based tools to tell stories, typically in the form of movies or interactive slide shows. These digital tales are created by the children, using a story structure basic to all narratives—a well-developed beginning, middle, and end. Instead of being read or told, however, these digital stories contain a mixture of computer-based images, text, recorded audio narration, video clips, and/or music. Many use Ken Burns's model of the genre as he first used it in the acclaimed "Civil War" series on PBS, with its archival photos mixed with sound effects, recorded narration, and period music.

Digital stories can vary in length, but most of the stories used in elementary schools last between 2 and 5 minutes. To begin their digital storytelling piece, Mrs. Nell encourages her students to apply what they have learned in language arts class: Writers and storytellers invariably compose narrative text using a predictable format, or *structure*. First, stories are structured into beginnings, middles, and ends. Second, nested within this story structure, most stories contain four traditional components that form the skeleton of the story: the structural elements of plot, setting, conflict or problem, and characters. The beginning introduces the main characters, the setting, and the problem or conflict. The middle describes one or more attempts to solve the problem. The ending presents the resolution of the problem or conflict. Most children attain a sense of the elements of story structure simply by listening to and reading stories. But it is helpful to review them when they are applied to digital storytelling through questions such as the following (Gunning, 2010):

- "When and where does your story take place?"
- "Who are the characters? Are they believable?"
- "What problem or conflict does the main character face? How can you build suspense?"
- "What does the main character do about the problem or conflict? How do you think he/she felt about it?"
- "How is the problem resolved? Is it a surprise?"

The elements of story structure can be used as a framework for composing stories, digital or otherwise. Students begin the digital storytelling experience by brainstorming story ideas and gradually narrowing them down to one idea. Mind mapping helps to create a story framework; storyboarding is often recommended as an organizational strategy for organizing digital stories. By illustrating a story panel by panel, much as in a comic book, storyboarding allows students to visualize how the story can be put together before they actually compose the digital story on a computer. Simple illustrations are commonly drawn in pencil; stick figures and basic shapes will do. Using index cards or sticky notes allows students to move parts of the story around. Students can also cut out pictures from magazines or use the organization chart software that comes with Microsoft Word to create a storyboard. Next, the students develop a script, working with short sentences to describe each of the storyboard panels. The digital story will be accompanied by images, music, and sound effects, so there is no need for a lot of words.

Once the students have developed a script, they are ready to move into the production phase. You can use a number of computer tools, including Windows Movie Maker, Apple iMovie, or Microsoft Photo Story. Web-based tools such as Digital Storyteller (http://www.digitalstoryteller.org) also offer teachers and students access to digital images and materials that enable them to construct compelling folktales, myths, legends, and other story genres.

COMPUTER-ASSISTED INSTRUCTION

Available online or as commercial software programs, computer-assisted instruction is designed to teach. Quite often, teachers will project the images onto a large electronic whiteboard at the front of a class and/or run the program simultaneously on a network of desktop computers in a classroom. Computer-assisted instruction has generally been classified according to the categories of instructional assistance it offers:

1. *Drill-and-practice.* Game-style activities motivate students to answer questions about information that has been previously learned.

2. *Tutorial.* Tutorial programs do the same things as individual tutors—they teach on a one-to-one basis. Tutorial software consists of interactive programs that present new content or skills in a step-by-step instructional sequence. Most tutorials have practice and review features to help ensure comprehension of the material. The multimedia instructional design presents instructional material in an engaging way, prompts quick responses, evaluates the responses, and guides students through the material on individualized paths.

3. *Educational Games.* Educational games, sometimes referred to as "edutainment," are programs designed to make learning fun through a game format—a competitive activity where success requires a set number of points, accumulation of coins, or some other such earned reward.

4. ***Simulation.*** Computerized programs often take the form of simulations, or authentic representations of real-life situations. One of the most noteworthy simulations available for upper-grade elementary school classrooms is the traditionally popular and critically acclaimed SimCity (Maxis). The objective of SimCity is to build and design a simulated city from scratch, converting an untouched landscape into the world's greatest city. Students plan residential, commercial, and industrial sectors; they build roads, bridges, and railways. In return, people flock to the city and start paying taxes. Having to contend with the constantly shifting demand for the three zone types (residential, commercial, and industrial) while continuously adding better services and transportation for the citizens, and also maintaining a monthly budget, adds up to some intense decision-making experiences.

Simulations offer several advantages: Simulations are often cheaper to create than their real-life counterparts. A simulated trial during which your students can see the legal process at work is less expensive than attending a real trial. Most are also easier to carry out. How could your students more realistically experience the plight of fugitive slaves than through realistic role-playing software? Simulations remove the element of danger from the situation. Are your students afraid to climb mountains, forge river rapids, or face an angry grizzly bear in real life? You can help them do so in the safety of your classroom, where they can take time to hit the "pause" button and assess what is going on.

5. ***Problem Solving.*** Problem-solving software presents highly complex situations in which students confront a problem, search for potential causes of the problem, identify alternatives, and select an approach to solve the problem. One traditionally popular problem-solving program for children in grades 3 to 8 is "Where in the World Is Carmen Sandiego?" In the original and most of the many remakes, the format remains the same: Students become crime fighters for the ACME detective agency and search the world for Carmen Sandiego (an ex-secret agent turned thief) and her gang of V.I.L.E. henchmen. Program developers have added other adventures, such as Where in the USA Is Carmen Sandiego? and Where in Time Is Carmen Sandiego? The series has grown in popularity so much that it has now branched out into math, literacy, and other school subjects.

6. ***Specialized.*** Specialized software for social studies is abundant. Lever-Duffy and McDonald (2011) explain that

> software for the social studies ranges from software that creates timelines, to CDs of famous speeches, to software that provides multimedia reenactments and information of specific historical events or ages. . . . In our changing political world, map software offers teachers and students the most accurate possible world atlas on CD. Software is available to create virtual dioramas of historical periods . . . , experience and practice the decision-making process related to current events, and examine the implications of population on [Earth's] resources. (p. 225)

An example of specialized social studies content software is Talking Walls (Sunburst Technologies). It is an excellent literature-based software program that helps students discover the stories behind some of the world's most fascinating walls—such as the Berlin Wall and Nelson Mandela's prison walls. The Complete National Geographic (National Geographic) allows students to browse articles, photographs, and maps from more than 122 years of *National Geographic* magazine—exactly as they appeared in print. Additional reference materials are available on CDs or DVDs; many have Internet links to even more information. They include encyclopedias such as *Encyclopedia Britannica*, almanacs such as *The Time Almanac*, atlases such as *Google Earth* (Google), and newspapers such as the *New York Times*.

Reflection on Learning

You may simply scribble rough notes or jot down something more polished and complete. The point is to simply start recording your ideas spontaneously and candidly.

Some technophiles regard technology so positively that they see it as a magic potion to improve all aspects of life, even suggesting that computer-based learning will soon replace teachers. They claim that teacher obsolescence will undoubtedly be hastened by the Internet and innovations in online instruction. Does that alarm you as a teacher? How important are good teachers? Do you think a good teacher could (or should) be replaced by a machine?

Digital Peripherals

While the computer has revolutionized classroom instruction, it was just the forerunner of several other digital devices that have followed. Lever-Duffy and McDonald (2011) elaborate:

> Once you have computer systems in the classroom, the possibilities for expanding their capabilities by the addition of digital peripherals are enormous. You can add input devices that let you scan leaves from your nature walks and load photos from your field trips, let students operate a computer by touching a display projected onto the classroom whiteboard, or let you dictate input via voice instead of keyboard. Or you can add output devices that allow you to share what's on your monitor with the whole class, that can turn segments of a videotape into digital pictures, or that can read sections of the textbook to your auditory learners. (p. 145)

Various types of technologies are frequently integrated into tech-oriented curricula. Among these are digital projectors, interactive whiteboards, digital cameras, and wireless devices.

DIGITAL PROJECTORS

It is possible to hook up a digital projector to a computer or video source to project onto a whiteboard or screen a larger image of anything that can be displayed on a computer (educational software, websites, etc.). This makes it easier for students to see a larger version of a PowerPoint or a Word document, or even to follow the teacher as he or she visits educational websites. Enhance your classroom presentations with detailed charts, virtual field trips, and presentations from guest speakers in a high-tech, multimedia environment.

INTERACTIVE WHITEBOARDS

An interactive whiteboard is a touch-sensitive screen that is connected to a computer and digital projector. When the projector displays a computer image on the interactive whiteboard, a teacher or student can draw or write over the image in digital ink, using a pen, stylus, or finger. A teacher or student can interact with the projected display, visit websites, and access databases directly from the board. Everything can then be saved in printed or electronic format. Interactive whiteboards are used in many schools as replacements for traditional chalkboards, whiteboards, or chart paper. You may often hear interactive whiteboards referred to as SMART Boards. That is because the first interactive whiteboard was manufactured by SMART Technologies, Inc., in 1991. Since that time, SMART Technologies has been such a formidable force in manufacturing interactive whiteboards that the company's name has become synonymous with the product line.

DIGITAL CAMERAS

Digital cameras (digicams) can do things the old film cameras could not; they have several advantages over their analog counterparts. In the past, you would need to drop off film at a photo processor to get it developed; with digital cameras, you display images on a screen

The potential of digital cameras to improve student learning in social studies is virtually limitless.

Sementinov/Fotolia

immediately after recording them by simply uploading the pictures to a computer or storing them in the camera to be uploaded at a later time. Then they can be edited with photo editing software, published online, or emailed to other classrooms. You can print hard copies of the photos using a printer or an online printing service. Students can document class projects and special events with the cameras, and the children enjoy incorporating their photos into their reports and multimedia presentations. An especially useful feature that helps young photographers capture that perfect image is the small LCD screen that shows a live preview of the image—whether documenting a field trip, taking digital photos of work to include in a portfolio, displaying work on classroom websites, or giving a personal touch to a class newsletter. The unique applications of digital cameras are limited only by the cleverness and creativity of the students and teachers using them.

WIRELESS DEVICES

Wireless devices, in several different forms, are quickly becoming commonplace in contemporary classrooms. They include smartphones and tablets. With their ever-expanding possibilities of texting, taking photos and videos, web browsing, and game playing, these devices are much like walking around with a computer in your pocket. Their potential as learning tools must be recognized by our schools. Using a smartphone, for example, students can research an interesting question during a "teachable moment" that arises in the middle of a field trip rather than waiting until they return to their classrooms. Learning should literally be at the student's fingertips.

In addition to smartphones and other cell phones, many school districts have experimented with online electronic reading devices, also known as *e-books*, or electronic versions of conventional print books. Rather than having heavy hard-copy textbooks and other print sources, students will use a single lightweight device on which multiple texts can be stored and easily updated without having to publish new editions. The capacity to embed audio and visual enhancements in text adds to the appeal and instructional value of e-books. An e-book reader is used for reading digital books and periodicals. The term *e-book reader* refers to any device that enables someone to read digital text, but the term is more often used to refer to a specific kind of device, such as an Amazon Kindle or a Barnes & Noble Nook, that has a special display screen suitable for reading.

Student response clickers are a lot like TV remote controls. They are wireless response systems that students click to immediately transmit answers to a small, transportable receiving station, where they are immediately received and tallied. Each clicker is registered to a particular student, so teachers know who has answered correctly and who has not. Clickers provide instant feedback, so teachers are aware if students are confused about material that is being presented. "With clickers, you don't have to wait until you see how they do on a paper test to know whether or not they're 'getting it'!" said one satisfied teacher.

Every teacher must understand the importance of active learning and realize how interactive technology can help get students personally involved in learning. However, even though technology intimately touches almost every part of our daily lives, a number of schools appear to lag far behind when it comes to integrating technology into the curriculum. That trend seems to be reversing itself as tech-savvy teachers have begun to explore the potential technology offers for teaching and learning. Properly used, technology will help students develop the insights required to prosper as productive citizens in a complex, highly technological society.

 CHECK YOUR UNDERSTANDING 6.1 **Click here** to check your understanding of this section of the chapter.

Reflection on Learning

You may simply scribble rough notes or jot down something more polished and complete. The point is to simply start recording your ideas spontaneously and candidly.

Numerous examples have demonstrated how technology can be used to transform teaching and learning in social studies. These examples demonstrate that, when properly planned and carried out, the use of technology can stimulate and facilitate a wide range of project-based activities, student and teacher collaboration, and interdisciplinary inquiry. If you knew you couldn't fail, in what creative ways would you use technology to contribute to a more powerful social studies learning experience?

Learning Centers

Learning centers, also called *learning stations* or *interest centers*, are clearly defined, well-equipped classroom nooks that contain a variety of learning materials and activities designed to promote independence, foster decision making, and encourage collaboration; children participate at these centers with minimal teacher involvement. The classroom may be divided into any number of areas, each equipped for a distinct kind of learning. The resources and learning materials provided at the centers are planned with the goals and standards of instruction firmly in mind, so the possibilities for learning center activities are extensive and diffuse; they run the gamut from playing content-focused learning games to engaging in problem solving and inquiry.

Although you may think of learning centers as most appropriate for younger children, they are highly worthwhile for all students. Acknowledging the appeal of learning centers, it is assumed that nearly all elementary school classrooms will contain at least one dedicated to social studies. For social studies purposes, I find it most convenient to think of three categories of classroom learning centers: (1) *review/reinforcement*, (2) *enrichment*, and (3) *exploratory*. Whichever you select, you must be sure they have interesting activities, ample resources, and are designed with your students' needs and interests in mind.

Review/Reinforcement Centers

Review/reinforcement centers (sometimes called *skills centers*) are based on the old adage "Practice makes perfect" and are typically used when you determine that it is important for your students to work independently or to collaboratively review content or practice skills in a fun way.

Review and reinforcement has been a traditional strategy for helping students retain important knowledge and strengthen skills, and learning centers contain the kinds of activities that spark excitement in this all-too-ordinary process. Did any of your elementary school teachers ever adapt popular games such as *Jeopardy* to review subject matter content? If you enjoyed those games, then you will certainly appreciate review/reinforcement centers. Your students will look forward to these learning center review games in much the same way.

What kinds of activities do teachers like to include in a reinforcement learning center? They usually start with teacher-made games; children love all kinds of games—board games, television game shows, video or computer games, and playground games. Anyone who has spent time with children in "their world" will attest to the fact that games appear to be an instinctive and fundamental component of their lives. You can liven up your review and reinforcement process by using any of the following examples.

Ms. Walker (remember her unit plan from Chapter 2?) augmented her "Inventors and Inventions" thematic unit by designing a reinforcement center containing several review and reinforcement games; one was called "Inventor Concentration." For the game, Ms. Walker wrote the names of the inventors the students had been studying on index cards. She printed their corresponding inventions on index cards of another color. Center directions informed the students to combine and shuffle the cards before placing them face down in rows on the playing area. Taking turns, each player was to turn over two cards, one of each color. If the "Inventor" card matched the "Inventions" card, the player kept the cards and took another turn. If the cards did not match, the player returned the cards to their original positions. The game was over when all the cards were taken up. If the children wished to designate a "winner," it should be the student holding the most cards. (See Figure 6.1.)

Ms. Walker also liked to use websites to provide her students with learning center review and reinforcement activities. For example, she accessed "Learning Games for Kids," a site that includes several games and puzzles about inventors and inventions. The students were free to use this site at the center. Ms. Walker also selected a quiz show template for PowerPoint from Microsoft Office that she used to create her own learning center quiz games, including true/false, revealed-answers, multiple-choice, and matching questions. She often encouraged tech savvy students to consider creating their own PowerPoint games for their classmates to use.

FIGURE 6.1   Learning Center Activity

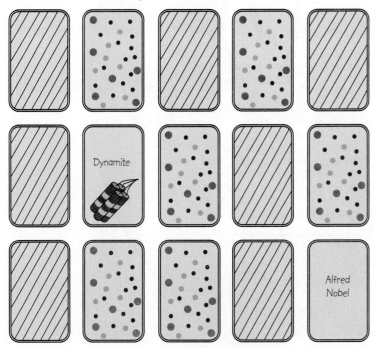

Enrichment Centers

Enrichment learning centers offer students an opportunity to expand their understanding of content and concepts through individual activities or experiences. These centers offer students more time to investigate content in greater depth and complexity and provide opportunities for them to pursue individual areas of interest and strength. Activities not only encourage curiosity and open new doors of learning, they also provide a context for applying knowledge and skills to real-life, meaningful contexts. Enrichment centers normally employ interactive, project-focused activities that include a variety of arts and crafts, puzzles, reading and writing, computer activities, and other experiences that help extend any topic. In contrast to review/reinforcement centers, which most often focus on practicing a specific understanding or skill, enrichment centers are often interdisciplinary, incorporating other subject areas such as art, music, science, math, reading, or writing.

> *In addition to teacher-made and computer games, Ms. Walker has found that learning centers help extend and deepen the subjects her students are learning about by creating artwork related to an area of interest. Who was their favorite inventor? Why? For her thematic unit, Ms. Walker invited her students to induct noteworthy inventors into a classroom "Wall of Fame." Each student selected an inventor, illustrated his or her invention on a plaque, and printed the inventor's name at the bottom. See Figure 6.2 for an example of Grace's plaque. The students were asked to write a two- to four-sentence summary of the inventor's contribution to complete the plaque. Each plaque was added to the learning center's rapidly growing "Wall of Fame."*
>
> *Ms. Walker also included a computer activity (there was a computer at the center) that challenged students to create sets of five clues that would lead to the identity of a famous inventor and send them via email to other classrooms studying the same unit in the school district, one clue a day for five days. Classes tried to be the first to identify the inventor in as few clues as possible.*

FIGURE 6.2 "Hall of Fame" Plaque as a Culminating Activity

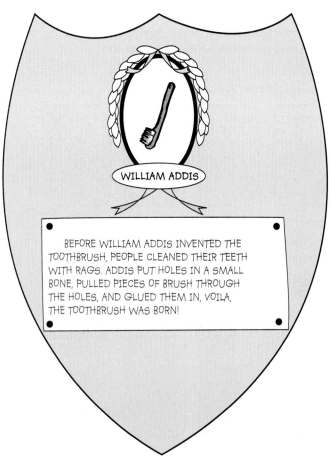

WILLIAM ADDIS

BEFORE WILLIAM ADDIS INVENTED THE TOOTHBRUSH, PEOPLE CLEANED THEIR TEETH WITH RAGS. ADDIS PUT HOLES IN A SMALL BONE, PULLED PIECES OF BRUSH THROUGH THE HOLES, AND GLUED THEM IN. VOILA, THE TOOTHBRUSH WAS BORN!

Enrichment centers help enhance student understanding and creativity with a wide variety of crafts, games, and other activities that will help your students dig deeper into any social studies topic. Sometimes you will post provocative questions to strengthen your students' thinking and extend meaning; at other times, your students will cook, build models, make crafts, explore online exhibits, listen to music, carry out art activities, and pursue other purposeful activities that engage them as active learners. Be careful to offer assignments and projects that extend what is going on during the regular unit of instruction instead of "piling on more of the same."

Exploratory Centers

Exploratory learning centers differ from both enrichment and review/reinforcement learning centers in that they contain the resources that allow students to search for and find answers to their own questions or to satisfy their personal interests. The outcomes of working at these centers may not necessarily match the targeted content and skill outcomes of the unit; instead, they provide students with opportunities to engage in meaningful new discoveries that have captured their interest, at their own pace and ability level. An awareness of your students' interests will help pinpoint the specific areas you can use in the design of exploratory learning centers. A paper-and-pencil inventory can often provide you with important information about student interests, as will classroom conversations. The stimulus for action is what distinguishes whether a classroom learning center is considered an enrichment center or an exploratory center. To clarify, if a teacher's stated purpose is to enhance student understanding of content and concepts of tropical rain forests by posting the question, "What can we do to help save the rain forests?" at a center, it would be considered an enrichment center because it is curriculum-centered and the impetus for research is provided by the teacher. However, if the same question arose spontaneously from students, the classroom location where they would be free to satisfy their genuine curiosity is an exploratory center. I like to think of exploratory centers as "Research Labs" where students produce knowledge that is meaningful to them by exploring technology tools, good books, newspaper articles, paintings, political cartoons, songs, diary entries, speeches, and an abundance of other sources.

> *To inspire her students to take active roles in saving Earth's endangered animals by applying inventive thinking processes, Ms. Walker read Lynne Cherry's beautifully crafted book,* The Great Kapok Tree: A Tale of the Amazon Rain Forest *(Gulliver Green). Cherry wrote and illustrated the book to give readers a look at the breathtaking beauty of the rain forest and to increase awareness of the ecological importance of saving the rain forests. The book opens as an unnamed man prepares to cut down a huge kapok tree. He tires and soon falls asleep at the base of the tree. One by one the animals enter his dreams to plead with him not to destroy their home and try to convince him about how important every tree is in the rain forest. When the man awakes and sees the silent, somber expressions on the animals' faces around him, he silently drops his axe and walks away.*
>
> *After spending several minutes conducting an intense informal discussion of the book, Ms. Walker called the students' attention to a large wall chart containing only a list of the speaking animals in the book. To complete the chart, she asked the students to fill in the reasons given by each animal for not cutting down the kapok tree. She asked, "Do you think the animals really talked to the man, or was it all a dream?" Ms. Walker also asked the students to talk with a partner about the meaning of several of the animals' comments. For example, they discussed what the anteater meant when he said to the man, "Senhor, you are chopping down this tree with no thought for the future. And surely you know that what happens tomorrow depends upon what you do today." Ms. Walker concluded the discussion by asking, "What do you think would have happened if the man had not listened to the animals?" The students added their own question: "What can WE do to save the rain forest and its animals?"*
>
> *Once the discussion was completed and the students' feelings remained high, Ms. Walker introduced them to an exploratory center where they would have the opportunity to brainstorm creative solutions to their rain forest question. The students knew that inventions usually solve a problem and often make the world a better place. They also understood that inventions can be things (a cookie or*

automobile) or an idea (a better way to eat lunch). Any new way to do something is considered an invention. They would now have an opportunity to apply these understandings at the exploratory center by brainstorming creative solutions to the problem and using tools, materials, and techniques to invent workable solutions.

Exploratory center activity is driven by the students. Your role is that of a facilitator ("curiosity scaffolder") who lends a hand whenever needed to assist the students as they go about the process of coming up with something new to them.

Reflection on Learning

You may simply scribble rough notes or jot down something more polished and complete. The point is to simply start recording your ideas spontaneously and candidly.

Suppose you were assigned to teach about the three branches of the United States government. How would you help promote student interest and understanding of the topic through the use of learning centers? What types of learning centers would you consider most appropriate?

Learning Center Organization

Whatever type of learning center you use in your classroom, organization is essential to ensuring that all students have an opportunity to work independently or in a small group on the learning tasks available. There are many ways to do this, but a simple weekly schedule chart will do the trick and enable you to keep records of your groups and tasks. If you believe that children function best within an individualized, self-paced curriculum where learning is integrated into meaningful activities, then a sound organizational plan will not only help your students develop a sense of belonging and ownership, it will also influence their ability to extract meaningful learning from the activities and materials contained in the classroom learning centers.

Select a learning center title and caricature that are attention-drawing and descriptive. An illustrated representation of a cartoonist standing beneath a colorful banner announcing "'toon in to History," "It's No Laughing Matter: Political Cartoons," or "Getting Cartoonish" has greater potential for attracting students to a learning center than simply making a sign with the words "Political Cartoons." Children, like most of us, respond positively to the allure of a package that catches their eye, so the center's design, layout, and appearance serve to pull students to the center and provoke them to learn more about it: *The higher the perceived quality of the package, the higher the students' interest.* The package should not be so elegant that it causes distraction or sensory overload, however. Long messages, too many bright colors, and ostentatious illustrations can easily distract even the most focused child. At the other extreme, students will often dismiss learning centers if they suggest low quality: messy or faded lettering and colors, crude designs, outdated illustrations, and cheap construction. "Educational" and "eye-catching" do not have to be mutually exclusive design responsibilities; excellent learning centers are educational and reasonably eye-catching.

As you arrange the centers in your classroom, be sure to separate quiet and noisy areas (as well as active and quiet areas) and strategically arrange your furniture to eliminate long, straight runways that encourage running. Give the centers a cozy touch with plants, art, rugs, posters, and perhaps some comfy pillows for a relaxed reading corner. And, of course, leave plenty of room to feature displays of the children's work. It is best to keep a center in operation only as long as interest remains high and it continues to fulfill the theme's instructional goals and standards.

Include a variety of learning alternatives within and among learning centers. Sometimes students benefit from opportunities to work independently on learning center activities, but they also enjoy working collaboratively with their peers. Sometimes they benefit from learning activities that provide structure; but they also flourish when doing activities that allow creative freedom. Sometimes uncomplicated center activities provide necessary review of basic skills and knowledge, but students also enjoy higher-order thinking activities that challenge their questioning and investigative skills. Sometimes students create complex technology-based productions to represent what they have learned; at other times, they are satisfied to draw pictures with crayons. Your curricular requirements, as well as the needs and interests of your students, will dictate the kinds and numbers of activities you provide at the various learning centers.

Since students will be working independently, centers must be self-directing. That is, students must be able to enter a learning center and determine what to do by themselves. For that reason, it is important to post signs at each learning center that clearly list the steps required to accomplish the activities. Center signs not only inform your students of what is expected, but also inform parent volunteers, classroom aides, and visitors of the center expectancies. The signs should be neatly handwritten or machine printed and supported with visual illustrations (a pencil for a writing task, a computer for an online research task, etc.); it may be helpful to provide an audio version of learning center directions for some students. Write the instructions in a clear, step-by-step format that can be read quickly. For example:

> *In this activity, you will be reviewing a number of current political cartoons, either with a partner or individually.*
>
> 1. *Look carefully at the cartoons that are in the blue box.*
> 2. *Select three cartoons that you understand best and find the most interesting.*
> 3. *Determine the message in each cartoon.*
> 4. *Complete the "Cartoon Analysis" sheet for the cartoon that interests you most.*
> 5. *Add your cartoon and "Cartoon Analysis" sheet to the center display.*

Plan time to discuss each set of directions with your students, either when you are first acquainting your children with a learning center or when adding a new activity to an established center. Presenting a brief (3- to 5-minute), focused "mini-lesson" is a productive way to explicitly inform the students of the expectancies for the center.

Elementary school students work best when they have a clear idea of classroom expectations, so in addition to knowing how the learning centers work, students must also understand the procedures for selecting centers and center activities. Will you assign students to selected centers and activities? Offer them opportunities to choose on their own? Provide two or three alternatives and let them pick one? Although each possibility has its pluses and minuses, I have found that students welcome learning centers most enthusiastically when they feel a sense of attachment—when *the students* have some choice and control. Although there will be some center activities you will want all your students to try, it is helpful to provide degrees of choice. While many traditional classroom tasks are not optional, learning centers offer a venue that allows students an opportunity to experience freedom. A system of organization helps you to monitor the choices of your students, especially if you want to ensure that they encounter a rich variety of experiences.

 Video Exploration 6.2

 CHECK YOUR UNDERSTANDING 6.2   Click here to check your understanding of this section of the chapter.

Pictures and Study Prints

A rich storehouse of social studies content can be uncovered in the endless supply of pictures and study prints (large, commercially prepared posters) found in sources such as informational books, textbooks, prints, newspapers, travel brochures, calendars, and magazines. Pictures help students envision people, places, events, and other phenomena impossible to experience in any other way, thus proving the truth of the old expression, "A picture is worth a thousand words."

As you display and discuss pictures, it is important to note that your students will vary in their ability to read and comprehend them, much as they vary in their ability to read and comprehend print. While "reading" picture images, some may function only at the *literal level*, being able to simply name, list, and provide specific details about what is being observed. As they get older and accumulate experiences, they will extend their abilities to the *inferential level*, being able to answer more than the directly stated information: Who, What, When, and Where. They do not simply respond with basic facts, but form conclusions or perceive relationships drawn from a combination of their personal background knowledge and the new information. Ultimately, your students will approach the *critical level*, where they are able to use some criteria to judge the quality or value of what is being observed.

As you share pictures and study prints with your students, structure related discussions with questions and prompts of varying sophistication, giving students of varying abilities the opportunity for success at their individual levels of competency. By exposing less mature students to the higher-level thinking of their peers, they learn by example and gradually develop the ability to perform higher-level tasks without help. Sample discussion questions and prompts are shown in Figure 6.3.

 CHECK YOUR UNDERSTANDING 6.3 **Click here** to check your understanding of this section of the chapter.

Although the phrase, "A picture is worth a thousand words," has been overused to the point that it now seems trite, rich high-interest pictures and study prints actually do help students learn far more than a thousand words can hope to match.

Windzepher/Fotolia

FIGURE 6.3   Levels of Picture Interpretation

Literal Level

Describe the people.

Describe the setting.

Describe the activity.

What do you see that makes you say that?

What does the picture remind you of?

Inferential Level

How does this fit into or challenge what you already know?

How is this the same or different from _____?

Could you tell what is happening in your own words?

What will happen next?

What surprises you about the scene?

Critical Level

Why did this happen?

What do you like/dislike about the picture?

What questions do you have?

How can you find the answers?

How might you use the information in this picture?

What is the value of this picture to the topic under study?

 Video Exploration 6.3

Simulations

Activities are considered authentic if they are established in contexts that mimic the way they are performed in real life. That is why the use of simulated activities in social studies classrooms is widely becoming recognized as an important instructional tool. What are simulations? Think of simulations as staged likenesses or impersonations of an event, idea, or process in order to enhance student understanding. Simulations can be found in all aspects of our lives: the military uses them in boot camp, flight simulators help train airline pilots, and a race car arcade game gives you the chance to sample racetrack competition. All are just like the real thing. Even many video games are simulations, with one of the most popular ones using a variation of the word *simulation*—SimCity. Teachers at all levels use simulations; they can be as simple as the teacher role-playing during the introduction of a lesson to get a response from the students:

> *Entering the classroom appearing every bit a space alien in her metallic-type fabric shirt and pants, Betty Hunter introduced herself as a citizen of Zaxton, a planet 25 light years from Earth. "We Zaxtons have been tracking you Earthlings for some 300 years now. We have had a very difficult time understanding your language, but even more difficulty learning about you. In the 6 Earth years*

Simulations can be fun and playful activities during which children act out a role or a real life context.

Zokov_111/Fotolia

I've been observing your planet, I've had a chance only to learn a few things." She continued, "My studies of geography have informed me about such primitive things as trees, dirt, and running water. These are things I've only read about or seen in pictures on my viewing screen. Such things are a pleasure to see because our planet became so polluted that Zaxton is now depleted of them." Then, peering at the classroom globe, Ms. Hunter continued, "Because of what happened to Zaxton, my favorite kinds of lessons about Earth are lessons about geography. What can you Earthlings teach me about this planet you inhabit?" Ms. Hunter then went on to a unit that she called Geography 101, Life on Planet Earth.

Reflection on Learning

You may simply scribble rough notes or jot down something more polished and complete. The point is to simply start recording your ideas spontaneously and candidly.

I have heard many people say that teaching is a lot like acting. They see teachers and actors as high-energy, spirited performers who easily transition among numerous, often disparate, roles. But the performance aspect of our profession is rarely emphasized in teacher preparation programs. Can you visualize yourself as Betty Hunter, feeling comfortable and safe using the skills and talents that are often associated with actors and other live performers? As you think about it, what would be one of your biggest, wildest simulation ideas for bringing surprise to student learning?

Social studies simulations are most often complex learning experiences that involve students as participants; they can last for several days. Classroom simulations replicate the actual circumstances so well that there is scant deviation between the simulated setting and the real one. For example, in her unit on "Regions of the United States," Carmie Latimore used tasks and instructional resources simulating those used by adults in real settings (the workplace) to design an authentic, simulated classroom project.

Ms. Latimore's students liked to take virtual trips on the web and showed a lot of passion for learning about other places. She decided to capitalize on their enthusiasm and put them to work as intern travel agents for the classroom-based World Wide Travel Agency. To create interest, Ms. Latimore and her students received a pretend email correspondence one day from Mr. John Doe, a fictitious client who planned to take a border-to-border tour throughout the contiguous United States in the near future and wished to arrange his itinerary through the World Wide Travel Agency. The students were impressed with the potential business Mr. Doe could bring to the agency, but were a little uncertain if they had the expertise to handle it: "What do travel agencies do?" No problem here; Donyelle's mother ran the local travel agency and was more than happy to arrange a visit to her place of business. The students returned to the classroom laden with posters, pamphlets, guidebooks, and brochures. These materials helped the students understand the kind of information tourists need. They learned firsthand about the travel business and what it takes to promote trips to different places.

Ms. Latimore and her students agreed that it would be in their best interest to designate sections of the classroom as separate "travel agency offices"—one to deal with each region of the United States. After the students were divided into small groups, each came up with its own office name and displayed a business sign: Middle Atlantic States, Great Lakes, and so on.

The travel agency offices thought they were ready to design an advertising package for their respective regions, with resources similar to those they brought back from their trip to the real travel agency. They decided it would be best to produce a guidebook, a travel poster, a travel brochure, a magazine advertisement, and a radio/television campaign for each office. Before they began their work, however, Ms. Latimore asked the students in each travel agency office to focus their research activities on the kinds of attractions the region was noted for—sandy beaches, scenic mountain trails, historic sites, industry, or agriculture. Some groups found information in magazines and books and others decided to watch a video, but all found a wealth of information on various Internet sites. After they finished, each group illustrated a large poster and used a few well-chosen words as a caption (for example, the group investigating America's Southwest focused on the Grand Canyon and used the caption "A Grand Adventure!").

The brochures were eye-catching, too. Patterned after commercial brochures, each was created with Microsoft Publisher and contained colorful graphics, photos, maps, and captions. For example, a steaming loaf of bread dominated the front page of the brochure from the group responsible for the Midwest: "The Central Plains: Our Nation's Breadbasket." The children chose six important features of the region to highlight on the inside, each one accompanied by text and illustration. The back of each brochure included a small map of the region, directions on how to get there, and sources of further information.

The purpose of the magazine ads and radio/television campaigns (a 30-second spot using the classroom video camera) was similar: to draw visitors by describing the important features of the region. Students were advised that each form of advertising needed a concise message so potential customers wouldn't be bored by excessive detail.

The guidebooks were much more comprehensive. Each guidebook had these features:

- *A preface that briefly promoted the region.*
- *An introduction that served as a slightly more comprehensive guide to the region's attractions, climate, geographical features, chief products, and so on.*
- *A history section that included significant dates and events as well as the important people who have lived in the region.*
- *A calendar of events that highlighted fairs, celebrations, and seasonal attractions.*
- *A places-to-see section that included information about the capital, major cities, museums, parks, zoos, recreational activities, historical sites, and businesses.*
- *A food and shelter section that provided information about hotels, restaurants, and campsites, including their costs.*

To culminate the experience, Ms. Latimore requested that each travel agency office share its advertising campaign with the other offices in the World Wide Travel Agency. Parents were later invited to visit the classroom to enjoy the students' work. The children learned a great deal about the various regions through participating in this enjoyable, creative project.

The basic idea behind simulations is to allow students to assume the roles of real-life people and act out scenarios in order to gain deeper insight into people and life situations. Several software companies specialize in designing simulations and the Internet is loaded with possibilities. However, some of the best simulations have been created by teachers in their effort to address the unique needs and interests of their students. You will find that topics for simulation are practically unlimited—from slave ship experiences to the first shot fired at Lexington to planning cities in response to various policy decisions. Some topics are controversial, however—loaded with underlying emotion and controversy—especially those related to racial and ethnic matters. For example, teachers have developed simulations over the years to encourage students to think and act as Holocaust victims or passengers on a make-believe slave ship. Some cite these as among the most powerful and memorable elementary school experiences while others claim these oversimplified experiences are dangerous and unnecessary, especially for emotionally vulnerable elementary school students. Because such simulations are risky and can often go awry, it may be best to focus on the countless emotionally safe simulation possibilities and infuse your entire social studies curriculum with segments on bias, bigotry, and discrimination.

 CHECK YOUR UNDERSTANDING 6.4 **Click here** to check your understanding of this section of the chapter.

A Final Thought

Children develop at different rates and in different ways. Some walk at 10 months of age, while others take their first wobbly steps at 18 months. Some say a few words at 1 year; others take a bit more time. Those variations are normal. But some variations are more serious than others and have a profound effect on how children grow and develop. Some children may have developmental delays or difficulties right after birth, while others experience extreme delays a little bit later. In some cases, the delays are associated with ethnicity or culture or language; still others may involve physical health factors, mental health issues, a traumatic event, abuse or neglect, poverty, poor nutrition or health care, or gender expectancies. And, although they have not been recognized as "special needs" students, gifted children require as much support to grow to their fullest potential as those with distinctive physical, behavioral, or emotional disabilities. Understanding individual differences in growth and development, as well as their causes, helps us to accept the idea that children differ in the way they learn and that the idea of "one size fits all" has no place in the elementary school social studies classroom.

The best social studies teachers have been differentiating instruction for as long as social studies has existed as a school subject; these teachers have learned to accommodate a wide range of student abilities and unique learning needs in their social studies classrooms. They have realized that there is no "how to" recipe for differentiation because respecting the individuality of students means that diversity can be translated into classroom practice in many ways. These teachers select a variety of effective instructional resources to maximize learning for each student. They know that teaching key concepts using only abstract or only concrete representations of those concepts leads to less productive knowledge acquisition than teaching students with a range of instructional representations. The message of this chapter, therefore, is that there is no single means of representation that will be optimal for all learners; providing various options for representation is essential for successful social studies instruction.

References

Dodge, B. (1995). *Some thoughts about WebQuests*. Retrieved from http://edweb.sdsu.edu/courses/edtec596/about_webquests.html

Gunning, T. G. (2010). *Creating literacy instruction for all students* (7th ed.). Boston, MA: Pearson.

Lever-Duffy, J., & McDonald, J. (2011). *Teaching and learning with technology* (4th ed.). Boston, MA: Pearson.

March, T. (2003). New needs, new curriculum. *Educational Leadership, 61*, 42–47.

National Council for the Social Studies. (2006). Technology position statement and guidelines. *Social Education, 70*, 329–331.

Beyond the Ordinary:
Teaching and Learning with Informational and Persuasive Text

Learning Outcomes

You will come across various definitions of the terms *literacy* and *language arts* as you go through your methods courses; some even use the terms interchangeably. But I will use their relatively traditional meanings. *Literacy* will refer to reading and writing while *language arts* will comprise listening, speaking, reading, writing, viewing (understanding visual images), and visually representing (presenting information through images). Since the current educational climate draws primary attention to *literacy* across the curriculum, Chapters 7 and 8 will emphasize the importance of reading and writing in social studies. Reading and writing (along with mathematics) has always been at the heart of the elementary school curriculum. Through the years, it has traditionally been accepted that reading and writing know-how was the restricted domain of reading specialists and language arts teachers. But the good news is that social studies has moved on up the status ladder as schools have begun to value the importance of integrating reading with social studies instruction. What influenced that change? What role will reading and writing play in your social studies classroom? The purpose of this chapter is to help you find simple answers to those complicated questions.

After completing this chapter, you will be able to:

- Define the term informational text.
- Identify the strengths and weaknesses of textbook use in social studies.
- Explain how informational books benefit learning.
- Summarize how to incorporate biographies into the social studies program.
- Indicate how to use newspapers as a way to engage students more effectively in authentic learning.
- Explain the comprehension strategies that help students make sense of informational text.
- Define the term persuasive text.

Classroom Snapshot

Today, Elias Rose planned to introduce his students to the life of the rough, hard-working vaqueros (cattle workers) who rode the ranges and cattle trails of South America and Mexico during the 1700s and 1800s. He will help them explore the life of these proud cowboys by reading the book Vaquero by James Rice (Pelican). In the well-illustrated book, Chi Chi, a Chihuahua who has watched the vaqueros herd cattle and use their other special talents, relays information in both Spanish and English about the history, skills, and special gear of these "cowboys." After a short discussion of the book, Mr. Rose will help the students use what they have learned to compose a cinquain about these hard-working herdsmen; although there are many ways to write a cinquain, Mr. Rose has chosen to follow this pattern:

> Line 1: One word naming the title, theme, or topic (noun)
> Line 2: Two words that describe the title (adjectives)
> Line 3: Three words ending in "-ing" that express action (verbs)
> Line 4: Four things associated with the title (nouns) or a sentence describing feelings
> Line 5: One word that gives the title a similar name (synonym)

Mr. Rose used a technique called Carousel Brainstorming to help them recall and organize key information. He followed this procedure:

1. Identify 3–5 key questions. Write each question at the top of a large piece of chart paper, and tape the papers to the wall in equal intervals around the room.

2. Separate the class into equal groups based on the number of questions. Because this activity has four questions, there will be four groups: "What are some vaquero things (nouns)?" "What words describe both vaqueros and vaquero things (adjectives)?" "What words (ending in '-ing') express a vaquero's actions (verbs)?" and "What is another word for vaquero (synonyms)?" Write one question on each chart.

3. Send each group to one of the charts. Give each group a different color magic marker, and have one student in each group serve as the recorder. Explain that the groups will have 2 minutes to write down on their chart paper all the words they can think of that relate to the question on their sheet.

4. When the 2 minutes are up, the groups take their colored markers and rotate to the next chart to read what the previous group has written. Then they take 2 minutes to add their own ideas.

5. Continue until each group has had a chance to visit each chart.

6. When groups return to their original charts, give them up to 5 minutes to review and summarize all the contributions. The different colors will indicate which contributions were made by the separate groups. Then, depending on its chart, the groups will circle the two best adjectives, three best verbs, four best nouns, and one best synonym.

Lively discussion continued for some time as the students argued strongly for their personal choices. Key information bubbled forth as they sought to convince their group partners of the value of their personal selections. By creating a lengthy list for each chart, Mr. Rose not only helped the students organize a rich word bank from which to select words for their cinquains, he also helped them to review and organize the subject matter content under study into meaningful categories. The process of collecting, thinking about, organizing, and talking about the content was an important initial prewriting step for Mr. Rose's young authors, for they will structure their writing project on relevant facts and details.

When each group circled the appropriate number of selections from its assigned chart, Mr. Rose began the third phase of the writing activity—composing a group model. He posted a large sheet of chart paper, which exhibited a writing guide.

On the top line, Mr. Rose printed the word identifying the central topic—Vaquero. He then asked the "Describing Words" group to reveal the two adjectives it had selected and to write them in the appropriate blanks: hard-riding and proud. In the same way, the "Doing Words" group revealed its three verbs for the third

FIGURE 7.1   Vaquero Cinquain

Vaquero

hard-riding   proud

roping   riding   driving

rancho   mustang   reata   silla

Cattleman

line (roping, riding, and driving) and the "Things" group shared its choice of four vaquero things for the next line (rancho, mustang, reata, and silla). "What synonym for vaquero did you select for the last line?" was Mr. Rose's challenge to the fourth group. After considering all suggestions, the group decided on "cattleman" over "cowboy" and "buckaroo" because they thought it was an accurate English translation of the Spanish word. The group composition is shown in Figure 7.1.

During the fourth stage of the content writing activity—editing and rewriting—Mr. Rose encouraged the students to read the group-generated cinquain with him; they revised the text appropriately. Commas were added to separate items in a list and the first word of each line was capitalized. After the corrections were made, the class read the selection out loud together once again.

To begin the final stage of the writing activity—individual writing—Mr. Rose helped his students analyze the pattern of the group cinquain: "How many blank spaces do you see on each line?" "What kinds of words were used on each line?" "How have the words helped to paint a picture in our minds of what we have been studying about the life of a vaquero?" The students used their charts as word banks and referred to them as needed.

The final phase of the writing activity—publishing—involved sharing their individual written pieces with an audience. In this case, rather than stapling the cinquains to a bulletin board or reading them aloud in front of class, the cinquains were posted to their classroom web page.

Mr. Rose fully understands that the ability to read and write in social studies does not come about naturally; it is the result of careful planning and deliberate instruction. With that in mind, he followed a systematic series of six interrelated steps as he helped his students create their finished pieces:

1. *Explore the topic.* Offer a series of meaningful social studies learning experiences (including reading from informational text), through which the students uncover useful information on which to base their writing.

2. *Brainstorm and organize the information.* Help students recall what they have learned and chart relationships among the data.

3. *Compose a group text.* Use the organized data to cooperatively compose a whole-class or group model to serve as a sample.

4. *Edit the sample and rewrite, if necessary.* Reread the written piece to determine whether ideas are expressed clearly and accurately, and whether there are any errors in spelling, grammar, or writing mechanics.

5. *Create individual written pieces.* Offer an opportunity for each student to write a unique piece by applying the strategies used to create the group-generated model.

6. *Publish the individually written pieces.* Share what the classroom authors have created by asking them to read aloud to their classmates, contribute a page to a class-made book, post their work on a bulletin board, and so on.

Mr. Rose embraces *literacy integration* for his social studies program because it breaks from the practice of teaching literacy and social studies in isolation from each other. "I don't really understand those who think that integrating literacy with social studies is something new," remarks Mr. Rose. "I can't remember teaching social studies without incorporating reading or writing in some capacity. Can you imagine teaching *any* subject without using some pieces of literacy? It's impossible!" By encouraging his students to explore and experiment with reading and writing in social studies contexts, Mr. Rose helps them become aware that print symbols can be used for two complementary purposes—to either acquire meaning (reading) or impart meaning (writing) in a variety of ways. He explains:

> *I have no doubt that a child's overall literacy development is influenced by a strong connection between reading and writing. But, in order to help children truly develop as learners, I find it necessary to apply this literacy connection when teaching social studies. That is, you cannot activate the learning process without having something important to read and write about. Here's where social studies comes in; reading social studies content furnishes the subject matter—the people, places, and events—the ingredients for writing. In my social studies program, I don't even think about teaching reading and writing separately.*

Mr. Rose likes to portray the shared connections between literacy and social studies as a form of *mutualism*, a type of *symbiotic connection* between two different things in which both of them have something to gain. For example, a mutualistic relationship exists between bees and flowers; bees buzz from flower to flower gathering nectar, which they make into food. As they gather nectar from the flowers, pollen brushes onto the bees' short-haired bodies. They transport the pollen from one plant to another, resulting in pollination and eventually new plants. The bees get food and the flowers become pollinated—a "win–win" partnership. Social studies and literacy have a symbiotic connection, too. Literacy strategies and skills are used as students acquire and impart social studies learnings; specialized social studies content and skills bring application and purpose to literacy—a perfect symbiotic relationship! What better way is there to teach literacy skills and strategies than through interesting and relevant content about the world in which the students live?

 Video Exploration 7.1

There are many ways to integrate literacy and social studies, but *text* (any print source from which students derive meaning) appears to be receiving the greatest attention. Text may be represented in a variety of different forms known as *text types*. For the purposes of this book, we will consider three main text types—informational (sometimes called expository), persuasive, and narrative. How can you tell if text is informational, persuasive, or narrative? There are certain features you can look for. *Informational text* provides knowledge in a way that is educational and useful; it explains or describes something. Informational text is true; it is factual and intended to enlighten and, obviously, to inform. Social studies textbooks, informational books from the library, biographies, and newspapers are all examples of informational text. The purpose of *persuasive text* is to influence others that one idea, action, or opinion is more reasonable, proper, or correct than any other. Advertisements, editorials, and political cartoons are varieties of persuasive text. Generally, you will find that there are many kinds of narrative text. *Narrative text* may be categorized into fictional (occurring in an imaginary world), nonfictional (occurring in the real world), or a combination of both. Narratives run the gamut from personal diaries and journals to folktales and poetry. Although the primary purpose of narrative text is to entertain, the books your students will read will also be informative. You can expect your students to use these three text types to read and write for different purposes in social studies; consequently, you will need to understand how informational, persuasive,

Students apply literacy strategies as they acquire information and communicate what they have learned in social studies.

WavebreakMediaMicro/Fotolia

and narrative text works. For that reason, strategies for reading and writing informational and persuasive text will be explored in this chapter; narrative text will be dealt with in Chapter 6.

What Is Informational Text?

The purpose of informational text is to reveal information about our physical and social world. The content of informational text is endless: suggestions for preparing deep-fried Twinkies; driving directions to Zzyzx, California; how to groom your pet capybara; the climate of Tristan da Cunha; or the title of the book holding the record for being most often stolen from public libraries (the *Guinness Book of World Records*). Informational text will inform you of these bits of important information as well as other factual must-haves; for example, that Sherlock Holmes never said, "Elementary, my dear Watson," or that the first couple to be shown in bed together on primetime TV were Fred and Wilma Flintstone. What a fascinating genre . . . informational text includes all topics and all knowledge known to humanity!

Reflection on Learning

You may simply scribble rough notes or jot down something more polished and complete. The point is to simply start recording your ideas spontaneously and candidly.

If you're like me, you like to know things like, "Donald Duck comics were once banned in Finland because he doesn't wear pants." There are so many amazing things to learn and discover. Thankfully, as a college student, you've got a lot of free time to research information like this. So what amazing information about the world around us can you and your classmates uncover and collect into the "World's Greatest Compendium of Amazing Facts and Information"?

Despite its controversy, the Common Core State Standards (National Governor's Association, 2010) has produced at least one favorable end result—a call for an increase in the amount of time spent teaching students how to read and write informational text. Specifically, the standards recommend that fourth-grade students should spend half of their reading time with informational text, with the expectation that there will be even more focus on informational text in the later grades. Despite such recommendations, informational text is rarely found in first- through third-grade social studies classrooms. Gambrell and Marinak (2009) reported, "On average, only 3.6 minutes per day were spent with informational text during classroom reading and writing activities. In low socioeconomic status schools, almost no time was spent with informational text. As students progress into the upper elementary grades, the problem persists or worsens" (p. 4). Gambrell and Marinak (2009) explain that, despite our lack of interest in using informational text, many young readers are fascinated with informational books. Christine Pappas (1993) supported this contention with her often-cited study which showed that children as young as kindergarten age preferred informational books to storybooks. And, more recently, Mohr (2006), too, found that informational books were the overwhelming choice of primary-grade students. Informational reading and writing skills are best developed by using texts that contain worthwhile and absorbing content and by teaching students effective strategies that help them acquire and impart information with text. We will explore how to do that by examining the kinds of informational text commonly used in social studies classrooms: textbooks, informational books, biographies, and newspapers.

 CHECK YOUR UNDERSTANDING 7.1 **Click here** to check your understanding of this section of the chapter.

Social Studies Textbooks

Many teachers are sold on social studies textbooks; they feel the books are easy to use and offer a carefully researched instructional package including manuals complete with goals, CDs, DVDs, maps, lesson plans, activities, and tests. "Our school's social studies program is based on the social studies textbook," explains a fourth-grade teacher. "It's the whole package; the various resources it contains offer marvelous instructional support." When elementary school teachers are expected to use productive instructional strategies and activities for every subject they teach, the thought of having specially "packaged" help in social studies greatly reduces the pressure and anxiety of daily planning. Furthermore, textbooks provide subject matter that is organized sequentially from one grade level to the next; each teacher from kindergarten through Grade 8 knows what was done in earlier grades and what will be expected in later grades, thereby minimizing gaps or repetition. A textbook program is especially appreciated by beginning teachers who find it helpful to have a textbook's organized content, concise lessons, and recommended instructional strategies as they navigate a maze of first-year expectations. Although textbooks virtually take teachers "by the hand" and guide them through the instructional process, beginning teachers must eventually loosen their grip on the textbook, spread their teaching wings, and use their developing abilities to try new and exciting things. (This may not be popular with my professional colleagues, but I'm really not sure if it's the pedagogical method itself that brings about greatest learning or if it's the individual carrying out the pedagogy. For that reason, I have often said that if I had a choice, I would prefer a great textbook-based social studies teacher over a poor activity-oriented teacher.) Teachers who do well with a textbook approach consider the varied reading abilities of their students; they encourage collaboration and cooperation; they make sure that conceptual and experiential backgrounds are connected to the new material prior to reading; they confront students with challenging problems; and they supplement the textbook with a wide variety of literature sources and hands-on materials.

On the other side of the coin are teachers who feel that textbooks are written too unimaginatively for their students; the heavy load of facts and carefully controlled vocabulary result in bland and expressionless reading. And in their effort to compete with mass media glitz, some teachers complain that textbook publishers have gone overboard in using photos, charts, graphs, diagrams, boxes, study exercises, and other peripherals that cut available space for meaningful narrative content: "Just the size and weight of the text are turn-offs for my students," grumbled one teacher. "I can't imagine any of them being excited enough about their social studies text that they would want to curl up in a comfortable chair to read it!"

Whether or not you become a textbook devotee, the reality is that textbooks have traditionally been and continue to be a familiar source of instruction in elementary school social studies classrooms and stand a good chance of being the starting point for instruction as you begin your career. If that's the case, consider that even the finest textbook package is insufficient by itself; it is best to think of a textbook as fundamental teaching and learning tool that must be supplemented with videos, trade books, projects, and other activities and materials in order to maintain student interest and to satisfactorily address targeted learning goals.

 CHECK YOUR UNDERSTANDING 7.2   Click here to check your understanding of this section of the chapter.

Informational Books

Anyone who has spent time with children knows they are curious souls. Naturally attracted to new things in their lives, they waste no time questioning, exploring, speculating, and discovering. That is the way children learn about how our world works. Every new discovery brings them satisfaction and fuels a desire for further exploration. So when children experience the joy of discovery, seeds for deeper understanding are sown. I remember Kenneth, whose explorations of schoolyard rocks led to a fascination with rocks of all sizes and shapes; each and every day, he played with his extensive collection. Although only in third grade, Kenneth could tell me their names and which of the three main classes of rock they belonged to—sedimentary, metamorphic, or igneous (and he could explain the likenesses and differences among them). He read informational books about rocks incessantly and impressed everyone with his knowledge of rock cycles, rock formations, erosion, and the difference between rocks and minerals. The level of curiosity sparked by those playground rocks meant question after question . . . but it also created an innate drive for Kenneth to find just the right kinds of answers.

Like Kenneth, students will explore and discover all kinds of things in your classroom and, through their observations, they will learn a lot. But they will also need to know where and how to look for additional information. You must help them do this by providing informational books whose purpose is to teach readers about a topic. In a nutshell, informational books reveal content and concepts in absorbing and appealing ways, and help students learn about things that are difficult or impossible to experience directly. There are scores of informational books that adhere to finer literary standards and catch our eyes and hold our interest just like a good novel. And the illustrations provide strong clarification for technical vocabulary and complex concepts. Even when they have access to direct experiences, informational books help students deepen their understandings and help them see things in new ways. Young students find informational books interesting; many enjoy them as much as or more than storybooks. Make sure your school library and classroom library have strong collections of good informational books for children.

Text Structures

It is important to introduce the idea that informational books use distinct organizational patterns called *expository text structures* to present and explain information. The recognition and use of these expository text structures is basic to comprehension and retention of the

The content of informational text is interesting to almost all elementary school students, and many actually prefer informational texts to storybooks.

WavebreakMediaMicro/Fotolia

content. Meyer (1985) was among the first to categorize these expository text structures. His system follows:

- *Description.* Define a topic by describing its attributes, features, or characteristics. Examples are often used: "An ecosystem is a community of living organisms (plants and animals) interacting with themselves and also with their environment. There are many examples of ecosystems—pond, forest, river, desert, tundra, coral reef, and grassland."

- *Sequence.* Use numerical or chronological order to list items or events. For example, "In ecosystems, a food chain describes how different organisms consume each other in order to survive, starting out with a plant and ending with an animal. You could show a food chain like this: **grass → rabbit → fox.**"

- *Compare/contrast.* Describe how two or more concepts, events, topics, or objects are alike or different. For example, "Ecosystems can be very tiny, like a puddle or a tree trunk, or they can be as large as the Pacific Ocean."

- *Cause/effect.* Present ideas or events as causes, and then describe the effects that happen as a result. "When humans disrupt one part of an ecosystem, other parts will be affected as well. Cutting down trees and burning fossil fuels are just two of the ways that humans have upset the balance of nature. Can you think of others?"

- *Problem/solution.* Present a problem or question and then offer one or more possible solutions. For example, "Human activities cause changes to ecosystems. Deforestation has many harmful effects on the environment. A possible solution is to completely stop cutting down trees, but a more reasonable solution is to carefully control logging operations."

When students know what to look for in terms of text structure, they are better able to comprehend the subject matter content. Tompkins (1998) suggested the following steps to teach expository text structures:

1. *Introduce an organizational pattern.* Introduce signal words and phrases that identify each text structure and give students a graphic organizer for each pattern.

2. *Give students opportunities to work on the text.* Provide students with chances to analyze informational text structures. Students learn the signal words and phrases that identify each text pattern. They should use graphic organizers to illustrate these patterns.

3. *Invite students to write paragraphs using each text structure pattern.* Initial writing experiences should be a whole-class activity, followed by small-group, partner, and independent writing opportunities. This involves selecting a topic and using a graphic organizer to plan the paragraphs. Finally, the students write a rough draft using signal words and phrases for the text structure pattern, revise, and edit the paragraph to produce the final product.

 Video Exploration 7.2

Informational Books as Models for Informational Writing

Comprehending informational text involves understanding what has been read. Strategies for effective comprehension skills development were discussed in Chapter 3 and will be elaborated upon toward the end of this chapter under the heading "Strategies for Reading Informational Text" on page 231. Review those sections to help readers become proficient in literal, inferential, and critical comprehension. Because reading comprehension was treated in those sections, we will consider only informational writing here.

Informational writing (sometimes called expository writing) is perhaps the most common form of writing assigned in social studies classrooms and is also a major component of writing assessment on state standards-based tests. The goal of informational writing, logically, is to impart information by explaining, describing, defining, clarifying, or giving directions. Although informational writing has wide acceptance for all grade levels in social studies programs around the country, you cannot expect students to write informational text simply by telling them, "A report on Sitting Bull is due next Tuesday." Assigning reports like that only frustrates many students and encourages them to copy information directly from a book or website. Good teachers know that informational writing, like all other writing, must be supported by models to emulate so, adhering to Tompkins' previous advice, they offer their students quality informational books as good examples. It is widely accepted that good models produce good results.

IN THE EARLY GRADES

Neil Pennington, for example, knows that successful first informational writing experiences for younger elementary school students should be collaborative efforts. So he organized small groups of students to work together to write sections of a report that were later combined into an informational "book." Capitalizing on the wealth of informational books as *models* for student writing, Mr. Pennington selected *Bread, Bread, Bread* by Ann Morris (HarperTrophy).

Mr. Pennington began his instructional project titled "Bread Makers," by showing his children an assortment of real bread: bagels, pita, baguette, tortillas, and rye bread, to name a few. Bakeries were happy to donate sample breads, particularly day-old leftovers. Mr. Pennington did this not only to provide his students with a direct experience, but also to generate enthusiasm and interest—to prime the pump for the flurry of activity that would follow. The children tried the samples and made a graph of their favorites.

Mr. Pennington invited the children to label the country of origin of each bread sample on a large map. He added another interest-generating experience by giving the children an opportunity to bake their own bread. He gave them small balls of prepared bread dough (available in supermarkets) and asked them to place the dough balls on sheets of aluminum foil labeled with their names. Before they put their dough into the oven, the children shaped the balls any way they wished. The bread was baked according to directions, and the children discussed their sensory experiences as well as the physical changes they observed from start to finish. Everyone responded to this activity with enthusiasm and interest; a wealth of questions and comments followed the activity.

To begin the actual content-centered phase of the project, the next day Mr. Pennington assigned committees the task of writing their own information booklets on different breads. He specified the form the writing would take, but the children would eventually determine the content. To show the form that their booklets were to take, Mr. Pennington brought to class a very simple model of expository writing: Bread, Bread, Bread *by Ann Morris (HarperTrophy). The book contains impressive photographs and short descriptions of various breads from cultures around the world. As the class and Mr. Pennington surveyed the book together, they paid particular attention to the way the photographs and text were used on each page. Mr. Pennington and the students agreed that their forthcoming information booklet would include a drawing and a sentence with some information about the drawing (the culture, country, and main grain)—just like the model.*

The children worked on their bread books for about three days. Most of the committees decided that their books should be about six pages long (two pages for each child), but a few committees wrote more. To help the committees find information about bread, Mr. Pennington located additional expository text and inserted bookmarks at the proper places. He also encouraged the children to use Google's KidzSearch, a free, safe search engine for children, using the keywords "breads around the world." At the end of the first day, Mr. Pennington and the children sat in a circle to discuss how things had gone for them. Most had gotten as far as locating something they wanted to write about and starting their illustrations. The second day was spent completing the illustrations and the associated text.

On the third day, Mr. Pennington talked to the children about book titles and discussed how the covers of several of the books the children had been reading contained illustrations that represented the main idea of the text. The children illustrated the covers of their own booklets, added titles, listed their names as authors, put the pages in order, and stapled them together. The committees shared their books with one another, and the final copies were ceremoniously added to the classroom library.

One committee titled its booklet, The Bread Book; *it contained the following pages:*

> *Page 1: Navajos eat fry bread almost every day. It is fried in shortening, not baked.*
> *Page 2: People from France eat baguettes. They are long loaves of bread with a thin golden crust.*
> *Page 3: Paska is a round Easter bread decorated with fancy dough. It is very special bread from the Ukraine.*
> *Page 4: Mexican people like to eat a thin, round, flat bread called tortilla. Tortillas can be made from flour or corn.*
> *Page 5: Chapati is bread from India. It is flat and round like a pancake and baked on a hot griddle.*
> *Page 6: Bagels were first made in Poland. They are first boiled for a short time in water and then baked.*

Some of the final informational pieces showed only minor changes from the literature model, but others were truly creative. More important, however, was the fact that all the children were learning something about cultures around the world. Mr. Pennington summarized the booklet presentations by asking: "Which of these breads have you eaten?" "Which would you like to try?" "Why are breads so different from one another?" "What did you learn about bread?" The class made a bread bulletin board using a world map as the focal point. Students found pictures of their breads, labeled each picture with the name of the bread, and used yarn to connect it to its country of origin. Sarah summarized the experience perfectly, "This was fun and I learned a lot about bread. Maybe we can study different soups next!"

IN THE LATER GRADES

Isabella Rogers and her fifth graders assemble at a bright yellow rug they call their "Conversation Station." They are meeting to begin a new unit of study, History of the American Flag. *Before starting any new topic, Ms. Rogers makes sure her students are able to connect their previous knowledge and experiences to the new information, so she unfurls the current flag of the United States and asks the students to discuss what they already know about it.*

Since the major emphasis of this study was going to be research and informational writing (finding out and informing), Ms. Rogers knew a good place to start was with a model of related informational writing; students tended to write better original pieces while modeling what they saw in books.

Therefore, she selected the informational picture book The American Flag *by Elaine Landau (Children's Press). Ms. Rogers then read aloud Landau's short history of the American flag and helped her students analyze the text structure.*

Realizing that the history of our American flag was too broad a topic for a single student's writing project, Ms. Rogers broke it down into small, manageable subdivisions that would be researched through small-group investigations: "British Union Jack," "Grand Union Flag," "Betsy Ross's Flag," "Star-Spangled Banner," "Flag of 1818," "Flag of 1912," and "Today's Flag." The plan was for each small group to investigate its own flag, write a short informational piece, share their works orally, and compile them as separate pages of a class book, Flags throughout American History. *Of course, the pages of their class book would replicate Landau's book.*

The next stage of the research project involved developing a list of questions to guide research into the assigned flags. The class decided that each group should answer the same questions as modeled in Landau's book: What colors were used? What symbols were used? When was it adopted? Why was it changed? These questions provided a starting point for research and served as a focus for the students' writing.

Next, the students searched through a variety of informational books and websites for answers to their research questions. Ms. Rogers monitored this portion of the research process carefully, because students must learn to choose relevant information and avoid word-for-word copying from any source of information. "In too many classrooms, informational writing has been equated with copying facts from a book or cutting and pasting paragraphs from websites. Nothing can be more deadly," Ms. Rogers warns, "than to allow a child to stand in front of a classroom and read a report that was copied word for word. If the students don't give their reports a personal touch, you'll hear frequent pauses, the child will speak in a monotone, and he or she will often struggle to pronounce unfamiliar words."

To help them organize their reports, Ms. Rogers gave the students a number of index cards. She explained that these would be referred to as "information cards" because each would be divided into two major sections: a large circle at the top of the card representing the dot of the letter "i" and a bottom rectangular section representing the stem. The students then printed the main idea (usually the first sentence of a paragraph) on the top section (the dot of the "i"); in the bottom section they listed all the supporting details (see Figure 7.2).

FIGURE 7.2   A Sample Information Card

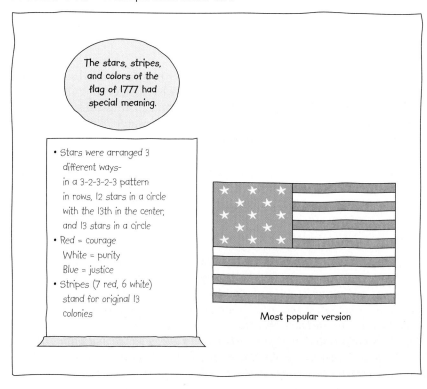

The information cards helped the children select interesting and appropriate information for their paragraphs. The groups shared their drafts with each other and revised them on the basis of the feedback they received. They edited their paragraphs for spelling, grammatical errors, run-on sentences, and other problems. It was helpful to have peers read the paragraphs, since they noticed things that the writers did not. Students then completed the separate sections of the complete report and, as a class, designed the cover and added an introductory page.

For the last stage, each research group set up an area of the classroom where they shared the written pieces. They donned simple costumes and used props to help the audience get a feel for the historical era. For example, the reporter presenting the "Grand Union Flag" wore a pair of glasses pulled down over his nose like Benjamin Franklin, and the reporter who told of the "Betsy Ross Flag" arranged a number of five-pointed stars among some simple sewing implements. As part of its presentation, each group displayed a model of its selected flag and read a short report describing the flag's historical significance. Figure 7.3 shows an example of the report that was read aloud by the first group for our colonists' earliest flag, the "Grand Union Flag."

A fascinating aspect of our profession is that, although instruction is focused on the same instructional goals, teachers creatively "customize" instruction to meet their students' various needs. For example, Angelo Gracia, Ms. Rogers' fifth-grade teaching partner, was responsible

FIGURE 7.3   Student Flag Report

for carrying out the same American flag writing project with his students, but personalized it by using a different graphic organizer and alternate end result. Instead of information cards, he selected a graphic organizer he called the "Main Idea Hamburger," and in place of a book, his students completed a computer presentation program.

> *Mr. Gracia's class was divided into several small groups; each group identified the main idea or theme of the report and wrote it on the top portion of the hamburger bun (see Figure 7.4). Then the groups listed details supporting the main idea on the meat patty of the graphic organizer. Finally, on the bottom section of the bun, each group wrote a personal statement summarizing what the symbol meant to its members.*
>
> *Mr. Gracia agrees that taking students beyond the content of what they have learned by having them either rewrite something in their own words or writing a new version reinforces the learning that has taken place. So after reading Landau's book about the American flag, Mr. Gracia's class made a Kid Pix Deluxe presentation to help pull together all that they had learned. Kid Pix Deluxe is a simple computer drawing program that has an array of art mediums (paint, watercolor, airbrush, pencil, crayon, marker, chalk). Text can easily be added to the children's drawings, formatted, edited, and even turned into speech. Each student in Mr. Gracia's class wrote one interesting thing about the historical evolution of the American flag and added an illustration. The class combined and organized all the slides into a "Symbol of Freedom" slide show. The students included patriotic music to complete their remarkable video production.*

Reflection on Learning

You may simply scribble rough notes or jot down something more polished and complete. The point is to simply start recording your ideas spontaneously and candidly.

A teacher made this comment to me recently: "For what reason does the Common Core State Standards dislike fiction? It seems like they're trying to remove from our classrooms the richness and power of good children's literature. I just can't imagine a developmentally suitable classroom without delightful picture books, fantasy, novels, and just plain old fun stories." How would you respond to that teacher?

FIGURE 7.4 Main Idea Hamburger

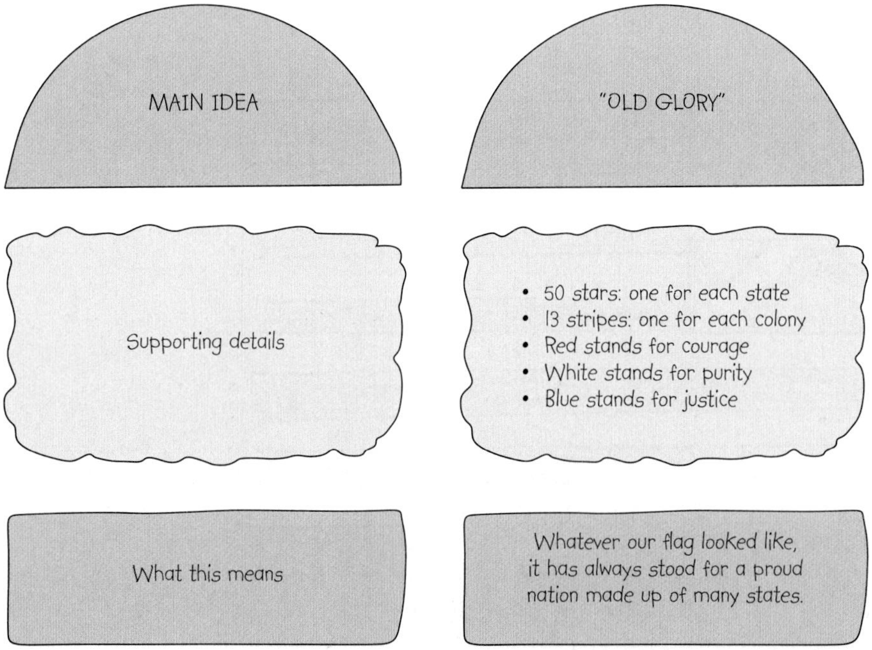

CHECK YOUR UNDERSTANDING 7.3   Click here to check your understanding of this section of the chapter.

Biographies

A biography tells the true story of somebody's life; it is a detailed written account of the life of a president, athlete, artist, entertainer, political activist, world leader, Supreme Court justice, inventor, chef, educator, activist, reformer, or other notable person. (An autobiography is a story of a person's life written or told by that person.) Biographies can be only a few sentences long or as extensive as a book. Your students may experience only brief encounters with the lives of extraordinary people in their social studies textbooks, but biographies turn ordinary individuals into vital, high-powered human beings students can personally respond to and identify with. When students read about their strengths and accomplishments, as well as their failings and weaknesses, famous figures often escape the realm of embellished, extreme versions of reality to a world of "down-to-earth" people with a strong grip on reality.

Because biographies are true, informative accounts of notable people, the authenticity of time and place must be accurate. In addition to painstaking accuracy, biographies must engage young readers in a riveting story that brings to life the main character portrayed in the book; biographies must be entertaining. Most good biographies written for elementary school students seem to meet these criteria and often become the favorite genre of many young readers.

Jack Jarrett, a fifth-grade teacher, searched for enjoyable and productive strategies that might personally involve his students in the lives of people from the past. Mr. Jarrett was aware of the power of superbly written biographies and of their enduring themes—sacrifice and responsibility, power and oppression, failure and achievement. And he knew that these stories vicariously engage students in the lives of others, help them see the world through others' eyes, and make them aware of human potential. But his major stumbling block was finding a "hook" that would grab the children's imagination and draw them into the stories of people who made a difference throughout history.

Mr. Jarrett's quandary was resolved as a result of a discussion of children's favorite heroes one Monday: "Superman," announced Bradley, "because he's really strong." Others suggested names like Peyton Manning ("he's an awesome football player") and Jennifer Lopez ("she's really cool"). "Lots of kids used sports and entertainment figures as heroes," says Mr. Jarrett. "I'm convinced that kids must learn to rethink their choice of heroes. I have to work to expand what they think is heroic. So, that's it—heroes. That's exactly the hook I was looking for!" He then pulled together a series of dynamic learning experiences that included a text set of five different biographies on the theme "Heroes in History."

> *Mr. Jarrett kicked off "Hero Week" in his classroom by inviting real-life local heroes to visit—among them a retired teacher who was also a Holocaust survivor and a former member of a 1960s nonviolent Civil Rights group who once was jailed for 21 days for his activities. Then, convinced of the power of good biographies to provide additional examples of wisdom, courage, and inner character, Mr. Jarrett collected five copies each of five different books about people who made a difference—male and female; from various cultures; famous and not-so-famous; adults and children. Mr. Jarrett introduced these books to his children during a short mini-lesson. The mini-lesson began with Mr. Jarrett's oral reading of Barbara Cooney's picture book* Eleanor *(Puffin). The book tells how Eleanor Roosevelt overcame a difficult childhood to become one of the 20th century's most influential and admired women. When Mr. Jarrett finished reading, the children talked at great length about how Eleanor's difficult childhood helped her grow into a brave and loyal adult.*

After the discussion, it was time for the students to select their own hero books from the text set Mr. Jarrett had pulled together:

- *Ruby Bridges with Margo Lundell,* Through My Eyes *(Scholastic)*
- *Natalie S. Bober and Rebecca Gibbon,* Papa Is a Poet: A Story About Robert Frost *(Henry Holt)*
- *Malala Yousafzai with Patricia McCormick,* I Am Malala *(Little, Brown Books for Young Readers)*
- *John B. Severance,* Gandhi: Great Soul *(Clarion)*
- *Maira Kalman,* Thomas Jefferson: Life, Liberty, and the Pursuit of Everything *(Nancy Paulsen Books)*

Mr. Jarrett gave a brief description of each book and then turned the students loose. His simple directions were that they were to look at the different books but not select the first one they came to. They were to sample the different offerings to see which ones they might eventually like to read. (He called this a "gallery tour.") After they completed their gallery tour, students were instructed to list their first through third book choices. Then, after school that day, Mr. Jarrett spread out all the slips and began assigning books according to choice. The next day, the children got their books, sat together in groups with others reading the same book, and began reading about their historical heroes. Mr. Jarrett employed the Literature Circle approach developed by Harvey Daniels (2003). Patterned after discussions associated with popular adult book clubs, literature circle discussions are guided by a list of roles that assign a thinking task to each group member. In Mr. Jarrett's case, the roles were:

- ***Discussion Director-*** *who comes up with thoughtful questions to guide discussion;*
- ***Word Finder-*** *who checks unfamiliar or challenging vocabulary words;*
- ***Literary Luminary-*** *who chooses two interesting or notable passages from the selection;*
- ***Illustrator-*** *who draws a picture, graph, chart, or other graphic response to the selection; and*
- ***Connector-*** *who makes text-to-self, text-to-world, or text-to-text connections.*

To bring together the literature-based experience, Mr. Jarrett organized the construction of a "paper bag time line." He modeled the process by showing the students a completed bag he had constructed for Eleanor Roosevelt. Each text set group was then given a strong paper bag and asked to print the name of its hero in bold letters at the top. The groups were to use this bag to show what they had learned about their heroes through writing, drawing, and collage. The students were first given an outline of a coat of arms with four blank segments. They were directed to draw an appropriate picture or symbol (or print a word) in the segments that best answered the following questions:

1. *"What is your greatest personal accomplishment?"*
2. *"If you could compare yourself to an animal, what would it be?"*
3. *"What is one lesson others can learn from you?"*
4. *"What is one word you would most like people to use to describe you?"*

The coats of arms were taped to the fronts of the bags. The students labeled the bags with dates underneath the hero's name to show when their hero had lived and printed two questions at the bottom of the bag. The students were to use questions that could be answered by looking at the coat of arms on the front of the bag.

One group completed the coat of arms in Figure 7.5 for Ruby Bridges, who, in 1960, at 6 years of age, was the first African American student to enter William Frantz Elementary School in New Orleans. The students explained that they drew a school in the first section because it showed that Ruby helped integrate the elementary school by passing through a mob of racist protestors shouting insults and threats. They selected a sheep as an animal to represent Ruby in section two because they felt Ruby had a wonderful smile and remained calm and peaceful throughout this unusual challenge. In the third section, the students explained that they chose to depict an African American child holding hands with a White child because Ruby Bridges would want to teach others that White people and Black people should respect and love each other. Finally, the students wrote the word "courage"

FIGURE 7.5   Coat of Arms for Ruby Bridges

in the last section because they felt Ruby had bravely faced a difficult situation with strong character. The story of Ruby Bridges showed that even small children can be heroes for each other.

When all the bags were finished on the outside, the students were asked to consider three important events from their heroes' lives and explain their significance; then, they were to find an artifact, make a model, or draw an illustration as a representation of each event. The items were then packed into the paper bags. One item placed in the Ruby Bridges bag was a small, student-drawn sign reading "Whites Only" that signified the signs the angry White people carried in protest as they gathered outside Frantz Elementary School. A baseball, toy airplane, and can of food helped another group represent a part of baseball star Roberto Clemente's life when he died in an airplane crash trying to bring medical supplies and food to people in Nicaragua (whose city was destroyed by a terrible earthquake in 1972).

After each group chose three artifacts and placed them into the bags, they sequenced the bags in chronological order. Next, each group prepared a short story that told about the events represented by their artifacts and read the stories, with props, to their classmates. Afterward, everyone had a chance to explore the questions, coats of arms, and artifacts.

To consider the contributions of each hero a bit more deeply, Mr. Jarrett introduced a list of five traits, called the "five themes of citizenship," that seemed to capture the major attributes of the heroic people the students had read about: honesty, responsibility, compassion, respect, and courage. He offered examples and described these traits to the class, making sure they understood each one. Mr. Jarrett then taped signs labeled with the five themes to the classroom walls at even intervals around the room. The students were asked to go with their books to the area designated by the theme they thought best defined their heroes. It was interesting to see that students reading the same biography tended to split away from their partners to position themselves at different signs. For example, one member of the Ruby Bridges group went to responsibility, another went to honesty, and three went to courage. Knowing that open discussions often disintegrate into idle chatter, Mr. Jarrett directed their conversations with a printed conversation guide: (1) Briefly summarize the actions or values that made your person a civic hero; (2) explain why you selected this trait to associate with your civic hero, reading a short selection from the book to support your point; and (3) make a connection between what you read and your own life. Of course, Mr. Jarrett modeled these behaviors by first offering an example of what he would say, based on the book he had read aloud to the class, Eleanor.

Mr. Jarrett brought his biographical study of historical heroes to a close by asking the students to consider three questions. The first was, "If you could bring any real-life hero from the past into the present, which would you choose?" The second question was, "What five questions would you ask the *person?" The third question challenged the creativity of small discussion groups: "What kind of hero will our country need in the year 2050?"*

Writing Biographies

To begin writing biographies in your classroom, read a good biography to your students and use it as a model: Who was the biography about? What made the biography interesting? Then, follow the steps below:

- ***Choose someone interesting to write about.*** Select a person you are interested in or who you think is important. You will spend a great deal of time researching this person's life, so choose someone who inspires you or someone you are curious about.
- ***Find out some key information about the person's life.*** Explore the library or the Internet for information to help you tell an interesting story. Investigate different resources including books, newspaper and magazine articles, reference books, and websites about your person. What makes this person special or interesting?
- ***Write an introductory paragraph.*** All good stories need a "hook" that captures the readers' attention, informs them who you are writing about, and makes them want to keep reading. Figure out how to capture your readers with the very first sentence.
- ***Write a paragraph that familiarizes readers with the person.*** Briefly explain why this person is important. Do not bring in detailed information yet; you will do that in the next paragraph.
- ***Write another paragraph or two telling about the person's accomplishments.*** Fill the body of your biography with information that gives insight into this person's special accomplishments or the problems this person has overcome.
- ***Compose a final paragraph that tells why it is important to learn about this person.*** What can we learn from this person's life?

Student biographies can be as short as a paragraph or several pages long. One student's short biographical sketch of Sacagawea is shown as an example in Figure 7.6.

FIGURE 7.6 Early-Grade Biographical Sketch

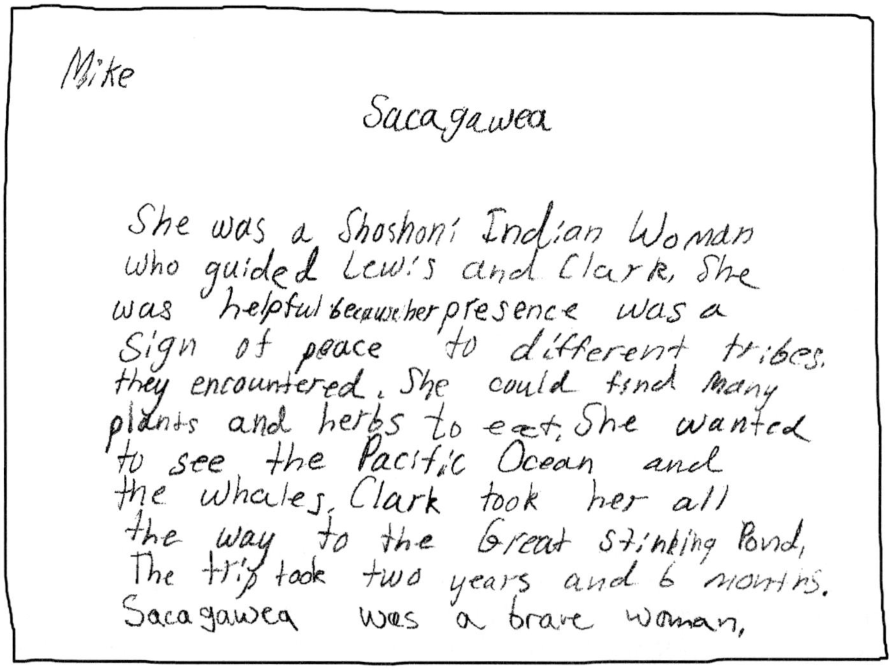
Mike

Sacagawea

She was a Shoshoni Indian Woman who guided Lewis and Clark, She was helpful because her presence was a Sign of peace to different tribes they encountered. She could find many plants and herbs to eat. She wanted to see the Pacific Ocean and the whales, Clark took her all the way to the Great Stinking Pond, The trip took two years and 6 months. Sacagawea was a brave woman,

Video Exploration 7.3

 CHECK YOUR UNDERSTANDING 7.4 **Click here** to check your understanding of this section of the chapter.

Newspapers

Many elementary school students find newspapers uninteresting or too difficult, in part because they do not know enough about how newspapers operate and how news articles are written. However, our schools share responsibility for preparing citizens who are willing and able to understand the issues in their lives, so a major goal of instruction is to help students understand newspapers, either digital or print. The more exposure students have to newspapers and current events, the more aware and interested they become in learning more about them. Also, including newspapers and current events in the social studies curriculum can go a long way toward developing lifelong newsreaders. Oldendorf and Calloway (2008) lament that reading the paper version of newspapers may well become a lost art, and they make a case for using actual newspapers as a resource in elementary social studies: "Newspapers provide an engaging, visual, hands-on resource to introduce young children to the world beyond the one they know and to help them become literate, well-informed citizens" (p. 18).

A trip to a newspaper publisher and a careful inspection of the local newspaper can help students understand how newspapers operate. Students always seem to enjoy their visit to a newspaper facility. Upon returning to the classroom, give each student a newspaper, hold up a copy, and discuss the different parts of a newspaper with them. (You don't need to buy a newspaper for each student in your classroom. Most newspapers have an online version, so you can either print out preferred articles or use your classroom computers.) The first page of a newspaper includes the title, all the publication information, the index, and the main *hard news* stories. The hard news is split into several parts—usually the *national*, *state*, and *local* or *regional* news; the editorials and political cartoons, too, can be found in the first section. The major story of the day is placed in the most noticeable position and is highlighted by a large, boldfaced headline. Students should apply the strategies they use for reading all varieties of text to comprehend the hard news. Those strategies will be presented later in this chapter.

It must be emphasized that you may risk turning students away from newspapers if all they are exposed to are routine comprehension activities or if instruction becomes dull and routine (such as assigning students to bring in an article for the day). However, if used in a stimulating way, newspapers can help students not only to develop reading skills but also to acquire important knowledge of and insight into a wide range of local, national, and international affairs. Below are some tips and activities that can help.

- Ask students to select a short item of news and to summarize it to a partner, changing some of the details. Partners need to try and guess which of the facts are accurate and which have been altered.
- On a wall or bulletin board, post categories describing different kinds of news articles the students need to find. Students cut out the articles and pin or tape them beneath the appropriate categories. Some possible categories include:
  - Some good news
  - Some bad news

You will be surprised at how interested and involved your students become once you invite them to read the newspaper regularly.

Ariwasabi/Fotolia

- News about an animal
- Weather in the news
- A funny news event
- A sad news event
- Kids in the news

● Cut up some popular comic strips and ask individual students or groups to put the strip back in the proper order. Then introduce the students to a current news event that has been cut apart into paragraphs, and ask them to rearrange the paragraphs in proper order.

● Give small groups of students a hard news article and an editorial on the same topic and ask them to identify the differences. Students regularly sense that a hard news story reports the facts while an editorial expresses an opinion.

Other than learning what is happening on local, state, national, and international scenes, a major reason for integrating newspapers into the curriculum is to acquaint students with using various types of informational text in their writing. It's easy to help your students learn about newspaper writing by creating a newspaper for your school. Working on a newspaper staff allows students to learn valuable lessons about writing, editing, and working as team members.

A Classroom Newspaper

The most helpful place to begin the process of starting a classroom newspaper is by studying your local newspaper to find out about the kinds of information it provides. This insight will help the children plan sections for their own newspaper. Divide the class into small groups and give each group a copy of the same newspaper. Hold up your copy of the newspaper and discuss the different parts of a newspaper with them. Students should understand that the ABCs of writing good hard news stories are *accuracy*, *brevity*, and *clarity*; newspaper reporters use the inverted pyramid style to achieve the ABCs. In the inverted pyramid style, the heaviest or most important information should be at the top—the beginning of the story. The lead paragraph(s) of the story answer six basic questions (*who, what, when, where, why*, and *how*). Then, moving from top to bottom, the information should gradually become less important. See Figure 7.7.

FIGURE 7.7   The Inverted Pyramid

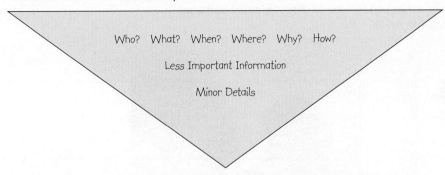

Who? What? When? Where? Why? How?

Less Important Information

Minor Details

Students should be aware that hard news stories must be factual; there is no room for editorializing (giving an opinion) in a hard news story. There is a section of the newspaper where writers are allowed to present their opinions. That section most often includes editorials, political cartoons, and letters to the editor. Political cartoons and editorials use words and illustrations to influence people's opinions about a particular issue. Children should know that this is okay; it is certainly appropriate to voice an opinion, even if it differs from someone else's, if it is backed up by reasonable facts and figures. Students should not view their main task as deciding whether a cartoon is right or wrong, though they often assess its bias. Read more about political cartoons and editorials in the following sections.

Your students should learn about other sections of the newspaper, which are often referred to as the *soft news*. These sections contain more light-hearted pieces intended to entertain or inform readers on topics of interest: a *lifestyle section* that features stories of interesting people, entertainment, travel, fashion information, cooking, useful household hints, advice columns, comics, puzzles, and reviews of movies and books; *classified ads*, including help wanted ads; and *sports*. Daily newspapers provide a wealth of information and, if they are not completely supplanted by online news sources at some point in the future, they will offer an informative, thoughtful, and even entertaining way to find out what's going on in the world for years to come.

Although staffs differ among newspapers, all generally include the following positions:

- *Editor-in-chief-* The person responsible for all phases of the production of a newspaper.
- *Editors-* The people in charge of each hard and soft news section. Editors read and edit stories, and they work out the layout of the sections. Editors assign stories to writers.
- *Copy editor-* A person who edits stories and works on the layout.
- *Reporter-* A person who researches and writes the news stories.
- *Feature writer-* Individuals who write soft news stories.
- *Photographer-* A person who takes photos for newspapers.
- *Political cartoonist-* A person who presents an idea or opinion in just a few words and a drawing.
- *Circulation manager-* The person who oversees the entire distribution process.
- *News artists-* People who create the graphics and other illustrations.

Once your students understand and appreciate what a newspaper does and how, they will likely be eager to start their own classroom version. The first thing they will do is name their newspaper. Allow them to be as creative as possible. The students in one of my fifth-grade classes at Main Elementary School, for example, came up with *The MESS* (**M**ain **E**lementary **S**chool **S**heet). Once they decide on a name, the students should design a masthead, or title block that goes at the top of the front page; it is often boxed with a border. Sometimes a logo or a motto is placed within the masthead. Next, the students must decide which sections

As they take on such roles and responsibilities as writers, reporters, and editors, students create authentic articles and features for their classroom newspaper . . . a valuable experience in group writing.

Syda Productions/Fotolia

they want to include. Ask them to think about the different types of information they can report on—things like classroom or school events, birthdays, a new classmate, pet advice, or a teacher's or child's interesting hobby. Some children may want to create comic strips, book reviews, sports, or movie pages. Assign students to a group (staff) for each section and have each group select an editor. Writers and reporters suggest story ideas to the group editor. The editors assemble their section's stories and submit them to the editor-in-chief. After the copy editors do their job, the students assemble the sections and organize the stories using a desktop publishing program. The artist and photographer add some clip art, original drawings, or stock and original digital photographs for clarification and variety. All that is then needed is to print, copy, distribute, and enjoy. Microsoft Office Publisher is an example of software that students can use to quickly and inexpensively publish a classroom newspaper. Teachers and students can choose from several templates to publish class newspapers from ReadWriteThink Printing Press. Newspaper worksheets for writing newspaper articles and for analyzing existing newspaper articles are available online from Enchanted Learning. Students would enjoy creating web versions of their newspaper to broaden their audience. Writing a classroom newspaper is an exciting way to share news with others, and you will find that each issue yields a delightfully impressive sample of informational writing.

One of the important consequences of a worthwhile newspaper program is to motivate students to become active and promote a cause or address a critical issue in the news, whether through a letter-writing campaign, petition, or volunteerism. Although some elementary school children shy away from civic engagement because they feel, "It won't make any difference," or "No one will listen to a little kid," most want to get involved in an issue and uphold their obligations as part of a democratic community. Denise Trainor, a fifth-grade teacher, illustrated how the local newspaper served as a valuable tool in spurring civic engagement in her social studies classroom.

Ms. Trainor's students became quite upset after coming across a newspaper story describing the accidental discovery of a mass grave while a construction crew was excavating a site for a new office complex. The front-page article described a local university professor's research indicating that these were the remains of 57 Irish immigrants who had died of black diphtheria while working as railroad laborers in the late summer of 1853. Their job was to use their picks and shovels to clear and straighten out a portion of hilly land through which a set of new train tracks was to run. It was grueling, dangerous work, and these men labored from dawn to dusk during their six-day work week. Unfortunately, a combination of unhealthy conditions and terrible accidents contributed to a sadly familiar expression of that time: "An Irishman buried under every tie." The 57 Irish immigrants had been working there only six weeks before they got sick with black diphtheria and died. They were callously dumped in a mass grave between two of the hills they had worked to clear. Today, this location is at the center of a busy crossroad where the office complex was going to rise.

"I can't believe it," blurted Charles. "Those poor men didn't mean anything to the company that hired them."

"Yeah," agreed Katrice. "They were wiped off the face of the Earth, and nobody even cared."

"It's like they were treated worse than animals. They were willing to work hard, and look how bad they were treated!" protested Tyreke.

"I wish there was something we could do to give them the respect they deserve," offered Diane.

"Maybe there is," suggested Ms. Trainor. "Let's think about it."

The students looked into the situation a bit more deeply and found that a group of interested people had already planned to gather at a dedication ceremony in about a month to honor the Irish workers. The group's goal was to locate as many of the workers' remains as possible and provide the men with a proper burial near the construction site.

Today, there is a small plot of land near the office site where the 57 Irish workers have been properly buried; the stones surrounding the tiny burial ground are the exact blocks the workers put down as the base for the tracks. The students attended the dedication ceremony and were given permission to plant an oak sapling at the site to commemorate the occasion. It now grows proudly next to a dignified historical marker that honors the workers.

"To know and to not do is to not know" is a very old Chinese proverb that sums up the situation that attracted the attention of Ms. Trainor's students. What the old saying means is that if these children were aware of this tragic injustice and failed to respond to it, then they may as well not have known about it at all. Children must be taught to become knowledgeable about current issues, pay attention to them, and embark on a path of participation that leads to constructive change through action: "I really didn't think anyone would listen to a kid like me. Now I know we can be part of something we care about right away," reflected Freddy.

Reading and Writing Period (Historical) Newspapers

As with contemporary newspapers, period newspapers offer interesting insights into the past. The pages of these historic newspapers contain a wealth of information—firsthand accounts of major events, fashion trends, real estate, government and politics, reform movements, businesses, sports and recreation, health and medicine, entertainment, industry, technology, and weather. Several online resources have made the availability of period newspapers much more effortless than in the past. One site of particular interest is the ProQuest Historical Newspapers site, which has digitalized newspapers dating from the 19th century to the present—in most cases, full runs of newspapers. Additionally, the Library of Congress and the National Endowment for the Humanities announced the availability of Chronicling America: Historic American Newspapers. Chronicling America is an Internet-based, searchable database of U.S. newspapers with select digitization of historic pages as well as information about newspapers from 1690 to the present.

Newspapers are a great way to teach students about life in the past, as each newspaper is filled with reports and information from eyewitnesses who were present at the time. Consider the newspaper advertisement for a runaway indentured servant from 1843 that is shown in Figure 7.8. Among such advertisements in old newspapers, you will often find reward notices that offer interesting clues to 19th-century life. Such advertisements usually include information such as the clothing the runaway wore and comments on appearance and temperament. With their "striped row trousers," "gingham roundabouts," "brown flannel jackets," "old straw hats," or "dark fustian pantaloons," these "remarkably ugly fellows" may have "lost two of their

FIGURE 7.8   Ad for a Runaway

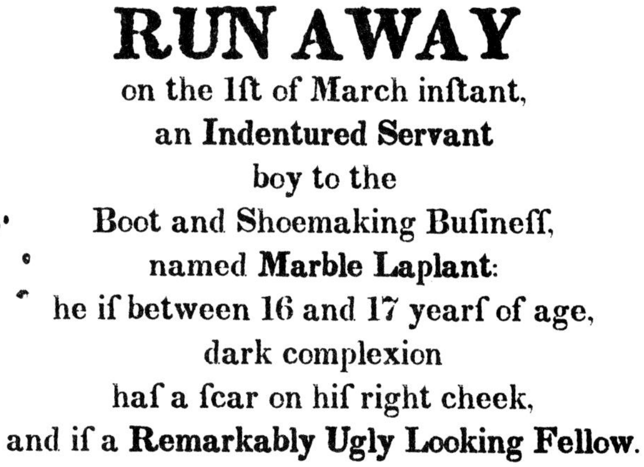

RUN AWAY
on the 1ſt of March inſtant,
an Indentured Servant
boy to the
Boot and Shoemaking Buſineſſ,
named **Marble Laplant**:
he iſ between 16 and 17 yearſ of age,
dark complexion
haſ a ſcar on hiſ right cheek,
and iſ a Remarkably Ugly Looking Fellow.

fore teeth" or "had three fingers cut off at the first joint on the right hand." These descriptions offer remarkable portraits of life during the colonial days.

Students must understand that, much as today, political cartoons, newspaper editorials, and advertisements were common outlets for persuasive messages and were often found on the front page. Take, for example, Benjamin Franklin's first-known political cartoon published in an American newspaper; it was first revealed in his *Pennsylvania Gazette* on May 9, 1754 (Figure 7.9). It was an image of a snake cut into eight sections, each segment labeled with the initials of an individual colony or region (New England was the region at the head of the snake). Written simply beneath the snake were the ominous words "Join, or Die." The cartoon helped Franklin make his point about the importance of colonial unity.

Like contemporary classroom newspapers discussed earlier, your students will be interested in using archival newspapers as a model for writing a simulated period newspaper. For example, Curtis Yannie's fifth-grade class produced a newspaper set in Revolutionary War times. Their *front-page stories* took form beneath these blaring headlines: "British Evacuate Boston," "Grand Union Flag Unfurled over Boston," "Redcoats Invade New York," "Congress Approves Declaration of Independence," and "Washington Stuns Hessian Fighters." *Feature articles* detailed items of interest such as quilting, candle making, and the steps of drying food for winter. An *advertising section* offered articles for sale (spinning wheels, bed warmers, teams

FIGURE 7.9   Replica of Franklin's *Join, or Die* Political Cartoon

of oxen, pewter tableware, flintlock rifles, wigs). An *employment section* listed jobs such as post rider, saddler, tanner, wigmaker, tavern keeper, chandler, mason, cooper, hatter, and printer. An *editorial page* displayed a *political cartoon* showing a crowd of Continental soldiers pulling down an equestrian statue of King George III as they celebrated the signing of the Declaration of Independence in Philadelphia, and an *editorial* solicited funds for the relief of widows and children of the patriots "murdered" at Lexington. There was a *book review* of Thomas Paine's *Common Sense*, and a *sports section* detailed the results of popular events such as stool ball, quoits, arm wrestling, and gunnysack races. When finished, the period newspaper was sent to the *production department*, where illustrations were created. The text was entered using a word processor, illustrations were added, and the stories were printed out on a laser printer, assembled, stapled together, and distributed to the other fifth-grade classrooms.

 CHECK YOUR UNDERSTANDING 7.5 **Click here** to check your understanding of this section of the chapter.

Strategies for Reading Informational Text

There is no doubt that phonemic awareness, phonics, fluency, and vocabulary are the foundational backbone of effective early reading instruction; repeated instructional experiences in specialized reading classes during the early grades heightens awareness of these essential skills and leads to reading success. But since the ultimate goal of reading in social studies is comprehension, you must learn to apply practical instructional strategies to help students understand and enjoy informational text. Social studies teachers accept a significant role in this process; after all, comprehension is the reason for reading in social studies: *literal comprehension* (understanding the subject matter), *inferential comprehension* (reading "between the lines") and *critical comprehension* (forming judgments and conclusions about the information). Much of what your students learn in social studies will depend on being able to read skillfully and strategically; obviously, struggling readers will learn a lot less social studies content than capable readers. Therefore, a major instructional quality that you must make part of your professional repertoire is the ability to plan and carry out comprehension instruction that will help your students become purposeful, active readers with ability to make sense of text.

What can you do to help students become competent readers of informational text? The following two major techniques are part of standard comprehension instruction in many elementary school social studies classrooms: (1) *directed reading*, a strategy that provides students with instructional support before, during, and after reading and (2) *close reading*, a strategy that requires careful, sustained investigation of a brief passage of complex literary or informational text.

Directed Reading

Directed reading provides students with scaffolded instructional support *before*, *during*, and *after* reading. Although the word "directed" is part of the technique's name, your role in this instructional strategy is more a "guide on the side" who engages students as active and thoughtful readers than a "sage on the stage" who dominates all aspects of learning and instruction. Although presented in a step-by-step fashion, the framework is a guide; it does not need to be followed inflexibly with every text or in every reading situation. The suggestions represent only a portion of the countless alternatives from which you may choose. Please bear in mind that variety is key.

BEFORE READING

Before reading, your responsibility is to activate the students' thinking about the text. What students bring to the printed page will affect what they read, so a guided discussion about what they are about to read can provide insight into their thinking and help you assess what they already know or expect to learn from the material. Because what is done before reading is critical for understanding the text, you must be ready to:

- *Pre-teach specialized vocabulary.* Understanding informational text depends a great deal on how familiar students are with words they will rarely, if ever, encounter in contexts other than the social studies reading assignment of the day: for example, *junta, shaman, boycott, cassava, longitude, tundra*. It is impossible to find informational text without such specialized vocabulary and, to comprehend what they are reading, students must first know what those distinctive words mean. For that reason, you will want to *briefly* pre-teach specialized words and phrases before actually beginning the reading. To start, it must be emphasized that asking students to write the words in a vocabulary notebook, find the definitions in a dictionary or the glossary of the textbook, match the words to definitions, or write the words in a sentence are *not* effective ways to introduce new vocabulary. The words you choose should be critical to comprehension of the passage and unfamiliar to most, if not all, students. Define the new words in context by writing them on the whiteboard and using the correct pronunciation as you read aloud. In order to activate prior knowledge, have the students brainstorm what they already know about the selected vocabulary. Then, help them define the words by searching what you have written to find clues about what the meanings might be. Sometimes you can insert a phrase or separate sentence following the sentence in which the word is used to offer an explanation: *The Mexican* **vaquero** *was very proud. A* **vaquero** *is a Mexican cowboy.* At other times, you can provide a direct explanation in parentheses: *The* **vaquero** *(Mexican cowboy) herded cattle and sheep on the range.* Or, a synonym, clause, or phrase that explains the meaning of a word may be inserted into the sentence: *The vaquero practiced cattle roping for many hours with a* **riata***, or long braided rawhide rope.* Be sure to include enough surrounding material so that students have sufficient context to figure out what the word might mean. And remember that visual reinforcement is an important contributor to vocabulary comprehension and retention. So whenever possible, it is extremely helpful to supplement words in context with real objects, pictures, or photographs to provide students with opportunities for purposeful learning.

- *Connect the text to students' prior knowledge and experiences.* Use an initial prompt, task, or activity that connects the new content to what the students already know. Ask students, "What do you already know about _____?" or "What experiences do you have with _____?" Teach students the *text to self, text to text,* or *text to world* strategy:

  - *text to self*—connections between the text and the student's previous experiences;

  - *text to text*—connections between the text being read and a text previously read; and

  - *text to world*—connections between the text being read and the real world—past, present, and future.

- *Make predictions about the text.* Start the prediction cycle by examining the title. Then look at the pictures and illustrations to get an overall idea of what the selection will be about. Then examine other text features including charts, graphs, and maps. Connecting these clues with students' prior knowledge and experiences should help students make predictions about the reading selection. ("Given this information, what do you think the reading selection will be about?") Predictions will help students focus on the text as they read or listen—actively refining, revising, and verifying predictions as they go along.

- *Establish a purpose for reading (or listening to) the text.* "Why is my teacher asking me to read this?" "What's in it for me?" Students are uncomfortable going into a learning experience without knowing what is expected of them. So after showing your students a ship's bell, having them handle and ring it, and sharing previous experiences with and knowledge of ship's bells, you can draw out predictions about how the bell is used on a ship, and then direct students to purposefully read the selection to check their predictions: "I wonder why bells ring every half hour on a ship."

The *before reading* phase usually culminates in a purpose-setting statement, a "launch pad" from which your students will propel themselves into a reading selection: "Why are bells rung every half hour on a ship?"

DURING READING

During reading, students will purposefully interact with the text using visualizing, summarizing, questioning, connecting, and word-attack strategies. You will find it helpful to stop students at strategic points in the story and asks them to verify, reject, or modify their predictions.

- *Visualizing.* Students form images or pictures in their minds based on text and are encouraged to imagine a story taking place as if it were a movie. After hearing a selection read aloud or after independent reading, you may ask your students to make an illustration or write a reading log or journal entry describing what they saw in their mind's eye—a character, setting, or event.

- *Determining text importance.* Stop along the way to help your students differentiate the important ideas from irrelevant information and to meaningfully note which predictions are being supported by the details: "Does the information match my purpose for reading?" "Is all this information equally important or is some more important?" Prompt your students to revise their unsupported predictions or make new ones. Recognizing important information is one of the most difficult comprehension strategies to teach; you must constantly model it and provide plenty of time and opportunities to practice it.

- *Asking questions.* Asking questions keeps students focused as they read and provides a way to monitor their comprehension. These questions can be as simple as "Do I understand this?" or "What do I know about . . . " to "I wonder why . . . ." It is helpful to encourage students to make questions out of the subheadings in the text. For example, it is constructive to look at the subheading "A Ship's Bell Time" and turn it into a question such as, "What is a ship's bell time?"

- *Connecting.* It helps students to understand new information if they are able to relate it to their lives. Encourage their continued use of the text-to-self, text-to-text, or text-to-world strategies described above.

- *Attacking new words.* Students will often come across unfamiliar words as they engage with text. In order to understand their meanings as they relate to the text, students must apply word-attack strategies to help decode, pronounce, and understand unfamiliar words. You can also model and instruct students in using context clues; examining familiar letter chunks such as prefixes, suffixes, and base words; sounding out the new word; reading past the new word and looking for clues; and connecting the new word to words the students already know.

AFTER READING

After reading, students discuss, either orally or in writing, their responses to the text. It is important to begin by asking the purpose-setting statement as a question: "What did you learn about the reasons why a bell rings every half hour on a ship?" As they come to grips with the purpose-verifying question, "What did I get out of this?" students will employ a range of activities. Four common techniques used in social studies classrooms include discussions, retelling, graphic organizers, and follow-up activities.

- *Discussions.* The kinds of questions we use have a great impact on the success of text-related discussions. But with well over 30 question classification systems dotting the education landscape, how can you choose the one that holds the most promise for your classroom? For content area subjects like social studies, I recommend that you use a system that prompts students to ask themselves, "Where can I find the answer?" While attempting to answer that question, students get a chance to revisit the text and think more deeply about the information in either or all of three ways: (1) *in the text*, (2) *the text and me*, and (3) *just me*.

- *In the text* questions (literal comprehension) can be answered with explicit information found right in the text. For example, suppose this sentence was in the text being read: "In July of 1945, allied leaders sent a message to Japanese leaders— surrender or be crushed—and waited anxiously for the Japanese reply." An *in the text* question can be, "In what year did the event take place?" The answer can be easily found in the text: "The event took place in July of 1945."

- *The text and me* questions (inferential comprehension) require inferential thinking; that is, the answer is not explicitly stated in the text, but the students figure it out by bringing together what they already know with new information from the text. For example, suppose this sentence was in the material being read: "Allied officials, seeing Suzuki's response ("mokusatsu") as another example of the Kamikaze spirit, decided within 10 days to drop the atomic bomb and Hiroshima was leveled." A *text and me* question could be, "Why do you think the author used the term 'Kamikaze spirit' in the sentence?" The answer, even though "Kamikaze spirit" is not defined in the text, could be: "The Kamikaze warriors sacrificed their lives for their homeland. Maybe the allied leaders thought Suzuki would rather die than surrender." *Text and me* questions are a great way to assess what your students are thinking and how they are comprehending the text through the lens of their life experiences.

- *Just me* questions (critical comprehension) require the application of all the thinking processes described to this point, but now students are expected to personalize the information by pulling it together in new or novel ways, seeking creative solutions to problems, or making reasoned judgments; their answers are personal and will not be found in the text. For example, the text being read debated the idea that the atomic bombing of Hiroshima and Nagasaki during the final stages of World War II in 1945 may have been a significant Allies mistranslation of the Japanese response ("mokusatsu") to their ultimatum. A *just me* question could be, "If the correct translation had been made, would atomic bombs have been dropped on Hiroshima and Nagasaki?" Students must trust their personal judgments, even if they are not in agreement with what others might say or believe.

- *Retelling.* A second way to bolster comprehension is to retell entire stories such as biographies. In order to retell, children must determine the important information and summarize in their own words details about character, setting, plot, dialogue, or content. *Five Finger Retelling* is a helpful reminder for students when they are asked to orally retell a story. Using this strategy, students think of one question per finger:

  - Who was the story about (characters)?
  - Where did the story take place (setting)?
  - What was the problem?
  - What were the events or episodes (two or more things that happened, including the problem)?
  - How did it end? How was the problem solved?

Younger children, especially, like to retell stories by pretending to be characters they have read about. The point is not to memorize the exact words, but for students to recall the story in their own words. To be a true comprehension activity, the retelling should be planned by the students. They should know the story and characters well enough that a written script is not needed; retelling works best when students improvise action and dialogue. Since most students will want a role, the retelling dramatization can be recast with different students so that everyone has an opportunity to have a part.

● *Graphic organizers.* In addition to encouraging attachment to new content through carefully planned discussion and retelling strategies, teachers often find it helpful to use graphic organizers such as diagrams, charts, drawings, and other visual displays. Graphic displays of information help students consciously connect their past experiences to the targeted skills or concepts under study. There are many kinds of graphic organizers, but one of the most widely used is shown in Figure 7.10—the KWL chart, a helpful device that can be started during the before reading phase and continued through the after reading phase. KWL is a thinking strategy that requires students to identify what they already know (**K**) about a particular topic, what they want (**W**) to know, and what they learn (**L**) as a result of the lesson. You could, for example, begin by leading students in a group brainstorming session that activates their prior knowledge of the topic. Students should list what they already know about the topic under **K**. Then ask students to come up with questions about what they want to know and write them under **W**. Throughout the subsequent lesson, students should note in the **L** column what they have learned from examining various sources of information. The information may be answers to the questions they wanted to know (**W**) or unexpected bits of new information. If questions in the **W** column remain unanswered, students can seek further information in appropriate text resources or on the web. Then the students can use the information to write a summary paragraph on what they have learned about the topic or represent their new understandings in other appropriate ways.

● *Follow-up activities.* You should always follow up your lesson with an after reading activity that gives students the opportunity to apply what was learned and support the skills and strategies that were taught. Sample activities may include:

  ● writing a new ending or a new title
  ● writing captions for illustrations or photographs
  ● writing a response to a text (for example, a letter to the allied commanders)
  ● drawing story maps with captions
  ● giving first-person news accounts as radio or television newscasters
  ● constructing a mural, model, or diorama
  ● making a historical period news magazine or newspaper
  ● creating multimedia presentations that express their ideas, experiences, and understanding to others

▶ **Video Exploration 7.4**

FIGURE 7.10   KWL Chart

WHAT I KNOW	WHAT I WANT TO LEARN	WHAT I LEARNED

Your goal in using directed reading is to help students apply the targeted comprehension strategies until they reach the point where they can use them independently. The following classroom episode illustrates how Karen Tenenbaum was able to use the guided reading strategies to engage her students' thinking, even when the sole source of written text was limited to a social studies textbook. The major goal of Ms. Tenenbaum's lesson was to help students understand the major factors that transformed many of the colonists from loyal British subjects to dissidents on the verge of revolution.

Ms. Tenenbaum began by announcing to the class that the school district budget had just bottomed out, and very little money was available to purchase the supplies necessary to finish out the school year. A committee of teachers had met to study the problem and decided that a good source of revenue would be to have students pay a small fee each time they carried out a routine activity such as putting something into the wastebasket, using the restrooms, getting a drink of water, or sharpening their pencils. Ms. Tenenbaum asked the students if they thought this was a fair solution to the district's money crisis, especially since they had never before been required to pay such a "tax." She also raised the question of whether teachers had the right to impose such a tax on students: "Does anyone feel upset? Why?" Ms. Tenenbaum involved the students in an active debate of the options available to them (avoid paying the fee, boycott classes, protest the plan, complain to the local newspaper) and the consequences of their actions.

Ms. Tenenbaum urged the students to recall that the Seven Years' War had drained the treasury of Great Britain, so the government was in desperate need of raising money, just like their teachers' dilemma. Britain began to do something it had never done before: It decided to impose taxes on the colonies. To bolster their background knowledge of vocabulary and word comprehension necessary for complete understanding of the textbook selection, Ms. Tenenbaum introduced the phrase "taxation without representation" and explained that this was the rallying cry colonists seeking independence from Britain had begun to use: "What do you think this slogan means?" she asked. The class drew parallels between the British taxation plans to their classroom "tax." Then, to begin the day's textbook reading assignment, Ms. Tenenbaum invited predictions about what the British might tax in the colonies and how the colonists could react to those British taxes. After the students had exhausted their ideas, Ms. Tenenbaum directed them to read a section in their textbooks to find out (1) what goods the British taxed, (2) the colonial reaction to each British tax, and (3) the British response to the colonists' reactions.

Directed reading encourages students to be active and reflective readers.

Monkey Business/Fotolia

Ms. Tenenbaum reminded the students to use the context to help make sense of any words they were unsure about. She used a think-aloud strategy to model how to do this by selecting two sentences and reading them aloud ("The Townsend Acts, passed in 1767, required the colonists to pay taxes on imported goods like tea. Not surprisingly, the American colonists chose to boycott tea."). She commented, "Hmm, I wonder what the author meant by 'boycott'? I really need to know that if I want the sentence to make sense." Ms. Tenenbaum then demonstrated how the context of a sentence or short passage can be used to figure out what would make sense: "I'm going to read the next sentence to see if it will help." ("The American colonists refused to buy the tea.") "That's it!" exclaimed Ms. Tenenbaum. "Boycott means that the colonists would not buy the tea as long as the British taxed it. Does that make sense?" By providing this kind of modeling, Ms. Tenenbaum encouraged the students to use context cues as they read.

After a short discussion of the reading selection, the students used charts to summarize the three British taxes: (1) the Stamp Act, (2) the Townshend Duties, and (3) the Tea Act (see Figure 7.11). (Note how the organizer directly relates back to the stated purposes for reading.) The information contained on the graphic organizers was used to address the questions: "How was our situation similar to what happened in colonial America before the Revolutionary War?" "In what ways were the British taxes fair or unfair?" "Was there a way the British could have made the taxes fair for all? If so, how?" "Do you think the British were smart to tax the colonists this way?" "Do you think the colonists were justified in their anger toward the British? Why or why not?" "How did the actions taken by the British Parliament and the responses of the colonists to these actions contribute to the outbreak of the American Revolution?" To carry through and apply their understandings of and feelings about the topic, Ms. Tenenbaum offered students a choice either to create a political cartoon or to compose a newspaper editorial expressing their feelings toward the British taxes.

Close Reading

Among the most significant of the current shifts in social studies education is the Common Core expectation that all students will be able to read increasingly complex informational texts proficiently as teachers apply extensive scaffolding, explanation, and support. Listed first on the 10 anchor standards for reading, for example, is a specific focus on "close reading."

CCSS.ELA-LITERACY.CCRA.R.1
Read closely to determine what the text says explicitly and to make logical inferences from it; cite specific textual evidence when writing or speaking to support conclusions drawn from the text. (National Governors Association, 2010)

Although the first anchor standard has been singled out here, each of the 10 anchor standards emphasizes that students must be taught to build a solid foundation of knowledge and to use increasingly challenging literary and informational texts to help develop comprehension skills, whether those texts are primary source documents, current events articles, folktales, or

FIGURE 7.11   Graphic Organizer

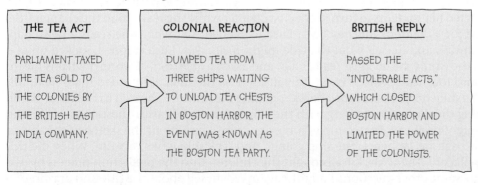

textbook pages. When students do a close reading, they carefully and purposefully focus on the facts and details contained in the text, with multiple readings accompanied by targeted instructional lessons. Students use a collection of detective-like schemes and skills to uncover and interpret facts and information (evidence) that lead to understandings about the text. Understandably, not every informational text you bring to your classroom goes through a close reading; that would only stifle student interest in both reading and social studies. Close-read texts must be relatively short and include complex ideas; that is why Lincoln's Gettysburg Address or a short newspaper column about choosing America's president in 2016 would be more appropriate for a close reading than a book about Nate the Great solving the mystery of the missing picture. Close reading is a multiday commitment to a brief text that offers rich enough vocabulary, ideas, and information to justify reading, examining, and discussing it over several days without making the students feel like they are beating a dead horse.

Successful social studies teachers use assorted strategies and a mix of learning situations; close reading is but one tool in a well-equipped teacher's toolbox. For that reason, there will be days well suited for close reading and other days when you will want your students just to sit back and enjoy a story—focusing on vocabulary and technical concepts will be the furthest thing from your mind. When your purpose for instruction is to build the necessary reading skills required to engage with complex text, close reading may be a good choice.

FIRST READING

How do you lay the groundwork for close reading success? To begin, consider four very important questions: (1) Are the outcomes that result from close reading sufficiently matched to the stated goals, objectives, and standards of instruction? (2) Is this a brief, challenging, high-interest informational passage? (3) Is the content suitable for building targeted skills, such as finding the main idea and details, identifying cause and effect, inferencing, or sequencing? (4) Is the material sufficiently challenging so that multiple readings are needed? Should your answers justify its use, you start the reading by *briefly* introducing the text. One of the ways close reading differs from directed reading is that students dive right in without any significant *before reading* activities. Instead, students are expected to blend their background knowledge with the text as they read. By design, your major responsibility during the first reading is mainly to help students establish a clear *purpose for reading;* a sufficient introduction to the first text reading would be something like, "We are going to read *Escape from the Ice*, a story about Ernest Shackleton, an Antarctic explorer." Take a minute or two to scan the title, chapter headings, and illustrations. Then ask the students to make predictions and to justify their responses to an *essential question* (one that gets to the heart of the reading): "In the face of danger, what will cause Shackleton to be successful while others might fail?"

If your students are new to close reading, or are struggling with how to do it, you can help them access the strategy by modeling how to think as they prepare to read. While the goal for students is to read complex texts independently, not all students will be able to carry out the process at first. Scaffolding instruction helps support students until they are ready to take over by themselves. There are many ways to scaffold instruction, such as reciprocal teaching, shared reading, QAR, or jigsaws, but teacher modeling is a solid strategy that involves showing students how to carry out inner conversations during their reading experiences. Nadya Luca, for example, directed her students to turn to the first chapter while she read aloud the chapter title, "Men Wanted for Hazardous Journey." Ms. Luca explained that when she reads a new chapter title, she always asks herself what the title might mean. Ms. Luca stopped, looked up as if reflecting on the words she had just read aloud, and asked a question, "I wonder what is meant by a 'Hazardous Journey'?" And, "What do you suppose the men are needed for?" Next, Ms. Luca asked the students to look at the chapter opening illustration. She said to the class, "I find that examining the illustrations along with the title before I read raises questions in my mind about what might be ahead. For example, some questions I had about the sketch of the ship at the top of the page are: 'Where is the ship going?' and 'The ship looks very old. When did this journey take place?'" Then, Ms. Luca brought the children into the prediction process by asking, "What are some other questions I might have asked myself about the title and drawing?"

In this Shackleton example, Ms. Luca chose only Chapter 1 of the book, which is just four short pages. During the first reading, students are expected to read the text independently with a *colored pencil* or *highlighter* in hand so they can underline or highlight key words and phrases, or make notes in the margins (some teachers prefer that students make notes on separate papers). When they come to something they don't understand, students slow down, reread, and then jot down a brief reminder in the margin; students appear to pay closer attention to a challenge and think more deeply about evidence when they record their thoughts. Questions and discussion during the first reading may focus on the author's word choices and repetition, specific sentences, literary devices, vocabulary, or particular passages containing information that is key to understanding the text.

Again serving as a model for those who needed it, Ms. Luca read aloud a sentence that created a question in her mind: "Sir Ernest Shackleton needed twenty-seven brave men. He placed an advertisement in English newspapers. 'Men wanted for Hazardous Journey. Small wages.'" (Roop & Roop, 2001, p. 1). Then Ms. Luca demonstrated how she would circle the words *Hazardous Journey* and write her question in the margin. She explained that she will continue to do this each time she comes up with a question about the content.

The students will now be expected to independently apply the modeled strategy as they continue reading about Shackleton. Two sentences particularly grabbed Shelly's attention: "The whalers on South Georgia Island had warned Shackleton of early ice. They told him he must force his way through heavy pack ice to reach land" (Roop & Roop, 2001, p. 10). Remembering her teacher's demonstration, Shelly stopped and circled the terms *early ice* and *pack ice*. Shelly thought to herself, "I wonder what those mean. I've never heard of early ice or pack ice." So, in the margin, she noted, "Pack ice?" "Early ice?" The pack ice question, conveniently, was answered on the next page, so Shelly discovered that questions are often answered when we continue reading. When they find an answer in the text, students should make a margin note to indicate where they found the answer. Through this process, the students will also learn that their questions are not always answered in the text; finding out about *early ice* will be left to group discussions or to independent research.

After the reading on day one, students are asked *text-dependent questions,* or literal, in-text questions that require them to return to the text to identify or recall relevant information that was explicitly stated in the reading selection. Students may be asked to recall or identify facts about the characters (name, traits, and feelings) or the setting. They may be asked to recall or

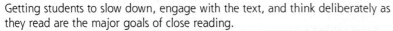

Getting students to slow down, engage with the text, and think deliberately as they read are the major goals of close reading.

Monkey Business/Fotolia

identify details about a specific event. Or they may be asked to recall explicitly stated reasons for certain actions or events. An example of a text-dependent question would be something like, "The chapter describes the journey as 'hazardous.' Give two pieces of information from the chapter that explain what made the journey 'hazardous.'" Discussions often focus on what the text means to the students and how it connects to previous learnings and experiences: *What were the most interesting words you came across in the chapter? What did the author mean by . . . ? What do you already know that helped you come to that conclusion? What did you previously read that helped you come to that conclusion? What do you understand now that you didn't understand before? Can you predict what will happen now?*

Since *Escape from the Ice* was driven by riveting character actions and situations, it inspired much discussion—students were eager to return to the text to find support for their responses to the story's events. Following the first read, have students *Think-Pair-Share* to assess what they have learned from the text. Divide the class into groups of two to rehash the information and share their reactions to the text. Pose a question, usually by writing it on the board or projecting it. First, have the students take a minute or two to consider the question on their own. Next, have the students discuss the question with their partner for two or three minutes, sharing their ideas and opinions. Then, come together again as a whole class to share responses from some or all the pairs. Their contributions will provide excellent assessment evidence and help to determine where to focus instruction during subsequent readings.

SUBSEQUENT READINGS

For a second or third close read, students reread the selection to thoroughly address additional targeted learning outcomes that could be met through text-based questions and discussion. Purposes for rereading include defining conceptual vocabulary; differentiating fact from opinion; analyzing cause-and-effect relationships; describing people, places, times, or events; determining an author's purpose; or facilitating the development of a number of other social studies/literacy skills and strategies such as learning to use organizational features (table of contents; chapter and section previews and summaries; headings and subheadings; photographs and illustrations, including captions; graphics; glossary; and index). Again, you will find it useful to introduce expectations through a think aloud for *text-dependent questions,* or questions that can only be answered by referring back to the text being read. A text-dependent question would be something like, "The book describes Shackleton's hazardous journey. Offer three pieces of information from the book that help us understand that the expedition was hazardous." As they become more skillful in reading, discussing, and analyzing text, you will want to gradually transition the responsibility for reading and thinking to the students. The key is to offer just the right amount of scaffolded assistance at the proper time. Throughout the entire process, students will continue to make marks on the reading material to indicate notes, questions, words, or evidence.

To provide an example of how teacher modeling during second and third readings helps foster deeper thinking about the text in regard to a targeted skill, suppose that your job is to focus on the skill of *inferring*, which involves using the text to figure out something the author does not actually say. Start by reading a brief passage or sentence aloud: "'What the ice gets, the ice keeps,' Sir Shakleton told Captain Worsley" (Roop & Roop, 2001, p. 17). Share your thinking: "I'm not sure I quite get this. I wonder what Shackleton meant by that comment. But based on what we have read so far, I can infer that the ship *Endurance* is trapped in the ice and might slowly be crushed." As you read through more of the narrative, continue to demonstrate inferential thinking with comments such as: "I can infer that . . . ," "I think . . . ," "Maybe this means . . . ," "I am guessing that . . . ," and "I predict . . . ."

Eventually, students will pick up on how to extract deeper meanings or ideas from the text. "I believe Shackleton did the right thing," declared one student, "because the story tells how he thought about all the dangers first." And with that first declaration, the groups began citing, selecting, and interpreting just the right evidence to back up their ideas. Discussion is a perfect way to bring a close reading to a satisfying conclusion, especially when students are challenged to use textual evidence to support their ideas and feelings.

Video Example 7.1   https://www.youtube.com/watch?v=HDfv3B_JZQo This video summarizes a complete lesson for a second close reading of a short social studies text. What are some major close reading instructional responsibilities that Wiley Blevins employed while carrying out this lesson?

Reflection on Learning

You may simply scribble rough notes or jot down something more polished and complete. The point is to simply start recording your ideas spontaneously and candidly.

A teacher complained, "My students once loved to read. Now, reading seems like work to them and they seem to hate it. It seems like reading is being reduced to the ability to navigate standardized tests and my kids don't like it. What can I do?"

 CHECK YOUR UNDERSTANDING 7.6   Click here to check your understanding of this section of the chapter.

What Is Persuasive Text?

It should come as no surprise that the main purpose of persuasive writing is to persuade—to express an opinion or to take a stance and then attempt to sway others to agree with your point of view. Unlike the factual nature of informational writing, persuasive writing conveys the opinions and biases of the writer. It is often used in letters of complaint, reviews (of books, movies, music, etc.), advertisements or commercials, and newspaper opinion and editorial pieces. A writer uses *persuasive writing* when he or she wants to influence the reader to agree with a particular viewpoint or take a desired course of action, and includes supportive facts that help argue a point.

Fact and Opinion

Students are introduced to the concept of persuasive writing as they learn to distinguish between fact and opinion. Although everyone naturally seems to have an opinion on almost everything, we must help guide and nurture this natural inclination by teaching students the basics of taking a stand on an issue and convincing others to agree with them. Establishing a personal opinion and supporting it with logical reasoning is how this is done, but the process is a challenge for many elementary school students. They must learn that effective persuasive writing is made up of three interrelated parts: (1) an introductory opinion statement that catches the reader's attention; (2) a body of facts that offers supportive evidence; and (3) a conclusion that restates the opinion and appeals to the reader to take action.

The purpose of informational writing is to explain and inform with accurate *facts*. For example, "George Washington was the first president of the United States" can be confirmed as being correct and factual by consulting any number of trustworthy sources. Likewise, "The American flag is red, white, and blue," can be verified by examining an actual American flag. On the other hand, *opinions* are personal views or beliefs that cannot be substantiated. For example, "George Washington was the greatest of all U.S. presidents," is an opinion. It is true that George Washington is considered by many to be distinguished among U.S. presidents, but the idea that he was "the *greatest* of all U.S. presidents" is a personal viewpoint of Washington's importance that cannot be proven.

To help children sort out factual statements from opinions, write a factual statement on the chalkboard. Explain that this statement can be considered a fact if someone can answer *yes* when asked if it can be proven. Here's an example:

"The Star-Spangled Banner" was made our national anthem on March 3, 1931.

Ask students if this statement is true: "Can it be proven?" State that you must find reliable sources of information to check if the statement is factual. Show them a page from a credible reference such as Elaine Landau's book *The National Anthem* (Children's Press), to prove that this statement is true. Continue by asking the children to volunteer additional statements of fact and to describe how their suggestions could be verified. Then explain that opinions differ from facts because they are personal beliefs or feelings that cannot be verified with reliable sources of information. Help the children spot opinions by encouraging them to look for words that are likely to express a personal feeling or belief:

If you ask me, "God Bless America" would be a better national anthem than our current one.

Have the students help you brainstorm other signal words that indicate that a judgment is about to be made, such as *I believe, I suggest, my point of view, perhaps, usually, bad, good, better, worse,* and *most.* Children must be led to realize that facts and opinions are all around them—in the books they read, on television, in advertisements, on the Internet, and in everyday conversations.

It is very important to expose children to different models of persuasive writing as you introduce them to this genre . . . advertisements, editorials, letters, book or movie reviews, and so on. It is important to have a good variety of texts so children can explore the assorted purposes of persuasive writing. Following is a small sample of persuasive writing opportunities.

ADVERTISEMENTS

Advertising is the primary tool of communication used by businesses to inform consumers about their goods and services and to convince consumers to buy what they have to offer. Youngsters are bombarded by such advertising everywhere they turn; it is wise to introduce your students to advertising techniques so that they will be better able to recognize persuasive text in its various forms. Start by looking through newspapers and magazines to uncover a variety of print advertisements. Talk about the different persuasive techniques advertisers use to target specific groups of people—men, women, boys, girls, young children, teens, senior citizens, and so on—to buy their products. See if students can find examples of each of the following techniques and who the advertisers are targeting with each ad:

- *Bandwagon:* an appeal to follow the crowd. You don't want to be left out, do you?
- *Buzz words:* words that have suddenly become popular with consumers (like "multitasking" or "eco-friendly")
- *Testimonial:* someone you admire or respect endorses the product (like a popular celebrity endorsing a certain brand of clothing)
- *Snob appeal:* an attempt to convince buyers that owning a certain product is a status symbol
- *Facts and figures:* trying to convince a buyer that "9 out of 10 families" prefer a certain product (without telling you who those families are)
- *Plain folks:* a suggestion that the product is a good value for ordinary people (such as an automobile manufacturer showing an ordinary family piling into a minivan)
- *Wit and humor:* giving customers a reason to laugh or to be entertained by clever use of visuals or language
- *Patriotism:* the suggestion that purchasing this product shows your love of your country (a company brags about its product being made in the United States by American workers)

So many things to think about and so little time!

Spass/Fotolia

- *Demonstration:* simply showing the product in action
- *Problems:* claiming that the product can help the buyer solve a problem (like cleaning out the rain gutters)
- *Card stacking:* distorting or omitting facts

Distribute a variety of magazines to small groups of students and ask them to find examples of each advertising technique and who each ad targets. Discuss the persuasive techniques used: "Which of the ads featured a famous person? An expert? Ordinary people? Monetary incentives? Buzz words?" "What's the message in each ad?" "Which messages 'grabbed' you?" "Which techniques do you think were most effective?" "Which were not as effective?" As a follow-up to the activity, it would be interesting to ask your students to design their own ads that would attract visitors to their school using one of the propaganda techniques.

POLITICAL CARTOONS AND EDITORIALS

Be sure to emphasize that political cartoons carry serious messages intended to influence a reader's opinion about an important issue, even though they use humor or sarcasm to make their point. Cartoonists use few words to express ideas because the illustrations themselves are intended to communicate the message. The cartoon characters tell the story. Show the students some political cartoons, making sure to choose ones that communicate the simplest ideas in the most uncomplicated style possible. Help the children analyze the cartoonist's point of view, determine the cartoonist's purpose, and decide whether they agree or disagree with the cartoonist.

Figure 7.12 is a political cartoon. You could lead a discussion about this particular cartoon with the following prompts:

- What do you see here? Do you recognize any of these people?
- What is happening? Describe what is going on.
- What issue do you think the cartoonist is trying to highlight? What point is he trying to make?
- What is the cartoonist's viewpoint on the issue?

FIGURE 7.12   Political Cartoon

Source: Courtesy of the *Daily Local News*, West Chester, PA. ©1963.

- What techniques or devices does the artist use? Caricature? Symbolism?
- What other techniques could the cartoonist have used to make her or his point?
- What is the purpose of the cartoon? What is its message? Is it effective?
- What contrasting opinion could someone have on the same issue?
- Do you agree or disagree with the cartoon's message? Why?

Newspaper editorials serve the same purpose as political cartoons, but editorials use words instead of illustrations to express a personal viewpoint. Writing an editorial is different than writing a news story. In a news story, the facts are paramount and opinions are left out; an editorial piece, on the other hand, is heavily grounded in opinion, with facts used to support a viewpoint. Explain to your students that an editorial is a form of persuasive text that expresses an opinion about a current issue or topic. Talk with them about attempts they have made to persuade someone to side with them on an issue they really cared about. Inform them that an editorial is a form of persuasion that advances an opinion or calls its readers to action. Share samples of editorials with your students that you have collected from newspapers and magazines (or online). Discuss the title and examine the topic sentence. Students may want to make annotations or use highlighters as they read the editorial. What is the issue or call to action? What factual evidence and background information are offered? What is the tone of the editorial? How persuasive is the editorial? Next, have the students select a topic important enough to apply what they have learned to writing their own persuasive editorial. That could involve reading newspaper articles, checking television news stories, searching reliable websites, or digging up topics in the most unlikely places.

John Kerrigan, for example, became deeply concerned about his principal's decision to remove the hallway door to the boy's restroom as a move to curb school vandalism. To express his concern about the principal's action, John wrote a biting editorial for his classroom newspaper. His friend Chris volunteered to draw an accompanying political cartoon. Their rough copy is shown in Figure 7.13.

Critical readers understand persuasive text and realize that writers have diverse purposes for writing. Therefore, they adjust their reading style to match the intended purpose of

FIGURE 7.13 John's Editorial and Chris's Political Cartoon

"Are bathrooms private anymore

Mr. Towson has a great scence of hummer, his last joke was the funnyest of of all. You better sit down for this Ready? Okay - He took... you sure your ready for this... Well, he took the bathroom door off. See! I told you should sit down. Now you propally think all the resonibillaty has gone to his head. Well for once I think he's absolutely almost right. Heres his side. Someone took three rolls of tolite paper in the toilet and flush it. It flooded the bathroom and the boys locker room. But taking the bathroom door off is to much. I mean you ever try and go in the bathroom with about 50 girls standing in front. But, there is a good part, the vandalism has gone down.
Now Mr. Towson has something to worry about that is weather the school board impeaches him and if the health board calls the school a health hazrd.

Har! A littel town with a littel school has there own Watergate. I can see the head of lines now "First Princepal to be Impeached." I thought Mr. Towson is a nice guy (sometimes). But the health hazard is yet a nother thing. But don't worry Mr. Towson will figure out some and we hop bathrooms are still private

Chris

OH The Bathroom, first open Door
on the right

a written piece, engaging with the text critically, for example, when it contains certain signal words or phrases, such as, "*I believe* that Franklin Roosevelt had prior knowledge of the Japanese attack on Pearl Harbor." Critical readers know that the purpose of these kinds of written pieces is to *persuade* them to consider different beliefs or to cement their existing beliefs. They ask the question, "Is this true?"

✓ **CHECK YOUR UNDERSTANDING 7.7** **Click here** to check your understanding of this section of the chapter.

A Final Thought

Although it is difficult to look into the future and imagine today's wholesome elementary school youngsters as adults, there is one thing we can count on. They will need to possess efficient and reliable literacy skills to succeed in life during the 21st century—that is, the ability to comprehend and appraise a variety of texts and to write and communicate effectively. How do you address the challenge of creating the environment required to nurture such learners and help them grow while simultaneously meeting state and national standards in social studies? To begin, engagement with text must start early in the elementary school years and develop across all disciplines, especially social studies. Social studies content knowledge is strengthened when you integrate literacy into content-rich teaching and learning; conversely, reading and writing skills improve as students acquire and impart their content knowledge. As their literacy skills develop throughout the grades, you will gradually shift the responsibility for reading and writing to students through guided assistance and encouragement during individual and collaborative social studies learning experiences.

You must provide your students with rich and varied opportunities over time to develop the complex reading and writing skills demanded for eventually carrying out successful 21st-century careers. These opportunities must include authentic learning tasks that help your students discover real-world connections between literacy and social studies. However, we must realize that we can no longer view literacy as being solely text-centered; we are part of a culture filled with images and messages that are not limited to words on a page. Now and in the foreseeable future, being literate means not only interacting with printed text, but also understanding wikis, blogs, tweets, skype, digital media, and other emerging technologies. Our responsibility in preparing the 21st-century learner lies not only in teaching about print media, but also in acquiring the ability to locate, evaluate, and use materials in varied formats from a wide range of sources, including electronic documents and multimedia texts.

References

Daniels, H. (2003). *Literature circles*. Portland, ME: Stenhouse.

Gambrell, L. B., & Marinak, B. A. (2009). "Sometimes I just crave information!" *Social Studies and the Young Learner, 21,* 4–5.

Meyer, J. B. F. (1985). Prose analysis: Purposes, procedures, and problems. In B. K. Britten & J. B. Black (Eds.), *Understanding expository text: A theoretical and practical handbook for analyzing explanatory text* (pp. 11–64). Hillsdale, NJ: Erlbaum.

Mohr, K. (2006). Children's choices for recreational reading. *Journal of Literacy Research, 38,* 81–104.

National Governors Association Center for Best Practices & Council of Chief State School Officers. (2010). *Common core state standards for English language arts and literacy in history/social studies, science, and technical subjects.* Washington, DC: Authors.

Oldendorf, S. B., & Calloway, A. (2008). Connecting children to a bigger world: Reading newspapers in the second grade. *Social Studies and the Young Learner, 21,* 17–19.

Pappas, C. C. (1993). Is narrative "primary"? *Journal of Reading Behavior, 25,* 97–129.

Roop, C., & Roop, P. (2001). *Escape from the ice: Shackleton and the* Endurance. New York, NY: Scholastic.

Tompkins, G. E. (1998). *Language arts: Content and teaching strategies* (4th ed.). Columbus, OH: Merrill.

Beyond the Ordinary:
Teaching and Learning with Narrative Text

Learning Outcomes

Reading and writing are the foundational skills required for success in social studies; they are the primary input and output sources for communicating social studies subject matter. It seems that most of our current instructional goals and standards emphasize the variety of text students must use to good advantage as they acquire and convey functional, accurate information and ideas. Although we often think of informational text as being the major push of literacy integration in social studies classrooms, narrative text also has a very important place. Successful social studies teachers make sure that their students read narrative text with understanding and reflection. They also make sure that their students write narrative text to explain ideas or to generate something new, something creative. Providing students with a chance to read and write exciting and interesting narrative text can heighten student engagement in the learning process and motivate those who may have been unenthusiastic about traditional classroom exercises.

After completing this chapter, you will be able to apply a wide range of strategies to help students comprehend and appreciate:

- The qualities of good personal narratives.
- How historical fiction accurately and authentically represents a historical time period.
- The unique themes, characters, and settings of folktales.
- The basic components in a work of fantasy.
- How to construct and express meaning through poetry.

Classroom Snapshot

When the children returned to their third-grade classroom after lunch, they were greeted by their teacher, John Ogborn, doing his best impersonation of a griot (pronounced "GREE oh"), an African village storyteller/oral historian. Mr. Ogborn was dressed in a dashiki (a loose, flowing tie-dyed shirt) and a brimless kente kufi cap, garments worn by some West African griots. In the background, the beautiful soft sounds of traditional kora music filled the classroom (a kora is an instrument with 21 strings that sounds like a harp). Griots often used the kora to accompany their stories. An African griot may have carried a net containing several small objects (or worn a hat with articles suspended from the brim); when someone selected an item, the griot responded with a relevant story. Today, Mr. Ogborn shouldered a small net containing miniature objects related to stories he was prepared to read: a mosquito (Why Mosquitos Buzz in People's Ears), a tiny book (A Story, A Story), a spider (Anansi the Spider), and a cotton ball cloud with a bolt of lightning sticking out (Bringing the Rain to Kapiti Plain).

After a good meal, the children of a village in long-ago Africa may have heard a kora, drum, or rattle and a powerful voice that called, "Listen to a tale! Listen to a tale!" announcing that a story was soon to be told. When they heard the call, the children ran toward it because they knew they were about to hear a wonderful story with music and dancing and song! Their favorite stories were about Anansi, the little spider who always seemed to get into a mess and used his wit and wordplay to escape. They all loved Anansi! So, modeling the griot storytelling tradition, Mr. Ogborn signaled for the children to join him on the group rug in the shade of a huge "African baobab tree" that was taped to their classroom wall. "Children, listen to a tale . . . for fun, for fun!" When they heard the call, the children knew they were about to take part in something special. As the children settled down to listen, Mr. Ogborn showed them a toy mosquito and asked them to venture a guess about its significance: "Does the mosquito give us any clue as to what the story could be about?" he wondered. After a short discussion, Mr. Ogborn asked the eager listeners to join him in a call-and-response storytelling chant common to many African cultures: "Are you ready?" he asked several times. The children responded each time, "Yes, we are ready!" The classroom griot then used a traditional West African story opening: "Then I will tell you a story which was told to me when I was a little boy. A story, a story, let it come, let it go. . . ." Mr. Ogborn then read the book Why Mosquitos Buzz in People's Ears, as retold by Verna Aardema (Penguin).

Mr. Ogborn read the story in a fluent, expressive voice that reflected the tone of the story and the nature of the characters. He used gestures at appropriate points in the story and involved the children whenever he could—especially with making predictions and joining in on repetition, rhymes, actions, and fun words. When he reached the end of the story, Mr. Ogborn closed with a traditional West African ending: "You see, that is my story. I heard it when I was a child. And now you have heard it, too!" Mr. Ogborn saved time to ask open-ended questions to evaluate and discuss the ideas encountered in the text, such as their favorite part of the story; which character they would most like to be; how the story made them feel at the end; whether they could think of a different ending; and what connections they could make to any personal experiences or other stories they had heard or read.

Because Mr. Ogborn's curriculum is driven by CCSS-based state standards directed toward fostering students' understanding and working knowledge of basic conventions of literacy, he knew that the story would be an excellent resource for teaching how sequencing (the order in which things happen) helps order story events and functions as a key comprehension strategy—"CCSS.ELA-LITERACY.RL.3.3: Describe characters in a story (e.g., their traits, motivations, or feelings) and explain how their actions contribute to the sequence of events." So, after completing their story conversation, Mr. Ogborn provided pairs of children with picture cards illustrating the key characters from the story. The dyads worked together to place the picture cards in the order they appeared to retell the story. Once each dyad agreed on its character sequence, it shared its results with one other team; each dyad was asked to agree or disagree on the other dyad's sequencing plan. Following that activity, Mr. Ogborn focused the students' attention on the story's onomatopoeic language, which comes from the African oral tradition. He presented the students with two additional sets of cards in random order: one set contained the sounds made by each animal from the book and the other set identified the corresponding actions. "Rabbit," for example, "bounded across the clearing," making the sound, "krik, krik, krik." The students were to work with one animal at a time until they made a story chain, sequentially ordering the three-card sentence strips—animal illustration cards, the sounds made by each animal, and the corresponding actions. This activity was not only enjoyable, it was also a type of formative assessment that easily informed Mr. Ogborn about the sequencing abilities of his students.

Finally, Mr. Ogborn introduced story theater, the dramatic presentation of a story told by a group of students who act out the text and provide narration. Before they planned their own story theater performance, however, Mr. Ogborn wanted his students to see that African storytelling, by and large, is an interactive oral performance; in most traditional African societies, everyone participates in the storytelling event. So, Mr. Ogborn shared a YouTube clip showing actual African griots using musical instruments to accompany their stories and summoning the listeners to join them with whatever musical instruments were at hand. Following the clip, Mr. Ogborn explained the story theater format to his students and encouraged them to volunteer for several roles: narrators, musicians, and actors. Once the parts were filled, Mr. Ogborn opened a large box that contained two balaphons (xylophones made of wooden keys with natural gourds as resonators), two thumb pianos (marimbas made from a dried gourd and wooden top with metal reeds that are plucked with the thumbs), tambourines, and a variety of drums and shakers (made from natural fruits, pods, and gourds, dried with their seeds inside). Mr. Ogborn gave the children a few minutes to explore the instruments and to each select one to represent his or her animal. The children who preferred not to use an instrument were told that they could instead clap their hands, slap their thighs, pound the upper arms and chest, or stamp or shuffle their feet to enhance the story (as shown on the YouTube clip). Known as "body percussion," these movements have traditionally been incorporated into Africa's storytelling routines. The students practiced over . . . and over . . . and over, with a "love to read" attitude, until they were ready to share their productions with each other and friends in the other third-grade classrooms.

For the much anticipated story theater performance, the narrators stood in a straight line with their scripts. A large index card with an illustration of a designated animal dangled from a piece of yarn around each reader's neck so the audience could better visualize the animal as its part was read. A student-created mural was attached to the wall behind the readers. It mimicked the woodcut design of the book's illustrators, Leo and Diane Dillon. In cartoon balloons above each animal, the students wrote its unusual sound ("wasawusu, wasawusu," "mek, mek, mek," "pem, pem, pem"). As the students read, the actors slithered, bounded, and moved in a variety of creative ways, and the musical instruments and body percussion mimicked the unique sound words of the story.

"Folktales have always had an important place in my social studies classroom," explains Mr. Ogborn. "They not only provide substantial information in an appealing way, but they also do a great job communicating a culture's morals and values. Verna Aardema has retold many African folktales, but *Why Mosquitos Buzz in Peoples Ears* has quickly become a student favorite . . . so much so that it is beginning to rival the appeal of that old trickster, Anansi. The interactive nature of *Why Mosquitoes Buzz* just seem to grab my students; they always love to participate, so when they were offered the opportunity to make sound effects and music, call out catchy words, act or move like an animal, and even to help retell part of the story, they jumped at the chance. The students especially like the way African folktales use animals to act like humans in order to teach a lesson. I like to follow up folktale reading with an assortment of activities including drama, art, and music, along with a strong comprehension and writing component, such as using the stories as models to write and tell folktales of their own. Although they are normally associated with language arts classes, folktales contribute immensely to our social studies program because of their historical, cultural, and geographic context. And children think the world of folktales; their entertainment value is as high as any other classroom tool. As icing on the cake, I find folktales to be among the best resources for integrating instruction across the curriculum."

 Video Exploration 8.1

Folktales are part of a literature category referred to as narratives. Very simply, the difference between the informational text discussed in Chapter 7 and narrative text to be discussed in Chapter 8 is that informational text is primarily intended to supply information while the

Narratives offer a superb opportunity for teachers and students to explore the many themes of social studies.

WavebreakMediaMicro/Fotolia

major purpose of narrative text is to tell a good story. Narratives explain and order events in a well-organized, meaningful sequence that makes them interesting to read and listen to. Most of us have shared our childhood with a menagerie of storybook friends, and there are many that we remember with special delight. It seems that very little burns itself so lastingly into our minds as the stories and story characters we were introduced to during our childhood. Good stories, however, are only a part of what makes narratives such a valuable component of first-class social studies classrooms; also included in this category are the documents and correspondence that people use to record daily events and experiences in their lives—that is, personal narratives. In this chapter, we will examine the several types of narratives commonly used in elementary school social studies classrooms: *personal narratives, historical fiction, folktales, fantasy, and poetry*.

Personal Narratives

Personal narratives are stories relating a significant personal experience told in the temporal sequence of that experience. Personal narratives include letters, diaries, interviews, or other personal accounts, either in their original forms or published in print or online. Show your students a copy of Jackie Robinson's letter to President Kennedy in which he expressed his impatience with what he regarded as President Eisenhower's failure to act decisively in combating racism (National Archives Website), and they will erupt with questions and comments about one of the most turbulent eras in our nation's domestic history. Poring over 12-year-old Eliza's diary and letters will enthrall your students as they read her narrative about running away from the cruel master who sold away her mother (Jerdene Nolen, *Eliza's Freedom Road: An Underground Railroad Diary* [Simon & Schuster]). Before the age of Twitter and Facebook, the best way for people to chronicle their lives was through a letter, diary, or journal; bringing such "stuff of history" to your classroom can give students a very real sense of what it was like to be alive during a long-past era. Personal narratives intrigue students because they are real and offer very personal insights into the lives of the people about whom history is written.

Books, especially textbooks and informational books, will probably be the major source of reading in your social studies classroom, but whether your class is studying the *Iroquois*

Confederacy or *How a Bill Becomes a Law*, a variety of personal narratives can strengthen your program. In addition to diaries, journals, letters, and other personal narratives, be sure to add quality literature as excellent sources of personal narratives. For example, the picture book titled *Back of the Bus* by Aaron Reynolds (Philomel) offers a fictionalized personal story told by a young child who describes riding on a segregated bus in Montgomery, Alabama in December 1955. Innocently, the boy rolls a marble down the aisle to the front and a smiling Rosa Parks rolls it back to him. As the bus fills with people, the driver tells Mrs. Parks to move to the back; she refuses and the driver calls the police. The child's firsthand perspective personalizes the well-known historical incident and will evoke strong emotions in your students. In addition to the possibilities mentioned, I like to include writing-to-learn tasks in this personal narratives category as they are short, informal, personal writing tasks that help students document their thoughts and feelings about something that happened to them during selected classroom learning experiences.

Letters

Letters give us a window into the past through the eyes of people who lived long ago. The events covered by historical letters are diverse; they can describe eyewitness accounts of famous battles, nuances of family life, or details of an invention. Fortunately, many have survived over the years and now help tell the tale of the lives of our ancestors, including both the famous and not-so-famous. Consider, for example, just how much Benjamin Franklin's letters have helped us gain insights into his life and the early days of our developing nation. Among other interesting revelations, Franklin's surviving letters reveal that he was vigorously opposed to adopting the bald eagle as our national symbol and considered the turkey a far more appropriate choice. Unfortunately for him, Franklin was in France in 1782 when Congress designated the eagle as our national symbol so he was unable to convince others to join his cause. Annoyed at their decision, Franklin wrote in a letter, "He is a bird of bad moral character; he does not get his living honestly. . . . Besides, he is a rank coward; the little kingbird, not bigger than a sparrow, attacks him boldly and drives him out of the district." Franklin continued, "The turkey is in comparison a much more respectable bird, and withal a true original native of America. . . . He is . . . a bird of courage, and would not hesitate to attack a grenadier of the British Guards who would presume to invade his farmyard with a red coat on." You may have heard stories of Franklin's dissatisfaction with the bald eagle, but don't you agree that reading his actual words adds a great deal of substance and interest to the matter? Think about the degree to which actual letters, or exact replicas of them, would enliven the investigative efforts of your students, too. A wealth of surviving letters appropriate for use in social studies classrooms is available online from the National Archives and other web sources. Responding to their availability in her classroom, Celia, a fifth-grader, commented, "I love the letters they have! They show us what people were really thinking about back in the old days."

In addition to their power to enlighten students about the past, simulated letters from the past help youngsters analyze the conversational style as well as the format of the times. Therefore, letter writing in the context of bygone days offer important first-person writing experiences for social studies classrooms. When writing a simulated letter to a parent during colonial days, for example, authenticity should be expected. A proper greeting might be *Honour'd Sir (or Madam)* and a proper ending would be *Your Dutiful Daughter (or Son)*. Also in keeping with authenticity, it would be interesting to have students write with the implements commonly used at the time. A letter during colonial times would have been written with a quill pen—a goose, peacock, pheasant, or wild turkey feather. Ink was made by crushing and boiling down natural vegetation such as cranberries or walnut shells. This may be difficult to do in typical elementary school classrooms; educational supply companies, though, sell small colonial writing kits containing a goose feather and dry ink for about three dollars each. There were no envelopes during colonial times, so letters should be folded and sealed. A blob of hot sealing wax was used during colonial days, but pressing a small ball of clay to seal the simulated letter would work fine.

Figure 8.1 shows an example of a simulated letter. While a group of fourth-graders was learning about Christopher Columbus, the students were asked to pretend to be Columbus writing a letter to Queen Isabella requesting support for his explorations.

Journals and Diaries

Journals and *diaries* have existed in one form or another for hundreds of years as personal records of personal experiences. Historians have recognized journals and diaries as being among the finest resources for adding to our understanding of the past: "What was it really like to ride on the Oregon Trail?" Just look how the following entry from the diary of Catherine Sager Pringle can help historians learn about the Oregon Trail experience. Catherine wrote the following entry in 1844 as her family journeyed across the plains from Missouri to Oregon:

> *August 1st we nooned in a beautiful grove on the north side of the Platte. We had by this time got used to climbing in and out of the wagon when in motion. When performing this feat that afternoon my dress caught on an axle helve and I was thrown under the wagon wheel, which passed over and badly crushed my limb before father could stop the team. He picked me up and saw the extent of the injury when the injured limb hung dangling in the air.*

Catherine and her six siblings were eventually orphaned along the Oregon Trail so he was unable to make his feelings known. Despite these misfortunes, Catherine maintained her diary throughout the entire trip, recording both the good times and bad. It is now available, along with many others, on a website specifically for teachers designed by Mike Trinklein

FIGURE 8.1   A Student's Letter, Written from the Perspective of a Historical Figure

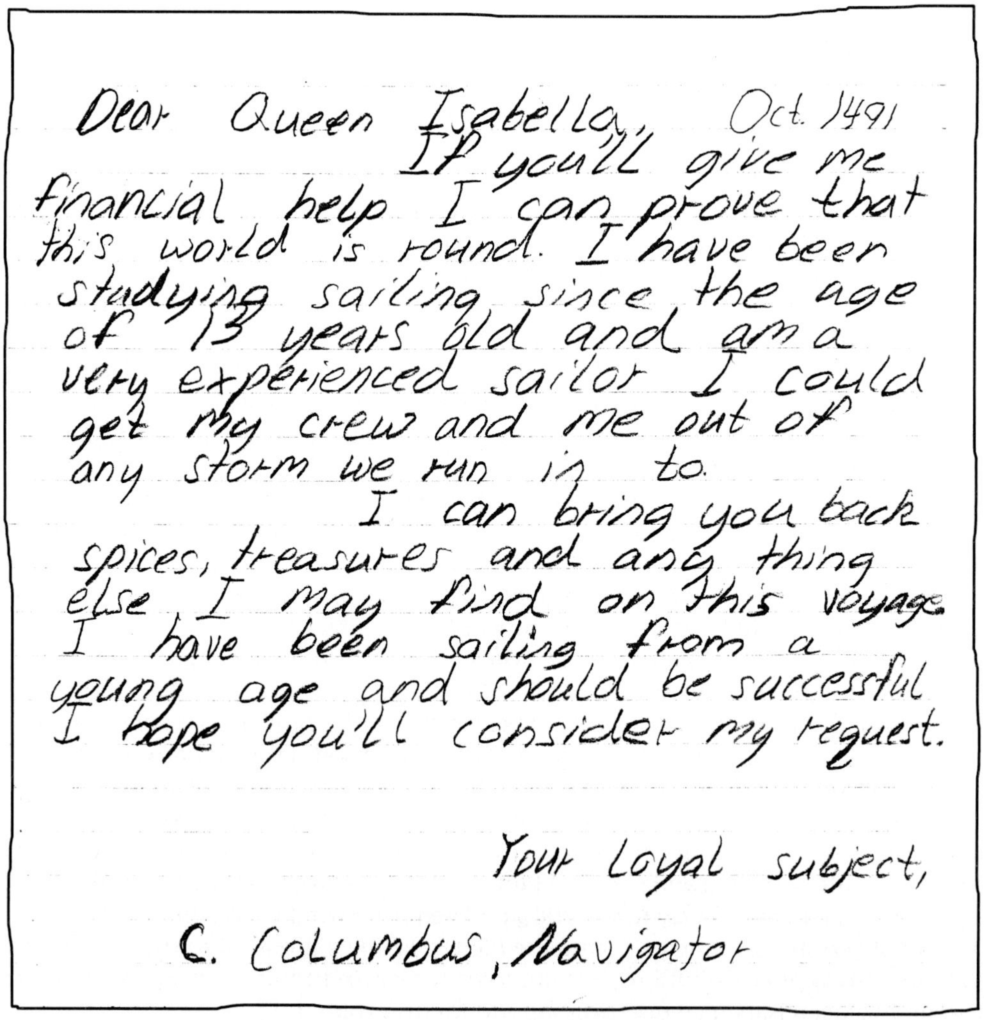

Dear Queen Isabella,   Oct. 1491
             If you'll give me
financial help I can prove that
this world is round. I have been
studying sailing since the age
of 13 years old and am a
very experienced sailor I could
get my crew and me out of
any storm we run in to.
          I can bring you back
spices, treasures and any thing
else I may find on this voyage
I have been sailing from a
young age and should be successful
I hope you'll consider my request.

                         Your loyal subject,

     C. Columbus, Navigator

and Steve Boettcher. During the three years they spent researching the PBS documentary film *The Oregon Trail*, they uncovered a wealth of great material for teachers and built the website http://www.america101.us/trail/Oregontrail.html.

There are many other good websites that offer original diaries for classroom use. The DoHistory website, for example, not only brings a diary's words directly to your students but also uses a special "magic lens" that changes the diary from a handwritten to a transcribed version as it moves over the handwritten version. This is a useful tool because many historical diaries have been written in a script that is difficult for elementary school children to read. This site also has many other unique historical documents that have been scanned and transcribed, along with examples of how historians use such documents in their investigations. In addition to quality websites, there are also many good examples of diaries and journals in children's literature.

Students can compose simulated journals and diaries from the viewpoint of individuals writing directly about themselves, accurately portraying what the characters think, feel, or experience. The students often refer to themselves using the first-person singular pronouns "I" and/or "we." The learning process starts as students learn about significant events, lives, times, and places. Then, applying what they have learned as background information, the students breathe life into historical figures by writing from the first-person perspective, thereby extending their learning and constructing personal meaning.

Using real diaries as models can serve as a strong guide for the children's own imaginary diary entries. The following entries were written by a student pretending to be a sailor on one of Magellan's ships that was unable to complete the circumnavigation of the globe in 1522:

> *Day 10. The storm lasted two days and two nights. I never saw waves so high or the wind blow so hard. Our ship was thrown against huge rocks and was smashed to bits. We held onto our lifeboats for longer than I could remember—every sailor was scared stiff. We finally spotted some land. . . .*
>
> *Day 11. Fresh water is disappearing. Our captain divided us into four groups. Each group was to go in a different direction to search for fresh water. In mid-afternoon the fourth group found a freshwater spring on the west side of the island. . . .*

Interviews

Quality social studies instruction must include authentic, real-life experiences that help students construct meaningful concepts and important skills. The process of conducting and recording interviews is a superb way of achieving that goal. Because most children are familiar with interviewing—they see people interviewed on television nearly every day—you can help them understand how to conduct an interview by discussing the interviews they have seen and observing you as you model an interview with a child in your classroom. Emphasize the types of questions an interviewer asks; some questions are designed to gather facts while others are intended to find out about personal feelings and opinions. Since children seem to ask many questions that elicit yes or no answers, point out that an interviewer asks very few, if any, of those questions because the answers to such questions do not yield much useful information. *Why*, *how*, and *what* questions produce much more information. You can provide your students an opportunity to act as interviewers by showing them an interesting object and encouraging them to keep asking you questions until they get at the story behind the object. Play the "interviewee" role as the children assume the job of "interviewers." When children are comfortable asking good questions, have them plan an interview with a person who might contribute new insights into a historical topic. In the following scenario, Mario Fiore placed his students in the role of interviewers to elicit life stories from family elders.

> *Intergenerational friendships can help students learn about their ancestors and develop a sense of pride in their heritage. Mario Fiore asked his students to brainstorm a series of questions their grandparents could be asked to find out what life was like when they were in elementary school. Each proposed question was written on an index card. The students examined the collection of index cards, discarding those requiring simple yes or no answers and keeping those which stood the best chance of drawing out the more detailed information they were looking for.*

Once the cards were arranged in a useful questioning order, the students were set to conduct their interviews. Some grandparents lived in the same community as the students, but others lived far away, so they were interviewed by phone, email, or Twitter. Carrying their special reporter's notebooks, students jotted down notes to help them remember what was said during the interview. Others carried digital cameras or recorders to capture special moments.

The students listened carefully to their grandparents' responses to determine whether the desired information was being gathered. If not, they asked probing follow-up questions to clarify points or elicit additional information. By creating their own personal narratives, students not only find a creative outlet for their inquiries but also begin to understand why history is a human construction that is, at times, prone to tentative and arguable judgments about the past.

Finally, Mr. Fiore's young historians wrote individual accounts of their interviews. Each was read in class, and one set of copies was bound into a class book. A sample is shown in Figure 8.2.

Uncovering a portion of a family member's life story provided the stimulus to learn about other people and subjects that interested them, just by asking questions: "Let's interview the mayor to see what's causing global warming!" suggested Regina. Obviously, in conducting interviews, a major aim is to use students' own questions, which are inspired by background experiences and natural curiosity about the world. Obviously, there will be times when judicious teacher guidance will be helpful in framing useful interview questions. In most cases, it helps to model how to come up with good questions. After he modeled essential question-asking skills, Mr. Fiore's students developed a list of "real" questions for their mayor—the things they really cared about and the specific issues they felt the mayor had authority over: "What important actions will you take in addressing . . . abandoned automobiles in our neighborhood . . . water quality in our community . . . and how we students can help initiate an anti-litter campaign?" The students obtained their mayor's Twitter account and sent out a Tweet introducing themselves and requesting an interview to discuss the important actions that the mayor would urge.

Personal Stories

Stories are a unique ingredient of what makes us human; human beings are the only Earthly beings who tell and listen to or read stories. Beginning in early childhood, stories play a vital role in every child's life. The picture books for the very young as well as the more complex novels for teenagers steadily introduce new concepts and new ideas into the lives of our youth. Stories stimulate their imaginations and expand horizons; they teach youngsters important lessons about the world around them.

In the early primary grades, personal stories—those that are self-written as well as those written by others—are among students' favorites. *Personal stories* are written or told for the purpose of providing a truthful, accurate account of an actual life experience. The story is often written from the first-person point of view, using an "I and me" (or "me and us") perspective; that is, the main character tells the story in his or her own words. Whether or not the personal story is told from the first-person perspective, the key to establishing that it is a personal story is that it divulges a real event that happened to you. The traditional acceptance of well-structured show-and-tell, where a child brings to school something from home and talks about it, illustrates the appeal of personal stories in the early primary grade classroom (although wise teachers take steps to diminish the competitive atmosphere it can create).

It is important to use stories in the personal writing voice during the early primary grades in order for students to gain confidence and competence in reading and writing in social studies. Personal stories are what our youngest children create when they scrawl a series of lines, loops, and squiggles and tell you about a personally meaningful event or experience. Those scribbles constitute children's initial attempts to convey their thoughts in print. Because these stories are true accounts about a brief, distinct moment of their lives and not an entire lifetime, I refer to them as personal stories rather than biographies or autobiographies. Teachers of kindergarten and first-grade children support their students' efforts to get personal stories down on paper in a variety of ways—most commonly either as *invented spelling stories* or as *dictated stories*.

FIGURE 8.2   A Student's Interview with His Grandfather

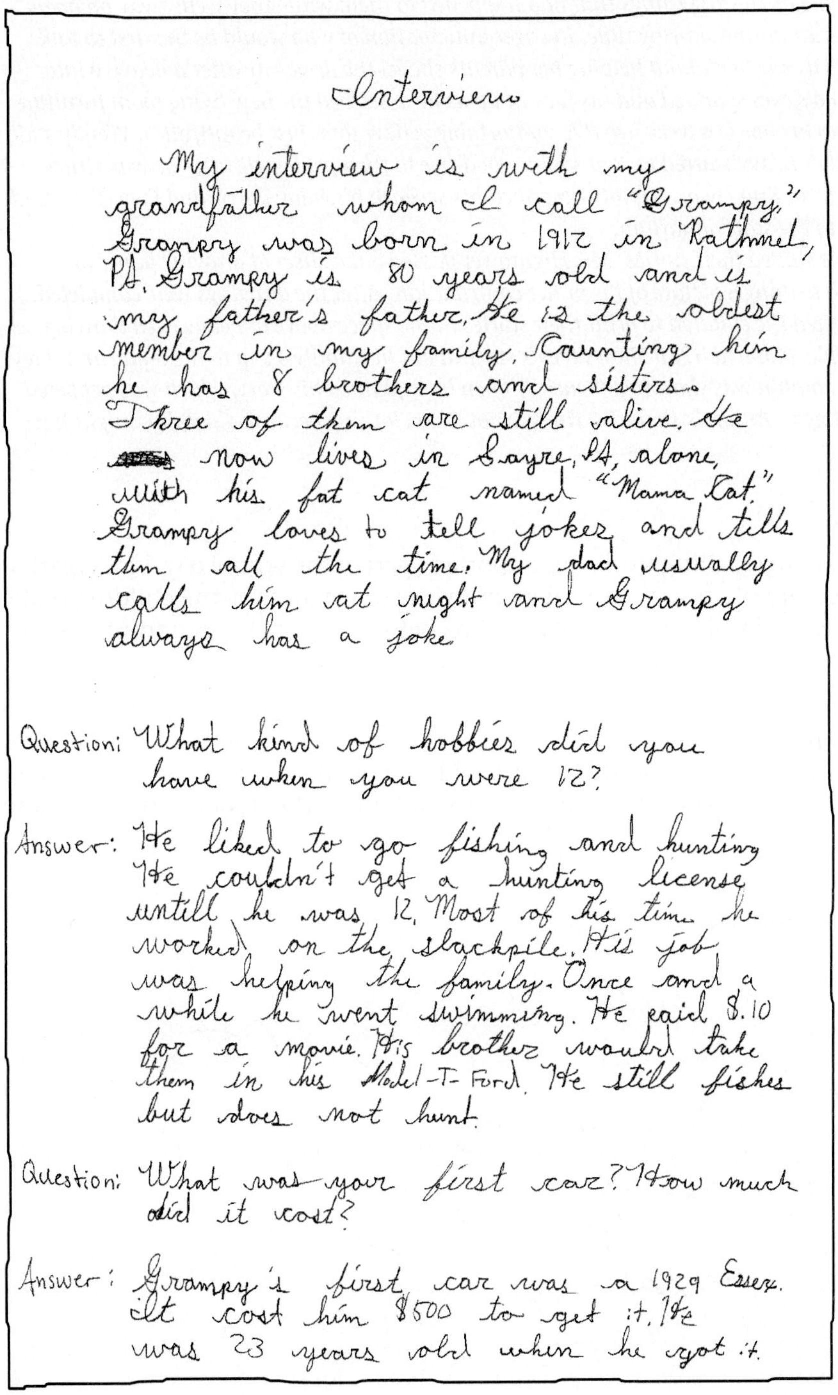

> ### Interview
>
> My interview is with my grandfather whom I call "Grampy." Grampy was born in 1912 in Rathmel, PA. Grampy is 80 years old and is my father's father. He is the oldest member in my family. Counting him he has 8 brothers and sisters. Three of them are still alive. He now lives in Sayre, PA, alone, with his fat cat named "Mama Cat." Grampy loves to tell jokes and tells them all the time. My dad usually calls him at night and Grampy always has a joke
>
> Question: What kind of hobbies did you have when you were 12?
>
> Answer: He liked to go fishing and hunting He couldn't get a hunting license untill he was 12. Most of his time he worked on the slackpile. His job was helping the family. Once and a while he went swimming. He paid $.10 for a movie. His brother would take them in his Model-T Ford. He still fishes but does not hunt.
>
> Question: What was your first car? How much did it cost?
>
> Answer: Grampy's first car was a 1929 Essex. It cost him $500 to get it. He was 23 years old when he got it.

INVENTED SPELLING STORIES

When you offer a piece of drawing paper or primary grade writing paper, most kindergartners and first graders will draw a picture of something they have experienced at school or elsewhere, tell stories about it, and then "write" a story about the picture with scribbles and "invented spellings." (For example, a child may initially scribble *d* or *dg* for *dog* before eventually using conventional spellings for simple words by the end of first grade.) When finished with their master works, kindergartners and first graders will delightedly share their "stories" with their teachers, classmates, and family.

When Ms. Hightower's first graders came back to school at the close of winter vacation, they were excited to share all the interesting things that had happened to them while they were away on break. Hands flew into the air during sharing time, in eager anticipation of who would be the first to talk. Teri's words erupted as she told about helping her parents shovel the driveway after a heavy winter snowstorm. Agostino's eyes sparkled and his face lit up as he described the new living room furniture that was delivered to his house a week ago ("A comfortable yellow sofa, just beautiful!"). Wendy sadly recounted her family's heavyhearted task of saying good-bye to their pet beagle after he was struck down by a speeding car. Kun Hwan happily described his seventh birthday party, and Frey (Free) told of his family's trip to the state aquarium.

After everyone shared their stories, Ms. Hightower passed out a sheet of drawing paper to each child on which to draw a picture of his or her contribution. After the drawings were completed, Ms. Hightower directed the children to print their stories in the space above or below each drawing. Figure 8.3 is a sample. (Cn u rd it?) It shows Frey's story about his family's trip to the aquarium. Frey explained that the dolphin was shouting, "Ouch!" Then he explained his story, which was peppered with invented spellings: "Animals should definitely not wear clothing because a dolphin might have trouble with its fin."

DICTATED STORIES

Along with making invented spelling stories an important part of the school day, kindergarten and first-grade teachers will often serve as scribes and write down ideas as the children orally tell their stories. The dictated stories help clarify the link between what children think and talk about with its written form. This is how the dictated story process works:

Step 1: A Shared Experience. The dictated story process begins with a shared activity to provide a common topic that students will want to talk about. It could be something the class does together, such as a field trip, or it could be students describing a sequence of events from real life. Take a good amount of time to talk about the students' thoughts and observations.

FIGURE 8.3   Invented Spelling Story

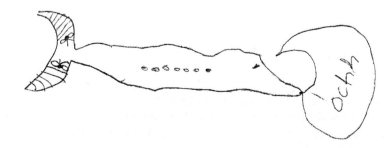

Step 2: Document the Experience. Students draw pictures (or use digital cameras) that help give an account of the experience.

Step 3: Create the Text. Students verbally recall the shared experience by volunteering a sentence or two about their pictures. Keep it short; you do not want to overwhelm the students with too much text. Transcribe the student's words beneath the picture to create the text.

Step 4: Read and Revise. From time to time, stop and read aloud to the child what you have written, pointing to the words, and having the child confirm that you are getting down his or her ideas accurately. Ask the students if they want to make any corrections or additions to the story.

Step 5: Read and Reread. At the conclusion of dictation, read back the whole piece, pointing to the words and encouraging the student to read along.

Step 6: Extension. This text can be used for a variety of extension activities like encouraging children to "read" their stories aloud. Some classrooms have an "Author Chair" where children sit when they share their stories.

Beginning with the early years and continuing throughout the elementary grades, I like to stress the importance of establishing a democratic *community of writers*, not only for dictated stories but for all writing experiences. Mirroring life in a democratic society, a community of writers recognizes the value of everyone's thoughts, upholds their right to express ideas in an open forum, and encourages support for one another through mutual and shared experiences. For example, when writing down children's ideas for dictated stories, you must be very careful not to constantly edit their contributions. If the child uses "was" for "were," write it as spoken. The idea at this point is not to require perfect grammar, but to show children that writing is their ideas put down on paper. Sometimes, however, children will utter words that test our ability to comprehend what they are saying. For example, I remember observing Vince, who confidently came out with this comment after a trip to the farm: "We saw a big halo!" "A halo," he repeated pensively as his teacher listened. "It holded lotsa corn . . . like the picture in our book. Remember?" Realizing what a wonderfully creative act had begun, his teacher invited him to tell more about the "halo" and finished by printing a sentence or two beneath a drawing on his writing paper. By listening carefully to what Vince had to say and asking him to tell more about it, the teacher discovered that he had ingeniously woven together two words he had heard on the trip—*hay* and *silo*—into a clever new word. Imagine the bitterness and harm that could

A community of writers comes together to support and encourage each other.

WavebreakMediaMicro/Fotolia

have resulted if the teacher had impatiently cut Vince short with a tactless comment such as, "I'm not sure what you're trying to say here. Farms don't have halos; angels have them. I'm confused about what you mean here . . . we'd better move on. Who's next?" (I hesitate to write this because it stings so much, but I once heard a teacher call a child "stupid" for volunteering a word like *halo*!) A sense of community not only facilitates communication among children and teachers but also helps develop writers who appreciate the freedom to produce new ideas and think creatively without the fear of humiliation.

 Video Exploration 8.2

SUBSEQUENT PERSONAL STORIES

As students flourish within a community of writers, they will begin to revise and edit their writing. Their scribbles will evolve into real letters and words as students write in a journal, diary, or learning log and compose stories of personal experiences—any personal story that can be jotted down with a pen, pencil, keyboard, typewriter (remember those?), papyrus scroll, or clay tablet. Language arts class will help students grow by teaching the *writing process*—prewriting, drafting, revising, editing, and publishing. With your assistance, students will apply the writing process to the various goals and forms of writing found in social studies.

In most cases, subsequent personal stories written by elementary school children will have relatively simple plots and contain a single episode. Emerging writers prefer to create visual images before setting down letters and words, however, so expect them to draw a picture before writing the text. They like to talk about their drawings and quickly show an interest in recording them in print, taking great joy in writing independently. And they take great pride in reading the written versions to their teacher or classmates and taking them home to share with their families. To begin the study of the Jewish traditions surrounding Hanukkah (the "Festival of Lights"), for example, Elizabeth Arya started by listing what the students already knew about the holiday on the whiteboard. She then read *A Picture Book of Hanukkah* by David Adler (Scholastic). Ms. Arya frequently uses picture books as a stimulus for personal story writing because the illustrations offer children something interesting to talk about. Talking not only presents children with an opportunity to explore content and ideas but also to rehearse what they are going to write. Amy, for example, proud of her Jewish heritage, drew a picture and retold the story of Hanukkah as depicted in Figure 8.4.

Children enjoy publishing their own books containing the writing projects in which their class has been involved. It was apparent that publishing was valued in Ms. Arya's classroom by looking at a corner of the room where the sign "GoodBook Publishing Company" was clearly visible. After the writers completed their holiday manuscripts, they took them to the classroom publishing company where they were polished and printed by a staff of expert workers. The class enjoyed being involved in these "behind-the-scenes" publishing departments:

- *Production department.* Puts pictures and stories together and gets them ready for printing. (Students who know how to use a word processor, or who have a desire to learn, can make special contributions here.)
- *Art department.* Designs book covers; illustrates stories, if necessary.
- *Advertising department.* Creates ads (with pictures) that highlight new books.
- *Mechanical department.* Runs the printer or copier, collates the pages, staples them, and gets them ready for distribution. Many books are produced with hard covers.
- *Circulation department.* Places the books in the classroom library and delivers first-printing copies to the principal, other teachers, and classmates.

Upper elementary grade students enjoy reading, writing, and publishing personal stories, too, and, as we saw with their younger counterparts, they need to hear what good personal

FIGURE 8.4   Early-Grade Personal Story

Amy L.
The BAd Gise
SaiD you CAn't
PrAy To god. You
hAve To PrAy To us
not god. And The
BAd reckT Their Houes

But thAt wAs not
nice. And A
Little Kid fouNd
some Oel And
The LiGHt stAd
for eiGHt DAys.

stories are like if they expect to make their own writing better. I like to recommend continuing the practice of reading aloud a picture book written in the first person as a model of personal narrative writing. For students throughout the elementary grades, picture books are excellent models of how stories are created. You can see how this works as I invite you into Mary Novak's fifth-grade classroom to experience her approach to a personal story project.

> After school one day, 10-year-old Graciela flew into her house and declared to no one in particular, "I know just what I'm gonna write about. This is gonna be so cool!" What Graciela was so excited about was a social studies personal story project that her teacher began that day as a way to explore, identify, and express the rich cultural composition of her classroom. That afternoon, Mary Novak read to her fifth graders Cynthia Rylant's enduring personal narrative When I Was Young in the Mountains (Puffin), a tale of her own childhood growing up in the Appalachian mountains of West Virginia. The engagingly repetitive picture book details Rylant's everyday life, from swimming in a swimming hole (among the snakes) to drinking cocoa made by her grandmother.
>
> After mapping the story events and discussing the author's style of beginning each page with the words, "When I was young in the mountains . . . ," Ms. Novak and the children talked about the idea that everyone has a family history and how interesting it would be to bring into the classroom something special representing each child's family heritage.
>
> The children brought home letters asking their parents to help them select a family artifact that had a special story. To help them consider what to bring, Ms. Novak showed her students a cloth doll dressed in traditional Polish garb that her great-grandmother (circa 1910) had brought from Poland when her ancestors emigrated to the United States. She referred to her relatives from the past as her "ancestors" and showed on a map where they came from. Then, holding up the cloth doll for all to see, Ms. Novak told a story to illustrate her point. Ms. Novak's story helped make children aware of how a family's history and culture can be rooted in an artifact. After her story, Ms. Novak went on to explain: "Almost all of your families came from other countries, too, and have interesting stories to tell about special family relics." Ms. Novak then assigned the children the responsibility of bringing an artifact to school and speaking about it for about 3 to 5 minutes, modeling her artifact story: where our ancestors lived before moving to the United States, why our ancestors came to the United

States, when our ancestors moved to the United States, what artifact holds special meaning for our families, why it is important, and a short story connected to the artifact.

On the day of their presentations, the students took turns sharing their family artifacts. Graciela told this story about the pair of colorfully decorated maracas she so anxiously planned to share:

> *My family lived for a long time in a tiny village in the Andes Mountains of Peru. They were farmers who planted gourds in a large section of the farm. When they are dried, gourd shells become very hard and can be used for many things such as bowls or bottles and containers for storing salt and spices. Artists carve and paint special designs on the gourds. These old maracas were made out of gourds. My grandfather told me why these maracas are important to our family. He said that around 200 years ago, people from his tiny village began making regular trips to other villages to trade their gourds, corn, and beans for stuff they needed. One day they met gourd carvers from another village. They taught my ancestors how to carve and decorate gourds. For many years after that, my family's gourds were thought to be the best in all of Peru. When my grandfather and his family moved to the United States, they brought along samples of their work, including these maracas.*

In like manner, other students came to the front of the class, presented a family artifact, and told about its significance. Included were a chunk of ceramic tile from Italy, kente cloth from Ghana, a vintage golf plaque from Scotland, a wood carving from Indonesia, an intricately embroidered shirt from Russia, an old toy from Ireland, a photo of a festival with Native American dancers, and a cookbook from Greece. The class sat spellbound as each item was shared; they spontaneously asked questions about each.

To complete the project, Ms. Novak explained that the class would use the pattern found in Rylant's book to create a digital story about their individual family artifacts. Their class story would be more than just a simple slide show of photos set to music; it would be an actual story made by interweaving different media. Students then drew and wrote down their script on a piece of drawing paper; all the pages were then organized in storyboard form to outline the sequence of events. Modeling Rylant's book, each student's storybook page contained a sentence that began, "When I was young and in . . . ." For example, Graciela drew a picture of a beautifully decorated gourd and wrote, "When I was young and in the Andes Mountains of Peru, I learned to make the best carved and decorated gourds." Each student did the same for his or her family's story. They chose to use a docudrama format to tell their story; it required the students to "step into the shoes" of an artifact's creator as a creative first-person approach for weaving together and telling significant story events.

Since their classroom had Mac computers, the students gathered materials for Apple's iMovie video editing software application. They used images and maps from the Internet, took digital videos and photographs of their family artifacts, scanned old family photos, and selected music to help create the right mood for both the overall story and the individual components. Creating a digital story provided Ms. Novak's students with important opportunities to practice and master a number of specific 21st-century skills, content, and technology standards.

The last part of the digital storytelling process was to share the story with others. They saved their story and watched it repeatedly; they invited other classrooms to view their production. The students were so proud of their digital story that they uploaded it to sites such as YouTube for others to enjoy. Ms. Novak explains that one of the most compelling outcomes of this personal story project was its power to build a sense of community in the classroom.

Teachers like Ms. Novak realize that family history projects can be extremely difficult for children whose families have been touched by adoption, divorce, or the death of a parent, or children who may be from blended families, families with same-sex partners, and so on. The very idea of a family's history can raise questions of belonging and relatedness and can cause divided loyalty, confusion, and, in rare cases, embarrassment. As a result, some youngsters may struggle with the assignment or refuse to participate. Ms. Novak anticipated these possibilities, so she made sure to telephone the parents of children who might have difficulties before she sent home the letters. The parents were appreciative of her consideration. One set of adoptive parents encouraged their daughter to research her birth family while another family refused its child permission to participate in the project. Students and their families have a right to choose how or whether they want to become involved. For example, Carl, whose parents are divorced, now has a stepmother. He decided to bring in two artifacts—one representing each family. By offering suitable help and understanding, teachers can demonstrate a deep respect for their students and for their family's privacy.

Reflection on Learning

You may simply scribble rough notes or jot down something more polished and complete. The point is to simply start recording your ideas spontaneously and candidly.

As children become aware of diverse family structures, they begin to ask a question such as, "Can someone have two daddies?" How can you help your children understand that our nation is becoming a mixture of families of different configurations, beliefs, cultural norms, and personal practices?

As children become more skilled, they will learn that good personal stories, like all stories, have a *setting,* which is usually described early and helps the reader create clear pictures of the physical surroundings. Good personal stories have *characters*: What are their physical and emotional attributes? How do they look, dress, and feel? What do the characters say? What do the characters think? Good personal stories have a *plot,* or sequence of events. The plot describes the action—what the characters do and what happens to them. The plot revolves around conflicts or problems that confront the story's characters and provides an account of the characters' attempts to resolve the problem. These events make up the *story structure*. A most basic three-step story structure is found in most children's stories—beginning, middle, and end. In the beginning the reader is introduced to the characters, the setting, and a conflict or problem that serves to "hook" the reader. The middle takes the reader through a series of complications and obstacles (events) related to the conflict or problem; three events are typical in most elementary-age stories. Tension increases and decreases as each crisis is encountered; the story leads inevitably to the main character's positive change of fortune (the climax). In the end, the tension quickly lessens and the main character's triumph (or downfall) is described. In most picture books, the plot is relatively simple with one main sequence of events, but in chapter books, the plot becomes more complex with one or more subplots that underlie the main events.

By developing an awareness of story structure, students are better able to analyze the plot, make predictions about what may happen from one event to the next, and make better sense of what they are reading. Story maps are popularly used to help whole classes, small groups, or individual readers work with story elements and story structure for better comprehension of narrative text. There are many types of story maps, or graphic organizers. The most basic ones focus on the beginning, middle, and end of the story (see Figure 8.5).

Writing-to-Learn Tasks

It is important for students to write in social studies for different purposes using a variety of standard written formats. Writing to learn involves a personal narrative not primarily intended to communicate facts and information or stir emotions; it is a completely private process designed to informally explore ideas and clarify thoughts associated with the subject matter content of social studies. Writing-to-learn tasks are 3- to 5-minute informal writing activities that call for students to stop, explore their thinking, and briefly note in writing the key concepts or ideas they have been learning about. Students are asked to write about what they have learned, problems they have encountered, what they liked (or did not like) about the lesson, and about how well they understood the concepts. The justification for including writing-to-learn tasks in your social studies program is that the act of writing about thinking helps

FIGURE 8.5   Story Map Graphic Organizer

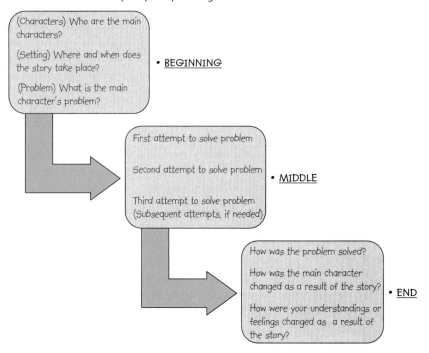

students become deeper thinkers and better learners. Attention is focused on personal ideas and reactions rather than conforming to any "correct" style, grammar, or spelling expectations. A writing-to-learn approach frequently uses journals, logs, responses to written or oral questions, summaries, freewriting, notes, and other writing assignments that align with ideas and concepts under study.

For years, teachers have used informal writing techniques to promote thinking during ongoing instruction. A few additional examples follow. It is important to understand that these strategies should not be used for grading purposes but to provide feedback about what is being understood so that adjustments to instruction can be made as needed:

EXIT TICKETS (INDEX CARD SUMMARIES/QUESTIONS)

1. At the end of the lesson, distribute an "exit ticket" to each student—a piece of paper that looks like a ticket but has space for writing.

2. Ask students a question that requires a summary statement, or the big idea, of the lesson. Determine what single question they should be able to answer to demonstrate that they got the big idea.

3. Give students 3 to 5 minutes to write their answers.

4. It is not necessary for the students to place their names on the exit tickets, but each student should give you one.

5. Review the tickets to learn how many students got the big idea and how well they understand it. This data can be used to guide future instruction.

ADMISSION TICKETS

"Admission tickets" work just like exit tickets except that they are used at the beginning of a lesson rather than at the end. They encourage students to reflect on what they have learned during the previous lesson by tapping into what has been retained from the previous learning activity: "What is an important thing you learned from the last lesson?" "What is a question from the last lesson that you would like answered today?" The students ask a question, hypothesize possible answers, and then summarize information gained through the learning experience.

When writing to learn, students focus on clarifying and organizing their thoughts.

WavebreakMediaMicro/Fotolia

ONE-MINUTE PAPERS

A bit more involved than the exit slip, this technique involves giving the students 1 to 3 minutes to write a brief summary of the key idea or understanding: "What is the most important thing you learned today?" "Take out a piece of paper and tell me what you have learned so far." "What was the most confusing idea presented today?" Collect the papers and use them for promoting discussion or identifying misconceptions. (Some teachers like to use the label "One-Minute Essay" for this assessment strategy, but I have found that the word "essay" often makes children nervous.)

LEARNING LOGS

Learning logs are basically personal journals in which students think about, reflect on, and jot down informal notes about what they are learning. In most cases, students keep these concise and factual records in a notebook, binder, or folder so the documentation is continuous. To begin, you may want to use guiding questions as a prompt to identify or summarize what your students consider to be the most important information from a lesson and to record any questions they may have:

> What did you learn today?
>
> What did you find most interesting?
>
> What did I do on our project today?
>
> How did today's lesson build on yesterday's?
>
> What questions do you have about what you learned?

Be careful not to make this list longer than one or two questions; some students may feel overwhelmed by a long list.

EMAIL OR TWEET

The contemporary nature of emailing or texting can be an attractive alternative to writing notes on paper. Students pause briefly before, during, or after the lesson to send an electronic message to summarize what they want to learn, what they have learned, or what they feel is especially important, interesting, or surprising (or to ask a question about something they are unclear about).

Writing-to-learn responses must be short; give students about 2 minutes to summarize and/or ask questions. Much of the time, their writing will remain uncollected and private; at other times, you will read their writing but not comment on it. If you do respond to the writing, provide only minimal feedback. Sometimes you will want your students to share their writing among peers to stimulate class discussion or to review subject matter content.

 CHECK YOUR UNDERSTANDING 8.1 **Click here** to check your understanding of this section of the chapter.

Historical Fiction

Do you like reading about former times . . . the imagined days of yore? If so, historical fiction is probably for you. Historical fiction can be defined as a literature genre in which stories reconstruct the past; although the facts are true, the story plot is purely a product of the writer's imagination. Inspired by people or events of bygone eras, writers of historical fiction go beyond the straightforward events, dates, and details of history by weaving a story that captures young readers and transports them vicariously to days gone by, helping them to easily make personal connections to the past. Historical fiction, then, sheds light on the past; enriches social studies learning and instruction; and helps connect realism and authenticity to the people, conditions, and events of the past.

Doris Cutler often begins history-themed units with an engaging and informative picture book or chapter book. Before she begins reading aloud, she makes sure to discuss what the students already know about the topic and establishes a sound purpose for reading: "As I read the story, your job will be to find examples of how the main character deals with some very important problems." For example, Mrs. Cutler used historical fiction to awaken the social consciousness of her students through the eyes of Nellie Bly (the penname of Elizabeth Cochrane), a pioneer for women in journalism having the passion to challenge inequitable social conditions and bring about social justice.

Doris Cutler employed a powerful account of sexism to help her students use critical thinking skills: Stop the Presses, Nellie's Got a Scoop! *by Robert Quackenbush (Simon and Schuster). The story centers on a boy and girl who stumble on an old suitcase in the attic. While rummaging through its contents, the two young investigators discover a relic telling of the life of Elizabeth Jane Cochran. Elizabeth was nicknamed "Pink" because she liked wearing that color as a child. In 1880, when Pink was 16 years old, she wrote an anonymous letter, signed "Lonely Orphan Girl," to the editor of the* Pittsburgh Dispatch. *The newspaper had published an article titled "What Girls Are Good For"; the columnist expressed his opinion that women should not be allowed to work because their dutiful place was at home. Days later, a rebuttal appeared in the paper. The response, by Lonely Orphan Girl, whose real name was Elizabeth Jane Cochran, argued how important it was for women to be independent and self-reliant.*

The managing editor of the Dispatch *was so impressed by Pink's forthright style that he ran an ad asking her to identify herself. Instead, she showed up in person and convinced the managing editor to hire her. Pink had landed her first job as a journalist! Since it was considered quite improper at that time for a woman to write for a newspaper, women commonly used pen names. After several suggestions from newsroom workers, Pink and the editor selected "Nellie Bly," the character in a popular song written 35 years earlier by Stephen Foster.*

Not interested in writing fluffy women's interest stories or columns about fashion, Nellie immediately took on meaty stories about social issues—working women, female prisoners, poverty, women's rights, divorce laws, and factory conditions. Her work, controversial at times, sparked social reforms that had been considered necessary for years.

As they learned about the tumultuous life of this vocal spokesperson for women, the children wrote entries in a double-entry journal. In the left column, they jotted down brief notes about significant events in Nellie Bly's life. Then, they recorded their feelings in the right-hand column (see an example in Figure 8.6).

Because children are more likely to become absorbed in history when it comes to them as a story, historical fiction should be a major component in all contemporary social studies programs. By presenting critical issues and multiple perspectives through powerful resources such as historical fiction, teachers help all children learn that people can truly make a difference. In addition to reading historical fiction, your students will enjoy writing stories to portray a time period or historical event. But we do not simply tell the students to open their word-processing programs and write a historical fiction piece. They must be taught the technique. I have found that one of the best ways to facilitate the production of high-quality historical fiction is through helping students construct Storypaths, or unique and engaging stories that students create within the context of particular social studies content.

Storypath

Storypath uses the basic components of a story—setting, characters, and plot—to help students from the second grade on up to actively and imaginatively write meaningful historical fiction. The *Storypath* approach to writing historical fiction was originally developed in Scotland during the 1960s (as *Storyline*) and it has been popularized in the United States by Margit McGuire at Seattle University (1999). *Storypath*'s narrative structure helps students understand concepts that they often find difficult to comprehend in the traditional social studies curriculum. Each *Storypath* unit begins by establishing the setting and

FIGURE 8.6   Double-Entry Journal for Nellie Bly

Nellie Bly's Life Events	My Feelings
Born in Cochran's Mills, PA	Look out world!
Nicknamed "Pink" as a child	I like the color pink, too.
Wrote a letter to a newspaper editor in Pittsburgh complaining about a sexist article	She was brave because women weren't respected then.
Editor asked her to join the paper	I'm glad he liked her "spunk."
Took the name "Nellie Bly"	Women writers could not use their real names.
Wrote articles about women factory workers	She was brave.
At age 21 she went to Mexico and wrote articles criticizing the Mexican government	I would be afraid to get arrested.
Nellie moved to New York City where she wrote about the horrid conditions in women's insane asylums	This brought Nellie lasting fame.
In 1888, Nellie took a trip around the world in 77 days—a world record back then	Nellie became a role model for women everywhere.
In 1894, Nellie retired from journalism and became an industrialist and was president of the Iron Clad Manufacturing Co.	Wow! Now she's a leading women's industrialist. What a woman!
Nellie died in 1922 at age 57	Nellie died young, but had a very full life.

characters for the story. Then, students are confronted with a critical problem that sets the plot in motion.

- *The Setting. The students* make a mural or other visual representation of the topic. *The teacher* reads a short description of the place under study; leads discussion about the place; organizes groups to create murals; facilitates discussion of setting and murals; helps students create a word bank; and asks students to compose a paragraph or two describing the setting.

- *The Characters. The students* add characters to the setting. *The teacher* leads a sustained discussion of the characters they would find in the selected place; facilitates research into the characters; manages the addition of characters to the mural; helps students brainstorm additional words for their word bank; and asks students to compose short biographical sketches of the characters.

- *Context Building. The students* think more deeply and learn more about the setting and characters. *The teacher* helps students develop a deeper knowledge base; scaffolds and facilitates learning; and models how to organize and write a report.

- *Critical Incident. The students* create a problem characteristic of those faced by people of that time and place. *The teacher* helps students think of an appropriate problem; guides thought and discussion about the problem; and asks students to add the problem and its solution to their growing narratives.

- *Concluding Event. The students* engage in an activity that brings closure to the *Storypath*. *The teacher* helps students reflect on their experiences; helps students conclude their *Storypath* experience; and helps prepare for an end-of-unit "happening."

Robert Turner imaginatively transported his students back in time to the bitter winter of 1777 when George Washington and his troops camped at Valley Forge. He asked a friend to visit class one day dressed as a ragtag Revolutionary War soldier named Captain William Howard. Captain Howard introduced himself and informed the students that he had come to tell them about the terrible conditions he faced at Valley Forge during the winter of 1777 when General George Washington marched his tired, beaten, hungry, and sick army to Valley Forge, a location about 20 miles northwest of British-occupied Philadelphia.

SETTING

Captain Howard helped students connect to the conditions at Valley Forge in an engaging and enjoyable way: "*After his defeats at Brandywine and Germantown, General George Washington led us, his army of about 10,000 troops, to Valley Forge, an out-of-the-way place on a hill along the Schuylkill River, about 25 miles from Philadelphia. From Valley Forge, Washington hoped to keep an eye on General Howe's British army camping in Philadelphia. A nearby small valley had once been the site of a blacksmith shop, also known as a forge, so that's why the place became known as Valley Forge. We arrived at Valley Forge on the 19th of December and, eight days later, the deepest snow of the season fell. The next few days brought the winter's bitterest cold. We had little food and not much clothing to protect us from the cold. Tents were our only protection against frost and wind. . . .*" Captain Howard went on to tell about men marching without clothes, blankets, or shoes—leaving bloody trails in the snow as they walked from one place to another. He described food so bad that on Christmas Eve the troops forced down a meal of rice and vinegar. "*Many soldiers ran away . . . deserted,*" he remembered. The students asked Captain Howard a series of questions about the strategic importance of Valley Forge and more about the hardships endured by the soldiers. Establishing a climate of curiosity, with opportunities for discussion, is an important initial component of successful story writing, so after listening to Captain Howard, the students met in small discussion groups.

Following their group discussions, the students designed murals illustrating what they knew about the setting at Valley Forge. Some students thought that the snow-covered rolling hills of Valley Forge would best represent the setting, but others insisted that tents, log huts, campfires, bare-branched trees, heavy gray clouds, and large boulders would make the scene more complete. Still others thought it would be a good idea to add the Schuylkill River in the background, the iron forge in a dell, and a few muddy roads. One group, setting its mural off from the rest, decided that a cutaway view of a crowded log hut would be a good way to portray the setting. The focus of this mural construction activity was not to make an exact replica of the military camp, but to help students express their current understanding of the setting. It is important to remember that the process of designing a mural and talking about it prior to writing is a "rehearsal" process for the actual writing act, not an end in itself. So accuracy is not a major concern at this point. Before many children write, they like to draw a scene and talk about it. Then they write about the scene they have drawn. Called *pictorializing*, this appears to be a useful preparation (or rehearsal) strategy that many young writers use before putting words on paper. Next, the groups brainstormed a list of words to clearly describe the setting depicted on their murals; suggestions ranged from "snowy" and "bitter" to "grungy" and "the pits." The cards were posted around the murals to create a sizeable word bank. To better connect his students to the setting each group had created, Mr. Turner asked each group to use its words and the scene depicted in its mural to write a paragraph or two about the setting. One group wrote this:

> *"The Army was camped on a flat hill overlooking a small valley. The place was called Valley Forge. It was wintertime and very cold. They lived in tents for a while but George Washington gave the troops orders to build log huts. Twelve men lived together in a 16 × 14 foot log hut. Each hut had a stone fireplace. They had dirt floors. The huts were drafty, cold, smoky, and awfully unhealthy."*

CHARACTERS

After describing the setting in picture and words, students moved on to thinking more deeply about their characters after Mr. Turner asked the question, "Who might we have found at Valley Forge?" The class brainstormed a list of people and went to work talking about what they looked like and what they might have been doing. When the students were satisfied with their lists, they added the characters and a descriptive word bank to their landscape murals. The groups named their characters and used their character word bank to write a short biographical description for each. Danusia wrote this character sketch, for example, to describe a pitiful character she painted on her group's mural:

> *Seth Jones is in pitiful shape. He looks like a skeleton sitting next to the smoky fire. No hat, or coat, or shoe—just wrapped in an old, worn blanket. He is pale, skinny, sick, and sad. Just after Christmas, one of his feet and legs froze. A doctor had to cut them off.*

Few descriptions were as heartrending as Danusia's, but most were quite descriptive of the squalor and suffering the troops were forced to endure. Mr. Turner went on to encourage the students to think about how these character descriptions might be connected with others to create interesting story ties.

CONTEXT BUILDING

The purpose of this phase is to help students develop a deeper and clearer understanding of the setting and characters. Mr. Turner chose to facilitate their efforts through the use of a KWL chart. He asked the students leading questions for each column of the chart, such as, "What do you already **know** about Valley Forge?" "What things do you **want to learn** about Valley Forge?" and "What did you **learn** from your research?" The students thought it would be a good idea to search the Internet by using keywords that took them to websites where information could be found.

To supplement the Internet research, Mr. Turner suggested, "I could have also used this interesting book, *The Winter of Red Snow: The Revolutionary War Diary of Abigail Jane Stewart, Valley Forge, Pennsylvania, 1777* by Kristiana Gregory (Scholastic). It's a diary written by an

11-year-old named Abigail Jane Stewart who describes the winter of 1777 when she witnessed the struggles of George Washington and his soldiers. I'm going to see if I could find how the soldiers handled daily chores such as cooking and laundry." Mr. Turner found the information and entered it on the chart under the **L** column. He encouraged the students to follow his example to uncover interesting and appropriate information to answer to their questions.

The students used their new information to add, delete, or change things on their murals and descriptive paragraphs. Below, one group tells about an interesting feature it added to its mural:

We were surprised to find that Washington's army was not just men soldiers. We found out that there were also women and children. And there were 755 African American soldiers at Valley Forge. Black and white soldiers fought together, got paid the same, and wore the same uniforms.

CRITICAL INCIDENT

Two major story elements were now addressed—setting and characters; all the students needed was a plot—an interesting sequence of events. To engage the reader, a good plot must provocatively engage the reader in the story's problem and solution. With their setting and characters firmly in mind, the students recalled the original visit from Captain Howard to identify and explore a major question in-depth and use supporting questions to gather details.

After careful examination, the students decided on the following *major question* (problem) on which to build their critical incident: "How did the conditions at Valley Forge affect the Continental Army?" Next, they prepared a list of *supporting questions* designed to pull out the information needed to address the problem:

- What were the weather conditions like at Washington's camp?
- How did the weather affect the living conditions?
- What was life like at Valley Forge?
- How might it feel to live in this camp?
- How did Washington's leadership help form a strong fighting force?
- Who helped Washington develop and carry out worthwhile change?
- What might a historian say about the events at Valley Forge?

Mr. Turner's students once again used their search strategy for locating web information by closely examining supporting questions for keywords and using the keyword pool to help locate useful information.

CONCLUDING EVENT

The culmination of *Storypath* is an inquiry-induced story that helps students make publicly known what they have learned; in this case, Mr. Turner used a dynamic approach to writing called *digital storytelling*. As the name implies, digital storytelling involves the use of computer tools to tell stories, typically in the form of movies or interactive slide shows. Digital stories employ a mixture of computer-based images, text, recorded audio narration, video clips, and/or music. They can vary in length, but most digital stories in elementary schools last from 2 to 5 minutes.

To begin their digital stories, the students searched for audio resources (such as music, speeches, and sound effects), image resources (such as pictures, drawings, and photographs), and text resources (from websites or their word-processed information paragraphs). They saved these resources in folders created on their desktops. Next, the students took the first step in composing their stories by using a process called *storyboarding*. They illustrated their stories panel by panel, much as in a comic book, with simple stick figures and basic shapes (or cut out pictures from magazines). Next, they wrote a script from their research, working with short but informative sentences to describe each of the storyboard panels. With script in hand, they moved into the production phase, selecting from among a number of computer tools, including Windows Movie Maker, Apple's iMovie, or Microsoft's Photo Story. Web-based tools such as Digital Storyteller also offer students access to digital images, music, and sound effects. Finally, the students shared their stories with their classmates, other classrooms, and parents.

Santiago's group created the digital story shown below, complete with inspirational sound and images, about the leaders who helped turn the Continental Army into a trained fighting force.

> *George Washington was a great general, but troop spirit was very low and there wasn't very much military skill at the Valley Forge camp. There was a lot of gambling and fighting. Some soldiers even walked away from camp and went home when they wanted to. The men were brave, but they didn't know how to march together or even how to move on the battlefield. Someone said that they knew how to use their bayonets more for cooking over a fire than for fighting. All this changed when Baron von Steuben came to Valley Forge in February. He made sure they kept the camp clean and sanitary. He drilled the men and trained them until they were a mean fighting machine. Their spirits grew. The men loved Baron von Steuben.*

 CHECK YOUR UNDERSTANDING 8.2 **Click here** to check your understanding of this section of the chapter.

Folktales

A genre as old as language itself, folktales are "stories of the people" that were originally passed down by the oral tradition from one generation to the next. A cherished practice of every culture since ancient times when people huddled around campfires sharing stories to explain and understand the natural and spiritual world, storytellers used many dramatic techniques

So much to think about. . . . Is the text interesting? Is the information accurate? Is it organized clearly and logically?

WavebreakMediaMicro/Fotolia

to bring their stories to life. Folktales reflect the values and customs of the culture from which they come.

Folktales include fables, fairy tales, and old legends—stories of giants, witches, ogres, magical helpers, heroes, and tricksters. They often contained moral "lessons," thereby effectively shedding light on a culture's traditional values, and customs: Tortoise teaches us that we should never give up despite the odds and Anansi teaches us that deceiving others is wrong. Folktales often include struggles such as good versus evil, wise versus foolish, beauty versus unattractiveness, age versus youth, stinginess versus charity, or rich versus poor—the message is key. As exemplified by Olga Danko, folktales are great resources for read alouds in your classroom. Using one of the books in her thematic unit, "Folktales around the World," Mrs. Danko reads Jan Brett's popular Ukrainian folktale, *The Mitten* (G.P. Putnam's Sons). The story is about a little boy named Nicki who asks his grandmother (Baba) to knit him a pair of snow-white mittens. She warns Nicki that white mittens would be hard to find if he loses one in the snow, and he promptly loses a fancy white mitten while in the woods looking for some firewood. The animals found his lost mitten and crawled inside to keep warm. The parade started with a mole, who was joined by a rabbit, hedgehog, owl, badger, fox, and bear. To everyone's surprise, all were able to fit inside the mitten until the tiny mouse joined them. The mouse's whiskers tickled the bear's nose, causing him to sneeze, "Aaaaa-aaaaa-ca-chew!" and the entire mass of animals took wing. As the mitten soared through the air, Nicki retrieved it and took it home to his smiling Baba. Mrs. Danko used the story to help her students learn about the Ukrainian culture as well as to teach reading skills such as predicting and sequencing.

To build a common background of knowledge prior to the start of the reading experience, Mrs. Danko reached into her story basket (a large picnic basket that holds a hidden surprise associated to the books she reads). Filled with anticipation, the children begged Mrs. Danko to open the basket so they could see what special surprises were waiting inside today. Because Brett's book contains detailed artwork with intricate borders and elegant embroidered details of Ukrainian tradition, Mrs. Danko decided that today's surprise must exhibit those kinds of ornate folk details. So, she cautiously reached into the basket and drew out a beautiful shirt from a Ukrainian folk costume that she had borrowed from a friend. The children were fascinated by the intricate adornment and elaborate embroidery. She showed the children a photograph of a Ukrainian family dressed in similar traditional attire. Mrs. Danko explained that this folk costume was from Ukraine, a large country in Eastern Europe, and together they located the Ukraine on a globe.

Mrs. Danko reached into the basket once more and carefully removed a pair of white mittens. She and the children talked about occasions when they wear mittens and why the mittens are important on a cold winter's day. She asked the children if they had ever lost a mitten and how the mitten on the cover might have gotten lost in the woods. Then, examining the expressions on the animals' faces, she asked the children to think about what might go through an animal's mind if it saw a mitten lying on the ground in the forest. She elicited several ideas and then went on to read the story.

After the story was finished, the discussion began. The children did not raise their hands in response to the teacher's questions, but joined in a natural, spontaneous conversation about the book. As they talked, Mrs. Danko listened and helped the children make connections. But the children, not Mrs. Danko, determined the flow of the conversation. The following day, Mrs. Danko reread the book and, using cutouts of the mitten and animal characters, she invited the students to help retell the story. Next, the class focused on the diverse animal life in Ukraine and even sang together a popular animal song from Ukraine while Mrs. Danko clicked on the digital projector to display animal names and animal pictures as they entered into the song. She focused on the action words Brett used to describe the animals' movements—swoop, lumber, trot, snuffle, bump and jostle—and asked her children to mimic these movements.

Sticking to the animal theme, Mrs. Danko then focused on the theme of the book— friendship and generosity. Capturing that theme, Mrs. Danko told the children about a group of compassionate animal lovers in Ukraine who have been concerned about a very serious animal-related problem there. It seems that there is a lack of everything needed to help abandoned household pets found roaming village and city streets—time, money, food, and people willing to help. Mrs. Danko described the plans of the animal lovers to build and staff animal aid centers where these unfortunate animals would be treated and helped back into a new life. Toward the end of this conversation, the children's interests turned into: "What can we do to help?"

The purposes of cultural folktales are to recognize the common elements of the genre, establish connections between folktales and the cultures from which they originated, and determine the relationship between the key ideas and the central message, or lesson. *The Mitten* not only triggered these outcomes in Mrs. Danko's students, but also aroused their empathy toward a very serious problem involving animals and the people of Ukraine.

As students are helped to analyze folktales, they will learn the characteristics of the genre and use them as models to create original tales of their own. Talk with your students about how they can use the story that was read as a model for their own version. Encourage them to brainstorm possibilities for a story that tries to explain something, help cope with the world in which they live, or teach a lesson or moral. Could they use the structure of *The Mitten* as a model to write an original story about another culture such as *The Sombrero* or *The Leprechaun Hat*? Once they make their topic choice, help your students organize a storyboard (a series of pictures like the panels of a comic strip) to organize their characters and setting as well as the plot—beginning, middle, and end. Next, ask your students to write several sentences or even a paragraph for each picture. They may read the sentences to a peer and request any feedback such as what information might be missing or what might make the story more interesting. After making the changes, the students will be ready to write a final version of the folktale complete with an illustrated cover informing readers of the title and author.

 CHECK YOUR UNDERSTANDING 8.3   **Click here** to check your understanding of this section of the chapter.

Fantasy

Fantasy is based on imaginative events or stories that lie outside the normal boundaries of the real world. The genre includes elements that are unrealistic, impossible, or unreasonable, such as talking animals, toys, or objects and magical powers. Fantasy stories are often filled with strange or different characters: Winnie the Pooh, Pinocchio, the Indian in the Cupboard, Harry Potter, James and the Giant Peach, or Bunnicula. When you read stories about these characters, it is easy to spot the major elements of fantasy: magical objects, imaginary places, invented languages, nonhuman characters, and a good versus evil plot line. There appear to be three ways fantasy stories take place: (1) some begin in a magical world and move to the real world, (2) some begin in the real world and move to a magical world, and (3) some take place entirely in a magical world. Using fantasy in social studies may seem inappropriate or frivolous to some, but these stories are highly useful instructional resources for the elementary school classroom; they challenge children's imaginations in powerful, constructive ways. One of the most obvious benefits of fantasy is that it is a perfect match with the imaginary life of young children; fantasy invites children to bring their natural fantasy world into the classroom.

George White and his students, for example, took a fantasy jaunt around the country without having to leave the confines of their classroom. Mr. White felt that a fantasy children's picture book would be a good way to introduce his fourth graders to the topography of their state—Ohio. It may seem like an odd match, but the book Mr. White selected was Lynn Cherry's *The Armadillo from Amarillo* (Voyager Books). Although Sasparillo's story deals with the landscape of Texas and not Ohio, Mr. White felt the book would serve as an excellent model for his children as they started exploring, and eventually writing about, their own state. He is convinced that quality social studies–themed literature can be an excellent model for a wide range of integrated reading and writing activities. Sasparillo the armadillo wants to know where on Earth he is, so he embarks on a trip from his home in San Antonio, Texas and treks northward through the state to Amarillo. There, he meets an eagle who gives him a true bird's eye view and helps him find an answer to his question. Stunning illustrations depict the distinguishing terrains of the Texas landscape—canyons, woodlands, prairies, and plains—and inset postcards that Sasparillo sends back to his cousin Brillo in the Philadelphia Zoo add further information and appeal. While the storyline of this book is obviously fantasy, the geographical information is accurate.

After Mr. White read the story, he helped the students chart the sequence of cities Sasparillo visited on his journey through Texas. As they analyzed The Armadillo from Amarillo, *the students began to sense how they might use it as a model to create their own stories about the topography of Ohio. Mr. White kicked off the study of Ohio by challenging his students to answer the main question from the book, "Do you know where on Earth you are?"*

Mr. White began this exploration by challenging his children to imagine they were Sasparillo flying high above their school: "What do you think Sasparillo would see if he flew on an eagle's back directly over our school?" After a short discussion, Mr. White directed the students to the classroom computers where they visited the TerraServer-USA website and NASA's Earth from Space site. Some students preferred Google Earth; it mixes satellite images with aerial photographs to provide interesting models of various locations, too. They visited the TerraServer-USA website, entered their school's address, and clicked on the "Go" button. The children were awestruck at seeing what their school looked like from high above. "You can actually see a picture of our school from a satellite camera high in the sky," the students marveled, "just like Sasparillo!" Their curiosity soared as they entered other addresses of interest, including their homes. At a key point, Mr. White challenged the children once more by asking, "What do you imagine Sasparillo would see if he flew over the entire state of Ohio?" Mr. White recorded each idea on large chart paper for everyone to see.

Mr. White divided the class into four research groups—one for each region. They discovered that Ohio has four distinctive topographical regions—the foothills of the Allegheny Mountains in the eastern half of the state; the Erie Lakeshore, extending for nearly three-fourths of the northern boundary; the Bluegrass Region trickling north from Kentucky; and the Central Plains in the western half of the state. Each group was responsible for writing, illustrating, and publishing a descriptive story of its region. The students got to work exploring a variety of resources, including the Internet, to find out about the topography of Ohio. Using Sasparillo's trip through Texas as a model for their project, the students decided that the northern part of the Appalachian Plateau should be illustrated with rolling hills and valleys. The southern part of the Appalachian Plateau would show steep hills and valleys because it is the most rugged part of the state. The Erie Lakeshore could be illustrated with fertile lowlands and beaches of clay and sand. The children decided that the Bluegrass Region, spilling north from Kentucky, would be represented by hilly and gently rolling land, but they couldn't decide how to show that the soil is thin and, for the most part, not very useful. The children found that the gently rolling landscape of the Central Plains is one of the most fertile farming regions in the United States. They had no trouble deciding that this gently rolling landscape would be represented by illustrations of thriving, productive farms.

The students reexamined the illustrations in The Armadillo from Amarillo *and decided that, in order to communicate the most information, they would model Cherry's technique of drawing features both as Sasparillo would see them as he flew over them and from the side. Continuing to model Cherry's book, the groups labeled and wrote a brief rhyme of what their drawing illustrated, added inset postcards that would be sent to Brillo in Philadelphia, and pulled each section together into a book describing what Sasparillo saw when he flew over Ohio. The class named its book* The Armadillo from Ohio.

A helpful resource for assessing and selecting quality narratives for elementary school students is *Notable Children's Trade Books for Young People*, compiled annually since 1972 by the Children's Book Council in cooperation with the Book Review Committee of the National Council for the Social Studies (NCSS). The annotated book list is published once a year in the NCSS journal *Social Education*.

After using narratives of any genre, children will react differently. Some will want to talk about what they enjoyed most about the book while others will focus on a favorite character, a similar book or event in their own lives, or whether or not the characters and setting were believable. Give children some time to express their feelings about a story they have read or listened to. Resist the temptation to pepper them with factual questions or other comprehension activities until they have had a chance to talk about their personal and emotional reactions to the text. Regardless of their choice, a good book draws out feelings and establishes a personal relationship with the reader. For that reason, the focus of initial discussion should not be on information but on eliciting personal images and emotions. I like to compare this experience to a discussion you might have with friends after viewing a particularly good movie. Chances are that your comments will focus on feelings and emotions ("The ending brought me to tears because . . . .") rather than someone asking ad nauseam a string of questions about specific facts ("Let's see, who played the title role? Where did it take place? When did it happen . . . ?). Facts will enter your discussion ("How sad, I didn't realize Lincoln was shot on Good Friday, just 5 days after Lee surrendered in Virginia."), but primarily because they affect your feelings.

In addition to encouraging students to share their personal reactions, teachers help them make sense of the text through environments that support active, purposeful reading. Text comprehension can be enhanced by instruction that helps students use specific comprehension strategies, such as the suggestions contained in Chapter 7 under the heading, Strategies for Reading Informational Text.

Reflection on Learning

You may simply scribble rough notes or jot down something more polished and complete. The point is to simply start recording your ideas spontaneously and candidly.

Current pressures on academic achievement are causing social studies teachers to move away from fantasy and traditional storybooks toward information texts. Should you resist the rush or join the crowd?

 CHECK YOUR UNDERSTANDING 8.4   Click here to check your understanding of this section of the chapter.

I love to write so much that I dream of publishing my stories some day!

WavebreakMediaMicro/Fotolia

Poetry

Carole Simpson, a fourth-grade teacher, has been captivated by the attraction of poetry. Her classroom echoes with the sounds of poetry several times each day. "We *need* poetry in our classrooms; our young children *need* poetry in their lives," declares Ms. Simpson. "We don't analyze it; we don't memorize it; we don't deconstruct it or try to uncover its deep meanings. We just *enjoy* poetry!" Unfortunately, poetry does not appear to receive the same attention in many classrooms. Most teachers appear to be much more captivated by other literature genres. I've often had informal discussions with classroom teachers about this state of affairs and have come to the conclusion that, because so many teachers have had personal experiences as students with giving only the "correct interpretation" of poems and dissecting the symbolism of selected poetry, they have developed a dislike for poetry and resist sharing it with their students. In professional workshops, I try to convince skeptics that there is much more to poetry than memorizing it or analyzing it, and try to help them sense the magic of poetry by demonstrating how enjoyable and powerful it can be. We start out by reading lots of poetry. I find light, humorous verse an especially appropriate way to begin. Shel Silverstein's and Jack Prelutsky's lighthearted poems about childhood seem to strike a sentimental chord in everyone's heart. Their rhythmic, light verse serves as a great bridge leading to appreciation of poetry in general. We continue sharing poetry and discussing how it can be connected to the curriculum with no overall goal in mind other than building appreciation. It is surprising to see how soon teachers are finding and sharing poems they want to use in their classrooms. Vardell (2003) explains, "That is the key: providing open access to poetry without roadblocks of formal analysis. Opportunity for in-depth responding and understanding can follow [after we] create an environment for spontaneous pleasure in poetry" (pp. 206–207).

Poetry fits exceptionally well into social studies. Vardell (2003) maintains, "Poetry is not just for reading, writing, and language arts. It's [sic] brevity, conceptual focus, and rich vocabulary also make it a natural teaching tool for the content areas, social studies, science, and mathematics" (p. 208). How do we go about sharing poetry in social studies? Vardell (2003) suggests seven strategies for making poems come alive with students by reading them aloud. The strategies are presented in order of difficulty, starting with greater teacher involvement and ending with increased student involvement. As with my workshop teachers, the first step in inviting children into the oral world of poetry is simply reading poems aloud to the class.

1. *Teacher modeling.* Select poems you enjoy personally; then share them with expression and enthusiasm. If possible, display the words on a whiteboard or with a projector. Seeing the words while hearing the words is additionally beneficial.

2. *Read the poem in unison.* Now that the students have heard the poem read aloud, invite them to join you in a "concert read aloud" (if they haven't already jumped in). Choose shorter poems with a strong rhythm, and read the poem aloud first as a model. Even nonreaders can join in because the text is very predictable.

3. *Students join in on a repeated line or refrain.* This third strategy requires that students consider timing and join in only when their word or line appears. However, they still participate as group members, with no obligation to perform individually. As always, the teacher models the process by reading the poem aloud first; in repeated readings, students join in on a line or refrain that is regularly repeated in the poem.

4. *Two student groups: call and response.* Once students are familiar with reading aloud parts of poems, divide the class in half to read poems in a "call and response" method where parts are read alternately (sometimes, parts may be read simultaneously). The best poems for this poetry performance strategy are those whose lines are structured in a back and forth manner or those with two clearly different points of view.

5. *Multiple groups; multiple stanzas.* As these group read-aloud strategies become familiar, the students will want to confront greater challenges. Using multiple small groups

is the next step. Obviously, with more groups, the number of students reading a part will become smaller. This puts the spotlight on fewer students; thus, the reading may take more practice. But since students have previously enjoyed unison and large-group read-alouds, adjusting to smaller reading groups is not usually a problem.

6. *Individual solo lines.* Some poems are listlike in their structure; these work well for "line-around" or "child-a-line" choral reading in which each line is read by a different student. As students become more experienced, they will enjoy suggesting which lines will be most effectively read by the whole class, small groups, or individuals.

7. *Singing poems.* One final strategy for performing poetry is to try singing the poems by matching them to familiar tunes that contain the same meter, such as "Row, Row, Row Your Boat" or "Mary Had a Little Lamb." This is not a particularly complicated process, but can be enchantingly fun. Students of all ages love the connection between music and poems.

One of the most enjoyable forms of writing in social studies is poetry, a genre that inspires children to put together words in refreshing, novel ways. Help your students recognize the power of poetry by reading lots of it. Since nursery rhymes are the first poems children usually listen to, it would be helpful to select from a range of funny and silly poems as well as poems with entertaining rhythm and rhyme. And children seem to love listening to and reciting poems loaded with nonsense words. Children love rhymes and quickly learn to identify rhyming words in stories. Even with wide exposure to poetry, however, you will find that they require help when venturing to write their own poems. Two forms of poetry are especially applicable for social studies classrooms: *free-form verse*, in which children choose words freely to express their thoughts without concern for rhyme or a particular structure; and *structured poetry*, using formal structures such as rhyming couplets, haiku, diamante, or cinquain to help students convey ideas about the topics they are studying. After listening to a number of poems, for example, Algonquin Patee developed an interest in writing his own poetry. He penned a *free-form poem* in which he expressed some of his positive (and maybe not-so-positive) characteristics. Notice in Figure 8.7 how he made several attempts to use rhythm and rhyme to bring his poem to life.

Your students should understand that not all poems rhyme, but many do contain rhyming words. As students develop as readers and writers of poetry, there are many more poetry

FIGURE 8.7 Young children enjoy rhythm, rhyme, and sound in poetry

activities that can serve to inspire their inate creativity. Here is an example of a *structured poetry* social studies experience:

As with all abstract concepts taught in her classroom, Rosa Muñoz knew that she must approach the topic of chronological thinking with materials and activities that were attention-grabbing, authentic, and understandable. To begin, Mrs. Muñoz drew the outline of a calendar on a large sheet of yellow paper covering a bulletin board. In the space where a picture or illustration normally appears on a commercial calendar, she simply attached a stick in which she had cut ten notches and this title:

Moon of Starting Winter
A Lakota Sioux Calendar

Mrs. Muñoz selected this title and notched stick because her students had been making headway through a unit on Native Americans and both are very significant in the moon-based calendar system of the Lakota Sioux. She often chooses a good book to introduce new ideas like these and, in this case, read Eve Bunting's sensitive picture book, Moonstick: The Seasons of the Sioux *(HarperTrophy). The book describes the 13 moons of the Sioux year and how they are marked on a "moonstick," a branch that has been decorated with painted symbols and beadwork. A new notch is cut into a stick as each moon passes, 13 notches marking the course of each year. Mrs. Muñoz was careful to emphasize how the Lakota Sioux marked time by naming the passing moons according to seasonal qualities: "Planting Moon," "Hunger Moon," "Thunder Moon."*

The students examined the bare calendar carefully and questioned Mrs. Muñoz about the whereabouts of their regular commercial calendar. "We're going to try something new this month," announced Mrs. Muñoz. "All we have to do is come up with some important things to say about the Lakota Sioux." The students generated a large chart summarizing what they had learned throughout the unit of study. After all the ideas were charted, Mrs. Muñoz informed the students that their information would be used for the calendar. Next, Mrs. Muñoz took a rectangular precut piece of white drawing paper (2" × 4") so that, when folded horizontally in the middle, the resulting squares would fit into the boxes on the calendar template (2" × 2"). On the top fold of her sample square, Mrs. Muñoz drew a Lakota Sioux thunderbird and printed the word "wanji" beneath it. She attached the drawing to the outlined calendar square immediately beneath the label Tuesday, the first day of the month of Waniyatu Wi *(Moon of Starting Winter), which corresponds to our month of November.*

"Here's how it works," she said. "First, look at my paper square with the word "wanji" (wanchi) on the front. In the Lakota number system, wanji is "one." I've decorated it with a thunderbird because it illustrates that the thunderbird was a powerful spirit in the form of a bird. Now I'm going to select something from our information bank that tells about the importance of the thunderbird in the lives of the Sioux and write a two-line rhyme about it on the inside . . . here it is." Mrs. Muñoz flipped up the top and revealed her rhyme:

Thunderbird is the mighty one
Who makes the thunder, blocks the sun.

Mrs. Muñoz explained that a rhyming couplet is a pair of lines that rhyme. Usually they have the same meter, but not always. After working with the students to examine the rhythm and rhyme of her couplet, Mrs. Muñoz gave the students a blank piece of paper like hers and assigned each a number. "Use the information chart to come up with an idea for your date," she instructed. "First, however, we must review the Lakota number system." Stressing the unique vowel sounds and other special intonations, Mrs. Muñoz and her students took a fresh look at the Lakota numbers.

The air grew still as the eager young minds went to work. After a few minutes, Hannah's hand shot into the air as she proudly announced:

"Today is saglogan, or November nine,
My arm band is made from quills of porcupine."

"Good thinking!" Mrs. Muñoz and the children declared. "And it rhymes just like some poems do!"

"Wait . . . I've got one, too," shouted Harry with great pride:

> *"I am yamni—also known as day three*
> *Old time Lakota Sioux ate about three pounds of buffalo meat a day, dear me!"*

"What an interesting choice," beamed Mrs. Muñoz. "I like the way you used the amount of buffalo meat to match the date."

The students continued to work on writing their Lakota number poetry and creatively illustrating their assigned dates on the paper squares. In a short time, all were finished and the Waniyatu Wi calendar was complete. Each day, the students marked the date by taking turns reading their poems from their calendar. Buoyed by her success, Mrs. Muñoz expanded the poetry social studies calendar curriculum each month to include calendars from other cultures: a Roman version complete with Roman numerals for the dates and Latin names for the month (Februarius) and days of the week (Dies Saturni for Saturday), a Mayan calendar adaptation, and an Egyptian version.

Without doubt, the most important reason for writing in social studies is to accurately and convincingly communicate ideas. But there are other matters that must be addressed before a written piece is considered complete: Is the student's writing interesting, authentic, and believable? Does it have accurate content that is well-organized and reasonable? What about proper grammar, spelling, and punctuation? Yes, the ideas are very important in content-area writing, but grammar rules and the mechanics of writing are also critical components of learning to write in social studies. Good writing skills and mechanics allow students to convey their ideas in a clear and understandable way.

Let us assume that your students have worked eagerly to complete their heartfelt writing in a clear and understandable way. Is there anything else for you to do other than have them hand in their masterpieces for a grade? You bet there is! You are now confronted with the responsibility

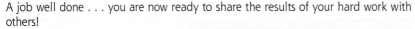

A job well done . . . you are now ready to share the results of your hard work with others!

AVAVA/Shutterstock

of helping your students share their finished writing with an authentic audience; sharing assigns a strong sense of importance to the students' writing. Sharing can be accomplished in a variety of ways, and with the help of computers, their writing can even be printed or published online:

- read it orally to classmates or to other classrooms (an author's chair is a genuine and delightful way to do this)
- tack it on a bulletin board
- send it to someone (for example, a pen pal)
- make it into a book to be kept in the school library
- publish it on the Internet or classroom website
- share with other classrooms around the country (or the world) through collaborative Internet projects
- combine it with other works and print it as a class book
- post it on the refrigerator (just checking to see if you're paying attention!)

 Video Exploration 8.3

Reflection on Learning

You may simply scribble rough notes or jot down something more polished and complete. The point is to simply start recording your ideas spontaneously and candidly.

Some of your students will not have developed the literacy skills sufficient to be successful learners in social studies; others will have very advanced skills. How will you differentiate instruction for such diverse learners?

 CHECK YOUR UNDERSTANDING 8.5 **Click here** to check your understanding of this section of the chapter.

A Final Thought

Would you feel comfortable teaching your students about life in ancient Egypt without reading books? What about having your students share the results of their social studies investigations without writing a word? Your answers to both questions are quite obvious. Literacy is an irreplaceable component of learning in social studies, an intricate element that no other resource can ever hope to supplant. That is why teaching in ways that integrate literacy and social studies is acknowledged as a major goal of the contemporary elementary school curriculum. Regrettably, however, the connections between these two naturally affiliated subjects are not often as clear as we would like them to be. Forced connections outside of meaningful contexts occasionally hinder the curriculum integration process and diminish the value of integrated learning.

Much like some marriages, I've seen curriculum integration start out with exuberance and passion only to end in bitterness and estrangement. Those that have succeeded, however, seemed to start out by knowing as much as possible about the partnership, including the potential of each participant to contribute to the union. If curriculum partners were similar, the union may have started out comfortably, but it may not have been what the students needed to experience success. Conversely, it seems that each component of successful curriculum partnerships brought something important and something different to the table; each participant complemented the other's character and individuality and had a desire to make the union work. As far as the social studies/literacy partnership is concerned, each brings something important and complementary to the table; social studies has its content orientation and literacy brings its skills emphasis. And neither ally in this winning partnership is averse to being dependent on the other . . . they each have the other's back! Literacy and social studies seem to blend together without a glitch; merging social studies with literacy is fundamentally natural and uncomplicated. By properly blending their power and worth, both literacy and social studies will be seen by students as jointly permeating life and not as unrelated entities subsisting in isolation.

It seems that as you begin to steadily deepen your understanding of how to support student learning through curriculum integration, you will identify more and better ways for social studies and literacy to jointly contribute to students' understanding of our world. As you do this, both subjects will take on a livelier, more accessible nature and become more personally meaningful for the students. By understanding the sophisticated interactions of literacy and social studies, you will learn to build creative learning activities that help students acquire and communicate key ideas rather than just providing them with disconnected facts and skills. In considering those activities, however, you must first maintain the strength of the curriculum bond by judging whether or not the activity has the potential to deliver goal-relevant benefits and then deciding whether or not the students will find the activity interesting and enjoyable.

References

Fulwiler, T., & Young, A. (Eds.). (2000). *Language connections: Writing and reading across the curriculum.* Retrieved from WAC Clearinghouse Landmark Publications in Writing Studies: http://wac.colostate.edu/books/language_connections/

Hughes, R. (2013). Why historical fiction writing? Helping students think rigorously and creatively. *Social Studies and the Young Learner, 26,* 17–23.

McGwire, M. E. (1999). *Storypath foundations: An innovative approach to teaching social studies.* Chicago, IL: Everyday Learning Corporation.

Vardell, S. M. (2003). Poetry for social studies: Poems, standards, and strategies. *Social Education, 67,* 206–211.

SECTION FOUR

Lenses on Learning: Six Social Sciences

Section 4 focuses on the six core disciplines and their respective content, tools, and investigative processes from which your students will draw as they attempt to uncover and discover significant curricular content about human beings and the way we function: history, geography, civics, economics, anthropology, and sociology. Each has its own set of *content lenses, tools lenses,* and *process lenses* through which your students will filter and focus the unique story of our human experience. Content lenses refer to the subject matter knowledge required of students to be active and engaged citizens. Learning about the Magna Carta, for example, will require the use of two content lenses—history and civics, while exploring forms of government will require only one content lens—civics. Tools lenses are the specialized implements or devices students will use as they investigate the disciplines. Application of a geography tools lens is activated as students search a product map to locate the most productive coffee-growing region of Colombia; sociology tools lenses lead students to creating a questionnaire to find out what their peers think about the need for a community swimming pool. And process lenses help your students find just the right intellectual operations that help students-citizens become sophisticated users of knowledge from each discipline—inquiry, decision making, problem solving, critical thinking, reasoning, and so on. You are encouraged to help learners apply these three unique lenses to attain a clear view of the world in which they live.

Young Historians:
Learning to Unlock the Past

Learning Outcomes

History provides identity, helps us understand the past and present, assists us in making wise decisions, presents models of good citizenship, teaches us how to learn from the mistakes of others, and provides a context from which to understand how the world works and how human beings behave. Despite these positives, history is perhaps the most contentious of all school subjects. Some people regard history as a useless school subject while others feel it is indispensable to our democratic society. There are many ways to discuss this quandary, but for now, we will use the argument put forward by those advocating a central role of history in our schools: If we want our students to see ahead more clearly, they must learn to assess where we've been. Why is it important to study history? How can we make history a subject that everyone likes? What can we do to make social studies more interesting and enjoyable for our students? After completing this chapter, you will be able to:

- Describe what students should know or be able to do in history and use that knowledge to make appropriate instructional decisions.

- Select strategies appropriate for helping students develop concepts of chronology.

- Describe how to utilize comprehension strategies with historical text.

- Explain historical analysis and interpretation strategies designed to make students thoughtful readers of historical narrative.

- Devise approaches that enlarge and enrich students' historical research capabilities.

- Create pedagogically sound techniques for developing historical issues analysis and decision-making skills.

Classroom Snapshot

Kathleen Anderson uses biographies quite extensively in her social studies program because she feels that this literary genre offers children one of the best sources for learning about the extraordinary accomplishments of important people from the past. So, while planning for the upcoming Presidents Day federal holiday in February, Miss Anderson wanted her children to learn that there is a lot more to the holiday than being a great weekend for sales. Presidents' Day began as a holiday honoring the February birthday of George Washington (the holiday is still officially known as Washington's Birthday) and then added the February birthday of Abraham Lincoln, but has now changed to become a day commemorating all presidents. So, Miss Anderson decided that Presidents Day would be an excellent context to help her children learn about the life and achievements of a number of America's past presidents.

To open their classroom's Presidents Day celebration, Miss Anderson read Catherine Stier's book, If I Were President (Albert Whitman). It is a simple but informative picture book in which children describe what their lives would be like if they became president of the United States. Then Miss Anderson grouped together five books as a text set of presidential biographies and assigned a text set to each group:

Group 1: George Washington: First President 1789–1797 by Mike Venezia (Children's Press);

Group 2: Abraham Lincoln—Lawyer, Leader, Legend (DK Publishing, Author);

Group 3: Meet Thomas Jefferson by Marvin Barrett and Pat Fogarty (Random House);

Group 4: George W. Bush: Forty-Third President by Mike Venezia (Children's Press); and

Group 5: Theodore Roosevelt: Champion of the American Spirit by Betsy Harvey Kraft (Clarion).

The groups finished reading their books independently, discussed them, and created charts highlighting the major accomplishments of their respective presidents. Normally, Miss Anderson stops there for she maintains that young readers do not want to experience elaborate responses to every book they read. "If they were assigned to do a project for every book they read, they'd quickly lose interest in reading!" Miss Anderson contends. However, she decided this presidents learning sequence was one that needed to be expanded on this important federal holiday. The stories not only motivated her students' thinking and cognitive development, but the students became deeply involved in the stories and connected with their presidents. Therefore, Ms. Anderson tapped her store of successful strategies and ideas to bring the stories closer to the children's lives. Ms. Anderson considered several alternative possibilities, but settled on having her students plan a "dinner party" where the presidents (role played by student volunteers) would be the honored guests.

To prepare, the students addressed some very important issues of protocol, or code of etiquette. Their tasks were divided among several groups:

Invitations. This group designed dinner invitations for the guests. The invitations included not only the typical "what," "when," and "where" information, but also informed the guests of the dress code (formal, informal, or casual), suggested time of arrival, where to park (their car or horse), and that they would be expected to deliver a few brief remarks.

The Menu. This group planned the entire dinner with several courses. Their biggest dilemma was whether to serve food from present day, consider the historical periods of the presidents, or provide a mixture. They eventually settled on a mixed menu with different courses representing varied historical periods.

Toast. Because this was to be a glorious affair, this group felt a toast should be given (with sparkling grape juice, of course) to honor and celebrate the significance of the event. They wrote a toast for each guest.

Message of Greeting. This group was directed to write a "message of greeting" to the presidents that would be delivered orally just before dinner.

Gift. This group suggested a special gift that would be given to each president before dinner.

Seating. To avoid confusion, this group felt that seating should be pre-assigned rather than random. Deciding how to arrange the guests to stimulate good conversation was a special challenge: Who will click and who will clash? Do any presidents have common interests? Will spouses be present? Should the presidents take their places randomly or should they be seated according to their importance? After much deliberation, they made a diagram of the seating assignments and designed name cards to specify where each guest would sit.

Conversation Starters. The students had to come up with a question or two for each guest that would stand a good chance of getting a good conversation going. Miss Anderson offered a few examples, such as: "Tell me a favorite childhood memory." When you were a child, who was your hero?" "What games did you enjoy as a child?"

Guest Speech. It is customary for a president to offer brief remarks just before dinner or immediately after. This group was assigned to compose what the presidents would be likely to say. Sample topics included "What it's Like Living in the White House" and, "How Tough the Job of President Is." As part of their responsibilities, students were required to research what their president looked like and the clothing he wore. They would then create a simple costume that represented each president, adding props to enhance the presentation.

Music. This group was assigned to create ambiance for the dinner party by selecting background music appropriate for Presidents Day. They planned to keep the volume low enough so that it would not interfere with the conversation.

Have you ever tried to lecture a classroom full of energetic fourth-graders about an event from the past, say the Constitutional Convention? Then you certainly must have learned that, to engage young learners, you must do something more than simply lecture. History can be quite fascinating, but students often find it boring when it is taught as an unconnected collection of names and dates to be remembered. However, after taking a peek into Miss Anderson's classroom, you will discover a more effective thought-provoking approach that engages students in historical events by connecting the past to their personal lives. As Miss Anderson actively engages her students in history, she shifts the responsibility for learning to them and, consequently, instills a greater interest in and love for history.

Historical role-playing, as in the simulated dinner party, is one strategy that has become very well received in Miss Anderson's classroom. It uses good children's literature as a basis for recreating a specific event from the past or breathing life into a character from history. In Miss Anderson's school district, teachers are encouraged to meet social studies standards by involving their students in participatory activities such as role-play that not only stimulate cognitive development, but also engage and motivate them. Unfortunately, some teachers refuse to employ historical role-playing because they are uneasy about such potential difficulties as time limitations, reluctance by some students, fooling around, and other classroom management issues. Miss Anderson counters, however, with her feeling that, "Historical role play is extremely engaging and is perfectly suited for elementary school students. All you need to provide is a bit of careful preparation and planning to effectively utilize children's natural affinity for creative dramatics."

Miss Anderson bases her overall approach to history on a conviction that instruction cannot be confined to memorizing "who did what to whom, when, and where" or to recalling a chronological series of dates typically archived in social studies textbooks. History can be found everywhere—homes, museums, or newspapers. It can be uncovered in a box of old receipts; in games children play; in stories people tell; in paintings, clothes, tools, furniture, books, letters, and diaries; wherever we look, we find history. History in Miss Anderson's classroom begins with the assumption that even our youngest elementary school children are able to engage in active historical inquiry, such as collecting and analyzing data, examining the perspectives of people in the past, and creating historical narratives. She will tell you that children are much like relentless detectives looking for evidence to solve life's mysteries: Why is the Liberty Bell cracked? How did a Revolutionary War battle end and what determined a winner? Why did they fight Civil War battles mostly on farmlands?

While social studies textbooks are often used to provide a good overview of what happened in the past, Miss Anderson has found that they are not as effective in telling the full story of the lives of people from long ago. Aligned with professional and state standards, Miss Anderson's active history curriculum uses a hands-on strategy that invites students to explore, analyze, and interpret historical evidence to gain insight into the past.

History in Focus

Of all the disciplines making up today's social studies, history seems to provoke more disagreement than any other. On the one hand, Henry Ford was once said to have commented, "History is more or less bunk." And, speaking tongue-in-cheek to a historian's craft, Winston Churchill boasted, "History will be kind to me, for I intend to write it." Describing history's value, on the other hand, George Santayana warned, "Those who cannot learn from history are doomed to repeat it." And Sigmund Freud made this plea in support of history: "Only a good-for-nothing is not interested in his past." In the face of these opposing points of view, one of the most hopeful signs during the past decade has been the widespread and growing support for more history in our schools. State standards, most of which are based on the Common Core State Standards (National Governors Association, 2010), have inspired teachers to teach history as a significant investigative process instead of a storehouse of facts to memorize. The C3 Framework (NCSS, 2013) argues that history goes beyond simply asking, "What happened when?" to acquiring relevant knowledge from a variety of sources and explaining why and how events occurred and developments unfolded.

What Is History?

What is history? Actually, there is no clear-cut answer but, simply put, consider *history* to be a written account (narrative) of significant events from the past in the order in which they occurred, along with an accurate and objective interpretation of their causes and effects. In more recent times, history is also documented on film, video, audiotape, and through digital technology. Because it is difficult, if not impossible, to piece together different versions of the same event into a truthful written narrative on which everyone agrees (just ask a police officer interviewing several witnesses to an accident), we may never fully understand what really happened in years gone by. That is because evidence from the past cannot tell its own story; it is difficult to know whether a historian's narrative is accurate and truthful or deceptive and dishonest. Historians, on the whole, are conscientious social scientists who examine evidence through a clear lens and try to tell us how the past really was. However, historians throughout the world have different belief systems and come to the material with contrasting lenses, so it is not surprising that they arrive at contradictory stories about the same evidence. Therefore, we say that history is *subjective*; it is told from a point of view and involves personal analysis and evaluation. Because interpretation is an extremely tenuous process, our views of history constantly change as new findings are uncovered and interpretations of old evidence are revised. Was Christopher Columbus a heroic explorer or a liar and a crook? Did Mrs. O'Leary and her cow cause the Great Chicago Fire, or is that merely a 19th-century legend? Did John Hancock help organize the Boston Tea Party to protest lack of representation or because British taxes threatened his tea business? Did the redcoats really fire the first shot at Lexington? Did Edwin Stanton, secretary of war at the time of Lincoln's assassination, actually plot to kill President Lincoln? Was Mary Todd Lincoln bright, vivacious, and politically astute, or was she high strung, hot tempered, and not especially sold on the concept of honesty? Did James Earl Ray act alone in assassinating Martin Luther King, Jr.? Our views of history constantly shift as the interpretation of new and old evidence disputes the legitimacy of perceived truthfulness.

Despite these misgivings, history is important. Granted, few written narratives will offer us a completely truthful story of what really happened in the past. That is why the study of history as a school subject requires processes similar to those employed by practicing historians: comprehending and questioning written narratives of past events, examining evidence with a critical eye, and asking new questions. To carry out such instruction, it is important to understand that historians use a wide variety of tools to answer questions about the past, both primary and secondary. *Primary sources* are original objects or documents; historical evidence that was written or created during the time under study is considered a primary source. Anything produced later than the time under study is called a *secondary source*. Secondary sources are considered secondhand evidence; they interpret or draw conclusions about primary sources. A number of primary sources are written documents, but historians also learn about the past through *artifacts* such as tools, weapons, clothing, jewelry, and photographs.

In addition to relying on primary and secondary sources, it important to know the skills historians use as they carry out their investigations. Is there any method that is recognized as *the* method? Actually, historians study the past with an investigative approach referred to as the *historical method*, a process based on three fundamental steps, each having its own primary tasks:

- Encountering a historical problem or experiencing a need for specific information about the past.
- Collecting, organizing, and verifying historical evidence.
- Reporting findings in an objective narrative.

Reflection on Learning

You may simply scribble rough notes or jot down something more polished and complete. The point is to simply start recording your ideas spontaneously and candidly.

W. R. Inge once commented, "History could be divided into events which do not matter and events which probably never occurred." What do you suppose leads some people to doubt or reject huge moments in history, such as the holocaust or the first human landing on the moon?

The historical method, then, is a systematic course of action to interpret historical evidence for the purpose of composing narratives of the past. Students must be offered an opportunity to dig into history as a historian—engaging problems and interesting documents, hands-on artifacts, exciting biographies and historical fiction, and technology and authentic products. When taught well, children love history. "I like learning about all the cool stuff that happened in the past," remarked Oliver, an astute third grader. "Like how I saw on the Internet that Voyager 1 has traveled farther than anyone or anything in history. It was launched in 1977 and is now flying toward the stars. That's what I call exciting!"

Why Is History Important?

Suppose you woke up today only to discover that you had no memory! You cannot recall your name, who you are, where you went to school, who your friends are, the things you've done with your life, and even what you are doing here. You cannot recognize members of your own family, and would not be able to communicate with them if you could since you no longer recall words and their meanings. Do you prefer pepperoni pizza or veggie wraps, surfing the Internet or reading a book, riding your bike or jogging? What is happening? Just as this frightful experience has robbed you of a sense of our own identity, having no historical memory deprives us all of a sense of our nation's and the world's traditions, central ideas, values, dreams, failures, successes . . . the entire record of times past. The past serves as humanity's most direct evidence in its need to understand why people behave as they do and why they make the decisions they make.

History, then, provides us models of good and responsible citizenship as well as a context from which to analyze the present and envision the future. History connects children to their roots as well as to the customs and traditions of diverse cultures and civilizations. Without this connection, children will find it difficult to acquire either a sufficient sense of self or of shared community that is essential for responsible citizenship in our democratic nation. The C3 Framework (NCSS, 2013) offers an astute summary: "Developing historical knowledge in connection with historical investigations not only helps students remember the content better because it has meaning, but also allows students to become better thinkers" (p. 45).

What Should Students Know or Be Able to Do?

Unlike the past, memorizing names and dates is not the central purpose of contemporary history, but significant facts and concepts do have a fundamental role in any history program. Information is the backbone of elementary school history. Children cannot be expected to think conceptually or critically about American history, for example, if they don't know who George Washington was or what events led to the signing of the Declaration of Independence. The reason is obvious—we can't teach our children how to think as young historians unless they have something worthwhile to think about. Historical knowledge should not be what many people think of as history—a memorized collection of names, facts, and dates. Instead, historians must think of themselves more as detectives, often unsure about what happened and what it means, but willing to sift through solid evidence (historical documents, journals, diaries, artifacts, historic sites, and other records from the past) in an effort to build and offer explanations for mysteries of the past.

The new approach revolves around the premise that historical thinking—like scientific thinking in science education and mathematical thinking in math education—is central to teaching and learning, and that students should become more competent as historical thinkers as they progress throughout the elementary school years. With this important perspective, the National Center for History in the Schools (1996) developed the *National Standards for History*, a set of standards considered suitable for an educated citizenry. The standards are of two types: *Historical Thinking* and *Historical Understandings* (see Figure 9.1). The tenets of the National Standards for History align superbly with the many state standards based on the Common Core State Standards (National Governors Association, 2010) by detailing how to develop not only historical literacy but also historical thinking and understanding.

The rest of this chapter explores the components of historical thinking and historical understandings in an effort to characterize quality teaching and learning of history in our elementary schools.

 CHECK YOUR UNDERSTANDING 9.1   Click here to check your understanding of this section of the chapter.

Chronological Thinking

In order for history to be meaningful, students need to know how to sequence events in time, examine the events in depth to learn about them, and know the names of the people and places associated with them. *Chronological thinking* is the process of arranging events in the order of their occurrence: What came first? What was next? What was the cause? What was the consequence? How significant was it? Without a sense of chronological order, events appear as a jumbled, bewildering mess. Chronology is a challenging task for most elementary school children because time is an abstract concept and young children are concrete thinkers. When you consider puzzling terms such as *seconds, minutes, hours, days, weeks, months, years, decades,* and *centuries*—as well as the concepts of *yesterday, today,* and *tomorrow; past, present,* and *future;* and *before* and *after* and *then* and *now*—it's not difficult to understand why the development of a mature sense of time and chronology is a slow, complex process. Yet, time concepts are at the very heart of historical thinking, for students not only learn about historical events as they occurred at a particular moment in time, but they must also fit those events into a temporal continuum where the causes and consequences of events are linked to each other. The foundation of history in your classroom, then, is to help your students learn the measures of time such as hour, day, week, month, year, decade, generation, and century. At the same time, they must learn and think about events as they occur in time—to understand how things happen and how things change.

FIGURE 9.1   History Standards for an Educated Citizenry

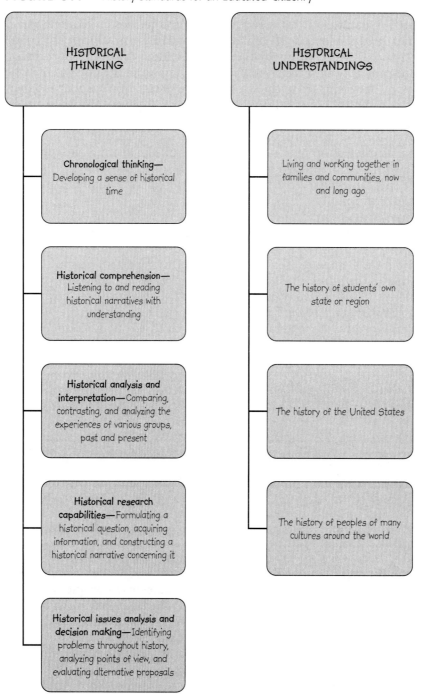

Chronology as a Natural Part of Life

Chronological time becomes a part of even the youngest children's lives as they experience the everyday world of people and things; time becomes integrated into their everyday lives and into their vocabularies as children take part in normal daily routines. These practical everyday experiences can be transferred to the classroom as teachers informally use the *language of time*, emphasizing words such as *before, after, sooner, later, early, yesterday, today, tomorrow, next week, morning, afternoon,* and *tonight.* Recognizing that events occur at predictable times during the day is another basic way younger children become aware of the passage of time. Kindergarteners and first graders like to know what time it is and that certain routines happen at an established time each day. Classroom routines typically have a set beginning, middle, and end; the children quickly learn these time sequences. The words *yesterday*, *today*, and *tomorrow* can be made more understandable by associating them with something observable and recordable; weather provides an ideal observable and recordable occurrence. Younger children can recall that *yesterday* was stormy and *today* is sunny. Some will be challenged to make a prediction for the weather *tomorrow*. Once they tackle these concepts, children can learn that clocks and calendars are tools to help us measure time. Children learn about time by observing and recording it. That is one reason why calendars are a popular part of the elementary school daily routine. Teaching early time concepts can be complicated and even frustrating at times, but hands-on materials and loads of practice will help learning transpire.

Chronology and Children's Books

Mastery of conventional chronology (clocks and calendars), then, is a prerequisite to learning any history at all. In addition, instruction should capitalize on the seemingly intuitive feeling for past and present (periodization) that children often display from a very young age. For example, when shown relevant pictures, children are able to differentiate objects in time; they will tell you that the horse and wagon appeared before the automobile, tricorn hats predated baseball caps, log cabins dotted the countryside much earlier than high rises. Therefore, picture books are an excellent resource to exploit while building on children's intuitive insights of the past. An important part of instructional time should be given to the use of fascinating biographies and historical literature containing accurate and compelling illustrations. Well-crafted, developmentally appropriate narratives have the power to grab students' attention and help them focus on the temporal structure of the events unfolding over time.

Chronological order can also be stressed by emphasizing organizational structure of books (beginning, middle, and end) during post-reading conversation or activity. For example, you may simply divide a sheet of paper into three-panel sections. Have pairs of students each write short summaries or draw illustrations, one part of the story in each panel. Each child cuts and separates the panels, challenging his or her partner to arrange the panels in the correct

Chronology can be very difficult for young children; calendars help them become aware of terms that describe the passing of time and also learn to place events in temporal order.

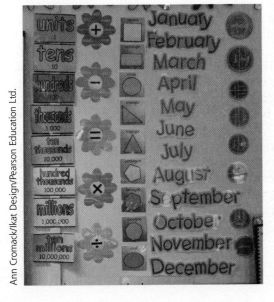

Ann Cromack/Ikat Design/Pearson Education Ltd.

Kolja/Fotolia

chronological order. The pairs can then summarize the story according to each chronology. Through good literature, children learn that authors often organize a story in chronological order so readers are able to follow the text—almost like a time line. In order to comprehend the story, readers must construct a "mental time line" of events to better understand the material and how the events relate to each other.

As historical stories are read, it is a good idea to search for context clues that offer meanings for time-sequence words such as *first, years ago, afterward, next, soon after, first,* and *finally.* Ask for volunteers to name the words that signal the order of the events in the story; tell them that words like these help them recognize the correct order of events in a story.

 Video Exploration 9.1

Chronology and Timelines

A *time line* is a sequential graphic representation of a series of historical events, constructed by dividing a unit of time into proportional subdivisions. Time lines provide students with a visual aid that helps them conceptualize and arrange event sequences—a day, a year, a lifetime. While time lines are often available as commercially made kits or displayed in textbooks, students become more actively engaged in learning if they construct their own time lines.

A good beginning time line is one that chronicles the stages of a human's life; for example, Maria Kim read Tomie de Paola's book *Now One Foot, Now the Other* (Puffin). It is a touching story that describes what it is like to be young, then old, and finally to die. To establish a context for the sequence of events in the story, Ms. Kim asked the students to describe their normal day in sequential order—wake up, have breakfast, go to school, come home, play with friends, eat dinner, do homework, watch some television, and go to bed. She was careful to call attention to the time of day when they did certain things. Ms. Kim then told the children to watch her as she tried to order events with the story because it was written in a sequential, or chronological, order: "Listen to me as I read the first part of the book and watch as I record the events in order on what is called a time line." Ms. Kim displayed a chart with a line drawn across it and began reading aloud from the book.

She read the first sentences and commented, "Tomie de Paola tells us that our lives start at birth (our "birth" day), so that will be the first step on our time line; I will add that to our chart first." Ms. Kim continued illustrating and labeling the key life stages in sequential, or chronological, order.

After a short discussion, Ms. Kim organized her students as small groups and asked each group to draw a sketch on a sheet of 8½"×11" drawing paper that illustrated significant life stages—"Birth," "Learn to Walk," "Learn to Talk," "Ride a Bike," "Go to Kindergarten," "Enter Fourth Grade," "Go to Middle School," "Enter High School," "Graduate from High School," and "Go to College" or "Go to Work." After they were done, Ms. Kim took the students to the playground. Those holding the "Birth" card were the starting point of the time line. Next, the children thought about the age at which they began to walk. Ms. Kim instructed the children holding the "Learn to Walk" card to begin at the "Birth" point and evenly walk off the number of steps it would take to get from birth to walking. She used the same process for each of the other life stage illustrations. When the chronological sequence was complete, Ms. Kim led the students in a discussion of the uneven distances among the various cards. Ms. Kim continued this approach as she helped her students construct time lines on topics having special meaning in the children's lives, such as children's toys and games, birthdays, and holidays (these may vary according to the cultural makeup of your school).

Later in the year, Ms. Kim selected interesting biographies from children's literature and helped her students create a time line about the life of a person of their choosing. She started out by reading Jackie Robinson's autobiography, *I Never Had It Made*, written with Alfred Duckett (Harper Perennial). Then, small work groups selected a series of short facts for important parts of Jackie's life, illustrated the major events, and sequenced the events as a factual time line. Ms. Kim took the students and their time line components to the playground where they walked off one step for each year between events. Returning to the classroom, the class completed the following tasks to create time lines of the significant events from Jackie Robinson's life:

- Make a list of events to be placed on the time line.
- Note the specific dates.
- List the events in chronological order—that is, in a sequence of earliest to latest.
- Decide on the units of time to use (days, months, years, decades, centuries). Then divide the time line into equal segments.
- Calculate the number of segments that your time line will need. (If students attempt to walk off years between events as they did on the playground, they will quickly learn that taking one step for each year will cause them to bump into walls. They will find that a smaller unit of measure is necessary for their classroom time lines, perhaps 1 or 2 inches to represent a year rather than one step. When working with smaller-scale time lines in the classroom, emphasize accuracy. An inexact scale distorts time relationships and interferes with true chronological thinking.)
- Draw a straight line and divide it into the number of equal segments that are required to include each significant event.
- Label the dates on the appropriate segments.
- Decide where each event should fall on the time line and how the events should be shown. For instance, a short summary could be written on the time line, illustrations could be placed at each important point, or students might elect to use a combination of text and illustrations.

Liam was quite an accomplished "computer whiz" and enjoyed using the computer for many social studies tasks, so he and his group decided to construct their version of a Jackie Robinson timeline with a web-based time line generator. Everything went smoothly until Liam encountered a slight problem as he attempted to transfer the data from his summary list to the time line. His group had selected 10 highlights to summarize Jackie Robinson's life, but the time line generator allowed Liam only 8 cells. The group members studied their 10 events carefully and eliminated 2 from the list so they could complete the computer-generated time line (see Figure 9.2). So, as you can see, the time line construction process involves much more than the perfunctory task of arranging events in sequence. Important problems must be solved, and critical decisions must be made all along the way.

Time lines are great tools for placing in perspective the accomplishments of a renowned historic figure or stories of important events. They not only help students bring chronological awareness to history but also establish a rich framework on which historical narratives can be summarized or created.

 CHECK YOUR UNDERSTANDING 9.2 **Click here** to check your understanding of this section of the chapter.

FIGURE 9.2   Biographical Time Line

The Life of Jackie Robinson	
1919	• Jackie Robinson is born
1941	• Won letters in four sports at UCLA
1945	• Jackie joins the Kansas City Monarchs
1946	• Jackie scores winning run in "Little World Series"
1947	• Jackie plays for Dodgers. Is named Rookie of the Year
1957	• Jackie retires from baseball
1962	• Jackie is inducted into the Baseball Hall of Fame
1972	• Jackie Robinson dies at age 53

Historical Comprehension

Historical comprehension is the ability to read and listen to historical narratives with under-standing. It entails skills such as recalling specific information; summarizing what has been heard or read; constructing understanding; interpreting the main idea of a narrative; pre-dicting outcomes; recognizing elements of story structure such as character traits, setting, sequence of events, and story plot; explaining the causes of historical events and their out-comes; making inferences about what the story may mean; and deciding whether a given piece of information is significant. While the development of most of these skills has been traditionally addressed in sound elementary school literacy programs, being able to read informational text has become a fundamental component of standards-based interdisci-plinary social studies instruction. Current standards documents place special emphasis on reading informational text as a quality of successful learners in all content areas. Suggestions throughout Section 3 of this text have highlighted the literacy methods and tools that can be aligned to the Common Core State Standards as well as NCSS's C3 Framework.

Acquiring historical comprehension skills begins in the earliest grades; superbly written historical narratives are staples of such a curriculum for young children. Historical literature should occupy an important place in the curriculum throughout children's schooling—from the earliest elementary school grades through the middle school years. Good historical literature not only serves to shed light on the past, it also helps integrate the curriculum. Historical com-prehension, then, begins with a rich supply of historical narratives; obtaining meaning from these resources must be facilitated through conscious and flexible comprehension instruction.

Historical Narratives

Historical narratives (stories) are crucial to elementary school social studies programs because they furnish one of the most inviting ways to enter the worlds of the past, meet famous peo-ple, and discover thought-provoking facts. Historical narratives have been looked on as the lifeblood of elementary school history programs for quite some time. Most historical narratives for young children are classified in a genre called *narrative nonfiction*, in which factually accurate information is presented as a true story. *Biographies* and *autobiographies* are specific types of narrative nonfiction that tell stories of a real person's life. Some historical narratives are written as *historical fiction*. These are stories that take place in a particular time period in the past; the basic setting is real, and the characters may be actual historical figures or a mixture of fictional and historical characters. Another popular genre is *nonfiction informational books*, or utilitarian books that deal exclusively with factual material designed to inform the reader. *Descriptive essays* are short literary works that vividly describe a person, place, object, or event at a particular moment in time. A type of written narrative that most children use in school is a chronological narrative, the *textbook*.

A helpful resource for assessing and selecting quality historical narratives for elementary school students is *Notable Children's Trade Books for Young People*, compiled annually since 1972 by the Children's Book Council in cooperation with the Book Review Committee of the National Council for the Social Studies (NCSS). The annotated book list is published once a year in the NCSS journal *Social Education*. The list may be downloaded from the Children's Book Council website.

Stories are powerful vehicles of communication. They not only inform, but they also move people (especially if the story is true). After your students have read a selection, you will need to help them derive meaning from the text. This can be accomplished through a variety of means such as class discussion, writing activities, graphic representations, or creative demonstrations as described in Chapter 8.

 CHECK YOUR UNDERSTANDING 9.3 **Click here** to check your understanding of this section of the chapter.

Historical Analysis and Interpretation

The ability to read historical narratives with meaning (*historical comprehension*) is the fundamental element of historical thinking; it forms the prerequisite starting point for the most closely associated, but more advanced level of thinking—*historical analysis and interpretation*. Historical analysis and interpretation calls for students to expand their skills of grasping and making sense of the content to judging the accuracy and fairness of the author's explanations. It involves the process of examining words and illustrations for the purpose of detecting accuracy, bias, fairness, or favoritism. In effect, the student asks, "What do I already know about this historical event or person that helps me decide whether the statements I am taking in are trustworthy and true?" So instead of simply accepting someone's ideas as accurate and dependable, students must critically examine the relevance of the sources as well as the perspectives of those involved in forming conclusions of any historical event. Gunning (2010) explains that these critical reading skills are more important today than ever, for it appears that many students "suffer from a malady . . . called the 'Gutenberg syndrome.' . . . If a statement appears in print, it must be true" (p. 388). He advises, "Students have to challenge what they read and realize that a printed or online statement might be erroneous or simply be someone else's opinion. . . . The idea is not to turn students into mistrustful young cynics but to create judicious thinkers" (p. 388).

Students who use skills of historical analysis and interpretation understand that historians have different purposes for writing and adjust their reading style to match the intended purpose of a written piece. They learn to read with healthy suspicion, for example, when the written piece expresses an opinion or point of view, such as, "I've concluded that Franklin Roosevelt had prior knowledge of the Japanese attack on Pearl Harbor." Critical readers know that the purpose of these kinds of written pieces is to *persuade* them to justify or change existing opinions or actions. Students ask the question, "Is this true?" when reading an *informative* piece; they must assess whether what is presented as fact is trustworthy. If we value children as thinkers, it is important to capitalize on their natural ability to probe and question as they try to construct meaning of their social world. If they ask you, either give them the information or admit that you don't know ("I don't know, but that's a good question."). Then encourage students to seek verification through authoritative evidence: "Let's look that up on the Internet." "Let's check that out in our textbook." "Who do we know that might help us answer that question?"

Judging a source of information can be very challenging for many elementary school children because information exists in such large quantities and is continuously being created and revised. There are many kinds of information (facts, opinions, stories, information books, textbooks) and information can be written down for many purposes (to inform, to persuade, to entertain). Whether the sources are found in print or on the computer, however, children should check their trustworthiness by using three main criteria: Does the source have expert knowledge about the subject? Is the information up to date? Is the source impartial?

How do elementary school teachers help build historical analysis and interpretation skills in their social studies programs? There are dozens of critical reading skills involved; most are treated in literacy texts and literacy methods courses. However, those having the most applicability to elementary school social studies programs have been detailed in Chapter 8.

 Video Exploration 9.2

 CHECK YOUR UNDERSTANDING 9.4 **Click here** to check your understanding of this section of the chapter.

Historical Research Capabilities

Historical research is the process of systematically uncovering and examining primary and secondary sources for the purpose of producing accurate accounts of what has happened in the past. New state standards often require students to conduct historical research while responding to a compelling question or prompt by examining primary and secondary data sources, interpreting and assessing information and ideas, and organizing and writing well-supported historical narratives or taking social action of some type. Whether used separately or in connection with each other, the Inquiry Arc (Chapter 4) and the history standards are intended to achieve a common goal—to promote the acquisition of disciplinary concepts and methods of inquiry. Therefore, the process of conducting historical investigations with the Inquiry Arc serves as a framework to support a research-based approach to history. To illustrate this connection, the *National Standards for History* (National Center for History in the Schools (1996) developed the following process (mirrored by the Inquiry Arc in Chapter 4) through which historical research and inquiry can take place:

- *Formulate historical questions* that lead to active investigation and decision making, not simply unquestioned information collection.
- *Obtain historical data from a variety of primary and secondary sources* including documents, art, artifacts, historical sites, diaries, newspapers, photos, documentary films, museum collections, resource people, and written text. The evidence used in historical research is known as *sources*. Sources are typically classified into two broad categories: *primary* and *secondary*. Historians refer to a combination of primary and secondary clues as a *historical record*.

- *Interrogate the historical data* by testing and evaluating sources for credibility, authority, authenticity, and bias.
- *Identify the gaps*; select what information to keep, enlarge upon, or discard.
- *Employ quantitative analysis* when exploring topics such as changes in family size or composition, migration, or changes in the economy.
- *Construct clear and appropriate arguments or conclusions* based on evidence.

You read in the previous two sections of this chapter (*historical comprehension* and *historical analysis and interpretation*) that students require thoughtful encounters as they unlock the meaning of, interpret, and analyze historical narratives (secondary sources). Despite the fact that secondary sources offer valuable, useful, and interesting interpretations of the past, children must be provided plentiful opportunities to encounter four major types of primary evidence: *written sources* (letters, diaries, newspapers, maps); *images* (photos, cartoons, film, video); *artifacts* (objects examined from many sources, including field trips and visits to "living museums" where life long ago is reenacted); and *oral testimony* (storytelling, interviews, oral history). Higgs and McNeal (2006) advise that if hands-on items are to be properly used, they should not simply be put on display with a "look but don't touch" warning. They recommend the following sequence of investigative strategies to guide children as they carry out research with objects from any collection or kit:

1. Assemble or obtain a kit of artifacts (or reproductions) that clearly represents an era or culture under study. Write a description of each artifact and keep it concealed from the children until a later time. Arrange a table display containing samples of modern implements so that comparisons to contemporary cultures or times can be made at a later time.

2. Pair up the children and place a different artifact on each pair's desk.

3. Invite the children to explore their artifacts. They should be encouraged to use all their senses, but the materials should never be placed into their mouths. Then, as young historians, direct them to write down their observations on an "observation log." The children should not "guess" what the artifacts are at this point; they should only record descriptions.

4. After the descriptions are recorded, the pairs brainstorm and record on their observation logs what they think their artifact might have been used for. The children must supply reasons for each assumption: "Why do you think this is so?" "What is your evidence?" Some, like a clay pot or coin from colonial times will be fairly straightforward to identify while others, like a Jacob's ladder or jackstraws, will be much more difficult.

5. Direct the children to retrieve a printed description of their artifact that you had previously arranged on a table. The descriptions may or may not verify the children's previous assumptions. The descriptions should be added to their observation logs.

6. The children must match their artifacts to the modern counterparts that would do similar work. If the children feel that none of the displayed counterparts fulfill this purpose, they are encouraged to suggest their own. The pairs discuss the comparisons and enter their interpretations on the observation logs.

7. Have the children speculate about the people represented by the artifacts: "Who used these artifacts?" "What evidence helped you come to this conclusion?" The children should record their findings and judgments and write a few sentences of explanation on their observation logs.

8. The pairs share their decisions with the class; the class deliberates as a whole to determine the actual event, era, or culture represented by all the artifacts. If they have difficulty arriving at a consensus, the teacher could add information to help the class arrive at a sound conclusion.

Think you've got the ancient Vikings figured out now? Primary sources provide concrete evidence pertaining to the topic under study.

Gareth Boden/Pearson Education Ltd

 Video Exploration 9.3

Reflection on Learning

You may simply scribble rough notes or jot down something more polished and complete. The point is to simply start recording your ideas spontaneously and candidly.

When efforts to improve learning in social studies fail, teachers take the blame. "It's impossible to teach teachers new tricks!" say school leaders. Instead of blaming teachers, it may be more productive to ask, "What can we do to make it easier for teachers to accept and carry out new instructional practices?" What do you suggest?

 CHECK YOUR UNDERSTANDING 9.5 **Click here** to check your understanding of this section of the chapter.

Historical Issues Analysis and Decision Making

This final element of historical thinking places students at the center of values-laden issues or dilemmas faced by individuals at critical moments of the near and distant past—*historical issues analysis and decision making*. Students may be asked to either judge the actions taken by historical figures to solve problems or to assess the consequences of alternative approaches to problem solution. This is the level of thinking that deals with personal principles, ethics, or codes of behavior. Students need help thinking at this level—developing the capacity to sort through the content, take multiple perspectives, make tough choices, and consider the consequences of their decisions.

Teaching historical issues analysis and decision making involves helping students make deep, personal evaluative decisions about problems faced by people in the past. Instruction tends to follow this basic pattern:

1. Identify and clarify the issue.
2. Collect evidence related to each side of the issue.
3. Determine alternative courses of action.
4. Consider potential consequences of each alternative.
5. Select a position or course of action.
6. Assess the choice from a variety of perspectives.

History subject matter contains untold numbers of issues and events that offer students an opportunity to weigh evidence and arrive at good/bad or pro/con judgments: Did the British government have the right to pass laws on its colonists in the Americas? Should the atomic bomb have been dropped on Japan? Who was the greatest American citizen ever? Answers to these kinds of questions involve analyzing available resources and evaluating the consequences of the alternatives. For example, during a unit on the Underground Railroad, fifth-grade teacher Amelia Reed opened a discussion with these questions: "How do you make a tough choice or a complicated decision? Have you ever made a choice or decision that resulted in something you did not expect?" She then read the following selection about a deep personal choice in the life of Harriet Tubman:

Harriet Tubman fell in love with John Tubman, a free black man. Since slaves were permitted to marry free blacks, Harriet and John married in 1844. Harriet remained a slave because slaves were still owned by their masters even after they were married to free blacks. Harriet and John lived in a small cabin by themselves, and Harriet never stopped dreaming about being free. She would talk to John constantly about how she would escape to freedom in the North, but John only snickered at her dreams. "I'm pleased with what I have here," John reflected. "I have no wish to go with you."

In 1849, Harriet jeopardized her own safety and escaped to freedom in Pennsylvania. Shortly thereafter she risked her life by slipping back to the cabin to rescue John. "I will not go back," declared John nervously.

Mrs. Reed stopped to lead a discussion of these questions:

- What is the issue?
- What are Harriet Tubman's choices?
- What do you think the consequences of her choices will be for herself and others?
- How do you feel about the situation?

Teachers have found that graphic representations are particularly useful in guiding students through discussions centered on a complicated personal decision. Mrs. Reed, for example, used a visual aid called the "Decision-Making Matrix" during her questioning sequence (Figure 9.3). The aid is especially useful when examining issues where there is more than one alternative (choice) involved. Mrs. Reed used this sequence of instruction:

- Write the problem or issue in the top box.
- Help students select the alternatives (choices or options) available to address the problem or issue.
- Have the students (in small groups) brainstorm the helpful and harmful consequences of each alternative (or positive and negative, or pro and con).
- Encourage students to examine and carefully consider each of the consequences.
- Ask students to choose the best, most useful, or most beneficial alternative.

After they share their ideas, it is not uncommon for students to ask, "What did Harriet Tubman really do?" When the students ask such unprompted questions, they will passionately

FIGURE 9.3   The Decision-Making Matrix

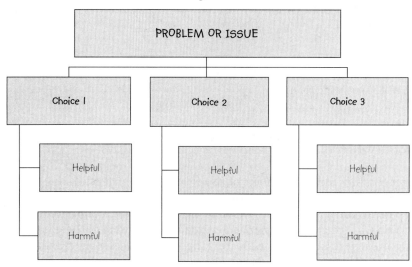

propel themselves into a search for more information. In Mrs. Reed's class, the students examined the Internet and a variety of print resources to learn that Harriet Tubman left her husband and, instead of taking him back North, she took a small group of slaves. Harriet repeated the process several times over a 6-year period, using the Underground Railroad to help more than 300 slaves escape to the North.

The interest in Harriet Tubman remained so high that Mrs. Reed reintroduced her "Decision-Making Matrix" to explore a linked real-life problem proposed by her students: "Should there be a national holiday recognizing the life of Harriet Tubman?" After completing this latest decision-making matrix, Eleanor dashed to a classroom computer and, fingers flying across the keyboard, launched herself into an intensive Internet search. "Look! I found it!" she called out to no one in particular. However, it was impossible to ignore Eleanor's excitement, so Mrs. Reed and a few students joined Eleanor to see what the commotion was all about. "Here!" Eleanor gestured passionately. "Look what I found!" Eleanor had discovered that the United States Congress had designated March 10, 1990 (the 77th anniversary of her death) "Harriet Tubman Day," to be observed with appropriate ceremonies and activities. "What a great discovery!" confirmed Mrs. Reed. "You taught all of us something special today." Eleanor's suggestion that the holiday should be celebrated as a national holiday each year propelled the class into yet another dimension of issue analysis and decision making.

Stories, an inherent component of history, pass on the passion, wisdom, and spirit others have experienced as part of a historical event. The stories draw students in to vicariously experience a moment in history and often provide them with a feeling of "being there" when it happened. Whether hiking through the 1800s wilderness or soldiering on the battlefield, a compelling story appeals to and draws out children's emotions; and, coincidentally, their emotions drive learning.

 CHECK YOUR UNDERSTANDING 9.6   Click here to check your understanding of this section of the chapter.

An Integration of Knowledge and Ideas

The following classroom scenario illustrates how Emily Barker used the recommendations made throughout this chapter to engage her students in historical thinking. How many examples can you find?

Having students write their own historical narratives helps to stimulate creativity and aids in the construction of historical concepts.

Wavebreakmedia/Shutterstock

To open a new literature-based topic of study on World War II, Ms. Barker displayed a large container on which the words "World War II Mementos" were inscribed. Together with the children, she opened it and inside they found eight pieces of primary source materials—a photograph of a group of World War II pilots, an aviator hat, a compass, medals, an identification card, a map, a newspaper article, and models of a World War II fighter plane and B-17 bomber. The students examined and discussed the objects as Ms. Barker activated their prior knowledge about World War II. Ideas were posted under the K column on a large, wall-mounted KWL chart and questions were written under the W column. Ms. Barker always makes sure to allow everyone time to share their thoughts and ideas as she is convinced that one student's prior knowledge often spurs the ideas of others. Finally, she pulled out Ian Graham's You Wouldn't Want to Be a World War II Pilot *(Scholastic), a humorous, but factual, book that explains the rigors and dangers of being a World War II fighter pilot. The book takes the students back to the 1930s where they learn about pilot school, air shows, joining the British Royal Air Force, fighter training, and actual combat. Ms. Barker asked the students to predict what the "Memento Chest" items had to do with the upcoming story and provided time for students to share their predictions.*

Ms. Barker next took her students on a quick "picture walk" through the book, explaining that the book is a form of historical fiction, a genre that includes real events infused in an imagined storyline, but the happenings are based on true events. The students enjoyed the comic book–like illustrations and were drawn in by their humorous appeal. Ms. Barker then began reading the book, pausing at the end of each page for students to check their predictions and make connections: text to self, text to text, and text to world. She also stopped at certain points during the story and invited the students to talk to one another about their predictions, connections, and any new questions that may have arisen in their minds. She asked the students to think about the significance of the items in her "Memento Chest" to see if and how they had been highlighted throughout the story. At the end of the story, Ms. Barker conducted a general conversation-type class discussion.

Ms. Barker and her students revisited their KWL chart, focusing on the L column: What did they learn about World War II airplanes and pilots? What conclusions could they draw based on the text and illustrations? Their suggestions were added to the L column. Ms. Barker made sure that all conclusions were supported by information in the book.

The next day, Ms. Barker helped the students take a new look at the clues in their "Memento Chest" and connect the materials to the information from yesterday's book reading experience.

The photograph was of an Army Air Corps eight-person crew taken during the closing days of World War II. The B-17 model was a model of the aircraft they flew; it was named "Miss Anthracite" for a coal mining connection to a pilot's hometown. The newspaper article was about Debra Pieri, a second-grade teacher who has been telling the story of the pilot, First Lieutenant Arthur "Dutchy" Sauler. The article detailed Pieri's account of the heroism that Sauler demonstrated in 1945 when, as a 21-year-old pilot, his B-17 was hit by anti-aircraft fire during a mission to bomb the rail routes of retreating German forces. It seems that two of the craft's engines were destroyed by enemy fire, but Dutchy stayed at the controls long enough to allow his crew time to bail out safely. Tragically, Sauler was the only crew member to perish. The map showed the location of these dramatic events.

The students carefully examined the artifacts and became intensely curious about each one and the story they told. There was no other information in the box or in the book, so the students decided to locate other resources to fill in the gaps. They found follow-up newspaper articles that told of exhaustive efforts by Pieri, as well as Sauler family members and friends, to have Sauler awarded the Medal of Honor. However, the Department of Defense had judged that Sauler's actions, although brave, merited only the Silver Star, our nation's third-highest decoration for valor.

"He sure was a fearless guy," offered Andrew. "I think he should be given the Medal of Honor."

"Yeah," agreed Anita. "How much braver can anybody be than to save seven lives and lose his own?"

"Just think of how many other brave soldiers there were in World War II," added Chaim. "I know it was a long time ago, but I wonder how many other heroes saved lives like Dutchy Sauler. It would be great to hear their stories, too."

Historical artifacts can knit strong and powerful links to the past. Each has its own story and effectively weaves a potent hands-on connection to people from other time periods. The students were mesmerized, for example, when Harry Novak visited their classroom the next day. Now in his 90s, Harry described how he developed an interest in airplanes when he was the students' age, building and flying model airplanes. Upon graduating from high school he joined the air force and ended up flying on the B-17 Flying Fortress. He displayed an obvious degree of pride in his past heroics, especially the time he and his unit fought to keep their plane aloft with just one of its four engines still working. "I always flew with a Bible in my pocket," Harry explained, "and in moments like that I'd pat it just so that my prayers would beam up faster!" The students were completely absorbed in the story of Harry Novak's heroism. Ms. Barker seized upon their undeniable interest and invited them to read selections from a text set containing true stories about flying heroes of World War II.

As the example clearly illustrates, Ms. Barker and her students capably incorporated the spirit of the C3 Framework, Common Core State Standards, and the National Standards for History to include higher-order thinking as well as mastery of basic skills:

- establishing a purpose for and interest in learning
- predicting (hypothesizing)
- asking questions
- using primary and secondary sources to seek out the most applicable information (evidence, content)
- clarifying, summarizing, and recalling facts and main ideas
- forming conclusions and making assumptions
- understanding and weighing implications
- collaborating effectively as a group member
- considering options of final products or performances

A Final Thought

History has long been a valued part of schooling in America; it continues to exert a major influence on what and how social studies is taught in our nation's elementary schools. Many have praised its value for producing good citizens over the years, but no one has done so more eloquently than Winston Churchill, who once proclaimed, "The further backward you look, the further forward you are likely to see." Such statements underscore the importance of developing the skills and sensitivities of historical consciousness in our schools. In a society steeped in triumphs and tragedies, knowledge of our past helps us to develop pride in our successes and discontent with our errors.

We cannot, however, expect children to become interested in the study of history when all we ask them to do is memorize facts from a textbook. Surely, content is an important part of history, but we must also be aware of the processes of history. Young historians must have regular opportunities to explore history rather than simply be exposed to it. We must lead students to perceive the nature of history itself. Those strategies will help students acquire a more balanced sense of history; it is not only something one knows but also something one does.

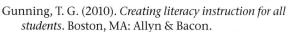

References

Gunning, T. G. (2010). *Creating literacy instruction for all students*. Boston, MA: Allyn & Bacon.

Higgs, P. L., & McNeal, S. (2006). Examining a culture from museum artifacts. *Social Studies and the Young Learner, 16*, 27–30.

National Center for History in the Schools. (1996). *National standards for history*. Los Angeles, CA: Author.

National Council for the Social Studies (2013). *The college, career, and civic life (C3) framework for social studies state standards: Guidance for enhancing the rigor of K–12 civics, economics, geography, and history*. Washington, DC: Authors.

National Governors Association Center for Best Practices & Council of Chief State School Officers. (2010). *Common core state standards for English language arts and literacy in history/social studies, science, and technical subjects*. Washington, DC: Authors.

CHAPTER 10

Geography:

Exploring the People–Place Connection

Learning Outcomes

Some people think of geography as simply locating places, but geography involves much more than that. Geography investigates relationships between people and their environment—how people adapt to the environment and how they change it. In a nutshell, geography deals with the physical and cultural characteristics of places in our world. After completing this chapter, you will be able to:

- Describe the powerful framework that geography offers for students to understand the people, places, and environments of Earth.

- Explain how to design and use instructional strategies that help students know and understand the world in spatial terms.

- Explain how to design and use instructional strategies that help students know and understand places and regions on Earth.

- Explain how to design and use instructional strategies that help students know and understand Earth's physical systems.

- Explain how to design and use instructional strategies that help students know and understand Earth's human systems.

- Explain how to design and use instructional strategies that help students know and understand how humans affect Earth's physical environment.

- Explain how to design and use instructional strategies that help students know and understand the uses of geography.

Classroom Snapshot

At the beginning of November, Gloria Robertson launched her third graders into one of their most enjoyable and instructive projects. She began by reading the book Flat Stanley by Jeff Brown (HarperCollins). In the book, Stanley Lambchop is a perfectly typical young boy until one morning at home he is flattened by a falling bulletin board. Although Stanley is very flat (he was not hurt), he discovers that there are many advantages to being 4 feet tall and a 1/2 inch thick. Stanley can slide under doors, go down into sidewalk grates, and even be folded up small enough so that his parents can stuff him into a large envelope and mail him off to California to visit some friends. Stanley fully enjoys his flatness until his brother finds a way to help him become well rounded again.

After reading the book, Miss Robertson kicked off the Flat Stanley project by asking her students to design, make, and send their own Flat Stanleys out from Rochester, New York, into other parts of the world, to cooperating classrooms around the country.

Each young geographer began the project by drawing, coloring, and cutting out a paper Flat Stanley and printing his or her name, school address, and classroom email address on the character's back. The children made a small notebook for their Flat Stanleys; on the cover they printed the words "Flat Stanley's Travel Journal." They wrote a brief statement on the first page, describing what the project was about: "I am sending you a Flat Stanley and his journal. Please write down some things about your community and school and what you do each day with Flat Stanley. Thank you." For two days, the children wrote about their community and some of the major events in Flat Stanley's school and home life. Their journal entries served as a model for Flat Stanley's hosts. For example, one day Jerome wrote: "We took Flat Stanley to the Susan B. Anthony House today. He learned about Susan B. Anthony's fight to gain voting rights for women." After two journal pages like this, the children wrote an instructional page for Flat Stanley's hosts: "Dear Friend: Please finish my journal. Include places I've been and sights I've seen. An inexpensive souvenir, or best yet, a photo of you and me together at a special place we visited would be nice! Sincerely, Flat Stanley. P.S. Would it be possible to send my owner a postcard from your town?"

Flat Stanley, a journal, a class photo showing the students holding their Flat Stanleys at the Susan B. Anthony House, an inexpensive souvenir (a "Failure Is Impossible" pencil from the Susan B. Anthony House), and a self-addressed envelope with return postage were inserted into oversized envelopes (just like in the Flat Stanley story) and sent from Rochester, New York, to participating classes around the country. A send-off party, which included music and food, was a huge success. Each student shared a moment alone with his or her Flat Stanley before saying good-bye. A small spray of confetti was thrown on the box holding all the envelopes, and a thunderous "Bon voyage!" was shouted before the students took the envelopes to the post office to be mailed.

Online and paper maps became important reference tools for Miss Robertson's young geographers as they sought out the route their Flat Stanleys would take to get them to their destinations. For example, locating Fargo, a small city in eastern North Dakota, wasn't a problem for Martel, but that didn't stop him from worrying about his little guy: "Look where my Flat Stanley is going," he remarked. "I should have dressed him warmer!"

After about a week, Margaret received the first return postcard. It was sent from Flat Stanley's host in Greenville, Mississippi; now the entire class wanted to know just where Greenville was located. They checked Google Maps, which provided a high-resolution satellite image for Greenville, and placed a pin on a wall map to mark the location of this first reply. Markers were added to identify the destination of each Flat Stanley. Some hosts sent email messages to Flat Stanley's original owners, detailing his new adventures as well as providing information about the weather and climate, local landmarks, population, industries, seasonal activities, and so on. After about three weeks, most of the Flat Stanleys had returned from their trips. The journals were full of marvelous information about their exciting adventures. The envelopes contained modest souvenirs, such as a small red plastic lobster from Bangor, Maine, and a miniature bag of peanuts from the site of the "World's Largest Peanut Boil" in Luverne, Alabama. Miss Robertson's social studies class spent an entire week of school reading through the journals and recording the path of each Flat Stanley's travels. The class honored the Flat Stanleys who had not yet returned with a "Missing in Action" poster, complete with photos of the absent Flat Stanleys and their owners.

The project ended as Miss Robertson's students wrote thank-you letters to Flat Stanley's hosts. This fabulous project helped the young geographers in Miss Robertson's room learn much about our country and its geography.

Have you ever thought geography could be <u>such fun</u>? While Miss Robertson's students were soaking up some basic geographic knowledge and skills, she tapped into their childhood passions—<u>curiosity, discovery, novelty, risk-taking</u>, trial and error, and pretense. She made learning *enjoyable* by capturing the children's interests and imagination. She made learning *meaningful* by presenting challenging learning activities in an authentic context. When children have opportunities to explore, experiment, and interact through activities like Miss Robertson's Flat Stanley project, not only do they learn about how the world works but they also derive a great deal of pleasure from it.

enjoyable and meaningful

Miss Robertson doesn't confine geography to memorizing facts such as, "Kansas City, Missouri is just east of Kansas City, Kansas." Although she concedes that it is important to know where places are (especially if you want to find your way back home after a movie), she feels it is even more important to understand why places are located where they are and how they got there. Miss Robertson constantly challenges her students to think about things such as how and why their school was built where it is, where the shoes they are wearing came from and how they got there, and why maple trees rather than coconut trees grow in their community. In Miss Robertson's approach to teaching, students are helped to think of geography not only as a source of information about the world but also as a way of thinking and acting. Although some teachers think it's proper to teach geography by handing out worksheet after worksheet, Miss Robertson is convinced that such uninspired "teaching" will not only fail to meet her district's geography standards but will also result in yet another generation of students who are oblivious to the excitement that geography can offer. Gilbert M. Grosvenor (2007), chairperson of the Board of the National Geographic Society, supports the contentions of teachers like Miss Robertson: "Young learners . . . find geography engaging. . . . I have seen it with thousands of schoolchildren in the classrooms I have visited for more than 20 years promoting the discipline across the country. Taught well, geography . . . should be the most popular subject in school" (p. 4).

Geography in Focus

You might not know where Turkmenistan is located or whether Zzyzx is a community in the United States or an animal at the zoo, but geography can help you find out. What is geography? The word *geography* was introduced in the 3rd century BC. by the Greek scholar Eratosthenes; it means "Earth description." Today, geography is commonly described as "an integrative discipline that brings together the physical and human dimensions of the world in the study of people, places, and environments. Its subject matter is Earth's surface and the processes that shape it, the relationships between people and environments, and the connections between people and places" (Geography Education Standards Project, 1994, p. 18). In short, geography can be thought of as the science of space and place—the study of Earth's natural environment and how it influences people. Did you notice that the first three words of our definition refer to geography as "an integrative discipline"? That is not an accident, because of all the disciplines in the elementary school curriculum, geography is probably the most open and accepting of integration with the content and processes of other disciplines. Through curriculum integration, teachers can make geography an important part of every classroom and, at the same time, help children find answers to the fascinating questions they have about the world around them.

Why Is Geography Important?

What's the point of teaching geography? There is no question that we are now living in an interconnected world and that virtually every aspect of life can be placed in a global perspective. It is therefore important to know <u>about people and places around the</u> world, and geography can help us effectively face the challenges of our time. All informed citizens must know geography. Grosvenor (2007) argues that today's young learners absolutely need geographic knowledge and skills to succeed in the future: "In a world increasingly defined by a global economy, cultural migration, and mounting environmental challenges, geography is an ever more important prerequisite to citizenship and success in the future" (p. 4). Therefore, in today's social studies, students learn how to describe places on Earth's surface, explain how those places came to be, and appreciate the delicate bond between humans and their physical environment. They learn geography by asking the same questions professional geographers ask: Where is it? Why is it there? How did it get there? What is the relationship between the people and this place?

It is rather easy to defend the need for geography in a 21st-century world where the very survival of our planet depends on understanding rapidly changing physical and cultural environments as well as the issues and problems that affect our nation and its neighbors. However, the results from the National Assessment of Educational Progress (NAEP, 2014) indicated that our nation's fourth and eighth graders have a limited understanding of their world within and beyond their country's borders (21% of the fourth graders and 27% of the eighth graders scored at the proficient level).

Why have our nation's schools failed so frightfully? Despite the fact that our nation's schools have faced pressure to prepare students for life in a 21st-century world, geography's place in the curriculum has become increasingly limited. More than one social studies curriculum supervisor has told me that spending the time and resources on geography has been difficult to accomplish since the emergence of the standards movement in the mid-1980s with its emphasis at both the national and state levels placed on reading, math, and science. However, geography has slowly begun to creep back into the curriculum in response to public concerns that students lack the essential geography understandings and skills that influence almost every facet of their daily existence in the United States and in the world—from global warming to terrorism, cultural diversity, and globalization.

What Should Students Know or Be Able to Do?

The most helpful steps to improve the teaching of geography have been those taken by the National Geographic Society, the National Council for Geographic Education, and the Association of American Geographers. Offering strong leadership and direction, these professional groups have published guidelines proposing what should be taught to our nation's children. The first significant advancement was the "Five Themes of Geography," proposed by the Joint Committee on Geographic Education of the National Council for Geographic Education and the Association of American Geographers (1984). Intended to facilitate and organize the teaching of geography in K–12 classrooms, the five themes are *location*, *place*, *relationships within places*, *movement*, and *regions*.

 Video Example 10.1   https://www.youtube.com/watch?v=7_pw8duzGUg In this humorous video, Jay Leno shows us that some Americans are pretty uninformed about the world around them. What do you think may have caused this state of affairs?

THE FIVE THEMES OF GEOGRAPHY

Given the option of anywhere in the world, where would you choose to live? It's a tough decision because all locations on Earth have advantages and disadvantages in regard to human habitation; one person's like is another's dislike. I once asked my college class this question and was surprised by their different responses. One student said Salt Lake City was her "dream location" because she was an avid skier. She loved everything about winter and had longed for years to live in such a "perfect" place. On the other hand, another student selected Santa Barbara, California, where *he* says everything is "perfect." He pointed out that days are usually mild all year long, with clear blue skies filled with golden California sunshine. Because there is no real "off-season," this student boasted that he'd be playing beach volleyball in January and enjoying temperatures in the 70s while the other student would be freezing on the snowy slopes of Utah.

Whatever location you've chosen as your "perfect" place to live, the key is that several factors will have played a huge part in your decision. Those factors are quite probably aligned with the five themes:

1. *Location: Position on Earth's surface.* Location answers the question "Where are we on Earth's surface?" Location may be absolute or relative. *Absolute location* refers to a specific position on Earth's surface by using identifiers such as latitude and longitude or a street address: "The Great Salt Lake is in northern Utah" pinpoints the location of a place, as does "Santa Barbara is 34° north latitude and 119° west longitude." *Relative location* means to locate a place respective to other landmarks—the direction or distance from one place to another. For example, "Salt Lake City is southeast of the Great Salt Lake" or "Beachside Santa Barbara is the hub of a large coastal California county lying northwest of Los Angeles, just off Highway 101."

2. *Place: Physical and human characteristics.* All places on Earth have unique characteristics that distinguish them from other places. *Physical characteristics* include features such as rivers, lakes, mountains, wildlife, soil, precipitation, beaches, and the like. For example, "Wasatch Mountain snow has been called 'The Greatest *Snow* on Earth'!" *Human characteristics* deal with the changes that people have made to the environment. For example, "Santa Barbara didn't exist until pioneers settled the area on a spring day in 1782, when the padre presidente of the California missions, Father Junípero Serra, founded the mission of Santa Barbara."

3. *Relationships within places: Humans and environments.* The physical features of a location affect people in different ways. An explanation of these ways can be divided into three parts: How people have been changed by the environment, how the environment has been changed by people, and how people depend on the environment. *How people have been changed by the environment* is often called *adaptation*. When people move into a location, they often make lasting changes there because of the nature of the environment. For example, if a city is located near a fault (i.e., a break, or crack, in Earth's surface), it may experience earthquakes. Therefore, people in Santa Barbara will explore different construction materials, shapes, and design options that affect the durability of their buildings. *How the environment has been changed by people*, or *modification*, is the way people alter their surroundings to satisfy themselves. In Salt Lake City, for example, large water projects are in the works to divert water from nearly 100 miles away because the growing population is exhausting the existing water supply. And in Santa Barbara, the Gibraltar Reservoir has been built on the Santa Yves River as a source of water for the community. *Depending on the environment* reflects the fact that people may rely on their environment for something important—for example, the use of trees as material to build new houses, or oil to run vehicles and factories, or rivers to transport goods and natural resources. Geographers look at all the effects—positive and negative—that arise when people establish relationships within places.

4. *Movement: Humans interacting on Earth.* The theme of movement helps students understand how they are connected with and dependent on other regions and other people in the world. Students should be able to recognize where resources are located, who needs them, and how they are transported over Earth's surface. For example, southwest of Salt Lake City are the Oquirrh Mountains, the site of the largest open-pit copper mine in the world. The mine produces copper that is shipped to all areas of the United States and throughout the world.

5. *Regions: How they form and change.* A basic unit of geographic study is the region, an area on Earth's surface whose characteristics make it different from other areas. The unifying characteristics may be physical, political, or cultural, but through the concept of regions, geographers are able to divide the world into manageable units for study.

Geographers may define regions according to types of land, climate, or characteristics of people. Therefore, we have land regions such as the Central Plains, Great Plains, Appalachian Highlands, and Pacific Coast. Using a land region classification scheme, then, we are able to assign Salt Lake City to our nation's Great Basin and Santa Barbara to the Pacific Coast region.

NATIONAL GEOGRAPHY STANDARDS

The five themes quickly gained broad acceptance and remain popular in curriculum planning today; however, 10 years after their introduction, an alliance of four professional organizations calling itself the Geography Education Standards Project (1994) released a set of recommendations titled *Geography for Life. Geography for Life.* They attempted to supplant the popular five themes with 18 standards grouped under headings titled *six essential elements*. The essential elements described what a geographically informed person should know and understand. Introduced during the ascent of the standards movement during the 1990s, the framework soon became a resource for creating state and school district standards. The standards became widely accepted, but fell short of its goal of replacing the five themes; school districts prefer to use the five themes jointly with the *Geography for Life* standards in developing their standards:

1. **The World in Spatial Terms:** Knows and understands how to use maps and other geographical representations to acquire, process, and report information.

2. **Places and Regions:** Knows and understands the physical and human characteristics of places.

3. **Physical Systems:** Knows and understands the characteristics of ecosystems on Earth's surface.

4. **Human Systems:** Knows and understands the characteristics, distribution, settlement, networks of interdependence, and migration of human populations on Earth's surface.

5. **Environment and Society:** Knows and understands how human actions modify the environment and how physical systems affect humans.

6. **The Uses of Geography:** Knows and understands how to apply geography to interpret the past and present as well as plan for the future.

Because the geography standards offer a useful outline of what students should know and be able to do, they will be used throughout the remainder of this chapter as major headings to describe what your students will be expected to learn and how you will be relied on to teach it.

Reflection on Learning

You may simply scribble rough notes or jot down something more polished and complete. The point is to simply start recording your ideas spontaneously and candidly.

Think back over your own schooling. Try to identify examples of what you now know as geography. What impact did these experiences have on you and your perception of geography as a school subject (positive and negative)?

 Video Example 10.2   https://www.youtube.com/watch?v=3IljIQ7t7nM
Geographic literacy is crucial for all Americans. Our daily lives are controlled by geography. This video offers testimony from several professionals as to why geography is important. Why is geography important?

CHECK YOUR UNDERSTANDING 10.1   Click here to check your understanding of this section of the chapter.

Essential Element 1: The World in Spatial Terms

Geography is considered a spatial science because its focus is on *where things are* and *why they are there*. Geography, as a spatial science, uses graphic representations (maps) of places to show where and how human and physical features are located, arranged, distributed, and related to one another. It is not surprising, then, that maps are among the most important tools of geographers. For young geographers, map work plays an important role in helping them comprehend spatial relationships; maps are among the most fundamental classroom tools.

What Is a Map?

What is a map? Although there is no standard answer, we will consider maps as *graphic representations of selected physical and human characteristics of a place, usually drawn on a flat surface. Designed to scale, maps use colors, symbols, and labels to represent Earth's features.* The oldest-known map is a 4-inch-high Babylonian clay tablet from about 2,500 years ago; it shows Babylonia as the center of the world, completely surrounded by water. Although map making has evolved from Babylonia's clay tablets to today's advanced technologies, a map's function has remained the same—to show locations of places and their relationship to other places on Earth.

ESSENTIAL MAP READING SKILLS

Much as learning to read books requires the application of several phonological and print awareness skills that are taught initially in isolation and gradually used in concert as children mature to the point where they are able to read independently with full comprehension, learning to read a map requires basic skills that are first learned in isolation and eventually combined until students become fluent, skilled readers and makers of maps. Therefore, your initial responsibility for crafting a systematic instructional program for reading maps is to identify the specific skills you will be required to teach in reading and making maps:

- *Locating places.* Identifying a point or an area on Earth's surface.
- *Reading cardinal directions.* Finding north, south, east, and west.
- *Reading intermediate directions.* Finding northeast, northwest, southeast, and southwest.
- *Recognizing and expressing relative location.* Determining the location of a place in relationship to another place.
- *Interpreting map symbols.* Understanding that shapes and colors represent real things, such as buildings, mountains, roads, bridges, and rivers.
- *Understanding map scale.* Understanding the relationship between a certain distance on the map and the distance on the ground (e.g., 1 inch equals 1 mile).
- *Knowing that the globe is the most accurate representation of Earth's surface.* Realizing that the most accurate world map is a globe.

In planning to teach children about maps, the first question you should ask is the same question I asked in the first paragraph of this section: "What is a map?" It is counterproductive to engage students in any sequence of map skills instruction before they have a good idea of what maps are. Some teachers try to convince 6- or 7-year-olds that a map is a representation of Earth that one would see if looking down from the sky, or "a bird's-eye view." This could be a

Maps for young children are simplified models of real places.

Artisticco/Fotolia

practical approach for older children, but for children in the early grades, this top-down image is quite confusing. Part of the confusion results from the children's natural egocentricity during the early grades; that is, they see things pretty much from one point of view—their own! They just can't understand that not everyone else can see things the same way they do. Piaget and Inhelder (1969) used a number of clever strategies to study this childhood *egocentrism* (explaining their environment only by their own point of view). One strategy used a three-dimensional table model of three distinctively different plaster mountains. Piaget asked children to choose from a selection of four drawings a picture that showed the scene they were observing. Most children were able to select the proper picture with little difficulty. Next, children were asked to select pictures showing what a doll would observe when looking at the mountain from different stops around the table. Overwhelmingly, the children selected the picture of their view of the mountain scene and not the doll's. According to Piaget, children experience this difficulty because they are unable to conceptualize another person's perspective.

SPATIAL THINKING SKILLS

Christina Riska (2014) illustrated how children's spatial thinking skills (visualizing, interpreting, and reasoning using location, place, distance, direction, relationships, movement, and change in space) develop across the elementary grades; below is an example of one spatial concept—map symbols—at different developmental stages. Because classroom learning activities should align with your students' developmental characteristics, it is critical to be aware of how your children develop these spatial skills and to recognize their probable misconceptions.

- *Grades PreK–1 (ages 3 to 6).* Because children at this stage are learning about letter and number symbol systems, many conclude that they are also ready to learn about spatial and geographic symbols. However, understanding that map symbols represent an object or place in the world is a difficult concept for most young children. Some may understand that concrete symbols represent an object or place in the real world (such as a popular restaurant sign), but it depends on how recognizable the symbol is to the child.

- *Grades 2–4 (ages 7 to 9).* By age 9, children are starting to better understand symbols; picture-like symbols begin to make sense to 7- and 8-year-olds (a lion to represent places in a zoo), but abstract symbols (a square to represent a house) remain a challenge until a child reaches about age 9. During this transition from pictorial symbols to abstract symbols, students will benefit from explicit guidance on what symbols mean and from your modeling of how to read maps and how symbols are developed and used. It is critical during this developmental stage to involve students in collaboratively constructing their own maps while making decisions about certain elements, such as symbols, on maps.

- *Grades 5–6+ (ages 10 and older).* Nine- to ten-year-olds show that they understand that symbols do not always "look like" the actual thing, but can stand for it. In these grades, then, students are able to use maps with different symbol systems including color and abstractions, different projections, and different themes.

The Building Blocks for Map Reading

Long before they can read maps, then, young children need to master key skills that will help them make sense of all those mysterious marks on the page. But asking children younger than 7 to 9 years old to think of a map as a representation of Earth from a bird's-eye point of view simply will not work. Because abstract thinking does not emerge until about 8 years of age, it is difficult, if not impossible, to communicate the concept of representing real-world, three-dimensional places on flat paper as abstract symbols. As Riska (2014) emphasized, kindergartners and first graders benefit from informal concrete activities rather than formal instruction to lay the groundwork for the symbol system of maps. Gandy (2007) also advises that, "Playing with toy trucks and cars on the carpet or in the sandbox, moving furniture around in a dollhouse, and building designs with blocks develop perceptions and skills that can apply to more abstract concepts in later years" (p. 31). Experienced builders explore patterning, balance, and symmetry as they build cities, roadways, castles, houses, and act out pretend play scenarios related to real-life experiences. Playing with blocks is both fundamental and crucial to constructing the "spatial thinking" required for map work. Many hands-on play materials—blocks, boxes, wooden or plastic people and animals, simple machines, vehicles, paper and crayons—must be made available even in your kindergarten and first-grade classroom so that young children can develop the kind of spatial thinking they need to represent their expanding world with maps.

You will often find that interesting questions and situations come up during informal experiences with blocks. While pretending to fight a fire in their complex block shopping center, for example, a group of first graders suddenly wondered aloud, "Hey, how's the water get in

As their dramatic play with blocks becomes more complex, children often make maps and may ask you for signs and labels for their structures.

iMAGINE/Fotolia

the hose?" The investigation resulting from this spontaneous question took them to the street to look at the fire hydrants, and eventually to the town's reservoir where they saw the source of water and the massive pumps that send the water through a pipeline maze to their streets. Naturally, when they returned to the classroom, the students were determined to represent the reservoir with a large sheet of blue bulletin board paper and add a series of plastic drinking straw "pipes" that carried the water to their building block "hydrants." Their block structure became an increasingly detailed symbolic representation of real places in their environment and, in essence, that's what a map is. The structure became a connection to something real; therefore, these children, like all children, found it helpful to build and play before abstract map concepts were introduced. Cognitive development does not happen independently of physical action for young children.

Skillful teachers know that their primary responsibility is not only to arrange an area with plenty of hands-on building materials and get out of the way but also to be aware of times when children need assistance in searching for clarity and understanding. You can learn a lot about children by watching and listening. Then, by offering suitable prompts, you can help them to think more deeply about their structures and find new relationships among established ideas.

Teaching Map Skills through Explicit Guidance and Modeling

If there is a single area of controversy that stands out above all others in map reading instruction, it is agreeing on the most appropriate time to move from unstructured, open-ended block play activities to more systematic instruction that enables children to comprehend the abstract concepts related to the symbol systems of maps and globes. Although social studies textbooks and scope-and-sequence charts often include various map basics as early as kindergarten or first grade, Piaget's description of egocentricity fuels considerable disagreement about whether children are cognitively ready before second grade. With strong consideration of the disagreement about the best time to begin map instruction, and keeping in mind individual differences, my contention is that when instruction is developmentally suitable, children are normally capable of learning about maps and globes at about second grade.

A SMALL WORLD APPROACH (CLASSROOM MAPS)

Constructivist learning principles inform us that map skills instruction must be tied into the children's lives and that teachers must help children build connections between familiar places and intended map concepts and skills through authentic learning experiences. Sobel (1998) calls this the *small world approach,* whereby children learn about maps by using environments that are emotionally important to them, and since children spend around 6 hours a day in school, the classroom is the most logical place to start. Launch your classroom map-making project (it usually works best with middle-of-the-year second graders) by obtaining white half-pint dairy cartons available online from packaging companies or from specialized milk distributers. Direct the children to cut off the peaked top so that they end up with a square, open-top box. Turn the box over so it is standing on the open end and then cut away parts along the sides with scissors so that the cartons appear to have legs (see Figure 10.1). Discuss the cardboard desks with the children, focusing on how they serve as models, or symbols, of their actual desks.

FIGURE 10.1   Milk Carton Desks

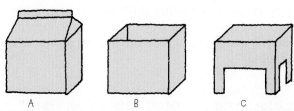

A   B   C

When the desks are finished, ask one child to locate her desk on a large sheet of cardboard (e.g., a side of a refrigerator packing box) that you have arranged on a worktable or on the floor. Explain that the cardboard represents the classroom floor but on a smaller scale. Encourage the child to carefully locate her desk in the actual classroom and then study the sheet of cardboard to determine the most appropriate spot for her milk carton desk. Once this first desk has been placed correctly on the sheet of cardboard, the rest of the construction process will move along quickly. To start, a child who sits next to the first child will be invited to place his desk "next to Margaret's." As children take turns placing their desks on the classroom model (as you use terms such as "in front of," "next to," "in back of," and so on), they are primarily using three of the basic map-reading skills:

1. Understanding that their milk cartons represent their real desks (*interpreting map symbols*).
2. Deciding where their desks should be placed (*locating places*).
3. Determining the placement of individual desks in relationship to the other desks (*recognizing and expressing relative location*).

Next, ask the children to bring to school empty boxes they might have around the house, from small jewelry boxes to boxes about the size of a toaster. Divide the class into small groups for the purpose of selecting boxes they think most closely resemble the piano, bookshelf, teacher's desk, and other classroom features. Since some young children find it difficult to work with others, you might want to assign small individual projects, such as representing the classroom wastebasket or computer. Keep a careful eye on the children as they select the boxes to represent their classroom features. It seems that the group responsible for the teacher's desk always selects the largest box, even though the teacher's desk may be far from the largest actual classroom feature. The children consider their teacher to be such an important person in their lives that anything less than the largest box would be discourteous! If this happens, you should persuade the children to look carefully at their own real desks and compare them to the teacher's real desk; then discuss the relationship between them. In due course, they will select a box that more closely represents the true size relationship. The children will explore, investigate, manipulate, test, and adapt the whole way through the process of selecting and designing the boxes to represent real classroom features. This is a primary advantage of using the classroom as the children's first mapping experience; basic skills are acquired and deepened as children go back and forth from map to real classroom, deciding how the features should be represented.

Sometimes students' painstaking struggles generate the kinds of humorous anecdotes that all teachers hold dear. For example, one teacher found that everyone had finished his or her assigned classroom feature, and it was time to place them on the growing three-dimensional map. But Alice was still at her workstation, busily working on a model wastebasket. When the teacher approached Alice to see what was causing the holdup, she found that the little girl was cutting, folding, and crunching dozens of tiny pieces of paper for her wastebasket. The job was taking forever! It seems that the actual classroom wastebasket was packed with scraps from the mapping project, and, in her drive to accurately represent the original, Alice took it upon herself to miniaturize each piece.

As the students complete their assigned features, they will be ready to add them to the three-dimensional classroom map. This phase of map construction is critical, as it contributes to the emergence of the previously discussed "bird's-eye view" concept—forming a mental picture of something as if it were viewed from above, much the way a bird might view something as it flies over. Instruct the children to examine their model classroom features from directly above as they arrange them on the map; they will see only the tops of the features and will begin to understand that paper maps are created from an analogous viewpoint of Earth. Notice that during this phase of construction, the three previous map-reading skills are being extended and reinforced, while a new skill has been introduced: *developing an idea of relative size and scale*.

Once the model classroom has been accurately arranged, you can further extend and reinforce map skills by using the map as a learning tool:

Locating Places

"Point to the box that shows the puppet stage . . . the worktable . . . the teacher's desk."

"James, can you find Michelle's desk? Put your finger on it."

"Put your finger on the aquarium. Now trace the path you would take to answer the door."

Recognizing and Expressing Relative Location

"Whose desk is closest to the coatrack?"

"Trace the shortest path from the reading corner to the door."

"Which is closer to the door, the science center or the teacher's desk?"

Interpreting Map Symbols

"Pick up the box that represents the puppet stage."

"What does the red box stand for?"

"How can we show the coatrack on our map?"

Developing an Idea of Relative Size and Scale

"Which is larger, the file cabinet or the piano?"

"Which box should be smaller, the teacher's desk or the worktable?"

"Point to the smallest (or largest) piece of classroom furniture."

TRANSITIONING TO FLAT MAPS

One of the best ways to introduce flat maps to young children is to extend the use of their three-dimensional classroom map. The model can be easily transformed into a flat paper map by following a few simple procedures. First, cut a large sheet of craft or butcher paper exactly the size of the cardboard base of the three-dimensional model and lay it next to the model. Ask the students, one at a time, to stand directly above their model desks, slide a piece of construction paper beneath the desk, and trace around the perimeter with a crayon or pencil. The children cut around the resulting outlines and label them with their names. Have the children compare the construction paper desks with the desk models and notice how a flat symbol can represent an object when looking from above. Then have the students glue their flat desks in the appropriate places on the large sheet of craft paper. Be sure not to hurry the children through this process; use the same prompts to help them place their desks on the flat map as you did with the three-dimensional model. Follow the same procedure while working with the remaining three-dimensional classroom features—file cabinet, piano, computer center, and so on. The three-dimensional map gradually becomes transformed into a flat map, as colorful traced symbols replace the three-dimensional figures. For the children to understand how the flat map functions in the same way as the three-dimensional map, ask questions and model thought processes like those used for the three-dimensional map. Effective discussion and modeling is as important for this flat map phase as for the three-dimensional phase.

STORY MAPS

Good children's books offer valuable opportunities to reinforce meaningful hands-on mapping. For example, in Eric Hill's popular "lift-the-flap" story *Spot's First Walk* (Puffin), a curious puppy meets all kinds of new animal friends as he wanders behind fences, by a chicken coop, and near a pond on his first venture away from home. As you read the story, invite the students to predict who they might meet under each flap. When the story is finished, have the students draw pictures of the snail, fish, bees, hen, and other friends Spot met along the way. Their simple illustrations can be arranged as a floor display, creating a sequence map of Spot's travels. The students can retell the story by explaining what happened at each point as they walk along their "map." It might be fun to cut out "puppy footprints" from construction paper and have the children place them on the floor to trace Spot's footsteps (pawsteps?) as they travel from place to place. Other stories I have observed teachers use for this purpose include *Katie and the Big Snow* by Virginia Lee Burton (Houghton Mifflin), *Rosie's Walk* by Pat Hutchins

(Macmillan), and *Harry the Dirty Dog* by Gene Zion (HarperTrophy). A sample story map for the traditional tale *The Three Billy Goats Gruff* is shown in Figure 10.2.

NEIGHBORHOOD AND COMMUNITY MAPS

Using the small world approach to map instruction should not stop at the classroom door or during the early grades. As their social environment widens during late second or early third grade, your students' ability to represent places on maps will expand from pictorial classroom- and home-centered maps to other meaningful places in the local environment such as the neighborhood and community. As with the classroom map and reinforcement maps, students can make a model of the neighborhood or community with packaging items easily found around the house. Oatmeal boxes, toilet paper rolls, and paper towel rolls are excellent building materials for trees,

FIGURE 10.2 Story Map

cylindrically shaped buildings, silos, and structures such as large oil storage tanks; cereal boxes, tissue boxes, candy boxes, and pasta boxes can represent tall buildings, apartment houses, or stores; and different sizes of milk or juice cartons make nice houses with peaked roofs. All you need to do is provide the proper work materials (i.e., construction paper, tempera paint, crayons, marking pens, school glue) and the children will get right to work.

MENTAL MAPS

The visual learning tool most commonly used in geography is the mental map. A *mental map* is a person's internal perception of the world, a visualization "in one's head" of the features of the person's known physical world. People use mental maps when they give directions to a location, draw a rough map of an area, or describe a location. Mental maps represent what a person knows about locations and the characteristics of places, from the layout of a student's bedroom to the distribution of continents and oceans on the surface of Earth. As students accumulate experiences with the world around them, they gradually add detail and structure to their mental maps.

One way mental maps help children is with the process of *wayfinding*. Wayfinding helps us use environmental cues to orient ourselves ("Where am I?" "Where am I heading?") and to figure out how to move from place to place ("How can I get to where I want to go?"). So, in a way, we can define wayfinding as a spatial problem-solving process. Wayfinding can also involve the process of developing maps, signs, technology, and other support that help people navigate from place to place—finding our way to school knowing that we walk past the fire station and pizza shop, and that we must pass the gas station and post office.

The development and refinement of mental mapping is an important part of geography instruction because it reflects a student's ability to observe the environment and conceptualize it in spatial terms. Young students will add detail and structure to their mental maps as they progressively learn more about the world around them. Therefore, mental maps for young children are usually limited to sketching maps of their small world: schoolroom, school, bedroom, home, neighborhood, or community. This includes children's home environments (both inside and out), the routes children take to school (especially if walking or biking), and the play spaces they inhabit, such as playgrounds and tree houses. As their world expands, children build mental maps of far-off geographic locations and features such as oceans, continents, countries, or mountain ranges.

Map Skills for the Upper Grades

We do not yet fully understand all the factors involved in learning to read maps, but one thing we know is that when children move through the upper elementary grades, their *lack of success in reading maps* becomes one of the most evident outcomes of map skills instruction. Bednarz, Acheson, and Bednarz (2006) report, "Assessments indicate that students are not competent map users. An analysis of the National Assessment of Educational Process (NAEP) geography exam revealed that at every grade level (grades 4, 8, and 12) test items that required students to use and interpret maps were the most challenging" (p. 399). Some suspect that this dismal showing is brought about by the increasingly abstract symbols and more highly complex maps found on upper grade maps. Surprisingly, Bednarz et al. (2006) explain that this is not the case. For some reason, upper grade children become confused even when confronted with highly pictorial symbols. For example, you will find that some children will explain a drawing of a cow as the home of one enormous cow rather than as a cattle-raising region. An automobile drawing, intended to symbolize automobile manufacturing, is explained as a parking lot or traffic jam. Color, too, is often mistakenly translated. Mark Twain's *Tom Sawyer Abroad* (2001), originally published in 1894, brings this problem to light with the kind of humor we can associate only with the author. In the book, Tom Sawyer and Huckleberry Finn set sail for Africa in a professor's futuristic hot air balloon. As they awake on the second day of the journey, the boys share some interesting ideas regarding maps.

". . . we ought to be past Illinois, oughtn't we?"

"Certainly."

"Well, we ain't."

"What's the reason we ain't?"

"I know by the color. We're right over Illinois yet. And you can see for yourself that Indiana ain't in sight."

"I wonder what's the matter with you, Huck. You know by the color?"

"Yes, of course I do."

"What's the color got to do with it?"

"It's got everything to do with it. Illinois is green, Indiana is pink. You show me any pink down here, if you can. No, sir; it's green."

"It ain't no lie; I've seen it on the map, and it's pink."

"Indiana pink? Why, what a lie!"

You never see a person so aggravated and disgusted. He says:

"Well, if I was such a numbskull as you, Huck Finn, I would jump over. Seen it on the map! Huck Finn, did you reckon the States was the same color out-of-doors as they are on the map?" (pp. 42–43)*

* Tom Sawyer Abroad. by Mark Twain. New York, NY: Charles L. Webster & Company, 1894

Bednarz et al. (2006) go on to say, "One explanation for . . . low assessment scores is that few social studies teachers . . . are prepared and motivated to teach about and with maps" (p. 399). Unfortunately, textbook or workbook maps control what goes on in many elementary grade classrooms; teachers rarely use supplementary materials or hands-on activity to introduce and reinforce new map skills. Despite this disheartening state of affairs, the writers suggest that informed instruction can make a difference. One suggestion is to continue the practice of constructing three-dimensional maps, for they can be effectively tied to the subject matter under study. Coleman Henderson's fifth-grade social studies curriculum used this approach, integrating geography, history, literacy, and technology during a unit about the major regions of the United States.

The region currently under study is the Great Plains. Students have enjoyed stories of how settlers pushed west into the Great Plains during the 1860s and settled in the area that is now known as Kansas, Nebraska, South Dakota, and North Dakota.

One of the major resources for their study was the collection of "Little House" books by Laura Ingalls Wilder. Most recently, the class had been reading Little House on the Prairie *(HarperTrophy), a story filled with the challenges faced by the pioneering Ingalls family as they moved to the Kansas prairie in the late 1800s. Wilder creates a lasting image of pioneer life by describing trips from the farm to Independence, the nearest town. Laura makes it seem like the town is much farther away from the farm than the 13 miles it truly is, but to a little girl seated on a bone-jarring buckboard, 13 miles can seem like a long way to go. Today, Mr. Henderson's primary instructional aim was to help his students explore the kinds of buildings the Ingalls family might have seen as they arrived in Independence: "Imagine that you are going with the Ingalls family on a trip from their farm to Independence, Kansas. What do you expect to find in Independence?" Mr. Henderson divided the students randomly into teams of two. Each team became "experts" on pioneer buildings after examining a website Mr. Henderson had selected beforehand: one-room school, church, hotel, general store, livery stable, blacksmith shop, jail, lumberyard, barbershop, cooper (barrel maker), and saloon.*

After the students completed their research, they wrote a short paragraph on index cards, detailing what they had learned. The "One-Room School" team, for example, wrote this narrative:

Schools in early prairie towns were one-room schoolhouses. There you could find students ages 6 to 16 and eight grades in one room. There was one teacher for all of them, and older students often helped the younger ones.

The index cards were displayed on a large chart to summarize the kinds of buildings that would be found in small prairie towns of the 1860s. Next, the teams were instructed to use an array of materials to construct a model of their buildings—cardboard boxes that Mr. Henderson had collected beforehand, construction paper, paint, crayons, and other art materials. The students went right to work constructing the buildings and then arranging them along streets on a tabletop display (with the index card information chart behind them). The groups were eager to function as tour guides, telling "sightseers" about their pioneer town as other classes came to visit throughout the day.

As you read about how these fifth graders mapped their pioneer town, did you sense how their construction was similar to the representations, or models, built by the younger children? Teachers do not abandon basic map skills instruction after the early grades but rather adjust instruction within appropriate contexts in an effort to help children refine and strengthen their thinking and comprehension processes: same skills, different contexts. Upper grade map skills are best acquired through continuous, developmental instruction by teachers who are ready to reinforce and extend what has been accomplished during the early grades.

MAP SYMBOLS

We have a vast array of symbols in our world—drawings, pictographs, printed alphabet letters and words, numerals, Braille tactile systems, vocalizations, gestures, American Sign Language (ASL) symbols, and informational signs, to name a few. Map symbols are a special kind of symbol that cartographers use to represent Earth's features. A map symbol is a figure or color that represents something in the real world. The types of symbols depend on the map being produced. As they use increasingly complex maps through the elementary grades, students will come across three major classifications:

- *Point symbols:* Stars, dots, or triangles to represent place location such as a city.
- *Line symbols:* Road, railway, boundary (dots and dashes), river, or canal.
- *Area symbols:* Forest, lake, town, or continent boundaries.

Suppose you will be teaching the symbol for *bridge*. First, write the word *bridge* on the chalkboard and carry out a short discussion about your students' experiences with bridges. After the children have shared their thoughts, emphasize that the written and spoken word *bridge* are two different kinds of symbols that stand for a real bridge. Ask the students to think about how a bridge might be shown in the special language of maps and to draw their idea on an index card. Don't be overly concerned if their suggestions do not conform to standard map symbols; at this point, you are more concerned with the overall concept of symbolization than the conformity of representation. Display a toy bridge (e.g., from a toy train set) or photo, print

The notion that a piece of paper with symbols on it represents a place in the real world is a gigantic leap for many students to take. As often as possible, construct three-dimensional models, even into the upper elementary grades.

Pearson Education, Inc.

its word symbol on an index card, and place it next to the bridge. Now follow this chain (*a small model or its photo/picture—map symbol—printed word label*) whenever you introduce new map symbols in your classroom.

Even during the earliest grades, children should be shown that maps use a *key*, or *legend*, to explain the meaning of each of the symbols used. A map legend is usually positioned in a small box in the corner of the map; it shows a small picture of each symbol used on the map, along with information about what the symbols mean.

PLACE LOCATION

Place location can best be understood by analyzing the two words that make up its name. *Place* refers to the physical and human characteristics of a geographic area. *Physical characteristics* include features such as mountains, rivers, forests, deserts, and animal and plant life. *Human characteristics* include the human-designed or cultural features of a place—land use, architecture, religion, transportation, or communication networks. All places have features that distinguish them from other places. A classroom is a place, for example, because of its unique walls, windows, students, teacher, books, maps, computers, whiteboards, bulletin boards, desks, dust balls, and everything else within the four walls, including the languages spoken.

When we ask the question "Where is this place?" we learn about its *location*. Location can be either absolute or relative. Whenever you've used a road map, an atlas, a software program or website such as Google Earth, or a GPS device, you've applied the map skill of finding a place's absolute location. *Absolute location* is the position of a place designated by a specific coordinate system, such as latitude and longitude. *Relative location* describes the relationship of a particular place to other places—how places are connected.

Video Example 10.3 https://www.youtube.com/watch?v=2RSI6M8IQ0I
With just a little encouragement and some direction, young children rapidly acquire the concepts and curiosity required to help them understand maps. How did the activity shown in this video help the young students learn important map skills?

Absolute Location (Latitude and Longitude) Geographers use a system of imaginary lines to describe the absolute location of a place on Earth. The grid system divides Earth into halves, each of which is called a *hemisphere*. Earth is round, and it can be divided in two different directions—north and south or east and west. The *equator* is the imaginary line that divides the north and south halves; these halves are called the Northern and Southern Hemispheres. Lines of latitude are often referred to as *parallels*. *Latitude* is the distance, in degrees, of a point north or south of the equator. The equator is the line of 0° latitude, the starting point for measuring latitude. The latitude of the North Pole is 90° N, and that of the South Pole is 90° S. The latitude of every point in between must be some degree north or south, from 0° to 90°. One degree of latitude covers about 69 miles (111 kilometers).

The *prime meridian*, or *Greenwich meridian* (because the line runs through Greenwich, England), is an imaginary line that divides Earth into a second set of hemispheres; these are called the Eastern and Western Hemispheres. Lines of longitude are often referred to as *meridians*. *Longitude* is the distance, in degrees, of a point east or west of the *prime (Greenwich) meridian*. Longitude is measured in degrees east or west of the prime meridian. This means one-half of the world is measured in degrees of east longitude up to 180° and the other half in degrees of west longitude up to 180°. See Figure 10.3 to better understand latitudes and longitudes.

How do latitude and longitude lines provide us with the *absolute location* of a place on Earth's surface? If we examine a map, we will find that the absolute location of the White House is 39° N and 77° W, a set of coordinates referred to as its *map address*. A location's map address is one

FIGURE 10.3 Latitude and Longitude

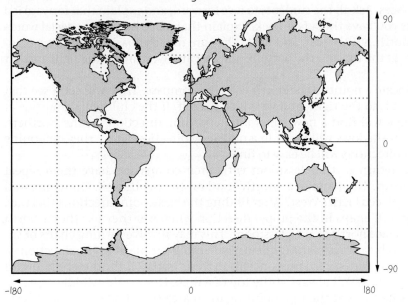

kind of absolute location. Often people regard street address as another kind of absolute location, but others argue that grid coordinates should be considered the only exact form of absolute location. For elementary school purposes, I like to recommend using both map addresses and street addresses as types of absolute location. In addition to its map address, the absolute location of the White House could also be established as 1600 Pennsylvania Avenue NW, Washington, DC 20500.

Relative Location *Relative location*, in contrast to absolute location, is determined by positioning one place in relationship to another place. For example, if we say that the White House is located in Washington, DC, situated on the banks of the Potomac River and bordered by the states of Virginia to the west and Maryland to the east, north, and south, we're describing the city's relative location. Relative location describes the location of one place in relationship to one or more other places. Relative location is not as precise as absolute location, but it is useful for describing where places or things are or to offer a general idea of their geographic locations.

Determining absolute location by using actual degrees of latitude and longitude may be beyond the capabilities of most fourth- and fifth-grade children. Guide them, however, in using latitude and longitude for locating general geographic areas, such as the low latitudes (23 1/2° north and south of the equator), the middle latitudes (between 23 1/2° and 66 1/2° north and south of the equator), and the high latitudes (between 66 1/2° north and the North Pole and 66 1/2° south and the South Pole). Children can generalize about the climatic similarities within these areas. In which latitudes are most cities located? Where is the weather warm (or cold) throughout most of the year? Show them how to find places east or west or north or south of their location by using meridians. After careful observation, they may find many surprising facts. For example, Rome, Italy, is nearer the North Pole than New York is; Detroit is north of Windsor, Ontario; Reno, Nevada, is farther west than Los Angeles, California; the Gulf of California does not touch California at any point; and the Pacific Ocean is east of the Atlantic Ocean at Panama.

CARDINAL AND INTERMEDIATE DIRECTIONS

The best method of introducing young children to the concept of cardinal direction is the same one we have discussed for all other related map concepts—through direct experience. Primary grade children enjoy going outdoors with simple compasses to find the cardinal directions (north, south, east, and west). Explain to the students that a direction is the point or line toward which something lies or faces. Ask all the students to face forward, and explain that forward is a direction. Do the same as you have them face back. Explain that maps have very special words to describe directions—north, south, east, and west. They are the four basic points on a compass. North and south are at the top and the bottom, and east and west are on the right and left sides of a compass.

Help the students locate a point to the north with the compass. They will soon see that south is behind them, east is to the right, and west is to the left. If the children are outside at noon on a sunny day, they will find a new clue for determining direction: In the Northern Hemisphere, at noon, their shadows will point in a northerly direction. Once they determine north this way, the other directions will be easy to find.

When the children return to the classroom with their compasses, have them repeat the process for finding north. Then attach a "north" card on the north wall. On which wall should the south card be placed? East? West? After finding the classroom directions this way, teach the children to "orient" maps in the proper direction whenever they use them. North on the map should always face north in the classroom. This may involve turning chairs or sitting on the floor; however, by always turning themselves and their maps in the direction of true north, children avoid the widespread misconception that "north" is the direction toward the front of the room. (North wasn't always at the top of a map. During the Middle Ages, for example, European maps had east at the top, pointing to an area then known as the Orient; that is how the term *orienting a map* was born.)

In the upper elementary grades, children should be introduced to *intermediate directions* (also called *ordinal*, or *intercardinal*, *directions*). There are four intermediate directions, just as there are four cardinal directions; the intermediate directions are located between the cardinal directions: *northeast*, *southeast*, *southwest*, and *northwest*.

Most of the maps children use in the lower elementary grades have the cardinal directions printed on the four sides of the map. In the upper grades, most maps do away with those direction tags and instead supply a direction indicator called a *compass rose*. A *compass rose* is a small figure on a map with an arrow indicating north and words indicating the cardinal directions and sometimes the intermediate directions. An illustration of a compass rose is shown in Figure 10.4.

The *compass rose* is one of the three basic features children must familiarize themselves with as they get ready to study a map. The other two are the *title* (which tells what the map

FIGURE 10.4 Compass Rose

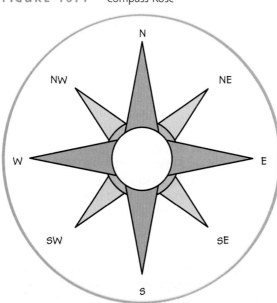

is about) and the *legend* (which explains the symbols used to represent Earth). For example, if the students are going to work with a political map of their state, they should start by reading the title and then discussing what they think the map will show. Then they should look at the legend. They will notice that on a political map, the legend will show different lines that indicate county, state, or international borders, as well as the symbols used to indicate major and minor cities. Finally, the children should locate the compass rose and determine north on the map. The map should then be oriented so that north on the map is facing the same direction as north on the compass.

MAP SCALE

Cartographers draw maps to scale when they reduce the size of every real feature an equal percentage to accurately portray places on Earth. Simply defined, then, *scale* is the relationship between distance on a map and distance on Earth. The scale of a map is determined by the amount of real-world area covered by the map and the size of the paper used to render the map. The idea of map scale should be handled in a general way rather than in a mathematical sense during the early primary grades. Map scales can be extremely confusing to young children who find it difficult to associate the size of a map to the real dimensions of Earth.

Upper elementary students learn that map scale can be expressed in three major ways. One way is the *verbal scale*. Verbal scales are spoken or written statements that tell what distance on the map is equal to what distance on the ground, such as "1 inch equals 5 miles" or "1 centimeter equals 5 miles." Though verbal scales may appear to be fairly uncomplicated, they are not often found on the maps upper elementary grade children use. Instead, a second type of scale, the *graphic scale* (sometimes called the *bar scale*) is more common. The graphic scale is simply a bar or line indicating the known distance on the ground. There are usually marks along the line that help measure the ground distance (Figure 10.5).

The third approach to map scales is the *representative fraction* (or ratio) *scale*, which indicates how many units on Earth's surface equal one unit on the map. It can be written as 1/100,000 or 1:100,000. In the metric system, the representative fraction could be interpreted as 1 centimeter on the map equaling 100,000 centimeters (1 kilometer) on Earth. Or, in standard measure, it could indicate that 1 inch on the map is equal to 100,000 inches on the land (about 1.6 miles). With representative fractions, the scale does not necessarily need to be represented by regular measuring systems. So a child could invent a scale where 1 paper clip on the map is equal to 100,000 paper clips on Earth, and this system would be entirely proper and useful. Although the representative fraction scale is useful on many maps, it can be confusing to many upper elementary children because they have difficulty understanding mathematical ratios at this age.

THE GLOBE

Since an early primary grade child's concept of Earth in space is rather undeveloped, formal instruction in globe-reading skills can often be difficult. Nonetheless, you should not ignore globes in a primary grade classroom. With simplified 12-inch globes, children can understand that a globe is a representation of Earth, much as the three-dimensional models they made earlier are representations of their classroom.

FIGURE 10.5 Graphic (Bar) Scale

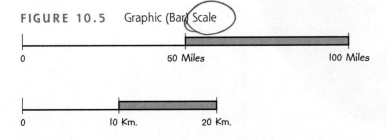

Have the children examine their three-dimensional classroom map and talk about how their classroom map is a model of their classroom—a place in the real world. Next, discuss how it would feel to be an astronaut and to be able to look at Earth from way above, as if they were able to view their classroom model. Show a satellite image of Earth and ask the children to describe what they see. Focus on broad attributes such as how the clouds, landmasses, and bodies of water look. Show the children a globe and discuss how it is a model of Earth, just as their three-dimensional representation is a model of their classroom. The globe should include a minimum amount of detail and, if possible, should show the landmasses in no more than three colors and the bodies of water in a consistent shade of blue. Only the names of the continents, countries, largest cities, and largest bodies of water should be labeled. Globes that show more detail easily confuse very young children.

When reading stories, children may wish to know where their favorite characters live; you can show them on a globe. For example, if you and the children are reading a story that is set in Mexico, you might want to show them where Mexico is located in relationship to your community. Say, "A globe tells you where places are. Pictures tell you what the place is like." After pointing out where Mexico is located, show some photos or illustrations of familiar features or landmarks. You can use times like these to familiarize young children with the globe and with the fact that they can use the globe to locate special places.

The basic globe concepts for development in the primary grades are: (1) to understand the basic roundness of Earth, (2) to understand the differences between land and water areas, and (3) to understand that Earth is mostly made up of water and seven large land areas known as continents. Students should know that our country is called the United States of America and that it is located on the continent of North America. North America is made up of several countries: north of the United States is Canada; south is Mexico; the Atlantic Ocean is east of the United States, and the Pacific Ocean is west. The United States is made up of 50 states, most of which touch each other. The two states that don't touch any others are Alaska and Hawaii. By the end of the primary grades, children should be able to locate their home state on a map of the United States.

During the upper elementary grades, students learn that a globe is the only accurate map of Earth and is an even better tool for studying locations, directions, or distances than a flat map. To emphasize this, you might want to show a satellite image of Earth and compare it to

Earth as seen from *Apollo 17*.

Fisherss/Shutterstock

a classroom globe. It is fairly easy to find satellite photographs; one option is to request them through the U.S. Weather Service. NASA has a useful searchable directory of images and animations of Earth on its website.

MAP PROJECTIONS

Globes help show shapes of areas exactly as they would appear on Earth's surface. Unfortunately, maps are unable to do this. Representing a curved surface precisely on a flat map has challenged cartographers for years. Students should try peeling an orange and pressing the peel flat on a table. They can clearly observe the peel crack and tear. The same thing happens when we try to flatten Earth's shape. This is called *distortion*. Distortion is the reason cartographers use *map projections*, or attempts to portray Earth's physical features on a flat surface. This was originally done with the use of a strong light to project the shadow of a wire-skeleton globe onto a flat surface. That is how the term *projection* originated. Various distortions, however, always result from this process. Well-known projections for world maps are the Mercator and Robinson projections. Until recently, most elementary school social studies textbooks used the *Mercator projection*. It maintains accurate direction and distance, but area in high latitudes is distorted. You might remember looking at a Mercator projection map and wondering why Greenland looked much larger than India, even though India actually has a larger land area than Greenland. Another well-known projection is the *Robinson projection*, which many newer social studies textbooks and reference books use (see Figure 10.6). In the Robinson projection, Earth is shown with a flat top and bottom. Area is represented accurately, but the distances and compass directions are somewhat distorted.

Each map projection has advantages and disadvantages; there is no "best" projection. The appropriate projection for a map depends on the scale of the map and on the purposes for which it will be used. Some projections are good for small areas, some are good for mapping areas with a large east–west extent, and some are better for mapping areas with a large north–south extent.

In modern cartography, the projection method has been largely replaced by computer-assisted programs; however, as shown in Figure 10.7, even these projections have one of three forms—cylindrical, planar, or conical—as their basis.

Essential Element 1 addresses wide-ranging considerations that are fundamental to effective map and globe skills instruction in elementary school. Because specific grade-by-grade expectancies vary greatly from one school district to the next, they are not outlined in this chapter. Targeted understandings and skills that children are expected to know or be able to do can be found in school district standards documents and curriculum guides. Those guides also offer activities and resources that are considered useful to the social studies program.

FIGURE 10.6 The Robinson Project

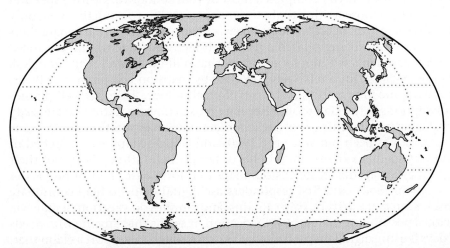

Source: IDL Astronomy Users Library, NASA. Online (http://idlastro.gsfc.nasa.gov/idl_html_help/images/map_robinson.gif).

FIGURE 10.7   Three Projection Forms

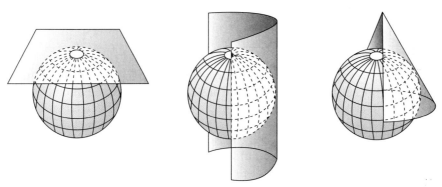

Source: FedStats, http://www.fedstats.gov/kids/mapstats/concepts_projections.html.

Maps for the Classroom

Commercial classroom maps usually fall into two categories: base maps and thematic maps. *Base maps,* also known as mother maps, depict basic features of Earth's surface, such as streets, mountains, coastlines, city locations, and oceans. A *thematic map* reveals a particular attribute connected to a place, such as votes in an election, population density, vegetation, or climate and weather. All thematic maps begin as base maps; their specific themes are then layered onto base maps via different mapping programs and technologies. Maps become increasingly abstract with each succeeding grade level, reflecting the growth of children's abilities to represent spatial information.

WALL AND DESK MAPS

It is important to provide a wide variety of maps, both as sources of information and as models for map construction. Your students will need quality geographical tools to understand and inquire into their community, state, country, and world. A good selection of quality maps will provide valuable lessons in using fundamental spatial concepts. There are several types of maps, each of which reveals different information; see Figure 10.8.

DIGITAL MAPS

Can you remember the days when you completed most of your schoolwork with paper and pencil? Although you still use those writing tools, the chances are that you pull them out only when you lack access to some form of technology. Likewise, the paper maps that geographers have used for centuries are now being phased out by high-tech instruments and advanced computer software. Your students will not be surprised that pull-down wall maps and desk maps are slowly being replaced, for a relatively low cost, by maps on cell phones or iPads, created using the geographic information systems (GIS) technology. Although cell phones can cause serious disruptions in the classroom, they have passed novelty status and are ready to be turned into valuable map teaching tools; teachers are now incorporating digital maps at a brisk rate. MapQuest has been out since the 1990s and Google Maps was launched in 2005; now, almost everyone has a digital map in his or her pocket. Airline pilots plot their course with iPads, real estate agents create custom maps to inform customers of properties and surrounding neighborhoods, and first responders use digital maps to help coordinate emergency responses. Even truck drivers, ship captains, and families on vacation operate via digital maps and global positioning systems (GPS) location. It seems that anyone who needs to use maps these days is using digital maps. Isn't that reason enough to support a claim that, for 21st-century citizenship, we must include digital maps at least as much as paper maps?

FIGURE 10.8   Maps for the Elementary School Classroom

- **Political maps.** Political maps show the line boundaries between countries, states, cities, and other human-made features.

- **Physical maps.** Physical maps show landforms and waterways, such as deserts, islands, forests, rivers, lakes, mountains, straits, and bays.

- **Product maps.** Product maps show agricultural or manufactured goods in a region— for example, dairy, corn, oil, wheat, or automobiles.

- **Tourist maps.** Tourist maps show the major attractions in an area—resorts, hotels, entertainment, buildings, and other sights. A tourist map is usually rendered as a three-dimensional view of a place and looks more like a work of art than an actual map.

- **Raised-relief maps.** Raised-relief maps are molded vinyl three-dimensional maps with bumpy surfaces that help children feel and see the differences in mountains, hills, plateaus, and plains. They are ideal for tactile learners.

- **Topographic maps.** Topographic maps include contour lines that show the shape and elevation of an area. Lines that are close together indicate steep terrain; lines that are far apart indicate flat terrain.

- **Climate maps.** Have you ever wondered why one area of the world is a desert, another a plain, and another a rain forest and why there are different types of life in each area? The answer is climate. A climate map shows a region's general pattern of weather conditions, seasons, and weather extremes, including hurricanes, droughts, and rainy periods.

- **Historical maps.** Historical maps show what places were like long ago and how they have changed over time. A historical map may show the routes of the explorers to North America, for example, or what the original 13 colonies looked like. Or a historical map could show the United States in 1861, when the Civil War began. This map might show the states that wanted to break away from the Union and become their own nation (Confederate States of America) and the northern states (the Union). The 1861 map might also show that not all the land was yet organized into states (e.g., The Dakota Territory and New Mexico Territory).

- **Road maps.** A road map is a map that helps us figure out a good route between two places. If you want to travel from Boston to Atlanta, a good road map will tell you how far and in which direction you must travel.

Maps provide an abundance of information for all grade levels.

Monkey Business Images/Shutterstock

Some envision children growing up with Google Maps on their wireless devices and never carrying a paper map again. Are paper maps becoming obsolete? Although digital maps have carved out a substantial niche, the reality of their totally displacing paper maps is rather unlikely. The same people who may have suggested that the convenience and reliability of computers and e-books would hasten the demise of libraries and bookstores may be the same skeptics predicting that the future points to students finding their way exclusively with a GPS device built into their phone or computer. "Sad to say, all my students can do with maps on their electronic devices is simply follow directions in moving from one point to another," complains one fifth-grade teacher. "They're lost when you ask them to read a wall map or a map in their textbook; they are completely befuddled! Many don't have a true understanding of what a map is. Paper maps are obviously losing out to electronic maps, but they just cannot be replaced. I still teach my students map skills and know other teachers do the same. Like paper books and magazines, paper maps will be here forever!" Certainly, when it comes to digital and paper maps, it is a mistake to consider one as better than the other. They must exist side by side in classrooms preparing students for life in the 21st century.

In order to acquire "21st-century skills," students must become familiar with innovations in computer cartography, computer-based geographic information systems (GIS), and global positioning systems (GPS). These new technological advances are transforming the way we look at Earth. Google Earth, for example, is one of the most popular advances in *computer cartography*. Its satellite images of Earth's surface allows users to view features such as cities, houses, maps, and terrain from directly above. Students can explore everything from three-dimensional buildings and structures to galaxies in outer space and canyons of the ocean. A *geographic information system* (GIS) integrates a variety of hardware and software for the purpose of storing, using, and displaying all forms of geographic data. Such systems are becoming increasingly common in homes and schools; children will soon use them in their classrooms as purposefully and as often as they use traditional printed materials. It is essential that students be exposed to as many forms of geographic data processing as possible and come to understand the role of computer systems in both the study and practice of geography. The *global positioning system* (GPS) consists of 24 satellites orbiting over 12,000 miles above Earth in 12-hour orbits. The satellites send radio signals to Earth from their high orbits. The signals are then detected by GPS ground-based receivers; the signals are used to pinpoint the receiver's position on Earth (latitude, longitude, elevation, and time).

Having access to digital maps is like having a huge library of printed atlases; through digital maps, students are connected to an immense storehouse of information that cannot be conveniently represented by traditional, printed maps. Elementary school social studies programs must be devised to exploit the full potential of digital technology.

Judy Clough brought in an array of commercial maps to show her third graders. She took some from her classroom supply and also used maps from the library, travel agencies, and informational books and atlases. She introduced the maps by asking the questions "What are these things?" and "How are they used?" Mrs. Clough challenged the children to examine the maps carefully, focusing attention on their likenesses and differences. Her main instructional goal was to have the children grasp the idea that maps display information in different ways, but they have a number of like features, such as symbols, scales, and legends.

Mrs. Clough then asked her students to share any previous map-making activity experiences. Some said they made imaginary treasure maps with their friends; others described earlier classroom mapping projects. Mrs. Clough informed them that they were going to make a special map today—a map of their school property. Then she passed out images of the school property that she had downloaded and printed from Earth Explorer. The students were fascinated by the image and spent quite a bit of time examining it. "There's our kickball field!" exclaimed Ellie. "Look at the long shadow from the flag pole out front," pointed out Tad. The children found grassy fields, blacktop areas, buildings, surrounding streets, trees, bushes, playground structures, and other features.

    After allowing sufficient time for the students to explore, Mrs. Clough passed out tracing paper and directed the children to carefully place a sheet on top of the image. Then she told the children to work in pairs for the next step: As one child held the papers in place and the tracing paper on top, her or his partner attached a 1-inch piece of transparent tape to the top-left edge of the papers and then repeated the process for the right side. When finished, the two papers worked together as if they were attached by hinges. The children were now able to lift up the tracing paper to look at the image beneath while keeping the two pages in alignment.

    Next, Mrs. Clough demonstrated how to trace outlines of the features in the computer image onto the tracing paper. (If children have trouble seeing through the tracing paper, you can have them tape their papers to the inside of a window.) Together, Mrs. Clough and the students began by tracing the tops of buildings. They talked about what the school features looked like as they were looking down from directly above. Everyone decided it would be a good idea to fill in the building outlines with brown crayon. The students repeated the process as they traced the trees, colored them green, and then added different colors for the remaining features.

    After they completed the last feature, the children carefully cut apart the tracing paper and computer image to reveal their impressive maps. "Look at mine!" yelped Hank. "It looks just like a real map!" The children were excited to compare their maps with those Mrs. Clough had showed them earlier, and they decided that they needed to have a legend. "Otherwise, people won't know what the colors mean," advised Ruthie. When Mrs. Clough asked Ruthie how they should do this, Ruthie suggested that everyone could start by drawing a small brown square at the bottom of their maps and printing the word "building" next to it. Ruthie went on to propose that they do the same thing for the other features.

    Ken directed their attention to something else that was missing on their maps: "Hey, we need to show the directions." The children added a compass rose to indicate north. Finally, they gave their maps a title and signed their names to let everyone know that they were authentic "cartographers."

Students must be helped to understand that they can learn many things about our planet from different types of maps and also that they are able to communicate to others what they know about a place by constructing many kinds of maps of their own. If elementary school students are to acquire geographic competency, they must acquire the necessary tools and techniques to think geographically. Geographic information is compiled, organized, and stored in many ways, but in thinking geographically, maps are central to understanding and analysis. If we expect children to use increasingly complex maps successfully, we must help them to arrive at deeper understandings of and insights into the six basic map skills.

 Video Exploration 10.1

Reflection on Learning

You may simply scribble rough notes or jot down something more polished and complete. The point is to simply start recording your ideas spontaneously and candidly.

    Most teachers who are going to teach geography to elementary school students have never had a course in geography during their college studies. How might a teacher's knowledge of geography influence his or her effectiveness?

It is important to infuse into your program the latest innovations in geographic technologies.

Oleksiy Mark/Fotolia

 CHECK YOUR UNDERSTANDING 10.2 **Click here** to check your understanding of this section of the chapter.

Essential Element 2: Places and Regions

All places have physical and human characteristics that distinguish them from other places on Earth. Studied together, physical and human characteristics provide clues to help us understand the nature of places on Earth. Physical characteristics include landforms, oceans, rocks and minerals, soils, animals, vegetation, the atmosphere, water, and climate and weather. Human characteristics include population, language, architecture, communication networks, political systems, migration, agriculture, transportation, and urban systems. A *region* is an area on Earth's surface that is defined by natural or artificial unifying properties. Language, government, or religion can define a region with artificial properties; deserts, lakes, wildlife, or climate are examples of regions with natural properties. A common way of classifying regions in the United States is grouping them into five regions according to their geographic position on the continent: the Northeast, Southwest, Northwest, Southeast, and Midwest; other physical or cultural similarities may be used to distinguish among areas. Figure 10.9, for example, is a map that shows one way to classify regions of the United States—by climate.

Geographers recognize three types of regions: formal, functional, and vernacular. The first type is the *formal region* characterized by a common human property, such as political, physical, language, cultural, and economic areas. Formal regions may be as large as a hemisphere or as small as a city block; some familiar examples include Canada, the Rocky Mountains, the Great Plains, the Islamic World, or the coffee-growing areas.

The second type is the *functional region*. It is organized around point-to-point activities such as transportation systems and communication systems. For example, New York City, with its highways, railways, ports, airlines, and telecommunications systems, is a focal point in the north-central region of the United States.

FIGURE 10.9   Climate Regions of the United States

Source: U.S. Department of the Interior Museum, Online (http://www.doi.gov/whatwedo/climate/strategy/images/CSC-Map-LTG02.png).

The third type of region, the *vernacular region*, is based on peoples' perceptions and feelings about an area and therefore varies from person to person. The vernacular region is designated by a common name in the everyday language of an area, as opposed to the accepted scientific name. Examples include Amish Country, the Sun Belt, the Coal Region, and the Bible Belt.

Because the social studies program in her school district is standards-driven, Becca Jones, a fifth-grade teacher from Flagstaff, Arizona, has developed new ways to think about geography and its key skills. As a dedicated teacher, Ms. Jones was eager to incorporate the standards into her instructional plans. This semester, Ms. Jones chose to focus on the second essential element— *places and regions*, the basic units of geography. Her goal was to meet this standard by offering her students interesting, hands-on activities and by encouraging them to think deeply about their surroundings as well as the physical and human characteristics of other fascinating places on Earth. One way she accomplished this was through an activity Ms. Jones called the "Exchange Package."

> To begin, Ms. Jones asked her students to assemble a number of inexpensive objects that could help explain life in Flagstaff. The objects would be placed together in a package and sent to fifth-grade students in a friend's classroom located in Elmira, New York. The students deliberated for quite some time until they selected a small chunk of volcanic cinder to represent Sunset Crater; a branch of ponderosa pine and a pine cone to represent Coconino National Forest, the world's largest contiguous ponderosa pine forest; a piece of wood, a toy train engine, and a plastic cow to represent lumbering, railroad, and ranching in the early economy of Flagstaff; a pair of mittens to represent the outstanding skiing and snowboarding at the Arizona Snowbowl; and a small piece of inexpensive silver costume jewelry with turquoise stones to represent native culture. Everyone seemed content with the collection until Claire shouted, "I just thought of something!" The children stopped what they were doing and peered at Claire in anticipation of her great revelation. "The Purina Company has a big pet food factory here," she said. "We should put something in the package to show that a lot of people from Flagstaff work there." The children breathed a collective sigh. "Not bad, Claire," they responded with a level of enthusiasm a few notches below hers. "What do we put in, a dog biscuit?" Marvin asked drolly. "Good idea!" Claire agreed, as Marvin stared in disbelief. "The dog biscuit is perfect." The dog biscuit received a place among the other relics as the students wrote a letter explaining each. Figure 10.10 shows one paragraph of the letter; it describes the significance of including the pair of mittens. The students from Elmira also arranged a package of items and an explanatory letter about their city and region and sent it to their new friends in Flagstaff.

☑ **CHECK YOUR UNDERSTANDING 10.3**   **Click here** to check your understanding of this section of the chapter.

FIGURE 10.10 Student Letter

> In flagstaff it snows a lot during wintertime.
> Sometimes it snows as much as 2 feet.
> There are many winter sports in Flagstaff.
> People especially like to go to the mountains
> to snow ski. I like to go snowboarding.
>   Jeffwan

Essential Element 3: Physical Systems

The National Geographic Standards (Geography Education Standards Project, 1994) divides Earth's system into four interacting physical spheres: the *lithosphere* (land), *hydrosphere* (water), *atmosphere* (air, climate, and meteorology), and *biosphere* (plant, animal, and human life). Although they are often discussed as four distinct components, no part of the whole Earth system should be considered in isolation from any other. Geographers want to know how these spheres work to shape and reshape Earth and what impact these changes have on plants, animals, and people. An erupting volcano, for example, causes changes to the land (lithosphere), affects the living things nearby (biosphere), and adds gases to the air (atmosphere). By understanding these physical processes, our young geographers must be able to ask and answer questions such as "What clothes must I pack for a trip to Caribou, Maine, in November?" "What is the value of grasses and rushes in the wetlands?" "What does the surface of Earth look like, and how did it get that way?" "Why is the Great Barrier Reef shrinking?" "How will China's position as the world's largest emitter of greenhouse gases affect global warming?" Students must be aware that, since the physical environment is the catalyst for all human activity on Earth, it is necessary to understand how the Earth system works through the interactions of its four independent components:

- The *lithosphere* (geosphere) is the solid, rocky shell covering Earth, including the crust and uppermost mantle. The lithosphere is broken into huge sections called *tectonic plates*. Their movement, called *plate tectonics*, causes natural phenomena such as earthquakes, mountain ranges, ocean trenches, and continental drift.
- The *hydrosphere* includes water in all of its forms (liquid, solid, and gas): oceans, lakes, rivers, ice, clouds, glaciers, and water vapor. The hydrosphere covers about 70% of Earth's surface.
- The *atmosphere* is the gaseous envelope that encircles Earth. It is made up of various gases (mostly nitrogen and oxygen) that act as a protective shield for Earth and helps sustain life on the planet.
- The *biosphere* includes all living organisms. These distinct communities of plants and animals living together in ecological communities, or *ecosystems,* are called *biomes*. Five common biomes studied by students in K–6 geography programs include aquatic, desert, forest, grassland, and tundra.

Earth, then, can be thought of as a dynamic planet with many separate but interactive spheres. When geographers and other scientists study how these spheres are interconnected, their aim is to understand Earth as a system made up of numerous interacting parts. Elementary school students often think that only human actions can seriously affect the Earth system. However, natural events such as volcanic activity and earthquakes can also have widespread harmful effects on the environment. Humans, though, are a critical part of the Earth system.

Often, topics related to Earth's four physical spheres, such as the *water cycle*, are included in content standards for both physical geography and Earth science. Because geography studies our planet in relationship to both human and environmental processes, it has often been described as a "bridge" of the disciplines, integrating the natural and social sciences. Therefore, some of the topics you will see overlapping with geography and science are the hydrologic cycle, weather and climate, tectonic forces, wave action, earthquakes, volcanoes, soil-building processes, and seasons.

 CHECK YOUR UNDERSTANDING 10.4   Click here to check your understanding of this section of the chapter.

Essential Element 4: Human Systems

Human systems are composed primarily of population, culture, and settlement and the relationships among these factors. Human systems continually fluctuate. To be geographically informed, advises the Geography Education Standards Project (1994), students must understand "the interaction of the human and environmental factors that help to explain the characteristics of human populations, as well as their distribution and movements" (p. 79).

From the beginning of humanity's story in Africa through the thousands of years it took to give rise to Earth's earliest civilizations, hunters, gatherers, and fishers adapted and continually moved to changing locations throughout Africa, Eurasia, Australia, and the Americas. Known as nomads, these communities of people moved from one place to another, searching for edible plants, game, and water and competing with birds and other animals for their nourishment. Eventually, the nomads learned how to cultivate crops and domesticate livestock such as cattle, sheep, yaks, and camels. Together, these changes allowed people to live in self-sufficient settlements instead of wandering from place to place looking for food, shelter, and other resources.

Early civilizations began as farming settlements in fertile river valleys between the Tigris and Euphrates (Mesopotamia), along the Nile (Egypt), near the Indus and Ganges (Pakistan and India), and beside the Yellow River (Huang He Valley of China). Eventually, agricultural surpluses made it possible to feed many people, so men and women were freed to develop nonagricultural trades such as tool making, weaving, pottery, and the like. These first permanent settlements grew into villages, and the villages grew into vibrant communities. By 1000 BC. Earth witnessed the dawn of its first complex societies having these five basic features:

1. A stable food supply
2. Specialization of labor
3. System of government
4. Social levels
5. Highly developed culture, including art, architecture, religion, music, and law

The movement and growth of populations has continued into modern times in two forms: *voluntary migration* within one's region, country, or beyond and *involuntary migration*. Migration is one of the most distinctive characteristics of human populations. Initiated for whatever reason, human migration has forever changed the demographics of lands throughout the world. Migrations may be temporary or seasonal, but for many people they are a permanent movement prompted by *push factors* that drive people away (such as overcrowding and lack of employment) and/or *pull factors* that draw people to a place (such as better housing and jobs). The major pull prompting migration today, for example, is economic; many people are drawn to new locations in search of jobs and higher wages. A major push factor is just the opposite of pull factors; people tend to migrate today because of a lack of economic opportunity. Pushes and pulls, therefore, are interrelated. That is, people migrate only if the reason to move (the push) is improved by the corresponding pull at the desired destination. In a geographical context, then, the push and pull factors explain both why people leave and why they choose where they go.

Migrating people carry their *culture* with them. Although it can be defined in many ways, culture is considered as the total way of life of a group of people—their values, goals, and practices. Language is a cultural component, as are religion, literature, and architecture. These components give cultures unique identities, as do technology, agriculture, medicine, modes of transportation, clothing, music, food, dance, sport, etiquette, and scores of other patterns of everyday life. *A cultural region* (such as urban, suburban, and rural) establishes the location of distinct communities having common cultural elements; *cultural diffusion* helps explain how groups with common traits got there. Generally, cultures originate in a particular location and spread outward into a larger territory. Thus, the presence of Starbucks or Burger King outside the United States is a type of cultural diffusion, and so is the appearance of Baja Fresh Mexican Grill in the United States. And, while most of early California was Christian, there has been a rapid growth of local cultural communities in which Judaism, Islam, or Buddhism is dominant. Because geography focuses on cultural traits and the impact of human culture on the environment, *culture* is one of the leading concepts taught in interdisciplinary elementary school social studies programs.

CHECK YOUR UNDERSTANDING 10.5 **Click here** to check your understanding of this section of the chapter.

Essential Element 5: Environment and Society

Suppose you were among the first group of settlers to step onto the shores of this land. Undoubtedly, you would have been overwhelmed by the incredible beauty of the vast, unspoiled environment. You would have marveled at the sparkling clear water in the streams, observed abundant natural wildlife, peered into the bright blue skies, and inhaled a lungful of pure fresh air. In just over 300 years, we have turned that pristine terrain into a natural time bomb that poses an explosive threat to the survival of life and beauty on this planet. Burning fossil fuels in our vehicles releases toxic air pollutants; across the Americas, the last snippets of wild nature are being wiped out by chain saws and bulldozers; Earth's atmosphere has become congested with heat-trapping carbon dioxide, threatening large-scale global warming; our streams and lakes have become contaminated; and uncluttered landscapes are rapidly becoming a memory. Every day, Earth becomes more and more polluted. It is apparent that we are passing on to our youth a planet that is markedly unhealthy.

This is where Essential Element 5 enters the picture. Education is the key to raising awareness of environmental challenges and shaping attitudes that can make a difference in the future. Children must be helped to recognize that Earth is a habitat shared by people and other living things and that its survival depends on a complicated relationship between delicate human and physical systems. Margaret Mead (1978), a distinguished anthropologist and social activist who wrote about many contemporary issues, hoped that schools would help children learn about a more humane and socially responsible society: "If children feel themselves as part of the living world, learn respect for it, and their uniqueness in it, they will have a foundation for growth into responsible citizens who will be able to discriminate and make decisions about science used for constructive purposes and the science used for destructive purposes" (p. 114). Therefore, contemporary social studies programs, through sound interdisciplinary planning, must enhance our students' understandings of the complexity of contemporary natural problems and help them achieve a sense of responsibility for restoring and preserving our natural environment. Cultivating an awareness of and a respect for Earth's systems must be integrated throughout the entire curriculum.

Many teachers capitalize on the annual celebration of Earth Day, celebrated around the world in an effort to increase awareness and appreciation for our planet, as a wonderful opportunity to teach children about the environment. Earth Day was first celebrated in San

Francisco on March 21, 1970, but eventually April 22 was adopted as the date for worldwide celebration. From humble beginnings, the Earth Day movement has grown considerably, with official Earth Day celebrations being held in 175 nations. Check the Green Schools Initiative and the United States Environmental Protection Agency websites for downloadable lists of Earth Day activities.

To prepare her students to celebrate Earth Day, Michele Burns taught a series of lessons about human impact on the environment prior to April 22. She divided her students into groups, each of which was assigned to produce an Earth Day brochure designed to increase awareness and appreciation of a specific environmental issue. In addition, each group constructed a "booth" and set it up on the school playground. Parents and other visitors were invited to the Earth Day celebration; the students handed out their brochures when visitors came to their booth and discussed their particular environment issue. The students took great pleasure in showing how much they had learned and how important it was to share that knowledge with others.

Our youth today must be convinced that saving Earth is important and that they can make a big difference in preserving our planet. Through appropriate learning experiences, students must be helped to realize that many of the things they can do will be fun, but others will require a lot of serious work. Regardless of whether their efforts are thought of as being fun or work, it is important for them to muster the courage and passion to step forward and make a difference.

Reflection on Learning

You may simply scribble rough notes or jot down something more polished and complete. The point is to simply start recording your ideas spontaneously and candidly.

Geography can be a useful interdisciplinary subject; however, most states have left geography off the list of "tested" elementary school subjects. This omission has pushed geography to the back burner of many schools' curricula. Why should geography move to the front burner?

 CHECK YOUR UNDERSTANDING 10.6   Click here to check your understanding of this section of the chapter.

Essential Element 6: The Uses of Geography

As the uncertainties of the future confront us, thinking geographically offers a vehicle for meeting and adapting to new challenges. What does one do to think geographically? The process involves five basic steps (Geography Education Standards Project, 1994):

1. Asking geographic questions
2. Acquiring geographic information
3. Organizing geographic information
4. Analyzing geographic information
5. Answering geographic questions

These skills are most often accomplished through question-driven inquiry and problem-solving experiences that engage students, with appropriate teacher support, in acquiring, organizing, and using geographic information.

Asking Geographic Questions

The process of geographic understanding begins with observing an actual geographic feature (e.g., pond, building, road) or a representation of an environmental feature (e.g., video, photograph, illustration) and asking these questions: "What do you see here?" "What is this place like?" "Why is it here?" "What is significant about this place?" "How is it like or different from other places you know about?" These questions help students describe and define places.

Alexis Little knew, for example, that in her thematic unit "Homes around the World," some types of homes were too far away (e.g., adobe homes, yurts) for field observations in those places to occur, but that it was possible to take a trip to Hoopes Park so the children could study the oldest still-standing structure in the community—a well-preserved stone farmhouse originally built in 1738. This stone farmhouse, built by Thomas Hoopes, using stone from an adjacent quarry, is very important to the community and can be found nestled in a grassy plot at the center of the park that bears his name. The children enjoyed visiting this site and learned a great deal about the property's charm as they examined its original architectural details.

When Ms. Little's young geographers go to a field site, they always take field notes and make sketches of what they observe and would like to learn more about. Sketches or field notes become the basis for detailed illustrations or for the construction of models; field notes are used to write summary accounts of or narratives about the trip.

Geographic investigations begin with observation, but they don't stop there. Observation lays the foundation for more complex understandings, such as why things are where they are and how they got there: "Where is it located?" "Why is it there?" "What do you think has caused it to look this way?" Students must not stop the process of learning about a geographic location simply by looking at and describing it; they must speculate about possible answers to "where?" and "why there?" questions.

Ms. Little, continuing with her "Homes around the World" unit, asked her young geographers to look for clues about how climate, natural resources, and other physical features might have influenced the selection of building materials as well as the design of a home. She asked the compelling question, "How have people adapted their homes to the environment?" This process should not be pure guesswork but rather a systematic form of deductive reasoning that calls on students to use previously acquired understandings and experiences to make reasoned inferences. These inferences, in turn, will be tested by the students while they uncover supportive data.

Acquiring Geographic Information

Skills used in acquiring geographic information include locating and collecting data, systematically recording information, and reading maps of places on Earth. In this second phase of geographic inquiry, Ms. Little subdivided the class into specialized research groups such as "yurts" (Mongolia), "tepees and wigwams" (Native American Indian), and "leaf huts" (Central African rain forest). Her students were expected to locate and gather information from primary and secondary sources to address the compelling question "How have people adapted their homes to the environment?" and the supporting questions "What kind of homes are these?" "What are they made of?" "How were they made?" "Why are they made this way?" "What do you think has caused it to look this way?" As the students worked, Ms. Little visited each group and used timely questions and prompts to direct and extend their thinking. For example, while visiting the adobe group, she offered prompts like these: "How do these homes compare with ours?" "Why are adobe homes so popular in some parts of the world?" "Do you think that homes in those areas will always be built this way?"

Organizing Geographic Information

Once the geographic information is located and gathered, it must be organized and displayed in such a way that it can be shared with others. Students may use charts, graphs, models, illustrations, narratives, time lines, maps, or clear written and oral summaries. Ms. Little, for example, asked the students to record on a chart all the facts they had uncovered about adobe homes. The students had been learning how to write effective informational paragraphs in language arts class, so this was a perfect opportunity to apply what they had learned: form a paragraph with a good topic sentence, supporting details, and a closing sentence.

After deciding on its topic sentence and the order in which the supporting details should be written, the "tepees and wigwams" group drafted this paragraph for wigwams:

Some people think the words "wigwam" and "tipi" mean the same thing. But they are very different kinds of houses that were built different and had different uses. Wigwams are round, domed huts that the Northeastern tribes called wigwams and the Southwestern tribes called wikiups. To build a wigwam, the men found many young tree saplings that were about 10 to 15 feet tall. They would make a big circle on the ground and space the saplings evenly around the circle. The saplings were bent toward the middle and tied at the top to form the frame of a small home that was 8 to 10 feet high. Then the women would cover the frame with materials that were found near where the tribe lived. Some were birchbark, others could be grass, reeds, animal hides, or even cloth. If the wigwams were not destroyed by the winter, the wigwams would be used for another year. If they did not survive the winter, new ones were built.

Next, the group studied its paragraph and edited it. For example, the students realized that "different" in the second line was used incorrectly so they changed it to "differently." They also felt the sentence would read better if it did not contain the word "different" three times. So they rewrote the sentence: "But they are very different kinds of houses that were not built the same and were used for dissimilar purposes." They went on to edit the rest of the paragraph and wrote the final copy on chart paper. Then they added appropriate illustrations of wigwams in their typical environment. They did the same for tepees. Finally, the group drew a map and used it to show the geographical distribution of wigwams and tepees.

Analyzing Geographic Information

The fourth geographic skill is interpreting and analyzing the information. It asks questions such as these: "Have the people been wise in using the environment in such a way?" and "Is this the most productive use of the land or its resources?" All personal opinions must be supported with sound reasons: "If not, why not?" "If so, why?" Since so many conditions of our world are intimately associated with the judicious use of Earth's physical environment, skills in this realm are of primary importance to children, the adult citizens of the future.

Geography helps students explore the ways Earth's environment influences the design and construction of homes such as wigwams ans tepees.

123RF

Waddell Images/Shutterstock

The wigwam and tepee group, for example, learned that tepees were used by hunting parties or nomadic tribes of the Great Plains. They needed shelters that could be put up, taken down, and easily moved from place to place. Other tribes had a different lifestyle. Some, like the Iroquois and other Northeastern tribes settled in villages and farmed the land. They wanted a more permanent home.

Answering Geographic Questions

Successful geographic inquiry culminates either in presenting geographic information in engaging and effective ways or extending the information that was collected, organized, and analyzed. Skills include sharing information in oral or written form while accompanied by maps, graphs, models, and other visuals. For example, Ms. Little's students organized a display that integrated maps, graphs, models of homes found around the world, and short paragraphs presenting answers to their geographic questions.

One group demonstrated the process of adobe brick making to accompany its presentation on adobe houses (pueblos)—the Native American house complexes built and used by the Pueblo Indians of the Southwest. The students explained how the Spanish introduced adobe bricks to the Pueblo Indians and then they showed an adobe brick-making process they had learned about on the web. To prepare, they mixed earth, straw, and water to create the mud (*zoquete*), packed it tightly into a wooden mold, and placed it outdoors to thoroughly dry in the sun for three or four days. On the day of their presentation, the students brought the hard brick into the classroom, took the form by the handles, and released the adobe brick. "Congratulations," commended Ms. Little. "Only 6,000 more, and we'll have enough to construct our own casita!"

✔ **CHECK YOUR UNDERSTANDING 10.7** **Click here** to check your understanding of this section of the chapter.

A Final Thought

By preparing students with the geographic knowledge and skills they need to make wise judgments about their environment, you will help develop caring citizens and powerful decision makers. That's certainly a worthy ambition for the future of our nation and the world, but one very important question must be answered before we can hope to achieve that ambition: How does a society that has not learned geography well teach it to a new generation? A step in the right direction would be to make the subject more interesting and more worthwhile for students. Professional education is the key to helping teachers master the specialized content of geography and the distinctive teaching methods that engage students in active learning. If teachers do not receive the necessary training in the content and processes of geography, they run the risk of teaching it like they might have been taught in elementary school—memorizing state capitals and the major exports of a country. As one of a new generation of teachers, you must stand ready and willing to take on the role of "expert" in the field. But there is more than knowing the content and processes of geography and mastering the recommended strategies for teaching them. You must help children understand that our Earth is shared by people and other living things, and it must be carefully maintained. You must also recognize the need for geography in a contemporary world where our continued existence hinges on the attitudes of our nation's young citizens toward our fragile planet.

From creating community maps to deciphering road maps and satellite images, this chapter offered simple, enjoyable suggestions for teaching young geographers the fundamentals of geography. As the power and beauty of geography are unlocked in dynamic social studies classrooms, children can much more clearly see, understand, and appreciate the web of relationships among the people and places on Earth.

References

Bednarz, S. W., Acheson, G., & Bednarz, R. S. (2006). Maps and map learning in social studies. *Social Education, 70,* 398–404, 432.

Committee on Geographic Education. (1984). *Guidelines for geographic education: Elementary and secondary schools.* Washington, DC: Association of American Geographers.

Gandy, S. K. (2007). Developmentally appropriate geography. *Social Studies and the Young Learner, 20,* 30–32.

Geography Education Standards Project. (1994). *Geography for life: National geography standards 1994.* Washington, DC: National Geographic Research & Exploration.

Grosvenor, G. M. (2007). The excitement of geography. *Social Studies and the Young Learner, 20,* 4–6.

Joint Committee on Geographic Education of the National Council for Geographic Education and the Association of American Geographers. (1984). *Guidelines for geographic education: Elementary and secondary schools.* Washington, DC: Author.

Mead, M. (1978). Creating a scientific climate for children. In C. Charles & B. Samples (Eds.), *Science and society: Knowing, teaching, learning.* Washington, DC: National Council for the Social Studies.

National Assessment of Educational Progress (2014). *The nation's report card: 2014 geography assessment.* Retrieved from http://www.nationsreportcard.gov /hgc_2014/#geography/

Piaget, J. & Inhedler, B. (1969). *The psychology of the child.* New York: Basic Books.

Riska, C. (2014). *Map It! with Children.* Retrieved from http://education.nationalgeographic.org/news /map-it-young-children/

Sobel, D. (1998). *Mapmaking with children: Education for the elementary years.* Portsmouth, NH: Heinemann.

Twain, M. (2001). *Tom Sawyer abroad.* Retrieved from http://books.google.com/books?id=hI8DGkScAvUC&vq =Tom+Sawyer+Abroad

CHAPTER 11

Civics:
Young Citizens in Action

Learning Outcomes

Young children start developing citizenship skills by living and practicing good citizenship in democratic classrooms. It is in this democratic classroom community that students will learn to make choices and take responsibility for their actions; to give and receive respect; to express ideas freely; to experience the rights and responsibilities of good citizenship; and to experience the strength of positive social relationships within a cohesive community. From this informal beginning, teachers infuse a formal social studies program with content and experiences designed to engage students' minds in probing the deeper questions of the duties, obligations, and functions of citizenship in our democracy. After completing this chapter, you will be able to:

- Define the term *civics* as a primary source of citizenship knowledge, skills, and attitudes.

- Explain how to design "best practices" that lead to an understanding of government and what it should do.

- Explain how to create classroom experiences that help students understand the basic values and principles of American democracy.

- Describe how the government established by the Constitution embodies the purposes, values, and principles of American democracy, and how to design strategies that help children construct associated concepts.

- Clarify the relationship of the United States to other nations and to world affairs.

- Explain the roles of the citizen in American democracy and describe how to teach the meaning of citizenship in the United States.

Classroom Snapshot

Claire Boyer enjoyed taking the study of local government beyond the textbook to where the action was, so she turned her students loose on a civics adventure that was firmly grounded on the district-wide recommended standards:

> *I.A. "What is government?"*
>
> *I.C. "Why is government necessary?"*
>
> *I.D. "What are some of the most important things governments do?"*
>
> *I.E. "What are the purposes of rules and laws?"*
>
> *III.D. "What are the major responsibilities of local governments?"*

For her special standards-driven project, Mrs. Boyer challenged her young citizens to build a town for themselves and run it. To start, Mrs. Boyer asked her students to pretend to be adult citizens in their community, called Media, 30 years in the future. To simulate the future, she read them a "letter from the Environmental Protection Agency" dated 30 years from now, demanding that all citizens move from Media as soon as possible due to severe and irreversible toxic waste problems. The students took on the role of the citizens, traveling together in search of a new place to settle. They were led to a large, empty room in the school basement where, to keep track of the victims of this unfortunate plight, the "citizens" were required to fill out Official Community Census Forms. After they completed the census, the citizens of this new town ("New Media") built homes for themselves from large packing boxes. The citizens painted and pasted until they were satisfied that the boxes looked like "real houses." Streets were laid out and named: A street sign bearing the name "Dunlap Street" was a tribute to Mr. Richard Dunlap, the principal of Media Elementary School, but no one was quite sure of the inspiration for Grape Road or Ice Road. A town newspaper was launched to chronicle the daily progress of New Media's citizens and to keep its populace informed. "Toxic Waste Forces Townspeople to New Land," blared the headlines on January 7, the first day of the project. An accompanying story read, "Townspeople Paint the Town," in reference to the construction of new homes.

The day after the families completed their homes, they held a town meeting to discuss potential community problems, with Mrs. Boyer presiding for the first meeting only. As is often the case with youngsters this age, they could foresee no particular problems. However, Mrs. Boyer was quick to suggest some—fires, crime, and problems that might arise if she could not lead future town meetings. Discussion led to the establishment of police and fire departments and an election for mayor. The children quickly set up minimum qualifications for voter registration and went about soliciting candidates for the mayoral position. Campaigning and debating began as students forged their platforms: Alex promised a cleaner environment, and Curtis vowed gun control. Candidates then planned campaign strategies, showing that political make-believe often mirrors political reality. There was, to be specific, the "great cookie caper," involving Alex and her closest opponent, Curtis. On the last day of campaigning, Alex distributed "Vote for Alex" pamphlets, decorated with paper hands grasping real chocolate chip cookies. Curtis's followers quickly cried "Bribery!" and complained that Alex was trying to buy votes. The matter went to the election board, which found that "No influence was obtained through the distribution of the cookies."

Following her landslide 14–2 victory, Alex immediately appointed Curtis as chief of police and presented him with his first book of tickets. Using his tickets to control the breaking of laws such as speeding (running in the halls), littering ($100 fine), and loitering (daydreaming), Curtis eventually learned the powers of his position. Through it all, Alex made new friends, was subject to the pressures of old ones, and generally learned that a position of authority has rewards as well as pitfalls. "I learned I'm never gonna be the real mayor," she reflected. "Even just pretending to be the mayor is a tough job."

Alex and her council members provided crucial leadership as the town began to grow through its hectic early days. Other classrooms acquired a sense of civic responsibility and offered to contribute to the growth of New Media. The first graders, studying the topic "Needs of People," contributed a food store and displayed the products themselves (Bob's California watermelon: $20 a pound). The third graders, studying "What Towns Need," built an electric power station, stringing yarn lines from one cardboard tube light pole to another all around town. The fourth graders, not involved in a relevant social studies topic at the time, demonstrated the interrelatedness of the physical and social sciences. They wired up streetlights by connecting batteries to light *bulbs, thus applying their knowledge of energy to making lives better for people. The fifth graders, anxious to contribute with the rest, made a trash truck (complete with oatmeal-box "trash cans" for the customers) and a bus from cardboard boxes. Finally, the kindergarten class spruced up the entire town with pink, white, and red paper flowers.*

The village of New Media grew through the remainder of the school year as the children added new features to coincide with what they were studying. The students served as perfect hosts as visitors from area elementary schools came to Media Elementary School to witness the expansion of New Media.

For a democracy to flourish, its citizens must acquire skills, values, and behaviors that are in accordance with its foundational principles. They must know enough about its governmental mechanisms to be able to access them when their interests are at stake. They must accept the responsibility to participate in local and national politics, improve community conditions, and participate in other civic initiatives. They must believe in the democratic ideal of participation and certain key democratic values, such as liberty, justice, equity, and the rule of law. Mrs. Boyer is convinced that active civic education can lead to positive change along these dimensions but that it is not enough to expose children to just any civic education program; children must experience their roles as young citizens in the classroom. For that reason, Mrs. Boyer finds great value in a recommendation for civics instruction made by the National Council for the Social Studies in its position statement *Creating Effective Citizens*: "Students are provided with opportunities to participate in simulations . . . and other activities that encourage the application of civic knowledge, skills, and values" (NCCS, 2001, p. 319). Simulations mimic the actual social conditions so well that there is little difference between the simulated environment and the real one, and the same kinds of learning outcomes can be brought about. So if you were to step into Mrs. Boyer's classroom, you would find her students voting, proposing public policy, establishing and enforcing their own rules, and making sound judgments for the good of the classroom; they are getting firsthand experience that will prepare them for the challenges and opportunities of adult life in American society.

Mrs. Boyer refers to her students as *young citizens*. She chose that term because, as young citizens, her students take on a classroom role that Alexis de Tocqueville called "an apprenticeship in liberty" and that Thomas Jefferson referred to as "office of citizen." She seeks to accomplish this mission through both a formal civics curriculum and an informal civics curriculum that makes the teaching and learning process a democratic experience for everyone. The primary aim of the *formal civics curriculum* is to facilitate the acquisition of basic and realistic knowledge of our rights and responsibilities as citizens and how governments work. The *informal civics curriculum* addresses the governance of the classroom community and the relationships among those within it; through the informal curriculum, students experience the dynamics and relationships that embody the fundamental principles and values of a democracy. So a teacher's role is to use integrative, creative, and active strategies not only to help construct meaningful subject matter content but also to establish an environment in which children have firsthand experience with the values that are part of democratic citizenship—liberty, equality, justice, freedom, tolerance, responsibility, and community.

Civics in Focus

The term *civics* comes from the Latin *civis*, which means "citizen." Civics education is considered the piece of the elementary school curriculum primarily responsible for developing and nourishing good citizenship. When they study civics, students learn about three major components of effective citizenship: *citizen rights* (e.g., understanding the guarantees of the First Amendment to the Constitution), *citizen responsibilities* (e.g., being an informed voter), and *how governments work* (e.g., knowing that the executive branch of the government is responsible for enforcing the laws of the land). While family, media, and other institutions share in the mission of developing good citizens, public education has always taken on the primary responsibility of preparing informed and engaged youth who are committed to the preservation of our democratic republic.

Why Is Civics Important?

By the late 1700s, education was considered a fundamental element to guide this new nation and its people into the future. Thomas Jefferson, for example, has been widely acclaimed for emphasizing the importance of education in a democracy, believing that education for all was necessary to ensure the success of the "Grand Experiment" undertaken in 1776—the first country that was formed "by the people, for the people" and based on democracy and liberty. Jefferson had faith in the ability of common people to elect wise and virtuous leaders and participate in government; informed citizens were considered the lifeblood of a democracy. Our educational leaders agreed with Jefferson, fearing that ill-informed students would soon become ill-informed citizens. That is why, from the beginning of our nation's history, Americans have been supportive of the idea that education is essential to sustaining our constitutional democracy and that there is no more important educational responsibility than developing informed, effective, and responsible citizens.

What Should Students Know or Be Able to Do?

Obviously, the goal of civics education is to help produce citizens committed to the principles of American constitutional democracy. But finding the time to accomplish this goal, given all the accountability measures presently heaped on teachers, is challenging. It seems that civics instruction, as other nontested subjects in today's standards-based testing era, is considered by many to be relatively less important than tested subjects such as math, science, and reading. Because civics has been considered "less important," it has been de-emphasized to such a degree that, when it *is* taught, it is often done superficially with content too far removed from the children's lives. Unfortunately, when it is taught like that, students struggle with topics such as the Constitution, election processes, and the steps involved in making laws because many children have a tough time understanding them and have little interest in learning about them ("Why do we have to study this stuff, anyway?"). Interestingly, when children have the opportunity to participate meaningfully as citizens in supportive democratic learning communities, they tend to develop a deeper interest in exploring the content of civics and in acquiring the knowledge essential to eventually becoming involved in the civic life of their local, state, national, and global communities.

The Center for Civic Education (1994) established a set of standards to help guide teachers in building high-quality formal civics curricula designed to nurture effective citizenship. The standards define what content understandings the students should develop as well as the intellectual and participatory skills they should acquire. The five major content standards, framed as questions, will serve as the organizing framework for the rest of this chapter.

1. What is government, and what should it do?
2. What are the basic values and principles of American democracy?
3. How does the government established by the Constitution embody the purposes, values, and principles of American democracy?
4. What is the relationship of the United States to other nations and to world affairs?
5. What are the roles of the citizen in American democracy?

> ☑ **CHECK YOUR UNDERSTANDING 11.1**   **Click here** to check your understanding of this section of the chapter.

What Is Government and What Should It Do?

Throughout the formal civics curriculum, students learn about the primary functions of government—to maintain order, settle conflicts, and protect the community—and that governments around the world come in many forms. Other than democracies, some of the most common categories are:

- *Monarchy.* A government in which the supreme power is lodged in the hands of a king or queen (sometimes an emperor) who reigns over a state or territory, usually for life and by hereditary right.
- *Oligarchy.* A government in which control is exercised by a small group of individuals whose authority is generally based on wealth or power.
- *Dictatorship.* A form of government in which a single ruler wields absolute power (not restricted by a constitution or laws).
- *Totalitarianism.* A government that seeks to subordinate the individual to the state by controlling the attitudes, values, and beliefs of its population as well as economic and political matters.
- *Anarchy.* A condition of lawlessness or political disorder brought about by the absence of governmental authority.

Every government, regardless of form, exercises three main functions: making laws, executing the laws, and interpreting or applying the laws. These functions correspond to the legislative, executive, and judicial branches of any government. In some governments, the ultimate responsibility for exercising power is held by a single person or small group. Those are known as *authoritarian governments*. In others, the responsibility for exercising power is assigned to the people. Those governments are known as *democracies*. Authoritarian governments are perhaps the oldest and most common form of government. On the other hand, in democracies, the people hold supreme authority. A democracy can be either direct or indirect. In *direct democracies*, public policy is established by the people themselves, as in New England town meetings. Because this form of government can work only when the citizenry can meet together as a whole, it is effective only in very small communities. A more familiar type of democracy is called *indirect democracy*, or *representative democracy*. In representative democracies, the people choose a small group to act as their representatives to carry out the policies of government.

Our students do not need to wait until they reach the age of 18 to experience what it means to be a citizen in a democratic society; citizenship awareness must start in their classrooms. Parker (2006) commented that when children go to school, they are immersed in an informal curriculum that teaches a great deal: "Its power at least matches that of the school's formal curriculum because the children experience it day after day. It's the 'air they breathe' there, so to speak, in the classrooms, hallways, playground, cafeteria, the principal's office, everywhere. In key ways . . . it shapes who they become" (p. 12). The informal civics classroom embraces the lives of students as young citizens today—not just as a "breaking in" stage for some obscure, far-off tomorrow.

Building a Democratic Classroom Community

Some teachers prefer to "live" the democratic principles of governmental authority for all matters beginning on the first day of school and lasting throughout the school year. At no other time during the school year do optimism, anticipation, and hope soar so high as on the first day of school. Returning from summer vacation, most children are renewed and energized—raring to go and excited to start a fresh, new school year. A familiar picture is painted on the first day of school in every community around the country: children, most chuckling and shouting, some with blank stares on their faces, all toting an assortment of packs on their backs, excitedly stepping off a large yellow bus and parading through a set of welcoming doors. The day brings out a range of emotions in children, teachers, administrators, and parents; it's a huge day in everyone's life.

Sadly, one of the first things some teachers do to quash this early enthusiasm is to promptly notify students who is boss: "Read them the 'riot act' as soon as they step inside the door," they insist. "You've got to jump on them for any monkey business, no matter how small; if you don't, it only gets worse as the year goes on!" These authoritarian teachers demonstrate little regard for their students with their harsh and insensitive remarks: "I make sure I don't smile until at least Thanksgiving. . . . You've got to intimidate them, or they'll run all over you." These teachers expect nothing short of meek and obedient behavior, dealing out severe penalties for those who do wrong; fear is their power source. At an extreme, these *authoritarian teachers* show little outward sign of personal interest in or affection for their students.

I hope you never had a teacher at this extreme because the encounters they have with children are discomforting, and they slowly chip away at their fragile shell of self-respect. The effect of biting criticism and sarcasm is humiliation; children end up feeling bad, stupid, dishonest, or irresponsible. Throughout my career in education, I have met very few elementary school children who come to school with the deliberate intention of making their teacher's day as miserable as possible. Most seek the affection and support that caring adults provide in a nurturing environment. When they see an angry face, hear a sharp voice, or become the target of an icy glare, children feel more pain and heartache than we can imagine; hurtful feedback cuts deeply, especially because children are at a point in life when they very much need acceptance and support.

Not surprisingly, democratic teachers totally reject this insensitive approach. "That's ridiculous advice," they counter. "Children should see their teacher as a positive influence, not as someone to steer clear of. Teachers need to smile, not scowl. If you don't smile until Thanksgiving, neither will the children!" For some teachers, though, the idea of establishing a *democratic classroom community* is easier said than done. It seems that they often think of a democratic classroom as a "laissez-faire" classroom in which very few demands or controls are placed on the students; "Do your own thing" is often the message. Called *permissives*, these teachers are convinced that any corrective response has the potential to inhibit their children's behavior and cause them to fear or resent adult power. Not surprisingly, permissive classrooms are loud, confused, disorderly, and dangerous. In the long run, children lose respect for such a teacher and begin to wonder, "Will I be safe here?" and "Can my teacher protect me?"

An important point is that a democratic learning community is not a place where a teacher is powerless and without control. Because of legal requirements, teachers must be in control. However, as a democratic teacher, you establish the conditions for democracy to exist—a place where students are helped to establish the rules, take responsibility for their own behavior, and know that their teacher is there to help everyone work together. Taken a step further, a democratic teacher is an *authoritative* facilitator (not *authoritarian*)—an adult who can be trusted and turned to in full faith; a caring individual who knows how to say the right word or do the right thing at just the right time. Authoritative teachers do not use gruff voices, nor do they scowl at children to control them; they do not ridicule, yell, or threaten. Likewise, they do not seem so disinterested and so far removed from situations that the children feel alone. Authoritative teachers are neither feeble nor overbearing. Instead, they hold children in deep regard; they never shrink from the responsibility to lead when the children need their help. They are firm when they need to be, and they are gentle, too, placing limits and controls on the students while simultaneously encouraging independence.

The overall goal of authoritative leadership is to establish a democratic classroom community—a group of diverse individuals living in the same place; having common rights, privileges, or interests; and unified under common rules. The classroom will not become a democratic

Authoritative teachers develop positive and supportive relationships within safe, happy classrooms; students trust and respect authoritative teachers.

Gelpi/Fotolia

community simply because you want it to be one; the children must learn that it is a type of social structure where everyone has a connection to others and shares a commitment to tolerance, respect, and shared values: "We are all here to help each other live and learn."

Obenchain and Morris (2011) advise that democratic classroom communities develop from the first day of school through the use of authentic learning experiences. So, whether you are teaching kindergarten or fifth grade, there are many simple things you can do on the very first day of school to help prepare your students for this new adventure in life. Let your students know that you are eager to meet them by greeting them at the door, smiling (yes, even before Thanksgiving), using eye contact when saying hello, and offering a personal comment that shows you are interested in them ("I'm happy to see you. Welcome to *our* [not *my*] classroom.") A warm welcome goes a long way toward starting out the year right.

On the first day of school, it is important to find creative ways to help children learn about each other. A variety of get-acquainted games and activities will help; for example, many teachers choose to read children a book with a "first day of school" theme, such as Margaret Wise Brown's *The Important Book* (HarperTrophy). Using highly predictable text, the book explains the "important thing" about all sorts of objects such as a spoon, apple, or shoe. (The most important thing about a spoon? You eat with it.)

To model what her students will be asked to do after the book reading experience, Ms. Fleming shared her original illustrated written piece that was patterned after the author's style—her own "Most Important" page: "The most important thing about Ms. Fleming is that she loves to teach. Ms. Fleming has a pet basset hound, plays golf, and loves to garden. But the most important thing about Ms. Fleming is that she loves to teach." Next, the students wrote their individual "Most Important" text beneath digital photos (or you may ask your students to draw self-portraits) for The Classroom Important Book. *The students will love this first illustrated book of the year. It is also handy for substitute teachers who come to your class throughout the year. They will appreciate that this resource helps them match faces with names.*

RESPONSIBLE CITIZENSHIP: CLASSROOM RULES

Although the classroom rule-making process may not be the right time to introduce documents such as the Magna Carta or the U.S. Constitution and its Bill of Rights, it is instructive to help students understand that classroom rules, like rules associated with sports or family games, are made to guide behavior and establish conventional procedures and routines. Start the process early in the school year by soliciting help from the students in developing a set of classroom rules and responsibilities: What actions must we take to start a new classroom government? This process gives students ownership in the process and makes them more likely to hold each other accountable.

To start, help the children brainstorm ideas to describe a good classroom environment for learning: "What are some important rules that can help us live together safely and happily in our classroom community?" "How should we act so that our classroom is an orderly and safe place for everyone?" When the reasons, or justifications, for rules are a part of your question, students are more inclined to think about rules as positive and practical standards of conduct rather than as unnecessary and "picky" restraints. It is very important, then, that your students recognize that rules are based on shared values such as responsibility, truthfulness, respect, fairness, or justice and that a good classroom citizen is one who properly fulfills his or her expected role of establishing and following "the law."

When prompts for rule discussions are presented to children in positive terms ("What do we need to do so that everyone can be happy and safe in our classroom?"), chances are greater that children will respond with positive rules rather than lists of restraints. However, children may come up with a number of "Don'ts," such as "Don't talk unless you raise your hand." Challenge students to state the rules positively; children should try to say what they should do as opposed to what they should not do. In addition, it is important to make sure that the rules are stated in language that the students can understand. A small picture or illustration next to each rule can help younger children unravel any confusing words. Another critical consideration is to limit the final list to three to five rules. Students are much more likely to remember a shorter list of general rules than a lengthy list of very specific ones. To help the students trim down their original list, ask them to examine the list and try to group together the rules that mean close to the same thing. For example, the children might group together these suggestions: "Don't hit others," "Don't call anybody a bad name," and "No bullying!" The children should then suggest one big positive rule to replace all the little negative rules they grouped together: "Treat others respectfully." The next task is to design a final poster displaying the final list of general classroom rules. Here is a sample:

- Treat others the way you want to be treated.
- Respect school property.
- Settle disagreements ourselves. If we cannot, we will ask our teacher for help.
- Follow all classroom routines and procedures.

All students must understand that they are subject to the mutually established rules of their classroom community so, before the rules are posted in a prominent place in the classroom, students should sign the document indicating that they accept the rules and, if they break a rule, agree to accept the logical and appropriate consequences. Do not just display the poster and leave it alone; you must teach the rules and consequences just like any other curriculum content. You could have the most impressive set of classroom rules in the country, but if the rules are not fairly and consistently enforced with appropriate consequences, they will be useless. Chaos will ensue if students realize that they can break the rules and suffer no consequences.

The rule-making process is serious business, and the rules collectively apply to everyone—to you as well as to your students. Think about the rule of being respectful to others, for example, when you see a teacher sitting at his desk, head down, feverishly writing a note to a colleague. Meanwhile, a little child timidly approaches to ask for clarification about a task being worked on for a group project. The teacher seems highly irritated at the loss of private time and growls sharply: "No, I can't help you. I gave the directions once, and you chose not to listen!" Why do we so often demand politeness and consideration from students and grant immunity to ourselves? We should never forget that we are powerful role models for our students, and we must hold ourselves to the same standards for civility and respect that we expect from our students. If a classroom rule states, "Treat others respectfully," the rule applies equally to students and teachers. Teachers are mirrors for their students.

RESPONSIBLE CITIZENSHIP: CLASSROOM PROCEDURES

Cooperatively constructing classroom rules helps students operate as active, engaged, and informed classroom citizens, provides a sense of ownership that makes cooperation more likely, and helps students understand the shared values on which democratic rules are based.

Point out that, as in our democratic nation, each rule implies both a right and a corresponding responsibility. Explain that everyone at school has the *right* to learn, be safe, and be happy, but it is also everyone's *responsibility* to behave in a way that recognizes and respects the rights of others.

Although you play many roles in the classroom, one of the most important is that of classroom manager. So along with classroom rules, you must help establish procedures. Although some may think procedures and rules are the same, they are not. Rules are broad statements describing the classroom environment while procedures detail the many acceptable actions subsumed under each rule: "I have to use the restroom. When may I go?" "I'm finished with my work. What do I do now?" "Under what conditions can I use the classroom computers or look at a book all by myself?" Your students need to know these things.

Your students will appreciate the clarification, and will carry out specific routines much more compliantly once they have internalized the procedures. As you took time to explain the reasons behind particular rules, it is advisable to also involve students in establishing procedures. To begin the process, study all of your classroom routines: For what activities is a specific process necessary? Once you have generated your list, systematically outline steps to carry out each one. Then:

- Introduce the procedure by describing it clearly and modeling the process step by step.
- Ask several students to perform the procedure; provide additional explanation or demonstration, if necessary.
- Have everyone practice the procedure. Rehearse until the students can perform the procedure without teacher involvement. Be sure to communicate your approval when the procedure is successfully implemented.
- Reteach the procedure if called for and provide further explanation, demonstration, or corrective feedback.
- Periodically, review and rehearse the procedure.

Although breaking a rule may result in experiencing a consequence, forgetting a procedure brings only a reminder or a need for practice.

THE CONNECTION BETWEEN RULES AND LAWS

To connect the rule-making process to the powers of government, students learn about laws and about the main difference between *rules* and *laws*. Rules and laws are actually quite similar; the major purpose of both is to bring about a sense of order, fair play, and safety. They are so similar that children often have a tough time distinguishing between the two; in fact, even some dictionaries define "law" as a *set of rules*! I find it useful to think of rules as codes of conduct that are designed for specific situations—school rules, family rules, and rules for games and sports. Only the individuals directly involved in those enterprises are subject to their conditions. Laws, on the other hand, represent the legal regulations of our society and are applicable and enforceable to its entire population. So, just as we have rules at home and in our classroom, a local, state, or national government also has rules, called laws, for citizens to follow. For example, laws requiring people to stop at red lights or cross only at crosswalks help all of us exist safely on the streets. When you break a law, a more severe consequence (such as a fine, community service, or jail sentence) follows than if you break a rule. Think of laws as a constitutional version of rules that are created and enforced by governments.

To ensure the government is effective and citizens' rights are protected, the U.S. Federal Government is made up of three branches: legislative, executive, and judicial. Each branch has its own powers and responsibilities, including working with the other branches:

Legislative: This branch, made up of senators and representatives, has the power to originate and pass laws.

Executive: This branch, made up of the president, vice-president, and cabinet, has the power to administer and enforce laws.

Starting the school year includes involving students in creating a few simple classroom rules: "I think we should have a rule that says boys have to play on a separate playground!"

Spass/Fotolia

Judicial: This branch, made up of the Supreme Court and federal courts, has the power to interpret laws, settle disputes, and punish law breakers.

Whether local, county, or state, all governments in the United States have these three powers. For example, your local community council makes the laws, your mayor enforces them, and local courts uphold the laws. These powers are often described in a constitution—a written document that outlines the principles, structures, and processes of government.

MANAGING RULES THROUGH CLASS MEETINGS

Have you had a recent squabble with a friend? What about a confrontation with a member of a collaborative work group who fails to do his or her part? We've all have had experiences that make us realize just how stressful and complicated human relationships can be. If they are that difficult for adults, think about how complicated life can be for young children, who are egocentric and impulsive by nature. Picture the anxiety and stress children face daily—assignments that are too difficult, getting bullied, too much homework, wondering how to fit in . . . the list is monumental. One way to address particularly delicate classroom problems that need extra attention is through weekly or biweekly democratic class meetings. Students can use such meetings to clarify school rules and resolve interpersonal conflicts with the support of the group.

The younger children are, the more difficult it is for them to think of things from another's perspective, so it will take great effort for early classroom meetings to run smoothly. A teacher's role will vary depending on the grade level, but a few guidelines help make meetings function constructively. Class meetings are best carried out in an environment where children share freely and where they realize that what each has to contribute is worthwhile. A positive, supportive atmosphere is basic to smoothly operating class meetings. You must be careful to avoid using the class meeting as a platform for lecturing and moralizing about issues. This does not mean you lack input into the meetings; your input is important, too. However, you must remain as objective and nonjudgmental as possible. Children are very astute in recognizing teachers who use class meetings as a deceitful scheme to manipulate them.

Coming together in a circle, a semicircle, or an oval provides the greatest attention and maximum participation, as children are able to see one another when they talk and listen. It is helpful to use sentence starters as a springboard for interactive discussion if the children have never participated in a class meeting. Sample sentence starters include "Something I like about this classroom . . . " "Something I think would improve our classroom . . . " "An important decision I think we should make . . . " and "I wonder why . . . "

When the children get to the point where they can address important class problems through such prompts, a student can add an item to the meeting agenda by putting a piece of paper inside an agenda box or writing it on the board. The issue, which includes the student's name and date, makes up the agenda for the class meeting. A group leader, the teacher first serving as a capable model early in the year, helps the children grasp the class meeting procedure. After a few practice meetings, students will become interested in taking over; each interested student should have an opportunity to be a meeting leader sometime during the school year. The meeting script follows:

- *Clearly present the topic of discussion for the meeting.* Make sure everyone understands what the problem is. Problems are usually of two major types: (1) those dealing with schoolwork and (2) those having to do with difficulties among students. Class meetings should address only those problems affecting the entire class. Those that involve two or three children are best handled in other ways (unless they affect the entire class).

- *Implement recommended group problem-solving strategies.* Clarify the problem, analyze causes, identify alternatives, assess each alternative, choose a solution, implement the solution, and assess whether the solution was helpful.

- *Establish the rules of good discussion.* Signal when you want to speak, listen carefully to others, and be respectful of everyone's opinions (no put-downs, complaining, negative body language, or fault-finding).

- *Use active listening strategies.* Such strategies include paraphrasing a student's comments and asking clarifying questions.

- *Summarize what has been said.* All the ideas should be quickly repeated: "Let's go back and recall what was said."

The students should be helped to come up with constructive solutions to problems rather than suggest some type of penalty or punishment. You should have confidence in the students' decisions and make an effort to give their ideas a try, even if their proposals may have a good chance of failure. By doing this, teachers communicate a very important message: "I know you will do your best, and I have faith that you'll do what's right." However, if it is obvious that someone or something could be hurt or offended as a result of the class decision, you must exercise your "veto power." Because a major goal of class meetings is to help students make caring decisions, teachers should use their veto power only as a last resort. Students will learn from their mistakes.

Regardless of how they are used, democratic class meetings help students learn that their ideas are appreciated and valued and that they can benefit from working together as democratic citizens. Classroom meetings establish a feeling of trust and respect among teacher and students and help students accept responsibility for what goes on in their classroom—the ultimate goal of democracy in the classroom.

 Video Example 11.1 https://www.youtube.com/watch?v=FnWDN4neV2I
Class meetings enable students to share their thoughts and solve classroom issues on their own. The students and teachers in this video talk about the value of class meetings. In what ways do class meetings help build a democratic classroom community—a sense of group belonging?

CHECK YOUR UNDERSTANDING 11.2   Click here to check your understanding of this section of the chapter.

Reflection on Learning

You may simply scribble rough notes or jot down something more polished and complete. The point is to simply start recording your ideas spontaneously and candidly.

Democratic teachers can sometimes come across as being indecisive, especially during a crisis. Will there ever be any classroom situations that might call for you to take on an authoritarian, directive role and not be worried about fully addressing the thoughts and feelings of everyone involved?

What Are the Basic Values and Principles of American Democracy?

Interest in and concern about the values and principles that represent good citizenship are not new to America. These are among the most important reasons for establishing and expanding public schooling in Colonial America. During those early years, memorizing inspirational passages helped provide children with strict moral and religious lessons. Consider this passage from *The New England Primer*, a primary school text that was first published in the 1690s for the purpose of teaching children to read and to follow a pious life:

> *The idle fool*
> *Is whipt at school!*

Although values are taught much differently now, there is no doubt that learning the values we share in our contemporary American democracy continues to this day as a central goal of civics education. *Fostering Civic Virtue: Character Education in the Social Studies*, which is the position statement of the NCSS (1997), emphasizes the importance of teaching the civic values that we all share:

> *Preserving and expanding the American experiment in liberty is a challenge for each succeeding generation. No profession plays a more central role in meeting this challenge than the social studies teachers in our nation's schools. At the heart of social studies is the obligation to teach democratic principles and to inspire civic virtue in the young people who will shape our future.*

Character Education

The NCSS initiative is but one part of a widespread call for schools to be more active in teaching the fundamental beliefs and constitutional principles that unite all Americans—a process referred to as *character education*. Character education should not be thought of as the exclusive domain of social studies; rather, the entire elementary school curriculum provides the necessary conceptual framework for character education. Children participate in character education daily as they live and learn in democratic classroom communities where adults model good civic character and children experience the ideals of citizenship. Modeling and direct experience are among the most potent approaches to character education.

To help strengthen and reinforce those informal experiences, NCSS (1997) has emphasized:

In a society such as ours, where citizens have been divided and diverse throughout history, it is essential that schools and communities foster a reasoned commitment to the founding principles and values that bind us together as a people. A commitment to democratic principles, a willingness to engage in the democratic process, and the affirmation of core values are key elements of the bond that joins us as 'We the People.'

Implementation of character education programs with such aspirations can be contentious, however, because teaching values has historically been controversial. Some have argued that in a pluralistic society such as ours, there can be no common set of values; therefore, civics education must be free of objectives and values so that all viewpoints can be treated fairly. Others counter that the fabric of our democratic nation consists of fiber derived from honorable moral and ethical values and that the spirit of our nation requires commitment to the democratic principles and values so essential to the well-being of our nation.

Although the latter position is currently most popular, it does raise an inescapable question: *Which* values, or *whose*, should we teach? The Center for Civic Education (1994) answered this question directly by explaining that while there may be disagreement on certain issues, such as keeping the words *under God* in the Pledge of Allegiance, nearly everyone can agree on a list of basic democratic values that children ought to have and that schools ought to teach—civic virtues found in the U.S. Constitution and other documents. The center advised that students should be able to explain the importance for themselves, their school, their community, and their nation of each of the following fundamental values of American democracy: *individual rights to life, liberty, property, and the pursuit of happiness; the public or common good; justice; equality of opportunity; diversity; truth;* and *patriotism.*

Because traditional social studies subject matter provides the conceptual framework for an understanding and appreciation of the democratic way of life, it is important to highlight four techniques that are especially helpful in teaching and reinforcing character education and civic virtue: (1) reading and discussing books exemplifying civic character; (2) engaging in decision-making activities; (3) working to promote the values and principles of American democracy; and (4) recognizing the importance of symbols and holidays to national identity.

READING BOOKS EXEMPLIFYING CIVIC CHARACTER

Teachers frequently help children grasp the importance of democratic values and beliefs by reading and discussing biographies and other stories of notable characters who embody the core values of our culture. Basically, all literature deals with values, but especially appropriate for character education programs are stories of courageous women and men who display outstanding positive personal traits such as honesty, leadership, and compassion. Textbooks, with their distinctively informative approach, can define civil rights and describe its importance in a democracy, for example, but the effects of discrimination are much more explicit in a story about the early life of Martin Luther King, Jr., in *Marching to Freedom: The Story of Martin Luther King, Jr.*, by Joyce Milton (Dell Yearling, 1987). Readers can grasp the cruelty of racism as Milton's spellbinding words transport them back to 1943 and into the seats of a bus where they witness bigotry's horrors. It was in that bus that 14-year-old Martin Luther King, Jr., then known as M.L., first encountered the "Jim Crow" laws that he would never forget. M.L. and his teacher, Mrs. Bradley, were riding together on the bus as it pulled off to the side of the road to take on new passengers—white passengers. The bus driver ordered Mrs. Bradley and M.L. to give up their seats in a tone of voice M.L. had never heard before. The memory of that cruel encounter became permanently etched into M.L.'s memory. Although he was threatened and attacked repeatedly throughout his life, M.L. described that moment as the angriest he had ever been.

With increasing frequency, elementary school social studies teachers are making use of quality children's literature in their character education programs; children's books appear to be experiencing a second life as a basic resource for learning. Stories of civic virtue were at the curricular core of elementary school social studies well into the 20th century, but with the advent of social studies textbooks for elementary school classrooms, their popularity abruptly waned. Now, however, teachers are reconsidering good children's books to energize their social studies curriculum. This is not surprising, as children's books and social studies seem to be made for each other; literature makes it possible for children to connect on a personal level with characters, events, places, and problems.

ENGAGING IN DECISION-MAKING ACTIVITIES

In our nation's democratic system, who makes decisions is often established by rule or law. However, because the public has the right and responsibility to participate in the government, citizens also have the freedom and ample opportunity to become involved in the decision-making process. Therefore, decision making must be considered an essential citizenship responsibility. Since the lifeblood of our democracy is spirited debate over fundamental issues, those who know how to make good decisions tend to make better informed decisions when addressing public concerns.

Civic engagement is the process of applying decision-making skills to identify and address issues of public concern and to help improve conditions for others. Schools help foster civic engagement when they teach civic decision-making skills and provide an open classroom setting for discussing contentious issues. Therefore, students are helped to build decision-making skills and to effectively use those skills in real-life civic situations. The decision-making process is normally carried out in small groups where students investigate contestable issues. After presenting students with a significant civic problem, teachers implement a decision-making strategy in which the students (1) identify and describe the inherent values issue, (2) gather evidence to support both the positive and negative consequences of the decision, and then (3) make personal choices while attempting to resolve or take action regarding the issue. This is the same process active citizens use as they engage as decision makers in their own and the broader community.

The age-old art of storytelling, or story reading, is especially fitting for introducing students to civic issues. No special equipment beyond the power of listening and speaking is needed to draw the listeners into a character's life and the difficult choices confronting the character. After sharing the story, teachers help children visualize the three-step decision-making process with graphic organizers (visual diagrams based on a central issue or idea). During a unit on the Underground Railroad, for example, Thomas Morgan's fifth graders were learning about how the Underground Railroad helped assist runaway slaves.

Mr. Morgan enjoyed using dramatic stories to spur his students' interests and to discuss and reflect on actions that reflect the values of a culture at a particular point in time. He read a dilemma faced by Sie, a slave from Maryland in 1825, when his extremely troubled master burst into his cabin with an unusual request. It happened that the master had encountered severe financial problems and, in two weeks, was to lose everything he had, including Sie and all the other servants. In his extreme hysteria, the master threw his arms around Sie and begged him to gather up the other slaves and run away to Kentucky. The master planned to follow Sie in a few months to reestablish himself in Kentucky.

After discussing the dilemma to make sure the students understood what it was all about, Mr. Morgan commented, "Isn't it interesting that after being Sie's master for over 30 years, the plantation owner became so dependent on him? Should Sie help out the owner?"

Mr. Morgan divided the children into small discussion groups and asked them to decide what Sie should do. He provided a graphic organizer for them to organize their divergent viewpoints (see Figure 11.1). Each group was to consider the owner's request and discuss whether or not to help him. To encourage the students to consider each alternative equally, Mr. Morgan directed that every time they listed a reason to help, they had to follow it with a reason not to help; the students were required to have an equal number of items in both columns. When the groups finished their lists, they revealed their decisions and supported each with sound reasons.

FIGURE 11.1   Pro and Con Visual Organizer

PROS AND CONS

SOMETIMES AN ISSUE IS SO COMPLICATED IT'S HARD TO TAKE SIDES.
HERE'S A WAY TO HELP YOU MAKE A DECISION.

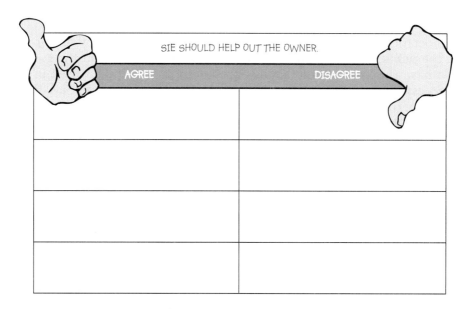

WORKING TO PROMOTE THE VALUES AND PRINCIPLES OF AMERICAN DEMOCRACY

The day you take your first step into your own classroom full of bright-eyed, bubbly elementary school students, their curiosity and ambition may leave you awestruck. They jump in and fight for the things they care about and are inspired when learning has implications that go far beyond the walls of the classroom. And students respond with interest and motivation to teachers who appear to share their enthusiasm and caring. When students come to you with an issue, help them develop exciting ways to build new understandings and solutions. Work together to define and analyze the issue, consider why it is something people should care about, and how it can be approached and worked out. Then students can take initiative and action. By doing their research and creating potential solutions, students will be carrying out the ultimate form of participatory citizenship right in your classroom—active, engaged, and informed.

This form of participatory citizenship should not be thought of as happening only during "civics class," but as something that winds its way throughout the total elementary school curriculum. For example, Donna Anderson reports that one issue that tends to absorb her elementary school students is the environment. She customarily seizes on this natural interest because as residents of planet Earth, she knows her students will share the responsibility for taking care of our land, water, and air for years to come. Consider this peek into Miss Anderson's classroom:

Donna Anderson's students gather around a worktable at the back of the classroom. Ashley carefully measures one turtle, while Bradley weighs another on an electronic scale. Miss Anderson's classroom is one of the first classrooms around the country to become involved in a long-term project to save Vietnam Pond turtles threatened with extinction. These Southeastern Asian turtles are now considered extinct in their home habitat, a very small area of central Vietnam. Their natural environment was either destroyed by Agent Orange, used during the Vietnam War, or has been converted to rice fields. Because there is no protection program for these turtles in their homeland, the Asian Turtle Consortium has tapped several schools in our country to help the turtles. The schools will help to breed a new generation of these turtles in the United States and send them back to conservation sites in Vietnam.

Miss Anderson's class received its 10 turtles in October and has been faithfully feeding, weighing, and measuring them since then. The turtles were about 1½ years old when they arrived, and the five largest turtles will be sent back to Vietnam at the end of the school year. "It's a big responsibility," commented Marisol. "I was really excited when I found out the importance of this project. When I was little, I always wondered what I could do to help animals in danger of extinction. Now I know I can make a difference."

Energized by an expanding sense of responsibility, Miss Anderson's students moved on from the turtle project to tackle other opportunities involving community volunteerism. They adopted a local park and pledged to keep it clean, packed breakfasts for the homeless as part of a Martin Luther King, Jr., Day service project, collected funds for the March of Dimes, and raised $200 for a classmate whose house was damaged by a catastrophic fire. Through their incredible thirst for involvement, Miss Anderson's young citizens took their first ambitious steps into the realm of real-life learning called *service learning.* Service learning encourages active assistance through student projects that meet the needs of groups or individuals in the community. Service learning helps students become engaged in community matters as conscientious citizens and helps to assure students that they can make a difference. Although service learning cuts across all curricular areas, it is a big part of civics.

RECOGNIZING THE IMPORTANCE OF SYMBOLS AND HOLIDAYS TO NATIONAL IDENTITY

Like every other country in the world, the United States depicts and celebrates its fundamental values with symbols and holidays that give its citizens a sense of national pride and cohesion. People strongly identify with the symbols of their country and feel tremendous pride when they see their nation's flag or hear their nation's anthem.

National Symbols   Among the actions that helped forge a sense of national identity and spirit following the Revolutionary War was the introduction of patriotic national symbols: the eagle as the symbol for America, the Great Seal of the United States, the "Star-Spangled Banner" as our national anthem, and the American Flag. These helped define the United States as a new nation and became representative of a new history and culture. There are many symbols associated with the United States, but elementary school social studies programs generally focus on the ones in the following list:

- *Flag of the United States.* The Stars and Stripes originated as a result of this resolution adopted by the Second Continental Congress at Philadelphia on June 14, 1777:

   Resolved, that the flag of the United States be thirteen stripes, alternate red and white; that the union be thirteen stars, white in a blue field representing a new constellation.

   Our current flag has 50 stars that represent the 50 states and 13 stripes that represent the colonies that became the first 13 states.

- *Seal of the United States.* The seal, adopted in 1782, was designed by the Founding Fathers to reflect the beliefs and values of the new nation. Above a bald eagle are thirteen stars representing a "new constellation." In its beak, the eagle grasps a scroll bearing the first motto of the United States:

   E Pluribus Unum.

- *National bird.* The bald eagle was declared the national bird of the United States in 1782. Its image represents strength and freedom.

- *National flower.* In 1986, the rose was proclaimed the "national floral emblem" of the United States. It was selected because it is considered a universal symbol of life and love and devotion.

- *National mottos.* "In God We Trust" was adopted as the official motto of the United States in 1956. It was the first official motto to be adopted since *E Pluribus Unum* ("from many, one") was adopted in 1782.

- *Liberty Bell.* The Liberty Bell gained fame on July 8, 1776, when it rang from the tower of Independence Hall in Philadelphia to summon people for the first public reading of the Declaration of Independence.

- *Statue of Liberty.* The Statue of Liberty, dedicated as a national monument in 1924, was a gift of friendship from the people of France to the people of the United States in recognition of an alliance established during the American Revolution.

- *National anthem.* During the War of 1812 (September 14, 1814), U.S. soldiers at Baltimore's Fort McHenry raised a huge U.S. flag to celebrate a crucial victory over British forces. Inspired by seeing the American flag still flying during the raging battle, poet Francis Scott Key wrote a poem entitled "Defense of Fort McHenry." The poem eventually became the U.S. national anthem—"The Star Spangled Banner."

National Holidays   National holidays are a significant part of every nation's culture, and the Congress of the United States has set aside a number of special days to remember and honor noteworthy historical events and individuals as well as to pay tribute to significant national or cultural beliefs and customs. Most of us look forward to the celebrations that are such an integral part of these patriotic national observances—including speeches, music, symbols, special foods, art, drama, or literature. Federal government offices are always closed on federal holidays; schools and many businesses close on some major holidays, such as Thanksgiving, Christmas, and New Year's Day, but may not always be closed on other days, such as Presidents' Day or Veterans Day. Currently, Congress has designated 10 legal holidays: New Year's Day, January 1; Martin Luther King Day, third Monday in January; Presidents' Day, third Monday in February; Memorial Day, last Monday in May; Independence Day, July 4; Labor Day, first Monday in September; Columbus Day, second Monday in October; Veterans Day, November 11; Thanksgiving Day, fourth Thursday in November; and Christmas Day, December 25.

Only legal federal holidays are listed here, but there are dozens of other holidays that various ethnic and religious groups in America look forward to each year—Halloween, Valentine's Day,

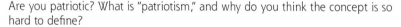
Are you patriotic? What is "patriotism," and why do you think the concept is so hard to define?

Jami Garrison/Shutterstock

Mother's Day, Father's Day, Earth Day, and Flag Day, to name a few. Various ethnic and religious groups also celebrate days with special meaning to them; they include Easter for Christians, the High Holy Days for Jews, Ramadan for Muslims, Day of Vesak for Buddhists, and Diwali for Hindus. Holidays can be secular, religious, international, or uniquely American. Critics of the proliferation of holidays complain that the sheer number of holidays often brings needless and potentially overpowering stimulation to the classroom. The result is a flood of holiday busywork that can result in trivial projects such as turkeys in November, hearts in February, and shamrocks in March. Often, very little significant information is connected to these holiday projects; month after month, the children cut, glue, draw, and paint long-established holiday prototypes. The emptiness of such an approach is epitomized in first-grader Victor's humorous response when asked why he was taping and gluing feathers on a stuffed brown paper bag to make a paper bag turkey: "Meh!"

Learning about holidays must shift the center of attention from the "20 turkeys on the window" type of arts-and-crafts projects to learning about how and when holidays are celebrated, their origins, and their meanings. However, in some cases, this is a highly sensitive topic loaded with a great deal of confusion. Take, for example, the legal issues related to the observance of our nation's only religious federal holiday—Christmas. How do public schools deal with associated religious themes or beliefs? To begin, it is important to understand that any instructional decisions must be based on a commitment to the constitutional guarantee of freedom of religion. That is, public school teachers must steadfastly support the idea that the function of public education is to neither promote nor thwart any particular religious belief. Does this mean that learning about religious holidays such as Christmas or Hanukkah should not be carried out in our public schools? To answer this question, we must first consider the influence of religion throughout history and its role in cultures. If we want to examine the significance of holidays while learning about cultural heritage, the instruction is considered appropriate. However, teachers must stay away from promoting any religion, religious celebration, or worship. Instruction must focus on the cultural aspect of the holiday, with an instructional focus on religious traditions only. With this perspective, it would seem wise to devise an instructional program that serves the needs and backgrounds of all students.

Recognizing religious holidays is one area of controversy, but even traditional, nonreligious holidays have had their critics. Take Thanksgiving, for example. Most of us think of this national holiday as a commemoration of the feast held in the autumn of 1621 by the Pilgrims and the Wampanoag to celebrate the colony's first successful harvest. Critics ask the question, "What did the Europeans give in return?" and tell us that within 20 years, European disease and treachery had decimated the Wampanoag. And most of us think of Columbus Day as a holiday to celebrate Columbus's stumbling on an entire continent that was mostly unknown to Europe when he had meant to find an all-water route to India. Critics of the holiday protest that Columbus and many of the Europeans who followed treated the Native American Indians cruelly and ultimately caused the deaths of countless people by spreading diseases that until that time had been unheard of in the Americas.

In a multicultural society such as ours, public schools try hard to be politically sensitive and make efforts to deal objectively with these issues. However, such controversy will continue to be passionately debated, for that is the nature of our free democratic society. Citizens have historically championed the worth and dignity of all individuals since our nation began: "We hold certain Truths to be self-evident, that all men are created equal, that they are endowed by their Creator with certain unalienable Rights, that among these are Life, Liberty and the Pursuit of Happiness." These words of our founding fathers still ring loud and true in our schools today.

Classroom observances of patriotic holidays help build a feeling of national pride and loyalty. The same can be said for classroom spirit; special classroom "holidays" help deepen students' appreciation for group cohesiveness. It is fun and instructive to immerse a class totally in its creative "classroom holiday" by gearing your curriculum to the theme, reading appropriate books, displaying suitable pictures, and playing fitting music. Book Readers' Day, Diversity Day, Animal Respect Day, and Native American Day (a day set aside to help children acquire a deeper appreciation for Native people and their contributions to our country) are a few creative classroom holidays that students have suggested, planned, and observed in some elementary schools.

 CHECK YOUR UNDERSTANDING 11.3 **Click here** to check your understanding of this section of the chapter.

> **Reflection on Learning**
>
> *You may simply scribble rough notes or jot down something more polished and complete. The point is to simply start recording your ideas spontaneously and candidly.*
>
> Consider this scenario: A Muslim student's parents complain to you about a "December Holidays" lesson you taught that was centered on Christmas, Hanukkah, and Kwanzaa. What should you do to address the parents' concerns?

How Does the Government Established by the Constitution Embody the Purposes, Values, and Principles of American Democracy?

Federal legislation requires that all schools receiving federal assistance teach students about the U.S. Constitution on Constitution Day, September 17 (when this is a Saturday, Sunday, or holiday, Constitution Day must be held on a day during the preceding or following week). Since the law does not specify what the educational program should consist of, social studies teachers are being looked to for their leadership; this is our opportunity to take the lead and provide guidance for those who would like to teach with appropriate and meaningful methods.

The Constitution Day directive notwithstanding, learning about the Constitution has been and remains an important part of an elementary school social studies program. Children learn that the Constitution is the cornerstone of our government—the basic and supreme law of the land. In 4,543 words, including the signatures, the Constitution outlines the structure of the U.S. government and the rights of all American citizens. It was written in 1787, when delegates from 12 of the 13 states met in Philadelphia in what is now called Independence Hall to express dissatisfaction with the weak Articles of Confederation and the need for a stronger federal government. (Rhode Island chose not to participate.) Initially, only delegates from Virginia and Pennsylvania showed up, and it took months for some of the other delegates to arrive. We now refer to the 55 men who eventually made it to the convention as either of two names—"founding fathers" or the "framers" of the Constitution. The delegates selected George Washington as presiding officer and spent four hot months, from May to September, hammering out a document that described a new, more powerful national government. On September 17, 1787, the secretive final draft of the new Constitution was completed and read to the 42 delegates remaining in Philadelphia; 39 framers attached their signatures to the document and notified the Congress that their work was finished. The current Constitution is divided into three parts:

- *Preamble:* This explains the purpose of the document.
- *Articles:* These describe the structure of the government (legislative, executive, and judicial branches) as well as the process for amending the document. There are seven articles.
- *Amendments:* These are the changes made to the Constitution. A careful reading of the First Amendment reveals that it protects several basic liberties—freedom of religion,

speech, press, petition, and assembly. Interpretation of the amendment is far from easy, as the Supreme Court has handled many disputes related to the limits of these freedoms. The first 10 amendments are called the Bill of Rights; a total of 27 amendments have been approved since 1791.

The U.S. Constitution established a new government based on the principle of "federalism," or sharing power among national, state, and local governments. While each state has its own constitution, all provisions of state constitutions must comply with the U.S. Constitution. Under the U.S. Constitution, both the national and state governments are granted certain exclusive powers and share other powers. For example, *powers exclusive to the national government* include the power to print money, declare war, provide an army and navy, and establish post offices. *Powers exclusive to state governments* include issuing licenses, conducting elections, regulating businesses within the state, and handling powers that the U.S. Constitution does not delegate to the national government or prohibit the states from using. *Powers shared by national and state governments* include the power to collect taxes, build roads, establish courts, and make and enforce laws.

 Video Example 11.2 https://www.youtube.com/watch?v=bO7FQsCcbD8
This entertaining and informative video by John Green teaches you all about the United States Constitution. What should every teacher know about how and why the Constitution of the United States became the supreme law of the land in 1787?

Despite its significance, we must recognize that unraveling the Constitution is not at the top of most students' "bucket" lists. One of the most daunting challenges encountered while teaching the Constitution is to arouse and appeal to the spontaneous interests of the children rather than focusing solely on a textbook account that often gives the Constitution substantial space, but presents a lifeless rendition of what was certainly a very provocative time in America's history. A productive way to deal with concerns like this is to carry out learning experiences in an active setting, using a literature-based approach enhanced by opportunities for cooperative and collaborative learning. Regardless of the strategy, however, nothing will work to its fullest potential unless you radiate enthusiasm, conveying the impression that you can hardly wait to dig into the lesson. When you bring sincere passion to any teaching responsibility, students will find your fervor infectious and approach their assignments in a pleasurable, productive, and stimulating way.

To discover what her fifth-grade students already knew about the U.S. Constitution, for example, Claudia March displayed a large picture of the framers working on the document and led a discussion about the kinds of things that might have been going on. Naturally, some of this information was accurate and some was quite off base: What comes to your mind as you look at this picture? What do you suppose is happening? When do you suppose this event took place? Who are these people? What is the U.S. Constitution? Why is it important? What's the difference between the Declaration of Independence and the U.S. Constitution? Who wrote the U.S. Constitution? Why? Ms. March recorded the children's responses on a large chart.

Then Ms. March passed out copies of Shh! We're Writing the Constitution *by Jean Fritz (Putnam). In a very engaging style, Fritz transports readers back to the Constitutional Convention in Philadelphia and tells the story of the birth of our Constitution. Smartly entwined into the account of how the framers carried out their task are some wonderful anecdotes that are sure to capture the children's imagination. And, of great help to Ms. March's plans, the text of the Constitution is conveniently reproduced in the book. Together, Ms. March and her students read the title of the book. She encouraged the students to come up with two or three predictions about what the book might be about, based on the large picture they had previously examined, the cover picture, the title, or all three clues. (If the clues were not helpful in giving the students a sense of what the story would be about, Ms. March would have provided a brief summary.)*

Fritz's simplified but accurate story of the Constitution makes Shh! We're Writing the Constitution *a superb option for introducing young readers to the intricacies of the document. Although the literary quality of this book by itself makes it an excellent choice, Ms. March's main reason for choosing it was to communicate important content in ways that made the "long ago and far away" seem more realistic. Because Ms. March is convinced that "every teacher is a reading teacher," she conscientiously teaches comprehension strategies whenever her children read books during social studies class.*

Some teachers implausibly try to aid comprehension by asking "dead-end" questions or simple questions that have no connection to the established purpose for reading. Nothing can cement boredom with the Constitution more than carrying out an "oral quiz" with a lengthy list of unconnected questions. Students caught yawning and shifting in their seats are frequently signs of the only real "activity" going on: "Where was the Constitutional Convention held?" "In what year was it held?" "How many states sent delegates?" "Which state chose not to attend?" "Name some famous framers who attended the Constitutional Convention." "How many states were required to ratify the Constitution?"

If, on the other hand, students are assisted in reflecting on and discussing important ideas, sharing reactions, rereading to achieve greater understanding, making connections between what they have just read and what they already knew (revisiting the prereading chart), and using what they have learned in a meaningful way, the selection can be considered a meaning-based activity.

When Ms. March's students finished reading, for example, she exploited the Constitution's importance and its potential as a learning tool by planning a role-play activity to strengthen student understanding of the issues faced by delegates at the Constitutional Convention. The role- play activity was intended not only to introduce new knowledge and understandings, but to extend and reinforce previous understandings once they were presented in Fritz's book. Therefore, in order to assist her students to more fully comprehend and carry out their roles, Ms. March helped them access several user-friendly Internet sites. Their research provided students an opportunity to become more familiar with the characters, places, and events surrounding the signing of the U.S. Constitution. Background knowledge of the time period is essential if students are expected to write meaningful scripts and accurately portray their roles; they must learn to think and act like their characters. The students focused on the following areas:

- *The setting: where and when the story took place.*
- *The characters: the main characters and the problems they faced.*
- *The events: the major story events; beginning, middle, and end of the skit.*
- *The major details and concepts: important information.*
- *Analysis: judgments and opinions using information from the story.*
- *Personal connections: connections between characters and events and contemporary life.*

The role-play project culminated with a presentation for parents and other fifth-grade classrooms. Ms. March feels that it is important for children to have opportunities to integrate new information, concepts, and skills into their own lives through greater engagement with the content, so she planned an interactive "Classroom Constitutional Convention" in which students practiced skills and applied knowledge gained from their research and role-play of the signing of the U.S. Constitution. In this instance, Ms. March's students used the U.S. Constitution as a model to build their own classroom constitution (see Figure 11.2).

Teachers who are serious about helping students understand the Constitution look for opportunities to relate its principles to the children's lives. Rather than limiting instruction to the memorization of First Amendment rights, for example, Ms. March encourages her students to compile a "First Amendment Diary" to show what they have learned about the rights guaranteed under the First Amendment.

Ms. March's students read Sy Sobel's *The U.S. Constitution and You* (Barron's Educational Series), a straightforward overview of the how the U.S. Constitution protects citizenship rights.

FIGURE 11.2 Classroom Constitution

Grade 5 Constitution

We the students of Grade 5, Room 14, in order to form a more perfect class, do establish this Constitution of the Fifth Grade.

Article I. Officials

1. There will be two branches of our government: the executive branch and the legislative branch.
2. The executive branch is made up of the President, Vice President, Secretary, and Treasurer.
3. The legislative branch is made up of all the rest of the members of the class.
4. Two candidates each for the offices of President, Vice President, Secretary, and Treasurer shall be nominated the Friday before the third Monday of each month.
5. Election of officers shall take place the third Monday of every month by secret ballot.
6. A student may hold a term of office only once.

Article II. Qualifications of Officers

1. Everyone automatically becomes a member of the legislative branch when entering Room 14 as a student.
2. Students must have these qualifications to be an officer:
   a. must be a member of Room 14 for at least two weeks.
   b. must be honest and trustworthy.

Article III. Duties of Executive Branch

1. President
   a. The President shall run all class meetings.
   b. The President shall take charge of the class in the teacher's absence.
   c. The President shall help the substitute (show him or her where things are).
   d. The President shall appoint class helpers.
2. Vice President
   a. The Vice President shall help the President when necessary.
   b. In the absence of the President, the Vice President shall take over.
3. Secretary
   a. The Secretary shall take notes at all class meetings.
   b. The Secretary shall take care of all class mail (letters, thank-you notes, and so on).
4. Treasurer
   a. The Treasurer shall take care of all class funds.

Article IV. Duties of Legislative Branch

1. To approve, by majority vote, class helper assignments.
2. To approve, by majority vote, any decision for which the class is responsible.
3. To volunteer for class helper assignments:
   a. clean chalkboard
   b. feed fish
   c. water plants
   d. pass out papers
   e. take lunch count

(Continued)

FIGURE 11.2 (Continued)

> f. serve as class librarian
>
> g. greet room visitors
>
> h. keep art materials orderly
>
> i. check attendance
>
> j. run errands
>
> 4. To approve, by two-thirds vote, any amendment to this constitution.
>
> **Article V. Presidential Vacancy**
>
> The Vice President shall take over if the President's office is vacant, followed by the Secretary, and then the Treasurer.
>
> **Article VI. Class Meetings**
>
> Meetings shall be held each Friday from 2:30–3:00 p.m.
>
> **Article VII. Amendments**
>
> 1. An amendment may be proposed by any member of the class.
>
> 2. An amendment must be approved by two-thirds vote of the legislative branch.
>
> **Amendments**
> Amendment 1.
> An elected official shall temporarily give up any classroom helper jobs held during his or her term of office. (Approved: February 10)

The students learned that the Bill of Rights is made up of 10 amendments, and they carefully examined each one. For an illustration of what they did, read the First Amendment below:

> *Congress shall make no law respecting an establishment of religion or prohibiting the free exercise thereof; or abridging the freedom of speech, or of the press; or the right of the people peaceably to assemble, and to petition the government for a redress of grievances.*

So that the students operated from a common conceptualization of the First Amendment, Ms. March helped them rewrite the Bill of Rights in their own words:

> *People are free to practice any religion they want. The government cannot stop citizens from saying or writing what they want. The people have the right to gather together to discuss problems they have with the government and to inform the government of their problems.*

To probe more deeply into the freedoms guaranteed by the First Amendment, Ms. March asked her students to list each freedom along the top of a grid titled "First Amendment Diary." Underneath each heading, students were asked to list the protected activities they were engaged in over a weekend, such as "Attended a soccer game" (peaceably assemble) or "Went to church with my family" (religion). On Monday, Ms. March helped her students compile a class list of all the entries and led a discussion of the data with questions like these:

- How many times did you rely on your First Amendment rights over the weekend?
- How might your weekend have been different without the First Amendment rights?
- Which rights did you exercise most? Least?

Through this activity, Ms. March demonstrated not only that civics knowledge is indeed important but that it also must have relevance to the students' lives. Civics education is more than studying flowcharts of how a bill becomes a law or reading a textbook chapter on the separation of powers. Should Ms. March use any of these activities again while they continue to study the Constitution, since they were so successful the first time? "Absolutely not," she declared. "Regardless of how well received it was the first time, the children will tire of any learning strategy if it is used repeatedly. I need to find something new!"

 CHECK YOUR UNDERSTANDING 11.4   Click here to check your understanding of this section of the chapter.

What Is the Relationship of the United States to Other Nations and to World Affairs?

What makes an independent state or country? Fundamentally, a state or country must have characteristics such as internationally recognized land and borders, and a national identity typically based on shared culture, religion, history, language, and ethnicity. Today, there are 195 independent countries or states recognized in the world. Kosovo, which declared independence from Serbia in February 2008, is the world's newest country. All nations have a system of political authority.

According to the Constitution of the United States, for example, the federal government was established for six specific purposes. These purposes include unity, justice, domestic tranquility, defense, promotion of the general welfare of the citizens, and securing liberty for all. While other nations may disagree on these purposes and how the government should serve its citizens, the fundamentals established over 200 years ago still hold true for the United States.

The ways that governments serve citizens of countries around the world vary greatly from one national political system to another. With an increasingly integrated global economy, however, political activity has been taking place more and more at the global level. Referred to as *globalization*, this trend is a process of interaction among the people, companies, and governments of different nations driven by international trade, human mobility, and information technology. Globalization affects political systems and also leaves its mark on the environment, on culture, on economic development and prosperity, and on human physical well-being in societies around the world.

Globalization is helping to erase old borders. *Multinational corporations* make products in one country, process them in another, and sell them to consumers throughout the world. Strong *multinational organizations* such as the European Union (EU) have increased interconnectedness among the countries of Europe, most notably in the areas of economics, politics, and culture. Powers once held individually by 25 countries have shifted to the EU capital in Brussels, Belgium. Citizens of one country can live, work, and even vote in another EU country with little trouble. *Intergovernmental organizations* such as the International Monetary Fund, the World Bank, and the World Trade Organization have assumed an increasingly important role in global economic affairs. *Nongovernmental organizations* (NGOs) such as Amnesty International, CARE, Save the Children, and Doctors Without Borders bring together people from around the world to deal with sensitive issues such as human rights, health, climate change, energy use, and child labor regulations.

Many believe that globalization can bring peace and prosperity to the world; they suggest that international cooperation can lead to the spread of democracy and help bring about greater respect for human rights. On the other hand, detractors warn that globalization has the potential to infringe on national and individual freedom; they caution that the most economically powerful countries may ultimately dominate the others. The clearest example is competition from foreign workers, which has especially infuriated America's working class. They contend that competition from China lowered wages and increased unemployment for American workers. Help your students understand that there are pros and cons to globalization. Begin by asking them to brainstorm what they feel some of the pros and cons may be; write them on a chart they can revisit later. Then share a story that represents an issue related to globalization.

For example, the main agricultural crop of a certain tribal community in West Africa is yams, which are grown using a farming technique called *slash-and-burn*. (The slash-and-burn technique is used in tribal villages throughout the tropics and, if done properly, enables people to derive a stable source of food.) Growing yams is so vital to the existence of the tribal community that an important ceremonial event is attached to their harvest. After harvesting yams in this West African village, the people hold a ceremony called *agwe*, which they carry out before anyone is allowed to eat the newly harvested yams. Should a world committee pass environmental laws banning the traditional slash-and-burn technique because, if done improperly, it can quickly degrade large areas of forest which will take decades to recover? Based on the comments contained on their chart, students should select the arguments that are most valid. Next, provide students with Internet websites to research and learn more about the debate over globalization. Finally, divide the class into two groups: students who focused on pros of the slash-and-burn scenario and students who focused on its cons. Have the two groups debate the slash-and-burn issue. Be sure your students support their claims and arguments with factual information from trustworthy resources.

Despite such concerns, it is probably safe to say that, in the coming decades, globalization will continue to be a powerful political and economic force. To accurately weigh the pros and cons of globalism, our young citizens must understand how globalization works and the policy choices facing them and their nation.

 CHECK YOUR UNDERSTANDING 11.5 **Click here** to check your understanding of this section of the chapter.

Reflection on Learning

You may simply scribble rough notes or jot down something more polished and complete. The point is to simply start recording your ideas spontaneously and candidly.

Globalization is one of the 21st century's most controversial issues. There are some who claim that globalization is a positive force because it helps build new industries and provide more jobs in developing countries. Others argue that globalization is a negative force because it pressures poorer countries to do whatever the big powerful countries order them to do. What do you think? Is globalization positive or negative?

What Are the Roles of the Citizen in American Democracy?

The 14th Amendment of the United States Constitution *defines* citizenship this way: "All persons born or naturalized in the United States, and subject to the jurisdiction thereof, are citizens of the United States and of the State wherein they reside." So, under current law, persons born in the United States automatically become citizens. A noncitizen may apply to become a citizen of the United States; that is, she or he can become *naturalized*. Naturalization is the process by which U.S. citizenship is granted to a foreign citizen or national after he or she fulfills the requirements established by Congress in the Immigration and Nationality Act (INA). An individual must pass a test of his or her ability to read, write, and speak English and of her or his basic knowledge and understanding of U.S. history and government.

Citizenship Rights

United States citizenship carries both rights and responsibilities. After the Constitution was ratified in 1787, there was widespread concern that it did not protect certain freedoms. Therefore, 10 amendments, referred to as *the Bill of Rights*, were added. The first 8 amendments specify individual rights; they are summarized below. The 9th and 10th Amendments are general rules describing the relationship among the people, the state governments, and the federal government.

Amendment 1: Freedom of (or from) religion; freedom of speech; freedom to assemble; freedom to petition the government.

Amendment 2: Right to bear arms.

Amendment 3: Freedom from quartering soldiers.

Amendment 4: Freedom from unreasonable searches and seizures; warrants must only be issued upon probable cause and shall be specific.

Amendment 5: Criminal indictments must be by grand jury; freedom from double jeopardy; freedom from testifying against oneself; right to face accusers; right to due process; right of just compensation for takings.

Amendment 6: Right to speedy trial; right to an impartial jury; right to be informed of the charges on which the accused is held; right to face accusers; right to produce witnesses for the accused; right to legal counsel.

Amendment 7: Right to jury trial in civil cases.

Amendment 8: Freedom from excessive bail or fines; freedom from cruel or unusual punishment.

Democracies are based on a belief that governments exist to support the rights of the people. While dictatorships constrain human rights, democracies continually attempt to support them. In tune with the concept of rights guaranteed by the Constitution is the democratic concept of equality, which implies that everyone is entitled to equal opportunity: No person should experience prejudice because of his or her race, color, religion, or gender. Teaching civic virtues involves nurturing the values and attitudes that lead to the support of those rights. To help his students unlock the specifics of the Constitution, Mike Randall used a strategy he referred to as a "Poster Session."

Mr. Randall divided his class into several groups of three and assigned them to the following parts of the Constitution: Preamble, Article 1, Article 2, Article 3, Article 4, Bill of Rights (first 10 amendments), and Amendments 11–27. Each group was directed to create a visual portrayal of its part of the Constitution on a large sheet of poster board. The portrayals could include drawn illustrations, words, pictures from magazines, printed images from the computer, or any other representations that communicated the associated content and spirit. The children taped the posters to the walls around the classroom and attached a short descriptive narrative to each. Other fifth-grade classrooms came to examine the display, circulating from poster to poster. Mr. Randall passed out sticky notes to the visitors and asked them to provide positive feedback for each poster. After this poster session, Mr. Randall brought the class together and led a discussion about what the children had learned and what they considered to be the most valuable outcome of the project.

While teaching the Constitution, Mr. Randall also helped his students investigate a variety of current issues involving the protection of individual rights and freedoms.

One day, for example, the local newspaper ran a front-page story about inhumane treatment of dogs. A photo accompanying the story depicted several incredibly undernourished, scrawny, sickly animals. The students spent some time discussing the ways these dogs in particular, and animals in general, are sometimes mistreated. "It's like they need their own Constitution!" blurted Charlie.

"Not a bad idea," chimed in Irina.

Seizing the opportunity, Mr. Randall divided the class into groups. Each group was to use a simplified U.S. Constitution as a model and work together to write a "Preamble" and "Bill of Rights" for an "Animal Constitution." When they finished, the groups compared their "Preambles" and "Bills of Rights," eventually merging them into a single document designed to protect the rights of animals.

Students more clearly understand civics by participating in the processes they are learning about.

Citizenship Responsibilities

The Constitution and laws of our nation, then, give many rights to its citizens. In addition to these rights, good citizenship also requires some important responsibilities. Although the U.S. Constitution does not specifically impose those responsibilities, it does, however, assume certain obligations of citizens to contribute to the common good of the nation. The following are a few of the basic responsibilities of citizens of the United States.

- The most important responsibility that citizens have is to exercise their *right to vote*. Before voting in an election, citizens have the responsibility to be well informed about the issues and candidates. The Constitution contains more than one amendment that has expanded the right to vote. Now, with few exceptions, all persons 18 and older can vote in any public election.
- Every person is expected to *obey the laws* of the community, state, and country in which he or she lives.
- The Constitution guarantees a citizen's right to trial by an impartial jury, and citizens have a responsibility to serve as jurors when summoned.
- All citizens living in the United States must pay income taxes and other taxes.
- The Constitution provides Congress with the power to raise armies, so citizens can be required to *serve in the armed forces.*
- Since the Constitution sets rules for treason against the United States, citizens have the responsibility to be loyal to their country.

VOTING

One of the best ways to teach children about what it means to be a citizen in a democratic nation is to get them involved in voting. Voting offers an excellent opportunity to learn civic responsibility and shared decision making in a meaningful and motivating context. By participating in the voting process (determining voting issues, suggesting possible choices, casting and tallying votes, and confirming the outcome of the vote), children directly experience how a democracy works.

First attempts at voting should involve issues of interest to the entire class. Unless they are interested in a voting issue, students will not be motivated to participate in the voting process and will likely come away from the experience with a feeling that voting is not important to them. Therefore, first votes should be taken on issues such as favorite storybook character, a class mascot, what to serve at a classroom party, which animal makes the best pet, or who will win the Super Bowl.

Children should be encouraged to carefully consider the issue before they take a vote, making arguments in support of the position they are willing to defend and trying to persuade their classmates to vote in their favor. It should be emphasized that opposing points of view should be presented with self-control and ease. The children must realize that it is normal for people to hold different opinions about things and that these differences should not break down friendly relationships.

Try to remember that young children do not understand the voting process as an adult does, so some of the measures we are comfortable with may be confusing to them. Take, for example, the common classroom practice of having children vote by raising their hands. Often, young children will let them fly as soon as a teacher says, "Raise your hands if . . . " even before they hear the options. Others will lower their hands before their votes are counted, and some may raise their hands more than once (even though they're directed not to).

Instead of raising hands, it might be better to:

- *Poll children.* You can list the children's names on a chart and ask each child how he or she votes. The children can then cast votes by placing a tally mark next to their names. The class can then count the votes for each option.

- *Construct name graphs.* Have each child print her or his name on a 3" × 5" index card. Ask each child how he or she votes and then place the index cards in a line or a stack corresponding to the option. Again, the entire class should be involved in counting the votes.

- *Use secret ballots.* If children exert excessive pressure on others to vote their way, it might be best to give each child one piece of paper, ask her or him to secretly make a choice, and drop it into a box. Again, the entire class should count the votes.

Voting should be a part of an older child's classroom, too, for it exemplifies one of the duties and responsibilities of citizenship in a democratic society and demonstrates why voting matters. In the upper grades, however, it is common to extend the students' understandings of the voting process as it applies to the election of officials at the local, state, and national levels.

Gordon Palmer, for example, helped his students understand the process of electing officials by holding a simulated election. In an effort to explain the processes associated with presidential elections, he turned his classroom into campaign headquarters. Rather than discuss the actual presidential candidates (and running mates) for each party—where they stand on the issues and what they plan to bring to office—Mr. Palmer decided to help the students gain an understanding of the electoral process. Focusing on the question "How does a person get to be elected president of the United States?" Mr. Palmer began the classroom simulation by randomly dividing the students into two political parties: "A. Pat Osaurus in 2012!" and "We back Rex!" Do these sound like strange election slogans to you? Not if you were visiting Gordon Palmer's fifth-grade classroom.

> *Mr. Palmer kicked off the election activities for the 2012 presidential election by having his fifth-graders browse through an easy-to-read version of the U.S. Constitution for the three requirements a candidate for the presidency must meet: (1) at least 35 years old, (2) a natural-born citizen of the United States, and (3) a resident of the United States for 14 years. "Knowing these requirements is great, but how does one actually get to be president of the United States?" challenged Mr. Palmer. Finding that his students were fairly uninformed about the election process, Mr. Palmer took advantage of his students' interest in dinosaurs to help them learn by simulating the election process.*

Having opportunities to vote from their earliest years in school teaches students about the voting process and about one of their most critical democratic responsibilities.

Monkey Business/Fotolia

Mr. Palmer reviewed with the children that dinosaurs can be classified in many ways, but two of the most popular are meat eaters (carnivores) and plant eaters (herbivores). By randomly picking slips of paper from a box, students quickly became members of the carnivore or herbivore "party." Each party met and selected a party name: The herbivores decided to call their party the Herbocrats, and the carnivores were the Carnublicans. Mr. Palmer explained that each party would meet to select a candidate for "dinosaur president." However, in order to vote, each student was required to register.

Mr. Palmer distributed 5" × 8" index cards to the students and asked them to print their names and addresses on the cards. The students then signed their cards. The Herbocrats and Carnublicans designed symbols for their parties and drew them on their registration cards. To be properly registered, the students went to a prearranged area in the classroom where an instructional aide checked their signatures on the class list, stamped their cards, and crossed their names off the list. They were told to put the cards in a safe place, as they would need to be presented as verification of registration when it came time to vote.

Each party was allowed to select three prospective candidates for dinosaur president. This process was compared to the primaries held during the actual presidential election process. During the primaries, party members vote for the candidate that would represent their party in the upcoming general election. The Herbocrats selected Stegosaurus, Triceratops, and Apatosaurus. The Carnublicans went with Tyrannosaurus Rex, Deinonychus, and Raptor. The party members were divided on the issue of which dinosaur would represent them best, so each party mounted a primary campaign, including buttons, stickers, and hats to wear at a rally. Of course, countless speeches, posters, and mock TV commercials extolled the virtues of each potential dinosaur candidate.

While the primary campaign was running its course, Mr. Palmer and his students made a voting booth from a large packing crate the custodians had rescued from the trash pile. They wrote "United States Polling Place" at the top and decorated it with various patterns of red, white, and blue. It was important that the students had a place to vote in privacy. At last, it was time to complete the first step of the election process, and each party selected its candidate!

Each party held its election, with officials making sure to check the registration cards and instructing each registered voter to pick up only one ballot. After the election committee tabulated the results, Tyrannosaurus Rex emerged victorious from the Carnublican Party, while the Herbocrats selected Apatosaurus. It was then time to focus on the national convention, the second step in the election process. During the national convention, the party finalized its selection for one presidential nominee, and each presidential candidate chose a dinosaur running mate.

Next was the third step—the general election process. Candidates campaigned in an attempt to win the support of voters in the other fifth-grade classrooms. In November, the voters were to go to the polls to cast their ballots. Each party published an election newsletter containing background information about the candidates. They made campaign buttons, bumper stickers, and posters. As in the primaries, they wrote campaign songs and slogans. Most importantly, each party was directed to formulate a platform for the candidate, describing the candidate's view on all issues of importance. The highlight of the whole experience was a spirited "dinosaur debate," featuring all the protocol observed during televised presidential debates.

On voting day, students in Mr. Palmer's class lined up at their packing box voting booth to elect the first dinosaur president. The other classrooms followed. They all clutched their registration cards and voted for their choices, again by secret ballot. The votes were counted, and the winner was announced later that afternoon. Tyrannosaurus Rex won in a landslide; the students felt that because this was the fiercest meat-eating land animal ever, it would be most suitable to rule the land of the reptiles. Of course, a huge victory celebration took place that afternoon (arranged and hosted by aides and parents). Everyone had a great time. In addition, the voting booth stayed in the classroom and was used for other important classroom votes that school year.

In November, the children were able to transfer their voting simulation to the U.S. presidential election; they understood the process much more clearly. They realized that Democrats and Republicans, not Herbocrats and Carnublicans, had voted for the candidates to represent them in the upcoming general election. The candidates were announced during political conventions, which are large meetings attended by delegates. After each party selected its candidate in these primaries, the general election campaigning process began. Finally, in November, the people were to vote for one candidate. Mr. Palmer understood that when a person casts a vote in the general election, she or he is not voting directly for a candidate. Instead, that person is actually casting a vote for a group of people known as *electors*. The electors are part of the Electoral College and are supposed to vote for their state's popularly elected candidate. However, the Electoral College system can confuse even many adult voters, so Mr. Palmer chose not to include it in his election simulation. If you try a voting-process simulation in your classroom, it would be interesting to find a way to make the Electoral College a part of the process.

Children should learn that one of the most important ways they can participate in their government is to exercise their right to vote. By voting, people have a voice in their government.

DIGITAL CITIZENSHIP

Digital citizenship is a relatively new concept; it is designed to help students use technology in appropriate, responsible ways—in other words, how they should act online. To help achieve this goal, Mike Ribble of the Digital Citizenship Institute (2016) has advanced nine themes of good digital citizenship (see Figure 11.3). You have the duty to lead when it comes to sound digital citizenship practices in the classroom. The moment your students turn on a computer or access any electronic device, they must be educated about digital citizenship (and their digital footprint). Ready-made lesson plans about digital citizenship can be found by checking Internet sites.

Video Example 11.3 https://www.youtube.com/watch?v=1FlU_y9Otns
Technology provides extraordinary opportunities for students to live and learn. Inherent in its use, however, are issues of privacy and safety that present real challenges for schools. Why is it important to teach your students to embody healthy attributes of *digital citizenship*?

CHECK YOUR UNDERSTANDING 11.6 **Click here** to check your understanding of this section of the chapter.

FIGURE 11.3 Nine Themes of Good Digital Citizenship

1. **Digital Access.** To become productive citizens, everyone must have access to digital technology.
2. **Digital Commerce.** Students must learn how to be effective consumers in a digital economy.
3. **Digital Communication.** Students must learn how to make appropriate decisions when faced with the plethora of communication options available today—email, instant messaging, and so on.
4. **Digital Literacy.** Renewed emphasis must be placed on how technology should be taught and how technology can be used in our classrooms.
5. **Digital Etiquette.** Everyone must be taught rules of behavior and standards of conduct in order to stop inappropriate use.
6. **Digital Law.** Students must understand that stealing or causing damage to other work is a crime (for example, hacking or downloading illegal music).
7. **Digital Rights and Responsibilities.** As rights and responsibilities are inherent in the U.S. Constitution, basic digital rights (privacy, free speech) and responsibilities (use technology in an appropriate manner) must be addressed.
8. **Digital Health and Wellness.** Physical (eye safety, muscle fatigue) and psychological (Internet addiction) well-being must be addressed.
9. **Digital Security (Self-Protection).** Users must protect their information from outside forces— personal information, virus protection, backups for data, surge control, and so on.

A Final Thought

The primary reason for educating our youth has been, and continues to be, developing good citizens—proud individuals who make up a unique combination of cultures we call American. Americans have come from everywhere and for every reason—some in chains as slaves; others to search for gold, to find land, to flee famine, or to escape religious or political discrimination. Even today, America continues to be a sanctuary for the oppressed as well as a haven for the ambitious. Forefathers of consummate wisdom created a new kind of government for America— of the people, by the people, and for the people. To maintain this prized inheritance, all elementary school teachers must stand up and accept their responsibility to protect, nurture, and renew our healthy democratic society. They can do this by supporting and enacting the influential declaration of the NCSS (1993): "The primary purpose of social studies is to help young people develop the ability to make informed and reasoned decisions for the public good as citizens of a culturally diverse, democratic society in an interdependent world" (p. 3).

Classrooms for young citizens should have a distinctly democratic flavor. Children should know what our country is now and envision the best our country can be. As a teacher of young children, you will be an important nurturer of maximum civic growth. You will help make society. You must have a vision of good citizenship—much the same kind of vision as Michelangelo had when he peered intently at a monumental slab of Carrara marble and saw within it *The Pietà*, waiting to be liberated. Will you work with the fervor of Michelangelo to release responsible democratic citizens? Should society expect anything less?

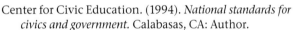

References

Center for Civic Education. (1994). *National standards for civics and government.* Calabasas, CA: Author.

Milton, J. (1987). *Marching to freedom: The story of Martin Luther King, Jr.* New York, NY: Dell Yearling.

National Council for the Social Studies. (1993, January/ February). *The social studies professional.* Washington, DC: Author.

National Council for the Social Studies. (1997). *Fostering civic virtue: Character education in the social studies.* Retrieved from http://www.socialstudies.org/positions /character

National Council for the Social Studies. (2001). Creating effective citizens: A position statement of National Council for the Social Studies. *Social Education, 65,* 319.

Obenchain, K. M., & Morris, R. V. (2011). *50 social studies strategies for K–8 classrooms* (3rd ed.). Boston, MA: Pearson.

Parker, W. C. (2006). Talk isn't cheap: Practicing deliberation in school. *Social Studies and the Young Learner, 19,* 12–15.

Ribble, M. (2016). *Digital citizenship: Using technology appropriately.* Retrieved from http://www.digitalcitizenship .net/Home_Page.html

CHAPTER 12

Economics:
Thinking and Choosing Responsibly

Learning Outcomes

Elementary school students are now, and will continue to be, confronted with economics issues as consumers, householders, jobholders, and voters. Those economic issues will require reasoned decisions, the consequences of which will influence their lives and the lives of others. Therefore, economics instruction must begin in the primary grades, with teachers who are knowledgeable in economic content and know how to employ quality economic education materials and activities. After completing this chapter, you will be able to:

- Describe what is meant by economics literacy.

- Delineate the basic principles that provide a framework for selecting desired economics outcomes.

Classroom Snapshot

"Econ" is a fuzzy toy spider that bounces on an elasticized string wrapped around Dorothy Yohe's finger and cheerfully invites the children to accompany him on a voyage to his kingdom, "The Land of Economics." Econ's kingdom consists of 26 towns, each beginning with an economic alphabet letter name. In each town live producers whose occupations begin with the town letter. A-Town, for example, is the home of artists, actors, and accountants; B-Town includes barbers, bankers, and butchers; and C-Town inhabitants are cooks, carpenters, and cartoonists. Econ and his fascinated travelers spend several days in each town, where children learn about occupations starting with that letter. Mrs. Yohe invites parents to class to describe their occupations—for example, Isaiah's mother, a landscaper, visited during L-Town week, and Rita's father, a computer programmer, told his story during C-Town week. Visiting parents become members of the VIP (Very Important Parent) Club.

Mrs. Yohe is occasionally challenged to stretch the limits of her creativity as she tries to make certain that each occupation has only one VIP guest (if there are two doctors volunteering to visit, for example, one could be the "doctor" and the other a "surgeon" or "physician"). VIPs are classified as either producers of goods or providers of services. Appropriate storybooks, videos, websites, field trips, and other sources of information help fill in the content while students visit a specific town; creative dramatics, art projects, writing activities, and reinforcement games supplement instruction and provide for information processing and enrichment.

As the journey through the economic alphabet comes to an end, usually before the hectic holiday weeks of early December, Econ welcomes the children to an empty shopping mall; unfortunately, the stores have not yet been completed because of an untimely strike. Even though the strike has now been settled, it will take more workers to complete the mall in time for holiday shoppers. Econ asks the children if they would be willing to work for him.

Children work and plan the shopping mall with Econ's help. He hires them to build the shops, paying them in play money. After the stores and shops are constructed, the children switch roles—they are transformed into consumers browsing through the shops at the new mall. One day, half the class is assigned to work in the shops, while the other students are consumers. The next day, the groups reverse roles. The shopping mall incorporates a bank in which students may deposit and withdraw the play money they have earned in class. Stores include a pizza shop, a card and gift shop, a travel agency, a bank, a flower shop, a food market, a jewelry store, a shoe store, and a clothing shop.

The students' first task in setting up the pizza shop, for example, was to arrange the tables and chairs for the customers and make sure the "kitchen" was ready to begin producing pizzas. Once that was finished, some children thought it would be important to add flowers to the tables, pictures on the walls, a phone for reservations, and wallpaper to brighten up the space. Crews went to work on each project, taping up their own artwork for pictures, using a play cell phone, sponge printing to create several sheets of patterned "wallpaper," making flowers from pipe cleaners and tissue paper, and selecting folkloric Italian music with mandolins, violins, and accordion.

Now the children were ready to use their pizza restaurant to dramatize the roles of producers and consumers. Some were customers and sat at the table ("Do you take credit cards?"). Others put on aprons to take orders ("Hello. My name is Chris. What may I get for you?"). No one seemed to notice that most of the orders were taken down in scribble writing. Two children donned chef's hats and pretended to flip and spin pizza dough.

As engrossed as they were in their pizza project, the children's interest quickly shifted from the restaurant to Gerald, who came to school one day proudly wearing new eyeglasses. You guessed it—a field trip to the ophthalmologist and the introduction of an eye care office to their shopping mall were next. An eye chart that was used for "eye exams" helped some children read and write the alphabet and another section displayed pipe cleaner "designer frames."

The restaurant and eye care center were two areas that the children came back to visit over and over again. As they added other stores, the students took great pride in giving tours to parents, other classes, and building visitors. Their mall became the catalyst and context for the study of economics throughout the year.

Dorothy Yohe was a dedicated and talented kindergarten teacher. Never having taken a college course in economics, Mrs. Yohe was intimidated by the subject matter of economics and reluctant to teach something she knew so little about. So for many years, Mrs. Yohe's kindergarten program could be described as "traditional"—one in which she believed wholeheartedly in helping children develop social and cognitive abilities through exposure to a variety of expressive, creative, communicative, and cognitive experiences. Economics in kindergarten? That was the furthest thing from Mrs. Yohe's mind. How and why did she make the change? Mrs. Yohe's story is about taking risks, and the results are fascinating.

Motivation to change can be found everywhere—from television to movies, to a good book, to magazines, to friends and family members. Often, your own children can get you going, providing just the right spark to drive you to analyze the way things are and reach out for something else. Mrs. Yohe attributes the changes in her teaching life to a single conversation she had with her son, who was about to graduate from college with a degree in economics. "As adults," he warned his mother, "your students will be confronted with economic decisions that will impact their lives and the lives of others. They will make decisions about what to buy, how much of their income they should spend, how much to save, and what careers to pursue. Even at this young kindergarten age, they are making decisions that can be examined with what economists call an 'economic way of thinking.' Did you know that spending by 8- to 12-year-olds has roughly doubled over each of the past three decades? In my mind, economics should be considered just as important as reading, writing, and 'rithmetic!"

"Teaching economics to 5-year-olds? I don't know about that," countered Mrs. Yohe. "First of all, I don't know much about economics. . . . It's always seemed like a high school or college subject to me. Besides that, kindergarteners don't know much about money; their parents may give them an allowance, but most kids that age are just learning how to count from 1 to 10, so how much can they actually understand about money?"

"That's the problem," her son countered. "Most people think economics is about money, when it's really about making decisions—thinking and choosing responsibly. Waiting until high school or college to teach our youth how to make those decisions is simply a matter of 'too little and too late.' Aren't your kindergarteners enthusiastic, spontaneous, and appreciative of hands-on activities?" asked her son. "To be truthful, economics can be very complex, but a lot of it can be broken down simply and concretely for young children. They can learn about economics and have fun doing it!" For the next hour or so, Mrs. Yohe listened, spellbound, as her son built a rationale for economic education during the early elementary school years, explaining how she could teach basic economics concepts and do so while meeting her school district's regular kindergarten standards.

Like a true decision-making economist, Mrs. Yohe weighed the costs of change against the likely educational outcomes. With a sound rationale clearly established, Mrs. Yohe faced two penetrating questions that she and her son spent the entire summer answering: "Which economic concepts are developmentally appropriate for the elementary school years?" and "How can those concepts be taught most effectively to young children?" Answering those questions naturally turns the focus of this chapter to the basics of economic education in the elementary school.

Economics Literacy

Most elementary school children go to the store and buy things. However, many have no idea how the merchandise was produced, how it found its way to the store, or what factors influence its cost—basic economic concepts frequently confuse young children. All they know is that parents have the means to pay for what they want and that there is no alternative other than to buy it for them . . . or deal with the consequences of refusing! According to Meszaros and Evans (2010), " . . . students don't understand why it is necessary for them to make choices. Nor do they realize that every choice involves a cost. . . . Others think the only reason they face scarcity

Even kindergarteners are able to learn basic economics concepts as teachers create a simulated functioning economy in the classroom.

Pavel Losevsky/Fotolia

is because adults are unfair" (p. 4). The authors go on to advise that teachers must be prepared to correct the economics confusion that young children bring to school; failure to do so may broaden misconceptions that will likely persist into the adult years.

Economics literacy, or an understanding of economic generalizations and concepts, is key to effective citizenship in our nation's democratic society. For that reason, basic economics concepts must be included in the social studies curriculum for all students during the early elementary grades. Meszaros and Suiter (1998) emphasize that,

> Students who are not articulate and well informed about economic principles and who lack the ability to apply economic reasoning skills will find the economic issues they face both as young children, and as adults, complex and confusing. Their decisions will be made based on incorrect assumptions, misunderstandings and misconceptions that could have been corrected during their school experience.

Any discussion of teaching economics must start with a definition: What is economics? Although many think of economics as the study of complicated tables and charts, statistics, and numbers, *economics* is, more accurately and simply, the study of how people satisfy their needs and wants. Although you will find a glut of definitions, in one way or another all of them tend to describe economics as a social science that investigates problems associated with the production, distribution, and consumption of goods and services, such as:

- unlimited wants,
- limited resources, and
- attempting to satisfy unlimited wants with limited resources.

Nearly every formal contemporary definition of economics includes the notions of *choice* and *scarcity*; because of *scarcity* (limited resources), various economic *choices* (decisions) must be made.

What Should Students Know or Be Able to Do?

What should students understand about economics, and how does this knowledge develop? National content standards provide us with an understanding of the fundamental economics concepts that professional economists single out for elementary school social studies instruction. School districts use the standards as a guide to determine placement of content across the grades so that economics can be taught in a systematic and sequential manner.

The most widely referenced set of standards is the *Voluntary National Content Standards in Economics* (Council for Economic Education, 2010). The standards specify what students should learn about basic economics in kindergarten through Grade 12 (see Figure 12.1). The Council's website provides extended explanations of the standards. Because students' reasoning about some economic concepts develops over time, the standards developers wanted to be sure that the expectations they had for a given age were realistic. Therefore, some content standards were not recommended for the elementary school years (i.e., interest rates, government failure, economic fluctuations, and fiscal and monetary policy).

The National Council on Economic Education (2007) reported that economics should be included, at least to some extent, in the educational standards of all states beginning at the kindergarten level. Economics has obviously gained a foothold in our elementary schools today, so the issue has shifted from *whether* to teach economics to *how* to teach it. Teaching economics requires you to understand the content, know how to scaffold the construction of useful concepts, and help students experience how economics is part of their everyday lives.

Do not allow a lack of confidence spawned by an inadequate understanding of economics to keep you from bringing economics to life in your classroom. When you design lessons that both accurately present economic content and engage students in the types of learning experiences that make economics come alive, the proverbial light bulb goes on. As a beginning teacher, your methods course will have provided you with a variety of opportunities to build the content knowledge and acquire the strategies and materials required to teach elementary school economics. In-service coursework, workshops, and graduate study are some possible starting points. In addition, you will want to investigate helpful online resources such as *The Council for Economic Education, The Federal Reserve Bank of St. Louis, The Foundation for Teaching Economics, State Departments of Education websites (especially the* Indiana Department of Education *which makes available a variety of award-winning online curricular materials),* and *online government sites.*

A sound knowledge background is crucial to good economics instruction, but it takes much more than knowledge of the subject matter to become a good economics teacher. You must also implement a variety of teaching strategies that help bring the subject matter to life. Lee Shulman (1986) referred to a thorough knowledge of the subject matter combined with

FIGURE 12.1   Voluntary National Content Standards in Economics

STANDARD 1: SCARCITY	STANDARD 11: MONEY AND INFLATION
STANDARD 2: DECISION MAKING	STANDARD 12: INTEREST RATES
STANDARD 3: ALLOCATION	STANDARD 13: INCOME
STANDARD 4: INCENTIVES	STANDARD 14: ENTREPRENEURSHIP
STANDARD 5: TRADE	STANDARD 15: ECONOMIC GROWTH
STANDARD 6: SPECIALIZATION	STANDARD 16: ROLE OF GOVERNMENT AND MARKET FAILURE
STANDARD 7: MARKETS AND PRICES	
STANDARD 8: ROLE OF PRICES	STANDARD 17: GOVERNMENT FAILURE
STANDARD 9: COMPETITION AND MARKET STRUCTURE	STANDARD 18: ECONOMIC FLUCTUATIONS
	STANDARD 19: UNEMPLOYMENT AND INFLATION
STANDARD 10: INSTITUTIONS	STANDARD 20: FISCAL AND MONETARY POLICY

a deep understanding of appropriate teaching practices as *pedagogical content knowledge*. As you acquire a proficient level of pedagogical content knowledge in economics, you will find that concepts such as "supply" and "demand" will be no more difficult to teach than the unique concepts and skills attached to other school subjects.

 CHECK YOUR UNDERSTANDING 12.1 **Click here** to check your understanding of this section of the chapter.

> **Reflection on Learning**
>
> *You may simply scribble rough notes or jot down something more polished and complete. The point is to simply start recording your ideas spontaneously and candidly.*
>
> Is it *possible* to teach economics to elementary school students without having taken at least a course or two in economics yourself?

Six Core Economics Principles

Students must interact with a wide range of materials in a variety of ways. That is why this section is organized around a highly useful and well-received set of six core economics principles described on a poster developed as an extension of the National Council on Economic Education (CEE) standards and resources by David Dieterele and John Noling of the Michigan Council on Economic Education and David Klemm of the Muskegon Area Intermediate School District. The principles integrate the *20 Voluntary National Content Standards in Economics* and provide a concise and manageable framework for selecting activities to help achieve desired economics outcomes. A poster explaining the six principles is now commercially produced and used by school districts throughout the nation for planning purposes. You can view the poster on the National Council's website. These are its *Six Core Economic Principles*:

1. People choose.
2. People's choices involve costs.
3. People respond to incentives in predictable ways.
4. People create economic systems that influence individual choices and incentives.
5. People gain when they trade voluntarily.
6. People's choices have consequences that lie in the future.

There are no particular teaching strategies that are unique to economics; the approaches to effective social studies instruction described so far in this text are applicable to economics instruction, too. The various styles range from those that are highly teacher directed to those that are indirect and student-centered. The teaching approach you select will depend on learning goals, student learning objectives, selected content, and assessment strategies; whatever approach you use, know that you will need to differentiate instruction in order to reach all students. If you want your students to come away from a lesson with factual knowledge or a specific skill, for example, you may choose to use direct instruction strategies. At other times, it might be more appropriate to use indirect practices such as computer simulations or gaming, group discussion, inquiry or problem solving experiences, or service projects outside the classroom. Whatever approach you select, it is important that the activity be directly linked to the desired outcomes of the lesson—*what you want your students to know or be able to do after they have completed the learning experience.*

An important issue that you must consider in incorporating economics into your teaching schedule is the already crowded curriculum. It is therefore important to find ways to integrate economics with the other social sciences, mathematics, science, reading, language arts, and technology. Infusing economics across the curriculum helps students make linkages among disciplines and provides a real-world context for learning. As you plan integrative experiences, remember that real-life experiences are superior to vicarious experiences as children attempt to unlock the essence of economics. Real-life experience makes the subject matter easier to understand and demonstrates the applicability of the content to real-life situations. Selections from children's literature offer another rich resource for economics instruction. Good books often "hook" children into the content of an economics lesson with the same excitement and interest as a hungry fish studying a juicy worm. With the global challenges that face us and our environment, there is a growing sense of the need for new, more integrative approaches that infuse economic analysis into science. Students enjoy using interactive online games and computer activities to learn about needs and wants, to make economic choices, and to learn almost everything about economics. And you can reinforce and deepen understanding of economic concepts by having students create and use simple graphic organizers. Free online graphic organizers can help students brainstorm, organize, and visualize choices and relationships.

 Video Exploration 12.1

The remainder of this chapter will be based on the *Six Core Economic Principles,** along with examples of associated teaching activities and strategies that will encourage your students to learn.

Principle 1: People Choose

We always want more than we can get, and resources (e.g., human, natural, capital) are always limited. Because of this major economic problem of scarcity, we usually choose the alternative that provides the most benefits at the least cost.

Perhaps the most customary way to introduce economics to elementary school children is through what is commonly referred to as "needs and wants." In its most basic sense, a *need* is something you *have* to have, something you cannot do without. Good examples include air, water, food, clothing, and shelter. These things are necessary for survival. A *want* is a good or service that you *would like* to have but that is not absolutely necessary for survival. For example, bikes, video games, televisions, designer clothes, cell phones, movies, and jewelry are all wants; we don't need these things to survive. People have unlimited wants, but they face limited resources; they cannot have everything they want and must make certain choices. This is especially true in times of *scarcity*, when people want or need more of something than is readily available.

Economics is concerned with the production and distribution of goods and services. *Goods* are things that are made or grown, and usually things you can see or touch. Examples include cars, toys, computers, shoes, sandwiches, and avocados. A *service* is something that someone does for you—like fix your car, treat your sore tooth, take your photo, or teach you about economics. Often, goods and services come together. For example, a restaurant offers food—a good. In addition, the food is prepared for the consumer by a cook and brought to the table by a server—both services. A *producer* is someone who provides goods or offers services. Farmers, carpenters, librarians, and store owners are examples of producers. A *consumer* is someone who purchases or uses goods and services. The distribution of goods and services is

---

* Based on Six Core Economic Principles poster created by Muskegon Area Intermediate School District. Contact Michigan Council on Economic Education (248-596-9560) or the Muskegon Area Intermediate School District (231-767-7227).

referred to as *marketing*. Marketing refers to advertising and other efforts to promote the sale of a good or service.

Because Principles 1 and 2 are closely associated, a classroom example in which both are highlighted is presented after Principle 2.

Principle 2: People's Choices Involve Costs

The relationship between needs and wants is an important lesson for children to learn and understand. It is Laney's (1993) opinion that if he were allowed to teach only one economic concept to elementary school students, *the ability to make choices about how to allocate scarce resources among competing uses* would be it. It almost seems as if the ability of children to grow into rational adult decision makers relies on their attainment of this important economics concept.

The *opportunity cost* of a decision is based on what must be given up (the next best alternative) as a result of an individual's choice. When you choose one thing, you forgo something else at the same time. An opportunity cost is not always a dollar and cents figure; it is often the next best alternative to any decision. For example, if your college decides to build student housing on a plot of vacant land, the opportunity cost involves comparing the overall impact of the housing units to other things that could have been done with that land. In building the student housing, your college has given up an opportunity to build a student center, or a parking garage, or a field house—or to sell the land and use the proceeds to reduce tuition. The opportunity cost of the decision to build the student housing is the loss of the student center *or* the loss of the money to be made from running a parking garage, *or* the loss of any other single alternative; opportunity cost is the cost of passing up the next best choice when making a decision, not a combination of all the possibilities.

Harold Brown provides an example of how the first two related economic principles can be taught in elementary schools by including children's literature as an integral part of the economics curriculum. Mr. Brown teaches his third graders economic concepts through his "Story-a-Week" program, which features a new children's book that contains basic economic concepts each week. Why does Mr. Brown use children's literature to teach economics? "First," he says, "my students and I love stories, so literature is a very satisfying approach. Second, economic concepts are introduced in the context of an interesting story, so the plot provides children with a better understanding of the concept. And third, using children's literature allows teachers to apply recent trends in education, such as an integrated curriculum. In an already crowded elementary school day, an interdisciplinary approach may be the best way to introduce economics into the curriculum."

Today, Mr. Brown is using Donald Hall's *Ox-Cart Man* (Viking), a picture book that provides his students with a glimpse of life in early 19th-century New England. It tells about a man who lives on a farm with his wife, daughter, and son. At the beginning of the story, the family is packing a two-wheeled wooden cart with the various *goods* the man will be taking to sell in Portsmouth—wool, a shawl, mittens, and candles. The man travels on foot to Portsmouth, where he goes to *market* and *sells* the *goods*, the cart, and even his beloved ox. (The children learn that the term *market* refers to any arrangement that allows people to *trade* with one another.) With *money* earned from the *sale*, the man *buys* an iron kettle, an embroidery needle for his daughter, a knife for his son, and two pounds of wintergreen peppermint candies. Finally, the man strolls home, where he is lovingly welcomed by his family. Together, as the seasons pass, they work on the new mittens, shawls, and candles they will *sell* again next year in Portsmouth.

> *To begin, Mr. Brown wanted to establish a context for the story. He displayed a large picture print of a home in the New England frontier, as it might have looked during the colonial period. He asked the students to talk about whatever came into their minds about life at that time and in that place. He listed their ideas on the whiteboard. The class concluded that, because of the wilderness surrounding them, people were required to provide food and shelter for themselves; they were remarkably self-sufficient.*

Mr. Brown read the story aloud to the class. As he read, he focused short discussions on the items the family gave up in order to get the things that they wanted and needed. Mr. Brown also focused on the concept of opportunity cost by discussing trade-offs that were made in order to receive something else. For example, the ox-cart man gave up wool, a shawl, mittens, and candles in order to get a kettle, a needle, a knife, and candy.

After Mr. Brown finished reading the story, the class discussed how the ox-cart man's family was both a producer and consumer of goods. Mr. Brown used a graphic organizer to help the students organize their ideas. Next, the class discussed the specialized work that the ox-cart man and his family did to manufacture, transport, and market their goods (e.g., carving, planting, weaving, shearing). Finally, Mr. Brown and the students developed a cycle chart, with examples, to explain the producing–transporting–selling–buying–producing yearly cycle:

- *The family produced the goods on their farm.*
- *The ox-cart man transported the goods to market in the cart.*
- *The ox-cart man sold the products at the market to make money.*
- *The ox-cart man bought things the family needed and wanted.*
- *The family continued to produce the goods in order to get the money they needed to satisfy their needs and wants.*

To extend the lesson, Mr. Brown directed the students to a website that provided information about needs that a colonial wilderness family had to meet in order to survive (e.g., shearing, carding, spinning, and weaving cloth for clothing and building furniture, tools, utensils, or other implements). Then the students drew pictures of things they might produce and give to the ox-cart man to take to the market to sell. The students wrote a description of the specialized work they would need to do to produce their goods and a description of what they would want brought back to them (as consumers) from the market so that they could continue to produce their products.

Principle 3: People Respond to Incentives in Predictable Ways

Incentives are actions, awards, or rewards that influence the choices people make. Incentives can be positive or negative. When incentives change, people change their behaviors in predictable ways. One of the most important questions that producers ask themselves is, "What can I do to interest people to buy my product or use my service?" The answer, in most cases, is emphatically, "Incentives!" Do you remember badgering your parents about buying you a fast-food meal just to get a free toy? How about demanding a box of "Crunchin' Good" cereal because you wanted the prize it contained? As a child, you, like a lot of children today, nagged your parents to buy those things because of *incentives*. Incentives are often used to influence consumer behavior. All of us, even teachers, respond to incentives: *Financial incentives* to increase student performance have become increasingly popular in education today. I once heard it said that most of economics can be summarized in four words: "People respond to incentives." Incentives are often connected with advertisements for products or services in an effort to influence us to buy them. In order to understand incentives, you must know that they may be one of two different types:

- *Positive economic incentives.* These incentives reward you for making certain choices. Advertisers know that the surest way to get people to behave in desirable ways is to reward them for doing so. Here is a positive incentive you may find in some classrooms: "If you finish your social studies assignment in time, you will receive extra time on the playground."

- *Negative economic incentives.* These incentives punish people for certain choices; they make people worse off. Here is a negative incentive you may find in some classrooms: "If your social studies assignment is not finished in time, you may not go out to recess."

In order to address Economic Principle 3, students must be able to identify the positive and negative economic incentives intended to influence our choices. Vera Kril, for example, focused on how advertising works in an effort to help her fifth graders make better, more informed choices when they shop and when they ask their parents to buy things for them.

Miss Kril was concerned that in today's world, advertising seems to be everywhere we look—online, on television, on billboards, in magazines, in newspapers, on public transportation, on grocery carts, and even on cell phones. "Advertising is all around you," she advised her students.

In an effort to increase their awareness about the amount of advertising and the pervasiveness of advertising directed toward children, Miss Kril used an activity designed to help her students understand and identify basic advertising techniques and appeals. She started by defining advertising (a type of persuasion) and describing, with examples, six common techniques:

- *Slogan or jingle: A short catch phrase, slogan, or tune that instantly makes you think of a product or company.*
- *Repetition: You hear something over and over until it is stuck in your head (sometimes it is the slogan or jingle; it can also be a phone number, name, or any "magic" word).*
- *Bandwagon: They convince you that everybody is buying or using it, and you should join the crowd. You don't want to be left out, do you?*
- *Promotion: Coupons, prizes, or gifts create the attraction of getting something "free" or at a greatly reduced price.*
- *Testimonial: A celebrity or famous person endorses the product.*
- *Plain Folk: Shows ordinary people using or supporting a product or candidate.*

Miss Kril then divided the class into groups, each group representing one of the advertising techniques. Each group was assigned the task of going through newspapers and magazines, looking for examples of its assigned technique and creating a collage of representative ads. As the groups shared their projects with each other, Miss Kril asked the students to respond to this question: "Who do you think is the intended audience? What makes you think so?"

Next, Miss Kril helped the students focus on the design elements of ads:

- *Use of color*
- *Amount and style of text on the page*
- *Text language*
- *Amount and types of images*
- *Facial expressions and body language*

Miss Kril asked each group to study ads representing its advertising technique and select one ad they thought was very effective in using the design elements and one ad that seemed deceptive. As a final assignment, each group was given a common object such as a drinking cup, pencil, shoe, or apple. Using the technique it was assigned, each group was to create a PowerPoint advertisement for its product. The groups presented their ads and discussed how their ads were alike and different from the commercially produced ads. The students also offered comments about the effective elements of each presentation.

Principle 4: People Create Economic Systems That Influence Individual Choices and Incentives

Written and unwritten rules determine methods of allocating scarce resources. These rules determine what is produced, how it is produced, and for whom it is produced. As the rules change, so do individual choices, incentives, and behavior.

An *economic system* is best described as the way nations resolve the connected issues of distributing scarce resources among producers and allocating scarce goods and services among consumers—in other words, how they manage the production and distribution of goods and services. To do this, all economic systems answer three basic economic questions: What will we produce with our resources? How will we produce these goods?

"What effect do you think the law of supply and demand will have on the price of our goods?"

Jon Barlow/Pearson Education Ltd

For whom will we produce these goods? The way that a nation answers these questions forms the basis of its economic system:

- *Traditional economy.* In traditional economies, answers to the three basic economic questions are based on *how they were addressed in the past.* There is little difference from generation to generation regarding who will do what and how it will be done; if your family grew wheat or potatoes in the past, you will farm wheat or potatoes, too. New ideas or ways of doing things are commonly rejected. Traditional economies are most often found in undeveloped rural regions where people grow their own food and build their own shelters.

- *Command economy.* In command economies, the government regulates the supply and price of goods and services. Government officials decide which goods and services are produced and how they are distributed. The government owns all property and controls all resources, including land, labor, and capital. Consumer needs are of minor concern in a command economy.

- *Market economy.* In market economies, the system is controlled by the nation's citizens and privately owned corporations rather than by the government. The exchange of goods, services, and information takes place in a free market governed by the law of supply and demand as opposed to governmental intervention or central planning.

- *Mixed economy.* In mixed economies, there is a blend of government regulation and private economic freedom. Individuals and businesses enjoy varying degrees of economic freedom, but they are also subject to a range of government regulation. Common examples of mixed economies include the United States, Canada, Australia, Japan, Germany, the United Kingdom, and Italy.

Anthony Kendall wanted to help his students understand the factors that must be considered as we search for answers to our three important economics questions: What will we produce with our resources? How will we produce these goods? For whom will we produce these goods? To begin, Mr. Kendall called the students' attention to four boxes that contained an assortment of inexpensive goodies that a parent had donated to the class—a colorful collection of noisemakers, bouncing balls, pencils, erasers, and much more. After distributing brown lunch bags to everyone, the students were told they could come to the front of the room, table by table, and help themselves to the toys and treats. Mr. Kendall called the first table of students and allowed them to take as many toys and treats as they wanted from the first box, giving them extra lunch bags if necessary. After two tables had their chance, one box of toys and treats was gone. The next table of students asked Mr. Kendall for the toys and treats from the second box. He opened the box and feigned shock upon finding nothing inside, apologizing to the students: "I can't believe it . . . . I thought all the boxes had toys and treats!"

Mr. Kendall suggested that if the first students had known there was a limited supply, they might have left enough for the rest of the class. But his explanation did little to dampen the disappointment and anger that some freely expressed about this seemingly unjust situation: "That's not fair, Mr. Kendall!" they bellowed in dismay.

Mr. Kendall responded by saying, "Let's talk about just the problem we have here."

"That's easy," several responded in near unison. "The first group hogged everything! There wasn't enough for everybody."

"Why do we have this problem?" Mr. Kendall asked in pretend confusion.

"Anybody could see that there just weren't enough toys for everybody. The kids that went first took everything!" grumbled Eunice.

Mr. Kendall asked what could be done about the problem. The students offered several ideas, including redistributing the toys, getting more toys, and, unfortunately, some going without toys. (And, yes, Mr. Kendall redistributed the cache of goodies so that everyone received his or her fair share.) Mr. Kendall used this opportunity to explain that this problem characterized a major economic problem that all societies face—allocation of resources. Scarcity occurs because people want many things, but supplies may be limited, so choices must be made about how scarce resources are distributed among producers and how scarce goods and services are divided among consumers. Mr. Kendall explained that people and societies make these decisions in different ways; the experience led to a computer scavenger hunt in which the students searched the Internet to research how different societies make allocation decisions. Mr. Kendall is sold on the idea that a solid academic foundation in economics is important, but that children also need to employ real-world skills, including decision making and problem solving. So, he often presents his students with situations in which they must make informed decisions. In this case, he divided the class into equal groups and assigned them the task of deciding what to do with this problem: "The Western states are experiencing a drought severe enough that there isn't enough water to satisfy the wants the people have for water. How should the water be allocated?"

Video Exploration 12.2

Principle 5: People Gain When They Trade Voluntarily

People specialize in producing goods and services because they expect to gain from their specialization. For example, people trade what they produce with others when they think they can gain something from the exchange. Some benefits of voluntary trade include higher standards of living and broader choices of goods and services.

Economic trade is not new; people have been trading since the earliest civilizations. Earth's earliest civilizations, obviously, had no money or credit cards, so to get goods, people traded items back and forth—that type of trade (bartering) has evolved substantially, and trade now involves complex processes such as buying and selling in the world's great financial markets. Despite the level of sophistication, the basic elements of trade have not changed over the years because, essentially, trade involves the simple concept of exchanging one thing for another.

In an elementary school social studies program, trade is treated as the voluntary exchange of goods and services between or among individuals and businesses. One example of international trade is *triangular trade*. During our nation's early days, for example, trade among England, the Americas, and Africa came to be known as the infamous *triangular trade*—the name given to the geometric shape of the trade route. The first leg was from England to Africa, where English merchants exchanged goods with Africans for slaves. The second leg, or "middle passage," was the transportation of the African slaves to the Americas. Once in America, the ship would unload the slaves and take on molasses, rum, sugar, and tobacco. Then the ship headed out on the third, and final, leg of the journey—back to Europe, completing the triangle. During their study of international trade, children learn that trading among nations is very important because no single nation can get all the services or goods it wants or needs within its own boundaries; there is no country that can produce enough of everything it wants or needs to survive. So trade is simply an exchange of things; countries (or people) trade things when they have too much of one thing for things that they lack.

Teachers often use graphic organizers to help their students manage their economics decision-making skills, including those dealing with the concept of trade. Graphic organizers assist students in arranging content or ideas in an orderly fashion, becoming aware of how ideas are connected, and participating in active, meaningful discussions. For example, suppose that you are going to be teaching the idea that a stable food supply was one of the prerequisites of early settled civilizations. The specific content you must first help the children understand is focused on the idea that as early gatherer-hunters learned to domesticate wild animals and to sow seeds, they gradually settled down and became farmers and herders. Then, as farming methods improved, people often found themselves with food surpluses. This unexpected bounty led to trade. A village with an overabundance of grain, for example, traded it for tools, pottery, cloth, or other goods from nearby villages. An overabundance of anything is called a *surplus*, and early civilizations had to learn how to face important decisions regarding surpluses because it wasn't always the best move to trade them for other goods. Theresa Padilla devised a way to help her students make economic decisions—decisions that depend on the economy at the time the decision is made.

> Ms. Padilla had her students assume the role of citizens of an ancient village, living on the land between the Tigris and Euphrates Rivers. Their village is fortunate; unlike others, whose farmland has been scorched by the sun, theirs has an irrigation system that has helped produce an abundance of grain. While other villages face a devastating famine, the students' village is thriving. Ms. Padilla held a discussion focused on the following questions: "How do you feel about having surplus food while your neighbors are starving?" "Is it fair that one village should have so much while the others face famine?" "Do wealthy civilizations have a responsibility to help those who have less?"

To delve more deeply into these issues, Ms. Padilla used a cooperative learning activity in which students were to address the problem of what to do with the surplus grain. She divided the class into base groups of three and assigned each student a number from one to three. Ms. Padilla directed all the ones, twos, and threes to move from their base groups into expert groups, with each expert group assigned to examine the positive and negative consequences of one of these alternatives: All the ones would study the "store the grain" alternative, twos would study the "sell the grain" alternative, and threes would study the "give it away" alternative. Completing a graphic organizer helped each group consider the positive and negative consequences of their alternatives. The "store the grain" group's completed organizer is shown in Figure 12.2.

After completing their graphic organizers, each member of the expert groups returned to his or her base group to share the results. Each base group listened to the positive and negative consequences of each alternative as it sought to arrive at a decision.

Principle 6: People's Choices Have Consequences That Lie in the Future

Economists believe that the costs and benefits of the economic decisions we make and, sometimes, our decisions themselves may lead to unintended consequences. Whenever people judge whether the advantages of an economic decision are likely to outweigh its disadvantages, they are participating in a form of economic thinking referred to as *cost/benefit analysis* (also called *benefit/cost analysis*). Although a cost/benefit analysis can be used for almost any decision, individuals, governments, and businesses most commonly conduct such analyses to assess the relative value of a proposed economic decision. Prior to buying a house, building a new bridge, or introducing a new product, for example, a cost/benefit analysis should be completed to determine whether the benefits resulting from the course of action outweigh the costs and by how much. How does this talk of cost/benefit analysis carry over to a social studies classroom? First, students must learn that, as wise consumers, they need to make good decisions. Also, basic to good economic decision making is the ability to think about the negatives and positives of any problem. Despite its importance, we use a necessarily simplified version of cost/benefit analysis in elementary school economics since real-life cost/benefit analysis can be an extremely complex and sophisticated process.

The social studies standards of Eugene Snyder's school required that students make economics decisions by systematically considering alternatives and consequences. So to start his creative

FIGURE 12.2   *Decision-Making Graphic Organizer*

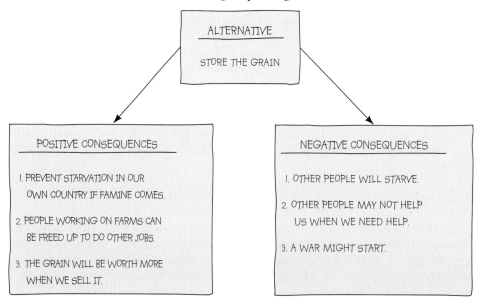

problem-solving (CPS) strategy, Mr. Snyder used a group problem-solving simulation involving an imaginary community environmental tragedy, as described in Figure 12.3. He divided the students into five-member groups and asked each group to stand in line in front of charts that were spaced evenly around the room. The first student in line was instructed to write a word, short phrase, or statement about the "mess" in which the community found itself—facts or feelings about the issue. In turn, the rest of the students rotated to the chart, writing as quickly as they could the things they knew, felt, or thought about the "mess." Some groups wrote more than 20 entries in the 5 minutes allotted for this task. After examining the lists, Mr. Snyder directed the students to talk together and select the one item that bugged them the most or seemed to capture the situation best. Each group then rewrote the selection as a problem statement. One group was mainly concerned about the unspoiled magnificence of the forestland; its problem statement read "In what ways might we control the junk that is being dumped in the forest?" Health concerns were the most worrisome facet for another group; its problem statement read "In what ways might we avoid infestation by dangerous vermin and avoid contagious diseases?"

After they articulated and selected their problems, the next step involved brainstorming possible remedies: "What are all the possible ways we might solve the problem?" Using a clean sheet of chart paper and employing the same group "relay" strategy that they had used to pinpoint the problem, Mr. Snyder encouraged the students to write whatever came to mind, even if the idea seemed at first to have nothing to do with a possible solution. No idea would be critiqued until all ideas had been written down. Suggestions included:

1. **Pick it up.** *Litter can be picked up by volunteers or by paid employees. Businesses can have their employees pick up litter from parking lots, entrances, and landscaped areas.*

2. **Adoption program.** *Encourage group volunteers to "adopt a spot" that they clean periodically. Any group that would like to participate will be provided gloves, trash bags, brooms, rakes, and shovels. They pick a day and a place, round up a few people, and go to work!*

3. **Educate people about the need to dispose of waste properly.** *Signs, messages printed on packaging, personal messages, and presentations about the harmful effects of litter may decrease some littering behavior.*

FIGURE 12.3   Environmental Littering Simulation

Green City is a small village in rural Forest County with a population of just over 5,000 people. It is a vibrant community that combines the beauty and charm of a rich 150-year history with an exceptional quality of life. Green City provides the best of all worlds, boasting excellent schools, tree-lined streets, a bustling downtown, public parks, a library, an award-winning museum, small stores and shops, restaurants, zero shopping malls, and a few thriving businesses. Green City is surrounded by unspoiled nature where deer run free and fishing is world-class. Hiking trails and lakes surround the community.

The problem with this idyllic place is what the residents describe as a "new breed of vermin"—illegal garbage dumpers. Village officials have identified 17 illegal dumpsites in the 85,000 acre forest surrounding Green City. They have witnessed rubbish and junk accumulating along the roadsides, stream banks, and hollows.

The problem has escalated in part because communities surrounding Green City have grown in the past few years and with the population increase comes stresses on the environment—people don't seem to care or are too lazy to dispose of trash properly. "We not only have a litter problem, we have a real dumping problem," one resident lamented. "People are putting refrigerators, tires, air conditioners, and mattresses out there! We're concerned about the disease and pests these things can bring."

Hoping to solve the problem, a local interest group (the Unspoiled Forest Club) organized a campaign that prompted the village council to post "No Dumping" signs that threatened fines or arrest for those caught dumping or littering illegally. However, the junk kept spreading. Residents are now quite concerned that their once unspoiled environment faces the possibility of becoming a toxic eyesore.

The condition of the environment is a topic of daily conversation among Green City's residents. They are convinced that the village and the county should look into different, more drastic, methods to deal with the dumping and litter problem. The mayor of Green City has talked with school officials about studying anti-littering and anti-dumping concerns in the classrooms. Do their fresh young minds have any suggestions that might help protect the health and safety of Green City and help support the general welfare of the environment?

4. **Provide receptacles and trash cans at key points of buildings, bus stops, and other areas where people frequently need to discard their trash.** *These are the places most people seem to discard their trash, before entering buildings or getting on a bus. Providing trash cans at these locations can dramatically reduce litter.*

5. **Anti-litter taxes.** *Consumers can pay a small "anti-litter tax" when they purchase a canned or bottled beverage. These funds can then be used to support anti-litter efforts.*

The students looked over their lists and determined which one or two items might best be made into a workable solution; they used a cost/benefit analysis strategy that involved simply adding up the value of a course of action and subtracting the costs associated with it. They restated the problem and narrowed the list of suggestions by asking questions such as these: "Will this idea actually solve the problem?" "Will it create new problems?" "What are the chances that it will work?" "Is it financially practical?" "Will we be able to use it in the near future?" "What are any strengths and weaknesses?" For example, one group found out that hiring people to pick up litter can cost a business or the community a great deal of money; a neighboring community spends $150,000 on picking up and disposing of litter each year. This phase of the problem-solving exercise required the groups to narrow the list of suggestions and work toward an agreed-upon decision. The ultimate choice might contain a single idea or a combination of ideas.

One group suggested making big signs such as "Spruce Up Around Here!" (Spruce was their play on words!) Another thought it would be fun and helpful to establish a periodic community "cleanup festival." A third group announced that it would install surveillance video cameras in secret locations throughout the most affected areas, with the goal of identifying and prosecuting violators and forcing them to pay fines or spend time in jail.

The final step in Mr. Snyder's problem-solving simulation involved expanding the interesting idea or combining interesting ideas into an action plan that detailed the steps necessary to implement the solution: "What course of action will we take?" "Does this plan depend on someone else's approval or support?" "What steps are needed?" "Who will do what?" "When must the steps be completed?" The video camera group, for example, suggested that its program would need to be approved by the village council and could be paid for with a grant from the State Department of Environmental Protection.

Mr. Snyder likes to use group problem-solving simulations to teach economics because, if they are carried out in the right way, groups bring a broad range of ideas, knowledge, and skills to the process of studying a problem, which results in a wider range and better quality of solutions.

Meszaros and Evans (2010) advise that,

> *"Economic instruction needs to start early to ensure that students are well prepared for their adult roles as consumers, producers, investors, U.S. citizens, and global citizens. Young children can learn the basics of economics if teachers are knowledgeable about the content, are provided with quality instructional materials, and receive guidance on what concepts to teach and at what age children are likely to be able to comprehend them"* (p. 7).

As a result of such instruction, students will not only have the ability to make informed economic choices but they will also understand how the consequences of their choices will influence their lives and the lives of others in the future.

Reflection on Learning

You may simply scribble rough notes or jot down something more polished and complete. The point is to simply start recording your ideas spontaneously and candidly.

Should controversial issues (e.g., that giving government assistance reduces an individual's incentive to help themselves) become a part of the elementary school economics curriculum? Do 7- to 10-year-olds have too many cognitive restraints that prevent them from making rational decisions on controversial real-world issues?

CHECK YOUR UNDERSTANDING 12.2 **Click here** to check your understanding of this section of the chapter.

A Final Thought

Economics instruction is based on the premise that authentic activities help students not only to develop a greater awareness of economics decisions in their current lives but also to acquire the insights and reasoning skills they will use when ultimately facing economic issues as adults. Economics education places students in classroom settings where they are initially introduced to the concepts of "needs and wants." From there, concepts such as production, distribution, exchange, and consumption are steadily introduced through a combination of explicit and student-centered instruction. You will find that your role includes explaining concepts to students, scaffolding their learning, reading stories, carrying out simulations, arranging problem-solving experiences, assessing advertisements, and developing a wide repertoire of teaching strategies to help promote economics learning and develop economics understandings. Through the economics curriculum, then, students will apply skills in critical thinking, decision making, and problem solving, not only to school learning situations but also to real-life circumstances.

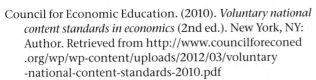

References

Council for Economic Education. (2010). *Voluntary national content standards in economics* (2nd ed.). New York, NY: Author. Retrieved from http://www.councilforeconed.org/wp/wp-content/uploads/2012/03/voluntary-national-content-standards-2010.pdf

Laney, J. D. (1993). Economics for elementary school students: Research-supported principles of teaching and learning that guide classroom practice. *Social Studies, 84,* 98–100.

Meszaros, B., & Evans, S. (2010). It's never too early: Why economics education in the elementary classroom. *Social Studies and the Young Learner, 22,* 4–7.

Meszaros, B., & Suiter, M. (1998). The case for economics in the elementary classroom. Retrieved from https://www.minneapolisfed.org/publications/the-region/the-case-for-economics-in-the-elementary-classroom

National Council on Economic Education. (2007). *Personal finance and entrepreneurship education in our nation's schools, 2007. A report card: Survey of the states.* New York, NY: Author. Retrieved from www.ncee.net

Shulman, L. S. (1986). Those who understand: Knowledge growth in teaching. *Educational Researcher, 15,* 4–14.

CHAPTER 13

Sociology and Anthropology:
Social Structures and Culture

Learning Outcomes

Sociology is the study of group life; it teaches children about the social and cultural forces that shape people's behavior, beliefs, and relationships. Anthropology is the biological and cultural study of humanity. Anthropologists employ a holistic approach to the study of likenesses and differences among human beings, past and present. The combination of anthropology and sociology in this chapter presents a unique breadth of exposure to the study of how cultures address human needs and concerns. After completing this chapter, you will be able to:

- Define the term anthropology.

- Explain the role of anthropology in the elementary school social studies curriculum.

- Assess the importance of multiculturalism in the United States and plan instruction in ways that fairly represent various racial, cultural, and social class groups.

- Define the term sociology.

- Explain the role of sociology in the elementary school social studies curriculum.

Classroom Snapshot

Cliff Howard's fifth graders slipped on their "archaeologist's vests," safety glasses, and gloves and began working at the sand table (borrowed from the kindergarten classroom). They were digging up, sifting through, and brushing off "ancient artifacts" hidden beneath the soil. For the kindergarteners' sand, Mr. Howard had substituted layers of screened topsoil (organic humus); unscreened dirt; and a mixture of dirt, sand, and crushed gravel to create stratifications of different colors and textures. (Mr. Howard did not use a layer of sand only because sand is too loose to keep objects in place.) Mr. Howard had concealed a number of artifacts within each layer—fake coins, miniature plastic objects, beads, imitation gemstones and jewelry, replicas of artifacts (or laminated images of artifacts), and other puzzle pieces from the past that his students were to examine, analyze, and incorporate into a story. Their work tools included plastic sheets, spoons and miniature trowels for digging, wire screen, brushes, magnifying glasses, digital cameras, containers for excavated dirt, small zippered plastic baggies to hold the clues, waterproof markers for labeling, clipboards and pencils, and a recording sheet for each layer.

Mr. Howard began the project by reading to his class Kate Duke's Archaeologists Dig for Clues (Collins). As part of the Let's-Read-and-Find-Out Science series, the book tells the story of a boy and his friends who go on a dig in a local cornfield with their archaeologist friend Sophie. Within this context, Duke explains what archaeologists look for, how they find things, and what their finds reveal. (Some upper-grade teachers hesitate to use picture books, but the concepts are introduced so well in this book that even Mr. Howard's upper-grade students found the story enjoyable and informative.) The students concluded that archaeologists are multifaceted—part scientist, part social scientist, part detective, part reporter.

Mr. Howard then asked his students to imagine that they were skilled archaeologists who recently chanced upon several artifacts from around 2,000 years ago. So far, no one had been able to identify the source of the artifacts; the students were chosen for this job because they were the foremost experts in the world.

Mr. Howard's students learned that not all archaeological fieldwork requires excavation, but when it is used, a grid must be laid out over the area to be excavated with stakes and cord; archaeologists always dig neat, organized, square holes. So, using Duke's book as a guide, they began their "dig" by dividing the surface of the site into squares with grids made from yarn. Once they completed the stringing phase, team members took turns digging, drawing, recording findings, and putting artifacts into correctly labeled bags. Each team carefully removed the soil from its own section, layer by layer, to dig up remains from the unknown past culture. "We have to dig carefully so all the artifacts we find can be mapped and photographed," cautioned Mr. Howard.

"Look at this!" shouted Jenny. The others left their stations to see what Jenny had unearthed. Jenny proudly held up something that looked like an old coin. "That's the best ever!" She brushed it carefully, examined it closely, and searched for information that could tell her where the coin might have been from. She noticed what she thought was a likeness of a Roman emperor wearing a laurel crown. The word AUGUSTUS was printed above the likeness. "Hmmm," reflected Jenny. "Where could this coin be from?" Before she ventured to answer the question, however, Jenny carefully recorded the exact location of her coin on the site map.

The students were finding different things in different parts of the excavation. Kiesha found an almost complete pottery vessel. Another team found rocks used for a campfire, with bones around it. However, the students became dismayed that the excavating time for that day was quickly coming to an end. They wanted to keep digging; at the end of the day, one group had just exposed a part of what looked like a small plastic replica of a Roman soldier's "gladius" (sword). Mr. Howard told them not to be concerned as they still had several days to complete their digs and write their reports.

"That's it! I'll prove to Mr. Howard that this mystery coin is from ancient Rome!" Jenny trumpeted the next day. The excitement in Jenny's voice was as clear as the pleasure reflected on her face. She saw what she believed to be a Roman emperor wearing a head decoration that looked like leaves. Based on this observation, Jenny guessed that the coin could have come from ancient Rome. Jenny searched through a series of reference books that Mr. Howard had arranged beforehand and learned about the history of Roman coins. She also consulted an electronic encyclopedia available on the classroom computer. She found that Roman coins were decorated with the likeness of the person who was emperor when they were minted, *although emperors also were inclined to depict war victories and other achievements of their reign on their coinage. Jenny learned that laurel crowns were used to adorn emperors and that the title AUGUSTUS was given to the popular Roman leader Octavian when he succeeded Julius Caesar following his death at the hands of Brutus. There was no date on the coin, but Jenny compared her information about Roman coins and emperors with what was on the coin she uncovered and made an educated guess that this coin was made in Rome between 31 BC and AD 14.*

Jenny was somewhat sure the research evidence supported her initial thoughts about the Roman coin but, working with an open mind, she stood ready to alter her initial conclusions should further evidence demand it. She compared her coin with something found by a classmate, Russell. He had dug up a miniature banner with the letters SPQR. Russell's research indicated that these are the initials for Latin words that translate to "The senate and the people of Rome." Together, Jenny and Russell concluded that they had enough corroborating evidence to substantiate a contention that these items were from ancient Rome. However, they did not know whether these artifacts were found in Rome or whether they had been left behind in a foreign land as a result of trade, travel, war, or migration. Their field drawings and artifact descriptions would await the findings of their "expert colleagues" before they could make a definitive conclusion. (While they were digging, the students drew and photographed the artifacts, put them into zippered plastic bags, and wrote the number of the square where each artifact was found on its bag.)

After all the evidence was in, Mr. Howard and the students discussed how even the smallest archaeological site may contain a wealth of important information about cultures. They talked about how archaeologists study objects left behind by past cultures to obtain information about the people who made and used them. After excavating and cataloging the items from their dig, the "expert archaeologists" were challenged to come up with plausible explanations for their finds: "Based on the physical remains contained in this site, what culture once inhabited this region?" Mr. Howard smiled to himself as he listened to his students' ensuing discussion, for he derived great pleasure and satisfaction from watching them attempt to clear up the mysteries of the buried artifacts.

Mr. Howard supplemented the archaeological dig experience with an enrichment learning center designed to offer students an opportunity to expand their learning by engaging in self-directed learning activities. The enrichment center housed a computer-based game called *Roman Town*. Created by professional archaeologist Suzi Wilczynski, the game allows Mr. Howard's students to maintain their role as virtual archaeologists who now team up with a "professor" needing help uncovering the ancient city of Fossura, found near Pompeii circa AD 79. In the process of solving the mystery of what happened to the ancient city, students learn about the tools and processes commonly used by archaeologists. Wiping off dirt from the artifacts hiding in the ground while using a computer mouse is not as hands-on or messy as the real thing, but Mr. Howard's students will tell you that it is equally instructive and enjoyable.

Mr. Howard chose to involve his students in this archaeology-based interdisciplinary unit in an attempt to address the NCSS standard that was part of his district's social studies curriculum: *Explore and describe similarities and differences in the ways groups, societies, and cultures address similar human needs and concerns.* But before he was comfortable with the idea of engaging his students in a "hands-on" experience, Mr. Howard felt that he needed to know more about archaeological excavation techniques. He searched a number of websites and found just what he was looking for at the Archaeological Institute of America (the primary professional organization of anthropologists) site. The site offers highly useful tips and essential information about the basic archaeological principles of excavation, teamwork required during an excavation, and evidence gathering and analysis. It includes a number of lesson plans that helped Mr. Howard organize his classroom dig.

Throughout this rewarding hands-on experience, Mr. Howard operated with a conviction that interdisciplinary, archaeology-based projects are a great way to get children interested in cultures of the past through material objects left behind. "It's unbelievable when you think about how many different disciplines can be natural parts of an archaeology project," he claims. "I'm able to integrate skills and content from a range of traditional subject areas into an inclusive, challenging framework of instruction. Interdisciplinary learning is not only great for the students but has a positive effect on me, too; I feel invigorated when I use such a fresh, new approach to teaching old content."

"My kids love archaeology," boasts Mr. Howard. "As 'archaeologists,' they get to solve puzzles every day and uncover new information; problem-solving activities seem to fascinate all kids at this age." The answers to archaeology's mysteries are not always easy for young children to unlock, but as they plug away, they discover that sticking to the task eventually pays off. I've heard people liken the work of archaeologists to that of detectives; both identify, collect, and process physical evidence and sort through clues to solve a complicated puzzle. An archaeologist might find a toy, a tool, or the ruins of a dwelling, but all these clues mean very little by themselves unless they can be connected together to tell a story of what life was like long ago. "Actually," explains Mr. Howard, "*archaeologists* are *anthropologists*. They are specialists in one of the four fields that comprise the discipline of anthropology. Each has a different set of research interests and generally uses distinctive research techniques."

What Is Anthropology?

Anthropology is the study of human beings and cultures, past and present. In the United States, anthropology is divided into four major fields:

1. *Cultural anthropology.* This field of anthropology examines the system of shared beliefs, values, customs, and behaviors common to societies all over the world, including gender relations, ethnicity, childrearing, religion, folklore, symbols, values, etiquette, sports, music, art, drama, dance, nutrition, recreation, games, food, festivals, and language (which is also studied in linguistic anthropology).

2. *Archaeology.* This field of anthropology systematically uncovers physical evidence of people and cultures from the past through excavation and analysis of their material remains.

3. *Biological (or physical) anthropology.* This field of anthropology studies humans within an evolutionary framework, examining how our ancestors changed over time to become the humans of today.

4. *Linguistic anthropology.* This field of anthropology considers the structures and functions of verbal and nonverbal communication, how languages developed over time, and how they differ from each other.

Despite having four wide-ranging and diverse fields, anthropology takes pride in describing itself as a "holistic" field of study. "Holistic" means that anthropologists study humanity in terms of the powerful interrelationships among all aspects of existence, across all times and all places. Of the four anthropology fields, elementary schools overwhelmingly pull from cultural anthropology; studying people and their cultures is a major part of elementary school social studies. When experiencing anthropology, students explore cultures through the examination of elements such as gender roles, governments, religious rituals, folklore and mythology, marriage, language, architecture, cuisine, technology, music, dance, visual arts, drama, literature, sports, medicine, dress, laws, education, agriculture, economy, grooming, values, work ethic, etiquette, courtship, recreation, gestures, cooking, games, jokes, sports, and even birth and death (because they are accompanied by different types of ritual ceremonies). So we can say that cultural anthropology is an interdisciplinary subject that infuses and draws on the resources of a variety of disciplines in an attempt to understand and appreciate cultures around the world. Teaching students about cultures helps them appreciate the likenesses and differences among people and their traditions. Unquestionably, that is a noble goal, but it begs the questions: "How do we teach it?" "How do we include cultures in our social studies program?" "Are some methods more appropriate than others?"

The National Council for the Social Studies (2010), in its *National Curriculum Standards for Social Studies*, recommends, "Social studies programs should include experiences that provide for the study of culture and cultural diversity" (p. 14). NCSS (2010) goes on to explain:

> Learners will understand how human beings create, learn, share, and adapt to culture. They will appreciate the role of culture in shaping their lives and the society in which they live. By recognizing various cultural perspectives, learners become capable of understanding diverse perspectives, thereby acquiring the potential to foster more positive relations and interactions with diverse people within our own nation and other nations." (p. 68)

 CHECK YOUR UNDERSTANDING 13.1 **Click here** to check your understanding of this section of the chapter.

Teaching Anthropology in the Elementary School

Whether talking about a group of college students, personal friends, or family members, we all have a culture—a unique system of behaviors, beliefs, and customs. A group's culture may be reflected in things such as its interpersonal relationships, language, clothing, or traditions. Differences among groups are widespread, in both the overt (clothing, hairstyle, language) and the subtle (how one addresses a peer or an elder). *Culture* consists of all the accepted and patterned ways of a group's behavior; it is the sum total of the group's ways of thinking, feeling, and acting.

An elementary school classroom must be a place where children not only experience pride in their own culture but also learn to understand and respect other ways of life; that is the role of anthropology. Since anthropology is considered a holistic study of the characteristics of the diverse cultures on Earth, we can assume it would be the ideal social science to pull from as we plan learning experiences that provide our students with a knowledge and appreciation of cultures filtered through a comparative lens: "What can be done to make our curriculum inclusive and respectful of all ethnic, racial, and cultural backgrounds?" "How might our curriculum become more multicultural and diverse within an increasingly tolerant environment?"

There are literally endless dimensions to culture, but Nitza Hidalgo (1993) has provided an important contribution to defining three levels of culture that are especially useful for planning elementary school instruction. Hidalgo's three levels are (1) *concrete*, (2) *behavioral*, and (3) *symbolic*.

 Video Example 13.1   https://www.youtube.com/watch?v=sMFsgPy1H5M
In this video without narration, educator and anthropologist Lauren W. Hasten shows how anthropology can provide students with tools for understanding the world. As you watch this video, consider an answer to its title: "What Is Anthropology and Why Should We Teach It?"

The Concrete Level of Cultures

The concrete level is the most obvious level of culture; it includes a group's unique material objects that can be experienced through the senses—clothing, music, art, food, games, and tools. You can expect to find these items used during routine daily activities as well

Teaching a culture in depth requires great effort and expertise in order for students to grasp its many elements—tangible elements such as the arts, artifacts, cuisine, or tools, and intangible elements such as language, religion, traditions, and core values and beliefs.

TheFinalMiracle/Shutterstock

as in special rituals or celebrations. There are many examples of using cultural artifacts to inform and inspire students—including strutting about in clogs from the Netherlands, pulling out one Russian matryoshka (nesting) doll to reveal a smaller figure of the same type inside, seeing how bad dreams will get caught in an Ojibwa dream catcher, and inspecting items such as a Nigerian calabash, a Korean 50-won coin, a cowboy hat, Buddhist prayer flags, genuine Navajo pottery, train tickets, newspapers, clothing, and so on. In fact, any object you can think of can be used to teach about cultures. Our "Classroom Snapshot" teacher Cliff Howard recognized that his students were more engaged and focused when they worked with hands-on materials: "There is nothing in the social studies classroom equal to activities that require learners to use their senses in partnership with their minds. Busy bodies help activate busy minds!"

A familiar Japanese folk toy that has been treasured for generations (since the 6th century) became a valuable primary artifact to help engage Mary Miller's fourth-grade students in anthropological inquiry during a unit on Japan.

Ms. Miller unveiled a Daruma doll and asked her students to inspect the sample (see Figure 13.1). She encouraged the students to talk about what they knew (or thought they knew) about the doll and made a list of their comments: What type of object is it (tool, toy, holiday item)? What color is it? What is its shape and size? What is it made of? What do you think it is? The next step was to make a second list that recorded what the students would like to know about the artifact. After completing the second chart, Ms. Miller challenged the students to locate sources that would help them find answers to the questions they had raised about the artifact: "What are the most useful and reliable sources?" The students decided that the best source at this time would be their laptop computers but, since they were not sure what the object was, they had a difficult time coming up with a keyword for their search. After a great deal of discussion, they decided that "Japanese doll" would be their first keyword try. A site on the first page helped the students learn that the toy was called a "Daruma doll," but it contained very little other useful information. Using their new keyword ("Daruma doll"), however, led to deeper and more complete information. They learned that the Daruma doll is a hollow, round traditional Japanese doll modeled after Bodhidharma, the Father of Zen Buddhism. Legend explains that Bodhidharma spent 9 years meditating in a cave, during which time he moved neither his eyes

FIGURE 13.1   *Daruma Doll*

nor his limbs. As a result of this inactivity, Bodhidharma lost the use of his arms and legs. Like Bodhidharma, Daruma dolls have neither arms nor legs, and they sit in a meditative pose with both eyes blank. The Daruma doll is weighted at the bottom much like "roly-poly" dolls in the United States; no matter how hard it is pushed over, the doll bobs right back up. Because it rights itself so effortlessly, the Daruma doll has become a symbol for not giving up.

The students made their own Daruma dolls by following Ms. Miller's directions. The process started with a blown egg having an enlarged hole at the bottom. The children put a small fishing sinker (sand works well, too) into the hole and covered the hole with masking tape. Next, they coated their eggs with four layers of papier-mâché strips. After the strips dried, the students painted on the doll's clothes. The clothes could be painted in many colors, but the most traditional is red (symbolizing the priest's red robe). Next, they colored in the face, leaving the eyeballs blank. The dolls are sometimes used by Japanese people while trying something new. When someone sets a goal, one eye is painted in; when the goal is accomplished, the other eye is painted in. Each student was asked to set a meaningful learning goal for the thematic unit and paint one eye. When he or she accomplished the goal, the student would paint in the remaining eye.

The Behavioral Level of Cultures

This second level has to do with a group's basic patterns of social interaction and conduct, such as verbal and body language, gender roles, family structure, education, and considerations such as when they sleep and how or what they eat. In a time-honored view of cultural behavior, sociologist Talcott Parsons (in Parsons & Bales, 1956) spoke of the birth of new generations of children as a recurrent barbarian invasion, emphasizing the point that human infants do not possess culture at birth—they have no conception of the world, no language, no morality. But because human beings cannot go through life behaving indiscriminately, their cultures prepare them with the training and education required to adapt to expected behaviors. The standards (unwritten rules) by which a culture guides the behaviors of its members are called *norms*; norms define expected, or "normal," behavior. *Enculturation* is the term used for the process of internalizing a culture's beliefs and values through experience, observation, and instruction. As individuals become enculturated, they learn culture-specific behaviors. For example, language is a cultural phenomenon guided by norms. While some cultural communities learn English, others learn Spanish, Japanese, French, Arabic, Russian, Aleut, Yoruba, or another of the hundreds of languages. Likewise, there is a world of cultural difference with respect to religion, education, cuisine, etiquette, technology, medicine, economy, law, government, music, dance, sports, courtship, grooming and hygiene, clothing, architecture, gender roles, work ethic, agriculture, and transportation. Since each cultural community has its own perceptions of what is acceptable within each of these cultural elements, norms vary from group to group—and this makes for an enchanting, culturally diverse world.

What does a national flag have in common with articles of clothing? Other than both being made of cloth, they are concrete artifacts that reveal much about the culture that produced them.

Daddy Cool/Fotolia

Ms. Miller, like many other teachers today, is rediscovering the power of storytelling as a source of passing on cultural beliefs and behaviors. To capitalize on this new point of interest, Ms. Miller included an authentic learning experience related to Japanese storytelling in her thematic unit.

Today, Ms. Miller pulled out a manila envelope containing a round-trip airline "ticket" to Tokyo for each child. She challenged the students to find Japan on the globe and a large world map. Ms. Miller asked them to name the ways people might travel to Japan, tracing the various routes on the globe.

She had the students prepare for a simulated air trip to Japan by filling out "passports." The pretend passports were small booklets that simulated the look of a real one. The students drew an illustration of the American flag on the cover; on the inside of the front cover, they drew a self-portrait. On the next page, the students printed their name, date of birth, sex, nation of citizenship, and date of issue. The blank pages that followed were filled in as students summarized unit activities; Ms. Miller used a date stamper to simulate the look of authentic passport entries.

After a simulated flight to Tokyo, a Japanese kamishibai *storyteller (Ms. Miller in costume) was the first person the children met as their plane "landed." Kamishibai, a unique form of Japanese street storytelling, is an authentic folktale strategy. Long ago, monks used picture scrolls to tell stories with moral lessons to mostly illiterate audiences. It endured as a minor storytelling method for centuries, but it experienced a major revival in the 1920s. The* kamishibai *storyteller, who was also a candy seller, rode from neighborhood to neighborhood on a bicycle equipped with a small stage for showing large story cards. He entered a neighborhood, striking together two wooden clappers, and everyone knew it was story time. The children ran from their homes so they could buy candy, and those who did were able to sit closest to the stage. The storyteller illustrated his stories with 12 to 16 story cards, on the back of which were written the corresponding parts of the story. He was sure not to read all the cards during one visit, for he wanted to capture enough intrigue by reading only three or four cards in order to entice the children to come back again (to, of course, buy candy). Ms. Miller used a number of illustrated* kamishibai *cards to tell a traditional, moralistic folktale,* The Tongue-Cut Sparrow. *(Authentic* kamishibai *cards can be ordered from the Kamishibai for Kids website.)*

FOLKLORE

Wherever people gathered—around a campfire, in the marketplace, or at tasks such as walking through the forest to pick nuts, fruits, and roots—stories were told not only to entertain but also to reveal the beliefs and values a culture considered important. These stories, referred to as *folklore* or *folktales*, are often referred to as the "mirror of a culture." Folktales are passed down and retold from generation to generation and have become well known because of their power to communicate a culture's values, as we find in Aesop's popular folktale *The Tortoise and the Hare*. The story has been interpreted in a variety of ways over the centuries, but the most popular moral of this story appears to be "Slow and steady wins the race." Folktales have no specific authors; they were passed down through oral tradition. However, after Johan Gutenberg's invention of the movable-type printing press in 1450, the emergence of the book publishing industry made it possible for people to print books containing folktales.

All cultures produce folktales, and there are striking similarities among their stories; similar plots have developed in different parts of the world from situations common to all people. For example, goodness is always rewarded, someone learns a lesson, people live happily ever after, monsters or villains are punished, wishes are granted, magic is involved, animals and plants have human characteristics, and many story events happen in threes. Folktales mirror the values and culture of the society from which they originate. A folktale offers a brief look into a culture and helps students gain insight into the values and customs of the society that produced the tale.

Third-grade teacher Mary Gilland is convinced that the study of folktales is one of the most instructive and enjoyable ways to teach students about cultures around the world because folk literature helps children discover universal qualities shared by all people. She will tell you that fairy tales, a part of the larger group of stories called folktales, are especially good examples of how cultures around the world share the use of a good-versus-evil theme to demonstrate morals to young, impressionable minds. Because the good-versus-evil theme is instilled in every child throughout the world even today, Mrs. Gilland felt that initiating a cross-cultural examination of Cinderella variants would be an entertaining and instructive way to explore and make connections among various cultures.

Estimates of the number of Cinderella variants range from 300 to 3,000. Some say the modern version of the story originated with Charles Perrault of France in 1697 (the Disney version is based on Perrault's story); others insist it emerged in China as early as 850, with a written version of Yeh-Shen. In any case, from its uncertain start, the story has somehow reached across countries and cultures to spread its message of goodness and virtue being recognized and rewarded through magical assistance.

Whether the central character is named Cendrillon, Rhodopis, Cap o' Rushes, or Rough-Face Girl, that common theme binds all variants. Mrs. Gilland identified two essential questions for her cross-cultural examination of Cinderella variants: "What changes take place as the Cinderella story is read from one culture to another?" and "What features remain the same?"

Mrs. Gilland selected six books for this cross-cultural experience (see Figure 13.2). Before reading the Cinderella versions aloud, the students located the country of origin for each on a big wall map and placed a marker identifying the version to be read that day. Mrs. Gilland first read the most common Cinderella variant to her students—the Charles Perrault version. She helped the children note the architecture, clothing, weather, time period, and other cultural characteristics depicted in the text and illustrations. To help the children with comprehension, Mrs. Gilland helped the class create a story map that summarized the major events and ideas in the story. They began at the starting point and moved through the story in sequential order, focusing on the key elements of characters, setting, problem or conflict, and resolution. Although there are many types of story map graphic organizers, Mrs. Gilland selected one with a basic focus on the beginning, middle, and end of the story.

Mrs. Gilland followed the same process with each of the other five Cinderella variants, reading one new variant each day. However, as each new story was read, it was added to a second chart that compared and contrasted the Cinderella variants (see Figure 13.3). After each variant was read, the students examined their summary charts and discovered several similarities and differences. Through this sequence, Mrs. Gilland helped the children learn to understand and appreciate those cultures and open up a wider view of the world.

FIGURE 13.2   Six Cinderella Variants

Folktale	Country of Origin	Reward
Cinderella (North-South)	France/USA	Marries prince
Yeh-Shen (Putnam)	China	Marries king
Mufaro's Beautiful Daughters (Lothrop)	Zimbabwe	Marries king
The Egyptian Cinderella (HarperTrophy)	Egypt	Marries pharaoh
Sootface: An Ojibwa Cinderella Story (Delacorte)	United States	Wins invisible warrior husband
Adelita (G.P. Putnam's Sons)	Mexico	Finds true love

FIGURE 13.3   Chart Comparing Two Cinderella Variants

	Cinderella	Yeh-Shen
Characters	Stepmother, 2 stepsisters, prince, fairy godmother, and beautiful Cinderella	Stepmother, stepsister, king, and beautiful Yeh-Shen
Setting	"Once upon a time" long ago in Europe	Long ago in China
Problem	Stepmother and stepsisters mistreat Cinderella. She is not allowed to go to the ball.	Stepmother forces Yeh-Shen to do the heaviest work. She kills Yeh-Shen's pet fish. Yeh-Shen is not allowed to go to the big festival.
Magic	Fairy godmother turns a pumpkin into a gleaming coach and rags into clothes, including glass slippers.	The bones of Yeh-Shen's dead fish give her a dress and slippers.
Events	Cinderella goes to the ball and loses a glass slipper while rushing to return home by midnight. Prince finds the slipper; Cinderella tries it on and marries the prince.	Yeh-Shen goes to the festival, loses a slipper, and returns home. King finds slipper and searches for owner; Yeh-Shen tries on the slipper and it fits. Her rags become a gown. Yeh-Shen marries the king.

Language and cultures are inseparable. Language helps societies communicate, and it also affects the way they think; it is through language that most of culture is learned and communicated; language is perhaps the most common form of cultural transmission. Lev Vygotsky (1978) theorized that language is the primary tool that facilitates the entrance into and preservation of cultures; once humans learn language, it becomes inextricably interwoven with the patterns and contents of their thoughts and actions—their behaviors. Culture is learned behavior that is passed on through generations by language.

The Symbolic Level of Cultures

This level includes a culture's beliefs and values, or the commonly held standards of what is good and bad, right and wrong, and fair and unfair. Every culture has a set of moral and social values that include ideals, goals, standards, customs, spirituality, religion, and mores. Every culture has a set of values. Valued principles and ideals are passed on from one generation to another, thus resulting in a continuum of traditions that are a part of the culture through the years.

BELIEFS AND VALUES EXPRESSED THROUGH RELIGION

An example of a symbolic component that is especially significant for elementary school classrooms is the question, "What is the origin of religion, and what is its function?" No one knows the answer to that question for certain, but anthropologists speculate that at some point in time very long ago, primitive humans, living without science, searched for answers to questions and fears about their mystifying, cruel, and unpredictable natural world: What controlled the seasons . . . rain . . . droughts . . . storms . . . the stars . . . crops . . . a good hunt . . . dreams . . . death? Some consider *animism*, or spirit worship, to be one of humanity's oldest religion-based attempts at creating explanations for these mysteries; its origin most likely dates to the Paleolithic age. Animism is based on the belief that life-spirits inhabit trees, rocks, mountains, seas, and other natural features, and these spirits have a consciousness and power that affect the well-being of humans. Rituals and celebrations were established to help build a favorable relationship with these spirits. Ancient tribal and hunter-gatherer cultures maintained animistic beliefs to explain the unknown, but animism, in various forms, still exists in the contemporary world. The traditional Shinto religion of Japan, some Hindu groups, and some traditional Native American religions are a few examples. The contemporary New Age religious movement in the United States and throughout the world purports that everything has a soul, that humans are intimately related not only to one other but also to animals, plants, and inanimate objects.

Another belief system that has been found throughout history and across the world's cultures is *polytheism*—the worship of multiple gods. The Egyptians had a highly developed belief system of religious worship that was based on multiple gods. The ancient Greeks had a system of myths that contained stories of multiple gods. When the Roman Empire conquered Greece, it assimilated much of the Greek culture, including its religion. As the Roman Empire continued to spread, it relished the idea of appending gods from the cultures it conquered. In addition to existing in Egypt, Greece, and Rome, polytheism was common throughout ancient Asia, Africa, Europe, and Native America. Unlike the monotheistic (belief in one God) religions Christianity, Judaism, and Islam, many of the world's religions today are polytheistic—including Hinduism, Mahayana Buddhism, Confucianism, Taoism, Shintoism, and contemporary tribal religions of Africa and the Americas. It is interesting to note that even in polytheistic religions, one god usually reigns supreme over the other gods, such as Zeus in Greek and Roman mythology and Brahman in Hinduism.

Monotheism, usually contrasted with polytheism, is the belief that there is only one God who not only created the world but developed the standards of good and evil. Human beings are God's creatures and are expected to live by His standards. Most monotheistic systems believe in and worship a single God, and most also reject the gods of any other religious faiths. The largest monotheistic systems today are Judaism, Christianity, Islam, and Sikhism.

Henotheism is the worship of one god without denying the existence of others. Most forms of Hinduism are henotheistic religions. Hindus generally worship one god yet acknowledge that there are many other gods that can be worshiped as well. The religion of the ancient Greeks and their worship of the Olympians is another well-known example, with Zeus being the supreme ruler of 11 other gods. Henotheistic and polytheistic religions have traditionally been among the world's most tolerant.

STUDYING RELIGIONS IN PUBLIC SCHOOLS

Severe consequences can arise from prejudice and antagonism related to religion, yet one of the most controversial issues today is the place of religion in public schools. Polarized battles over the place of religion incite deep passion; some want children to learn about *all religions*, others say *their religion* is most important and should be given priority, and some view public schools as *religion-free* zones. None of these positions, however, can be supported by the guiding principles of the First Amendment to the U.S. Constitution:

> *Congress shall make no law respecting an establishment of religion, or prohibiting the free exercise thereof; or abridging the freedom of speech, or of the press; or the right of the people peaceably to assemble, and to petition the government for a redress of grievances.*

The "wall of separation" is a common term to describe this concept of separation of church and state. Unfortunately, teachers and school administrators have become confused about the implications of the "wall of separation" doctrine and have taken the path of least resistance, turning religion into a forbidden topic of instruction. As a result, many public schools have become religion-free zones, and their students tend to remain largely uninformed about the immense impact, both honorable and destructive, that religion has had on world cultures throughout history. Have these schools missed the boat? Can and should religion be taught in our public schools? Since the 1960s school prayer cases (which prompted rulings against school prayer and Bible reading), the U.S. Supreme Court has repeatedly given its constitutional seal of approval to teaching about religions. In fact, it has recognized religious studies as a civic necessity. Although the 1963 *Abington Township School District v. Schempp* case struck down the use of daily prayer and Bible readings as exercises to open the school day, the U.S. Supreme Court declared the comparative study of religion in public schools an acceptable practice. In delivering the opinion of the Court, Justice Clark wrote (*Abington Township School District v. Schempp*, 374 U.S. 203 1963):

> *It might well be said that one's education is not complete without a study of comparative religion or the history of religion and its relationship to the advancement of civilization. It certainly may be said that the Bible is worthy of study for its literary and historic qualities. Nothing we have said here indicates that such study of the Bible or of religion, when presented objectively as part of a secular program of education, may not be effected consistently with the First Amendment.*

Reflection on Learning

You may simply scribble rough notes or jot down something more polished and complete. The point is to simply start recording your ideas spontaneously and candidly.

Countless families around the country send their children out on Halloween. It is a frequent debate among schools today as to whether the occasion should be observed in our nation's classrooms because of its religious underpinnings. What do you think?

The classroom implications of this ruling have been articulated well in "Religious Liberty, Public Education, and the Future of American Democracy," a statement issued by 24 national organizations, including the NCSS, National Education Association, and American Federation of Teachers (Haynes, 2008). In general, the influential statement explains that public schools may not *teach religion* in a devotional or doctrinal manner, although *teaching about religion* in a historical, cultural, or literary context is permitted. That is, public schools are forbidden to promote, inhibit, or denigrate any religion or lack of religious belief and, when *teaching about religions*, instruction must be carried out in an objective, factual manner. The National Council for the Social Studies (2014), in its position statement *Study About Religions in the Social Studies Curriculum*, echoes the joint statement made by the 24 national organizations. NCSS suggests that schools must:

- *approach religion academically, not devotionally.*
- *strive for student awareness of religions, but not insist on student acceptance of any religion.*
- *promote study about religion, not the practice of religion.*
- *expose students to a diversity of religious views, but not impose any particular view.*
- *educate about all religions, and neither promote nor denigrate any religion.*
- *inform the students about religious beliefs, but not seek to conform them to any particular belief.*

In summary, the courts have clearly prohibited public schools from using the *teaching religion* approach, a practice that violates the First Amendment. However, *teaching about religion* in a secular context is permitted and encouraged. This means that instruction must be geared toward the role of religion only in the historical, cultural, and literary development of cultures. *Teaching religion*, on the other hand, is considered religious indoctrination, a practice clearly prohibited in public schools. In addition to promoting or accepting any specific religion, a teacher may not denigrate any particular religion, religion in general, or lack of religious belief.

APPROACHES TO THE STUDY OF RELIGIONS

You must be fully informed about the constitutional and educational principles for the role of religion in public education, so it would be helpful to either obtain a copy of *A Teacher's Guide to Religion in the Public Schools* or examine it online (Haynes, 2008). The American Academy of Religion (2010), the world's largest association of scholars who research or teach topics related to religion, has advocated a cultural studies instructional scheme that incorporates these four approaches:

1. ***The historical approach.*** In this approach, the origins of a religion and its development are presented in historical context, with the political and cultural influences represented as central to understanding how that religion emerged, gained followers, and spread.

2. ***The literary approach.*** In this approach, students read religious texts themselves, or they read stories with religious themes. Teachers help students gain an appreciation of the way that religion infuses all aspects of culture as well as of the unique ways that individuals experience their religion.

3. ***The traditions-based approach.*** The focus of this approach is on specific categories that apply to many religious traditions, such as beliefs, texts, rituals, origins, and holidays, or on essential questions that religions address related to the purpose of life, how one should live, and various interpretations of identity. This approach can help students see common themes in religious traditions and can provide a useful framework for understanding the varieties of religious expression.

4. ***The cultural studies approach.*** This approach builds on and enhances the other three approaches by emphasizing the ways in which religion is embedded in culture and cannot be understood in isolation from its particular social/historical context.

In elementary schools, the study of religion generally centers on the cultural studies approach—the meanings of the holidays, customs, basic beliefs, and histories of the world's major religions. Only as they enter middle and high school will students be asked to think critically about religions and examine the conflicts between religious and secular ways of explaining our world.

CHECK YOUR UNDERSTANDING 13.2 **Click here** to check your understanding of this section of the chapter.

Multicultural Education

Respect for differences means weaving all facets of diversity into the school curriculum when comparing cultures around the world, not only religion. Groups speak different languages, eat different foods, play different games, and have different family roles. Some cultural attributes, however, are notably transcultural. People around the globe share the need to sustain themselves with food, for example, but what they consume, how they acquire it, who prepares it, and how it is served are factors fraught with cultural meaning. There is probably no one among us for whom at least one culture-specific food—its memory, taste, or smell—does not evoke a pang of sentimental nostalgia. Do foods like *deok* (traditional Korean rice cakes), or *dodo* (a Nigerian fried plantain or banana), or *gnocchi* (Italian dumplings served piping hot in a rich pasta sauce), or *Welsh rarebit* (a traditional English recipe of melted cheese poured over toast), or *homemade tortillas* (thin, flat pancake like bread made out of corn or wheat flour) tug at your heartstrings? Whether we choose to compare and contrast food, religion, holiday customs, clothing styles, or any other of the array of cultural traits, the unique beliefs and behaviors of any distinct culture provide its members with a feeling of group identity.

Over the years, a variety of strategies have been used to incorporate cultural perspectives into social studies programs. For most elementary school teachers, teaching about cultures is important and a substantial part of the instructional repertoire. These teachers resolutely persevere, despite the fact that the subject matter associated with cultures, the central focus of anthropology, is vast—to some, it is unmanageable. If you look carefully at the "four-field" definition of anthropology described earlier, you could say that the comprehensive discipline deals with human beings across all times and all places—the totality of a group's beliefs, behaviors, language, customs, values, arts, norms, mores, rules, tools, technologies, products, organizations, education, religion, and institutions. Upon considering this colossal body of content, it is easy to appreciate how culture and social studies are intricately related . . . and how difficult anthropology can be to teach. There are no simple prescriptions that can help guide your instructional practices; condensed versions of such a complex topic run the risk of oversimplification, misinterpretation, and inadvertent exclusion.

Dynamic social studies programs do not exist merely to transmit a massive data package that often results in a partial or shallow understanding of our world. Instead, they encourage comprehensive and interconnected experiences that enlighten students' understandings of cultures, past and present. To carry out this mission, it is important to understand how the three levels of culture—*concrete, behavioral,* and *symbolic*—can be incorporated into the curriculum.

Cultural Diversity

As a nation, we prize our cultural diversity. We are of many colors, speak many languages, and celebrate many unique customs and traditions. All of us contribute to our nation's rich and wonderful diversity; our ancestors are from any of the more than 100 ethnic groups represented in the United States. The United States experienced its first major wave of voluntary immigration during the colonial era when an overwhelming majority of immigrants arrived from Europe. European immigrants continued their domination into the 1860s as thousands sought to escape poverty and famine in their homelands. In addition, from the 17th to the 19th centuries, hundreds of thousands of African slaves were brought to America against their will. Fueled by the Industrial Revolution of the 1880s, Chinese, Japanese, and immigrants from other Asian countries joined the Europeans to form the largest group of immigrants in our nation's history. However, early in the 20th century, more than 80% of the immigrants arriving in the United

States were from Europe. Industrialization and urbanization in the United States helped stimulate immigration; people left their homelands to escape religious, racial, and political persecution, as well as famine and poverty. Eventually, the term *melting pot* (or *crucible*) gained popularity as the way to describe how people of different cultures could be dissolved, mixed, and blended into an existing society. The use of the term *melting pot* was popularized by Israel Zangwill in his play *The Melting Pot*, a hit in the United States during 1909–1910. In Act 1, David, a young Russian-Jewish composer, excitedly tells his uncle about how America's openness to immigration had inspired his music:

> *America is God's great Crucible, a great Melting-Pot where all the races of Europe are melting and re-forming! . . . Germans and Frenchmen, Irishmen and Englishmen, Jews and Russians—into the Crucible with you all! God is making the American . . . . No, uncle, the real American has not yet arrived. He is only in the Crucible, I tell you—he will be the fusion of all races, perhaps the coming superman. (Zangwill, 1921)*

The idea of a melting pot was that all ethnic groups possess strengths and that as the "crucible of America" molded them into a single alloy, a new and "super" culture would be cast. The melting pot, then, was not meant to destroy cultural diversity but to combine the strengths of many cultures into something new and unique: "The new emerging American culture must be built not on the destruction of the cultural values and mores of the various immigrant groups but on their fusion with the existing American civilization. . . . In the burning fires of the melting pot, all races were equal—all were reshaped, and molded into a new entity" (Krug, 1976, p. 12).

Today, our nation is experiencing a new wave of immigration, a movement of people with profound implications for our nation's schools. The new immigrants come to our shores not primarily from Europe this time but from Asia and Latin America as well as from the Middle East and North Africa, motivated mainly by political instability in their regions and better economic opportunities. Without doubt, the Hispanic population is the fastest growing ethnic group in the United States. The U.S. Bureau of the Census (2012) reported that the non-Hispanic white population is projected to peak in 2024, at 199.6 million. Meanwhile, the Hispanic population is expected to more than double, from 53.3 million in 2012 to 128.8 million by 2060. Therefore, in 2060, nearly one in three U.S. residents would be Hispanic, up from about one in six in 2012. As for other current minority groups, the Black population is expected to increase from 41.2 million to 61.8 million over the same period. Its share of the total population would rise from 13.1 percent in 2012 to 14.7 percent in 2060. The Asian population is projected to more than double, from 15.9 million in 2012 to 34.4 million in 2060; its share of nation's total population will consequently climb from 5.1 percent to 8.2 percent by 2060. Our nation is projected to become a majority-minority nation for the first time in 2043; that is, while the non-Hispanic white population will remain the largest single group, no ethnic group will make up a majority. By 2060, however, current minorities will be the majority in America.

This radical population shift challenges the suggestion of a melting pot; most observers now offer alternative analogies that allow ethnic and national groups to maintain their distinctive and rich cultural identities. For example, some liken our nation to a salad bowl, mosaic, pizza, or patchwork quilt, where each culture retains its unique characteristics that are still identifiable within the larger, overall structure. The foundation of social studies instruction is based on this idea of cultural pluralism—becoming aware of and sensitive to the various ethnic groups that make up society as a whole.

Ethnicity

What is an ethnic group? An ethnic group, according to Bennett (2007), "is a community of people within a larger society that is socially distinguished or set apart, by others and/or by itself, primarily on the basis of racial and/or cultural characteristics, such as religion, language, and tradition" (p. 55). Examples of ethnic groups in America are Turkmen, Mexican American, German, Polish, African American, Dutch Canadian, Igbo, Sante Sioux, and Greek. *Ethnicity* is a term often used to describe the deep feeling of personal attachment to one's cultural group; it greatly influences the standards used to judge group members and others—what is worthwhile, satisfying, or important. Strong feelings of ethnicity determine the ways we think, feel, and act. It is a positive cultural characteristic; ethnicity helps members value and respect their common community bonds, and it encourages and reinforces group togetherness. Sometimes, however, cultures become so convinced that their own behaviors and beliefs are superior that they view their culture as the standard against which all others are judged, a tendency anthropologists call *ethnocentrism*. Ethnocentrism simply means that cultures (and individuals) look at the world through the *cultural lens* they were raised with and they judge everything accordingly. It is impossible not to be ethnocentric to some degree, but carried to an extreme, ethnocentrism can have a negative impact, making it impossible to view another culture objectively. As a result, ethnocentrism can lead to a slanted perception of other cultures—a condition that is especially worrisome today in light of the need for interdependence among countries and the importance of establishing positive ties among all groups.

While considering the nature of ethnic and cultural group membership, it must be noted that the labels used to organize this chapter are merely social constructions, which cannot possibly embrace the defining characteristics of any single individual. For example, a person might not only be "White Anglo-Saxon Protestant" but also French, a Southerner, a farmer, hearing impaired, female, and lower-middle class. A person's group memberships include race, ethnic group, region, occupation, religion, ability or disability, gender, and social class. Many aspects of a person's life are shaped by membership in several groups, making the individual just described a much different person than an African American male doctoral student from a large eastern city who grew up in a crowded high-rise apartment, or a female Navajo teacher whose family makes its home in a pueblo in the desert Southwest. Groups can be defined along many different lines, and everyone is a member of an assortment of groups, each of which creates its own culture (knowledge, rules, values, and traditions that guide its members' behavior).

All of this is not meant to confuse you but only to emphasize that the children you teach are uniquely complex individuals who have become who they are through the interaction of many intricate genetic, cultural, and environmental factors. The labels we choose to describe the groups they belong to are not meant to stereotype but only to provide insight into the best practices for dynamic social studies instruction.

Banks (2009) advises teachers to view the curriculum from diverse ethnic and cultural perspectives so that feelings of ethnocentrism are minimized: "Educators need to foster the development of self-acceptance but discourage ethnocentrism. Diversity and unity in a delicate balance should be fostered by the schools" (p. 26). The National Council for the Social Studies (NCSS, 1991) has stated that multicultural goals should attempt to attain a delicate balance of diversity and unity:

a. *Recognize and respect ethnic and cultural diversity;*
b. *promote societal cohesiveness based on the shared participation of ethnically and culturally diverse peoples;*
c. *maximize equality of opportunity for all individuals and groups; and*
d. *facilitate constructive societal change that enhances human dignity and democratic ideals.*

Culturally Responsive Teaching

All children come to school with strong cultural and ethnic identities, whether those identities are typical or extreme. To provide effective and successful classroom instruction, you must understand and commit to practices that confirm and build on the ethnicity of your students. Such instruction is known as *culturally responsive teaching*, a process Geneva Gay (2000) described as having these characteristics:

- *It acknowledges the legitimacy of the cultural heritages of different ethnic groups, both as legacies that affect students' dispositions, attitudes, and approaches to learning and as worthy content to be taught in the formal curriculum.*
- *It builds bridges of meaningfulness between home and school experiences as well as between academic abstractions and lived sociocultural realities.*
- *It uses a wide variety of instructional strategies that are connected to different learning styles.*
- *It teaches students to know and praise their own and each other's cultural heritages.*
- *It incorporates multicultural information, resources, and materials in all the subjects and skills routinely taught in schools.* (p. 29)

With culture as the common thread, it is important that elementary schools design instructional programs that incorporate a respect for and understanding of cultures within the framework of cultural diversity and pluralism in the United States. Social studies programs that are responsive to cultural diversity and pluralism are commonly referred to as *multicultural programs*, or *multicultural education*. Although many definitions of multicultural education dot the educational literature, the following definition will guide content presentation in this chapter: *Multicultural education is an approach to classroom methodology and content selection that recognizes and values the complex dimensions of American cultures and society.* Banks (2009) suggests that this process could be most effectively accomplished by mixing and blending four approaches into teaching situations: (1) the *contributions approach,* (2) the *additive approach,* (3) the *transformative approach,* and (4) the *social action approach.* See Figure 13.4.

 Video Exploration 13.1

The cultural makeup of America is changing. Immigrants from Asia and Latin America have added a large measure of diversity to the American population in recent decades, just as free migration from Southern and Eastern Europe and forced migration from Africa did a century ago.

Fotolia

FIGURE 13.4   Four Approaches to Multicultural Education

CONTRIBUTIONS APPROACH	ADDITIVE APPROACH	TRANSFORMATIVE APPROACH	SOCIAL ACTION APPROACH
Ethnic or cultural content is limited to special days, weeks, months, or events such as Martin Luther King, Jr., Day, Black History Month, Women's History Month, or Cinco De Mayo.	The teacher adds content into the curriculum without restructuring it, but the content is still viewed from the perspective of the mainstream culture. For example, including a section on the Wampanoags while teaching a unit about the Pilgrims of New England.	Students experience concepts, issues, themes, and problems from several ethnic/cultural perspectives and points of view. For example, students learn how mainstream American culture emerged from a complex blend of diverse groups that make up American society.	Contains all of the elements described so far, but includes components that require students to make decisions or take actions related to concepts, issues, themes, and problems. For example, writing letters to agencies and organizations addressing the issue of racial tension in their community.

From U.S. Census Bureau, Population Division by U.S. Census Bureau.

THE CONTRIBUTIONS APPROACH

The approach to cultural study that is perhaps the earliest and is still the most widely used is variously referred to as the "tourist approach," the "heroes and holidays approach," or what James Banks (2009) calls the "contributions approach." This approach is characterized by observing special days or months that recognize ethnic heroes, ethnic events, or cultural celebrations, such as performing a dragon dance during the Chinese New Year, reading a book about Amelia Bloomer during Women's History Month, teaching a unit on Mexican Americans during early May (for Cinco de Mayo), reading books about important African Americans during Black History Month in February, or playing the dreidel game during Hanukkah. The contributions approach is characterized by offering special activities or projects only at the time when a significant cultural holiday or special observance takes place.

Banks (2009) suggests that the contributions approach can be the most convenient way to bring in cultural content because teachers are not compelled to invest the time, effort, and training needed to rethink and restructure the entire program of study. The primary purpose of this approach, which is especially used with very young children, is to help students understand that these days help us honor and respect our heritage and traditions; throughout the year, there are special days and observances we celebrate for various reasons and with specific rituals or rights. One of the characteristics of the contributions approach is to strive for inclusive excellence—awareness, respect, and appreciation for the beliefs and traditions that are important to a wide range of cultures and religions.

The major problem with the contributions approach, if it is the only way students experience cultures in their classroom, is that very little or nothing is studied about the cultural group before or after the special event or occasion. This may reinforce the notion that some cultural groups are not integral parts of mainstream society—that they are separate and apart from mainstream culture. Although learning about "holidays and heroes" is important and has a special place in dynamic social studies programs, we cannot reduce multicultural education to simply observing those events; doing so shortchanges the true multicultural spirit. Banks (2009) asserts that although it is "the easiest approach for teachers to integrate ethnic content into the curriculum . . . it has several serious limitations, including not helping students to attain a comprehensive view of the role of ethnic and cultural groups in U.S. society. Rather, they see ethnic issues and events primarily as an addition to the curriculum and thus as an appendage to the main story of the nation's development"(pp. 18–19). Most agree that the exclusive use of the contributions approach trivializes cultures; cultural understandings can be better accomplished by incorporating cultural observances into the total curriculum instead of simply making them add-ons.

THE ADDITIVE APPROACH

Banks considers the *additive approach* as the first forward-looking step of upgrading the contributions approach. In the additive approach, separate thematic units about minority groups may be appended to the existing curriculum, such as "Let's Explore Mexico" or "Women in World War II," without changing the curriculum's established structure. Or teachers may infuse fresh, meaningful cultural content to an existing unit; for example, they could include American Indian perspectives in a "Westward Movement" unit to balance the traditional pioneer viewpoint.

One of the strengths of the additive approach is that it expands the "special celebrations" method by integrating content, concepts, themes, and perspectives into the existing curriculum; the curriculum is not restructured, but it is broadened. While it is an improvement over the contributions approach, this approach has a major shortcoming: Because the curriculum is not restructured, the incorporated content is often viewed primarily from the perspective of mainstream culture rather than from the perspectives of the diverse groups under study.

The additive approach offers ethnically diverse learning opportunities by modifying the curriculum with culturally relevant instructional activities and materials. The content is expanded to include contributions from all groups so that the curriculum presents multiple perspectives from the community, the nation, and the world.

THE TRANSFORMATIVE APPROACH

The *transformative approach* makes a sharp deviation from the first two approaches in that it employs strategies that enable students to view cultural concepts and issues from contrasting ethnic perspectives and points of view. When students are studying the American Revolutionary War, for example, the perspectives of the British Revolutionaries, the British Loyalists, African-Americans, Native American Indians, and the British government are necessary for them to develop an objective understanding of this momentous event in our nation's history. Students must grasp the impact of these diverse groups to fully understand the American Revolution. To carry out the transformative approach, Banks (2009) suggests that students learn to use a pair of sophisticated problem-solving and decision-making skills he refers to as *insider* and *outsider* perspectives: "People who have experienced a historical event . . . such as discrimination [insiders] . . . often view the event very differently from people who have observed it from a distance [outsiders]" (p. 20).

Teachers who use a transformative approach to instruction weave a range of unique and important cultural perspectives throughout the social studies curriculum. The social studies curriculum no longer focuses on mainstream and dominant groups but on an event, an issue, or a concept that is examined from many different perspectives and contrasting points of view. To be successful at this approach, students must master higher-order decision-making and collaborative problem-solving skills. Without doubt, a critical mass of content is prerequisite for reaching higher-order thinking; the more knowledge your students gain about the world around them, the more they bring to the table when addressing complex cultural issues and problems. With this approach, you help students gain information, tap into what they know, and use their knowledge to confront a challenging question or problem. The challenge of this approach is that it requires a complete makeover of the curriculum.

THE SOCIAL ACTION APPROACH

The fourth approach to teaching about cultures blends together all the elements of the other three approaches but adds an additional component that requires students to make decisions and take social action related to the concept, issue, or problem under study. To do this, students must be able to gather and analyze pertinent information, identify alternative courses of action, decide what actions would be most constructive and effective, and explore and honestly acknowledge what they truly value at this time in their lives.

Reflection on Learning

You may simply scribble rough notes or jot down something more polished and complete. The point is to simply start recording your ideas spontaneously and candidly.

There are some critics of multiculturalism who argue that it tends to minimize or dismiss traditional Western customs and traditions and may actually unintentionally promote ethnic and cultural division. One critic, for example, commented, "I applaud our school district for adding two Islamic school holidays to its calendar, along with the existing two Jewish holidays. But the calendar shows the traditional Christian Christmas holiday and the Christian Easter holiday as Winter Recess and Spring Recess. This to me is biased and discriminatory." Do you agree or disagree?

Using a problem-solving approach to visual literacy, a fifth-grade classroom's social action approach started when Stephen Shudlick showed his students a large print of artist-adventurer Alex Bierstadt's 1888 painting, Last of the Buffalo. *The print depicted the cruel slaughter of buffalo (bison) at the time when these magnificent animals faced extinction. Mr. Shudlick began an investigation of the scene with a series of questions:*

> *"What do you see here?"*
> *"What is happening?"*
> *"Where is it taking place?"*
> *"When do you think it is taking place?"*
> *"Why is this happening?"*
> *"What do you think will happen next?"*
> *"What questions would you like to ask the artist?"*
> *"How does this relate to what you already know?"*

Mr. Shudlick encouraged active and thoughtful learning as he asked his students to jot down their "eyewitness accounts" of what they had just observed. Then each student exchanged his or her account with another student, and all dyads eventually came back together as a class to talk about their general ideas. Mr. Shudlick recorded their questions and impressions on a large sheet of newsprint. The students seemed to focus on two questions that would help them probe important social issues from the viewpoints of the Plains Indians and the European settlers: "How were bison a part of the Plains Indian culture?" and "How did European settlers affect that world?"

Mr. Shudlick found that a WebQuest was well suited to this unit of study; the first thing he did was to pull together a "hotlist" of good topic-related websites that would focus students' attention. Five links provided engaging photos that were similar to the subject matter of Bierstadt's painting; they were intended to give just a brief look into Sioux life with the bison. The students were to look at each of the five and pick the one that interested them the most. Then Mr. Shudlick asked them to respond to these prompts as they examined their selected picture more deeply: "What is happening?" "Where is it happening?" "Why is it happening?" "What does it make me think about?" "What do I need to find out more about?" Their questions focused on a number of topics for research, such as cultural beliefs and uses of the bison. However, most were fascinated by the destruction of the bison.

Next, the students conducted their "knowledge quests"—getting the basic information from the preselected websites that they needed to address their selected issue. Working in small groups or alone, the students visited at least three sites, found the five most important pieces of information related to their topic, and wrote an informative paragraph incorporating those five pieces. For example, a "Culture" group described how nearly all cultural activities, such as hunting, cooking, sewing, making art, teaching, praying, singing, dancing, and celebrating incorporated and honored the bison. The sacred buffalo became an integral part of the culture and religion of the Plains Indian. "Uses of the Bison" groups learned that the bison hunt was the central event of Plains Indian life and that every part of the animal had a use. The hairy hides could be used as bedding for them to sleep on or as warm robes, leggings, or mittens during the cold winter. The meat, of course, was used for food (sun-dried meat was called jerky). They made tools, weapons, and toys for children from the bones. Sinew was used to make bow strings and thread. The bladder served as a natural water vessel that was used to haul water; other organs were often used for medicinal purposes. The dried bison droppings were used as fuel. Even the tail was used as a flyswatter!

The "Destruction of the Bison" groups appeared to be the most emotionally connected to their research. They learned that, in the 1860s, the railroads brought over a thousand workers to the plains, workers who required fresh meat, which the buffalo herds supplied. The railroads also brought hunters who hunted the animals from trains as they passed the herds—the hunting was not for food, just for sport. In addition to railroad workers and hunters, farmers and ranchers also moved onto the plains. They did not want buffalo grazing on land their livestock needed, so they shot the buffalo to get rid of them. The herd that was once over 60 million was reduced to less than 1,000 by 1889. As the settlers destroyed the buffalo, they also dismantled the traditional Plains Indian way of life. The Indians were ultimately forced onto reservations where they could no longer roam the land to hunt.

Some people believe that elementary school students are incapable of dealing with difficult or controversial topics, but a visit to Mr. Shudlick's classroom the day his students shared the results of their research would quickly change their opinion: "I had no idea what greed has done to our nation. We destroyed a culture and almost lost the American bison! Can we ever make up for our disrespect?" The intense concern about a perceived wrong created a dilemma for Mr. Shudlick: Should he continue to follow the expected curriculum or seek further student engagement with legitimate social concern? Like all good social studies teachers, Mr. Shudlick chose to exploit this opening for engagement through a social action approach.

Because the students were so highly passionate about this particular issue, Mr. Shudlick provided opportunities for them to involve others beyond the classroom and to become advocates by raising the awareness of other students, teachers, family, and community members. First, he asked the students to "Imagine it is now the year 2050. You are looking at a painting somewhat like Alex Bierstadt's painting, Last of the Buffalo, *but it is being transformed to reflect recent efforts to bring bison back to the plains. What would you like your painting to say about those efforts?" Mr. Shudlick gave each small group a large sheet of paper and paint. He asked the students to work together to determine the most important ideas from their class conversation and to decide how they wanted to represent their ideas through drawings and symbols. Deciding to use the phrase "Showing Off" for an awareness campaign for the bison and Plains Indians, the students visually displayed their handcrafted paintings in the school hallway. They not only made a huge impact on other classrooms and teachers, but became a topic of discussion that encouraged inquiry into the question, "What else can we do?"*

Ultimately, the students learned that restoration of the bison has been going on for some time now and that several Native American tribes have been working together to bring the bison back to the American plains. With the overall hope that bringing back healthy bison populations would help reestablish hope for the Plains Indians, the students collaboratively wrote and everyone signed a group letter to encourage support from the National Wildlife Federation's Tribal Program as a vehicle to honor the sacredness of the wild bison and bring it back to its rightful home on the plains.

It is probably unrealistic to expect teachers to make an immediate jump from the contributions approach to a social studies curriculum that focuses on decision making and social action. Instead, it is more reasonable to use the contributions approach for a period of time and steadily move to the increasingly sophisticated demands of the other approaches.

 Video Exploration 13.2

If you plan to turn your classroom into a place where cultural responsiveness is a reality, start with a focus on the cultural and ethnic groups represented by the school population. You must understand that you cannot possibly offer equal treatment to the hundreds of microcultures in this country, so you must begin by developing an understanding of, sensitivity to, and respect for the various cultures of the families served by the school community; focus on the groups represented in your community.

Know the Students You Teach   The knowledge you gain about the community in which you teach and about the rich cultural backgrounds of the families served by your school should help make your teaching more effective and more meaningful. Acknowledging the home culture's practices and values significantly affects a child's feelings of dignity and worth. In turn, these feelings will lead to increased learning and an enhanced belief in self. Therefore, you should be especially willing to listen as well as talk to the parents of your students, to make sure that they understand your program's goals. Find out what they would like their children to learn about their own culture and other cultures. Teaching in a culturally responsive manner requires starting where students are. By finding out where the children are, you may find that the values and expectations of some families may differ markedly from your own.

Use Numerous and Varied Instructional Resources   Teachers can uncover abundant instructional resources by seeking input from students, parents, and the local community. Oral and local histories, family records, and cultural museums can be extremely useful. Furnish the classroom with multicultural dolls, tortilla presses, kimonos, cowboy boots, nesting dolls, bongo drums, serapes, art, music, authentic dramatic play props, games, and posters to create an aesthetically pleasing learning environment that fascinates children and encourages interest in people. Design learning centers that can be used in multiple ways; develop prop boxes containing multicultural items. Display family portraits, collages, and life-size drawings of the children and families.

Invite people from the community who are willing to come to your classroom and share something of their culture. Resource people can demonstrate a special craft or talent, read or tell a story, display and talk about an interesting artifact or process, share a special food or recipe, teach a simple song or dance, or help children count or speak in another language. Invite parents and elders to share stories, wisdom, and cultural traditions. Plan special activities that will naturally invite family participation, such as multicultural holidays, festivals, and celebrations.

Children, like adults, love to explore the Internet. Many websites offer fun and instructive cultural content. Good children's literature tells the story of the lives, culture, and contributions of diverse cultural groups in the United States. Through sharing carefully selected literature, students can learn to understand and to appreciate a literary heritage associated with many diverse cultures. Make every effort to expand your students' knowledge of ethnic and cultural groups by exposing them to quality literature—fiction, biography, and history. It would be enjoyable and instructive for everyone in your class to visit the library to find one good children's book with an interesting story about her or his ethnicity or culture. Celebrate the diversity in your classroom by presenting a brief book talk and a few sample illustrations or photos from each book. Classroom use of multicultural literature written in the students' native language helps strengthen cultural values and beliefs. Quality books are now being written for children in a number of languages and are becoming increasingly available throughout the United States. For example, Carmen Lomas Garza's bilingual book *Family Pictures: Cuadros de Familia* (Children's Book Press, with Spanish version authored by Rosalma Zubizerreta) is an authentic portrayal of what it is like to grow up in a Mexican-American family in southern Texas. Having a parent or other volunteer come to school and read from these books adds respect and appreciation for the native language.

All social studies programs have a responsibility to provide quality educational experiences that help children become compassionate individuals who feel comfortable with their identities and sense their unity with other people. We must create positive environments where children learn to accept others with cultural differences and begin to develop the skills of living cooperatively in a culturally diverse nation.

In addition to cultural diversity, our nation's schools must address issues related to various other special student needs. The concept of diversity is extremely broad and impossible to treat in one chapter of this text. For this reason, this chapter will focus only on students from various ethnic, cultural, special needs, and gender backgrounds. Although many definitions appear in the educational literature, this definition will guide our concept of culturally responsive teaching: *an approach to classroom interaction and instruction that recognizes and values the complex dimensions of diverse cultures and society.*

CHECK YOUR UNDERSTANDING 13.3   **Click here** to check your understanding of this section of the chapter.

What Is Sociology?

The content and processes of anthropology (especially cultural anthropology) and sociology are intricately mixed and matched; because both disciplines study the behavior of humans within groups, the lines between the two disciplines can be quite fuzzy. They share interests in the same social phenomena—such as family dynamics—and often use the same approaches to scientific inquiry. Because both anthropologists and sociologists study cultures and social phenomena, models of classroom instruction mirror the connection between the disciplines; considerable overlap between anthropology and sociology can be found in elementary school social studies programs.

Distinguishing anthropology and sociology as two disciplines did not gain much headway until about the middle of the 20th century; among those at the forefront of this effort was anthropologist A. L. Kroeber. Using the common assumption of his time that sociology was the systematic study of *societies* and anthropology the systematic study of *cultures*, Kroeber (1959) described how *society* and *culture* could be considered interchangeable concepts:

> It is . . . an inescapable fact, that . . . societies always exist in association with a culture; . . . cultures, with a society. Particular [research] studies can [take from] the social aspects of a situation to investigate the cultural aspects, or the reverse, or they can deal with the interaction of the social and cultural aspects. This is common doctrine of the two sciences. (p. 398)

Kroeber recognized that there were so many similarities between anthropology and sociology that they could be regarded as "twin sisters." Despite this "sharing of their basic concepts" (p. 398), however, Kroeber (1959) felt that differences were obvious. First, anthropologists work most actively to study humanity as a whole, while sociologists concentrate primarily on the behavior of people in social groups. Therefore, the scope of sociology was considered more limited; the scope of anthropology was thought to be more universal, or holistic. Second, Kroeber determined that the most obvious difference between the two disciplines was in how they carried out their research. A preferred anthropological research approach is participant observation, but anthropologists also investigate sources such as sites or digs to locate artifacts; they also carry out interviews, historical analysis, and cross-cultural comparisons. On the other hand, although a sociologist and an anthropologist may share some common research methods, such as participant observation, sociologists gather data through distinctive statistical methods such as survey research, case studies, interviews, and content analysis (analysis of media messages). Despite these differences, anthropology and sociology are more alike than unalike. Both are oriented toward the systematic study of beliefs and practices of diverse peoples and groups; that is why sociology is often combined with anthropology in college and university departmental units as a "Department of Anthropology and Sociology."

Here, we will consider sociology as the scientific study of social groups, as well as patterns of group interaction and behavior. The groups may be small, such as families, or large, such as cults, clans, and communities. Since all human behavior is social, the subject matter of sociology is immense; it covers topics as wide-ranging as social systems, marriage and family, social inequalities, gender studies, and sports and leisure. In actuality, when sociologists decide on which aspect of society they would like to study, there are endless possibilities.

CHECK YOUR UNDERSTANDING 13.4 **Click here** to check your understanding of this section of the chapter.

Teaching Sociology in the Elementary School

Expanding environments social studies curricula, although integrated with the other social sciences, typically center on sociology themes and concepts during the early grades (Grades 1–3): individual, home, school, and families in kindergarten and Grade 1; neighborhoods in Grade 2; and communities in Grade 3. In the Grade 1 social studies program, for example, students learn about their own and other *families* in safe, sensitive ways. Since the family is the most basic unit of care, affection, and belonging, it is most influential in shaping children's character and helps them learn about who they are in the world. Therefore, students must not think of families exclusively as the traditional two-parent family but must learn that parents today can be single, gay or lesbian, or grandparents; families can be blended, foster, or adoptive. Grade 1 content highlights family diversity to help create an atmosphere of equality and acceptance for all children. Social studies topics commonly expand to *neighborhoods* in Grade 2. As children grow, they move from being primarily family centered to building an awareness of different neighborhoods around them. Social studies in Grade 2, therefore, focuses on neighborhoods as places to live, work, learn, and play—starting with the children's own neighborhoods and expanding to others in the United States and throughout the world. In a Grade 3 social studies program, students typically explore rural, urban, and suburban communities in the United States and communities throughout the world. Students learn how different communities address their basic needs and wants and how they reflect the diversity of the world's peoples and cultures. Students' own communities serve as a basis for understanding and comparing communities—in other cultures, in other historical periods, and even in the animal kingdom. Although learning may take place within formal classroom settings, a great deal of valuable learning also takes place informally.

In primary grades, sociology content is derived from topics related to social institutions and social relationships—self, family, neighborhood, and community.

Monkey Business/Fotolia

Reflection on Learning

You may simply scribble rough notes or jot down something more polished and complete. The point is to simply start recording your ideas spontaneously and candidly.

Are young children better off learning about families, neighborhoods, and "community helpers" in the primary grades than extraordinary people and events during distant times and in faraway places?

Healthy Self-Esteem as a Prerequisite for Social Responsibility

Self-esteem is the value students place put on their importance, not in a boastful way but confidently and realistically knowing they are important and valued. "Self" is a thread running through the fabric of each of the early grade levels. It is important that children feel good about themselves because children with healthy self-esteem tend to enjoy interacting with others. They are as comfortable in social settings as they are in independent pursuits. Self-esteem is the foundation of a child's well-being and the key to establishing relationships with others; it is nurtured in warm classrooms by caring, compassionate teachers. During their primary grade years, children's self-esteem is based largely on their perceptions of how the important adults in their lives and their peers judge them. The distressing experience of Freddie, a third grader, illustrates the long-lasting effects of bullying on a child's self-esteem:

> *Freddie made a great bully target. He was frail, shy, and withdrawn; he chose to be with the girls rather than the boys. From his very youngest years, Freddie preferred dolls, playing house, and baking. While other boys were captivated by "boy games" with masculine attributes, Freddie selected "girl activities." From the time he entered kindergarten, Freddie knew deep inside that he was different.*
>
> *Sensing Freddie's vulnerability, Dennis started teasing him mercilessly from third grade on. Instead of defending himself, Freddie felt threatened and scared, his meek and passive demeanor informing Dennis that he would be submissive and compliant. Dennis and his fellow tormentors used a derogatory and "sing-songy" tone as they taunted Freddie with the humiliating moniker "Freddie the Faggot." They used homophobic terms like sissy and gay as weapons intended to hurt Freddie simply because he didn't conform to traditional gender roles. (At this age, bullies tend to use verbal teasing rather than violence to attack those who are different. However, words may turn to physical bullying in the upper elementary grades.) Dennis and his group often followed Freddie around the playground, shoving and tripping him. At one point, for several days in a row, one of the bullies would come up to Freddie, taunt him, and spit at him.*
>
> *Freddie didn't have the courage to complain. He feared retaliation; he was terrorized by the thought of getting beaten up. But when the stinging taunts turned physical, Freddie secretly shared what had been going on with his best friend Sheila. "They always say that gay word," Freddie complained. "They keep calling me gay, gay, gay. I'm so tired of hearing that word; they keep saying it over and over and over! I hate school. . . . I don't want to come to school anymore!" Sheila had noticed that Freddie had been very quiet the past few days. Yesterday, he'd even had a bruise on his chin.*

Like Freddie, other bullied children are afraid to go to school. They tend to have higher rates of depression and anxiety, low self-esteem, and other mental health conditions. Severe bullying can cause problems that last well into adulthood and affect one's personal and professional life. And, in extremely tragic cases, bullied children think about suicide.

Bullying is a serious and growing problem in our nation's schools. It involves aggressive, hostile behavior carried out intentionally for harmful and hurtful purposes. Bullying can be *physical* (such as hitting, kicking, or pinching), *verbal* (such as teasing, taunting, or name calling), or *social/emotional* (being excluded or ignored). Although not as prevalent in elementary school as it is in middle school or high school, bullying also includes *cyberbullying* (harassing emails, instant messages, or text messages).

Research suggests that children get locked into the role of victim at 8 or 9 years of age (Pepler, Smith, & Rigby, 2004) and may be bullied for many different reasons—and sometimes for no reason at all. Bullies often target victims who have a prominent distinguishing characteristic:

- Lesbian, gay, bisexual, or transgender individuals or those perceived to be lesbian, gay, bisexual, or transgender
- Frail, sensitive, quiet, withdrawn, passive, and shy children
- Children who have disabilities, are obese, wear glasses, or have other exceptionalities such as learning disabilities, autism, ADHD, or giftedness
- Children of different ethnicity, race, or culture
- Children who have specific religious beliefs
- Children who are not good at making friends and have little social support

If you suspect that a child in your classroom is the target of a bully, take the situation seriously. Learn to recognize bullying and know how to respond; early intervention can help prevent lifelong problems. Implement policies and practices that prevent student bullying; begin by providing a positive, inclusive climate in which all children enjoy a feeling of security, acceptance, and safety. Establish a classroom culture of acceptance, tolerance, and respect. All children, especially victims of bullying, look to their teacher for consistent, attentive, nurturing, and sensitive attention. Use your smile, your voice, and your total being to reassure each child that you are there to make everyone feel safe. In addition, it is important to add bullying prevention material and activities to your curriculum. For example, PACER's National Bullying Prevention Center offers several free creative activities and resources for K–12 students, teachers, and parents. The goal is to raise awareness and increase understanding of how to recognize and respond to bullying.

Although bullying is but one consideration, everything that takes place within a respectful classroom contributes to children's *sense of self*—that is, how much they value themselves, how important they think they are, and whether they believe they are worthy of high regard and acceptance. Most children achieve a healthy sense of self and visualize themselves as worthy, capable individuals. However, children such as Freddie are threatened when their sense of self does not match what they perceive as the school "norm"; something happens that makes them think of themselves as inept or unworthy. These are the children who often find their classroom to be the epitome of anxiety and frustration—"I'm stupid" and "I just don't fit in" are the kinds of comments that seem to capture their lack of confidence and loss of hope. And those agonizing thoughts are often accompanied by alarming feelings such as sadness, anger, or worthlessness. What can be done to help all children acquire a healthy sense of self?

Self-esteem, or sense-of-self, is an essential prerequisite to developing advanced social skills, so it is an excellent first step to any sociology program. From that beginning, the National Council for the Social Studies (2010) recommends that students at all grade levels be helped to address sociology-based questions such as: How am I similar to and different from others? What are groups and institutions? To what groups and institutions do I belong? How do groups and institutions influence me, and how do I influence them? What are the roles of groups and institutions in this and other societies? How do groups and institutions change? What is my role in effecting change? The NCSS social studies standards provide a framework for sociology not only the early grades, but for the upper grades as well. Recall that the standards framework consists of 10 themes, corresponding with one or more relevant disciplines. The fifth theme—*Individuals, Groups, and Institutions*—draws primarily from sociology, as is apparent in the theme's purpose statement:

> Institutions such as families, and civic, educational, governmental, and religious organizations exert great influence in daily life. Organizations embody the core social values of the individuals and groups who comprise them. It is important that students know how institutions are formed, maintained, and changed, and understand how they influence individuals, groups, and other institutions. (p. 42)

THE CLASSROOM ENVIRONMENT

The path leading to a positive sense of self begins with teachers who provide a classroom characterized as a warm, nurturing environment in which developmentally appropriate instruction takes place; these are clearly the essential elements of productive classroom life. A good place to start building such a classroom is to help students sense personal connections between their own lives and what is going on in school. So, at the beginning of each new school year, create an all-inclusive learning environment that nurtures trust and respect for all people—celebrating and valuing diversity—from the color of one's skin to intellectual or physical abilities to the language spoken. Children who understand and appreciate the glorious diversity among their peers will more likely grow up as wise citizens who respect our nation's rich mix of cultures, heritages, abilities, and interests. The overall goal of productive classroom life is to establish a trusting, caring, and supportive *classroom community* built on recognition of and respect for students' unique individual backgrounds and strengths. It is a given that all students present challenges from time to time, but students who have special needs could often present new challenges: What can I do to help this particular child reach his or her potential? In what ways can I help this student succeed in school?

Children with Special Needs

Aren't *all* children special? It is true that all children are special, but *children with special needs* have extreme differences in the way they develop or behave. Consider a "child with special needs" as any child requiring extra help because of a physical or mental challenge. A comprehensive list of all the conditions that are covered would be impossible to put together, given the variety of possible challenges. However, you may know of children with autism; Down syndrome; serious emotional and behavioral disturbances; mental retardation; attention-deficit/hyperactivity disorder (ADHD); epilepsy; cerebral palsy; feeding and eating disorders; learning disabilities; orthopedic, visual, speech, or language disabilities; traumatic brain injury; or other serious conditions. The definition of "special needs" is broad and includes many kinds of conditions. "Special needs children" may need Braille books to read, use wheelchairs or walk with the help of crutches or braces, or have serious problems storing and processing information. Children with special needs may require certain medical prescriptions, specialized therapies, corrective care, or concentrated help in school that other children do not typically need.

Inclusion of children with disabilities in regular elementary school classrooms has presented a major challenge for many teachers. The fundamental principle of inclusion is the valuing of diversity within the classroom community. While recognizing that there are no simple answers, just take a moment to think about how you would feel, and what you would do, if faced with each of the following classroom situations:

- Sarah has a convulsion, and you are the only adult around.
- Alejandro is lost and cannot hear you calling him.
- Noel flies into an explosive, lengthy, and destructive rage that is out of proportion with the issue.

It might surprise you that the way most people choose to "deal" with situations like these is to avoid them. How many of us tend to steer clear of children with disabilities because we feel inadequate or insecure? To effectively implement the spirit of inclusion, you must learn about how it operates; doing so may alleviate many fears and make those involved in the process feel more secure. The following suggestions are general and should be adjusted in consideration of each unique situation:

- *Seek professional support.* Talk to teachers and administrators who have worked with children with disabilities. They can help you find resources and information, and they can provide you with emotional strength.
- *Learn about the child's specific disability.* You have a good start toward understanding children with disabilities if you know about child development. After all, children with disabilities are still children. It is important to know that children with disabilities are

more like other children than they are different from them. Therefore, your first step in working with children with disabilities is to establish a framework of child development knowledge.

When a child with disabilities enters your classroom, take time to learn something about him or her; you will need a great deal of background information. Certainly, it is not possible to know everything about all the special needs children in your classroom; you have the support of a team that includes specialists in the field. To help in this regard, however, you will find it useful to search through professional journals, books, and videotapes available through professional organizations or publishers of special education materials. Go to the library and find out all you can or visit relevant Internet sites.

- *Support and nurture children with disabilities.* Often, children with disabilities require a great deal of emotional support. Show your belief in their potential by encouraging children with disabilities to do things independently or with the least assistance possible. Let them know that it is okay to take risks and make mistakes. Ask them to make important decisions; this will help them build self-esteem and confidence.

- *Arrange a suitable classroom environment.* Helping children with disabilities feel comfortable in a classroom involves some very critical considerations. Overall, an inclusive classroom should contain the same materials and activities suggested for general social studies programs, but with these offerings enhanced with opportunities to meet the needs of all children. It helps to include photographs or pictures of people with disabilities participating with nondisabled people on the job or in a variety of other activities. Be sure the learning materials are accessible to all the children. Some children will need Braille labels to help them locate things while others may require ramps to move from one area to another. Whatever the case, be sure to explain to the other children why these special adaptations have been made: "This ramp helps Francine get to the top level when she is in her wheelchair." Invite adults with disabilities to share their special talents and interests with your children. In short, the classroom should offer a safe environment where all children feel accepted, whatever their capabilities or special needs. Despite the fact that some adjustments must be made, each child should be enabled to gain skills and understandings in all areas and to reach her or his full potential.

- *Select books that help children learn about and appreciate disabilities.* Many good children's books offer information about disabilities, explain difficulties youngsters with disabilities often encounter, and tell stories about people who serve as positive role models for children with disabilities. Marc Brown's *Arthur's Eyes* (Little, Brown), for example, tells of how a little boy learns to cope with teasing about his new eyeglasses. Ada Basset-Litchfield's *A Button in Her Ear* (Albert Whitman) explains deafness and how hearing aids help children with hearing losses. Lucille Clifton's *My Friend Jacob* (Dutton Juvenile) tells about the friendship between a young boy and his older friend with a learning disability. Maxine B. Rosenberg's *My Friend Leslie* (Lothrop) is a photographic essay about a young girl with multiple disabilities.

Literature can be one very important path to understanding and acceptance. Keep many types of stories available and use them to promote questions, conversations, and empathy for children with developmental disabilities.

- *Maximize interactions among children with disabilities and nondisabled children.* Peers can be a big help by being friends. Children who are profoundly deaf, for example, want friends just like any other child does. But making friends can be a challenge. Some might tease them or make fun of them. You can help the situation by giving simple explanations about a child's disability when she or he comes to your classroom. Youngsters are curious; they want to know about a new child and will be satisfied with a short, open, honest explanation: "Russell's legs don't work well, so he needs a wheelchair." Encourage the children with disabilities to share their strengths. For example, Russell can help another child in a project that involves the use of his hands (such as building a diorama or drawing a picture), and others can assist Russell with his special needs. In his classroom, for example, Russell regularly plays outdoors with his classmates during recess. One of their favorite games is kickball. To play, Russell selects a "designated kicker" to kick the ball for him; after it is kicked, he speeds around from base to base in his wheelchair. Social acceptance and cooperation help support students with diverse abilities.

Inclusion involves changes in attitudes, behaviors, and teaching styles, but providing for the special needs of students will certainly bring some of your greatest challenges (and pleasures) as a professional educator. Plan your inclusive social studies program to fit your children's various abilities. No single section of a textbook can hope to give you a complete idea of the responsibilities involved in doing so, but if you truly want to be an outstanding teacher, you must plan to attend in-service training or professional development classes and pursue other educational opportunities that will hone your skills in curriculum modification and instructional techniques.

 Video Exploration 13.3

 CHECK YOUR UNDERSTANDING 13.5 **Click here** to check your understanding of this section of the chapter.

A Final Thought

Of all the "Final Thoughts" I've written, this one is the most personal. It's an emotional one because I want to use just the right words to encourage you as a beginning teacher. I don't expect all of you who have read this book to love it, but it does represent my best attempt to share with you my joys and hopes about teaching children. And, I have loved doing it! So, as I think about what to say, I would like it to be "stick with it!" A key quality of good social studies teachers is something I like to call "stick-with-it-ness." This is a persistent, intense devotion to what they are doing. For them, teaching is not only a job but an obsession. It leaves them starry eyed and eager to activate children for learning. All children must believe that their teachers are captivated by what they are doing. In social studies, this means that they view their world with fascination and inspire the children to look at their world as a never-ending mystery. To do this, teachers must plan significant learning situations in which there is a little mystery, a bit of magic, and a dash of magnificence. Elementary school children respond to these things; that is what makes their classrooms different from those of any other age group. You can achieve magic in your classroom when you deliver the best for each child and help them squeeze out the best that every day has to offer.

Good social studies teachers work hard to master their specialized professional responsibilities and realize that progress toward good teaching is deliberate. "Good teacher" is a status that takes time and hard work to achieve, much like running a marathon. Top-notch teachers know that the race takes a long time to complete but realize that once they reach the finish line, the greatest rewards of teaching are theirs. Satisfaction, however, comes not from arriving first but from the race itself. Some teachers train for but never start the race; others start but eventually realize it takes more time and energy than they are willing to invest. A select few will stride steadily and strongly forward until they break through as superbly talented professionals. Which will you be?

References

American Academy of Religion. (2010). *Guidelines for teaching about religion in K–12 public schools in the United States.* Atlanta, GA: Author.

Banks, J. A. (2009). *Teaching strategies for ethnic studies.* Boston, MA: Pearson.

Bennett, C. I. (2007). *Comprehensive multicultural education: Theory and practice.* Boston: Pearson Education.

Gay, G. (2000). *Culturally responsive teaching: Theory, research, and practice.* New York, NY: Teachers College Press.

Haynes, C. C. (2008). *A teacher's guide to religion in the public schools.* Nashville, TN: First Amendment Center.

Hidalgo, N. (1993). Multicultural teacher introspection. In T. Perry & J. Fraser (Eds.), *Freedom's plow: Teaching in the multicultural classroom.* New York, NY: Routledge.

Kroeber, A. L. (1959). The history of the personality of anthropology. *American Anthropologist, 61,* 398–404.

Krug, M. (1976). *The melting of the ethnics.* Bloomington, IL: Phi Delta Kappa.

National Council for the Social Studies. (1991). *Curriculum guidelines for multicultural education.* Retrieved from http:www.socialstudies.org/positions/multicultural

National Council for the Social Studies. (2014). *Study about religions in the social studies curriculum: A position statement of the National Council for the Social Studies.*
Retrieved from http://www.socialstudies.org/positions/study_about_religions

National Council for the Social Studies. (2010). *National curriculum standards for social studies: A framework for teaching, learning, and assessment.* Silver Spring, MD: Author.

Parsons, T., & Bales, R. (1956). *Family, socialization and interaction process.* London, England: Routledge and Kegan Paul.

Pepler, D., Smith, P. K., & Rigby, K. (2004). Looking back and looking forward: Implications for making interventions work effectively. In P. K. Smith, D. Pepler, & K. Rigby (Eds.), *Bullying in schools: How successful can interventions be?* (pp. 307–324). New York, NY: Cambridge University Press.

U.S. Bureau of the Census. (2012). *U.S. Census Bureau projections show a slower growing, older, more diverse nation a half century from now.* Retrieved from https://www.census.gov/newsroom/releases/archives/population/cb12-243.html

Vygotsky, L. S. (1978). *Mind in society.* Cambridge, MA: Harvard University Press.

Zangwill, I. (1921). *The melting-pot.* Retrieved from http://www.gutenberg.org/files/23893/23893-h/23893-h.htm

Author Index

Subject Index